The Music Producer's Ultimate Guide to FL Studio 2025

Third Edition

Create professional tracks using modern composing, mixing, and production workflows

Joshua Au-Yeung

<packt>

The Music Producer's Ultimate Guide to FL Studio 2025

Third Edition

Copyright © 2026 Packt Publishing

All rights reserved. No part of this book may be reproduced, stored in a retrieval system, or transmitted in any form or by any means, without the prior written permission of the publisher, except in the case of brief quotations embedded in critical articles or reviews.

Every effort has been made in the preparation of this book to ensure the accuracy of the information presented. However, the information contained in this book is sold without warranty, either express or implied. Neither the author, nor Packt Publishing or its dealers and distributors, will be held liable for any damages caused or alleged to have been caused directly or indirectly by this book.

Packt Publishing has endeavored to provide trademark information about all of the companies and products mentioned in this book by the appropriate use of capitals. However, Packt Publishing cannot guarantee the accuracy of this information.

Portfolio Director: Pavan Ramchandani
Relationship Lead: Larissa Pinto
Content Engineer: Mohd Hammad
Technical Editor: Vidhisha Patidar
Indexer: Manju Arasan
Production Designer: Shantanu Zagade
Growth Lead: Nivedita Singh

First published: February 2021
Second edition: June 2023
Third edition: April 2026

Production reference: 2200426

Published by Packt Publishing Ltd.
Grosvenor House
11 St Paul's Square
Birmingham
B3 1RB, UK.

ISBN 978-1-80638-441-9
`www.packtpub.com`

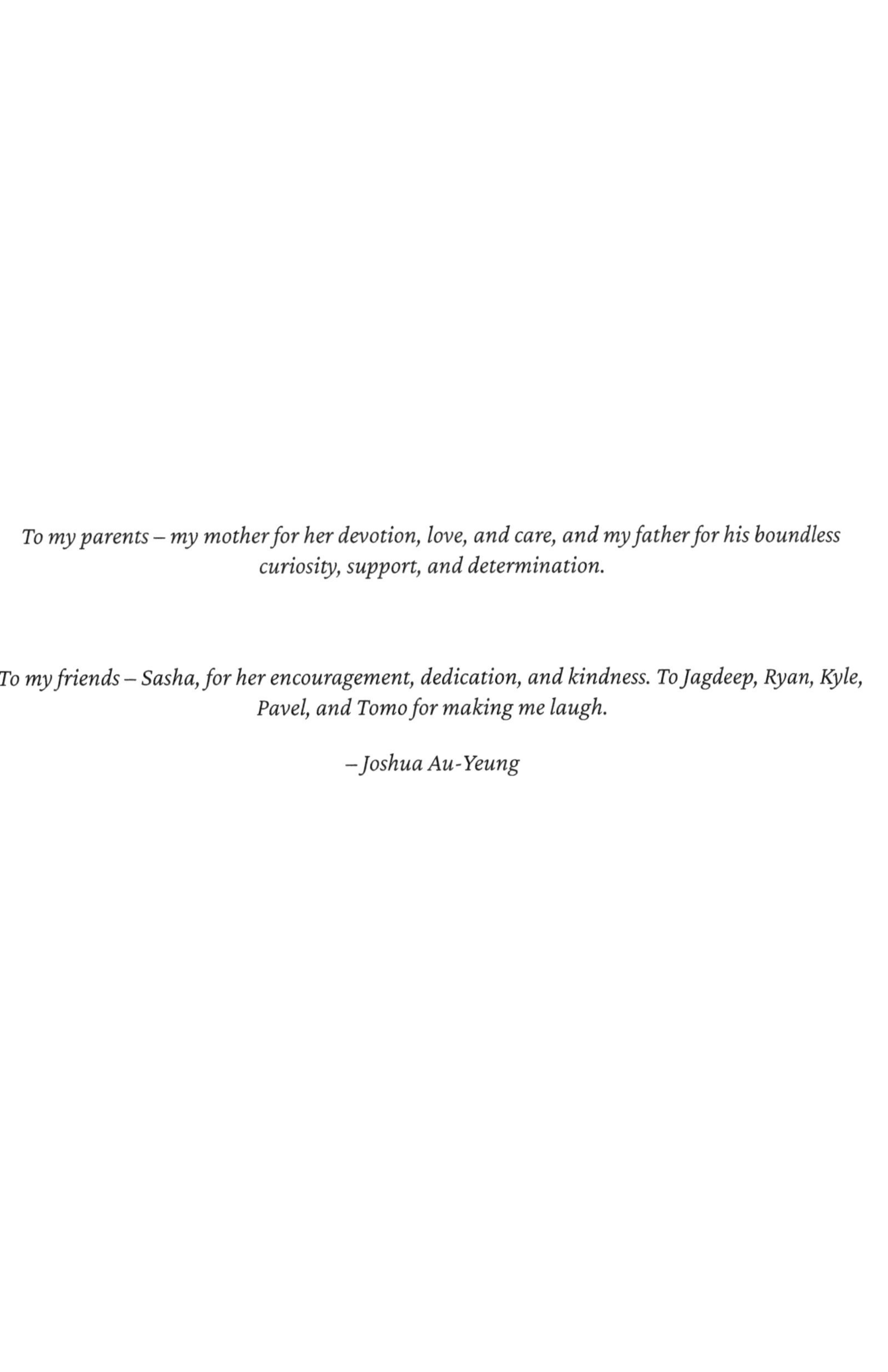

To my parents – my mother for her devotion, love, and care, and my father for his boundless curiosity, support, and determination.

To my friends – Sasha, for her encouragement, dedication, and kindness. To Jagdeep, Ryan, Kyle, Pavel, and Tomo for making me laugh.

– Joshua Au-Yeung

Contributors

About the author

Joshua Au-Yeung (professionally known as Chester Sky) is a music producer, composer, director, and software developer. He's published thirteen albums, directed and composed for short films, created board games, and hosts a podcast. He's an instructor for several online courses, including bestselling courses on music production and composing for films.

About the reviewer

Chris Noxx is a JUNO-nominated (2020 Rap Recording of the Year) producer, composer, and arranger with 12 Billboard chart entries to his name. A proud member of the multi-platinum, Grammy-winning songwriting and production team Tha Piecemakerz – alongside talents including Dr. Dre, Tory Lanez, Waka Flocka Flame, G-Unit, Talib Kweli, Xzibit, Bone Thugs-N-Harmony, and more – he has contributed to groundbreaking projects across Golden Globe-, BAFTA-, and Oscar-winning films, Emmy-winning television series, major sports associations, and high-profile advertising campaigns for global brands.

"When the student is ready, the teacher will appear."

I am deeply grateful to all my mentors and teachers who have guided me along this path. This book is a masterpiece in learning how to fully harness FL Studio's built-in tools and the latest upgrades, empowering the next generation of producers to create without limits. It has been an honor and a privilege to contribute to it.

Table of Contents

Chapter 7: Stereo Width – Panning, Reverb, Delay, Chorus, Flangers, and Distortion 227

Chapter 8: Recording Live Audio and Vocal Processing 279

Chapter 14: Publishing and Selling Music Online 515

Chapter 15: Unlock Your Exclusive Benefits 533

Preface

This book is the ultimate, all-in-one guide to mastering FL Studio and music production. It's meticulously designed to help you learn FL Studio fast and in depth.

This latest edition is fully updated to cover the newest FL Studio features and workflows, reflecting current industry standards and technologies. It organizes all the essential knowledge, from beginner fundamentals to advanced techniques. It's the authoritative book with everything in one place to save you time and frustration while you build your skills confidently and comprehensively.

Whether you're starting fresh or upgrading your knowledge, this book provides practical insights, professional tips, and creative guidance. It's your reliable companion on the journey to producing music that sounds great and stands out.

This book offers a practical, step-by-step guide to mastering FL Studio, combining in-depth software tutorials with essential music production techniques, creative sound design, and real-world insights on marketing and publishing. Unlike other resources, it covers the entire journey from composing and mixing to promoting your music, making it an all-in-one solution for musicians to create professional-quality tracks and build a successful music career in the digital age.

By the end of this book, you'll be able to utilize cutting-edge tools to fuel your creative ideas, mix and master music effectively, and publish your songs.

What's new in the third edition

Why do we need a third edition of FL Studio? Simple reason. FL Studio keeps getting better and better. Every year, FL Studio rolls out a new suite of plugins to improve upon its already outstanding software. There are so many fantastic new features coming out that we need a new edition to keep up with them.

In this third edition of the book, we include topics on FL Studio's newly added tools:

We added topics on the Kepler instrument, Kepler EXO instrument, Transporter effect, Low Lifter effect, Spreader effect, Channel Rack Loop Starter tool, FL Cloud Instruments and Effects, Gopher (AI Chat Assistant), the Piano Roll Chord Progression Tool, Fruity Slicer 2 plugin for vocal chopping, Emphasis mastering tool, Hyper Chorus effect, Stem Extraction using AI, Denoising using AI, Deverbing using AI, and FL Cloud AI Mastering. We've included additional topics on

Song creation using AI tools and getting more out of promoting on YouTube. We also updated existing topics from previous editions to ensure you're using the latest and greatest FL Studio features.

Who this book is for

This book is for musicians, music producers, composers, songwriters, DJs, and audio engineers interested in creating their own music, improving their music production skills, mixing and mastering music, and selling songs online.

How to use this book

This book is organized in a logical order, assuming you know nothing at the start, and gradually builds up skills and techniques as you progress.

Although you could read this book from cover to cover, I expect that many of you will not do so. More likely, you will jump around from topic to topic whenever you need to explore a tool in detail. For this reason, I've tried to compartmentalize topics so you can jump into any chapter and learn the topic without having to rely too much on other chapters. This way, you can quickly learn all you need and get back to making music.

My goal is for this book to act as an easy-to-use reference guide, regardless of whether you're new to music production or on your way to becoming a pro and just want to learn the ins and outs of a specific FL Studio feature.

What this book covers

Chapter 1, Getting Started with FL Studio, introduces you to FL Studio. Here we'll discuss a brief history of music production, the musician career path, and the overall process of song creation that you'll discover throughout this book. You'll create your first song and learn how to export music out of FL Studio.

Chapter 2, Exploring the Browser, Playlist, and Channel Rack, helps you learn about the main features in the Browser, Playlist, and Channel Rack. These, along with the Piano roll and Mixer, are the core tools of FL Studio. We'll learn how to use the Channel Rack loop starter tool to quickly assemble audio samples to get started with a song in a specific genre. We'll learn how to use Gopher, FL Studio's chatbot agent, to assist you with any music/plugin-related questions you may have.

Chapter 3, Composing with the Piano Roll, helps you understand how the Piano roll adds melody notes, arranges them, adjusts the inflection of notes, and easily moves notes between instruments. You'll learn tips for creating excellent chord progressions from scratch. Once you know how to use the Piano roll, you'll be able to compose melodies for any instrument. We'll learn how to use the Chord Progression Tool to use AI to help you come up with chord progressions.

Chapter 4, Routing to the Mixer, Applying Automation, and Freezing Audio, gets you familiar with the process of how audio is passed around the Mixer in order to apply effects to your music. We'll explore methods of automating effects and how to freeze audio.

Chapter 5, Fundamentals of Sound Design, lays the foundation of how sound works. We'll learn what it is, how it's manipulated, and how instruments create sounds. We'll learn how to extract vocal, drum, instrument, and FX stems from an audio sample using AI.

Chapter 6, Mixing Basics – Compression, Sidechaining, Limiting, and Equalization, teaches you mixing techniques with compressors and equalizers. We'll explore the Fruity Limiter and Fruity Parametric EQ 2 plugins.

Chapter 7, Stereo Width – Panning, Reverb, Delay, Chorus, Flangers, and Distortion, explores tools to increase stereo width. We'll explore the Reeverb 2, Fruity Convolver, LuxeVerb, Fruity Delay 3, Fruity Chorus, Vintage Chorus, Fruity Flanger, Fruity Phaser, Vintage Phaser, Hyper Chorus, Spreader, and Distructor plugins.

Chapter 8, Recording Live Audio and Vocal Processing, discusses the setup and preparation you need before recording. We'll learn how to record into FL Studio, how to mix your vocals, and best practices for applying effects to vocals. We'll explore microphones, record audio with Edison, and pitch correct with the NewTone plugin. We'll learn how to retime audio samples with the NewTime plugin. We'll learn how to denoise and deverb audio using AI.

Chapter 9, Understanding Vocal Effects, teaches you about special effects that can be used on vocals. We'll discuss how to create vocal harmonies and how to use vocoders to modulate your vocals with an instrument. We'll explore the Pitcher, Vocodex, and vocal chopping with the Fruity Slicer 2 and Slicex plugins.

Chapter 10, Glitch Effects and Creating Your Own Instruments and Effects, teaches you how to create glitch effects with sounds, transform samples into playable instruments, and create custom instruments and effect chains that can be reused in any project. We'll explore the Gross Beat, DirectWave, and Patcher plugins. We'll learn how to use the advanced arpeggiator called VFX Sequencer inside Patcher. We'll also learn how to use the Transporter plugin, a real-time relooping effect that triggers loops based on transients detected in the incoming audio.

Chapter 11, Intermediate to Advanced Mixing Topics and Sound Design Plugin Effects, introduces you to FL Studio's sound design plugins. We'll explore Pitch Shifter, adjust frequencies with Frequency Shifter, stretch audio waves with Fruity Granulizer, and use delay effects with Multiband Delay. We'll learn multiband processing with a frequency splitter. We'll learn how to use the Low Lifter plugin to control bass elements precisely within your mix. We'll learn how to use the Kepler and Kepler EXO synthesizer plugins.

Chapter 12, Mastering Fundamentals, helps you understand the mastering process. This will help your music reach production-level quality and be ready for distribution. We'll explore the Emphasis and Maximus plugins to master your music, as well as AI mastering with FL Cloud.

Chapter 13, Marketing, Content Creation, and AI for Music Production, will help you learn about developing your brand, marketing/promoting yourself, getting booked for music gigs, developing a show, suggestions for musicians to get more results out of YouTube, and tips for creating visuals for your music. We'll explore the ZGameEditor Visualizer plugin to create reactive visuals. We'll discuss AI tools for generating visuals and entire songs from scratch.

Chapter 14, Publishing and Selling Music Online, helps you understand how you can release your music online to the world and collect royalty revenue.

To get the most out of this book

You will need FL Studio to use the features explained in this book. Available for download at `https://www.image-line.com/`

Software/hardware requirements for the book	**Operating system requirements**
FL Studio	Windows, macOS

Download the color images

We also provide a PDF file that contains color images of the screenshots/diagrams used in this book. You can download it here: `https://packt.link/gbp/9781806384419`.

Conventions used

There are a number of text conventions used throughout this book.

`CodeInText`: Indicates code words in text, database table names, folder names, filenames, file extensions, pathnames, dummy URLs, user input, and Twitter handles. For example: "If you want to find only results that have the exact name, surround your text with quotation marks. For example, `"808 Kick"`."

Bold: Indicates a new term, an important word, or words that you see on the screen. For instance, words in menus or dialog boxes appear in the text like this. For example: "Alternatively, if you're starting from a fresh new project, you can open the **Create a chord progression** tool by loading a starter template by going to **File** | **New from template** | **Utility** | **Create a chord progression**, as shown in the following screenshot."

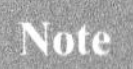

Warnings or important notes appear like this.

Tips and tricks appear like this.

Free benefits with your book

This book comes with free benefits to support your learning. Activate them now for instant access (see the "*How to unlock*" section for instructions).

Here's a quick overview of what you can instantly unlock with your purchase:

How to unlock

Scan the QR code (or go to packtpub.com/unlock). Search for this book by name, confirm the edition, and then follow the steps on the page.

Note: Keep your invoice handy. Purchases made directly from Packt don't require one.

Get in touch

Feedback from our readers is always welcome.

General feedback: If you have questions about any aspect of this book or have any general feedback, please email us at customercare@packt.com and mention the book's title in the subject of your message.

Errata: Although we have taken every care to ensure the accuracy of our content, mistakes do happen. If you have found a mistake in this book, we would be grateful if you reported this to us. Please visit http://www.packt.com/submit-errata, click **Submit Errata**, and fill in the form.

Piracy: If you come across any illegal copies of our works in any form on the internet, we would be grateful if you would provide us with the location address or website name. Please contact us at copyright@packt.com with a link to the material.

If you are interested in becoming an author: If there is a topic that you have expertise in and you are interested in either writing or contributing to a book, please visit http://authors.packt.com/.

Share your thoughts

Once you've read *The Music Producer's Ultimate Guide to FL Studio 2025*, we'd love to hear your thoughts! Scan the QR code below to go straight to the Amazon review page for this book and share your feedback.

https://packt.link/r/1806384418

Your review is important to us and the tech community and will help us make sure we're delivering excellent quality content.

Part 1

Getting Up and Running with FL Studio

In this first part of the book, you'll build the foundational skills needed to begin your music production journey with FL Studio. You'll start by exploring the music production landscape and creating your first song. We'll master FL Studio's core tools: the Browser for organizing sounds, the Channel rack for building musical patterns, and the Playlist for arranging your sounds together. From there, you'll learn to compose using the Piano roll, where you'll add melodies, create chord progressions, and use tools to refine your notes. Finally, you'll learn how to route your instruments into the Mixer and apply automation to bring evolving movement to your tracks.

This part of the book includes the following chapters:

- *Chapter 1, Getting Started with FL Studio*
- *Chapter 2, Exploring the Browser, Playlist, and Channel Rack*
- *Chapter 3, Composing with the Piano Roll*
- *Chapter 4, Routing to the Mixer, Applying Automation, and Freezing Audio*

1

Getting Started with FL Studio

Think about your favorite songs. What makes you like them? Is it the melody, the chords, or the catchy rhythm? Maybe it's a combination of a whole bunch of things that fit together perfectly. What if you could make music sound exactly the way you like? Perhaps you've already tried making songs at home and realized there's a big difference between the sound you're making and the level of professionalism you hear from your favorite musicians.

In the pages ahead, you'll learn the ins and outs of music production and be well on your way to making music like your favorite songs. You'll learn about tools used for composing, mixing, mastering, and publishing your music. By the time you've finished reading this book, you'll have all the tools you need to create music at a professional level.

In this chapter, you'll be introduced to music production and FL Studio. Here, you'll create your first song and export it from FL Studio.

This chapter comprises the following topics:

- Exploring the music production landscape
- The musician's career path
- Steps of composing a song
- What is FL Studio?
- Exploring the FL Studio workspace
- Making your first song

Note

Your purchase includes a free PDF copy + exclusive extras

Your purchase includes a DRM-free PDF copy of this book, a 7-day trial to the Packt+ library (no credit card required), and additional exclusive extras. See the *Free benefits with your book* section in the *Preface* to unlock them instantly and maximize your learning.

Technical requirements

In this chapter, we'll be using FL Studio. You can download a free trial version or a paid version of FL Studio from `https://www.image-line.com/`.

You can download a free trial version of FL Studio, which allows you to try out all the features of the software; however, it won't let you reopen your saved projects until you purchase a paid version.

FL Studio comes in several paid tiered versions, with more features available in the higher tiers. A user can upgrade from a cheaper tier to a higher tier to unlock more features at any time. If you are unsure of which version you need, you can start with the cheapest tier and upgrade later to a higher tier. There is a $10 additional charge for upgrading. Here are the different editions:

- The *Fruity Edition* is the cheapest. It includes all the basic features, such as access to the **Playlist**, **Channel rack**, and **Piano roll**. It includes the Autogun, BassDrum, BeepMap, Drumpad, FLEX, Fruity Kick, Fruity DX10, Groove Machine Synth, VFX Sequencer, Fruity Granulizer, Frequency Splitter, Distructor, and MiniSynth plugins. It does not include audio recording.
- The *Producer Edition* includes all features in the *Fruity Edition* plus audio recording and post-production tools. It includes the Edison, Slicex (loop slicer and re-arranger), Sytrus, Maximus, Vocodex, Frequency Shifter, Multiband Delay, Newtime, SynthMaker, and Spreader plugins. In this book, we include an introduction to the Edison, Slicex, Maximus, and Vocodex plugins.
- The *Signature Bundle* includes everything in the *Producer Edition* plus Fruity Video Player, the DirectWave sampler, Harmless, NewTone, Pitcher, Gross Beat, Vintage Chorus, Vintage Phaser, Pitch Shifter, and the Hardcore guitar effects suite. Fruity Video Player allows you to see videos in sync with your music, which is handy for film composers. In

this book, we include an introduction to the DirectWave, NewTone, Pitcher, and Gross Beat plugins.

- The *All Plugins Bundle* includes all FL Studio plugins and features, including a large selection of synthesizers.

To see a full comparison of features offered in the different tiers, visit `https://www.image-line.com/fl-studio/compare-editions/`.

Exploring the music production landscape

Music production has changed significantly in the last two decades. Before, a musician required the assistance of a music producer. You'd go to a studio to meet with a series of technicians who'd play around with mixing equipment that cost as much as your car or house. Then, you'd sign a deal locking you into a music contract for the foreseeable future. The studio would control how your album got released and what royalties you got paid.

Digital Audio Workstations (known as **DAWs**) changed everything. Software came out that revolutionized the music playing field. It became possible to be a music producer in your bedroom using just your computer. Nowadays, most music producers create music on their own long before they venture into a recording studio (if they do at all).

Studios started to decrease their investment in developing artists from scratch. They preferred artists who already had success and popularity with fans before considering them. iTunes appeared and disappeared, along with iPods that could hold an entire music catalog in your pocket. Then that was not good enough, and consumers wanted to stream online directly from their phones. Independent artists gained the ability to sell music online on their own. Artists could now release their own music and collect their own royalties.

Music streaming platforms such as Spotify, Apple Music, Amazon Music, and YouTube became mainstream. Why buy individual songs when you can access all of them, all the time, anywhere you go? Consumers now have their own personalized playlist recommendations, filled with songs that suit their personal taste. New artists can find their way onto a playlist by accident, subject to the whims of mystical algorithms behind the scenes.

In recent years, AI has come to significantly impact the landscape for musicians. AI tools are automating much of the manual tinkering with music tools and speeding up the song creation process. It's also made creating music visuals to promote music easier and faster than ever before.

All of this poses a powerful opportunity for the independent artist. You can promote yourself using tools equivalent to those that record companies use. You can produce a song on your own, get your music into households around the world, and market your own brand. That's what this book is about. It's a handbook to show you the ins and outs of music production and jump-start your musical career. By the end of this book, you will know how to compose songs, record vocals, mix, master, market your music, and sell it online. This can all be done from home on a minimal budget.

The musician's career path

Many of you reading this book will be looking for guidance on how to begin your music career. You've come to the right place. Whether you are a musician, DJ, composer, or music producer, this book will provide you with a how-to guide for making music.

Let's briefly look at your career path ahead. First, you'll spend some time getting familiar with your DAW. You'll come up with song ideas, record, and learn mixing techniques. You might invest in music plugins, synthesizers, hardware, and samples to play with.

At a certain point, you'll feel comfortable with your tools. It's here you'll realize that knowing how to use your tools is only one part of coming up with music. You need to develop a unique sound for yourself. To do this, you'll go out and listen to lots of music you like. You'll watch successful musicians and learn how to create similar sounds. You'll experiment with genres to find one or a combination that resonates with you. You'll begin to come up with ideas of your own that combine many influences.

You'll share your music with friends and colleagues. Likely, you'll want feedback from people who have some experience in the music business. You'll reach out to local musician groups in your community and attend their meetings. If you stay on course, this cycle of inventing and feedback will shift your music from amateurish to something that other people will enjoy listening to.

You'll get a few songs under your belt and have an album ready to go. You'll post your music online and come to the realization that even though your music is amazing, you don't have many fans yet. How come? People don't know about you yet. You'll need to cultivate a brand identity that fans can relate to and get excited about. You'll need to spend time thinking about the type of brand persona that you want to be recognized for. You'll look into artwork and visuals. You'll spend time on social media and websites, researching what other musicians are doing and trying out their marketing techniques yourself.

You'll have to figure out what kind of equipment you need to perform live. You'll also need to come up with something visually impressive to entertain audiences. Once again, you'll research what other musicians have done on stage and try out their techniques yourself.

Congratulations, you now have a show that you can take on the road! You're now a working musician. We've seen the big picture. It might seem like a lot now, but the good news is that most of the steps along the way are small and easy to do.

Steps of composing a song

Here's a roadmap that you can keep in the back of your mind as you journey through making your songs in this book. Rest assured, it's easier than it sounds and is actually a lot of fun.

First, decide what kind of song you want to make. What mood, genre, and emotion do you want? Or try to find something that inspires you, like a life event, a song you like, or an artist you know. Once you've got your criteria, come up with a melody and accompanying **chords**. Usually, the melody is experimented with on an instrument such as a keyboard or a guitar. You will likely go through a few iterations and drafts until you find a combination you like.

Now we have a melody and some accompanying chords. The melody notes are fed into a DAW as **MIDI** notes. From there, we select an instrument plugin to play the notes. This usually involves experimenting with different instrument plugins and possibly some sound design.

We add accompanying melodies and additional verses. We layer our instruments to *thicken* the sound. We add drums and percussion instruments to complement our melody. We add sound effects. This is a mix of single sound samples that could include percussion, rising and falling sounds, glitch effects, impacts, and drum fills.

If the song requires it, we record vocals. A vocalist is sought out (if you're not singing yourself), and the song's instrumental is sent to the singer to work on. Lyrics are written, and several vocal melody combinations are experimented with. The vocalist records the vocals. The singer and the music producer make adjustments to the song and go back and forth a few times, providing feedback to each other. The vocals are processed, usually separately from the instrumental at first, before adding the finished vocals back into the mix. Effects are applied to enhance the vocals.

We have our melodies, instruments, percussion, sound effects, and vocals. Now it's time to begin mixing. **Mixing** is the process of combining sounds to polish your music and give it a professional feel. It requires understanding how instruments and sounds complement each other in a song and knowing how effects can enhance them. This part gets very technical. This book will give you lots of tips and tricks to help you with mixing. Our song is exported and shared with all parties involved. We give feedback, collect feedback from each other, and make adjustments.

Now it's time for mastering. **Mastering** is what you do after you have a song that has been mixed. The goal is to make the song sound consistent regardless of what device you use to play the song. A song benefits from mastering in several aspects. It allows you to form a second opinion when listening to your song. It forces you to take a step back and re-evaluate your music from a distance, from an audience's perspective. Instead of tweaking individual notes and instruments, you're now forced to think about how the song sounds as a whole package. What is the overall effect of the song on a listener? One way to think about mastering is that you're thinking from a sales perspective. What will make this song have the widest appeal to listeners? This book will give you mastering tips and techniques.

Congratulations, you have a production-ready song! You register your music with the necessary organizations for your territory to prove your copyright ownership and ensure that any rights and royalties belong to you.

You create music videos and cover art to give your audience something to look at while listening. Often, a song's success is made or broken by the choice of visuals used.

You upload your music to an online distributor to sell your music on online stores and streaming platforms such as Spotify, Amazon, and so on. You upload your music videos to YouTube.

You leverage your social media and the existing fanbase you've curated ahead of time (hopefully). You self-promote your upcoming music release, tell everyone you know, and reach out to local outlets to play your music. Hooray, you've published a song!

Composing a full song may seem like a lot of steps and quite technical, but rest assured, by the time you've finished this book, you'll have a solid grasp of how to execute each of these steps. Hopefully, after going through this process, you'll find it intuitive, fulfilling, and profitable.

So far, we've learned about music production from a high-level perspective. Now it's time to get our hands dirty and start making music with FL Studio.

What is FL Studio?

FL Studio is a music software suite that contains all the tools you'll need to produce music. It's one of, if not *the*, leading music production workstation software currently on the market and is used by professional musicians all around the world.

FL Studio consists of tools, effects, and synthesizers designed to compose, mix, and master music. It's a collection of software plugins that can handle all your audio production needs, whether you are a musician, a film or video game composer, or a music producer. It has been designed to be quick to pick up and provides enough features to satisfy sound designers. Once you get comfortable with the main workflow, you'll find it intuitive and easy to use. Most importantly, in my opinion, using FL Studio is fun and a delight to play with. I frequently find myself losing track of time, having fun with it.

Exploring the FL Studio workspace

FL Studio is a software work environment. It comes equipped with tons of tools to assist you with your music creation. In order to create a song, you need to understand the basic workflow. When you first open FL Studio, you will be greeted with a workspace similar to the following screenshot:

Figure 1.1 – FL Studio workspace

It's possible that you may see a slightly different landing screen depending on what version of FL Studio you are using. To ensure that we are all seeing the exact same workspace, open a new template using **Basic with limiter**. Click on **FILE** in the top left corner of FL Studio and select **Basic with limiter**:

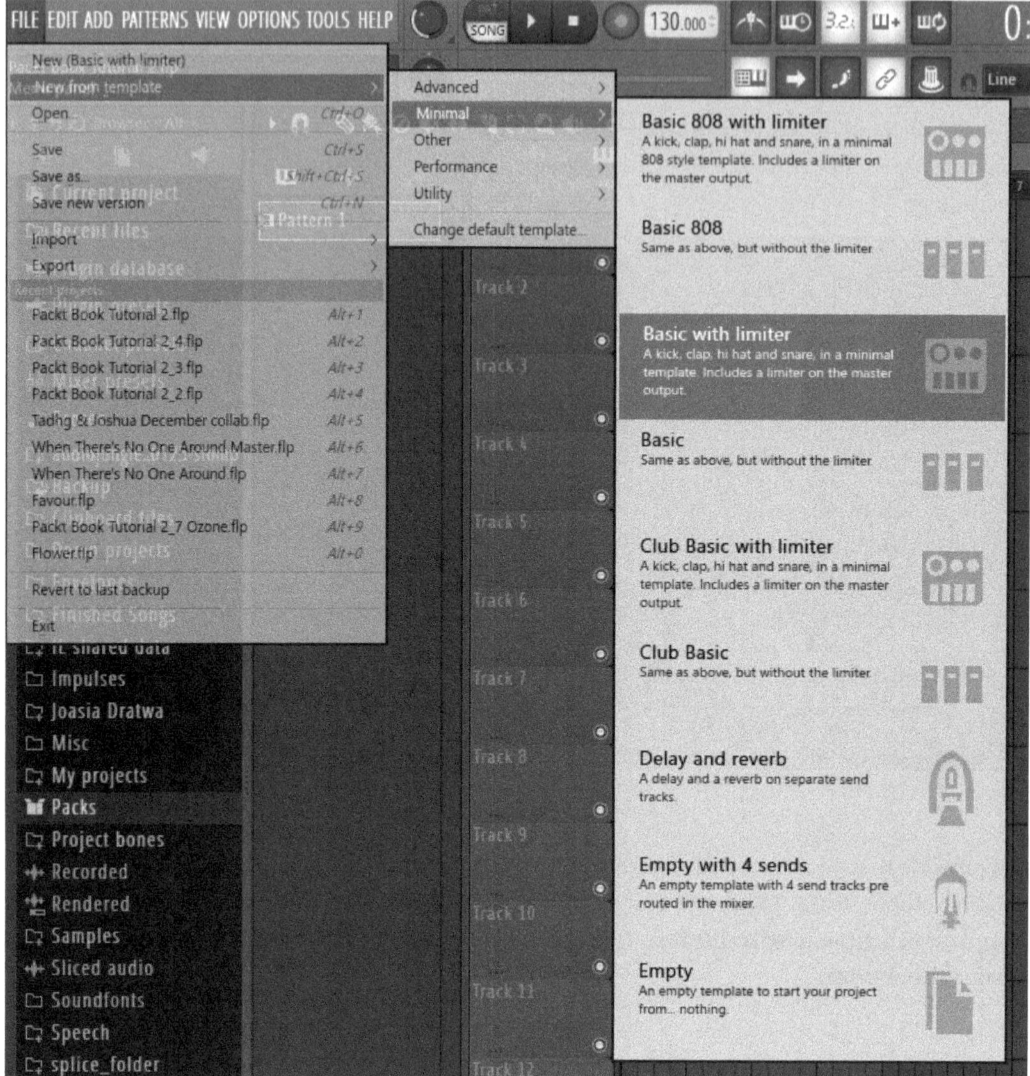

Figure 1.2 – Basic with limiter

You'll notice that there are lots of other templates to get you up and running quickly. I encourage you to explore the other available templates as well if you're curious.

The FL Studio workbench is divided into five panel sections.

Figure 1.3 – Toolbar

These panels can be opened or hidden by left-clicking the icons in the Toolbar. The first five buttons on the Toolbar open up the main sections of FL Studio. They can be opened or hidden by clicking on the tool symbol.

Here are the buttons in the order they appear from left to right:

- **Playlist**: Used to arrange your song compositions
- **Piano roll**: Used to compose melodies
- **Channel rack**: Used to load your instruments and compose percussive rhythms
- **Mixer**: Used to route your instruments and apply effects for mixing and mastering
- **Browser**: Used to organize all your files and navigate through your samples

The Playlist, Piano roll, Channel rack, Mixer, and Browser are the foundational building blocks of FL Studio. Using these five tools, you'll be able to create, organize, and apply effects to your music. In future chapters, we will explore these tools in detail, examining every control and effect. However, the best way to learn how to use FL Studio is to create music with it. So let's first create a very simple song in FL Studio.

Making your first song

FL Studio is a tool, and the best way to learn it is to just jump in and make something with it. To make our first song, we'll do the following:

1. Create a drum beat with the **Channel rack**.
2. Add an accompanying instrument.
3. Route the drum beat and instrument to the **Mixer**.
4. Export the song.

This will get you up and running with the bare-bones basics of creating a song in FL Studio. Let's get started.

Creating a drum beat with the Channel rack

One of the key features of the Channel rack is that it allows you to create percussive patterns with ease. To create a drum beat pattern in the Channel rack, you need drum sound samples and notes to indicate when to play the sound samples. To do this, take the following steps:

1. Open the Channel rack by selecting the **Channel rack** icon.

Figure 1.4 – Toolbar, including the Channel rack

2. Here, you'll see the following window. Since we used the template **Basic with limiter** when starting our project, we already have four sound samples (**Kick**, **Clap**, **Hat**, and **Snare**) preloaded into the **Channel rack** for us.

Figure 1.5 – Channel rack open

3. Extend the window by clicking the right edge to make it longer.
   The **Channel rack** allows you to view and load up all of your instruments and samples. Here, we can see that four instruments have been preloaded for us. In this case, they are single percussive sound samples.
4. Add notes by left-clicking on any of the gray and reddish buttons to the right of the instrument, so your **Channel rack** looks like the following:

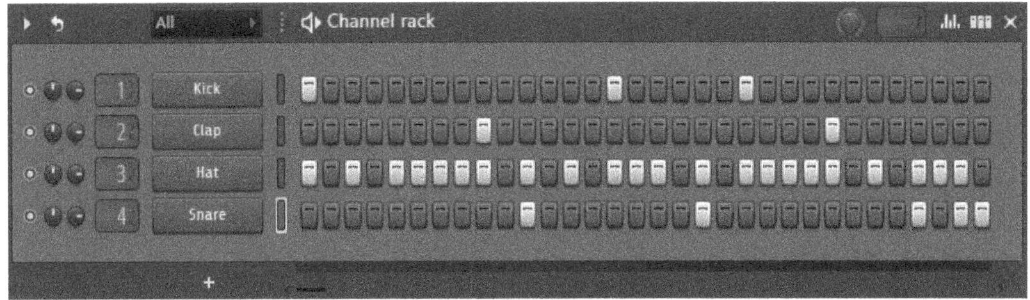

Figure 1.6 – Channel rack

5. Select **PAT** (short for **pattern**) and press play (the triangle symbol) or hit the *spacebar* so that you can listen to your drum beat.

Figure 1.7 – Player menu

So far, we have created a drum beat by adding notes for our percussion samples to play. In a real-life scenario, you'll want to swap out the samples used (for example, **Kick**, **Clap**, **Hat**, or **Snare**) with other samples. A drum beat on its own is pretty boring, though, so let's look into adding an accompanying instrument.

Adding an instrument to the Channel rack

We've created our first **drum beat pattern**. A drum beat isn't very interesting on its own. Music in general always needs a melody to give the song a sense of progression. To create a melody, we need an instrument that can play notes of different pitches. FL Studio has lots of instruments available. Let's add a simple bass guitar instrument to our composition:

1. To create a new pattern, left-click on the **plus** icon next to the word **Pattern 1** in the top Toolbar.

Figure 1.8 – New pattern

Give it a name such as `Bass melody` and press *Enter*.

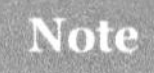

A **pattern** is the term that FL Studio uses to refer to a sequence of notes.

2. Back in the Channel rack, hover your cursor over one of the instruments (**Kick**, **Clap**, **Hat**, or **Snare**) and right-click, or select the **plus** symbol at the bottom of the **Channel rack**. A list of instruments will open up. Insert the one called **BooBass**. I'm using BooBass just because it's a very minimal instrument, so it should be very intuitive.

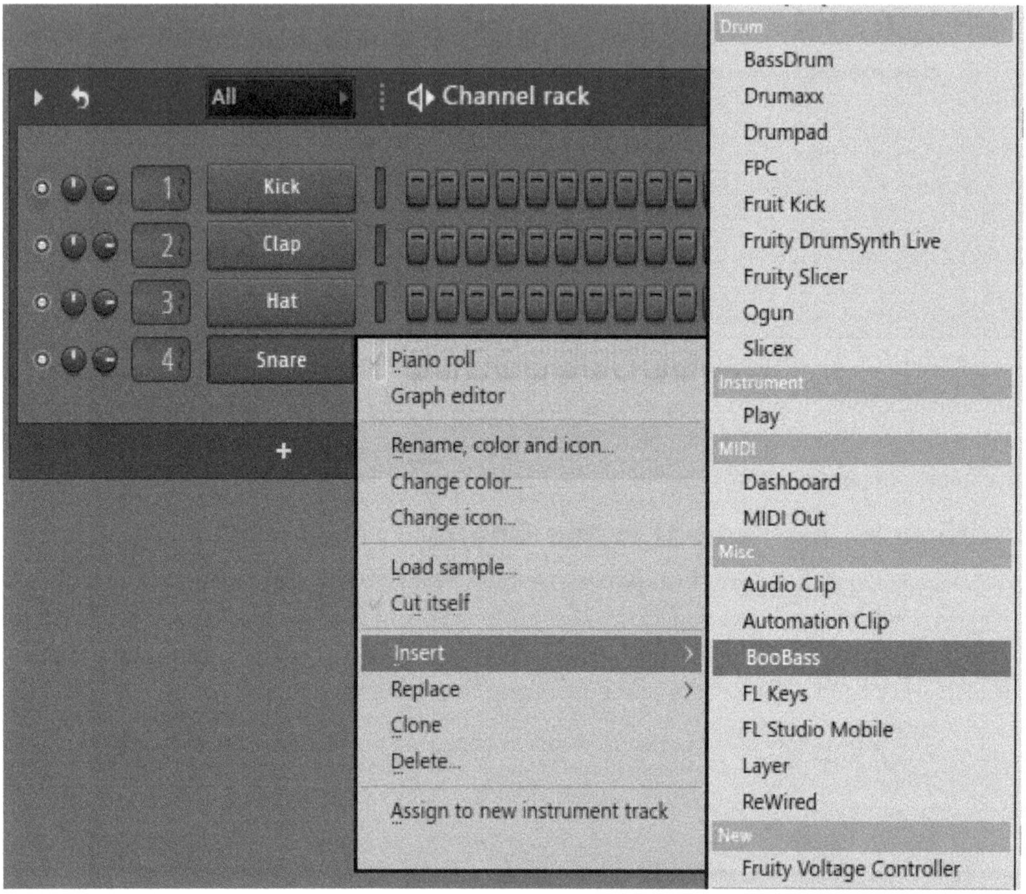

Figure 1.9 – Inserting an instrument

The **BooBass** instrument will load up, and you'll see the following:

Figure 1.10 – BooBass

3. Let's add some notes for our BooBass instrument to play. Right-click on **BooBass** and select **Piano roll**.

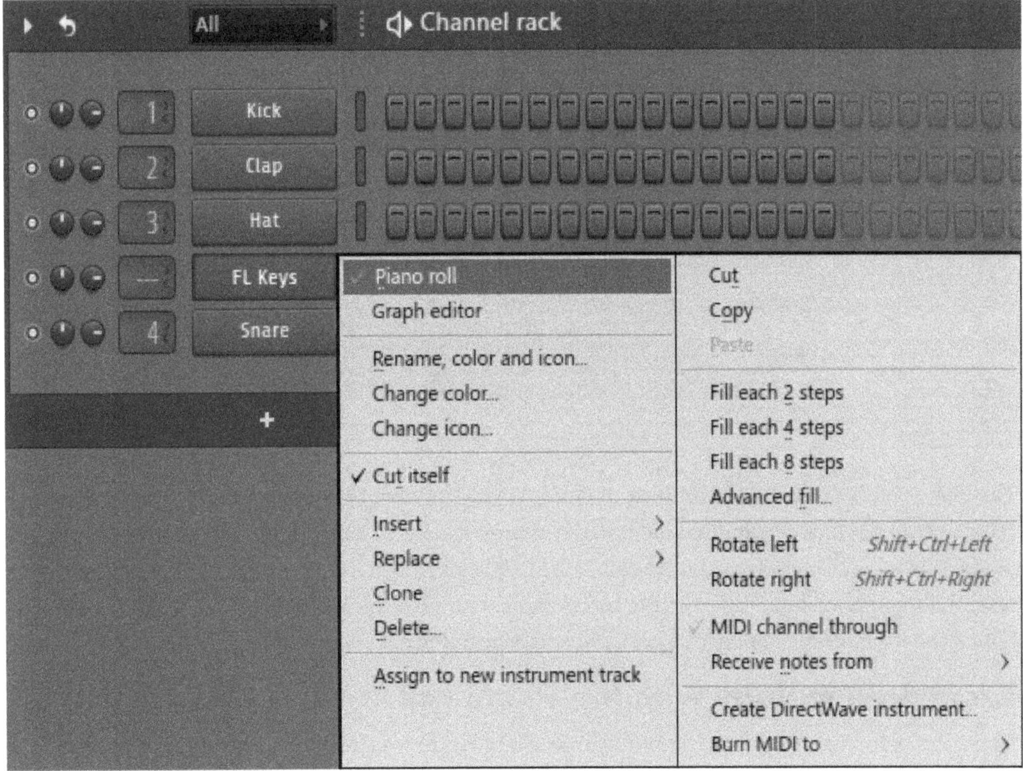

Figure 1.11 – Opening Piano roll

The **Piano roll** will open, and you'll see the following window:

Figure 1.12 – Empty Piano roll

The Piano roll is designed to combine a piano with a timeline from left to right. On the left, you'll see black and white rectangular boxes that represent piano keys. If you know how to play the piano, this will feel very intuitive to you. To the right of it, you'll see a series of blue boxes in what resembles a spreadsheet table. These boxes indicate a position in time. By adding notes, you are telling the instrument to play a certain pitch at a certain time.

Creating a melody with the Piano roll

So far, we've loaded up an instrument. It's time to give the instrument some notes to play:

1. You can add notes by left-clicking in the blue boxes. Add notes to the **Piano roll** to create a melody similar to the following:

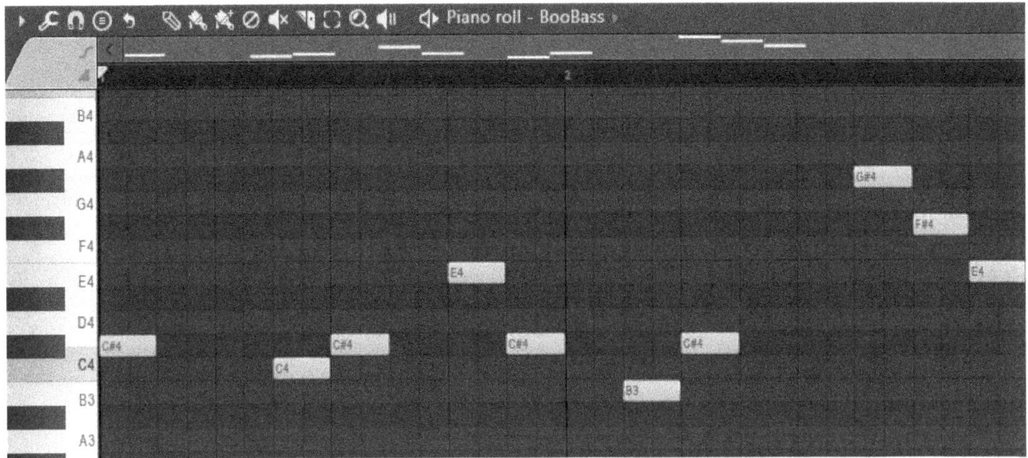

Figure 1.13 – Added notes to the Piano roll instrument

Great, we've now created a simple bass melody.

2. Let's add the drum beat and our bass melody to our **Playlist**. The Playlist is where you can arrange the timing of your music patterns. Open the **Playlist** by selecting the **Playlist** icon.

Figure 1.14 – Playlist icon

The **Playlist** will now open, and you'll see a window similar to the following:

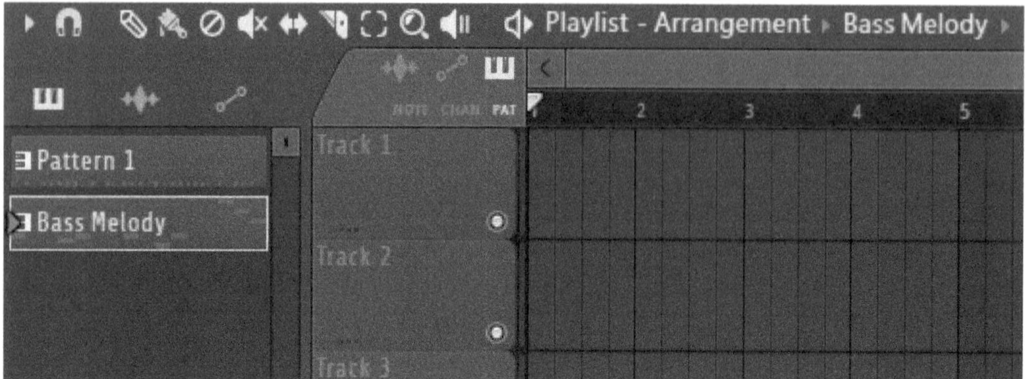

Figure 1.15 – Playlist

3. On the left side, you'll see **Pattern 1** and **Bass melody**. Pattern 1 is our drum beat. Bass melody is the melody that we just created. You can add the patterns to the **Playlist** by left-clicking the patterns on the left and dragging them onto the blue grid on the right. Once done, it will look like the following:

Figure 1.16 – Added patterns to the Playlist

4. Let's play our entire arrangement and see how the patterns sound when played at the same time. Ensure that the setting is set to **SONG** instead of **PAT** and press the **play** symbol (triangle symbol) at the top of the screen, as shown in the following screenshot. You will now be able to hear both of your music patterns being played at the same time.

Figure 1.17 – Player menu

So far, we have created a drum pattern, added an accompanying instrument, and added both patterns to the **Playlist**. Now, we need to route these instruments to the **Mixer**.

Routing channels to the Mixer

It's time to think about mixing our music. Mixing is where we can add effects to our music to enhance it. We need to send our sounds to the **Mixer** in order to apply effects to them. This is known as **routing** to the **Mixer**. We will go into the details of the mixing effects that we can apply in later chapters.

Let's *route* our instruments and samples to the Mixer:

1. Open up the **Channel rack**.

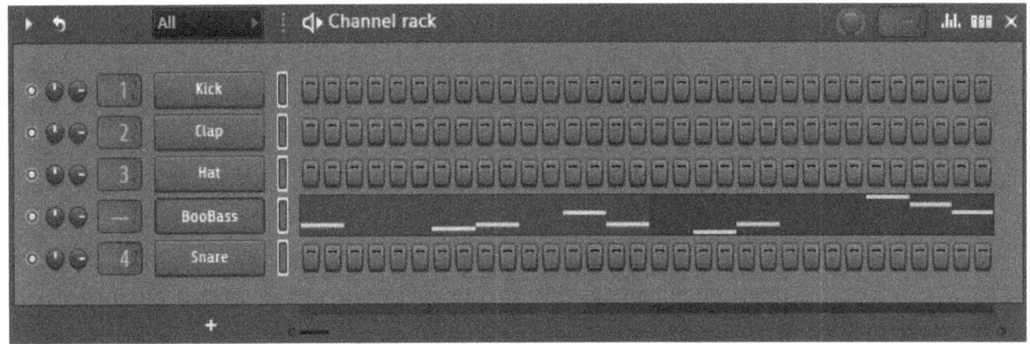

Figure 1.18 – Selecting channels in the Channel rack

   In the preceding screenshot, we can see that **Kick** has the number **1** beside it by default. This means that it is currently routed to **mixer track channel 1**. **Clap** is routed to **track 2**, and **Hat** is routed to **track 3**.

2. Our **BooBass** instrument has no mixer track channel number assigned. Let's route it to the **Mixer**. Double-left-click the rectangle buttons directly to the right of the instruments. This will highlight all of the available instruments with a green outline, as in the preceding screenshot, indicating that they are selected.

3. Next, press *Ctrl* + *L*. This will automatically assign **BooBass** and all other selected instruments to the **Mixer**, as well as any color properties given to them. Alternatively,

you can manually change the Mixer number by clicking on the number and dragging it up or down to increase or decrease the value. You'll see that **BooBass** now has the number **5** assigned to it. This means it has been assigned to mixer track 5:

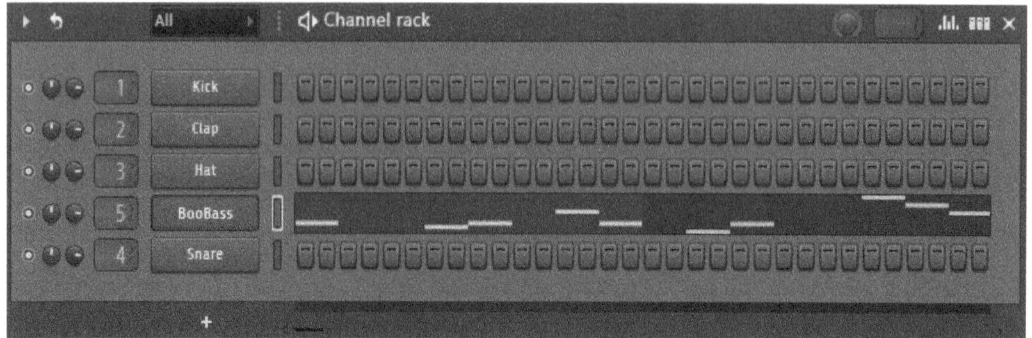

Figure 1.19 – Routing BooBass to the Mixer

4. Let's see our routed instrument in the **Mixer**. Select the **Mixer** icon from the Toolbar to open up the **Mixer**.

Figure 1.20 – Mixer icon in the Toolbar

In the **Mixer**, we can now see that our instruments from the **Channel rack** have been assigned channels in the **Mixer**. Notice how the numbers on the **Channel rack** correspond to the numbers on the **Mixer**. The Mixer channel track numbers can also be changed by selecting a Mixer channel, holding down *Shift*, and scrolling with your mouse wheel.

Figure 1.21 – Mixer

We have routed our instruments to the **Mixer**. At the moment, we won't do anything with the Mixer. Our goal was just to show you the overall flow of adding instruments and routing them. In future chapters, we'll learn how to apply effects to our instruments in the Mixer.

Exporting the song

Let's export our song out of FL Studio so that we can listen to it anywhere. Songs, when played on your phone or streaming online, are stored in the format of an MP3 or WAV file, so we need to convert them to one of those. To do this, follow these instructions:

1. First, check that the **SONG** setting is selected so we export our entire composition rather than just a single pattern.

Figure 1.22 – Player menu

2. Next, go to **FILE** | **Export** | **MP3 file...**, as seen in the following screenshot:

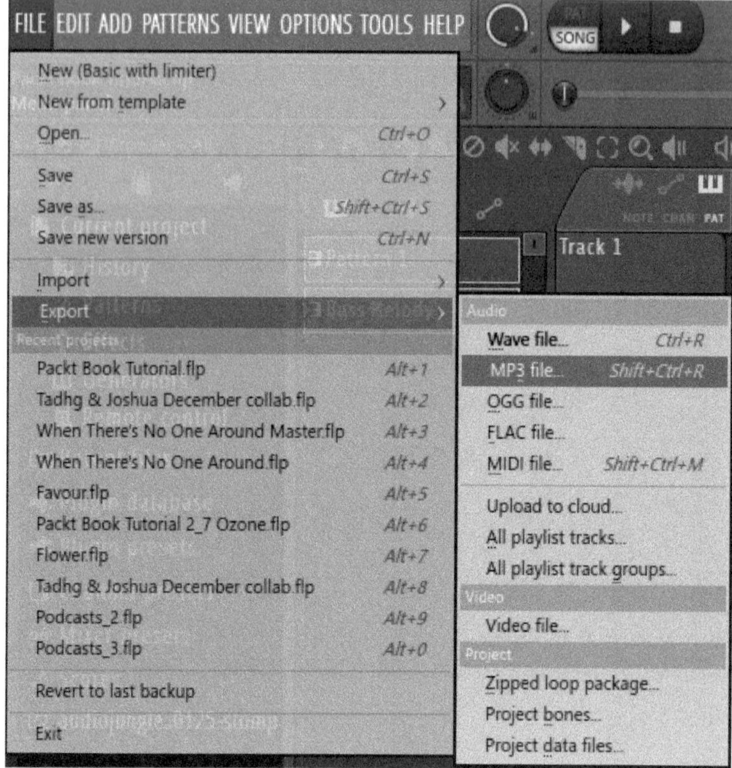

Figure 1.23 – Exporting the song

3. Choose a location on your computer to save your song.

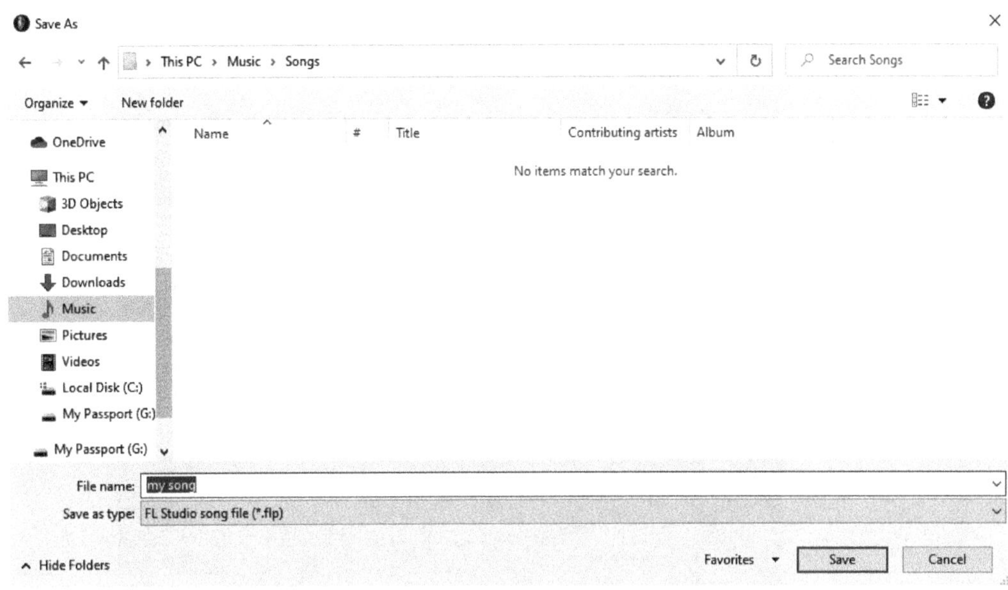

Figure 1.24 – Saving the song

4. Once you select **Save**, a window will pop up with information on rendering. This window gives you options on how to export your song. If you want to export quickly with the default settings, you can choose **WAV** or **MP3** and select **Start** to export your song.

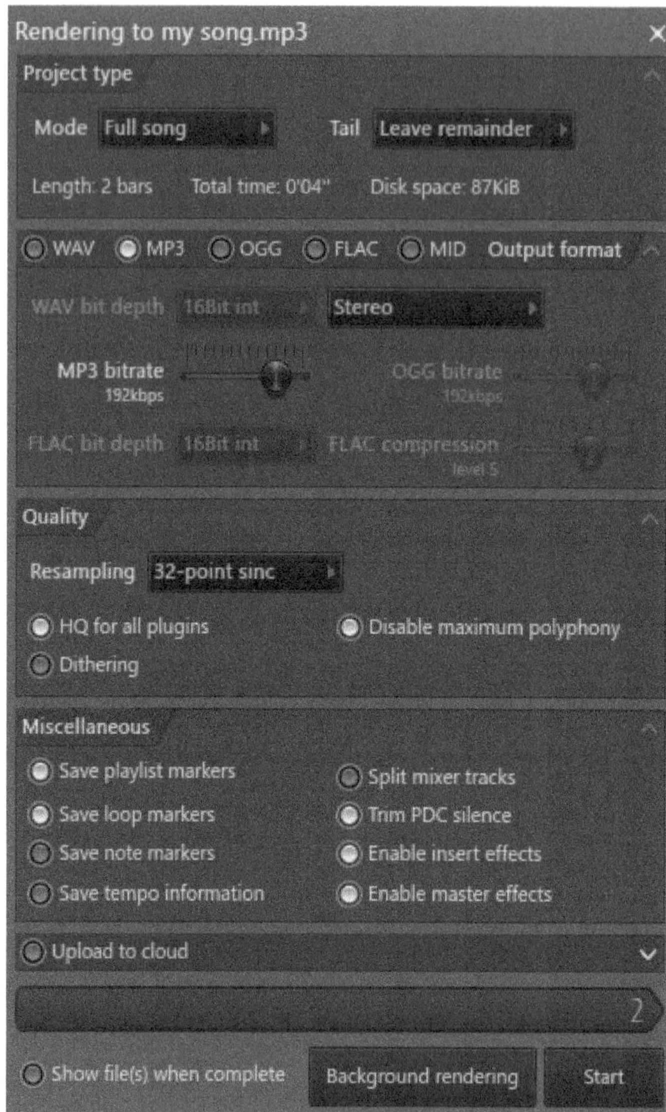

Figure 1.25 – Song render

Congratulations, you have successfully created your first song!

Song exporting options

If you're curious about the exporting features, here's a breakdown of the export settings. In the **Project type** options, you can choose to export your full song or just a single pattern.

The **Tail** option has three choices to pick from:

- **Cut remainder** abruptly ends the song the moment the sound and samples stop playing.
- **Leave remainder** allows synthesizers to naturally decay to silence at the end of your song. This is usually the choice you'll want in most scenarios.
- **Wrap remainder** takes any decay that would appear at the end of your song and places it at the start of your song. This is useful in circumstances where you are creating a loop and want the sound to repeat.

Underneath, you can see the song length, the total elapsed time of the song, and the size of the file the exported song will create.

You can choose between several output format types. You can choose to export as **WAV** or **FLAC**, which are lossless formats, meaning you will not lose any audio quality. Bit depth is the resolution you can choose to output. The options available are as follows:

- **16Bit**, the standard for CD quality
- **24Bit**, recommended for streaming
- **32Bit**, for sound archive size

FLAC uses data compression to reduce the file size; however, the sound will be identical to a WAV file. You can then increase the **FLAC** compression, which will make the file size smaller, but it still won't affect the sound quality; it will just take a little longer to export.

MP3 and OGG are formats that will lose audio quality when exporting. They throw away data while maintaining audio sound. MP3 bitrate determines the audio quality. A higher bitrate allows higher quality sound.

The MID format allows you to export your project as MIDI data, assuming that you created MIDI data in your project.

You also have the option of selecting output in Stereo or Mono. This refers to whether you allow different sounds to come out of the left versus the right speaker. You'll want to leave this as **Stereo**.

The **Quality** section refers to dithering, which is a highly technical topic, but as a general rule, leave it on because it improves audio quality.

Under **Miscellaneous**, you'll want to make sure that the **Enable insert effects** and **Enable master effects** options are selected so that your Mixer effects are applied. Leave **Trim PDC silence** on. This adds any necessary silence at the beginning of your track to ensure that the sounds are in sync. **Split mixer tracks** is what you'll use if you want to export a different sound file for each mixer track. You do this if you want to send your song to a third party for mixing or mastering.

Congratulations, you've just created your first song in FL Studio! That was quick and easy, wasn't it? In just a few minutes, you were able to create a drumbeat, add an accompanying instrument, compose a melody, and export your music.

Summary

You've had a glimpse of the journey ahead on your way to producing your own music. In this chapter, we created our first song in FL Studio. We made a simple drum pattern, added an accompanying instrument and melody, routed the instruments to the Playlist and the Mixer, and exported the song. All songs you make will use these steps.

Congratulations, you've taken the first step in your music journey and made your first song. This is only the tiniest taste of what FL Studio offers. In the pages ahead, we'll dive into the vast treasure trove and explore all the incredible tools FL Studio offers.

In the next chapter, we will explore some key FL Studio workbench tools in detail, including the Browser, Channel rack, and Playlist.

Get this book's PDF version and more

Scan the QR code (or go to `packtpub.com/unlock`). Search for this book by name, confirm the edition, and then follow the steps on the page.

Note: Keep your invoice handy. Purchases made directly from Packt don't require an invoice.

2

Exploring the Browser, Playlist, and Channel Rack

It would take a very long time to create a song if you had to learn how to play every single instrument in a band from scratch. Thankfully, FL Studio has five main tools you can reuse in every song you make, regardless of the genre or style. These tools are the **Browser**, **Channel rack**, **Playlist**, **Piano roll**, and **Mixer**. In this chapter, we will discuss three of these tools: the **Browser**, **Channel rack**, and **Playlist**.

The Browser is where you organize and access all your sounds, samples, plugins, and presets so you can quickly drag them into your project. The Channel rack is where you load those sounds or instruments and create patterns, such as drum loops, melodies, or basslines, using step sequencing. The Playlist is where you arrange those patterns, along with audio clips and automation, to build the structure of your full song. In short, the Browser helps you find your resources, the Channel rack lets you create musical building blocks, and the Playlist is where you assemble everything into a complete track.

If you are new to FL Studio, these tools may seem like a lot of information to process all at once. Don't worry, you don't need to know everything about these tools, especially not at the start. You can just have a quick skim through this chapter to get the basics. Once you've got a few songs under your belt, you can come back to this chapter and examine these tools in greater detail.

In this chapter, we will cover the following topics:

- Choosing FL Studio themes
- Using the Browser to manage your samples
- The Channel rack – organize instrument and program loops
- The Playlist – arrange your songs

- Using the Split by Channel tool to add instruments efficiently
- Version control to back up your projects
- Using Gopher chat assistant (ChatGPT for FL Studio)
- Getting sounds and plugins using FL Studio Cloud
- Introducing Loop Starter – the fastest way to get started
- Additional tricks and tips

Technical requirements

This chapter requires FL Studio. You can download a free trial version or a paid version of FL Studio from `https://www.image-line.com/`.

Choosing FL Studio themes

Before we begin explaining all the tools in FL Studio, let's make your FL Studio experience an enjoyable one. One of the neat aspects of FL Studio is that you get to choose how it looks. First, let's select a color theme for your FL Studio interface. The theme will color the tools you use in FL Studio. It won't change how the tools work, but it can make your FL Studio experience more enjoyable. Sometimes you need inspiration, and a different color theme may be all you need to get your creative juices flowing.

You can choose a theme by selecting **OPTIONS** | **Theme settings**, as shown in the following screenshot.

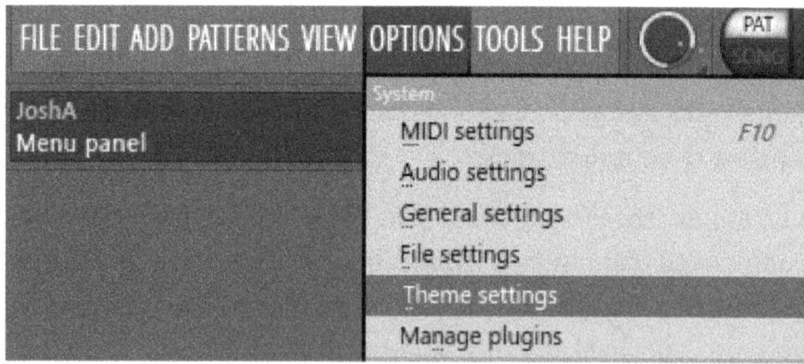

Figure 2.1 – Theme settings

A list of themes appears as shown in the following screenshot.

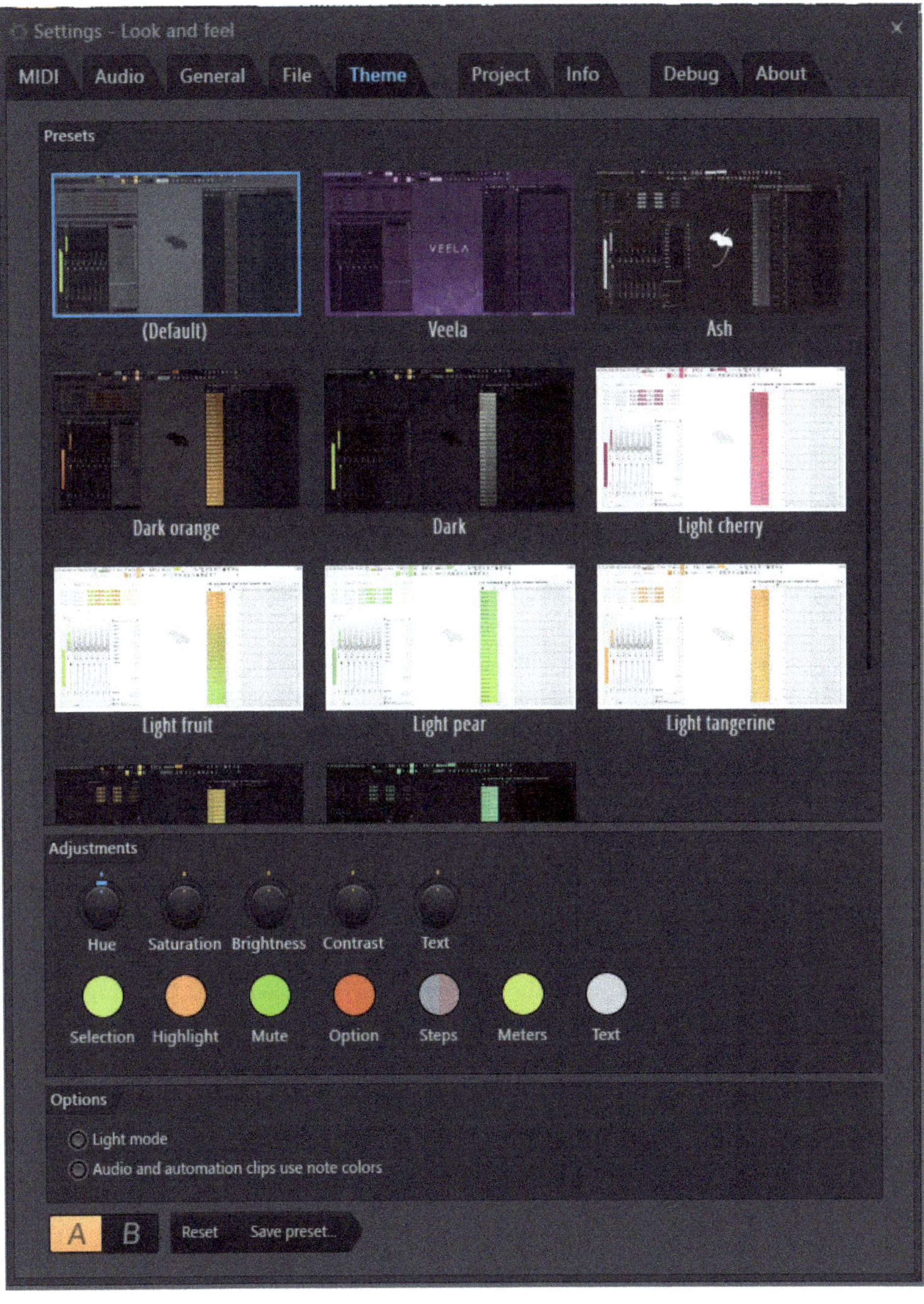

Figure 2.2 – Theme options

You can select a color theme for FL Studio. There is an adjustments section for further control if you want to change the color of specific elements. If you mess up, you can always go back to the **Default** theme preset. You now know how to choose a color theme for FL Studio.

Description text for every tool in FL Studio

There is a handy feature that tells you the name of everything your mouse cursor hovers over. At the top left, under **FILE**, you'll see some description text.

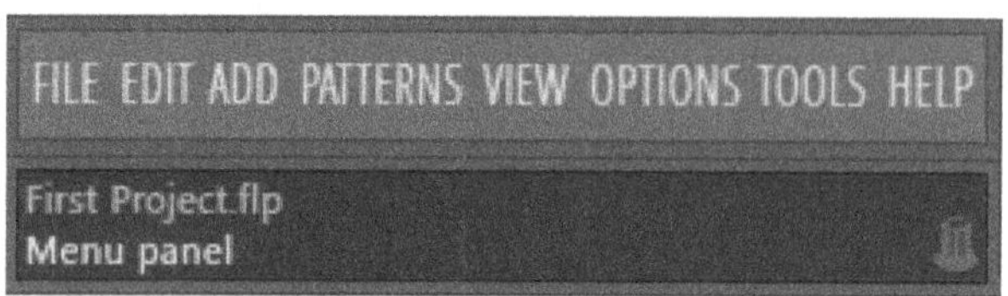

Figure 2.3 – Description text

For everything in FL Studio, if you hover over an item with your cursor, a description of the tool will appear here. For brevity's sake, we will describe only essential features—**player**, **metronome**, **tempo tapper**—that are not self-explanatory by reading the description when you hover over them.

To the right of the description text, you will see the **player**. This lets you play your compositions.

Figure 2.4 – Player

The player allows you to switch between playing a pattern and the whole song. It can play, pause, stop, and record input. You can control the global volume, the pitch, and the number of music beats that are played per minute (known as **BPM**). This is the speed or tempo of your song.

Directly to the right of the BPM number value, you'll see the **metronome** icon.

Figure 2.5 – Metronome

The metronome is used to give a timing reference. If selected, a click track will play, giving a click sound in time with the beat when a song or pattern is playing. To turn it off, simply click it again.

What if you're not sure what BPM number to use, but intuitively you know how fast the song is when you sing the tune? The **tempo tapper** is a useful feature to quickly get the desired tempo for the song.

Figure 2.6 – The tempo tapper button

The **tempo tapper** icon opens up the **Tempo tapper** plugin.

Figure 2.7 – Tempo tapper plugin

By left-clicking on the **tempo tapper**, the BPM of the composition will adjust to the tempo of your tapping. As you tap faster or slower, you'll notice that the BPM adjusts to the speed of the tapping. I find this very useful if I'm playing a live instrument and want FL Studio to match the same timing I'm playing at.

So far, we've seen how to play our song and adjust the timing of it, theme settings, and description text. Now, let's learn the first tool in creating your songs: the Browser.

Using the Browser to manage your samples

The Browser organizes your samples and instruments, and provides convenient access to easily insert and swap them in and out of your project. Before we understand how the Browser organizes samples, we need to know what samples are.

Samples are audio files that have been created for use in music production. Samples are usually sold in a bundle, known as a sample pack. There are many sample packs available for free online that you can easily find with a quick Google search. There are also premium paid samples for purchase.

When you're producing music, samples are useful. They can inspire you to get started. A sample pack may give you a head start in learning how to make sounds in a specific genre of music. For example, if you like house-style dance music, an **electronic dance music** (**EDM**) sample pack can give you sounds that are commonly used in EDM, such as EDM-style percussive kicks, FX impacts, and riser sounds. I personally have a collection of percussion and FX one-shot samples that I frequently use in my songs.

However, buying sample packs is an easy way to get sucked into spending a lot of money on products that you'll never use. In particular, I recommend avoiding buying sample packs that use the name *construction kit* and say they contain an entire completed song. A **construction kit** contains a fully created song that is fully finished, straight out of the box. I find these to be a waste of money. What you want to be doing is creating your own music, rather than copying what someone else has already made.

Sample packs may include MIDI note examples. These are note arrangements that can be loaded into your instrument plugin. These can then be tweaked to your liking afterward. If you're new to composing chord progressions, observing existing chord progressions can be instructive.

There are many sites out there that offer free and paid *royalty-free* audio samples for your compositions. Royalty-free means that the sample is legally allowed to be used without copyright infringement. **FL Cloud** contains samples available for download, which we will discuss later in this chapter. Other recommended sites with samples for purchase include `www.pluginboutique.com` and `loopmasters.com`.

Tip

A word of caution on samples: if you think you need to buy samples to become good at music producing, you're headed in the wrong direction. I personally made this mistake when I started and spent a lot of money on samples before realizing that I wouldn't be using them most of the time. Samples are most useful once you're already comfortable with producing music. If you're starting out and new to music producing, it's a much better investment of your time and money to master your instrument plugins and effects and create sounds yourself, rather than going out and buying samples. You want to be able to make original sounds from scratch so that you develop your own signature style.

We learned what samples are. Now, let's learn how to use them in our composition. For that, we turn to the Browser, which contains and organizes all the samples in our song.

Let's explore the Browser features:

1. Open the **Browser** by selecting the **Browser** icon, which is usually at the top center of FL Studio by default.

Figure 2.8 – Browser icon

The **Browser** window will open up with a list of folder names. You can see a list of various samples, instruments, and effects organized by folder name. You can think of this just like any other folder on your computer. They are simply there to provide you with convenient shortcuts to your files:

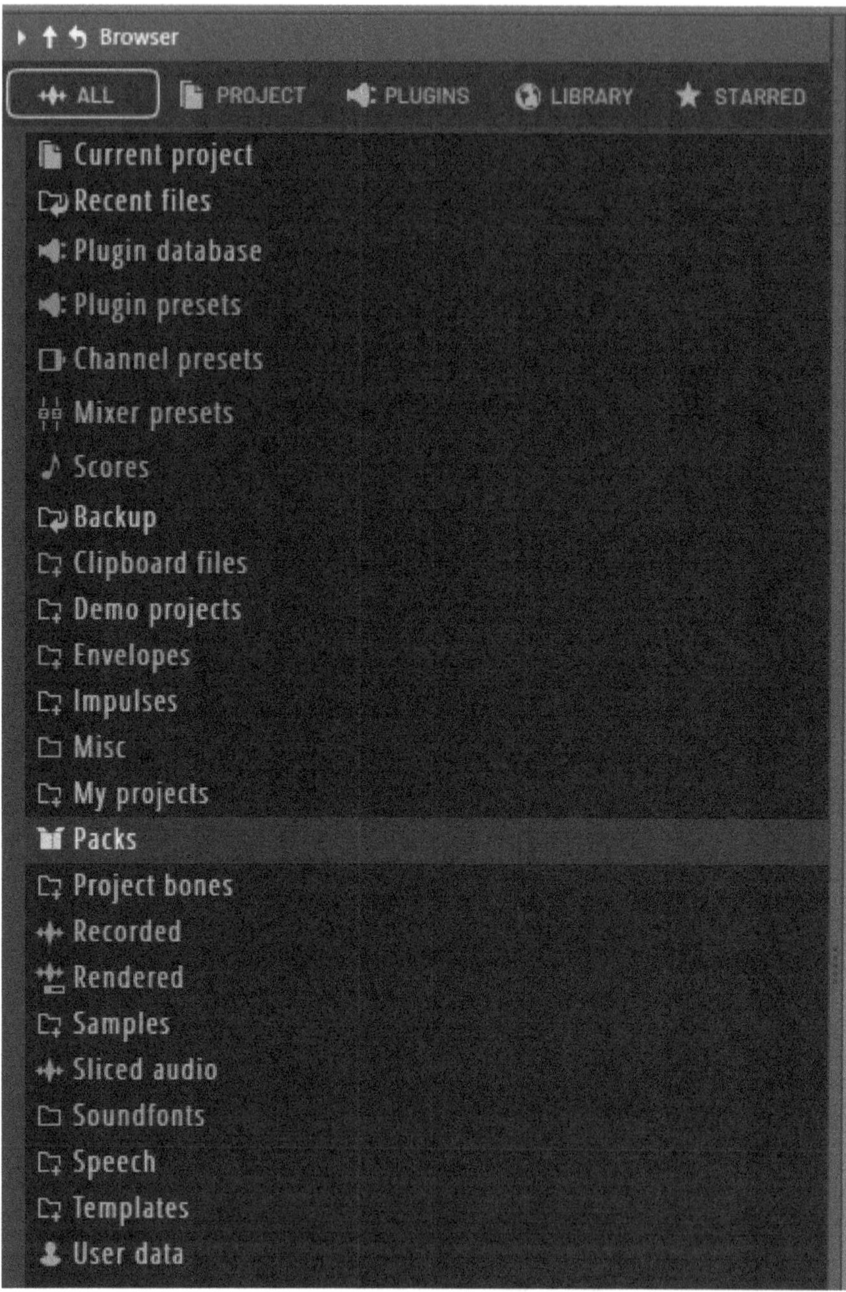

Figure 2.9 – The Browser

You can navigate the folders using the arrow keys on your keyboard. The right arrow key will open the selected folder, while the left arrow key will close the folder and move to the level above it.

2. Let's take a look at the samples inside some of the folders. Click the icon that says **Packs**. Within the **Packs** folder, we can see a list of folders with instruments and samples.

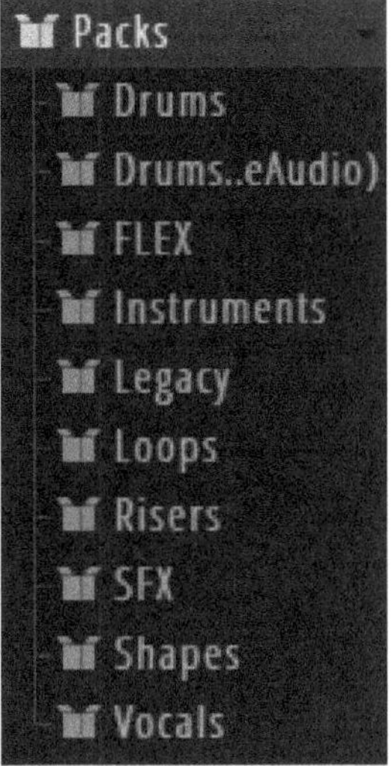

Figure 2.10 – Packs

3. Select one of the folders, such as **Vocals**
   A list of vocal sound samples becomes viewable. You can listen to any sample preview by clicking on it.

Figure 2.11 – Vocals

4. Let's bring a sample into the **Playlist**. You'll need to have the Playlist open to do this, which can be done by selecting the **Playlist** icon, which is usually at the top center of FL Studio.

Figure 2.12 – Playlist icon

By selecting the **Playlist** icon, the **Playlist** window will open up. The **Browser** and the **Playlist** are now both viewable side by side. The Playlist is where you'll combine all your samples together for your song.

5. Let's bring a sample into the Playlist. Left-click on a sample in the **Browser** and drag it into your **Playlist**, into an empty area of the blue grid.

Figure 2.13 – Adding a sample to the Playlist

We have successfully brought a sample from the **Browser** into the **Playlist**. You can now play the song and hear the sample play in time with your music patterns.

> **Note**
>
> You can drag multiple clips from the **Browser** into the **Playlist** at the same time.

Locating a sample's file location

At some point, you'll have a song with a bunch of samples, and you'll want to find where the samples came from to find similar sounds. FL Studio makes it easy to find the folder that samples were taken from:

1. First, double-left-click on the sample in your **Playlist**. A window will pop up that looks like the following:

Figure 2.14 – Vocal sample

Here, we can see a list of controls over the sample. We will explore these controls in detail later in *Chapter 5*.

2. Click on the **Locate sample in Browser** icon.

Figure 2.15 – Locate sample in Browser icon

This will navigate to the location of the sample in the **Browser**.

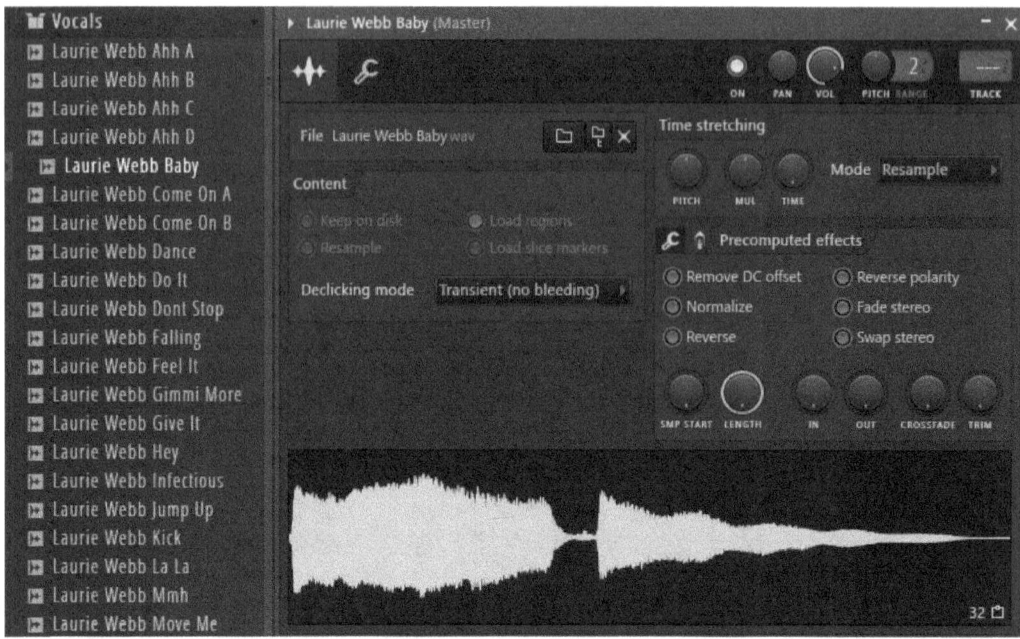

Figure 2.16 – Navigating to the sample location

We can now see the sample location in the **Browser** and any other samples in the same folder. This process makes it very easy to find similar samples.

As practice, drag a bunch of samples from the **Browser** into the **Playlist**. Then play your song and hear how the samples sound.

Next, let's look at how to search for samples by name.

Searching in the Browser

At the bottom of the **Browser**, you'll find the Browser search bar. You can type text into the search bar, press *Enter*, and the **Browser** will bring up any samples or instruments that have the included search text in the name. If you want to find only results that have the exact name, surround your text with quotation marks. For example, `"808 Kick"`.

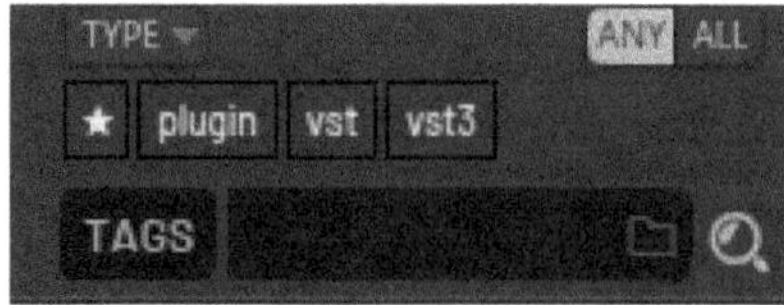

Figure 2.17 – Browser search bar

You can press the **TAGS** button at the bottom left of the search bar to reveal the additional search filter options, as shown in the preceding screenshot. You'll notice the following filters: **star**, **plugin**, **vst**, and **vst3**. These are filters that narrow your search results.

If you want to add a specific sample, **plugin**, **vst**, or **vst3** to your favorites tag list, right-click on the item in the **Browser** and select the option **Favorite** as shown in the following screenshot.

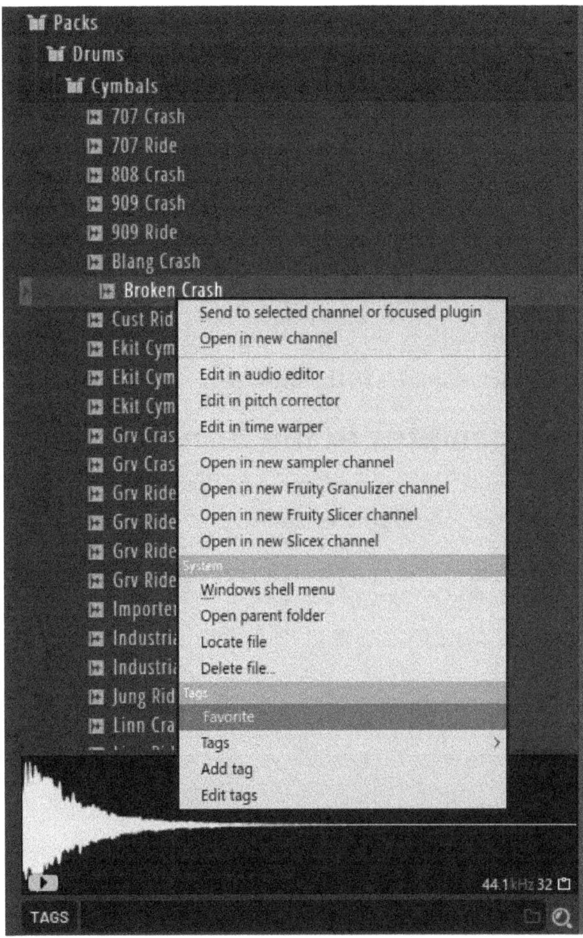

Figure 2.18 – Favorite tag

This will favorite the item. You can then quickly access it in the **STARRED** favorites section of the **Browser**. Alternatively, you can simply hover over the sample in the **Browser** and left-click on the star symbol that appears to the right of it.

Figure 2.19 – Browser STARRED samples

Now that you've found the sample, you can left-click on it to play a preview of it. If this isn't the sample that you're looking for and you want to see the next result, you can press *F3* to skip to the next search result. You can press *F2* to go to the previous result. You now know how to navigate the **Browser**.

Next, let's learn how to add new samples to the **Browser**.

Adding your own samples to the Browser

If you acquire additional samples online, you can add them as a new folder in the **Browser**. To add a new folder of samples, take the following steps:

1. Go to the drop-down arrow in the top-left corner of the **Browser** and select **Configure extra folders**.

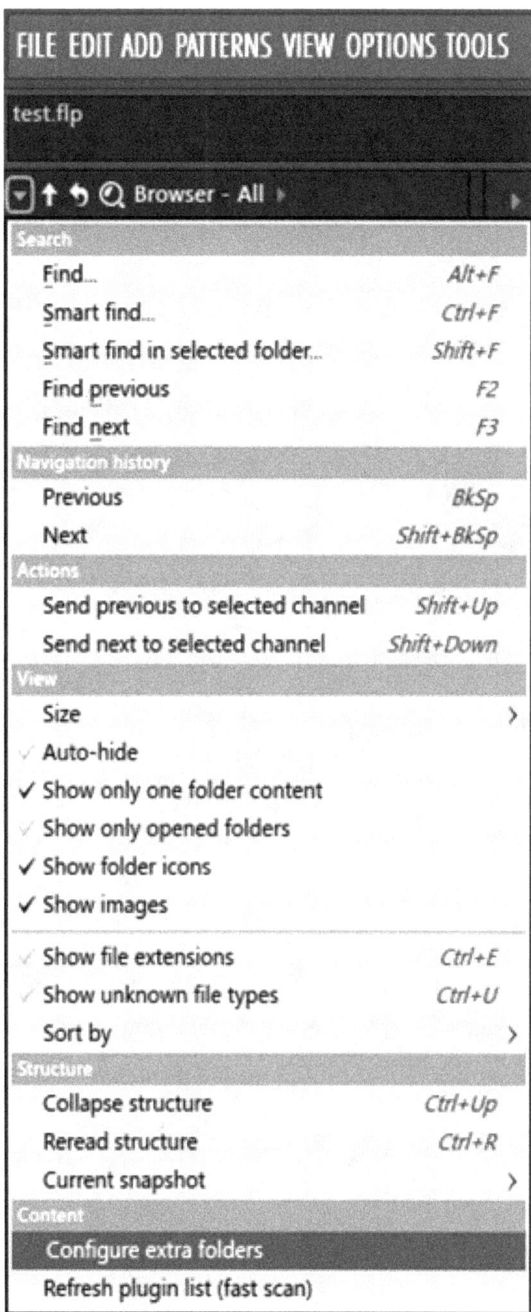

Figure 2.20 – Configure extra folders

2. This will open the **Settings - Files & folders** window.

Figure 2.21 – Settings - Files & folders window

Here, you can click on any folder icon under **Browser extra search folders** and navigate to the folder containing your samples. This will add your new folder to the **Browser**. You can now go back to your **Browser** and see the new folder with your samples.

You now know how to add samples to the **Browser**. Next, let's learn how to swap samples in and out of the **Playlist** from your **Browser**.

Swapping samples

Frequently, you'll insert a sample into your Playlist and realize it's not a sound you like, but you like the timing position of the sample in the Playlist. FL Studio makes it easy to swap one sample with another while retaining the timing position and **mixer track routing**.

You can easily swap out one sample with another. To swap samples, left-click on a sample in the **Playlist** that you want to replace, hover your mouse over the sample, then, using the scroll wheel of your mouse, select the sample you want to replace it with in the **Browser**. This will swap the sample in the **Playlist** with the sample in the **Browser**.

So far, we've looked at how the **Browser** can be used to bring in samples for use in our compositions. Next, let's look at how to load up instruments in the Channel rack.

The Channel rack – organize instrument and program loops

The Channel rack contains the instruments and samples you are currently using in a music pattern. It's here in the Channel rack that you'll add and remove instruments, create percussive rhythms, and flip between **music patterns**. A music pattern is a group of notes that are played by instruments on the Channel rack. Multiple instruments can play notes at the same time in a single pattern.

If you already have an existing project, you can use that. Otherwise, load up a template so that your **Channel rack** has some instruments preloaded to work with. Go to **FILE** | **New from template** | **Minimal** | **Basic 808 with limiter** as shown in the following screenshot.

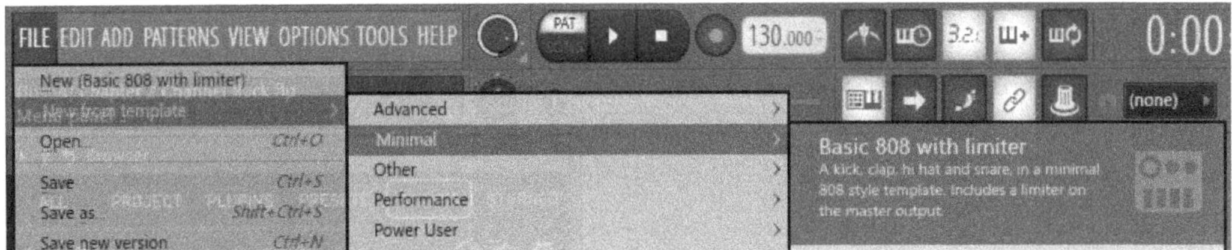

Figure 2.22 – Choose Minimal template

This will populate your **Channel rack** with some instruments. Open up the **Channel rack** by selecting the **Channel rack** icon on the main toolbar:

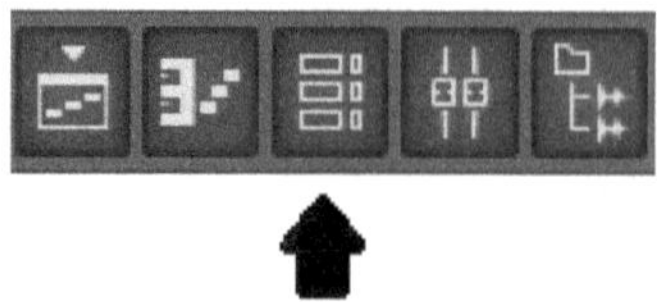

Figure 2.23 – Channel rack in the toolbar

The **Channel rack** will open up and show the currently selected music pattern. The following screenshot shows the **Channel rack**:

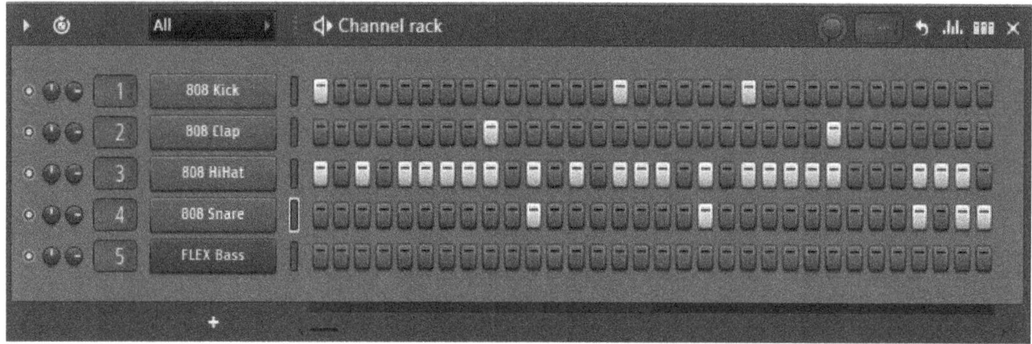

Figure 2.24 – Channel rack pattern

Moving from left to right on the **Channel rack**, first you see a green light to indicate whether the instrument is on or muted (deactivated). Instruments can be turned on or off by left-clicking on the light. If you want to listen to only a single instrument to focus on it, you can play it on its own (known as *soloing* it). To solo the instrument, hold down *Ctrl* and then left-click on the light of the desired instrument. All other instruments will become muted except for your *solo-ed* instrument (the lights will turn off). To unmute everything, hold down *Ctrl* and click the light again. The lights of all other instruments will become active again. This process works exactly the same in the **Playlist** and in the **Mixer**.

Next are the **panning knobs**, which control whether audio comes out of your left or right speaker. By default, audio is set to the middle. This means audio plays out of the left and right speakers equally. The panning can be changed by left-clicking on the panning knob and dragging up or down.

To the right of the panning knobs, you can see the **volume control knobs**. Volume can be changed by left-clicking on the volume knob and dragging up or down.

To the right of the volume knobs, you can see a number representing the Mixer channel that the instrument is currently assigned to. The Mixer channel the instrument is routed to can be changed by hovering over the number and scrolling with your mouse.

To the right of the Mixer channel numbers are the samples and instruments that are currently loaded. To the right of the instrument are the MIDI notes that are actively being played by the instrument.

You can shift instrument notes left or right in the **Channel rack**. This is done by selecting the instrument with notes by left-clicking on the rectangular button directly to the right of the instrument, and then pressing *Ctrl + Shift + the left arrow key* or *Ctrl + Shift + the right arrow key*.

So far, we've seen the components that make up the Channel rack and how to add instruments to it. Now, let's explore how to use the instruments.

Channel rack options features

By right-clicking on one of the instruments, you can see a list of **Channel rack** menu options. In this section, we will work our way through the menu options as shown in the following screenshot:

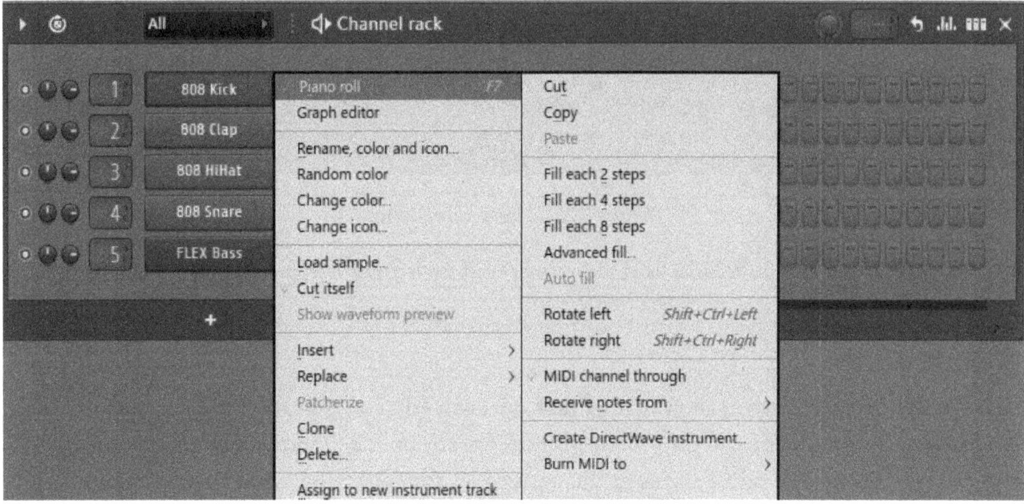

Figure 2.25 – Piano roll option

Let's take a look at them.

Piano roll

The **Piano roll** option opens the selected instrument in the **Piano roll** window.

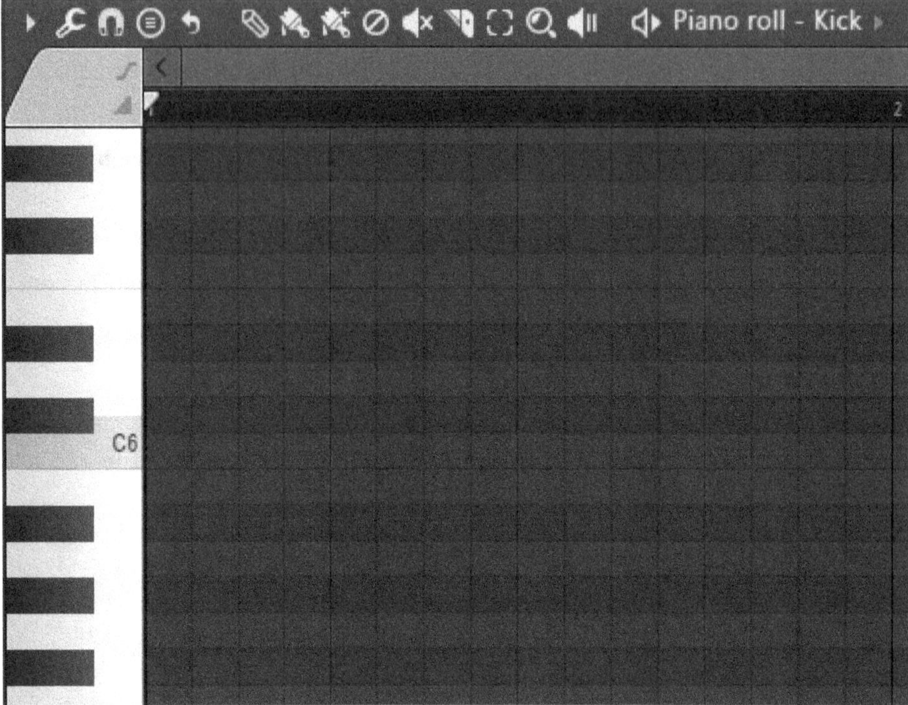

Figure 2.26 – Piano roll window

The **Piano roll** allows you to add notes for a selected instrument. We will explore the **Piano roll** in detail in *Chapter 3*.

Graph editor

Once you've created notes in the Channel rack, you can adjust the properties of the notes. Under the **Piano roll** option, you can find the **Graph editor** option. The **Graph editor** opens up a list of controls to edit the individual notes in the pattern. In the following screenshot, you can see the notes that are currently enabled for the **Piano roll** and the controls underneath to edit them:

Figure 2.27 – Graph editor

Here's a brief summary of the controls in the Graph editor:

- **Note pitch** is what note is being hit.
- **Velocity** is similar to how hard the note is hit. This will only be noticeable on instruments that have percussive volume control built into them. For instance, drum samples tend to have more explosive sounds at higher velocities.
- **Release velocity** is how quickly the sample volume fades away.
- **Fine pitch** allows you to shift the pitch of a sound up or down.
- **Panning** allows you to control whether the audio comes out of the left or right speaker. Used for stylistic effects.
- **Mod X** controls the cutoff of a filter.
- **Mod Y** controls the cutoff of a resonance.
- **Shift** controls the note start time offset.
- **Repeat** repeats the note.

Next in the **Channel rack** option menu list is the **Rename, color, and icon...** option.

Rename, color, and icon option

When you have multiple instruments playing, organization becomes more and more important to keep track of all your sounds, or else it can become a disorganized mess. Visual aids make organization much easier. You can give a custom name and color to your instruments by selecting the **Rename, color, and icon...** option, which will open up the following window:

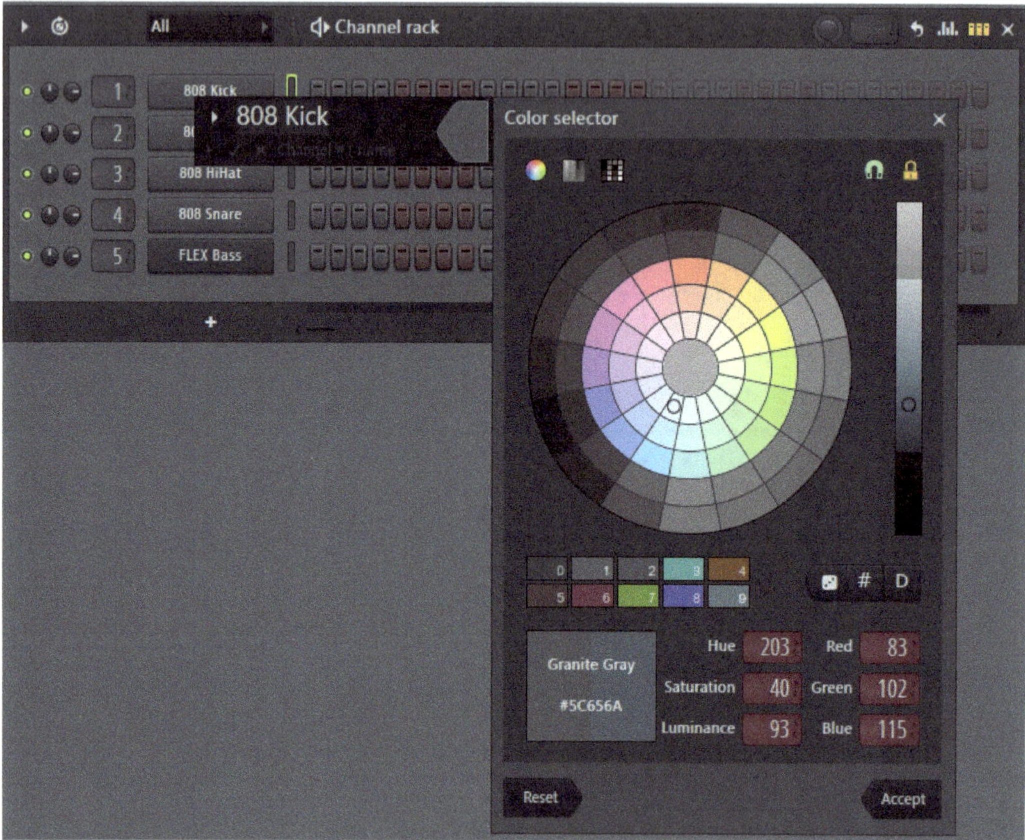

Figure 2.28 – Color selector

Here, you can click on a color to assign it to the instrument.

There is an easy way to quickly color all of your instruments at once, rather than manually choosing a color each time. Under the **Channel rack** drop-down arrow, there's a feature that lets you color all selected instruments at once using either a gradient or a randomly chosen color.

Figure 2.29 – Random color selector

Using **Random** or selecting a gradient is my recommended approach to giving all your selected instruments a color.

Instrument options

Let's return to the drop-down menu that appears after right-clicking an instrument or sample. In the following screenshot, we can see the list of available options:

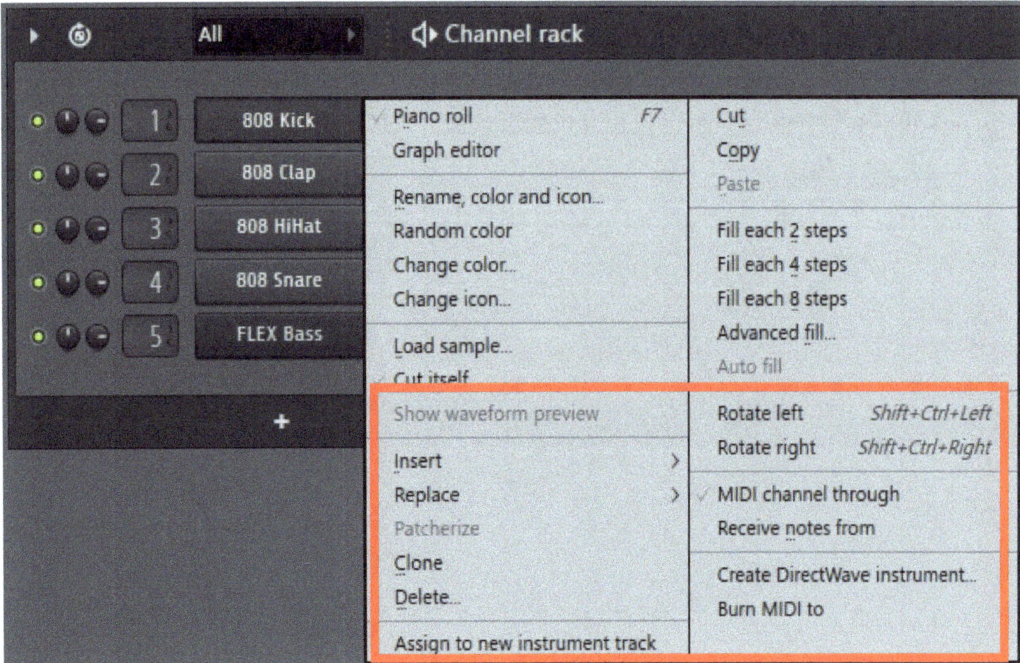

Figure 2.30 – Instrument options

Here's a brief summary of the options:

- **Insert** allows you to insert a new instrument.
- **Replace** works the same way as **Insert** for loading up instruments. It allows you to swap out your current instrument for another.
- **Clone** allows you to copy the instrument, audio, or automation currently in the Channel rack. This only copies the instrument, not the notes played by the instrument.
- **Delete...** allows you to remove the selected track. Alternatively, you can select multiple tracks in the Channel rack at once and press *left Alt* + *Delete* on your keyboard to delete them.

To move notes from one instrument to another, select a single instrument/sample that contains notes and press *Ctrl* + *C* or the copy option (or, alternatively, cut). Then, select a different instrument/sample and press *Ctrl* + *V*. This will paste the notes into the new instrument. You can paste notes into different patterns by switching to a different pattern first and then pasting.

- **Advanced fill** opens up a tool that generates a sequence of notes. Here, you can add notes by left-clicking on the circles around the dial or rotate the dial to move the notes left or right in the pattern. Selecting the die symbol will generate a completely random pattern of notes:

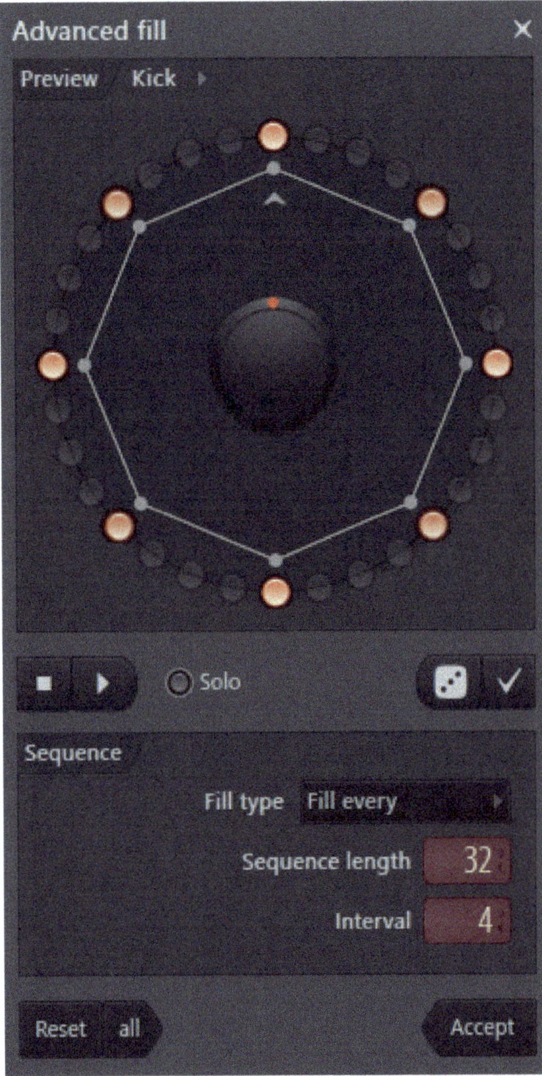

Figure 2.31 – Advanced fill

Detaching windows option

Often, you'll want to have the Channel rack open even while you're looking at other FL Studio tools, such as the Piano roll. You may have noticed that whenever you click away from the **Channel rack**, it tends to get hidden behind whatever else you clicked to focus on. That's annoying. You wanted to have both open at the same time. Luckily, FL Studio has a solution. For all instruments and plugins, you can make the window of the plugin detach so that when you click away from the window, it remains open. I use the **Detached** feature constantly when working, as I need to have multiple windows open at once to move stuff between them. To detach any window, simply go to the drop-down arrow at the top left of the plugin and select the **Detached** option:

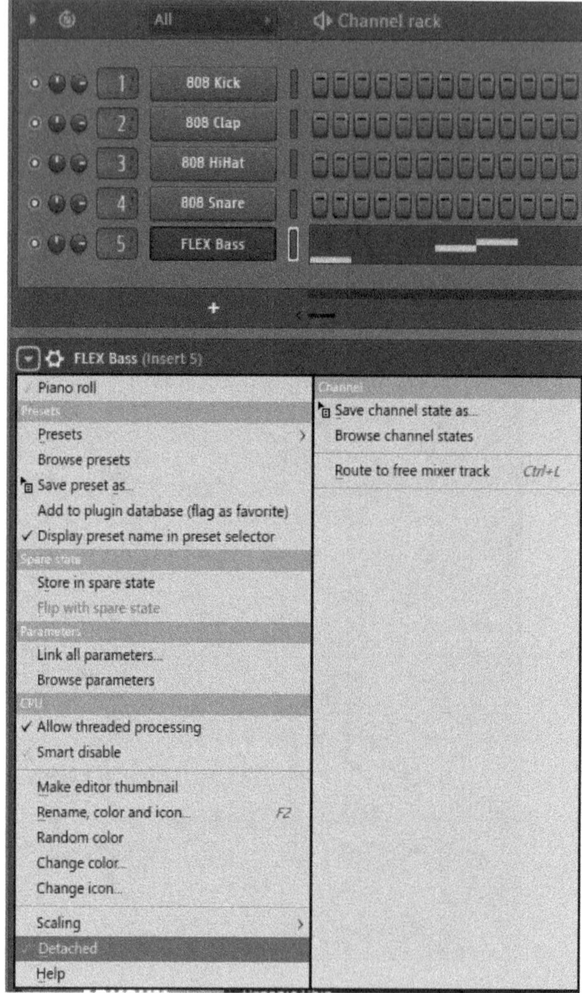

Figure 2.32 – Detached option

Using Channel rack layers

Layers allow you to play several instrument tracks at once. When a layer encounters the notes in the **Piano roll**, all instruments belonging to the layer will play the same notes. If you are stacking several instrument sounds together, this is an efficient way of having all the instruments play identical notes, rather than copying the same notes to all the instruments. To insert a layer, right-click on an instrument, then select **Insert** | **Layer**.

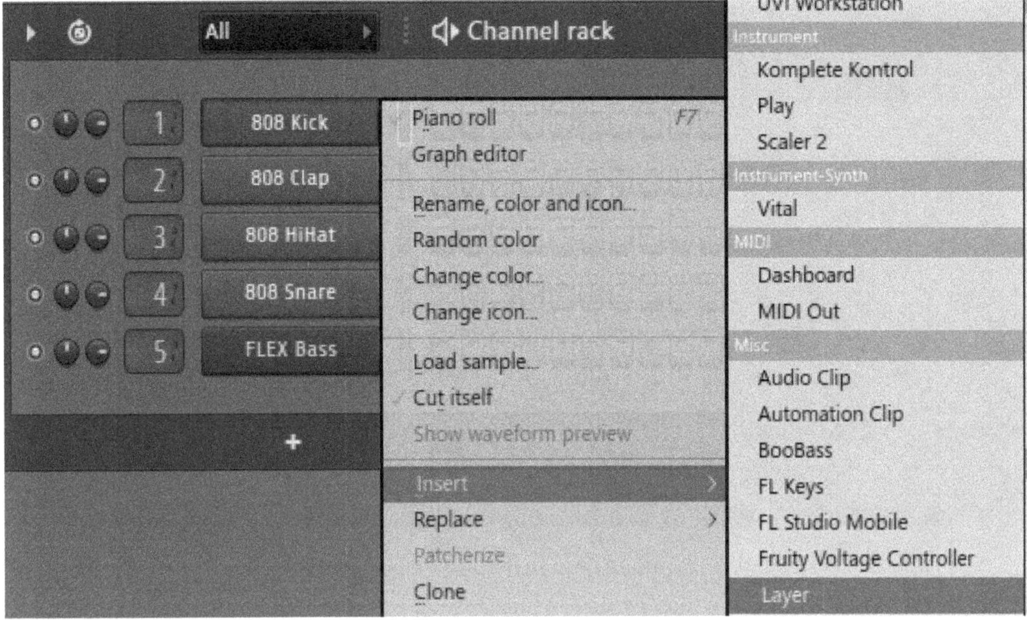

Figure 2.33 – Inserting a layer

A layer will now be created. If you left-click on the layer to open it, a window would pop up. Here, you'll see a button called **Set children**. This allows you to choose which instruments you want to include in the layer.

To use **Set children**, first select or highlight the instruments in the **Channel rack**. To select several at the same time, you will need to hold down the *Shift* key while left-clicking. Once you have your channels selected, return to the layer window and left-click on **Set children**. This will assign the instruments to the layer.

From here on, all instruments in the layer will play any MIDI notes that the layer receives.

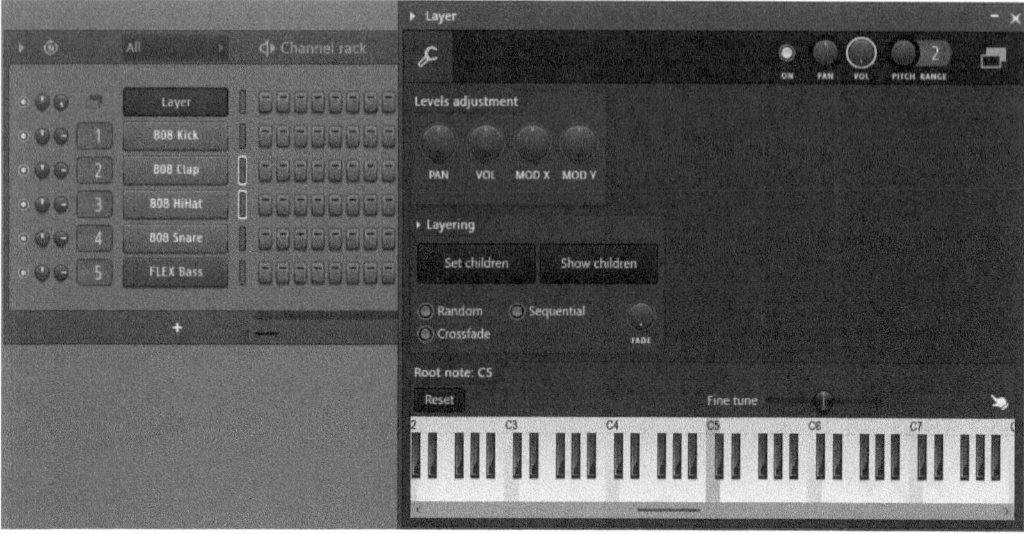

Figure 2.34 – FL Studio plugin manager

If you want to see all instruments currently belonging to the layer, the **Show children** button will highlight the related instruments. If you later need to change which instruments belong to the layer, simply reselect the instruments you want and press **Set children** again. You now know how to use layers to play multiple instruments at the same time.

Next, let's take a look at the Playlist to organize our music patterns.

The Playlist – arrange your songs

The Playlist is where you arrange the timing of all elements for your song. It holds patterns, Audio Clips, and the automation of effects. You can open the **Playlist** by selecting the **Playlist** icon.

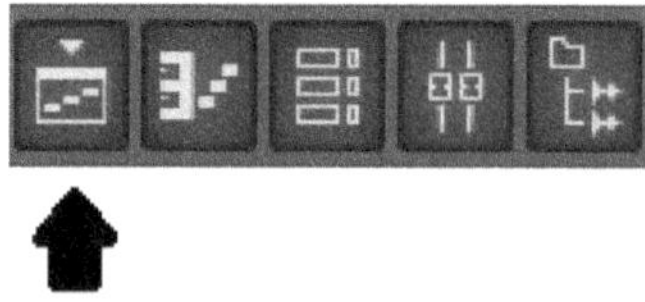

Figure 2.35 – Playlist icon in the toolbar

The **Playlist** will open up, and you will see a window similar to the following:

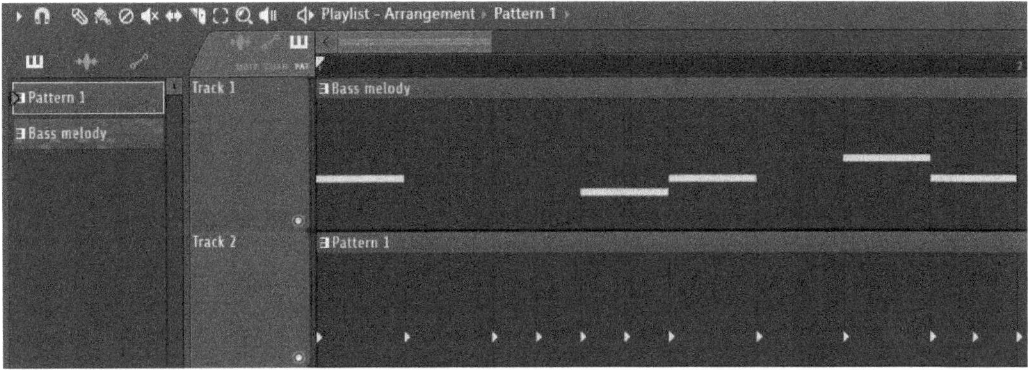

Figure 2.36 – Playlist

On the left-hand side, you can see the pattern, audio, or automation that is currently selected. In the preceding screenshot, we can see that **Pattern 1** is currently selected. We can left-click on patterns and drag them into the **Playlist**.

To the right of the patterns, you can see the name **Track 1** and a light to indicate that the track is active (not muted). You can mute the track by left-clicking on the light. You can customize the name and color of the track by right-clicking on it and selecting **Rename** and **Color**. In the following screenshot, we can see that we have left-clicked on **Bass melody** in the **Playlist** to select it:

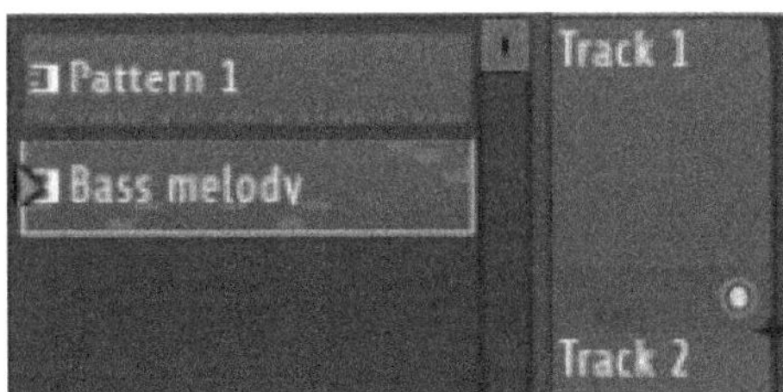

Figure 2.37 – Bass melody

There are several ways to switch between active music patterns. You can either left-click on a pattern to the left of the **Playlist**, as seen in the preceding screenshot, or choose a different pattern from the pattern selector at the top of the screen, as seen in the following screenshot:

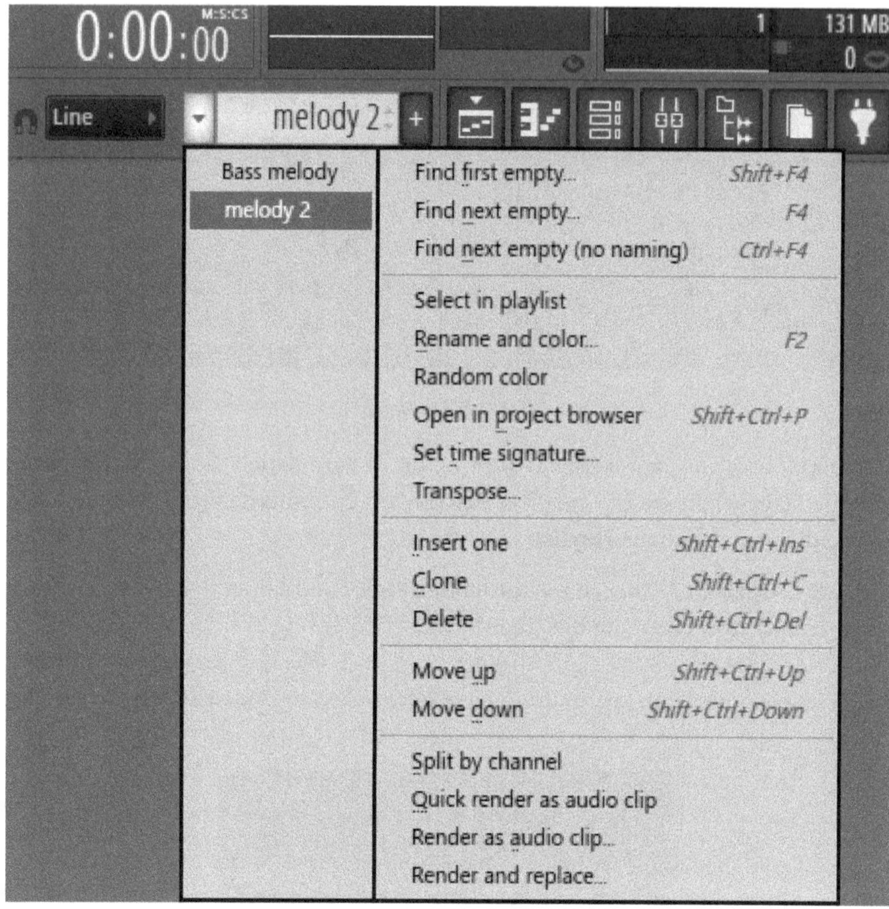

Figure 2.38 – Selecting a pattern

So far, we've looked at the components of the **Playlist**. Now, let's take a look at the tools it offers.

Playlist toolbar

Let's look at the tools available in the **Playlist toolbar**

Figure 2.39 – Playlist toolbar

In the Playlist toolbar, you can see a series of tool icons. Let's go through the tools from left to right, starting with the draw tool (we'll come back to the **Magnet** tool in the next chapter when we look into the **Piano roll** in detail):

- **Draw**: At the top left, you'll see a symbol that looks like a pencil. Selecting this allows you to add the currently selected pattern, sample, or automation to the **Playlist**. Once the **Draw** tool is active, you can left-click anywhere in the **Playlist** to place a selected element. While the **Draw** tool is selected, you can also left-click on any element in the **Playlist** and move it around freely. You'll want the Draw tool active by default most of the time.
- **Paint**: The paint tool is similar to the **Draw** tool except that it continues to add notes as long as you hold down your left click (as opposed to the **Draw** tool, which adds a single note per click).
- **Delete**: The **Delete** tool deletes anything you left-click on while active. You can also delete an element by right-clicking on any element in the **Playlist** while the **Draw** tool is selected.
- **Mute**: The **Mute** tool mutes (deactivates) any element you left-click on while active. If a pattern is muted, all instruments in that pattern are muted.
- **Slip**: The Slip tool shifts the position of notes in any pattern left or right. To do so, click on any pattern with active notes and drag left or right. The notes will shift accordingly.
- **Slice**: This allows you to split an element into pieces at the position clicked.
- **Select**: This allows you to select a group of elements. Another way to select elements is to hold *Ctrl* and left-click, and drag over the elements that you want to select.
- **Zoom**: This allows you to zoom in and out of any element on the **Playlist**. Another way to zoom is to hold down *Ctrl* and scroll with your mouse scroll wheel. This will zoom in or out on your patterns horizontally. To resize the **Playlist** to fit your screen, press *Ctrl* + right-click while hovering your cursor in the **Playlist**. To zoom into or out of your patterns vertically, hold down *Alt* and use the mouse scroll wheel.
- **Playback**: This plays the song starting at the position that is clicked in the **Playlist**.

Element pattern options

In the **Playlist**, you may notice that patterns, audio, or automation have a little symbol that looks like a piano. In my case, there's the text **Bass Melody** next to the symbol. By left-clicking on the symbol, you'll see a list of options available.

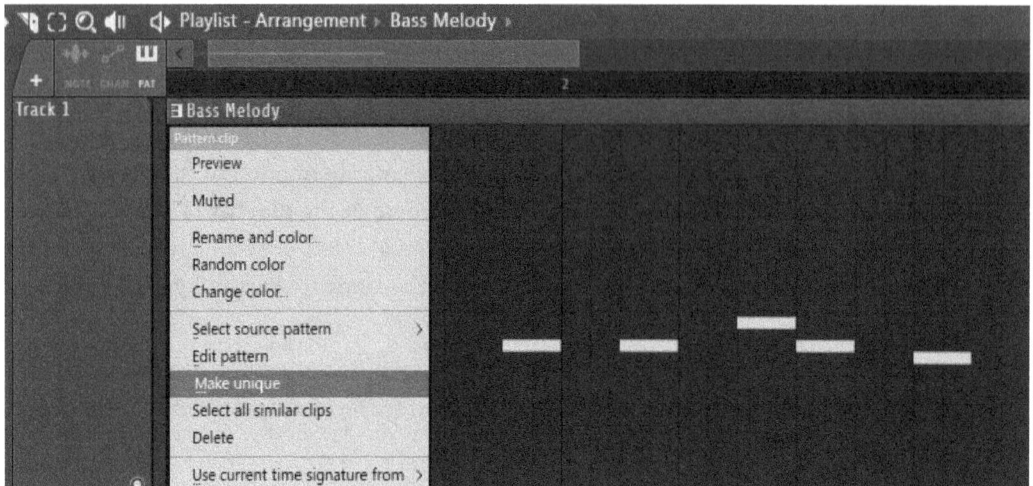

Figure 2.40 – Pattern options

Of importance is the **Make unique** option. This allows you to create a unique copy of your selected element. This is useful in a variety of situations. For example, say you had a pattern where an instrument played several notes. You now want to use the same pattern elsewhere in your song, but have it play a few different notes. If you make changes to the original, the pattern will be changed everywhere in your song. Selecting **Make unique** allows you to create a unique copy of the pattern, which you can then adjust without affecting the original.

So far, we've seen that the Playlist allows you to arrange patterns and samples. It gives you a bird's-eye view of your entire project, as well as the ability to zoom in and see precise details and edit them.

Recently, FL Studio added features allowing you to edit individual copies of samples without forcing you to make them unique clips. This is useful if you want to change the volume or pitch of an individual clip. Left-click the top left of a sample in the **Playlist**. Here, you'll see an option to edit the sample properties. An example is shown in the following screenshot, where we have two copies of an audio sample and want to make changes to just one of them.

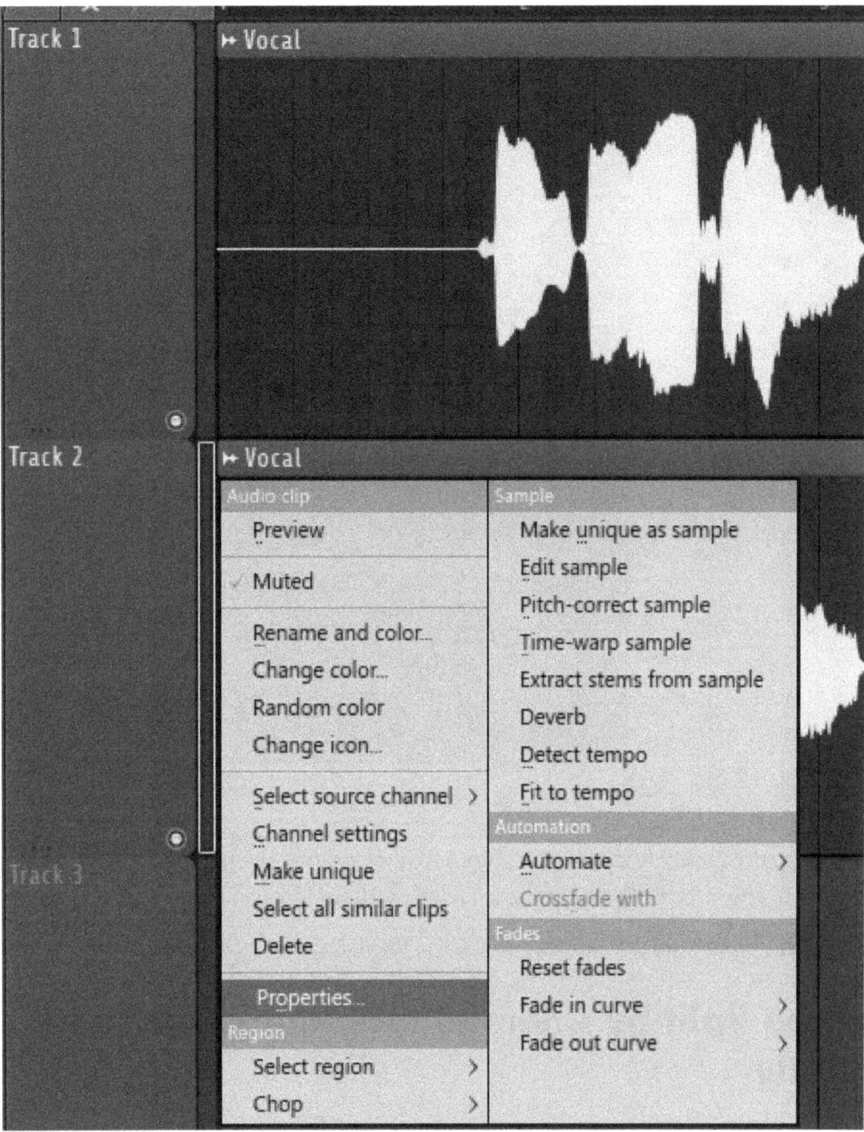

Figure 2.41 – Edit sample properties

After selecting **Properties...**, the **Clip properties** window will pop up.

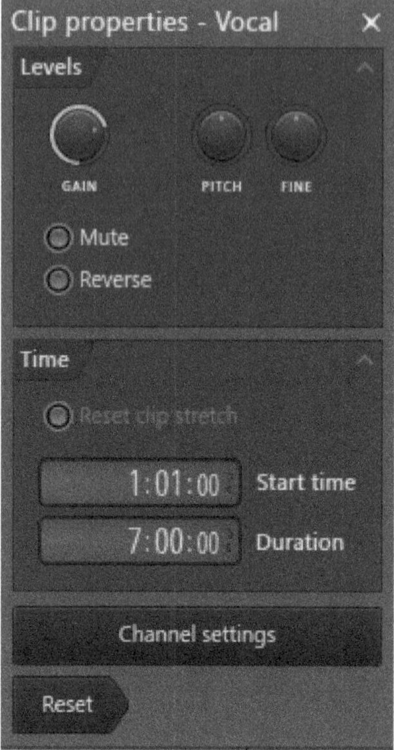

Figure 2.42 – Clip properties

Here you'll have the ability to adjust the gain, pitch, or reverse the playback of the audio sample. This change will only affect the single clip selected, without affecting any other copies.

Next, let's learn a tool to quickly add sounds to the Playlist.

Using the Split by Channel tool to add instruments efficiently

When you have multiple instruments in your Channel rack, how would you go about setting up patterns for the Playlist? Would you copy each instrument into its own pattern individually, one at a time? That would be tedious.

FL Studio has a super quick tool to name your instrument patterns for the Playlist. You can split all your instruments in the Channel rack for the Playlist in one step. For years, I was doing it the slow way, manually making patterns one at a time. Discovering this tool was a huge relief for me.

Let's look at the following screenshot example. Here we have a **Channel rack** pattern with five instruments that have already been color-coded and named (we discussed color coding and naming earlier in this chapter).

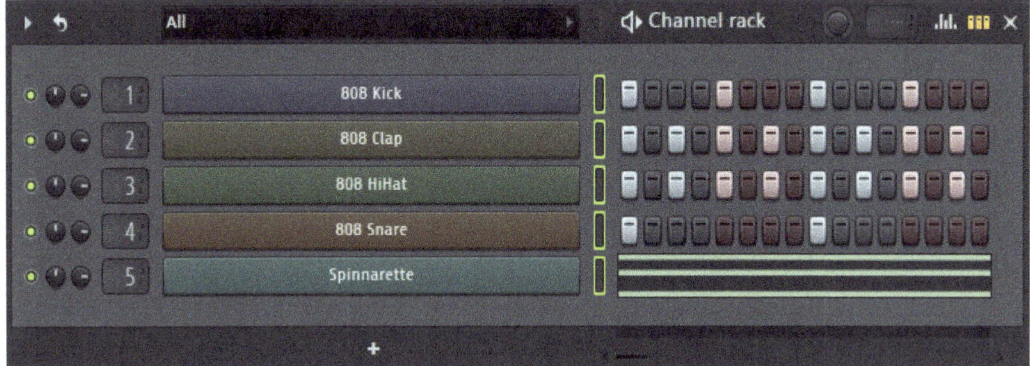

Figure 2.43 – Channel rack pattern

Currently, everything is grouped together in a single Playlist pattern. You can see what the pattern currently looks like in the following screenshot.

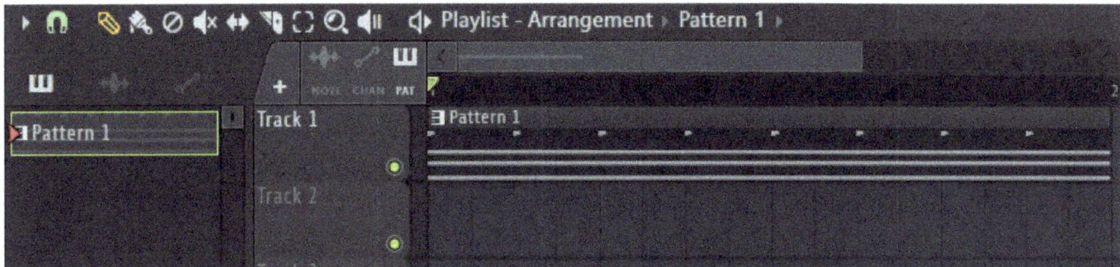

Figure 2.44 – Playlist with all instruments in a single pattern

Trying to figure out what instruments are in **Pattern 1** is not obvious from the Playlist view. **Pattern 1** contains all 5 instruments, but you wouldn't know it by looking at it. It's much easier visually and easier to understand if the instruments are split up into their own individual patterns. Let's fix this problem. Open the **Playlist** and right-click on the pattern containing multiple instruments. Then choose the option **Split by channel** as shown in the following screenshot.

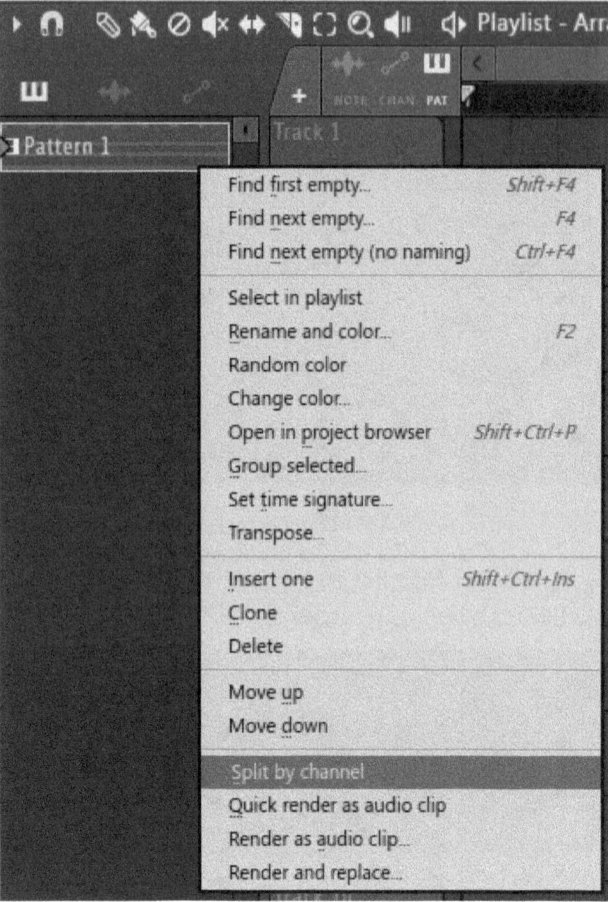

Figure 2.45 – Split by Channel

After splitting, the instruments in the **Playlist** will be separated into their own individual patterns and auto-named. You can see how **Pattern 1** has now become five instruments in the following screenshot.

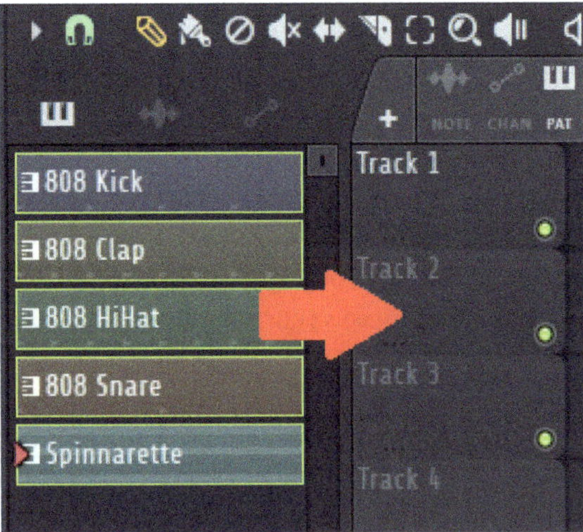

Figure 2.46 – Split by Channel and drop onto Playlist

We now have all our instruments split up. The hard part is over. Now we can drag them into the **Playlist**. Select all the patterns, left-click, and drop them onto the **Playlist** as shown in the preceding screenshot.

If you drag onto an empty track, you'll see that the patterns in the **Playlist** are also color-coded and named after the instrument, too. You can see the finished result in the following screenshot.

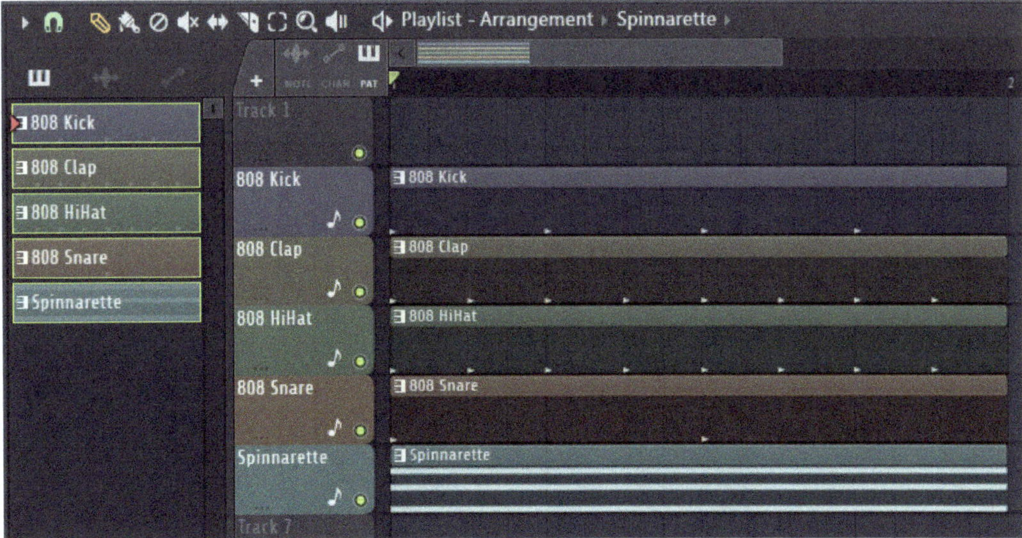

Figure 2.47 – Playlist showing the split instruments in their own patterns

> **Note**
>
> Note that if you want the auto-naming of instruments in the **Playlist**, you need to drag them onto an empty track, not just the general Playlist.

Splitting up your instruments this way makes using the Playlist much easier to visualize. Some of these steps sound a bit fiddly the first time, but once you've learned this trick, you'll be extremely grateful for how much more efficient it makes your workflow.

We've discussed how to use the Channel rack to add instruments and sound samples. Now, let's learn how to handle version control of your projects so you can safely make variations of your songs with backups.

Version control to back up your projects

When coding, it's a good idea to create your project in stages so that you can go back to an earlier stage (version) if you need to. So, it's good practice to save your project often. FL Studio has an option that will do this for you under **FILE** | **Save new version**.

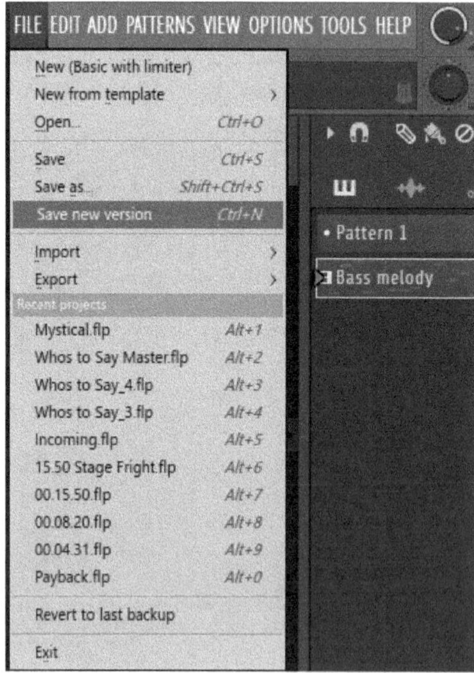

Figure 2.48 – Save new version option

This will save your file as a new copy of the project. If you ever need to go back, you can simply open up the original project.

You can also revert to the last backup. Sometimes, your computer might crash while you are working. In these cases, there is a way to go to the last autosaved version by navigating to **FILE** | **Revert to last backup**. This will load up the project's last autosave.

We've covered a lot of tools. What if you get stuck and need help, and you don't know where to look for assistance? Good news, FL Studio has your back.

Using Gopher chat assistant (ChatGPT for FL Studio)

FL Studio has an AI chatbot assistant trained on FL Studio documentation called **Gopher**. Whenever you want to do a deeper dive on an FL Studio feature or plugin, the first place you should look is Gopher. You can think of it as ChatGPT for FL Studio. There isn't a single way to use Gopher. It will provide custom answers depending on what request you give it. In this section, we'll explore a few useful ways that you can use Gopher to help you in FL Studio. We'll show you how you can use it to ask questions about FL Studio and how you can use it to brainstorm chord progressions and song lyrics.

To access Gopher, navigate to **Help** | **Gopher** or press *Alt* + *F1*, as shown in the following screenshot:

Figure 2.49 – Open Gopher

The Gopher chatbot will open up. Here, you can ask Gopher questions and make requests.

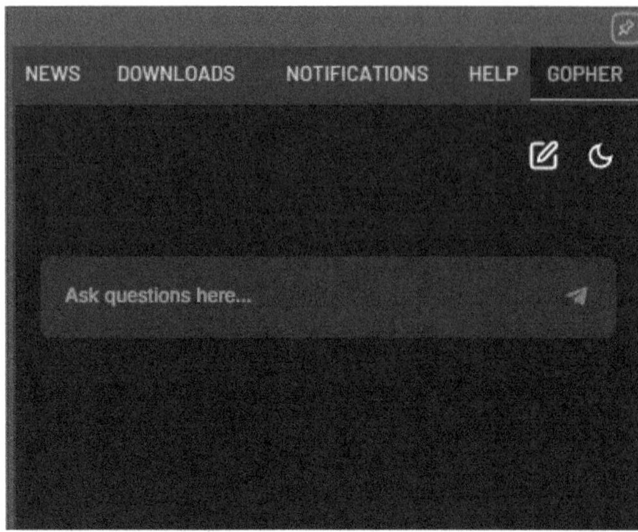

Figure 2.50: Gopher chatbot

You can ask Gopher any FL Studio questions. If you ask about an FL Studio plugin, it will provide you with links directly to the documentation topic. It's a smart AI, though, much more than just a reference index. It will give you customized answers to your questions rather than prepared responses. You can even ask Gopher for information on how to use Gopher.

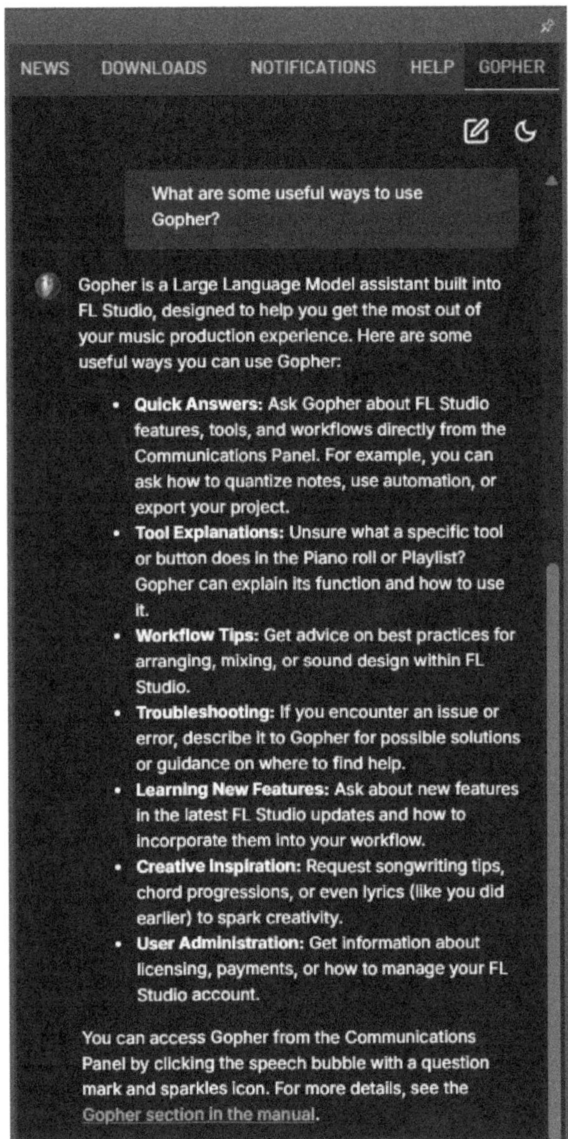

Figure 2.51 – Asking Gopher about its uses

In the preceding screenshot, Gopher suggested that you could use Gopher for creative inspiration, such as writing a chord progression. Let's try that out.

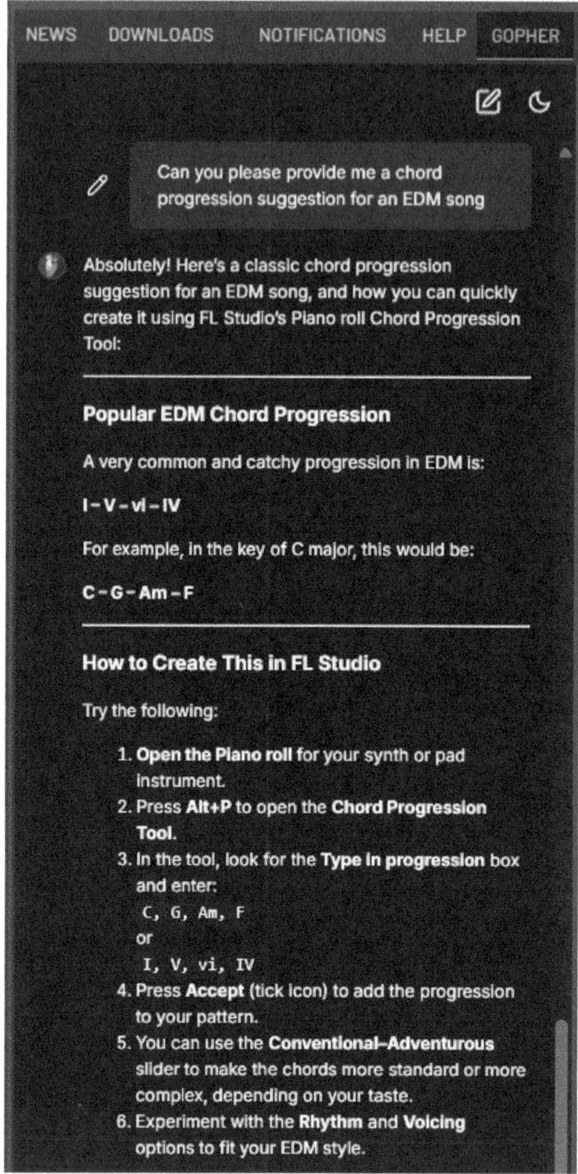

Figure 2.52 – Gopher chord progression suggestion

We now have some suggestions for chord progressions. Gopher can be used to generate original content, too, such as suggesting song lyrics.

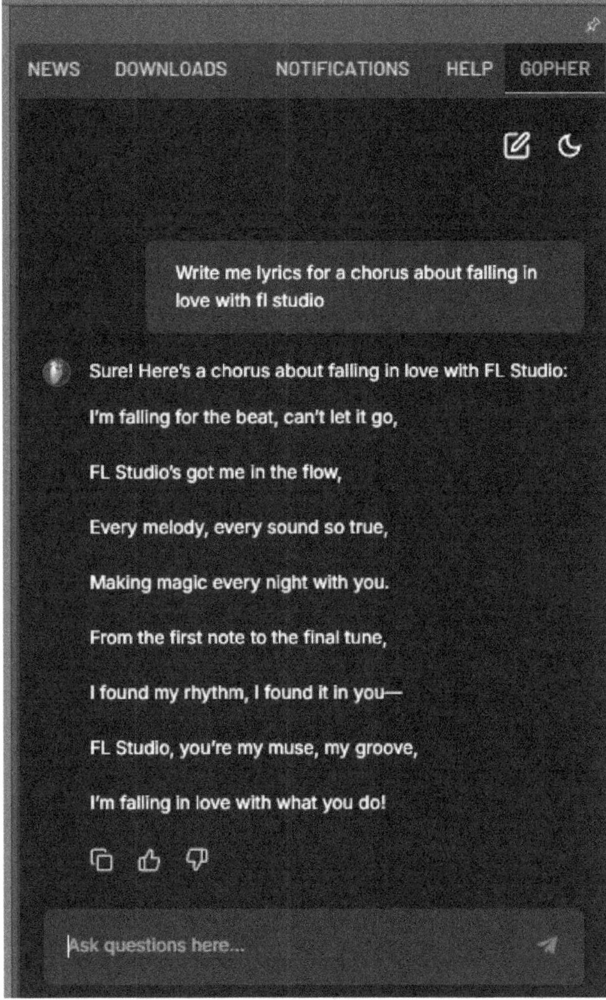

Figure 2.53 – Gopher content creation

You can ask Gopher to write lyrics for songs or give you suggestions for lyric variations of your existing lyrics.

How you use Gopher is up to you; perhaps you'll invent a new way to use it that hasn't been thought of yet. For example, here are some possibilities to get your creative juices flowing:

- **Synth presets & patches**: Describe the sound you want ("analog warm pad with airy reverb"), then use Gopher to generate ideas for synth parameters, waveforms, filter types, etc.

- **Chord progressions & voicings**: Feed it a key, scale, or mood, then use it to generate chord sequences.
- **Vocal melodies**: Suggest syllable replacement and phrasing based on lyrics.

We've learned how to use Gopher to provide troubleshooting advice and suggestions for your music production. Next, let's explore FL Studio Cloud.

Getting sounds and plugins using FL Studio Cloud

FL Studio offers a large selection of cloud-based features that are being updated all the time. They offer free and paid sound samples, plugins, and **mastering**. We'll discuss the paid sound samples and plugins in this chapter. We'll hold off on discussing mastering until the mastering chapters later in the book.

You can find the FL Cloud features under the **TOOLS** option, as shown in the following screenshot.

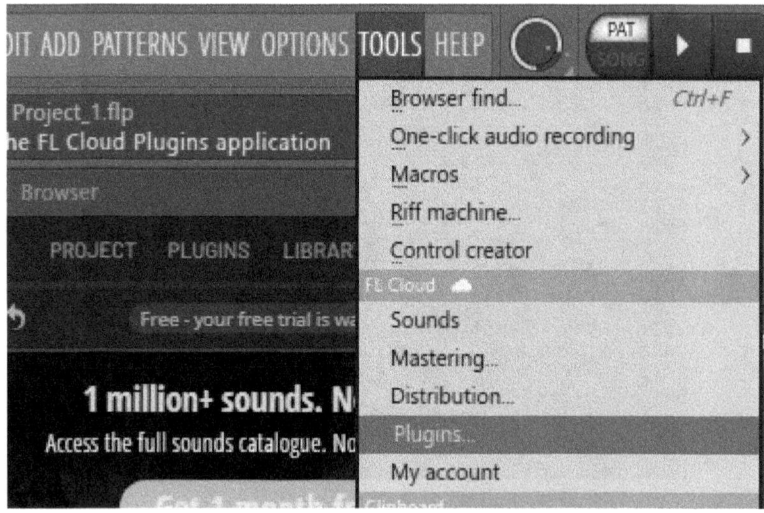

Figure 2.54 – FL Studio Cloud TOOLS dropdown

First, let's take a look at the plugins section of FL Cloud.

Plugins in FL Cloud

If you select the **Plugins...** option, you'll see a list of plugins that are available to install from FL Cloud Plugins.

Figure 2.55 – FL Studio Cloud plugins

In the top right of the **FL CLOUD** section of the preceding screenshot, you can see that I have the **Free** tier selected. This shows plugins that are included in your current cloud subscription. Everyone gets the free tier plugins included. If you want additional plugins, you can upgrade your cloud subscription, and you'll unlock lots more.

On the right side, you'll see an option to install the selected plugin. Once you've installed the plugins, they'll be available for you just like any other plugin in the Channel rack if it's an **instrument plugin**, or in the Mixer if it's an **effect plugin**.

In the upcoming subsections, we'll discuss how you can gain access to samples using FL Studio Cloud and easily drag them into your project.

Sound samples using FL Cloud

FL Cloud offers a library of sound samples that are easily accessible in the Browser. The samples are conveniently set up for drag and drop. Most sample packs offer a few teaser free samples to entice you to upgrade to unlock the rest of the pack. Let's take a look at the samples offered by FL Cloud:

1. Open the **Browser** by selecting the **Browser** icon.

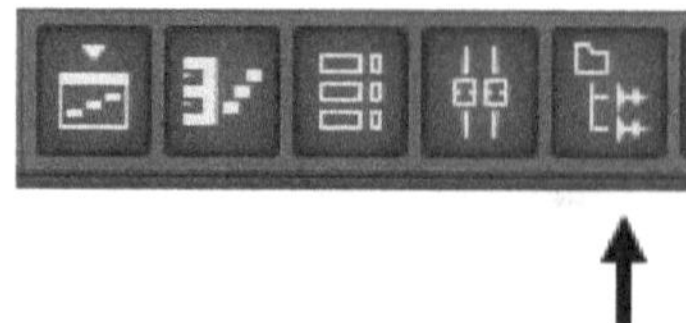

Figure 2.56 – Browser button

Inside the **Browser**, you'll see a tab called **SOUNDS**.

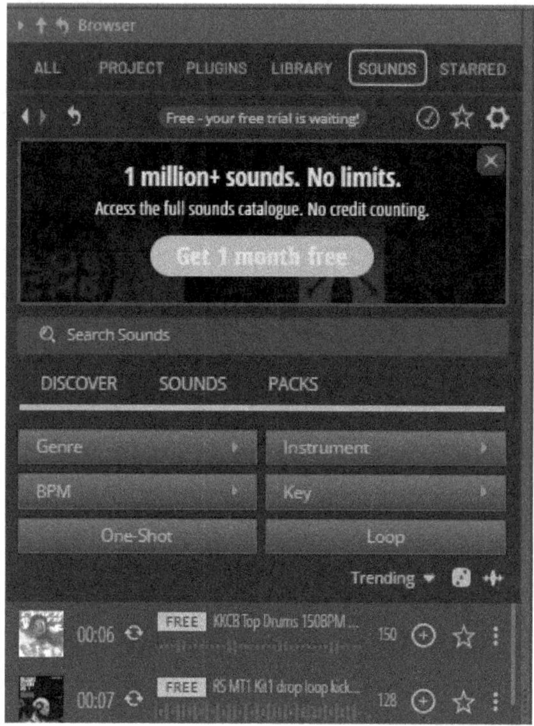

Figure 2.57 – SOUNDS tab

Here you'll find a section where you can filter through the sound sample. There are filter choices for **Genre**, **Instrument**, **BPM**, **Key**, and whether you want a **One-Shot** sample (single sound) or a **Loop**. For some samples, like vocals, you shouldn't worry too much about the BPM or key of the song because most samples can have their key and BPM adjusted to your project. We'll see how in just a moment.

Underneath the sample selection filters, you'll see a list of samples meeting the criteria you set. The samples have a bunch of button options, as shown by the following screenshot:

Figure 2.58 – Sample control

Starting from left to right, here's a description of the buttons:

- **Go to pack** navigates to the collection that the sample was taken from so you can see similar samples.
- **Sample length**
- **Play**
- **Download Sound**
- **Add to wishlist menu** adds a sample to a list of your favorite samples so you can easily find them later.
- **Options** menu displays several choices:
    - **Open/Edit in...** allows you to open the sample inside an FL Studio plugin for editing.
    - **Show in FL Studio Browser** shows you where the plugin has been downloaded to in the **Browser**.
    - **Locate File** shows you where on your computer the file has been saved.

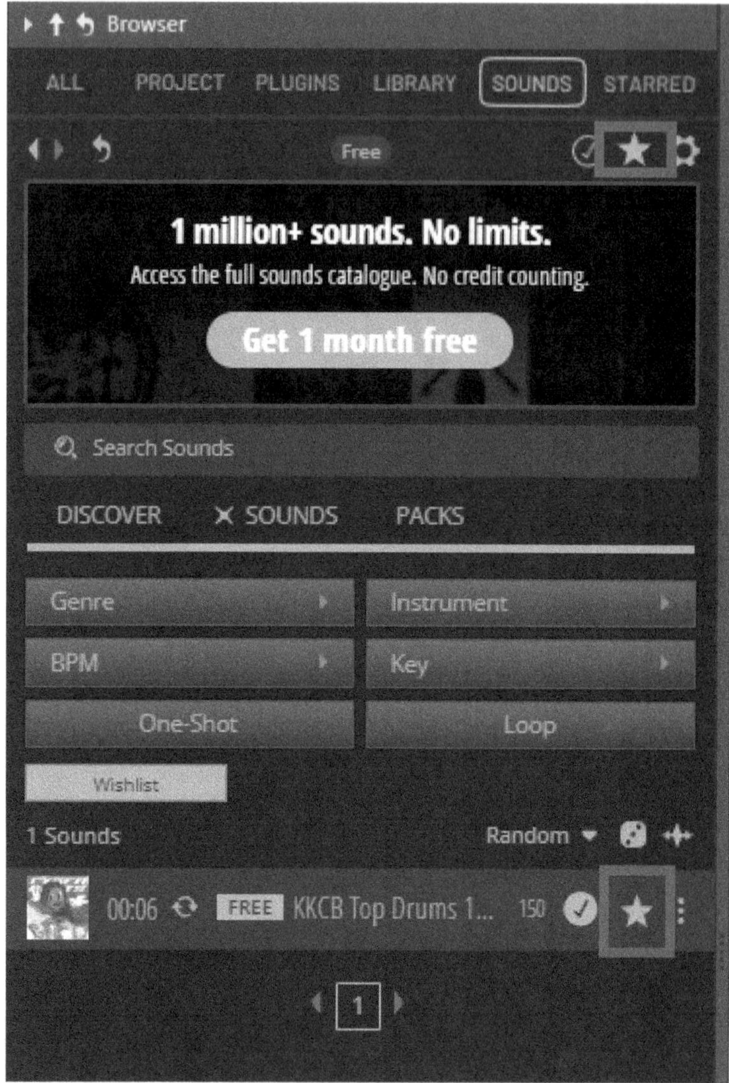

Figure 2.59 – Favorite a sample

In the preceding screenshot, in the top right, there's a **star** icon: **Show all your favorited sounds**. If that is selected, you can see all your favorite samples that you wish to be listed. This makes it easy to find samples that you already liked. The **star** icon is simply an easy way of saying "I want this sample to be favorited on my wish list for easy access."

At the bottom of the list of samples, you'll see the sample you currently have selected. In my case, I selected a vocal sample. Your screen might look a little different depending on which sample you have selected.

Figure 2.60 – Sounds customization

In the preceding screenshot, you'll see several controls:

- **Play previous**
- **Play preview**
- **Play Next**
- **Disable/enable looped playback**
- **Open playback speed menu** allows you to hear the song at different speeds, such as half speed or double speed.
- **Open key-transpose menu** allows you to quickly change the key of the sample to a different key. If the sample is in a different key from your song, no problem. Just select a different key that fits your song, and the sample will adjust. Not all samples have this ability to swap keys instantly, but for those that do, it's very convenient.
- **Playback volume**
- **Sync playback to project BPM** matches the speed of the sample to the BPM of your project.
- **Enable/Disable "Hot Swap" Mode** lets you quickly swap between other samples.

Once you're happy with your sample, you can left-click and drag the sample from the **Browser** into the **Playlist**. This will instantly bring the sample into your project.

Manually adding samples using FL Cloud sounds like it would take a long time to individually locate samples, right? Turns out FL Studio anticipated this problem and built a tool designed specifically to make it easier: the Loop Starter.

Introducing Loop Starter – the fastest way to get started

Loop Starter is a tool to automatically populate your Channel rack with samples. This is a super-fast way to jump-start a new project. The easiest way to learn it is to try it out. Open up the **Channel rack**.

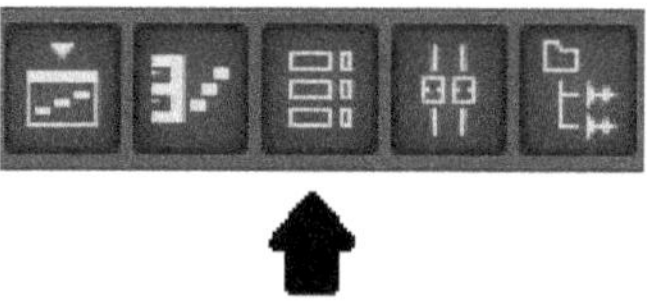

Figure 2.61 – Open Channel rack

At the top left of the **Channel rack**, there's a little symbol that looks like a die with a looping arrow around it. This is the **Turn Loop Starter mode** on or off button, and is shown in the following screenshot:

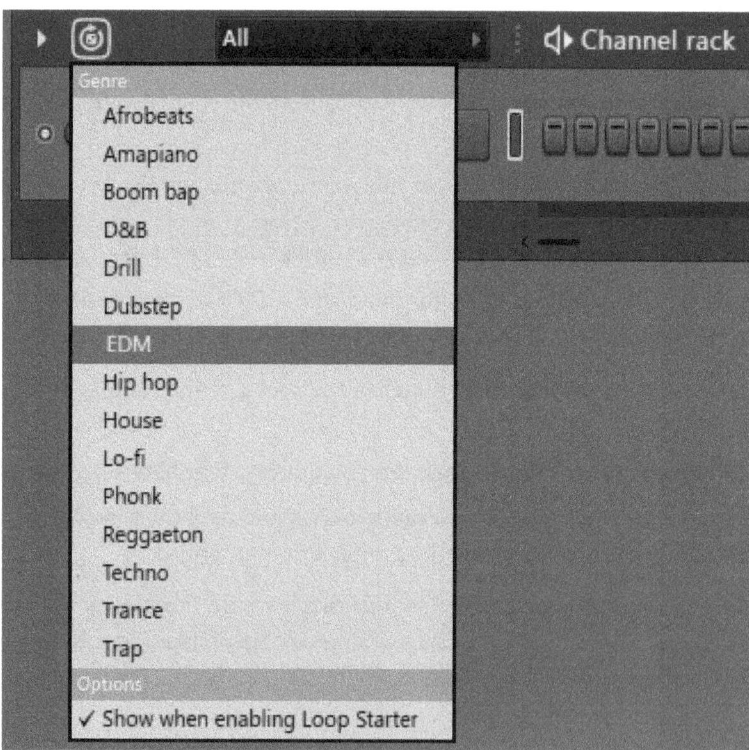

Figure 2.62 – Loop Starter

You'll see a list of song genres. Select the genre that you want to create. After you select a genre, the **Channel rack** will populate with sample loops and one-shot samples.

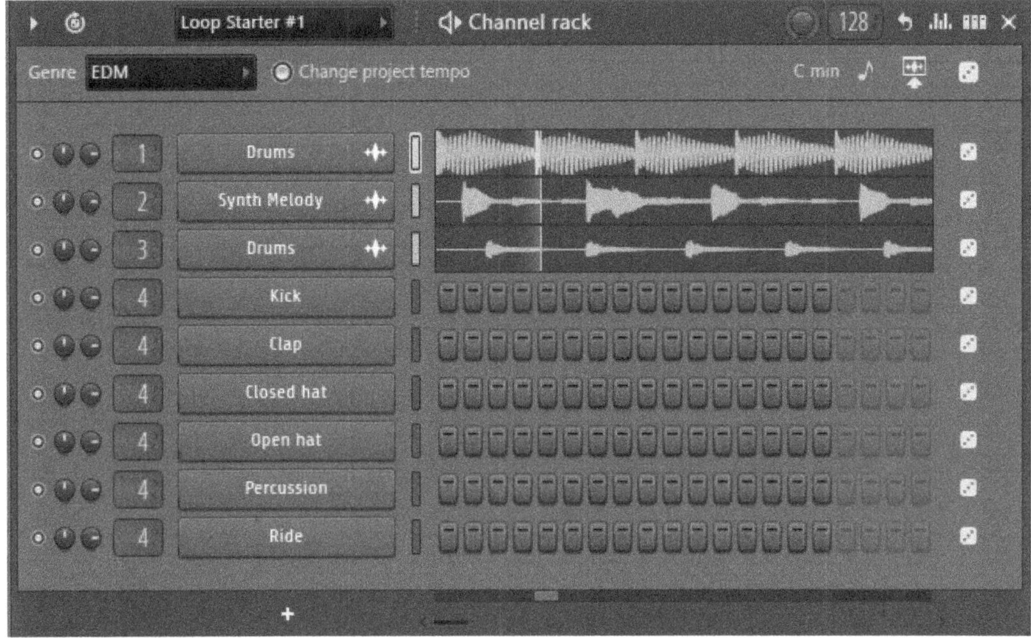

Figure 2.63 – Loop Starter samples

The **Channel rack** grabs samples from FL Studio Cloud and inserts them into your project.

The first three instruments on the **Channel rack** are looping samples. You'll notice that the one-shot samples (**Kick**, **Clap**, **Closed hat**, etc.) don't have any MIDI notes to play by default. Let's fix that.

To the right of the **Channel rack**, you'll see a button called **Replace all samples/Replace samples for selected channels**. Choose the option to **Generate steps for all channels**.

Figure 2.64 – Loop Starter – generate steps

Loop Starter will populate MIDI notes for all the one-shot samples in your **Channel rack**.

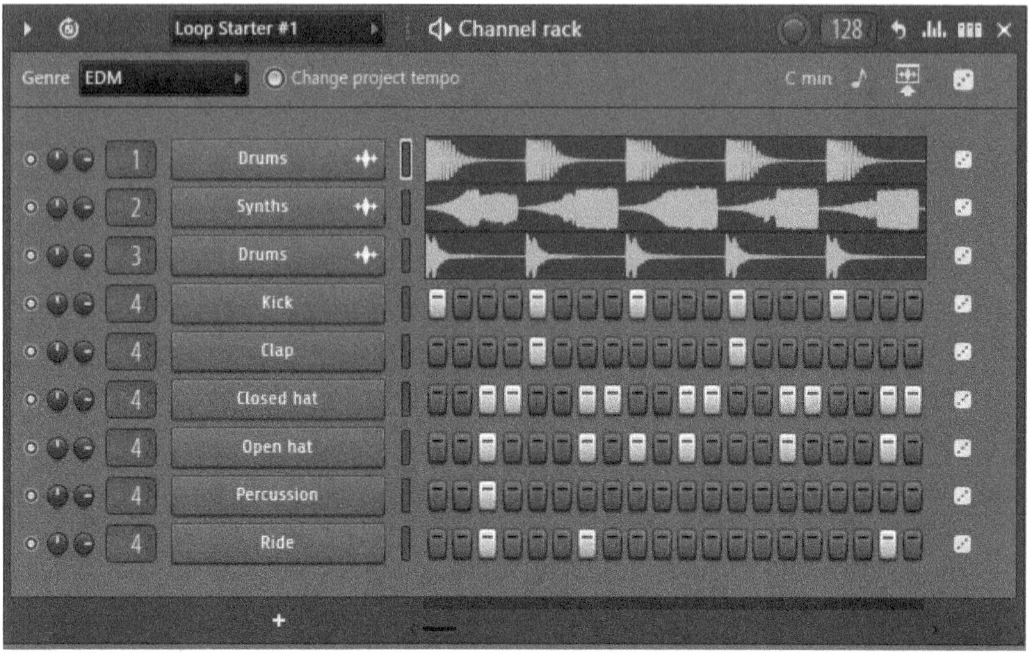

Figure 2.65 – Loop Starter steps generated

If you're lucky, the samples randomly imported will sound good together. But it's unlikely that they'll all sound amazing right away. More likely, you'll get a few samples that sound decent and need to replace the others. Luckily, there's a super-fast way to swap out the samples.

To the far right of every instrument, you'll see a little **dice** icon called **Replace the channel's sample**. If you click that, the sample will randomly be replaced with another sample from FL Cloud.

The sample that is replaced isn't completely random. You can specify the root note and the scale of the sample.

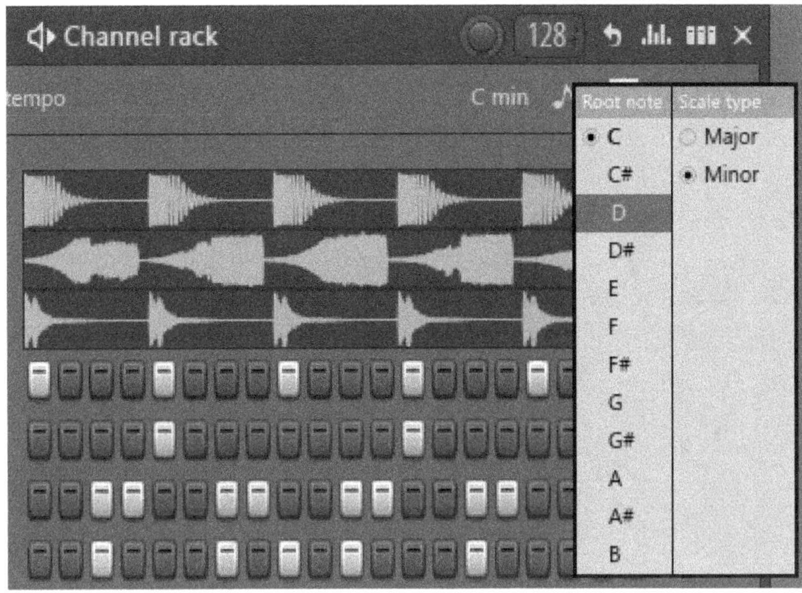

Figure 2.66 – Loop Starter – Set Pattern Key

The ability to specify the sample that gets grabbed is extremely convenient. Now, when you replace samples using the dice symbol, the sample grabbed will be much more likely to fit in with the rest of your song.

If you right-click on the dice symbol, you'll see additional options for the type of sample you want to replace with. For example, you can specify whether you want the sample to be replaced with a loop or a one-shot drum sample.

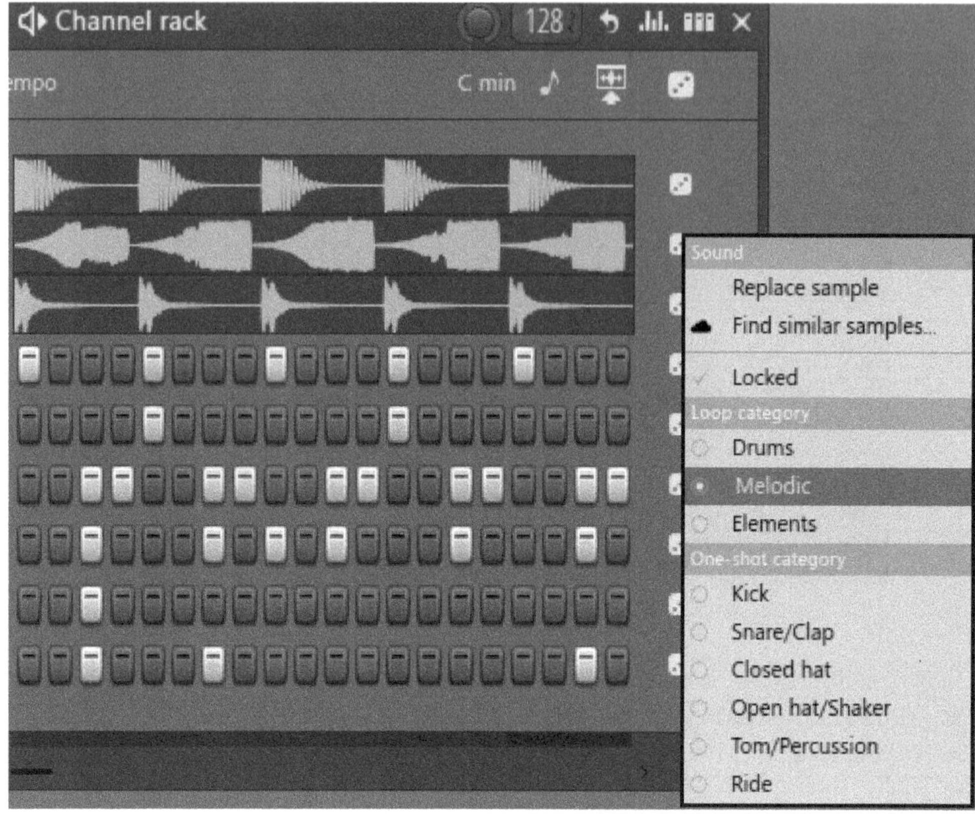

Figure 2.67 – Replace the channel's sample

When you're happy with the samples that Loop Starter created for you, you can send them to the **Playlist** using the **Send the audio loops and the pattern to the playlist** button.

Figure 2.68 – Send to Playlist

This will send all the samples to the **Playlist** and auto-name them. Any MIDI notes for your one-shot samples will also be added to a pattern. You can see an example in the following screenshot:

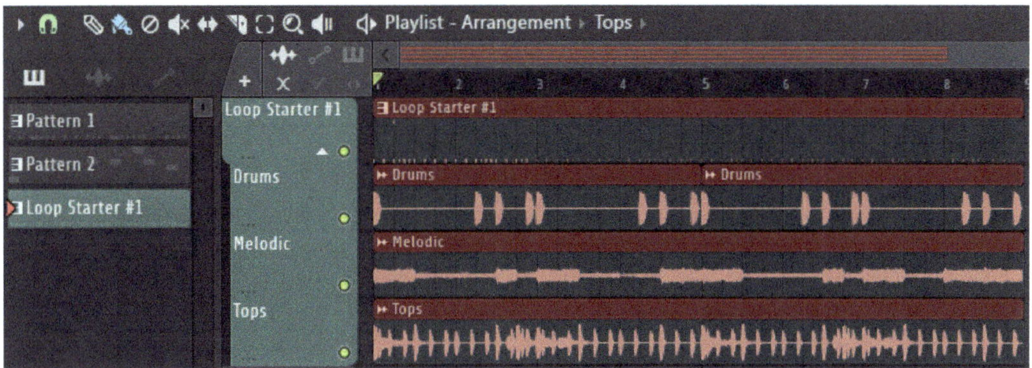

Figure 2.69 – Samples in the Playlist

Whoa, that was an easy way to get started making music. And good news, it's repeatable. Anytime you want more samples, you can go to the **Channel rack** and turn on Loop Starter again.

You've successfully jump-started your application with samples using Loop Starter. The samples in the pattern have also been added to the Playlist. Congratulations, you're well on your way to making a song.

Additional tricks and tips

Let's discuss a few tricks and tips that are handy and important to know. We'll discuss how to undo and redo your mistakes, how to fix projects that are lagging by changing the sound card driver, and finally, how to take notes throughout your project.

Undo and redo

When you make a mistake, it's easy to go back and fix it by undoing your last few actions. The undo and redo keyboard shortcuts allow you to go back and forward through the changes you've made.

To undo a change, use *Ctrl* + *Z*. To redo a change, use *Ctrl* + Shift + *Z*.

Audio Stream Input/Output (ASIO)

Is your FL Studio project running slowly and lagging? If so, FL Studio has a fix for you. **Audio Stream Input/Output** (**ASIO**) is a sound card driver for computer audio. ASIO drivers allow lower CPU overhead and buffering than your standard sound driver, and will make your project run faster. Under the **OPTIONS** | **Audio** settings, you can find some configuration settings. You'll see an option to change the device to **ASIO4ALL v2**.

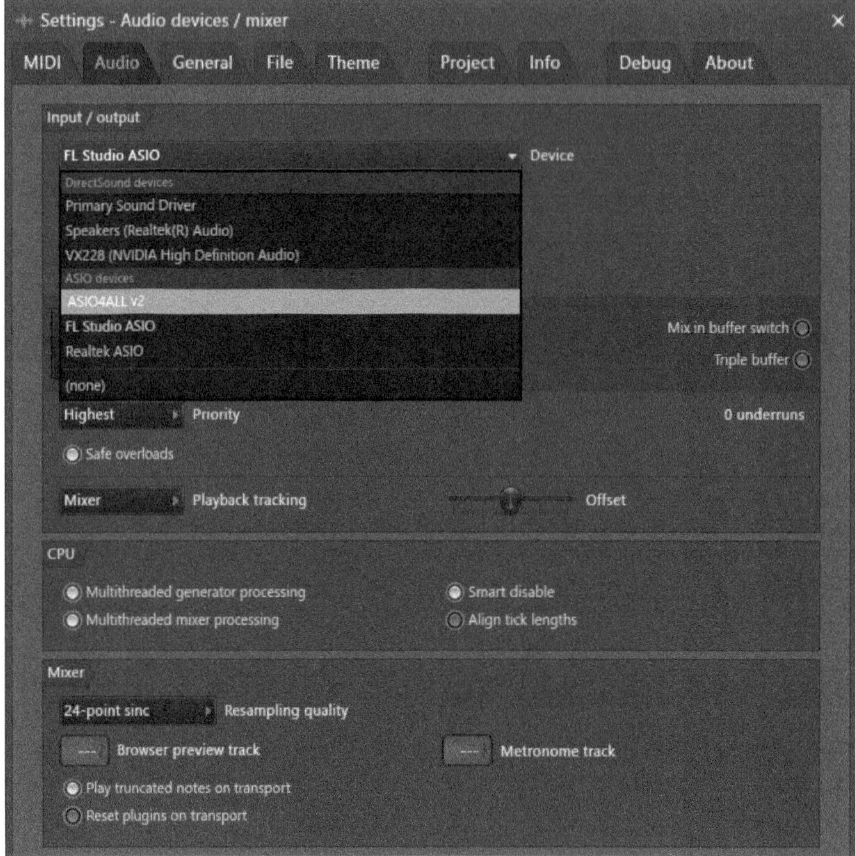

Figure 2.70 – FL Studio ASIO

This is a newer version of the sound card driver that tends to work better with FL Studio. If you find FL Studio is lagging, you may want to turn on **ASIO4ALL v2**.

However, turning on **ASIO4ALL v2** means that any other program you are running on your computer will likely no longer play audio and may possibly crash (YouTube, Netflix, and so on), so you'll need to turn this option back off when you want to have another program play sound. Many times, I'll find that my other programs that are running aren't playing sound, and I can't figure out what's causing the problem until I realize that ASIO4ALL v2 was turned on.

Taking notes on your project

If you want to keep notes about your project, there is a text record available for every song.

Figure 2.71 – Project Info icon

Clicking the **Project Info** icon will open the **Settings – Project credits** window.

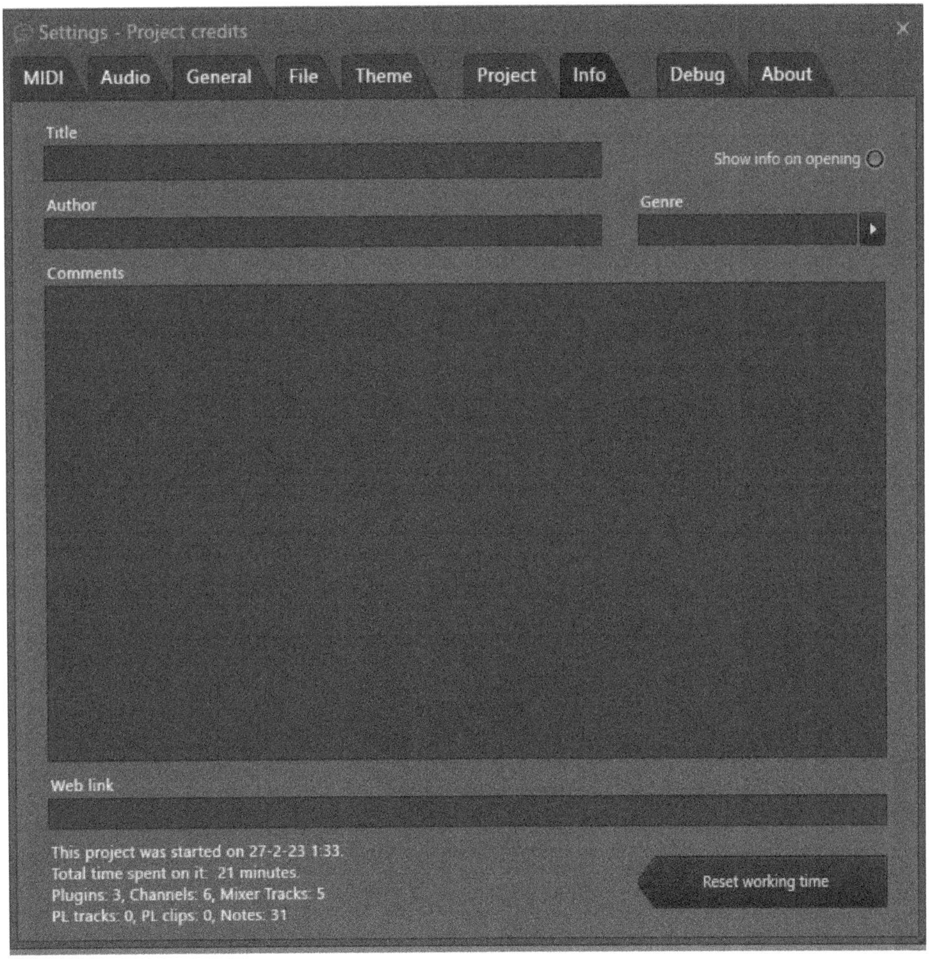

Figure 2.72 – Project Info

For example, I know some producers who like to use these note records to list the key of a song or links to YouTube or SoundCloud songs that they used for inspiration. You can use this for any notes that you want to have associated with the project file. The window also gives you some fun little statistics about your project, such as when you started working on it and how many hours you've spent working on it. I'm often surprised at how many hours I've spent working on a single project. I'm sure you will be too.

Summary

In this chapter, you learned how to use the Browser, Channel rack, and Playlist. You will use these tools again and again with every song you make. The Browser allows you to navigate through your samples and swap them in and out of your Playlist with ease. The Channel rack lets you load your instruments, navigate through them, and create percussive rhythms. The Playlist allows you to arrange the timing of your music patterns, samples, and automation.

We learned shortcut tips to streamline the process of adding instruments from the Channel rack to the Playlist using the Split By Channel Tool. We discussed how to use the Gopher AI Chatbot to get assistance with FL Studio tools. We introduced FL Cloud, which provides you with additional plugins and samples for your production. We discussed Loop Starter, a Channel rack tool to rapidly jump-start your project with samples from FL Cloud. Finally, we mentioned additional tricks and tips such as how to undo your mistakes, reduce project lag, and keep notes on your project.

In the next chapter, we'll look at the Piano roll tool so you can compose melodies for your instruments.

Get this book's PDF version and more

Scan the QR code (or go to `packtpub.com/unlock`). Search for this book by name, confirm the edition, and then follow the steps on the page.

Note: Keep your invoice handy. Purchases made directly from Packt don't require an invoice.

3

Composing with the Piano Roll

When you want to make a melody for your song, you need a tool to compose it. In FL Studio, that tool is the **Piano roll**. The Piano roll allows you to add melody notes, arrange them, adjust the inflection of notes, and easily move notes between instruments. This chapter will help you learn how to compose a **chord progression** on the Piano roll from scratch. Once you know how to use the Piano roll to compose chord progressions, you'll be able to compose melodies for any instrument.

In this chapter, we will cover the following topics:

- Compose melodies using the Piano roll
- Composing great chord progressions
- Using the chord progression tool
- Recording into the Piano roll with MIDI instruments
- Quantizing notes – fix the timing of your notes
- Humanize tool – make your notes sound like they were played live
- Editing note articulations with the Event Editor
- Exporting sheet music
- Using and exporting MIDI scores

Compose melodies using the Piano roll

The Piano roll is the tool for composing melodies. It is essentially a piano with a timeline. On the y axis, note pitches are shown, and on the x axis, time is divided into a grid of beats and smaller increments of beats. Notes are displayed as horizontal bars, as shown in the following screenshot:

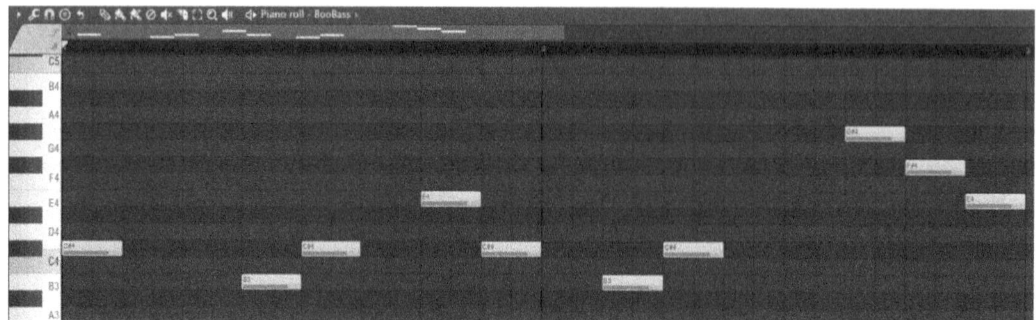

Figure 3.1 – Piano roll

The Piano roll is really good at taking a melody and mapping out the exact timing. It's easy to generate **chords** and experiment with notes that complement your melody. It's also good at comparing the timing of notes to other instruments playing in the same pattern and at jumping between instruments. We'll explore these in detail throughout the chapter.

Additionally, if you need help coming up with melody ideas, here are a few quick suggestions. I like to have a physical instrument nearby that I can use to experiment with chords or a melody. I play around with the instrument until I have a few chords that I like, and then think about recording the notes into the Piano roll. Alternatively, I'll listen to a sound sample or another song for inspiration to get ideas, or import **Musical Instrument Digital Interface** (**MIDI**) notes to experiment with (discussed later in this chapter). Once I have a basic melody, the Piano roll gives me the freedom to expand upon my idea.

The Piano roll offers a large set of useful tools for composing melodies. The Piano roll toolbar tools are the same as the Toolbar in the **Playlist**. So, once you learn the Piano roll tools, you'll know how to use them in both places. If you need a recap on the Playlist, we covered it in *Chapter 2*. Okay, let's learn how to use the Piano roll.

Choosing an instrument

Before composing a melody, we first need to choose an instrument to use in the Piano roll. You can choose the instrument you want to use by clicking on the **Channel rack** drop-down menu in the **Piano roll**, as seen in the following screenshot:

Figure 3.2 – Choosing instruments to use in the Piano roll

Alternatively, you can open the **Channel rack,** right-click on the instrument you want to edit in the Piano roll, and select the **Piano roll** option.

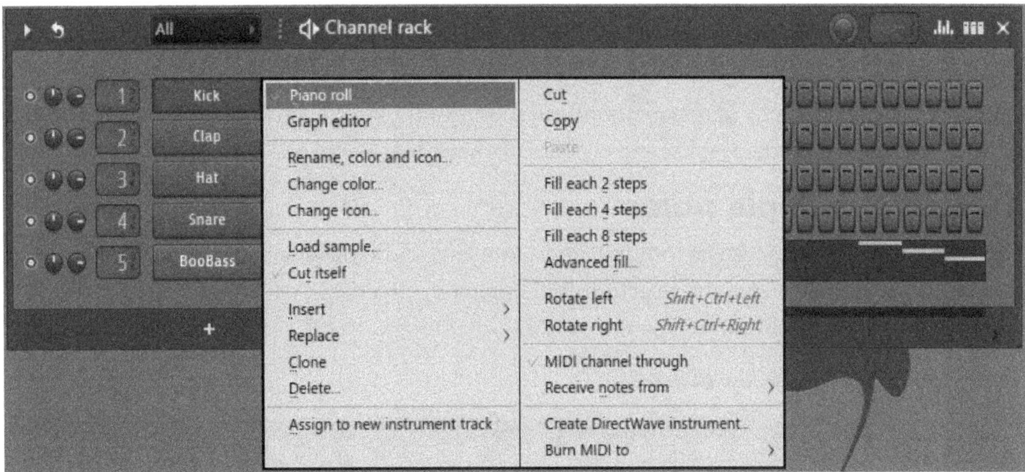

Figure 3.3 – Choosing instruments for the Piano roll

Now that you have chosen your instrument to compose a melody, we'll discuss the tools you use to interact with the Piano roll. You'll want to memorize the keyboard shortcuts for these tools. While manually clicking the tools is fine for beginners, it is not convenient. You want the keyboard shortcuts for repeated tasks like adding, selecting, and deleting notes to be so second nature that they're committed to muscle memory. This will make your composing experience much easier and more enjoyable. Let's check out the Piano roll tools.

Adding notes in the Piano roll

To add notes, first make sure that the **draw** symbol is selected.

Figure 3.4 – Selecting the draw tool

Then, left-click in the blue grid section of the Piano roll to add notes. It helps if you are playing the music pattern at the same time that you're adding notes, so that you can hear the melody being played and get the timings correct. To do so, make sure **PAT** is selected for the desired music pattern, and then press **play**.

Figure 3.5 – Play your Piano roll pattern

When **PAT** is selected, only instruments within the current pattern will play. However, if **SONG** is selected, all patterns in the Playlist and everything they contain will play.

Selecting multiple notes

Sometimes, you'll want to select multiple notes at a time and move them all at once or copy them to another instrument. You can select multiple notes by pressing *Ctrl* + *Shift*, then left-clicking and dragging over the notes.

Alternatively, you can use the **select** tool.

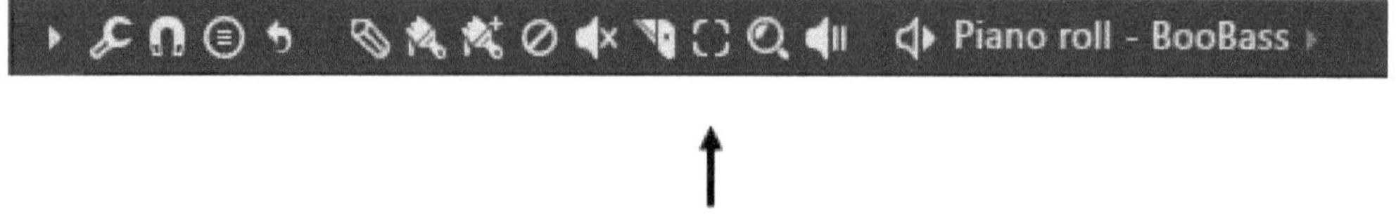

Figure 3.6 – Select tool

You now know how to select notes.

Deleting notes

What if you make a mistake and need to remove a note? There are multiple ways to do this:

- Right-clicking on the note you want to remove is the easiest way to delete notes.
- Selecting multiple notes at the same time and pressing *Delete* on your keyboard.
- Selecting the **delete** tool (shown in the following screenshot) and then left-clicking on the notes you want to remove.

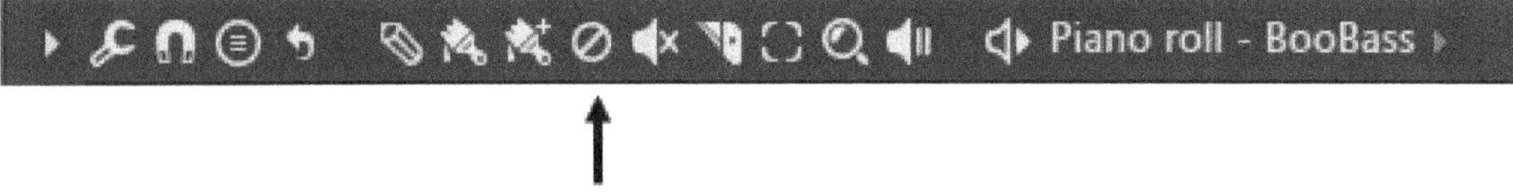

Figure 3.7 – Delete tool

If you delete more notes than you meant to, the undo (*Ctrl* + *Z*) and redo (*Ctrl* + *Shift* + *Z*) keyboard shortcuts are always there to help you.

Muting and unmuting notes

There's a way to use note placeholders to keep a reference of note positions without actively playing them. This is useful if you want to try out an alternative melody, but don't want to lose the original notes. You can mute notes without deleting them by double-right-clicking on an empty space next to a note and dragging over the note. To unmute, do the exact same steps.

Alternatively, you can select notes and then press *Alt* + *M*, or you can select the **mute** tool and then click on the notes.

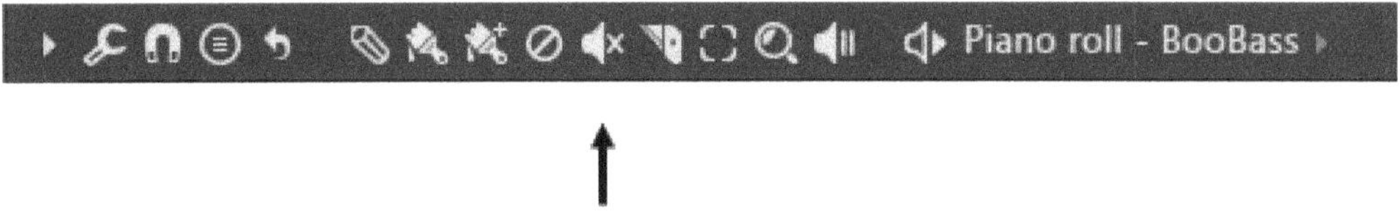

Figure 3.8 – Muting notes

You'll find muted notes very useful when you clone a music pattern and want to change some of the notes, but still want to remember the position of the original notes.

Slicing notes

From time to time, you'll want to chop up notes into several smaller notes. My preferred way to slice notes is by pressing *right Alt* + *right Shift* and then clicking on the notes that you want to slice. Alternatively, you can use the **slice** tool:

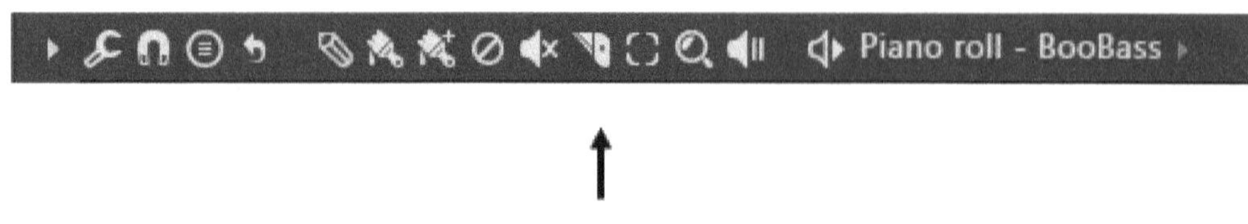

Figure 3.9 – Slice tool

The slice tool is most useful when you want to chop up several notes at once rather than change the length of an individual note.

Using the stamp tool to get assistance with scales

There are many musical scales. The most commonly known ones are major and minor, but these are only two scales out of many possible ones. Notes that fit within a given scale sound good together and consistent as long as you use notes that stay within the scale. Depending on the scale you pick, your music will have a different emotional feel and sound happier, sadder, lighter, darker, and so on.

> To learn more about scales, check out *Classic FM's* guide to modes with examples (`https://www.classicfm.com/discover-music/latest/guide-to-musical-modes/`) and this guide to piano scales: `https://pianoscales.org/jazz.html`.

When starting to compose a new piece of music, I find it helpful to force myself to use only notes that fit within a chosen scale. This reduces the choice of possible notes I can add and makes it easier to pick notes and chords that complement each other. The Piano roll provides several tools to assist you with choosing notes that fit within a scale.

The **Stamp** tool lists a series of chords, scales, and percussion rhythm examples to aid you in coming up with melodies. Choosing one of these will give you example notes. To use this tool, do the following:

1. Open up the **Stamp** tool, as shown in the following screenshot, and choose any one of the presets:

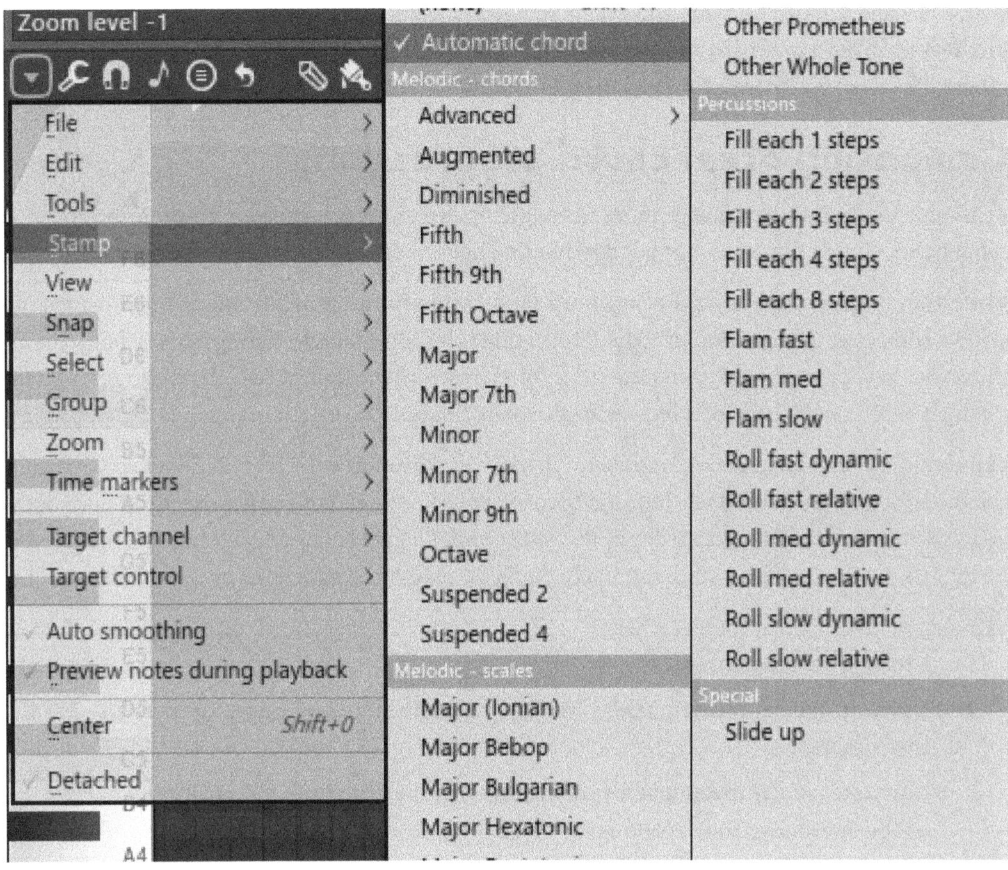

Figure 3.10 – Stamp tool

2. Next, left-click inside the **Piano roll**, and the example notes will be inserted.

Using the Stamp tool is a quick way to determine what notes are available in a scale. Let's say I was composing a piece of music for a film and needed a sound that was dark and emotional. I'd look up some example songs that were dark and emotional and figure out what scale they were using. If, for example, I found out that the scale used in a song was a *Phrygian* scale and I wanted a similar sound, I could use the Stamp tool to identify which notes are in the Phrygian scale by selecting the Phrygian stamp preset. I could then insert the example notes from the Stamp tool into the Piano roll and use that as my guide. The notes inserted would be my visual aid to knowing which note pitches are used in my scale.

In the preceding screenshot, you'll notice an option for **Automatic chord**. When this is selected, FL Studio will try to guess what chord might fit next in the Piano roll. If you then left-click in the **Piano roll**, a chord would appear.

We've learned about the tools the Piano roll offers. Next, let's learn how to compose a chord progression from scratch so you understand why some chord progressions sound better than others. Then, we'll explore a tool built into FL Studio that can help you build chord progressions.

Composing great chord progressions

A chord is formed when three or more notes are played simultaneously. A chord progression is a sequence of chords that sound good together and have a sense of movement throughout.

Understanding how to build a strong chord progression from scratch is one of the most valuable skills a composer can develop. It's the foundational building block of songs. It's usually the first thing that gets created, and it sets the rules for all instruments and vocals that follow. If you hear a song whose melody isn't very interesting, usually a subpar chord progression is the culprit.

Let's build a chord progression together. I'll walk you through each step in detail so you can see the thought process behind it – but don't worry, you don't need to copy it exactly. What matters is that you understand the key techniques. At the end, I'll give you a simple summary of the steps. As long as you grasp the overall approach, you'll be ready to create your own progressions. Let's begin:

1. Create a new music pattern.
2. Load up an instrument that can play multiple notes at once, such as the **FL Keys** instrument.
3. Add notes in the **Piano roll** by left-clicking in the blue grid and creating a pattern such as the one shown in the following screenshot:

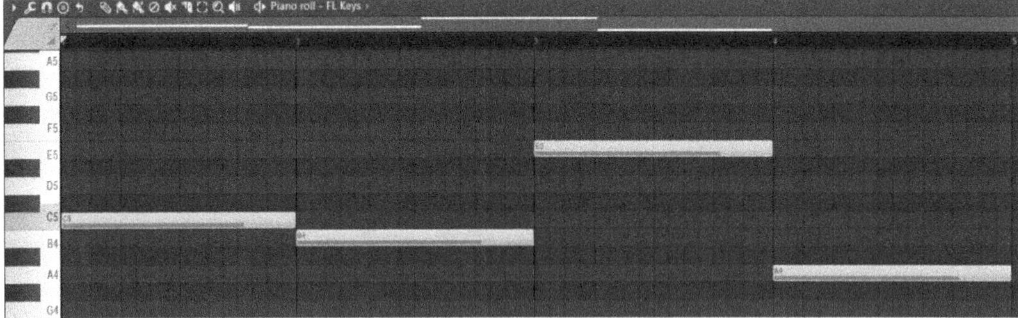

Figure 3.11 – Adding notes in the Piano roll

I've chosen the A minor scale, so the notes that we pick from here on will be within this scale. What we have so far is a baseline for our notes: C, B, E, and A. This is a starting point on which we'll build. The exact four notes that we pick aren't that important as long as they're within the same scale.

Our arrangement doesn't sound very interesting yet. One tool to add interest is to have the notes play a rhythm. At the top of the **Piano roll**, you'll see the numbers **1**, **2**, **3**, **4**..., and so on. This represents the number of **music bars**. Music bars are a measurement of relative time in music used to keep track of the beat. In pop music, baselines tend to be 4 or 8 bars long for a given song's verse or chorus. Right now, our notes are playing one note for four beats in each bar. This is boring to listen to, and breaking up the notes can help.

4. Let's break up the notes into a rhythmic pattern so that we can hear variation within the bar. Do it until they look like the following pattern:

Figure 3.12 – Added rhythm

What we've done is create a percussive pattern. Note the empty space between some notes. Deciding where to place silence is just as important as deciding where to place notes.

We're repeating the same general rhythmic pattern throughout each bar. This will make it clear to the listener that there is a cohesive theme that is easy to follow.

Let's form our chords. Playing multiple notes at once gives the sound some texture, which makes it more interesting. I want to add notes that will complement my baseline melody. For any baseline, complementing notes include notes that are a third or a fifth higher or lower than the root (original) note. In music theory, a third means three scale degrees of difference from the root note – in other words, three pitches away. A fifth is five pitches away.

5. Let's add some thirds and fifths to our root notes. Add notes as shown in the following screenshot. As long as we add notes that are within our scale (A minor), notes that are a third or a fifth will sound good in combination with the root note.

Figure 3.13 – Added thirds and fifths

We've added notes to complement our baseline. I've colored the new notes with a different color for visual convenience. Our arrangement is already sounding better. We're aiming for chords, though, which means we need to add another unique note to play at the same time. When I say *unique note*, I mean that we are playing a unique pitch. For example, if I play the note **A4**, when I add a unique note, the note I add will be a pitch other than an A pitch.

6. What notes could we add to finish our chords? This time, we need to use our ears and experiment until we find a sound that complements our existing two notes. There isn't an exact rule, but rather a series of attempts at trying out different notes until we find one that we like. Add notes such as those shown in the following screenshot:

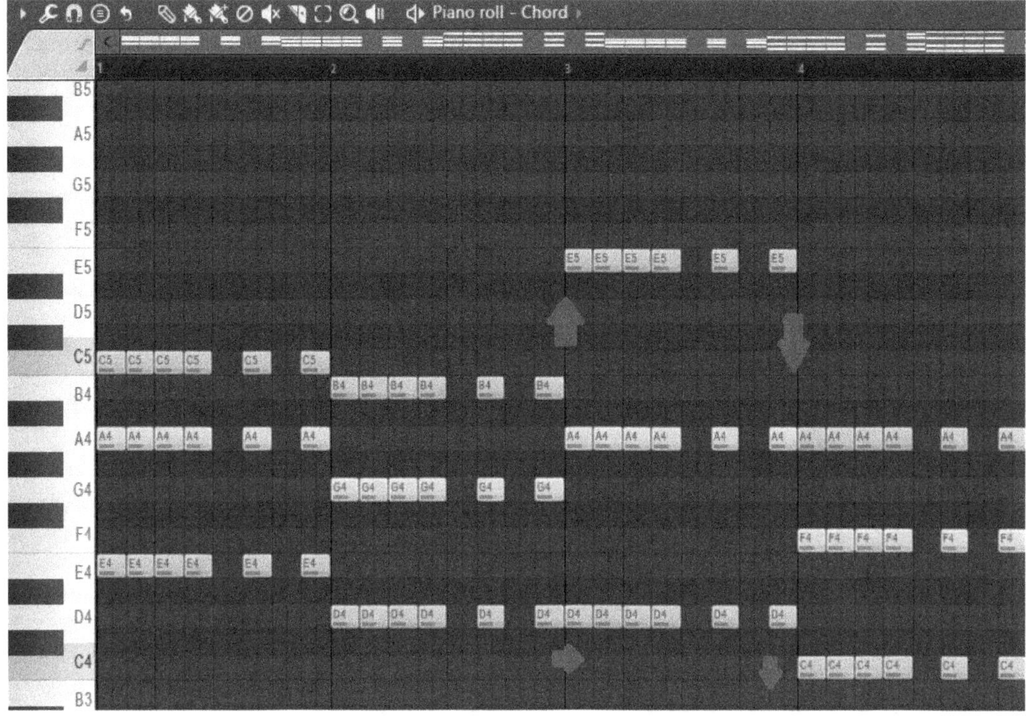

Figure 3.14 – Created chords

Here, we can see that all of our notes have now been turned into chords. It helps to think of the notes in a chord progression as separate melodies that are interacting with each other.

In our example, our original root notes are the highest-pitch notes. They start out moving in a descending direction, moving from C to B in bars **1** and **2**. In bar **3**, they change direction and move upward to E before descending to A in bar **4**.

The last chord notes I added are the lowest in pitch in the chord. The lowest melody moves in a downward direction, descending from E to D and then to C. In bar **3**, the highest melody and the lowest melody are diverging in pitch direction. The high-pitch melody is moving upward; the low-pitch melody is not. They then reunite in bar **4**, moving in the same direction again.

Chord melodies diverging in upward and downward pitch directions are interesting to your ears. If your chord melody sounds boring, consider making your high and low melodies diverge in pitch direction.

7. Bar **4** sounds a little bland and predictable. Let's fix this by giving it some variation to distinguish it from the other chords. Specifically, I want to change the last two notes in bar **4** so that they aren't playing the exact same pitch for the entire bar. I want the notes to feel like they're leading back to the beginning chord of the first bar. Replace the last bar with notes, as shown in the following screenshot:

Figure 3.15 – Adding variation to bar 4

In the last bar on the right, we can see two single notes that are not yet in a chord. Let's build chords around them.

8. We can repeat the steps of fleshing out individual notes into chords. Add a second note, using a third or fifth higher or lower in the scale. Then, experiment to find a third chord note that complements this. Add notes to fill out the chord in bar **4**, as shown in the following screenshot:

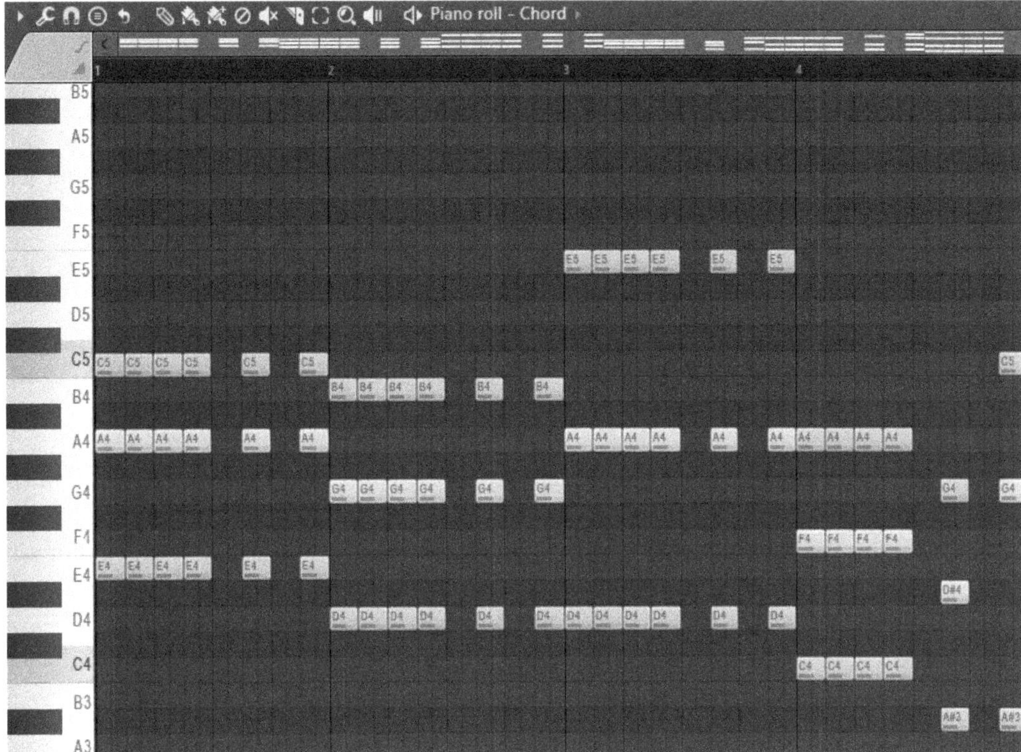

Figure 3.16 – Filling in the chord

Our chord progression is coming along now. It's time to polish our chords. One way to give our chords more texture is to add another unique note to the scale to make a four-note chord. The more notes, the more textured and nuanced our chords will sound.

9. Adding unique notes is something that needs to be done sparingly. Converting all three chords into four-note chords is not always a good idea. Creating all four-note chords will likely result in losing out on the overall melody of the chord progression. We only want to add additional notes if they don't detract from the overall melody. Deciding when to add more notes is something that needs to be done through experimentation. You tinker and play around to see whether it enhances or detracts. You add and take away notes until the chord sounds better. After playing around and experimenting, I've decided that bar **4** could be enhanced by adding a fourth unique note to the chords. Add notes to bar **4** as shown in the following screenshot:

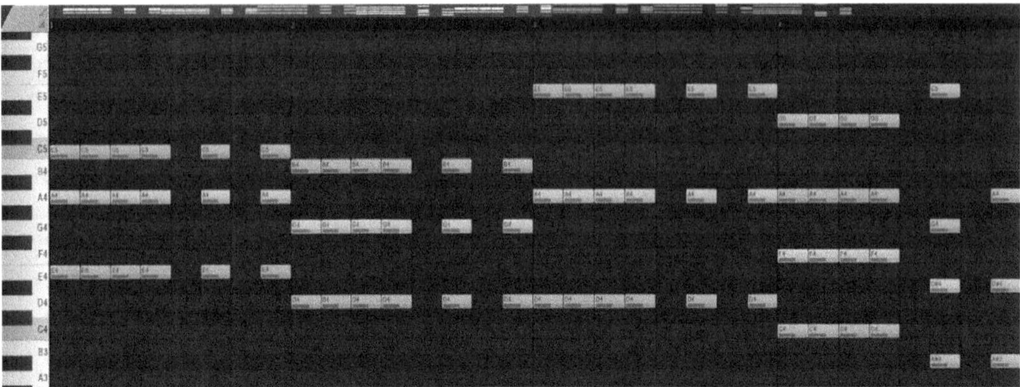

Figure 3.17 – Creating four-note chords in bar 4

We have the first four bars of our chord progression. It has a sense of momentum, where each chord sounds like it logically flows into the next chord. There is one problem, though: when this progression is played, it feels too short. When you listen to it, your ears want it to repeat again and reach some sort of conclusion. Right now, it resembles a cliffhanger in a book that is unresolved. Your ears want the chord progression to resolve itself.

10. Let's resolve the chord progression by expanding it from a four-bar to an eight-bar chord progression. Copy the notes from the first four bars and paste them directly after the four bars so that your **Piano roll** looks as in the following screenshot. You can quickly copy and paste notes by selecting notes and then pressing *Ctrl* + *B*.

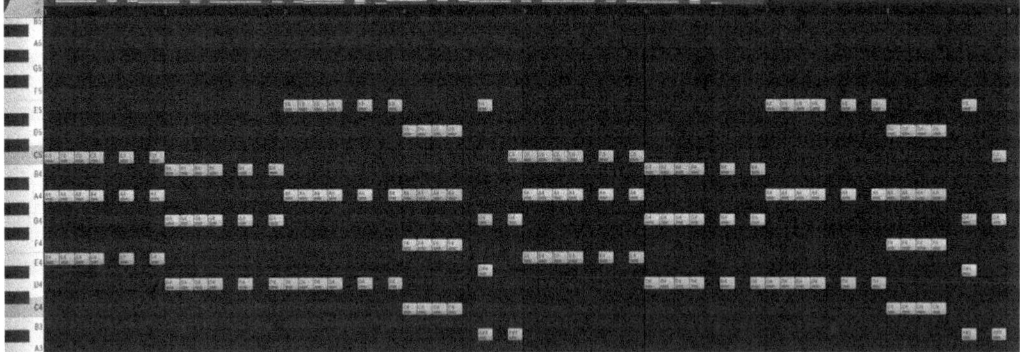

Figure 3.18 – Copied and pasted notes back-to-back

11. We now have the same chord progression playing twice, back to back. In the second iteration, we will create a melody variation and resolve the chord progression.

12. We're going to make some changes to the melody in bars **5** to **9**. Our ears naturally gravitate toward the highest-pitch notes and pay the most attention to them. These are the most noticeable. These are our main melodies. In other words, we want to manipulate the highest-pitch notes in our chord progression.

    When changing note pitches, you have three options:

    - Move an existing pitch note up or down to a new pitch.
    - Delete a pitch note.
    - Add a new pitch note.

    What to move, add, or take away is once again a series of trial and error. You experiment with adding and moving notes and see whether the melody is improved. A guideline is that the notes should fit within the notes of our chosen scale (in our case, A minor).

    Add notes in bars **5–9** so that the **Piano roll** looks as in the following screenshot:

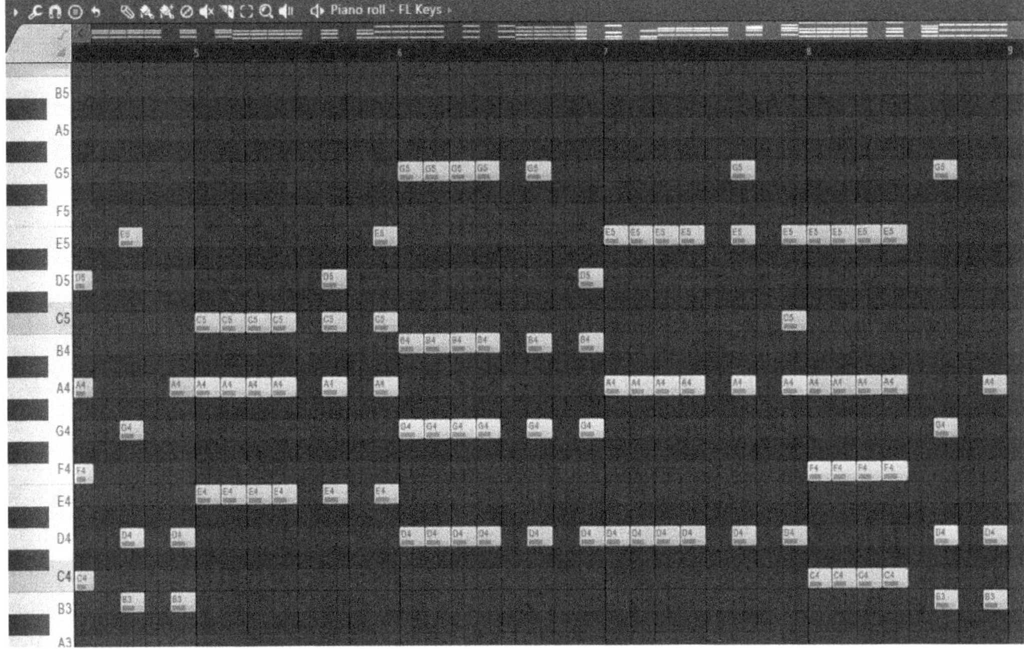

Figure 3.19 – Bars 5 to 9

In the preceding screenshot, we gave the second iteration of our chord progression variation by adding notes in bars **5–9**. Specifically, we focused on the highest pitch notes.

In bar **8**, we adjusted our four-note chord. We moved the highest-pitch note from **D5** to **E5**. By making this change, our chord has a slightly different texture than the chord in bar **4**.

In bar **6**, we added one of the same notes in our chord (**G4**), an **octave** higher, on the pitch of **G5**. An octave means a note of double the pitch, eight tones higher, but it still sounds like the same note. When you have a chord, you can add notes that are the same as existing notes in the chord, an octave higher or lower, and it won't change the chord. It will still sound good.

13. Knowing that you can add notes that are octaves higher or lower is another tool. We can transpose any existing notes in our chord progression to octaves higher or lower, and the chord progression will still sound good. When I say transposing, I mean moving a note pitch up or down an octave. By spreading out our chords across several octaves, we can unclutter our chords and give our chords a sense of space to make the sound feel larger.

    Take existing notes and experiment with transposing them an octave higher or lower. You can quickly transpose notes to a higher or lower octave by selecting notes and then using *Ctrl + the up arrow* or *Ctrl + the down arrow*.

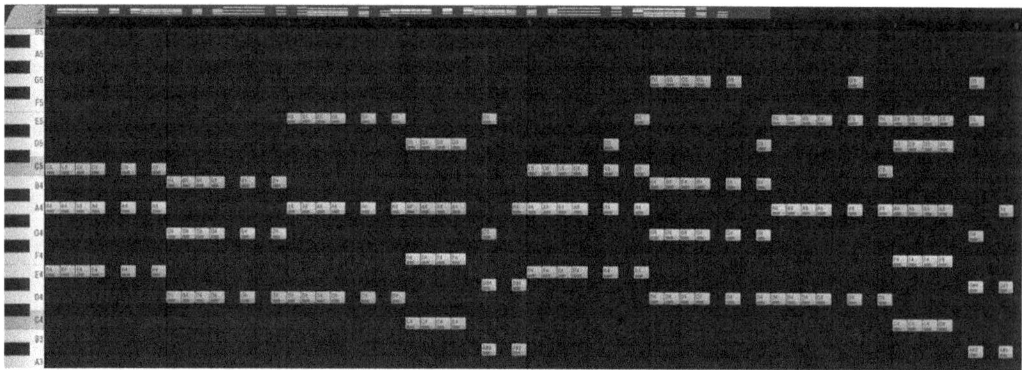

Figure 3.20 – Transposing notes

In the preceding screenshot, we can see that I've taken chord notes in bars **1**, **2**, **4**, **5**, **6**, and **8** and transposed them down an octave until they formed the lowest-pitch notes of the chords. Specifically, I transposed notes that were in the middle of the chords. The notes in the middle are generally the most cluttered sounds and benefit the most from transposing. By transposing these notes from the middle of the chords and spreading them down an octave, I've uncluttered our chords and given them a sense of space.

Our chord progression is now finished. Whew, that sounded like a lot of work. The good news is that the steps are easy to replicate for a variety of scenarios and can be broken down into a simple checklist. Let's summarize the steps we took:

1. Create a simple baseline melody with unique note pitches.
2. Add some rhythm by breaking up the notes and inserting breaks between some of them.

3. Add note harmonies by adding a complementary note, such as a third or fifth pitch higher or lower than the root note.
4. Add a third note to complete the chord by experimenting with pitches until you find one that fits
5. Polish your chord progression. Experiment with adding additional unique note pitches to your chords to form chords with four or more notes.
6. When repeating your chord progression a second time, give the second playthrough some variation from the first to distinguish it. The main melody is generally your highest note pitches. Your ears will look for this as your main melody, so the highest-pitched notes are usually the ones that you want to adjust.
7. Experiment with transposing notes in your chord progressions an octave higher or lower. Usually, the notes in the middle need to be transposed, as they will sound cluttered in the middle. This will add a sense of space and unclutter your chords.

You now have a solid base for building your song. Once you have a chord progression, the rest of the song is easy. It's just a matter of taking notes from your chord progression and assigning and layering various instruments to play them. For the lowest notes, choose a bass instrument. For the higher notes, pick instruments or vocals.

Another bonus is that coming up with vocal melodies becomes much simpler. Just by listening to the chord progression, your mind will naturally want to hum along with the chords and improvise melodies over them.

We've finished learning how to create a chord progression from scratch. Now, let's learn about tools that help us create chord progressions.

Using the chord progression tool

Making chord progressions from scratch can take a long time. The **chord progression tool** is here to take the guesswork out of building chords and help you get ideas flowing faster. Instead of sitting at the Piano roll wondering which notes to pick, you can use it to try out different progressions, swap chords in and out, and quickly hear how they change the feel of your song. It's great for sketching out a solid backbone for your track, whether you're aiming for something smooth and familiar or something more adventurous. Think of it as a creative partner that helps you set the mood and direction, so the rest of your music has a strong foundation to build on.

This tool is best learned by trying it out. Let's locate the tool from the Piano roll by going to **Tools | Generate chord progressions...** as shown in the following screenshot:

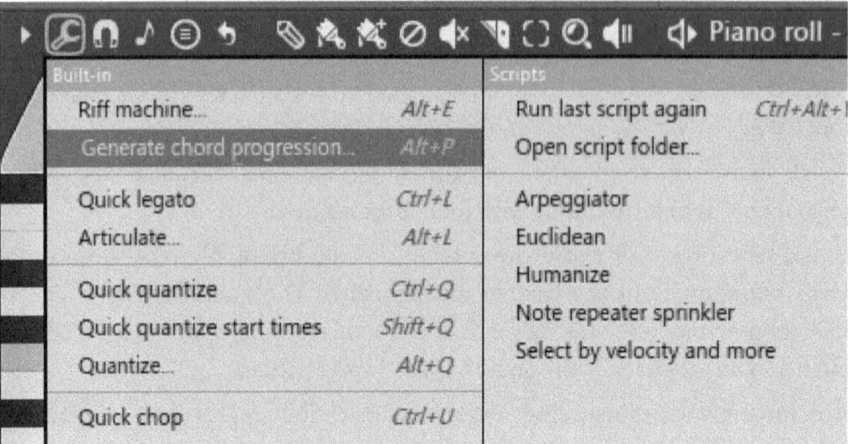

Figure 3.21 – Opening Generate chord progressions...

This will open the chord progressions tool.

Alternatively, if you're starting from a fresh new project, you can open the **Create a chord progression** tool by loading a starter template. Go to **File** | **New from template** | **Utility** | **Create a chord progression**, as shown in the following screenshot:

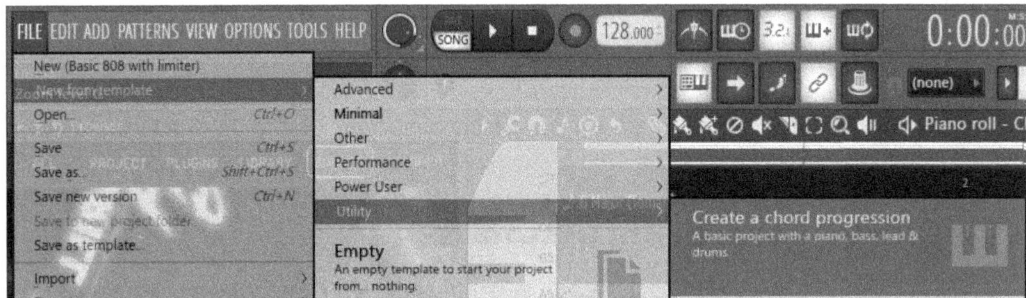

Figure 3.22 – Opening Generate chord progressions from a template

The chord progressions tool allows you to quickly generate and explore chord progressions.

The chord progression tool is divided into a top and bottom section. The top section gives you controls to play, create, and swap out the chords, and the bottom section gives you fine control over how the chords are created. In it, you select a scale. This sets the overall mood or tone that the chords will fit. You choose the length of the progression to build. You generate the chords. Once the chords are built, you can choose the chords you like and swap out any that you don't.

In the bottom section of the tool are three tabs: a **Presets** tab that contains a list of common chord progressions and rhythms, as well as a way to manually input a chord progression, a

Performance tab where you can break up your chords into smaller notes, and an **Advanced** tab that gives you fine-grain control over the chord-generating algorithm.

When it opens, by default, you'll see a list of 4 chords set up.

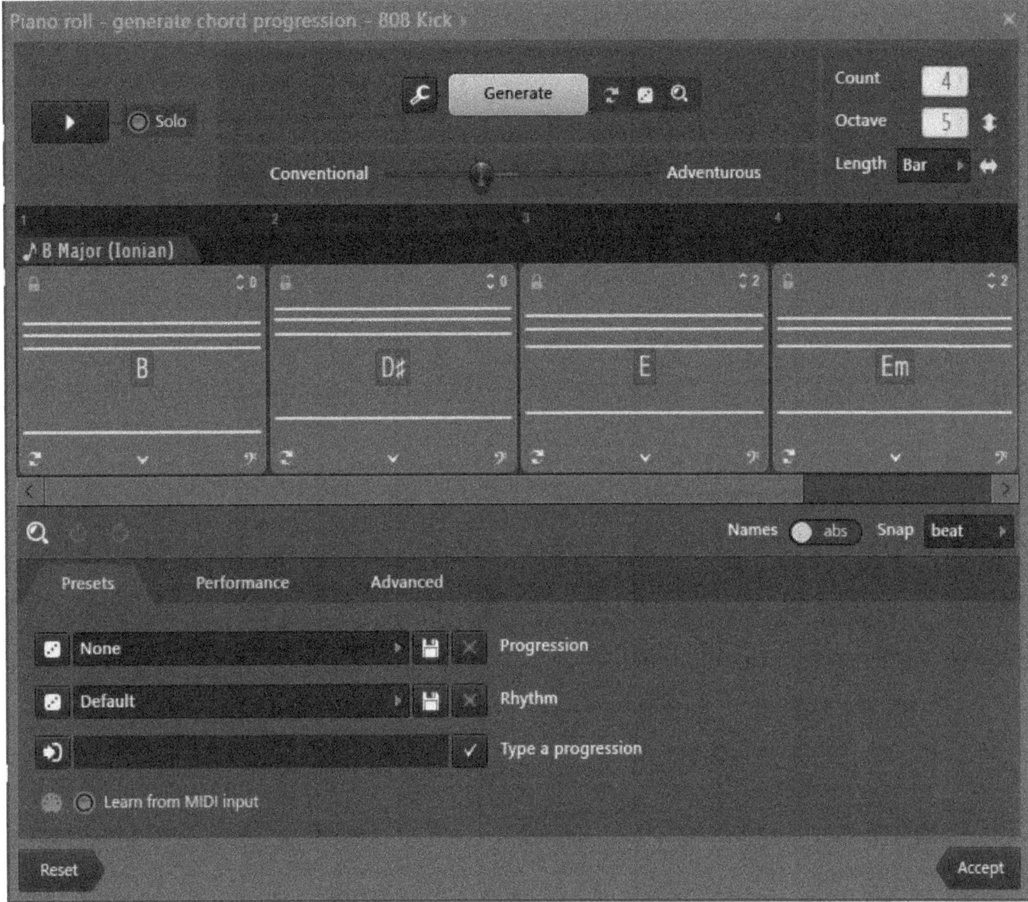

Figure 3.23 – Generate chord progressions

In the preceding screenshot example, the chords generated are **B**, **D#**, **E**, and **Em**. It assigns chords based on an algorithm, so you will likely see different chords in your setup. Later on in the plugin, you can tinker with the algorithm that generates chords if you choose.

If you hover over the chord notes (**B**, **D#**, **E**, or **Em**) and press *Alt/Opt* + *right-click* on the chord, you can hear the chord play. If you are happy with the chord progression, click **Accept** in the bottom right, and the notes are added to the Piano roll.

It is unlikely that the chord progression sounds good on the first try. Usually, you'll need to do a significant amount of swapping out chords before you find a good-sounding chord progression.

This plugin is intended to generate ideas. It's not expected to generate the final notes that you will use in your final project. You can spend endless time tinkering, trying to get the plugin to generate the ideal chords, but that's not the best use of your time. The smart way to use this plugin is to generate chords that are "good enough" to get started. Then you dive into the Piano roll, make adjustments, and do the editing heavy lifting.

There are a lot of features compacted into this plugin, so let's break it up into sections, starting from the top panel and working our way downwards.

Figure 3.24 – Generate button toolbar

- **Preview chord progression** (**Play** symbol) plays the chords.
- **Solo** plays just the chords (relevant if you have other instruments playing in the pattern).
- The **wrench** symbol lets you toggle on whether you want to generate the main notes and bass line notes.
- **Generate** creates the chord progression notes in the Piano roll.
- **Rework the existing progression** in **Generate** mode (the **rotating arrow** symbol), keeps the same existing scale when generating a new chord progression.
- **Start over** in **Generate** mode (the **dice** symbol), creates a new chord progression, ignoring the existing scale.
- **Analyze the notes found in the Piano roll** in **Generate** mode (the **magnifying glass** symbol), build the chords around the existing notes.
- Count the number of chords in the progression.
- Bass octave of the progression. Bass note refers to the lowest note that the chord is built on.

We've discussed the top panel. Now we can move on to the chords panel. Before you start generating chords, you'll first want to choose a scale. On the left side, just above the first chord suggestion, you'll see the scale that your chords are using. If you right-click on the scale, you'll see options for different scales. In the following screenshot, you can see that the scale currently is **E Major (Ionian)**. By right-clicking on the scale text (in my example, **E Major (Ionian)**), it brings up options for other scales.

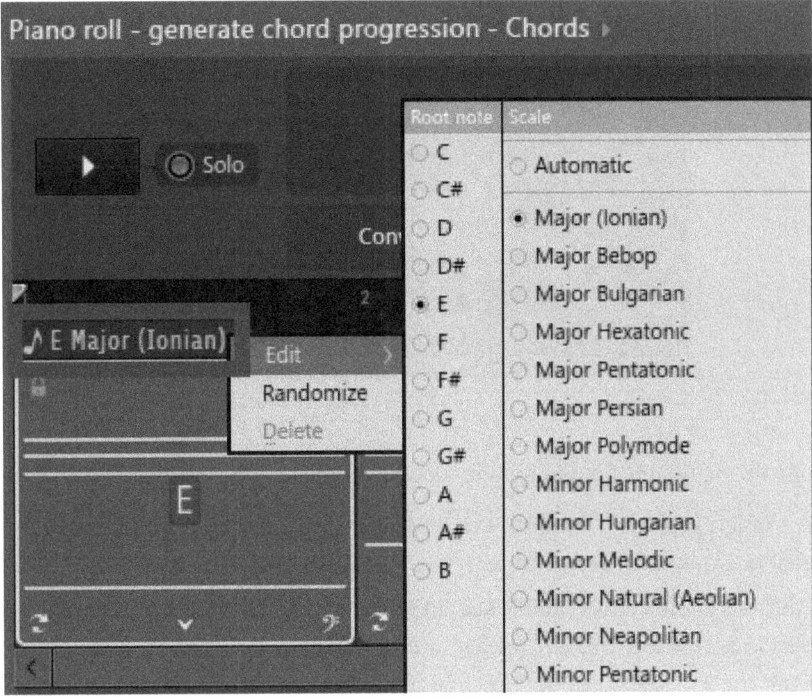

Figure 3.25 – Pick a scale

Once you've picked your scale, the chords you generate will use notes that fit into the scale.

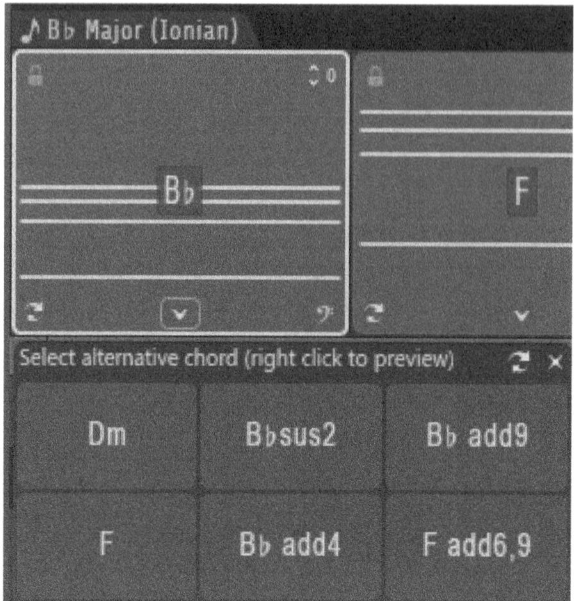

Figure 3.26 – Chord controls

Let's examine the highlighted chord in more detail.

- The top left **lock** icon lets you lock in a chord you like, so it doesn't change when you regenerate the chord progression.
- In the top right corner, you'll see an up and down arrow symbol called **Set Chord Inversion**. This lets you choose a chord inversion for the chord. A chord inversion just means you can rearrange the notes in the chord, trying out different chord notes on the top or bottom.
- In the bottom left corner, you'll see a rotating arrow symbol called **Regenerate current chord.** This lets you generate a new variation for just that specific chord.
- If you choose the center dropdown arrow called **Show chord alternatives**, you'll see a list of suggestions for chord alternatives to try out.
- In the bottom right corner, you'll see a bass clef symbol called **Set bass on/off**, which lets you turn on or off the bass note (the lowest note of the chord).

> **Tip**
>
> Here's a keyboard shortcut trick: you can hold *Alt* and *scroll on your mouse* while hovering over a chord to transpose the chord up a note.

Next, let's take a look at the chords below the bottom panel, as shown in the following screenshot. We're starting with the **Presets** tab selected.

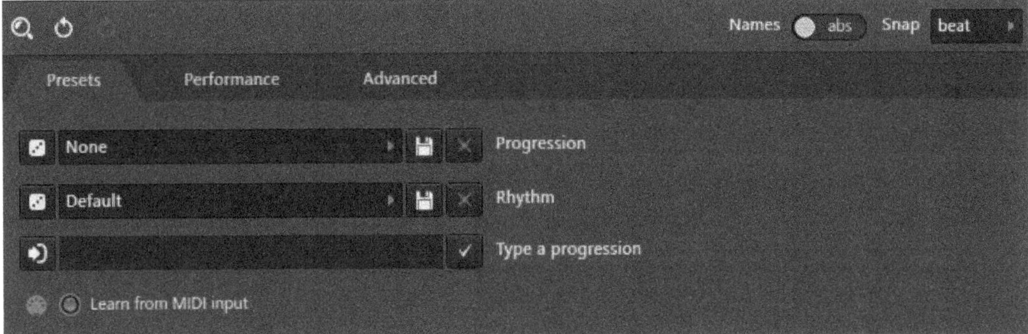

Figure 3.27 – Bottom panel and Presets tab

Let's discuss the controls at the top of the preceding screenshot and move our way to the right.

- **Zoom to fit all chords across the viewer** (**magnifying glass** icon) resizes the chord viewer if you scroll to the right of the chords and want to reset the view.
- **Previous Progressions** (circular **arrow** icon) reverts any change you make inside the plugin.
- **Redo** lets you redo, if you undo.
- **Names** toggles between absolute (standard letter names) and relative (scale-relative Roman numeral names).
- **Snap** set a snap resolution for chord movement.

Next, we come to three tabs: **Presets**, **Performance**, and **Advanced**. Let's take a look at the **Presets** tab first, as shown by the preceding image. Here you'll see several drop-down menus with the text **Progression**, **Rhythm**, and **Type a progression**.

- **Progression** allows you to choose a chord progression or randomly select from a list.
- **Rhythm** lets you choose the timing pattern for the chord progression. This will adjust the spacing for how long each chord plays.
- **Type a progression** allows you to type in the letters of the chord progression if you already know what chords you want.
- **Learn from MIDI input** allows you to override an existing chord.

To the right of the **Presets** tab, you'll find the **Performance** tab.

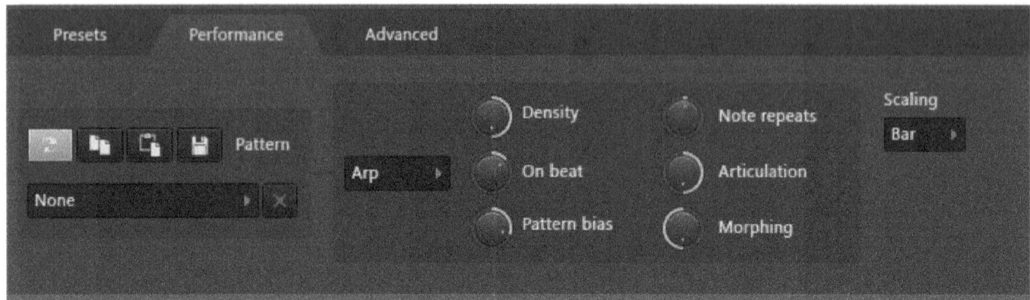

Figure 3.28 – Performance tab

The **Performance** tab is where you break down your chords into smaller fragments. On the left side, you'll find a section with the label **Pattern**. It contains a dropdown list of presets. In the preceding screenshot, it's the dropdown with the text **None**. If you scroll through the presets, you'll encounter a variety of ways to break up your chords into patterns.

The most important button here is the **Regenerate** button (the **circling arrow** icon). This will generate a new variation of the pattern each time you press it.

To the right of the **Pattern** label, you'll see a submenu panel of performance types. In the preceding screenshot, it's currently set to **Arp**. This submenu contains several options:

- **Arp**: Notes of a chord are played one after another in sequence instead of being played all at once.
- **Chop**: A group of two or more notes played at the same time.
- **Humanize**: Adjusts notes' timing slightly off the beat so that a performance feels less mechanical and more natural, like how a human would play.
- **Bassline**: Adjusts timing just for the bassline while leaving the chords untouched.

To the right, you'll find a series of knob effects to apply to the pattern. The knobs that appear there change depending on which performance type you selected (Arp, Chord, Humanize, Bassline). Let's explore these in more detail.

If **Arp** is selected:

- **Density**: Number of notes rather than rests.
- **Note repeats**: Frequency of consecutive note repetitions.
- **On beat**: How closely notes in the **arpeggio** start on the beat.

Note

An arpeggio is a musical technique in which the notes of a chord are played one after another instead of all at once.

- **Articulation**: Change note length.
- **Pattern bias**: How closely the Arpeggio reflects the selected **Pattern**.
- **Morphing**: How much the Arpeggio pattern changes across the chord progression.

If **Chop** is selected:

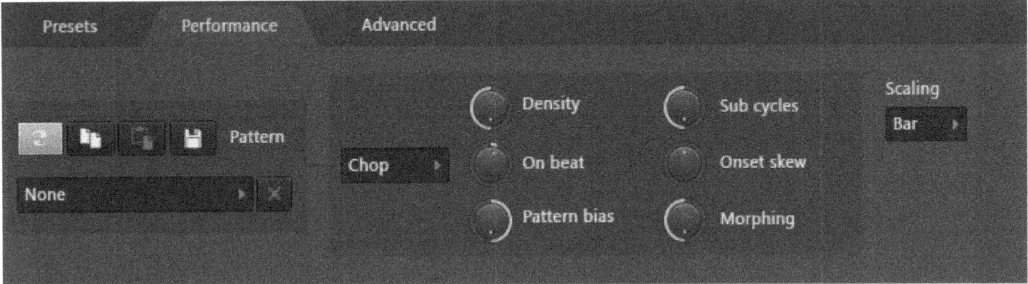

Figure 3.29 – Chop performance type

- **Density**: How many chops are created compared to the scaling setting.
- **Sub cycles**: How many smaller repeated patterns fit inside each scaling time interval.
- **On beat**: Higher values make chops start right on the beat. Lower values make them start off the beat. Tip: Turn this down for a more syncopated (offbeat) feel.
- **Onset skew**: Lower values pack more chops near the start of each scaling interval. Higher values pack them closer to the end.
- **Pattern bias**: Controls how closely the chops follow the chosen pattern.
- **Morphing**: Controls how much the chop pattern shifts as the chord progression moves forward.

If **Humanize** is selected:

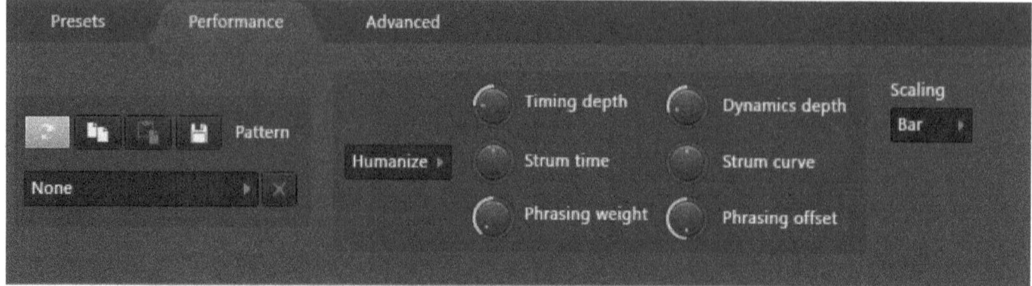

Figure 3.30 – Humanize performance type

- **Timing depth**: How much the start times of notes are shifted.
- **Dynamics depth**: How much the note volumes (velocities) vary.
- **Strum time:** How wide the spread is between notes in a strum.
- **Strum curve**: Changes the strum speed as it plays out.
- **Phrasing weight**: How strongly phrasing across the set time interval (Scaling × Lengths per loop) affects the dynamics.
- **Phrasing offset**: Phrasing works by applying a (morphed) sinusoidal push-pull to dynamics over a looped time interval. Altering the offset determines where in those loops the note velocities tend to increase or decrease.

If **Bassline** is selected:

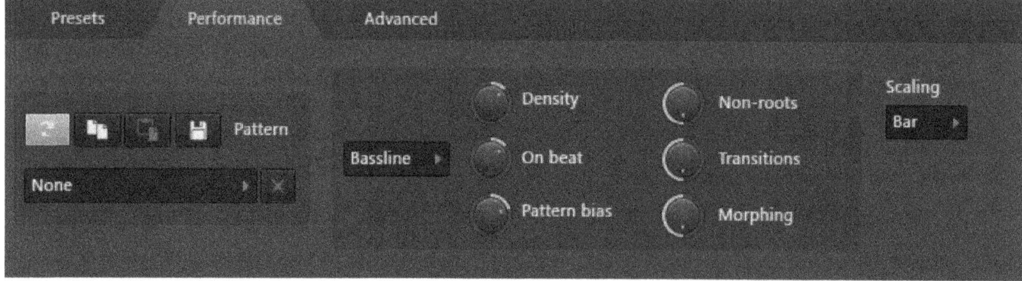

Figure 3.31 – Bassline performance type

- **Density**: Higher density means more chops are created compared to the scaling setting.
- **Non-roots**: Controls how much the notes move away from the root note.
- **On beat**: Controls how much the chops start right on the beat. Lower values make them start off the beat. Tip: Turn this down for a more syncopated (offbeat) feel.
- **Transitions**: Controls how likely the bassline is to react to upcoming chord changes.

- **Pattern bias**: Controls how closely the chops follow the chosen pattern.
- **Morphing**: Higher morphing makes the chop pattern change more as the chords move along.

Finally, let's discuss the final tab, the **Advanced** tab, for those who want fine control over the generation algorithm.

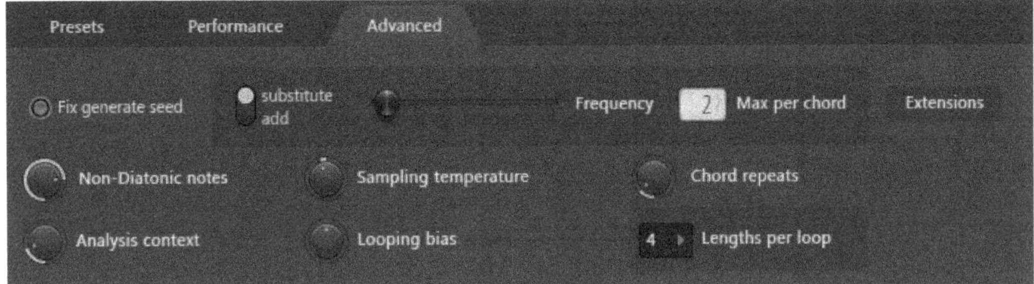

Figure 3.32 – Advanced tab

Here's a description of the controls:

- **Fix generate seed**: Turn this on to keep results the same while you change settings. Turn it off, and the AI will use new random seeds, which can make results change a lot each time.
- **Extensions**: Choose whether chord changes should *replace* the main notes or simply be added on top as extra notes.
- **substitute/add** (switch): Switch between replacing the main chord notes with the new ones or just adding the new ones as extras.
- **Frequency (slider)**: Set how often extra notes (extensions) are added.
- **Max per chord**: Set the maximum number of extra notes allowed for one chord.
- **Non-Diatonic notes**: Set how far notes can step outside the main scale.
- **Sampling temperature**: Set how normal or unusual the chords are. Lower values give you safe, common progressions. Higher values make chords sound more unusual, with stranger transitions and more dissonance.
- **Chord repeats**: Set how often the same chord is allowed to repeat
- **Analysis context**: Set how much the AI looks at the bigger picture of the progression, not just the single chord at that moment. At zero, it only looks at the notes in the current chord's time slot.
- **Looping bias**: Set how the AI chooses chords over each loop. Turn it right to keep chords more similar across loops. Turn it left to make chords change more and add variety.

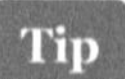

Works only if the progression has enough loops.

- **Length per loop**: Sets how many time intervals make up one loop. The AI uses this to shape the music – for example, progressions often finish or "resolve" at the end of a loop, and humanization can add variety across the loop's length.

We've learned how to generate chords inside the Piano roll both from scratch and using chord-creating tools. If you're looking for some next steps, I recommend checking out the chords used in songs you like and playing around with the notes in the Piano roll. It's easy to find and download MIDI notes online for any popular song if you search for them. Next, let's discuss how to record instrument notes directly into the Piano roll.

Recording into the Piano roll with MIDI instruments

If you want to play an instrument and capture what you play, you'll need to know how to record MIDI notes into your project. Recording MIDI is what lets you capture your performance – whether you're playing on a MIDI keyboard, pad controller, or even clicking notes in with your mouse. This section will walk you through the basics of setting up, recording, and editing MIDI so you can quickly turn ideas into something you can hear and build on.

MIDI is a way for software and electronic devices to pass music information from one device to another so that the new device knows what notes to play. You use MIDI to record notes.

If you already know how to play live instruments, you may want to look into acquiring a MIDI instrument. If you have MIDI instrument hardware, such as a MIDI keyboard, MIDI guitar, or another MIDI controller, you can play notes on the hardware instrument live, and FL Studio can record the notes directly into the Piano roll. This is a very efficient method of recording melodies.

I personally am a big fan of the instruments made by the company *Native Instruments*. I own a MIDI keyboard called *Komplete Kontrol* and their drum pad called *Maschine*. These can be used to play and record MIDI notes. If you're interested in learning more, you can learn more about their products at: `https://www.native-instruments.com/en/catalog/music-creation/hardware/`.

To record notes with your MIDI instrument hardware, take the following steps. If you don't have a MIDI keyboard, you can play notes by pressing keys on your computer keyboard:

1. Create a new pattern and select the instrument from the **Channel rack** that you want to play.
2. Select the **record** button and select the **Notes and automation** option.

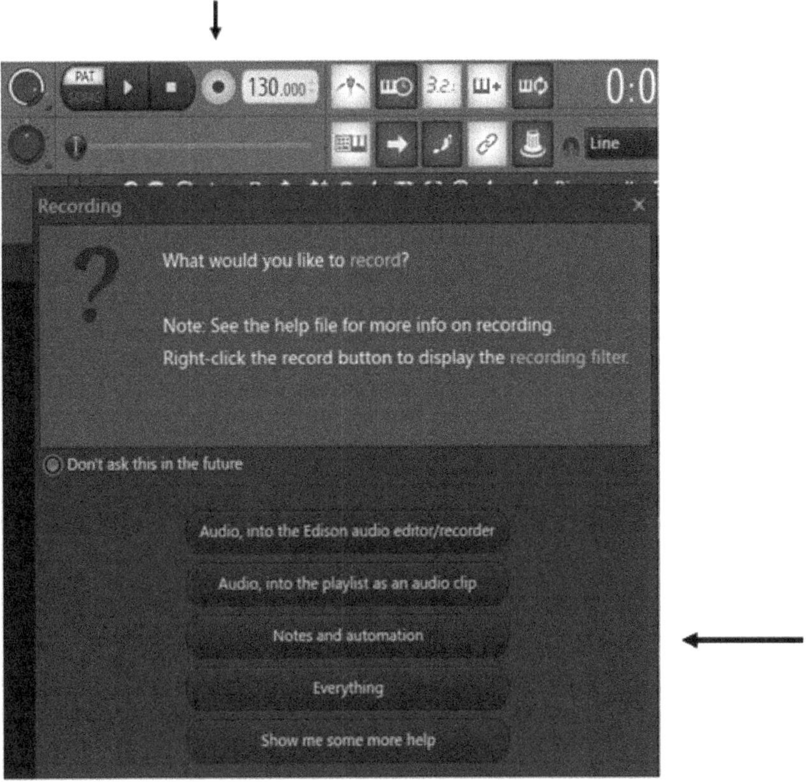

Figure 3.33 – Recording notes and automation

Once you press play, any notes that you play into the MIDI instrument are inserted into the Piano roll as the pattern progresses.

Once your music is recorded into the Piano roll, you'll need to adjust the timing of the notes to make it fit with the rest of your arrangement. In the next few sections, we'll learn about tools you can use to edit your recorded notes.

The snap to scale tool

FL Studio has a tool that can force your notes to fit into a chosen scale so that you don't hit incorrect notes outside of the scale. Once enabled, any new notes input into FL Studio will be forced to fit into the scale. This is very handy both when you're manually inputting notes with a mouse or when you're recording a MIDI instrument live.

At the top left of the Piano roll, you'll find the **snap to scale tool**.

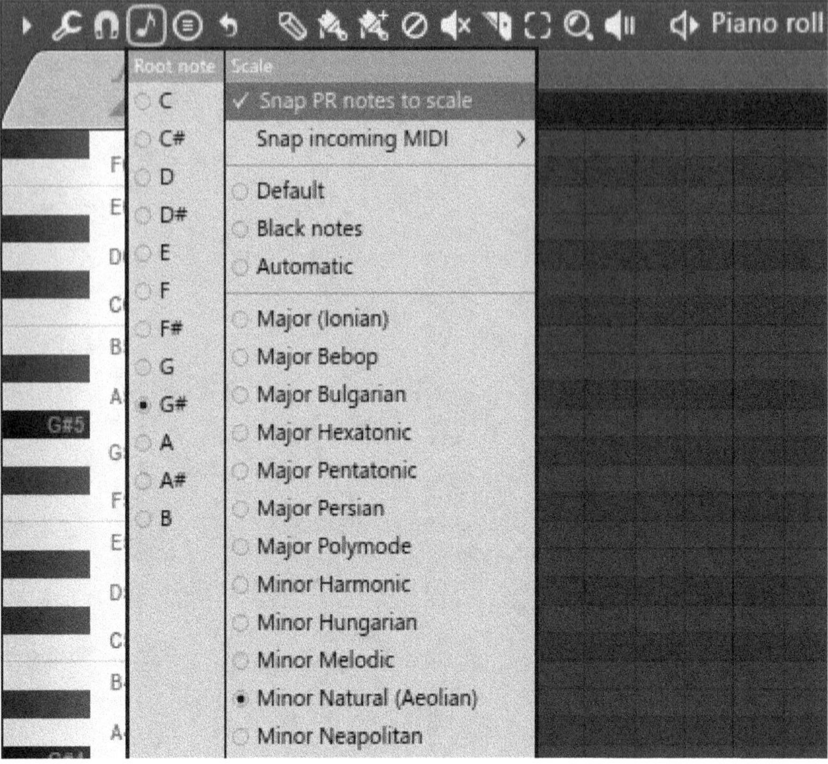

Figure 3.34 – Snap to scale tool

Make sure the **Snap PR notes to scale** option is selected. This will force your notes to fit your scale.

Then you can choose the root note for your scale, and then choose the type of scale you want your notes to fit.

You'll also see an option to **Snap incoming MIDI**; this is in case you are recording from a MIDI instrument and want incoming notes to be forced to fit the scale.

The snap to grid (magnet) tool

The snap to grid tool assists with making notes fit in the song tempo. The Piano roll segments notes in the Piano roll by beats. A beat is a basic unit of time and is the click you'll hear when you turn on the metronome. The number that you see at the top of the screen next to the record button is known as **BPM** (short for **beats per minute**). In the preceding screenshot, it's the number **130**. This is how fast your music is playing.

Using snap to grid (**magnet** icon), you can control what increments of a beat you want the Piano roll to divide into. By left-clicking on the snap to grid tool in the top-left corner of the Piano roll, you can see the timing options.

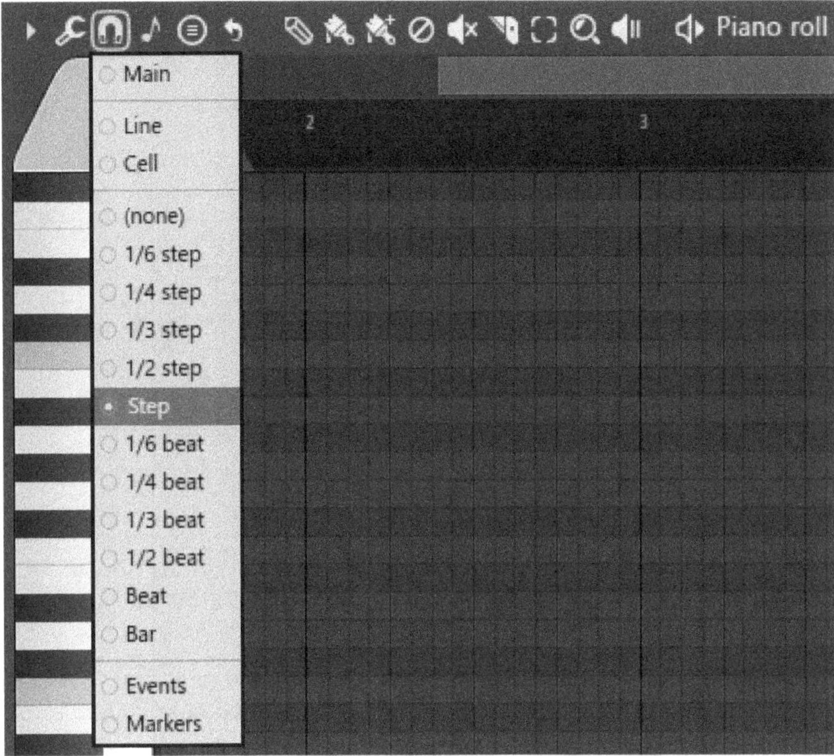

Figure 3.35 – Magnet tool

As you can see in the preceding screenshot, you can divide the Piano roll grid into increments of **Bar**, **Beat**, **1/2 beat**, and so on. Once you've selected an option, you'll notice that the number of increments in the Piano roll grid will increase or decrease depending on your selection. The snap to grid tool works the same way in the Playlist as it does in the Piano roll. Snapping to the grid is the precursor step needed in order to quantize notes, which we will discuss next.

Quantizing notes – fix the timing of your notes

If you record notes directly into the Piano roll with a MIDI instrument, you might notice your notes are out of sync with the timing of your song. You can fix this with a tool known as **quantize**. **Quantizing** means you're making your notes sync up with the Piano roll grid. The tool will adjust the start and end times of your notes to fit in time with the grid. You can quantize everything in the Piano roll or just the start times of your selected notes, as seen in the following screenshot:

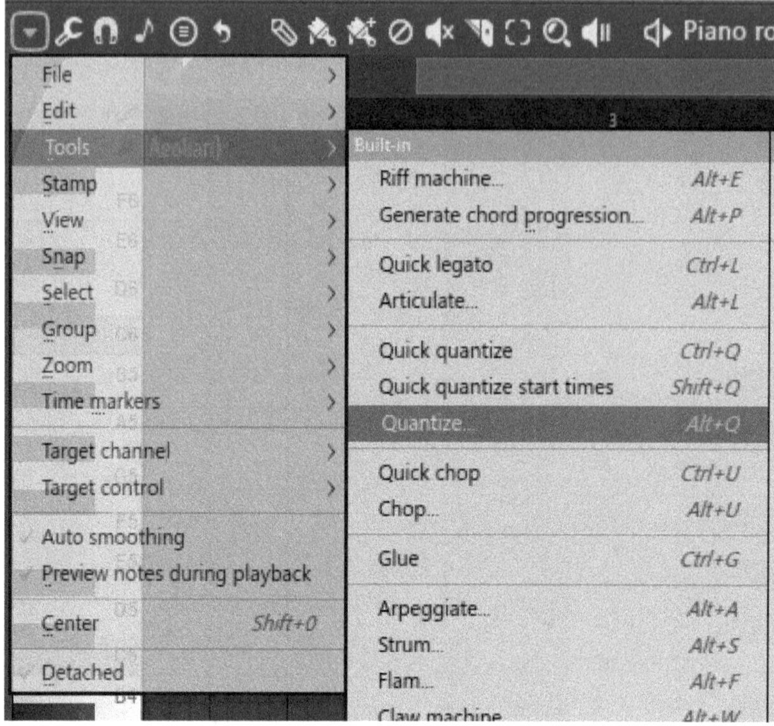

Figure 3.36 – Quantizing

If your notes are already in sync, you won't see any difference because your notes are already quantized. If your notes are out of sync, the quantize tool will slightly move your Piano roll notes forward or backward until they sync up with the grid timing. Making your notes fit perfectly with the grid is sometimes not the goal; in this case, we need a tool to help, which we will discuss next.

Humanize tool – make your notes sound like they were played live

FL Studio introduced a feature that I've been requesting for several years: the ability to *humanize* notes. **Humanize** means to adjust the timing of notes in the Piano roll so they are slightly off the beat. It shifts the notes slightly before or after the beat to add imperfection to a chord being played.

You can think of humanizing as the opposite of quantizing. Quantizing shifts everything to make the notes hit their marks perfectly. Humanizing shifts everything off the mark slightly.

So why would you want to humanize notes? Humanizing adds imperfection to your notes. Humans are not robots, so the timing with which they hit notes is not perfectly on the grid.

I personally find it useful when I've finished composing a song for an acoustic instrument and the notes sound a little robotic, perfectly hitting every single beat. Humanize can make it sound just a little bit imperfect, like it was a human playing and less like it was software playing it.

To use the Humanize effect, you'll first need to have some chords already existing in the Piano roll. Alternatively, you can quickly generate them with the Generate chord progression tool, which we discussed earlier in this chapter. Once you have some notes pre-existing in the Piano roll, you can find the Humanize tool by clicking the wrench symbol in the top left of the Piano roll, as shown in the following screenshot.

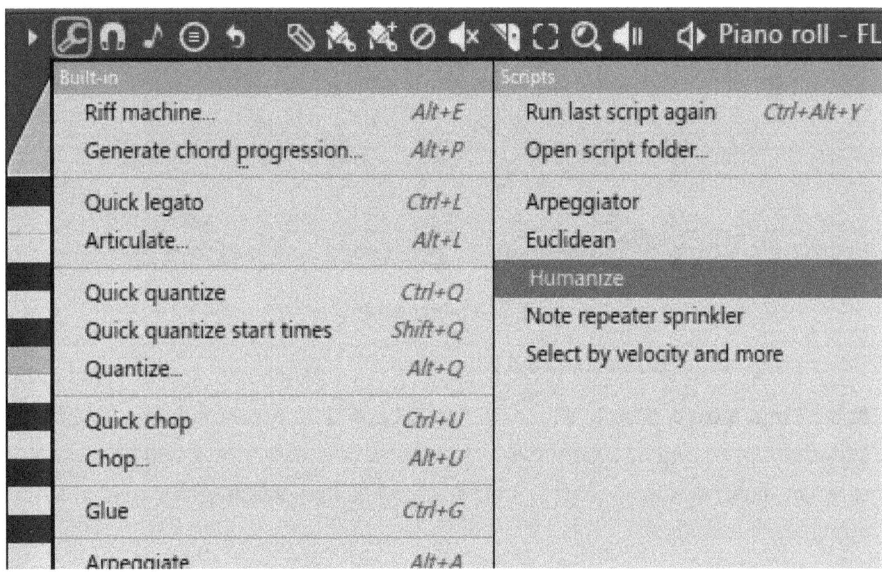

Figure 3.37 – Loading Humanize tool

Clicking **Humanize** opens the **Humanize Tool** tab.

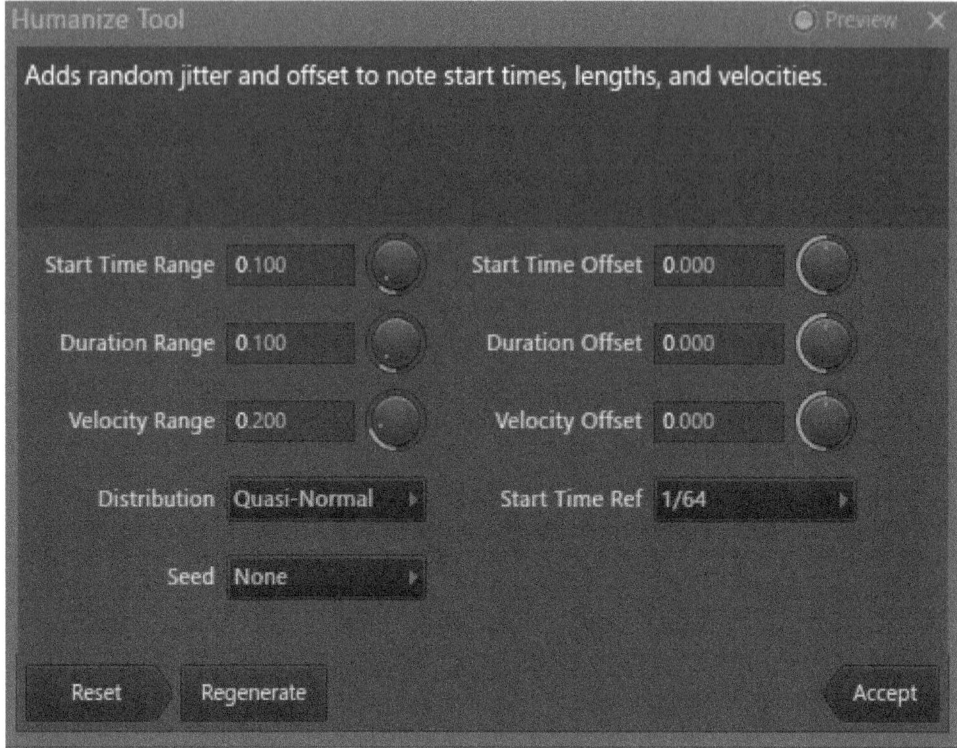

Figure 3.38 – Humanize Tool tab

Here's a description of the **Humanize Tool** controls:

- **Start Time Range**: This is the main "feel" knob. It controls how much randomness is added to the timing of your notes. A higher value means notes will be more noticeably early or late, adding a loose, human feel. A low value gives just a tiny, almost imperceptible nudge.
- **Duration Range**: This controls how much the length of each note will vary. Just like a real player doesn't hold every note for the exact same amount of time, this makes some notes shorter and some longer within the range you set.

- **Velocity Range**: This adjusts how much the volume (hit strength) of each note will vary. A real musician doesn't play every chord at the same volume; they add accents and softer touches. This setting brings that dynamic life to your pattern.
- **Distribution**: This is the "style" of randomness. Quasi-Normal (or often just "Normal") means most notes will be clustered very close to the original timing, with only a few notes being very early or very late. This creates a natural, believable human feel instead of a completely random, chaotic one.
- **Start Time Offset**: This lets you slide the timing of every note earlier or later by a fixed amount. It's a global nudge to make the entire part feel slightly ahead of or behind the beat.
- **Duration Offset**: This lets you change the length of every note by a fixed amount. Choose this if you want all the notes to be a bit shorter or longer.
- **Velocity Offset**: This lets you change the volume of every note by a fixed amount.
- **Start Time Ref**: This sets the grid size that the **Start Time Range** is based on. Setting it to 1/64 means the timing jitter can move notes by up to a 64th note's length (or whatever range you set). A smaller division (like 1/128) allows for finer, subtler timing changes.
- **Seed**: This is the starting point for the random number generator. None means it will pick a new random *humanization* pattern every time you click **Regenerate**. Typing a number here lets you lock in a specific random pattern you like and get the same result every time.
- **Regenerate**: The *roll the dice* button. It applies the same range settings you've chosen but calculates a new random pattern based on them. Click this until you get a humanization feel you like.

In addition to humanizing and quantizing notes, there are a series of other Piano roll tools available that I encourage you to try out.

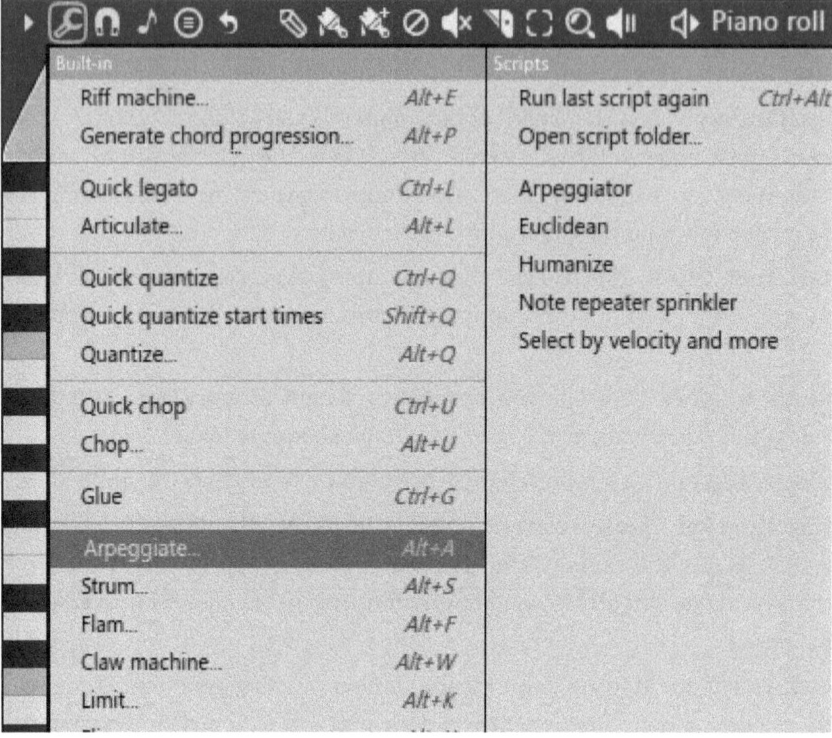

Figure 3.39 – Piano roll tool plugins

- **Chop...**: Slices your notes into smaller chunks based on the grid set by the grid magnets.
- **Glue**: Combines two adjacent notes into a single note.
- **Arpeggiate...**: Takes your notes, breaks them down into smaller pieces, and spreads the notes across several octaves.
- **Strum...**: Shifts the timing and velocity of notes to give the impression of strumming the way a guitar is strummed.
- **Flam...**: Allows you to play two notes very close together, blurring the sounds. This is a term mostly used with percussive instruments.
- **Claw machine...**: Removes notes, adds notes, and shifts the timing of notes to create new rhythms. This is good when used in combination with samples already sliced with the Slicex plugin, which is discussed in *Chapter 9*.
- **Limit...**: Allows you to choose a limit of pitches to which the Piano roll is confined. Any notes outside of the pitch range are transposed until they fit within the set range. For

example, if you set a limit to notes within C1 to C2, any notes lower than C1 or higher than C2 are transposed up or down in pitch until they fit inside the range.

- **Flip...**: Inverts selected notes horizontally or vertically in the Piano roll.
- **Randomize...**: Creates random notes. This can be confined within a set key.
- **Scale levels...**: Manipulates the velocity level of selected notes. Lets you adjust the overall volume of all your notes rather than individually for each note.
- **LFO...**: Controls the **Low Frequency Oscillator** (**LFO**). Lets you adjust the parameter of a control based on a sound wave.

So far, we've covered inputting notes into the Piano roll and adjusting the notes to better fit our song timing. Next, let's look at the bottom of the Piano roll in the Event Editor to learn how to fine-tune note inflection.

Editing note articulations with the Event Editor

The **Event Editor** gives you fine control over the inflection of notes in the Piano roll. At the bottom of the Piano roll, you'll find the Event Editor. Here, you can control a variety of parameters by clicking on the word **Control** in the bottom-left corner of the Piano roll.

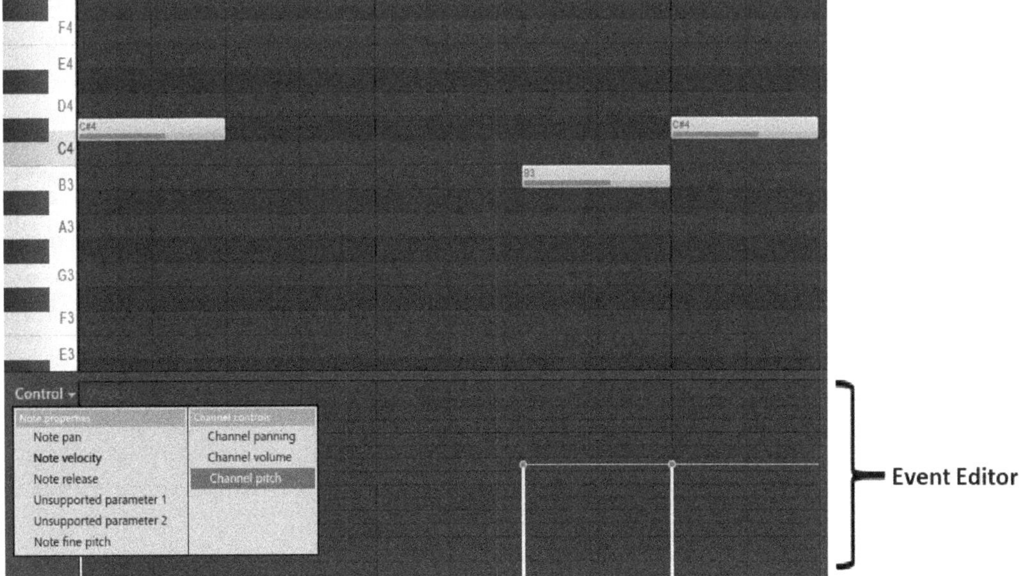

Figure 3.40 – Event Editor

Under the **Control** menu options, you can see controls for adjusting note inflections:

- **Note pan**: Determines whether you want sound to come out of the left or right speaker. By default, it comes out of both equally.
- **Note velocity**: Determines how forcefully a key is struck.
- **Note release**: The rate at which the sound of a note drops to no sound once a note finishes playing.
- **Note fine pitch**: The pitch of a given note. This can be changed on a note-to-note basis.
- **Channel panning**, **Channel volume**, and **Channel pitch**: The same as the note panning, volume, and pitch options, except that they affect the whole channel in the active pattern instead of the individual instrument selected. Any changes will affect all instruments in the pattern.

Next, let's discuss how to add variation to your individual note volume.

Using the Piano roll velocity

In the Event Editor, velocity is selected by default. **Velocity** is how forcefully a note is struck. For every note, you'll see a corresponding vertical line in the Event Editor. You can have a different velocity for each note.

My preferred way to adjust velocity is to hover over the note, press *Alt*, and scroll with the computer mouse. You can also adjust the velocity by left-clicking in the Event Editor in the grid section.

Here's a tip for how to use velocity. A real piano player wants to emphasize the melody. The main melody is usually high-pitched notes, and the lower notes are usually the accompaniment. To emphasize the main melody, the emphasized notes are played louder than the accompaniment. In the Piano roll, you can mimic a real instrument player by giving a higher velocity to notes of the melody you want to emphasize. Usually, these are the notes with the highest pitch. By playing around with velocity, you can add realism to synthesizer instruments.

Comparing instrument melodies with ghost notes

If you have another instrument playing notes in the same pattern, these will show up as faded-out notes, known as ghost notes. You can double-right-click on the grayed-out notes to switch to the instrument playing the notes.

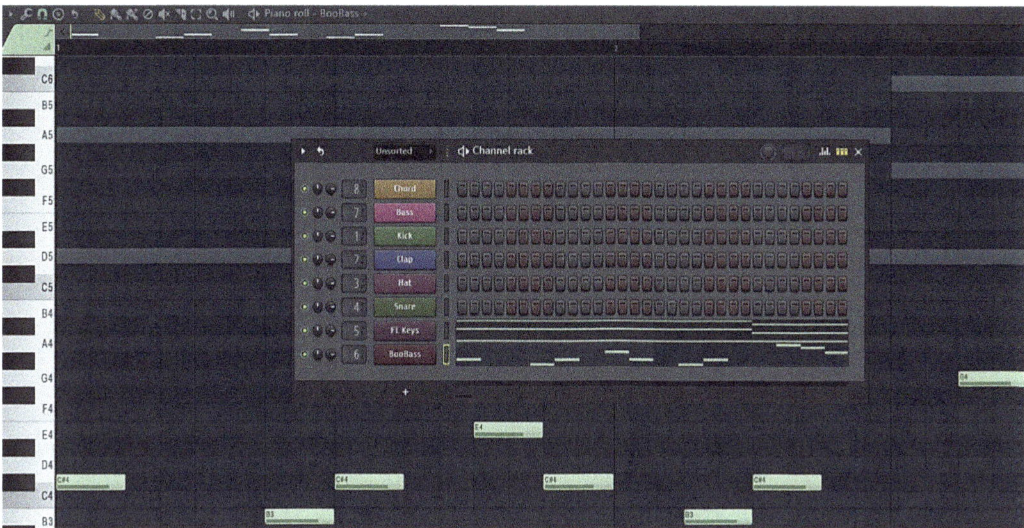

Figure 3.41 – Ghost notes

In the preceding screenshot, the **BooBass** instrument is currently selected, and we are seeing the BooBass notes in the Piano roll. In the **Channel rack**, we can also see that **FL Keys** has several notes. In the Piano roll, these show up as faded-out notes. What this means is that even though we have the **BooBass** instrument selected, we can still see the notes being played by **FL Keys** in the pattern. If we wanted to change from the **BooBass** instrument to the **FL Keys** instrument, we could easily do this by double-right-clicking on the grayed-out notes.

We've learned how to easily switch between instruments.

Creating sliding notes

Sliding notes are where the pitch of one note transforms into a new pitch. Sliding notes are very commonly used with sub-bass instruments. You can use the Piano roll to add notes that slide from one pitch to another. Only native FL Studio plugins are guaranteed to be able to use the sliding note feature in the Piano roll. External plugins often are unable to use this feature. To use sliding notes, we need to load up a plugin that allows sliding notes. To do so, execute the following steps:

1. Create a new pattern.
2. In the **Channel rack**, insert the **3x Osc** synthesizer.

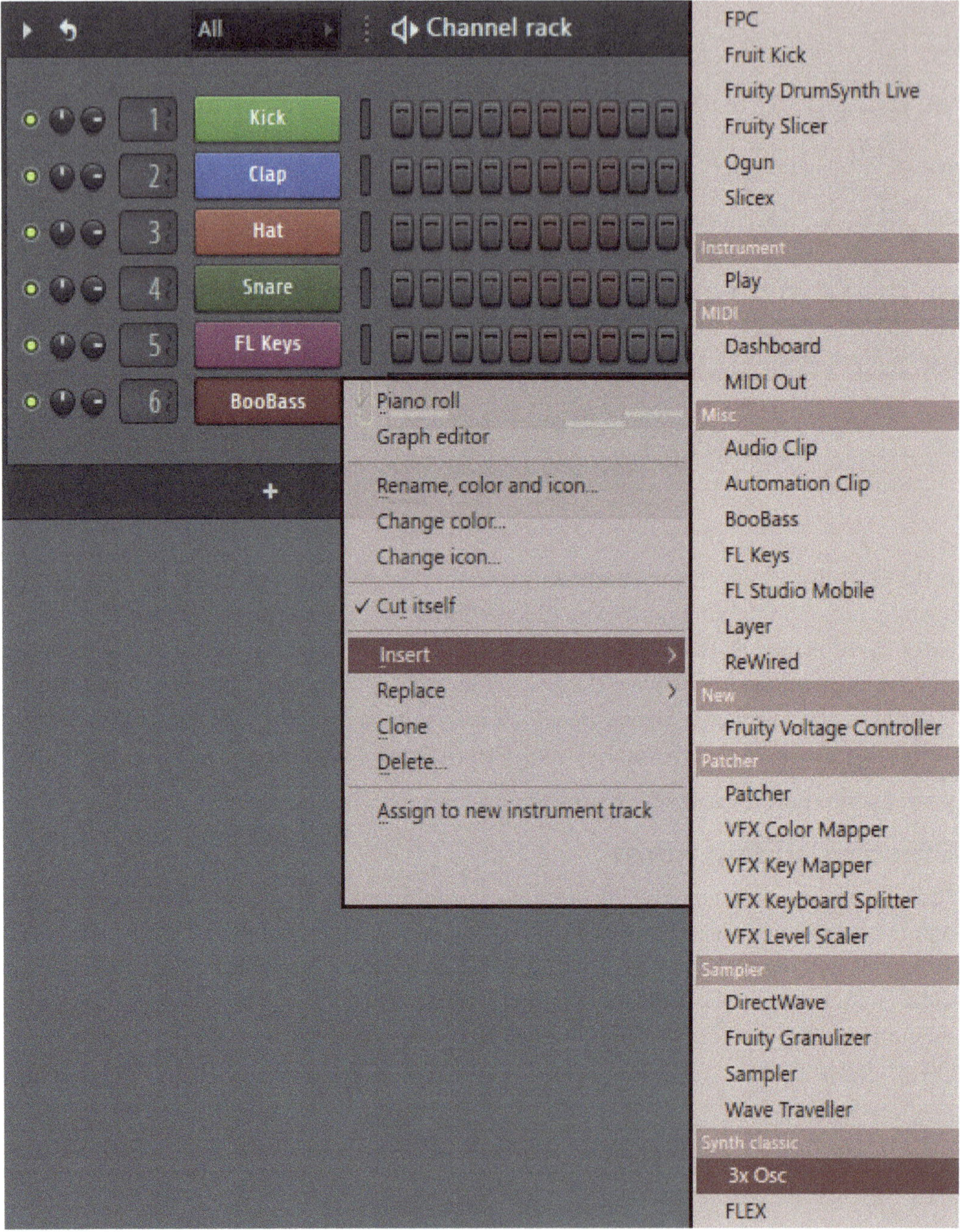

Figure 3.42 – Inserting the 3x Osc synthesizer

3. Using the **3x Osc**, we can create sliding notes. Open up the **3x Osc** instrument in the Piano roll.

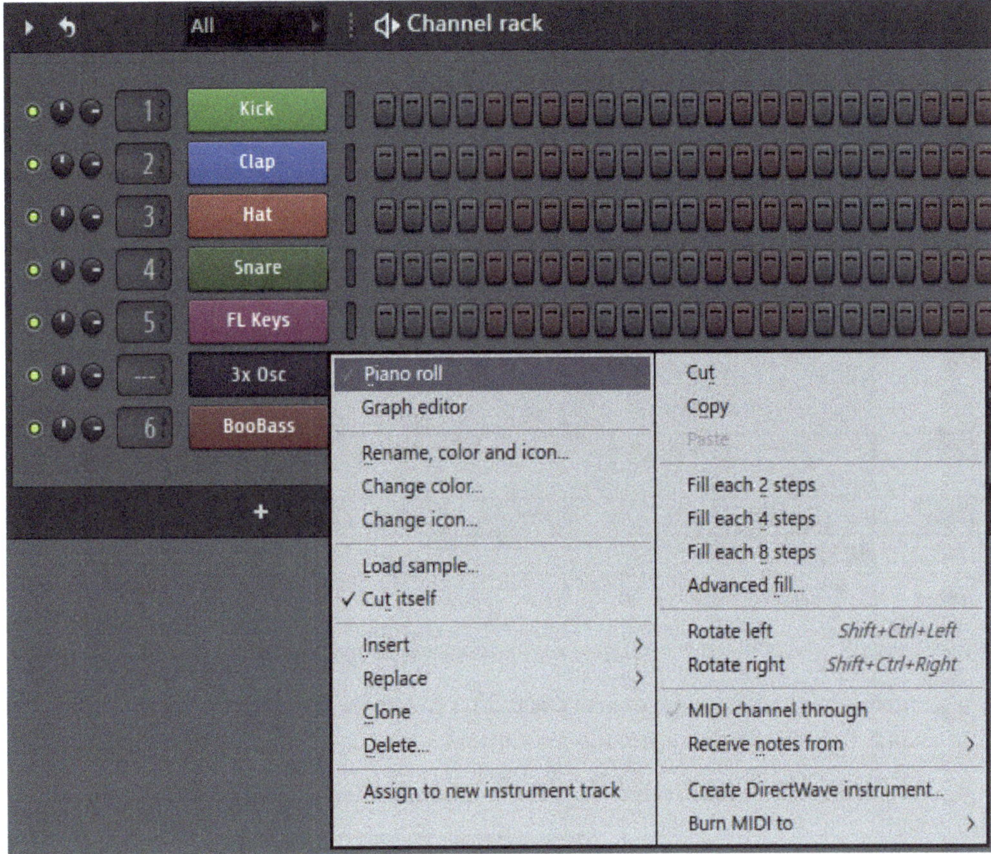

Figure 3.43 – The 3x Osc synthesizer in the Piano roll

4. Once in the Piano roll, left-click to add notes so that you have the following pattern.

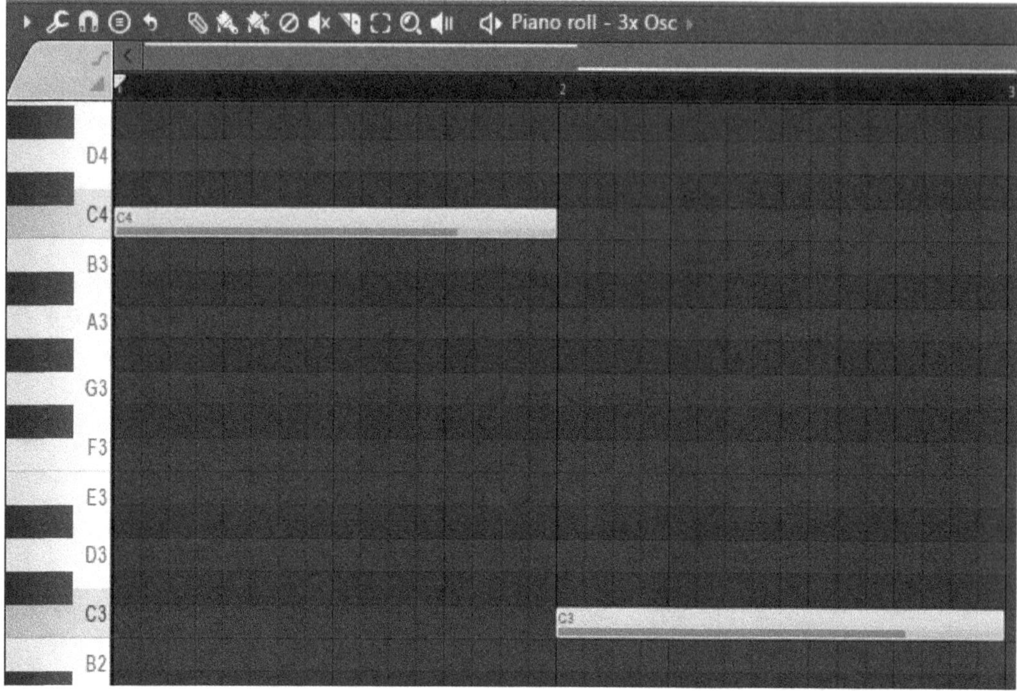

Figure 3.44 – Adding notes to the Piano roll

Here, we've added two notes to **C4** and **C3**. What we want to happen is for the pitch to slide from the first note into the second note.

5. To add a sliding pitch, select the **slide** tool from the top-left corner of the Piano roll.

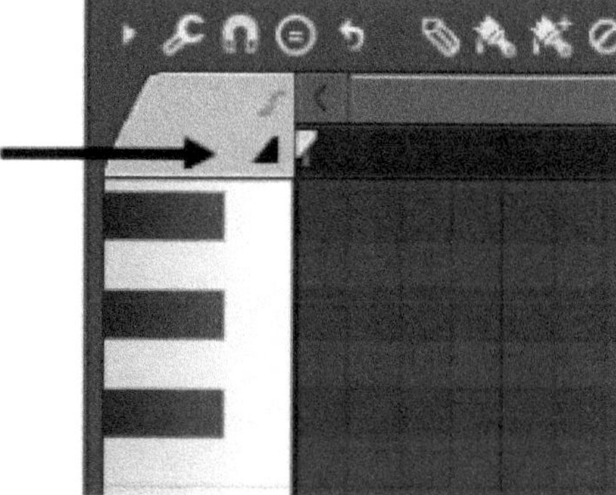

Figure 3.45 – Slide tool

When the **slide** tool is selected, it will add notes that slide from the current pitch into the new slide pitch. Add the **C3** note as shown in the following screenshot. You can tell that a note is a slide note by the **slide** symbol on the right of the note (**triangle** icon).

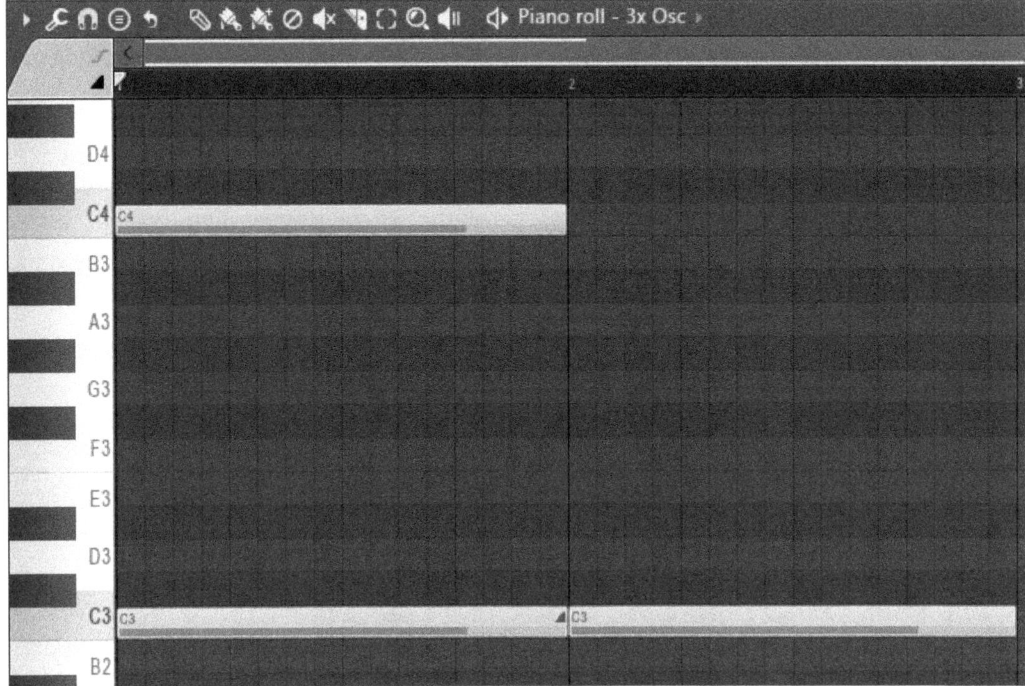

Figure 3.46 – Added sliding note

When you play the pattern, you'll hear the note with pitch **C4** sliding downward until it hits pitch **C3**. This technique can be used for sliding multiple notes at once.

Remember to click the slide tool again to turn it off when you're done, or else all notes you add going forward will be slide notes.

This technique can be used for samples as well as instruments. To do so, you can use samples in the **DirectWave** plugin (which we will explore in *Chapter 10*). You can then use the pitch slide effect on DirectWave. This is a big deal because you can turn any sound into a sample, even sounds from external VST instruments (**VST** is short for **Virtual Studio Technology**). In other words, with a little creativity, any sound can be turned into a slide note.

Exporting sheet music

Traditionally, when learning to play music, musicians learn to read sheet music. **Sheet music** allows musicians to transfer a musical idea to another musician so that they understand how to play the song. To read sheet music, they need to learn a large vocabulary of symbols and syntax so that they can understand what the other musician is conveying.

If you want to export your music in the form of sheet music so that a live musician can play it, select the **FILE** | **Export as score sheet** option. This will provide you with controls over the sheet music, such as the time signature and scale, as seen in the following screenshot:

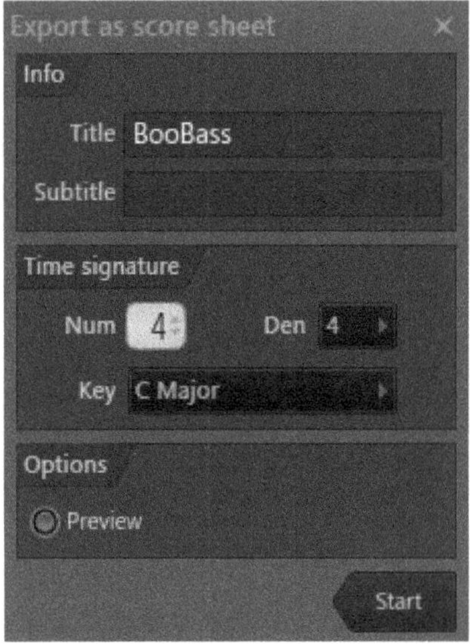

Figure 3.47 – Export as score sheet

After pressing **Start**, a PDF will be created with the sheet music, like the one in the following screenshot:

Figure 3.48 – Sheet music

For a professional musician, this sheet music may not provide enough syntax notation. If this is the case, you'll need to look into a more powerful music notation-creating tool. I recommend the open source music notation software MuseScore: `https://musescore.org/en`.

With MuseScore, you can copy in your MIDI file and create any kind of sheet music notation you desire. Next, let's learn how to export your MIDI notes.

Using and exporting MIDI scores

Piano roll has opened up the playing field for creating music to people who have not studied music theory. Reading music is now completely optional and not mandatory in order to make music.

If you wanted to copy music into FL Studio, do you need to manually write each note? No, there is a much easier method. You can copy MIDI notes directly into the Piano roll just by importing them. Doing so will require MIDI notes to copy. You can get MIDI notes for almost any song just by Google searching the name of the song followed by the words MIDI notes. Once you've found and downloaded the MIDI notes, you need to bring the MIDI notes into the Piano roll. You can do this either by dragging the file from anywhere on your computer into the Piano roll or by locating the MIDI note file in the FL Studio **Browser** and then dragging it into the Piano roll or Channel rack instrument. Once you've done this, the Piano roll will populate with notes from the MIDI file.

There are MIDI notes for songs available for free and for sale online, and these can be useful for getting song inspiration. An example of a website that sells MIDI note packs is `loopmasters.com`.

What if you wanted to export your music in a format that another musician can use? It's easy to export your MIDI notes or sheet music. To export your Piano roll melody as a MIDI file that another musician can then copy into their digital audio workstation, select the **Export as MIDI file...** option.

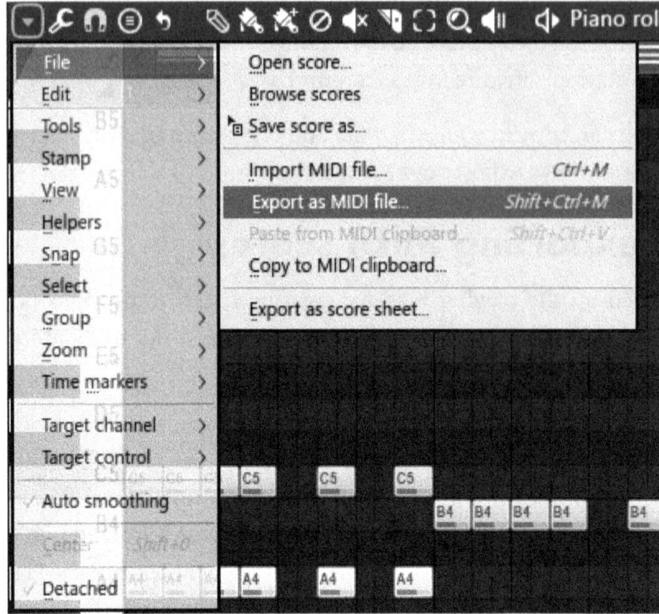

Figure 3.49 – Export as MIDI file

Exporting as a MIDI file will allow another music producer to copy the file into their digital audio workstation (regardless of whether they use FL Studio or another digital audio workstation) and receive the notes that you used in the Piano roll. We now know how to export music from the Piano roll.

Summary

In this chapter, we learned that the Piano roll is used to compose melodies. We learned the steps to create chord progressions from scratch.

We discovered how the chord progression tool can help bring songs to life. We saw that it's more than just a way to drop in chords; it's a guide that can spark ideas and give structure to your music. Presets offer an easy starting point, while the different settings let you shape progressions so they feel steady and familiar, or adventurous and unexpected. We also explored how small changes, like adding extra notes, shifting timing, or letting chords evolve over a loop, can make progressions feel more natural and alive. Put together, these tools give you the freedom to move from simple building blocks to rich, expressive progressions that can carry the mood of your track and inspire everything else you create around them.

You can insert notes into the Piano roll manually or by recording a MIDI instrument. The Event Editor allows you to edit individual note articulations. The Piano roll can use magnets and quantizing to get the timing of your notes in sync with the song tempo, as well as provide you with assistance when choosing notes in your scale. There's a tool called Humanize, which helps make note playing sound more natural and less robotic. The Piano roll makes it easy to compare melodies played by accompanying instruments and to copy notes from one instrument to another. The Piano roll also allows you to import and export MIDI notes and sheet music.

If you can learn to play the Piano roll, it means you can play any plugin that plays MIDI notes. This is a big deal, as it allows you to compose melodies for any instrument.

In the next chapter, we'll explore the **Mixer** and learn how to apply automation to controls.

Get this book's PDF version and more

Scan the QR code (or go to `packtpub.com/unlock`). Search for this book by name, confirm the edition, and then follow the steps on the page.

Note: Keep your invoice handy. Purchases made directly from Packt don't require an invoice.

4

Routing to the Mixer, Applying Automation, and Freezing Audio

Once you've arranged melodies for your song, you can begin **mixing**. Mixing is the process of combining instrument sounds and strategically blending them together. To mix music efficiently, you need to understand how audio is passed around the **Mixer**.

In this chapter, we'll learn how to get our sounds into the Mixer, known as **routing**. We'll also learn how to **automate** effects, which means having your effects change over time. Finally, we'll learn how to save sounds that come out of the Mixer, known as **rendering** audio. In future chapters, we'll dive into specific instruments and effect plugins, as well as best mixing practices that can be used to enhance your sounds.

In this chapter, we'll cover the following topics:

- What is mixing?
- Routing audio to the Mixer
- Navigating the Mixer console
- Applying automation to change effects over time
- Repurposing automation clips
- Editing automation clips
- Applying automation to external third-party plugins
- Freezing audio clips

What is mixing?

Mixing is the art of shaping sounds to achieve balance, space, and clarity in a recording, while also enhancing its emotional impact. It involves arranging each element so that every sound has its own place and purpose within the music. Traditionally, this was done in a hardware device called a **mixer control panel**. These devices were very expensive pieces of equipment, selling for thousands of dollars. In a **Mixer console**, you'd plug your instruments and microphones into the Mixer's ports and play sounds. The sound would be recorded on a recording device called a tape, which would store the audio information. The tape could then be played back and send the audio signals through the Mixer. The Mixer had knobs and buttons to finely adjust the volume, panning, and level of the input and output signals. You could then send the audio signals to effect plugins that manipulated the sound before sending the signal back to the Mixer.

Digital audio workstations like FL Studio replicate a Mixer console in looks and functions. Sounds are routed to the Mixer and given their own channel, known as a **mixer track**. The tracks allow you to process instrument sounds and apply effects to the audio. After the effects have been applied, the sounds are combined in a single channel called a master track. The master track is what gets exported as the finished song as an MP3 or WAV file.

From a high-level perspective, mixing is a very simple task: send signals to a Mixer, add effects, and export the song. Knowing what effects and where to apply them to improve a song is what distinguishes an amateur mixer from a seasoned mixing engineer.

Let's learn how to get your sounds into the Mixer.

Routing audio to the Mixer

Before we can mix our music, we first need to get our audio into the Mixer. The following is a screenshot showing the **FL Keys** and **BooBass** instruments in our **Channel rack**, which we are going to route to the **Mixer**. You can use any instrument you like in the Channel rack; the process will be the same:

Figure 4.1 – Channel rack and Mixer

In the preceding screenshot, we can see four samples and two instruments in the **Channel rack**. Our **Mixer** has no information mentioning instruments or samples yet. At this moment, the **FL Keys** and **BooBass** are being routed directly to the master channel. When we're done routing, all instruments and samples in the Channel rack will have their own assigned channel and will visually show up in the Mixer.

There are two ways to route an instrument in FL Studio to the Mixer. The first way is using the Channel rack, and the second is using the individual instrument itself.

Let's look at the Channel rack method first. This is the shortcut way:

1. In the **Channel rack**, select all instruments by double-left-clicking the rectangular button directly to the right of an instrument.

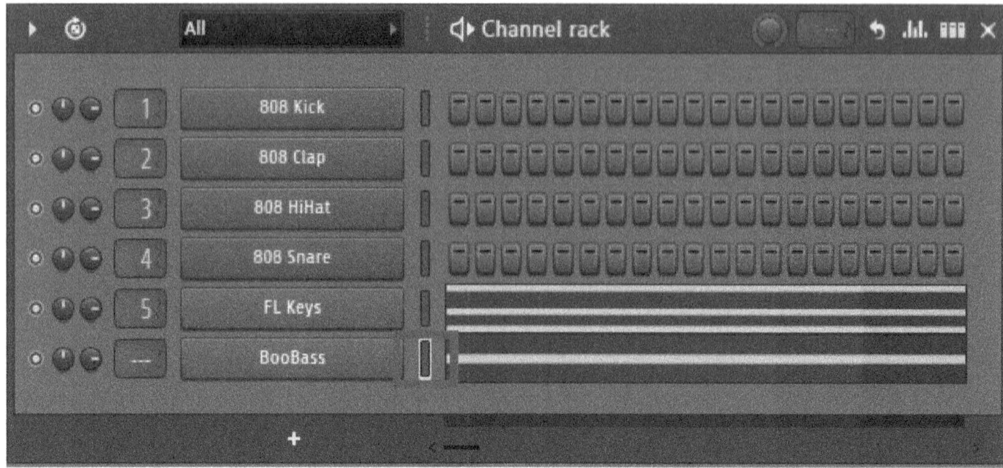

Figure 4.2 – Selecting Channel rack instruments

2. Next is an optional step, but it will be helpful for visual clarity. Go to the Channel rack option menu using the drop-down arrow, and select **Color selected** | **Random**.

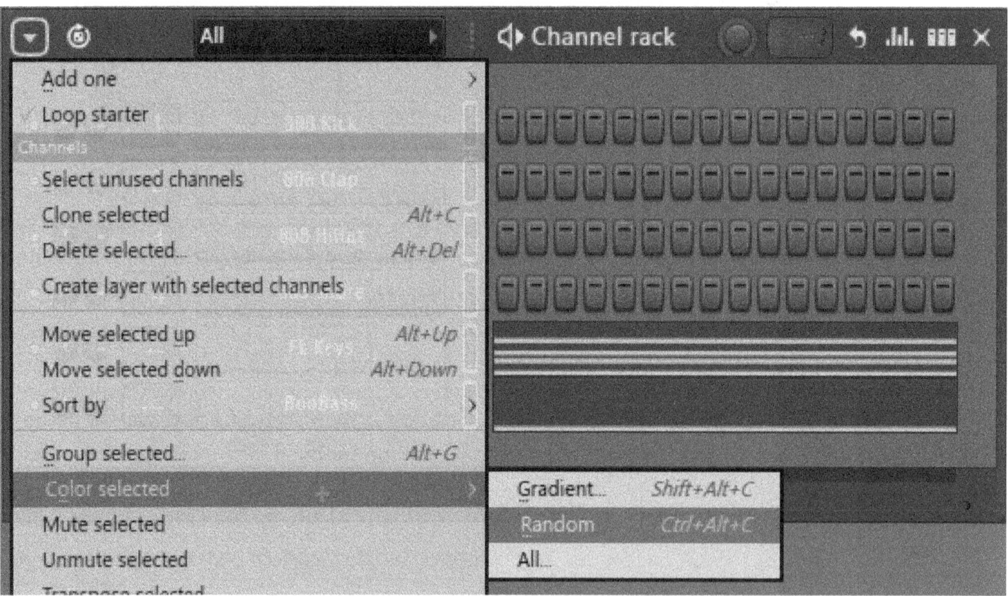

Figure 4.3 – Assigning color to instruments

Once selected, your instruments will be assigned a color at random. This will make it easy to visually distinguish your instruments in the Mixer.

3. Next, we assign the instruments to mixer tracks. Select all the instruments in the **Channel rack** that you want to route to the **Mixer**, as shown in the following screenshot. Open up the **Mixer** and left-click on **Insert 1** in the **Mixer**.

Figure 4.4 – Preparing to route instruments to the Mixer

Then, press *Shift* + *Ctrl* + *L*. This is a shortcut method for routing the instruments to the mixer track.

Figure 4.5 – Instruments routed to the Mixer

Your instruments have been routed to the **Mixer**. You can see that any names and colors in the **Channel rack** were transferred to the **Mixer**. This is the easiest way of routing your tracks to the Mixer.

Although I recommend the first approach, there are other methods too. An alternative method is to right-click on a single instrument in the **Channel rack** and select **Assign to new instrument track**.

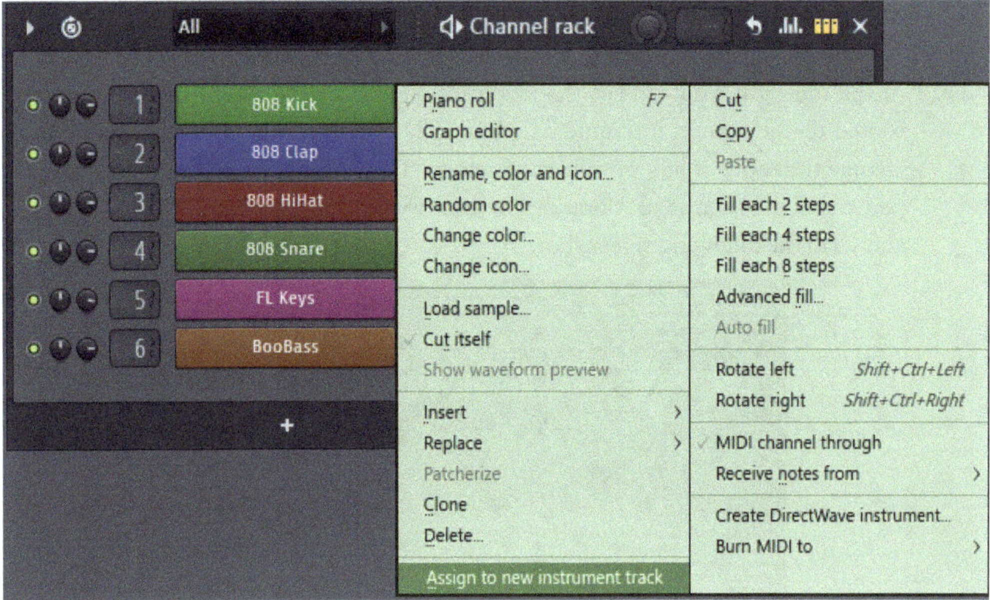

Figure 4.6 – Assign to new instrument track option

The **Assign to new instrument track** option will route the instrument to the **Mixer**. However, this second approach will not include the color, so I don't recommend this alternative.

Another way to route an instrument is to route from the instrument directly, as follows:

1. Left-click on any instrument in the **Channel rack**. I've chosen **BooBass** for its simplicity, but you should feel free to use any instrument you like. You can see **BooBass** in the following screenshot:

Figure 4.7 – Detailed settings gear Icon on BooBass instrument

Click the **gear** icon at the top left of the plugin, as shown in the preceding screenshot. The plugin will open up with a series of controls at the top of the plugin.

2. At the top right, you can see the mixer track number that the instrument is currently routed to. By default, instruments are usually routed to mixer track 1. So, if you don't change the route of any of your instruments, they will all be routed to mixer track 1. If you want to assign it to a brand-new track, you can left-click on the **TRACK** box, as shown in the following screenshot:

Figure 4.8 – Routing to a new track

BooBass will now be routed to a new track on the Mixer. If you hover your mouse over the track number and scroll with the mouse wheel, that will allow you to choose a specific mixer track to route to.

Any of the three methods shown will route instruments to the Mixer. I recommend the first approach because it's the fastest, but they all do the same thing in the end. Now that we have our instruments routed, let's take a detailed look at the Mixer console.

Navigating the Mixer console

I like to think of the Mixer console in terms of three distinct components:

- The **master channel**: A channel that all other channels eventually route to. Audio exiting this channel is what gets exported as the final song.

- The **insert mixer tracks**: Where audio is routed to from each instrument.
- The **effects rack**: Lists effects that are applied to each mixer insert channel.

In the following screenshot, we can see the **Mixer** and its components:

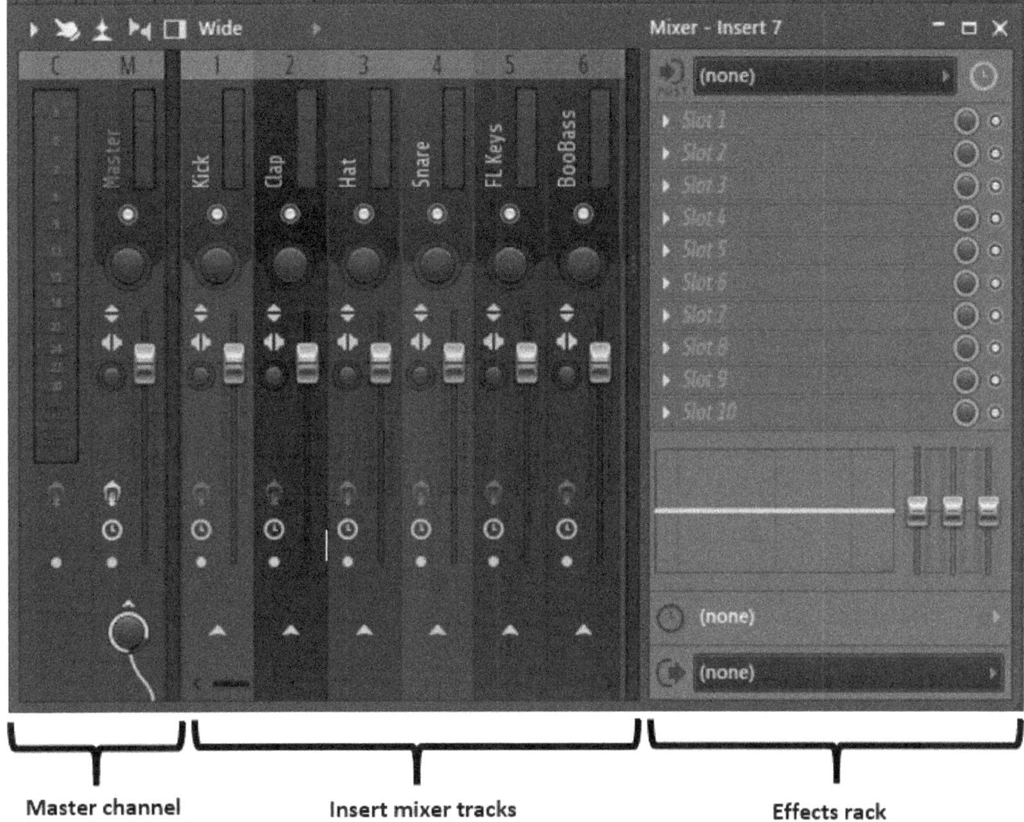

Figure 4.9 – Mixer console

Audio signals flow from the Channel rack into the insert mixer tracks. For each insert mixer track, effects from the effects rack are applied. Audio then leaves the insert mixer track and is either sent to another insert mixer track or to the master channel.

> **Note**
>
> The words *track* and *channel* can be used interchangeably.

Understanding the insert mixer track

It's called an insert mixer track because in the old days, these used to be individual pieces that you connected like LEGO bricks in the Mixer console. You literally inserted the track into the Mixer. The figure shows the parts of an insert mixer track:

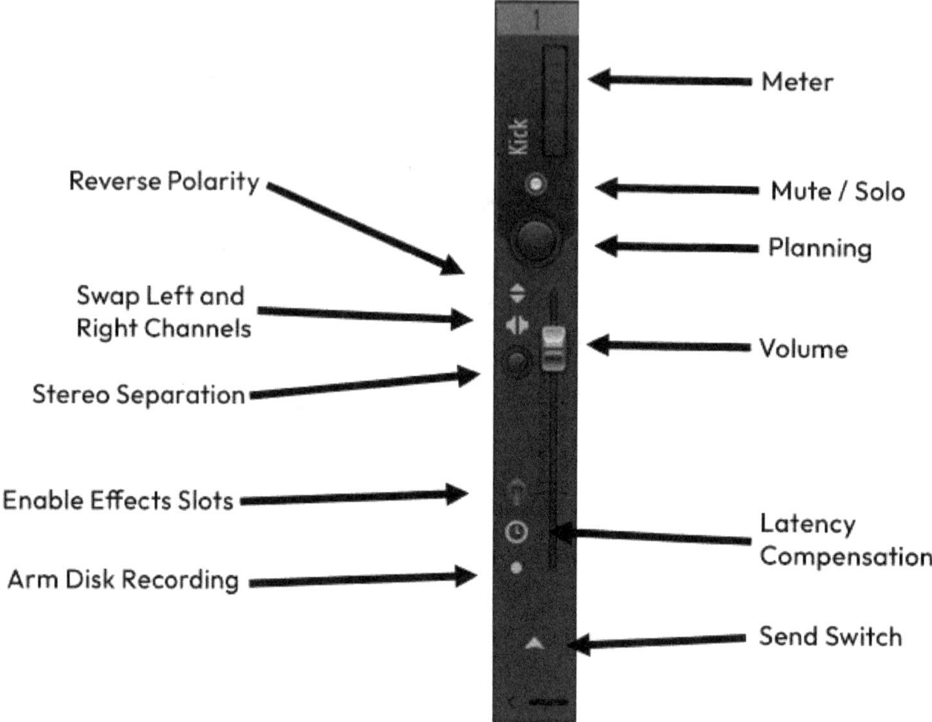

Figure 4.10 – Insert mixer track

Here's a breakdown of the insert mixer track from the top down:

- **Meter**: The volume of the audio signal received.
- **Mute / Solo Button**: Allows you to stop audio from exiting the mixer track. Useful for soloing individual tracks so that you can hear one sound at a time.
- **Panning**: Allows you to choose whether the audio comes out of the left or the right speaker.

- **Reverse Polarity**: Flips the audio waveform so that positive peaks become negative and vice versa. When playing two sounds simultaneously, sometimes audio waveforms can cancel one another out. If this is the case, you can invert the phase of one of the audio waveforms to resolve this issue.
- **Swap Left & Right Channels**: Swaps any panning effects from the left to the right and vice versa.
- **Stereo Separation**: A filter that allows you to increase or reduce any stereo effects. Stereo means that sound is coming out of both speakers and may have different sounds coming out of each speaker. The alternative is called mono, which means that all speakers have the exact same sound coming out of them.
- **Volume**: Controls how much audio input exits the insert mixer track after effects are applied. This controls the volume of the sound.
- **Enable Effects Slots**: Allows you to turn on and off all effects applied to the track at once.
- **Latency Compensation**: Adjusts for latency issues. Latency is an unwanted time delay, commonly known as lag.
- **Arm Disk Recording**: Turns on to receive audio from external microphones or devices.
- **Send Switch**: Allows you to choose where you want to send audio signals from this track. By default, it is set to send the audio signal to the master channel.

Understanding the master channel

The master channel has all the features of an insert mixer track. The only difference is that all insert mixer tracks eventually route into the master channel. The master channel is what eventually gets exported into the finished song.

Understanding the effects rack

For each insert mixer track, you can apply effects. Let's take a look at the effects rack:

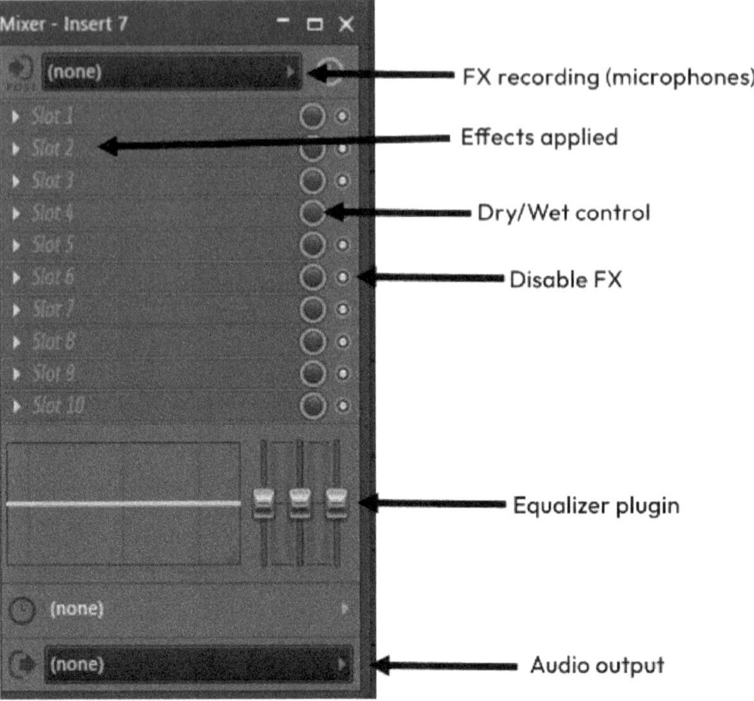

Figure 4.11 – Effects rack

Here's a brief breakdown of the effects rack:

- **FX recording**: Allows you to choose which input device you want to use, such as a microphone.
- **Effects**: Allows you to add effects. By left-clicking on an empty slot, you can add effect plugins.
- **Dry/Wet control**: Controls how much effect is applied from 0 to 100%. Dry means off, wet means on. If you hear someone talking about playing with the dry/wet of a plugin, it just means how much you turn it on. A fully dry signal is the original, unaffected sound, while a fully wet signal is the sound with the effect applied at its maximum.
- **Disable FX**: Turns the effect on or off.
- **Equalizer plugin**: Allows you to apply equalization effects to the audio signal.
- **Audio output**: Allows you to send the audio signal to another audio interface.

Next, let's learn how to apply an effect to our sound.

Applying an effect

Let's apply an effect to our sounds on a Mixer channel:

1. Select the **FL Keys** mixer track by left-clicking on it.
2. In the effects rack, left-click on an empty slot.
3. Select a plugin, such as **Fruity Delay 3**.

   The following screenshot illustrates adding an effect plugin:

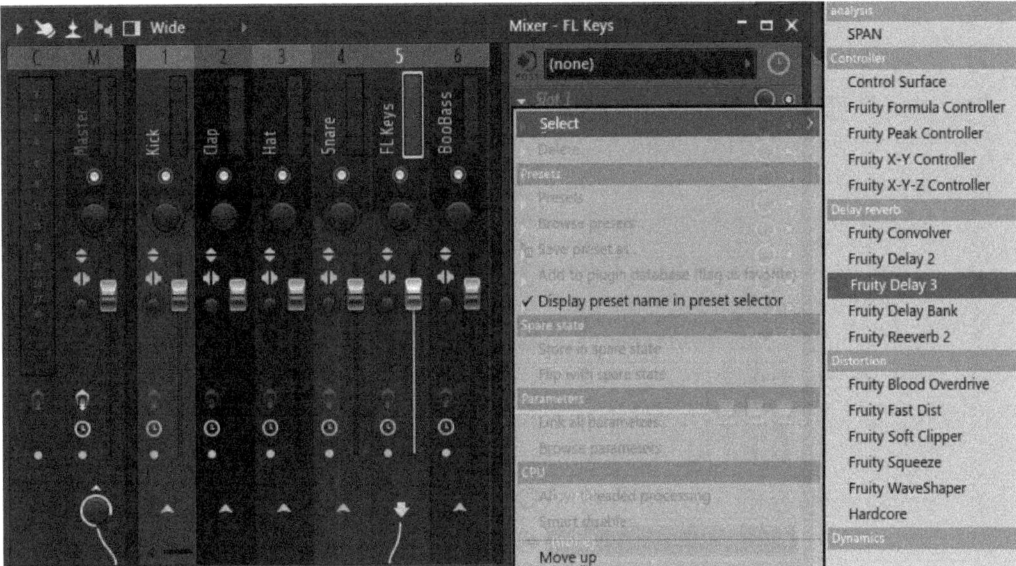

Figure 4.12 – Adding Fruity Delay 3

4. Play your song. You will be able to hear the delay plugin effect applied to your FL Keys sound. You will use this same process to add effects to your song, constantly going forward.

So far, we've taken a look at the Mixer console. Next, let's look at how to automate controls in the Mixer over time while the song is playing.

Applying automation to change effects over time

You can make effects change over time. This is called automation. **Automation** allows you to have fine control over your instruments and effects. In the following example, we look at applying automation in the Mixer; however, it should be noted that automation can be applied to any effect plugin, the Channel rack, the **Playlist**, and any instrument plugin. This is a big deal, as you can have sounds evolving throughout the song.

Essentially, any time that you want to have a sound transition from one state to another, you use automation. Here are some examples of automation that you hear in music:

- Sounds gradually getting quieter or louder. Any time a sound fades in or out, it's using automation.
- Any time in a film that you hear footsteps or the sound of a car appearing to move from left to right, you hear panning effect automation.
- Rising or falling effects can be created through the use of automation. A riser effect usually involves increasing the pitch of a sound over time, while a falling effect is usually decreasing the pitch over time. These pitch changes are usually combined with moving a high- or low-pass filter over time.
- When you want a synth instrument to gradually become more or less intense, you use automation. Progressive house music often involves gradually building up layers of plucks and synth chords over time. Changes in intensity and the fading in of instruments are done through automation.
- Vocal effect automation is used to create dubstep monster growls.
- Pretty much all dubstep bass instruments require automation to create the filtering instrument effects.

We're going to create an automation of an instrument effect. Let's illustrate automation through a simple volume change scenario:

1. Right-click on **BooBass** or any other instrument level fader (volume knob) and select **Create automation clip**. In the following screenshot, I've right-clicked on the volume fader in the Mixer.

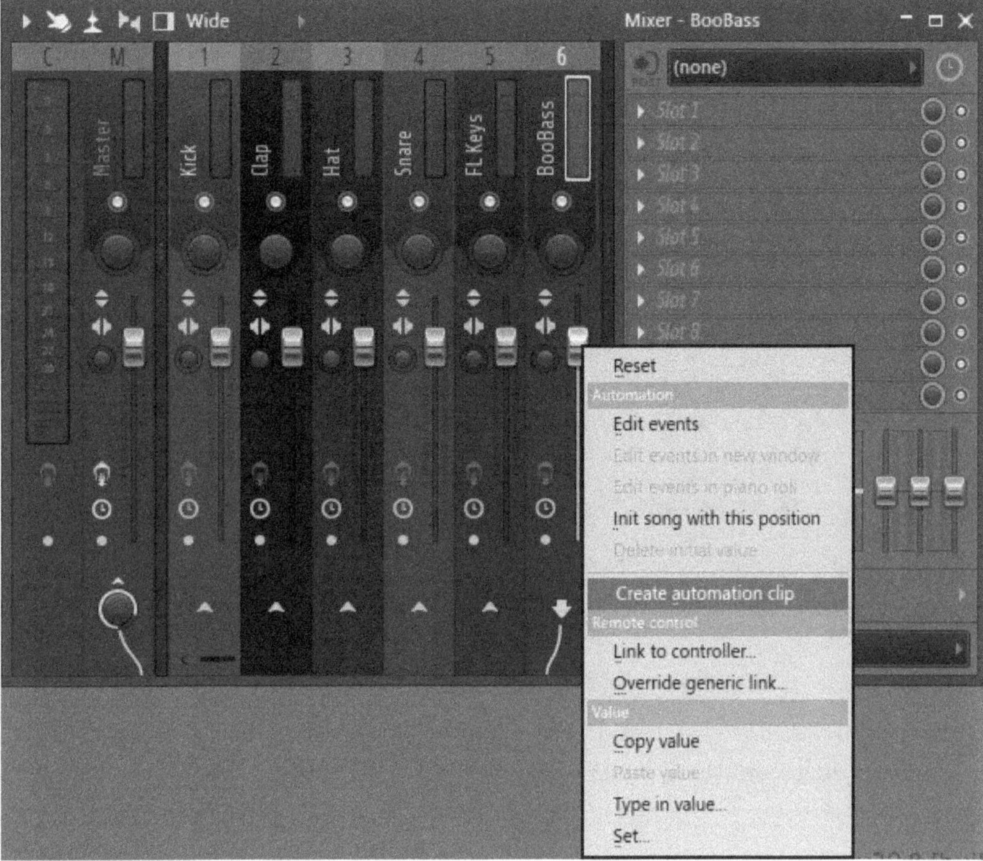

Figure 4.13 – Create automation clip

In the **Playlist**, you'll see an **automation clip** created for the selected parameter at the top left of the **Playlist** and in the grid section. In this case, the parameter that we are automating is volume. The automation clips consist of a line and a keyframe at the beginning and end. By default, the value is set to 80%, and correspondingly, the volume is set to be 80% of its maximum.

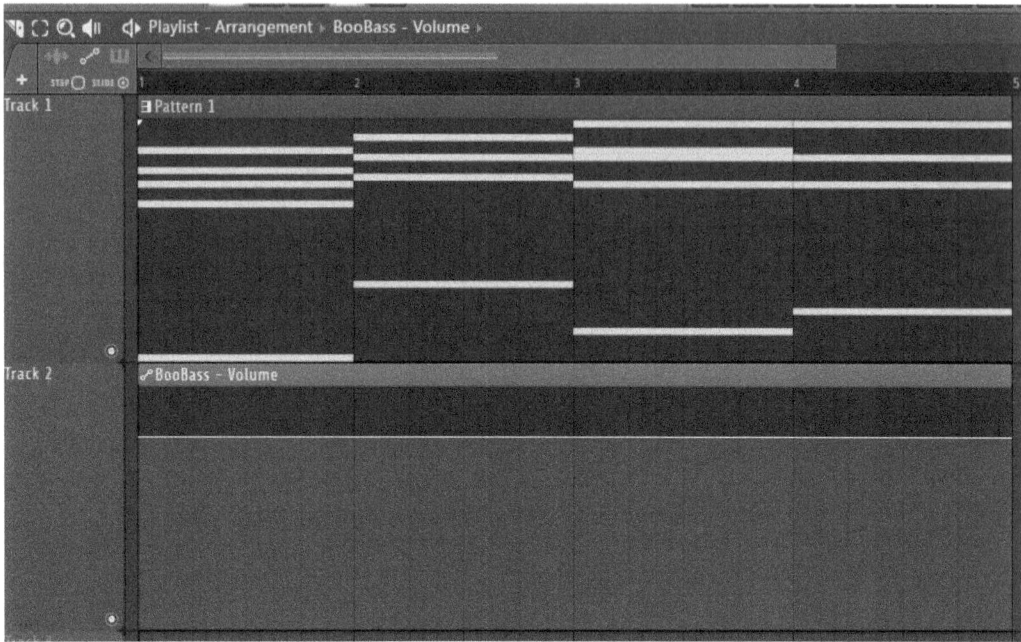

Figure 4.14 – Automation clip created

2. Right-click anywhere inside the automation clip. You can see an example in the following screenshot where I've right-clicked at the bottom. This creates an automation clip keyframe.

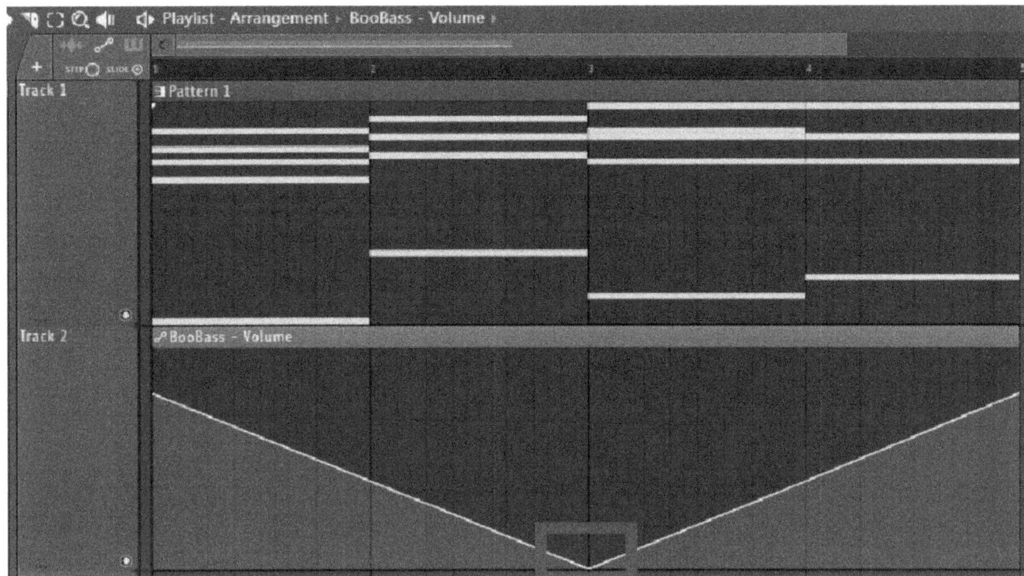

Figure 4.15 – Keyframe created

By adding the keyframe, the level of the volume fader for the BooBass instrument has been set to decrease over time until the middle of the clip and then increase again toward the end of the clip. Play the song to hear the volume automation.

3. There are several automation presets. Right-click on the keyframe that we created in the automation clip. You'll see a menu of available automation presets.

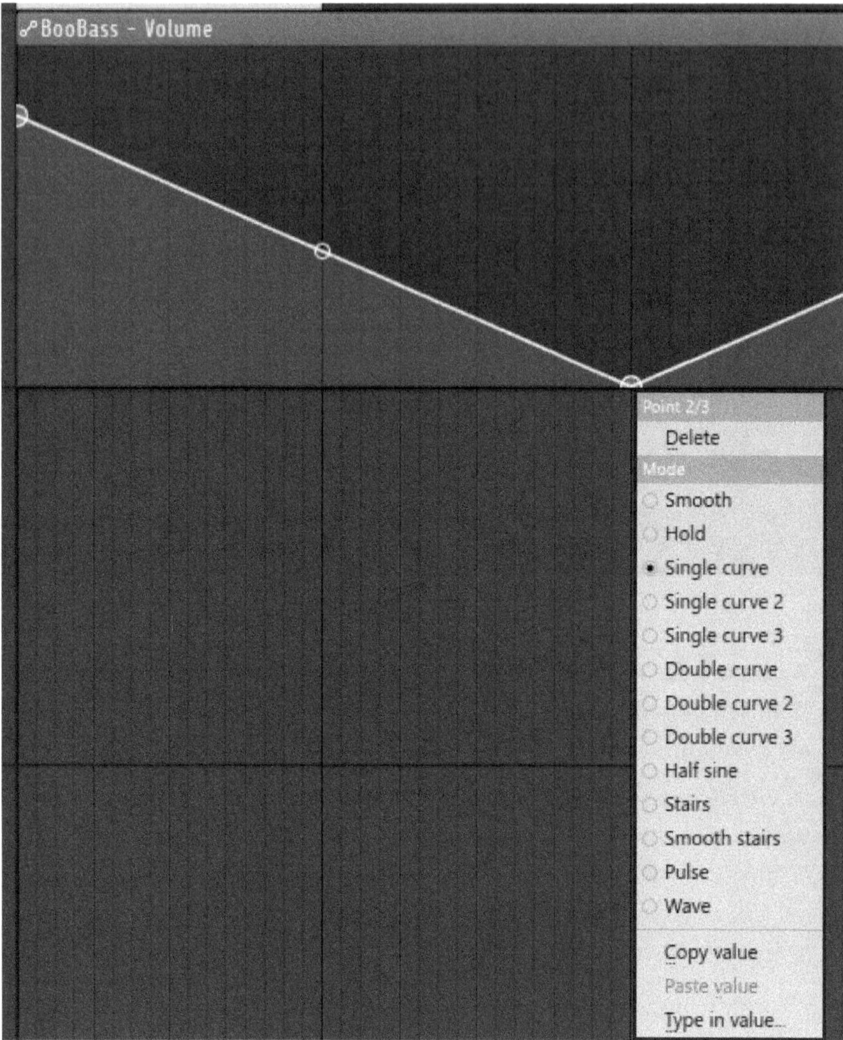

Figure 4.16 – Automation presets

These presets give examples of automation curves to choose from. If you select a curve, you'll see a new kind of automation clip curve. At the bottom of the menu, there is also an option to type in a value to specify the automation point. Feel free to select any one of the presets.

4. Open up the Mixer again and play the song.

Figure 4.17 - Volume automation

As you play the song, you'll see the insert mixer volume fader adjust as the automation clip progresses throughout the song.

Automation can be applied to any knob or button in FL Studio, and you can change it over time. Next, let's learn how to reuse your automation clips.

Repurposing automation clips

What if I like the automation curve that I created, but decide that I want to swap out the effect that is being automated? Or another scenario, I want to have multiple effects doing the same thing at the same time. Maybe you want multiple effects to turn on gradually at the same time.

It turns out you can repurpose automation effects over and over again for different effects very easily. Essentially, you can create an automation once and have control knobs on different plugins copy the automation.

So far in this chapter, we have created an automation clip for the volume of the BooBass. Now, let's reuse the same automation clip, but this time link it to a different effect control. For the sake of simplicity, we'll use a very simple effect: **Panning**. Panning effects control whether the audio is coming out of the left or the right speaker. So, if audio is panned completely to the left, audio will only come out of the left speaker. If audio is panned completely to the right, audio will only come out of the right speaker. We are going to automate the effect so that the audio copies the automation we set for the volume onto the panning effect. This will cause the audio to change back and forth between coming out of just the left speaker and just the right speaker.

1. In the **Mixer**, right-click on the **panning knob**. This is the control that we are going to add automation to. This will open a set of options. Choose the **Link to controller...** option. An example is shown in the following screenshot.

Figure 4.18 – Link to controller for panning

This will open up a window called **Remote control settings**.

Figure 4.19 – Remote control settings

2. Under the **Internal controller** tab, choose the automation clip that you want to copy over to the panning. In my example, the only automation clip that we created was an automation clip for the **BooBass – Volume**, so select that option.
3. At the bottom of the window, you'll notice a button that says, **Remove conflicts**. If that is selected, then it will remove the automation clip from the initial effect. If you leave it unchecked, then the automation clip will now power both effects. In other words, if it is checked, it will remove the automation for the volume and now solely just automate the panning effect. If you want both effects to continue to be automated, then leave this

button unchecked. In my case, I will leave the button checked as I want the automation clip to replace the volume change with a panning change.

4. Click the **Accept** button.

We have now replaced the automation clip of the **BooBass – Volume** with a panning effect for the BooBass, as shown in the following screenshot. The volume knob no longer moves, but the BooBass panning knob is moving.

Figure 4.20 – Panning effect automated

You'll notice that the **BooBass – Volume** automation clip hasn't changed its name. So that may be confusing down the road. In your projects, I recommend that you rename the automation clip to a name that makes sense. Otherwise, you'll have misleading automation naming.

Congratulations, you now know how to repurpose automation clips.

Editing automation clips

Once you've created an automation clip, you can edit the automation. You won't need to do this all the time. Usually, a simple increase or decrease in automation value is good enough. But it's useful to know how to gain fine-grained control if you want it. Let's see this through an example.

1. Create an automation clip, as discussed previously in this chapter. Right-click on any automatable control and create an automation clip in the **Playlist**.
2. Double-click on the automation clip name in the **Playlist**. The **Automation editor** will appear as shown in the following screenshot.

Figure 4.21 – Automation editor

In the automation editor, you can refine automation curves. You can play your clip in the Playlist simultaneously to see how your song is affected by the automation.

In the automation editor, you'll see a grid of points indicating automation. Higher points mean an increase in control value, and lower points mean a lower value. The value depends on the type of control used.

On the right of the window, you'll see the **step editing**, **snap to grid**, and **slide succeeding points** controls. The description is as follows:

- Step editing (the **pencil** icon): When enabled, allows you to add automation points by drawing on the grid. Right-clicking and dragging over automation points deletes them. When the step editor is disabled, you can drag points around the grid and add points by right-clicking on the grid.
- Snap to grid (**magnet** icon): Snaps automation points.
- Slide succeeding points/regions (**double arrow** icon): Allows points to slide around the grid when dragged.

At the top of the automation editor, you can enable the **LFO** button to view a series of LFO controls available for automation.

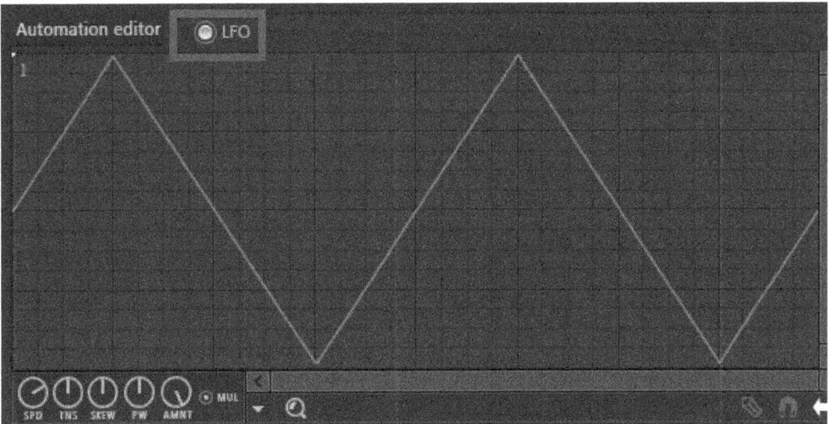

Figure 4.22 – Automation editor LFO button

You'll notice that the automation points change into a sine wave. On the left, you'll now see a series of control knobs that can be used to adjust the LFO, such as speed, tension, skew, and pulse width. This is useful if you want to create repeating automation.

Let's untoggle the LFO again. At the bottom, you'll find the **Target links** controls.

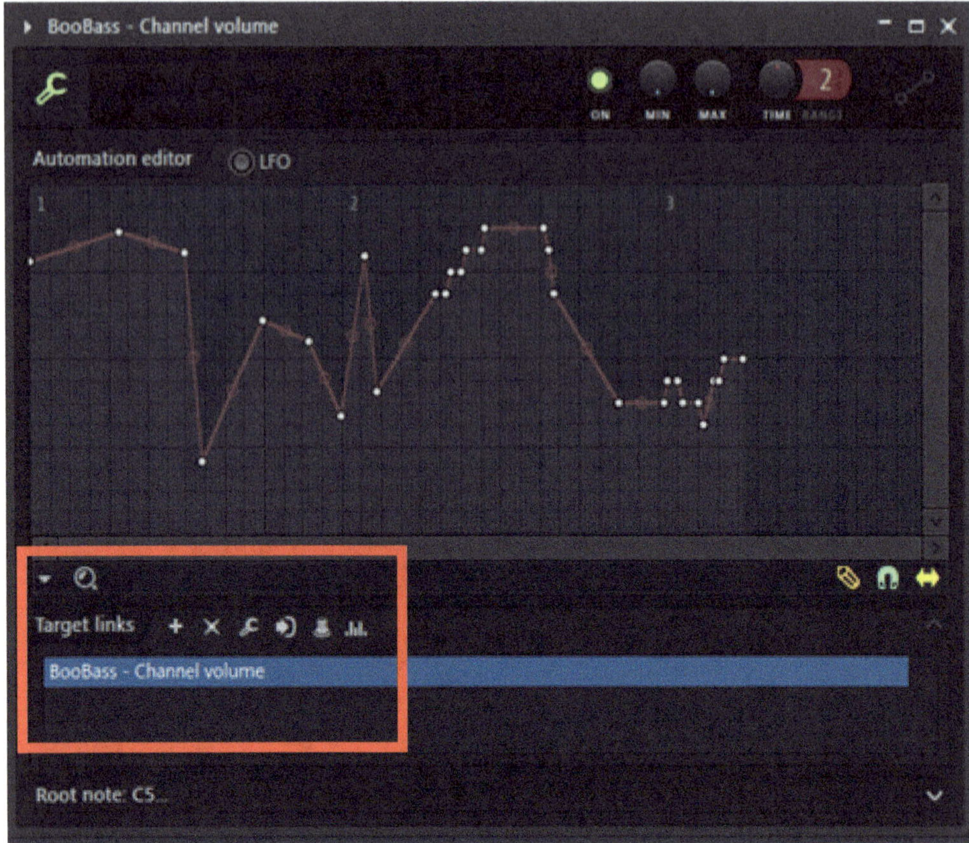

Figure 4.23 – Target links controls

Here's a description:

- **Add Target links**: It allows you to assign controls to follow the automation pattern. After clicking this button, you will be prompted to select controls to be assigned to this automation clip. It will continue to add controls until you click it again. Afterwards, all of the controls you selected will have their values affected by this automation. This might sound a little confusing to read, but if you try it out, you'll find it intuitive.
- **Remove Target link**: It removes a control from being assigned to the automation.
- **Edit Target link**: It opens up a window for additional control options.
- **Locate Target link parameter**: It opens up the plugin with the assigned control.

- **Animate Target link parameter**: It lights up when the **Add Target links** is used to indicate that it's waiting for a control to be selected.
- **Convert target to events in the current pattern**: It takes all of the automation points used in the automation editor and copies them into the **Event Editor**.

You may be thinking...what's the difference between **event automation** and automation clips? Event automation is bound to a specific pattern, **pattern clip**; automation clips are not. Event automation means you can open up the Piano roll and view the event automation in relation to the MIDI notes of the pattern. You can then view event automation in the Piano roll by selecting the **Control** drop-down and finding your event automation. The following shows an example in the **Piano roll**.

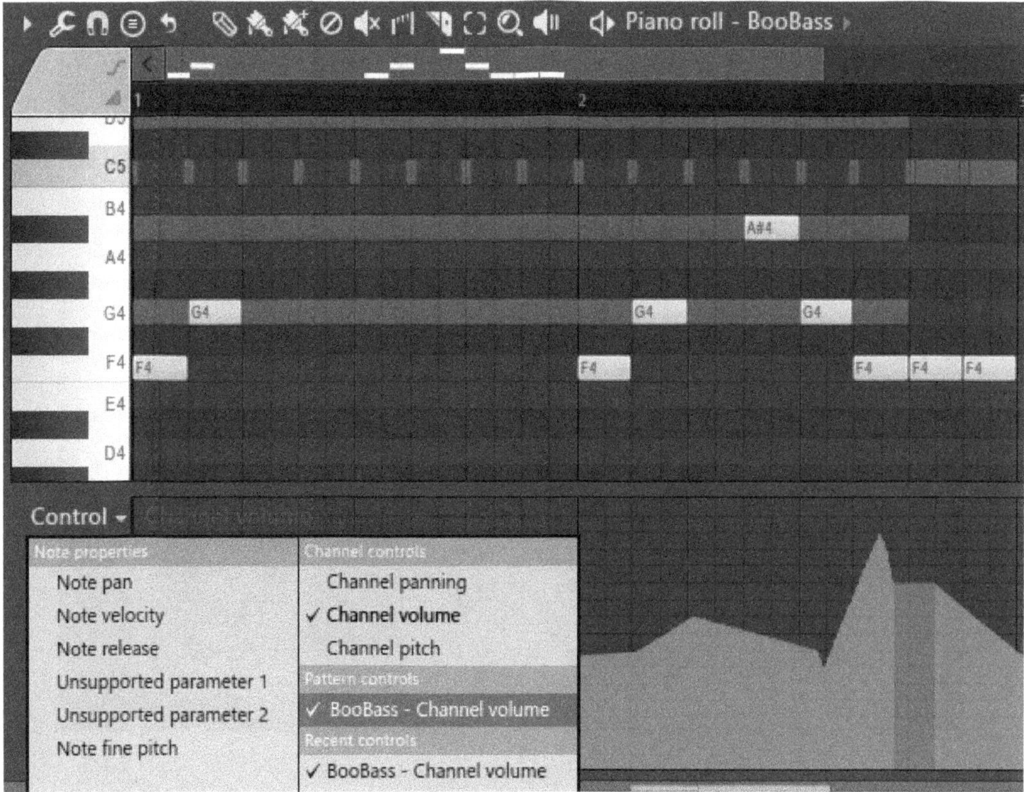

Figure 4.24 – Event automation

In the preceding screenshot, we can see MIDI notes in the **Piano roll**. Below in red is the event automation. In this example, the **Channel volume** is automated to change throughout the pattern.

In case you want even more control over your automation clips, there are additional options as shown in the following screenshot.

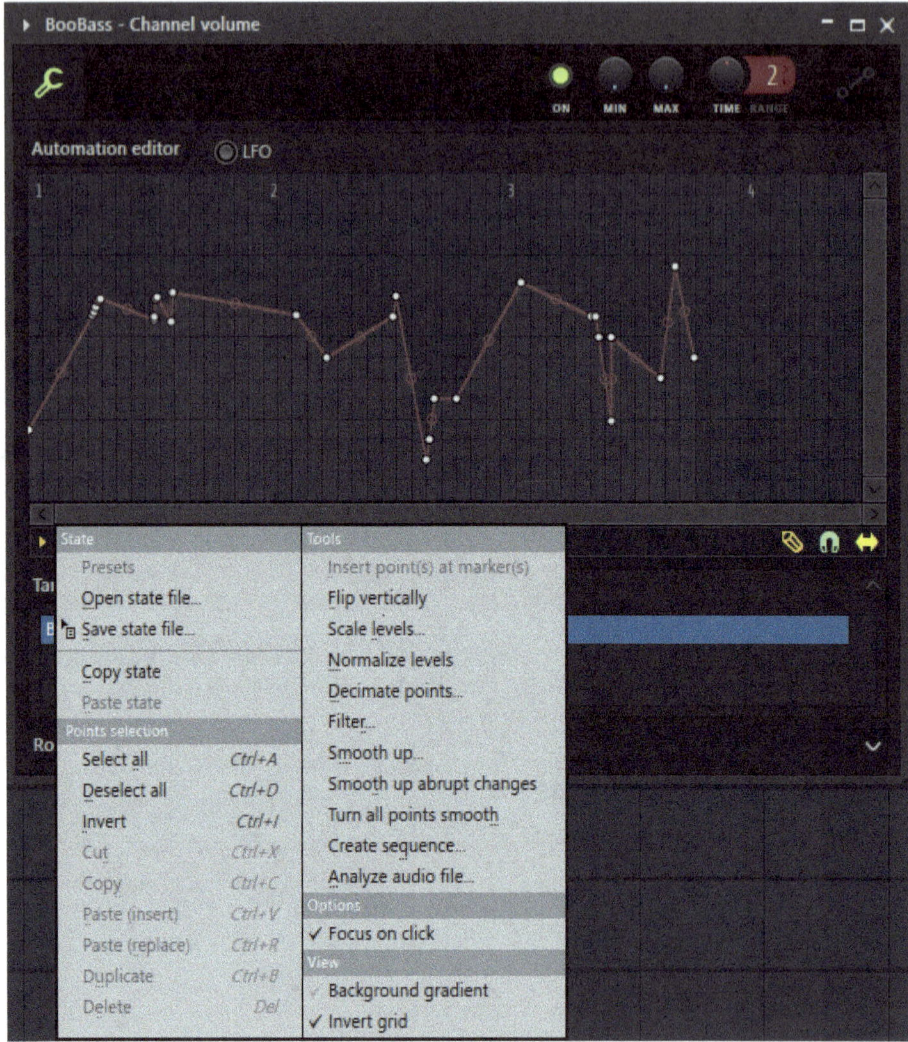

Figure 4.25 – Automation editor options

Here you'll find additional tools to adjust your automation clips: flipping, scaling, normalizing, decimating, filtering, smoothing, and creating an automation sequence.

We've learned how to create automation clips and how to edit them. Next, let's learn how to create automation clips for third-party plugins.

Applying automation to external third-party plugins

If you want to apply automation to an external plugin (not a native FL Studio plugin), you won't be able to right-click to apply automation. In order to apply automation for third-party plugins, you need to use another method.

We're going to explore two techniques for adding automation. The first approach, **MultiLink to controllers**, is the easiest and most intuitive. The second approach, **creating an editor thumbnail**, is more of a legacy technique, but it can still be used.

Using Multilink to controllers to add automation

There's an easy way to add automation clips for any plugin using the Multilink to controllers feature. The plugin doesn't have to be a native FL Studio plugin. It can be an installed **virtual studio technology** (**VST**) instrument or effect. This technique also works for adding automation for hardware controller controls.

You add automation by enabling the MultiLink to controllers feature. Once this is enabled, it listens for any control that is touched next. You touch the control of whatever plugin or hardware feature you want to change. The Multilink to controllers feature now remembers the last control touched. You can then use the Multilink to controllers feature to add automation. This feature will save you a ton of time and make adding automation for plugins easy. Let's explore the Multilink to controllers with a simple example:

1. Enable the **MultiLink to controllers** button by left-clicking it. An example is shown in the following screenshot.

Figure 4.26 – Multilink to controllers

   If you see the **MultiLink to controllers** button lit up, you know it's enabled and listening for you to adjust a control for automation.

2. In the Channel rack, load up any instrument plugin where you want to automate a control. In my example, I'll use the **FLEX** plugin for illustration purposes.

3. Change a control that you want to add automation to. In the following screenshot, an example is shown where I am changing the **PITCH**. All you need to do is slightly move the control.

Figure 4.27 – FLEX pitch controller

By moving the pitch controller, the **MultiLink to controllers** button will store the pitch controller. You can adjust multiple controls at once. In fact, I encourage you to adjust a few of the controls.

4. Right-click on the **Multilink to controllers** button, and you'll see the ability to add an automation clip.

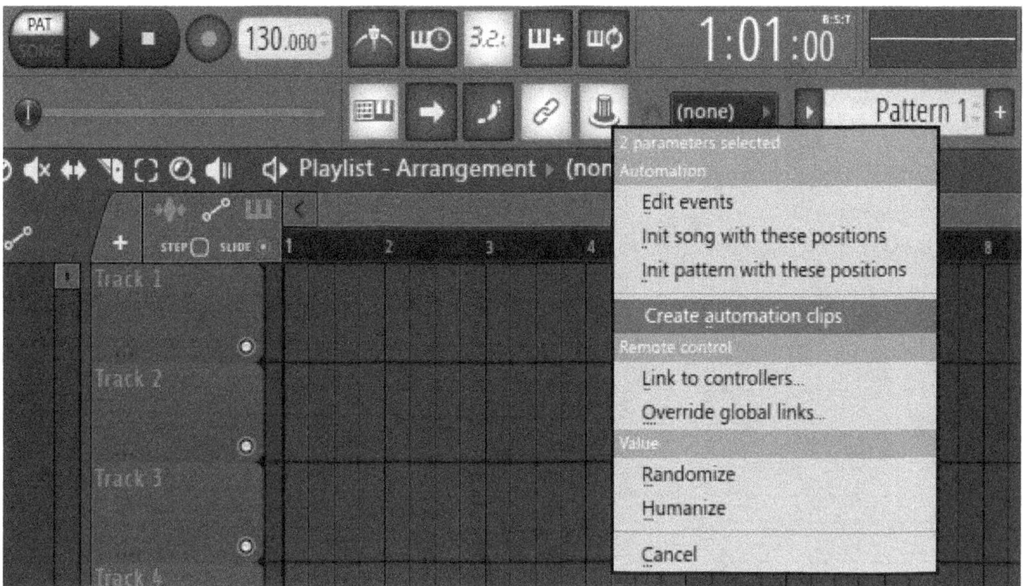

Figure 4.28 – Multilink to controllers button

After selecting the option **Create automation clips**, FL Studio will generate an automation clip of the control that was adjusted. An example is shown in the following screenshot.

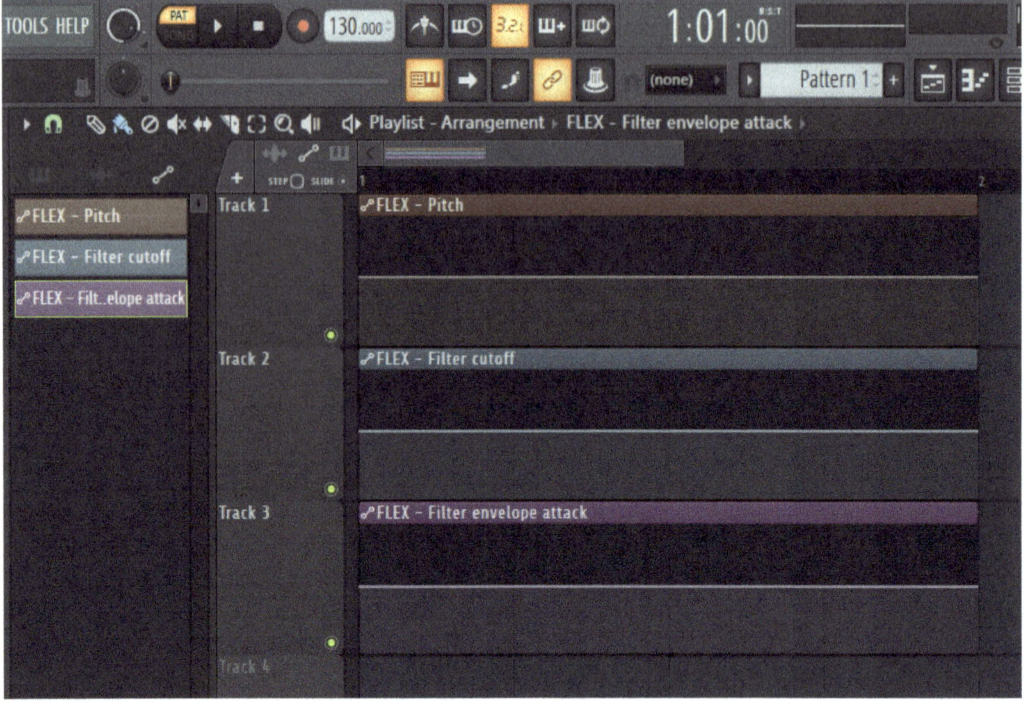

Figure 4.29 – Automation clips created

Automation clips have been created for every control that was adjusted. In my example, I adjusted the **Pitch**, **Filter cutoff**, and **Filter envelope attack**, so it created three automation clips. You can now adjust the values on the automation clips to however you see fit.

This technique works for hardware controllers connected to FL Studio. Simply enable **Multilink to controllers**, jiggle whatever knobs you want to on your hardware, and then add an automation clip. You now know how to use Multilink to controllers.

Creating an editor thumbnail to add automation

You can add automation to third-party plugins by creating what is known as an **editor thumbnail**. This is an alternative technique if you don't want to use, or can't use for some reason, the Multilink to controller method to create automation clips.

When you create an editor thumbnail, you're telling FL Studio to take a look at the plugin and analyze it for controls for use in automation:

1. To create an editor thumbnail, open your external plugin, go to the top-left drop-down arrow menu, and select **Make editor thumbnail**, as shown in the following screenshot.

I'm using FLEX again, but you can use any plugin, including those that don't come natively with FL Studio.

Figure 4.30 – Select Make editor thumbnail

2. The **Browser** will open up the instrument plugin. Click on the instrument in the **Browser**. In this example, I am using the **FLEX** instrument plugin.

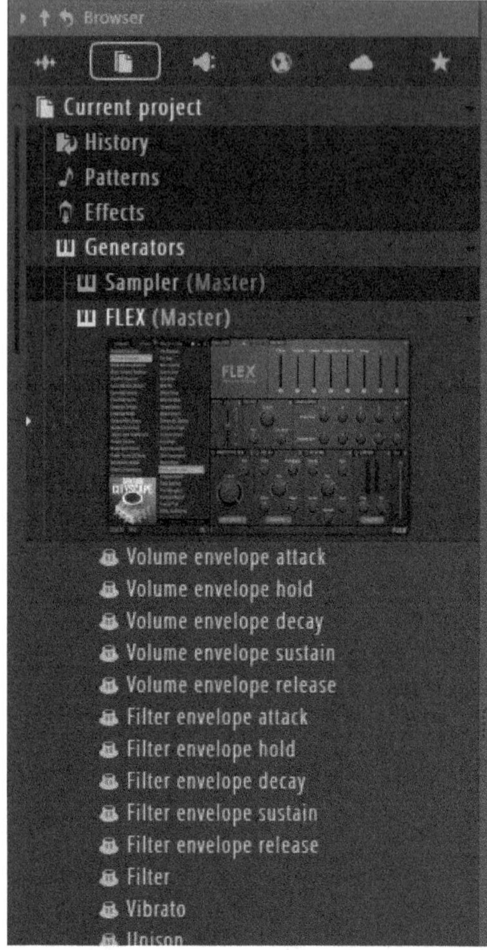

Figure 4.31 – Clicking on an instrument in the Browser

3. A list will appear of all the automatable controls of the plugin, as shown in the following screenshot:

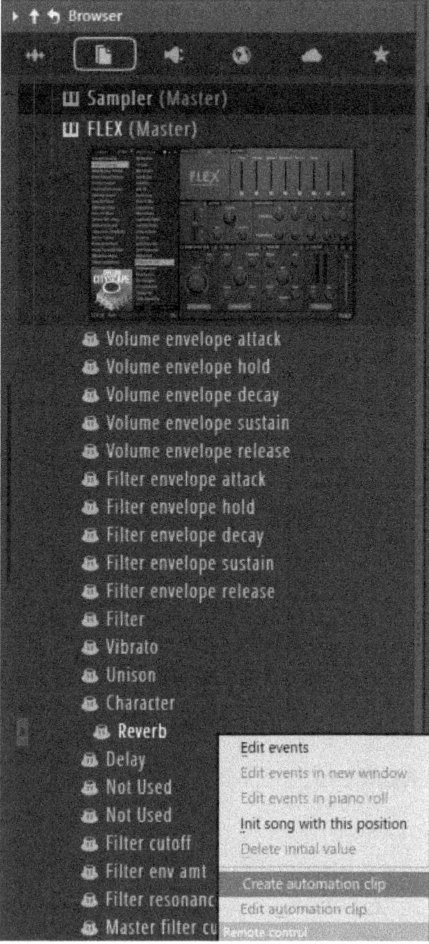

Figure 4.32 – Automation clip for a plugin

4. Right-click on any of the controls listed below the instrument and add an automation clip for the effect. An automation clip will appear in the **Playlist**, as shown in the following screenshot. I added some keyframe movements for illustration; yours will be just a horizontal line initially.

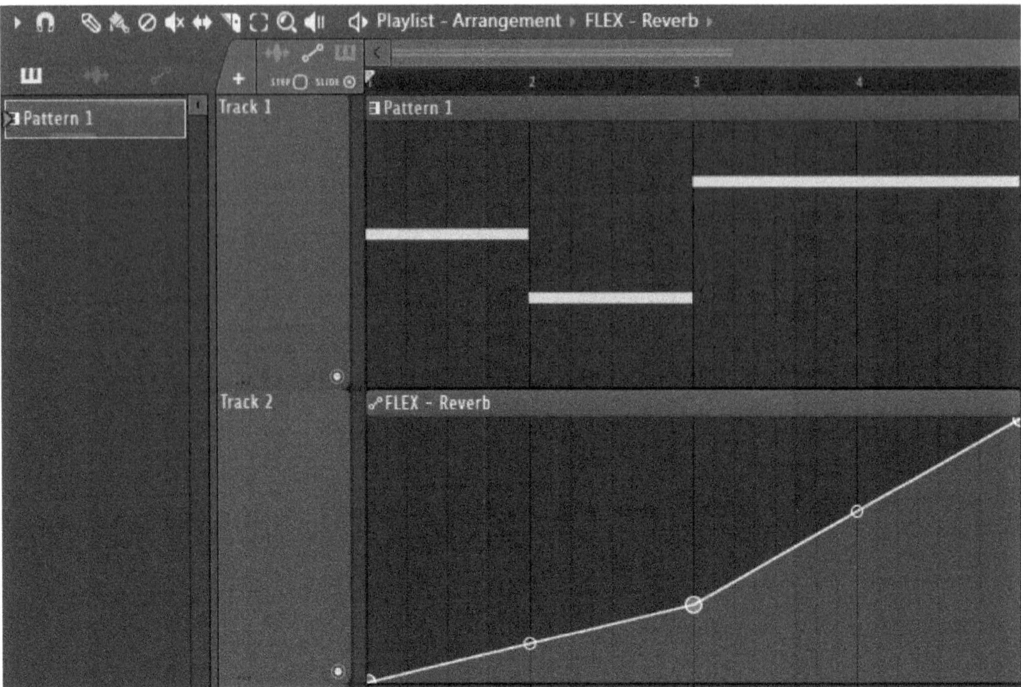

Figure 4.33 – Automation clip in the Playlist for an external plugin

You've successfully added automation for an instrument plugin.

5. If you want to automate another control parameter of the plugin, it's much easier the second time, as you've already taken an editor thumbnail. To automate another control of a plugin where you've already taken an editor thumbnail, go to the **Browser** and select **Generators**. This will list all currently used plugins in your project. Then you can click on any of the effects and add additional automation clips.

We've learned how to apply automation effects. This allows you to add variation to your sounds, making them more interesting to the listener.

We've learned how to manipulate effects on plugins. What if we want to manipulate the sound after it has already come out of a plugin? For that, we need to learn how to freeze audio clips.

Freezing audio clips

You can render any audio into an audio clip. Rendering to audio is commonly known as **freezing**. Rendering to audio or freezing means creating an audio clip sample out of any sound that passes through a mixer track. Freezing audio clips into samples has several benefits:

- Like version control, it gives you a version of your sound that will not change.
- Once in an audio clip format, you can manipulate the sound in ways that aren't possible with the original instrument, such as reversing, time-stretching, or slicing the audio.
- You gain all the benefits of being able to use the sample envelope controls and use the sample in other plugins, such as in **DirectWave**.
- A minor benefit is that a sample is less CPU-intensive than an instrument with effects. If you notice your computer lagging due to the usage of lots of plugins, you can speed up your computer by freezing CPU-intensive mixer tracks into audio.

If you're a beginner, you probably won't need to use track freezing right away. It's more useful later on when you want finer control over your sounds. If you find this overly complicated, feel free to skip it for now and revisit it once you're ready for more advanced control.

I mostly find myself freezing tracks when I need to process vocals, as these often require a lot of effects, and I want to have several versions of vocals to compare. Let's do an example and render our sound to an audio clip:

1. To freeze tracks, select the **arm disk recording** button on all the mixer tracks that you want to freeze, as shown in the following screenshot. The **arm disk recording** buttons will appear red after selecting.

Figure 4.34 – Arm disk recording

As we can see in the preceding screenshot, insert mixer tracks **5** and **6** are now ready to record audio input. Arming disk recording for a track tells the Mixer to get ready to record any input that comes through the tracks and to export it as a new audio file.

2. Next, select the drop-down menu from the top left of the Mixer and select **Render armed tracks to wave file(s)...**, or use the *Alt* + *R* shortcut. A dialog box will pop up, where you can then select the default option of **Start**. An example is shown in the following screenshot:

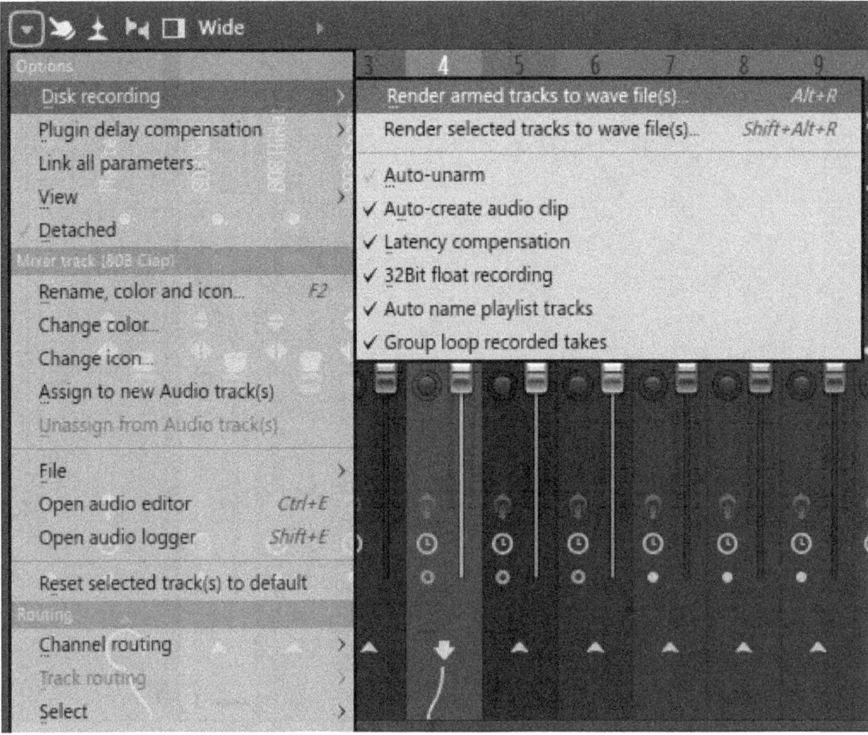

Figure 4.35 – Render to wave file(s)

Once the rendering is finished, you will see new audio sample clips appear in your **Playlist**. You have successfully rendered your audio to a new audio sample, as shown in **Track 4** and **Track 5** of the following screenshot:

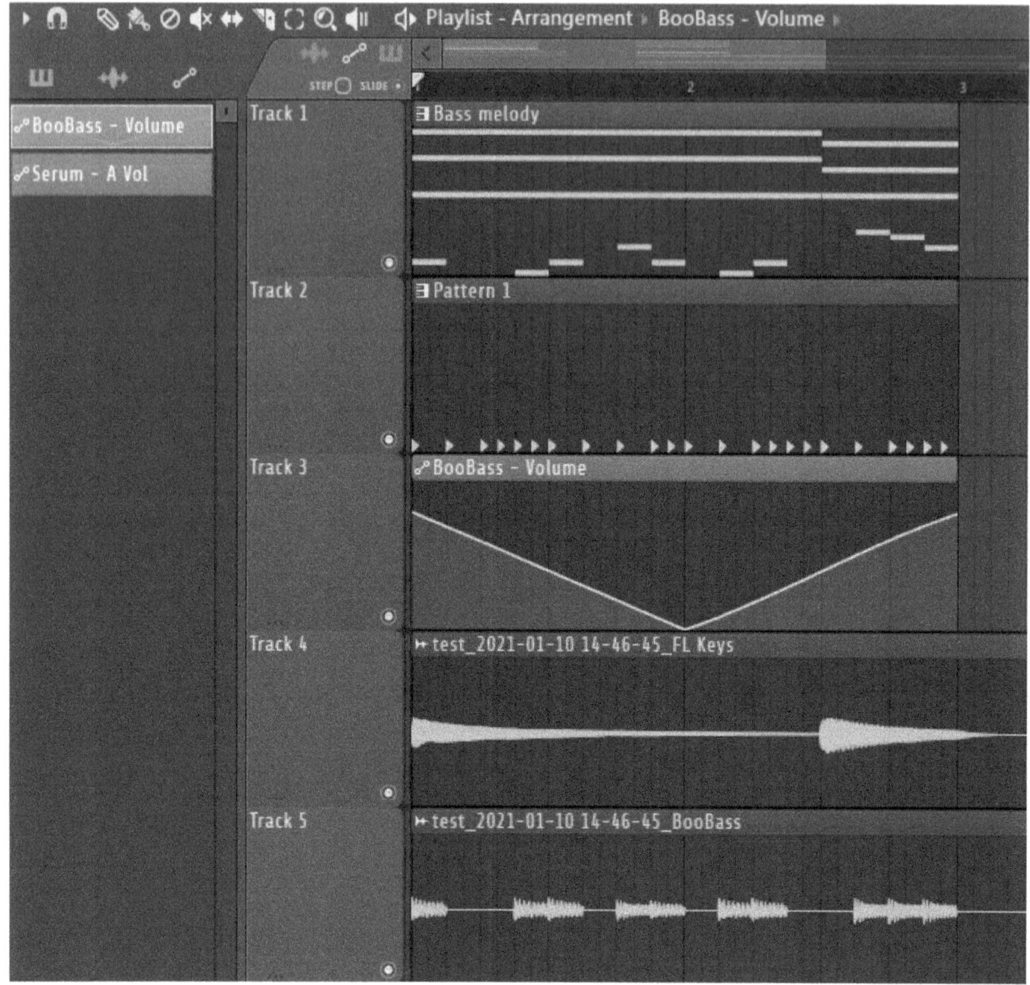

Figure 4.36 – Rendered audio

In this example, the BooBass instrument and the FL Keys instrument mixer tracks have been rendered into audio samples. If you play the song in the Playlist, you'll be able to hear the samples playing.

Once the tracks have been rendered, you can mute the original mixer tracks and disable any plugins that were applied. This will save CPU processing.

There is an alternative express way to render tracks to audio that doesn't involve using the arm disk recording buttons. It's essentially the same technique as the one just described, except that you no longer need to designate a track to be armed.

Simply select multiple tracks on the Mixer by holding down *Ctrl* + *Shift* and left-clicking on tracks. You'll know the tracks are selected because they'll be highlighted. Then select the options dropdown arrow in the top left corner of the Mixer. An example is shown in the following screenshot:

Figure 4.37 – Select tracks

When clicking the Mixer options, a list of options will appear. Select **Disk recording** | **Render selected tracks to wave file(s)...** as shown in the following screenshot. Alternatively, you can use the shortcut *Shift* + *Alt* + *R*.

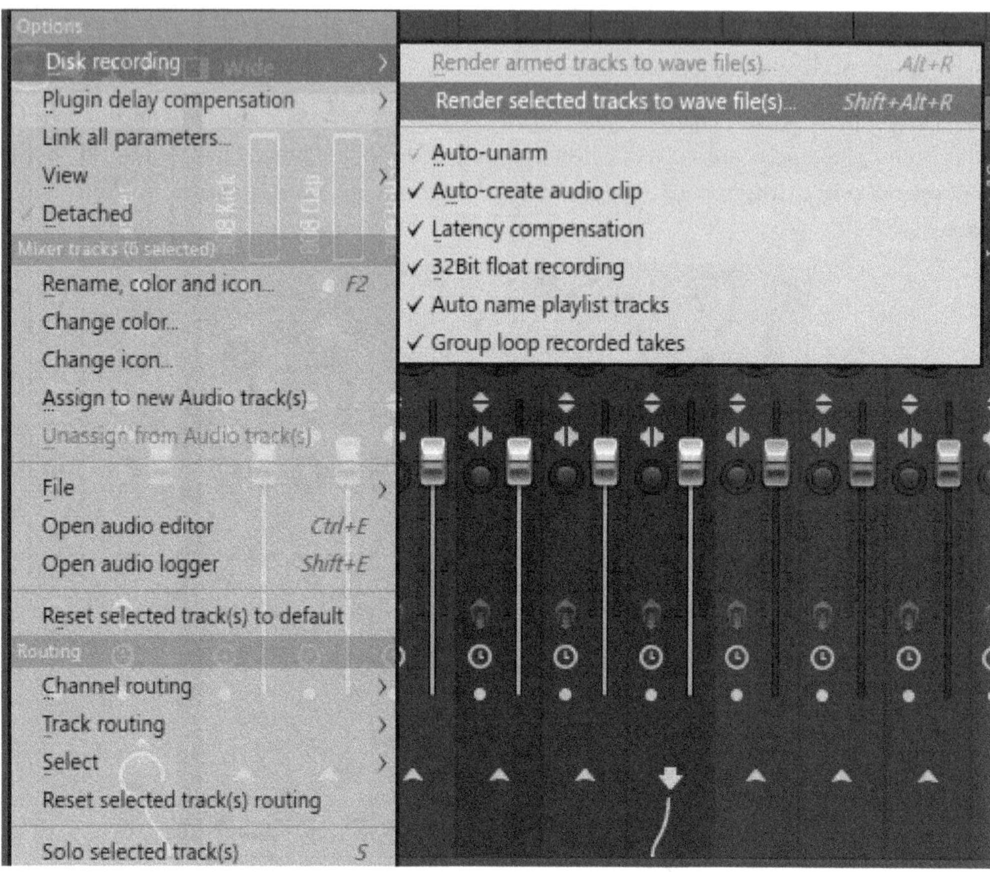

Figure 4.38 – Render selected tracks to wave file(s)

Rendered audio clips will be created. To view the audio clips, navigate to the **audio clips** tab of the **Playlist**, as shown in the following screenshot:

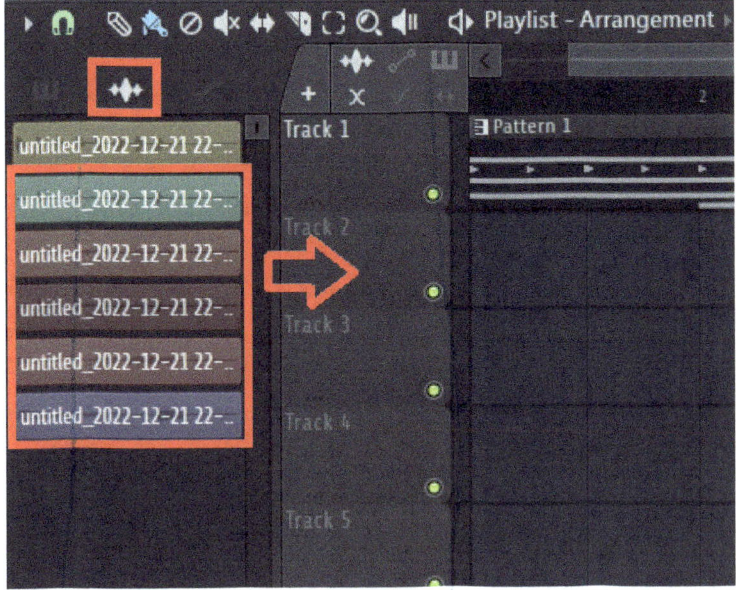

Figure 4.39 – Audio clips tab of the Playlist

You can then drag the clips onto the **Playlist**.

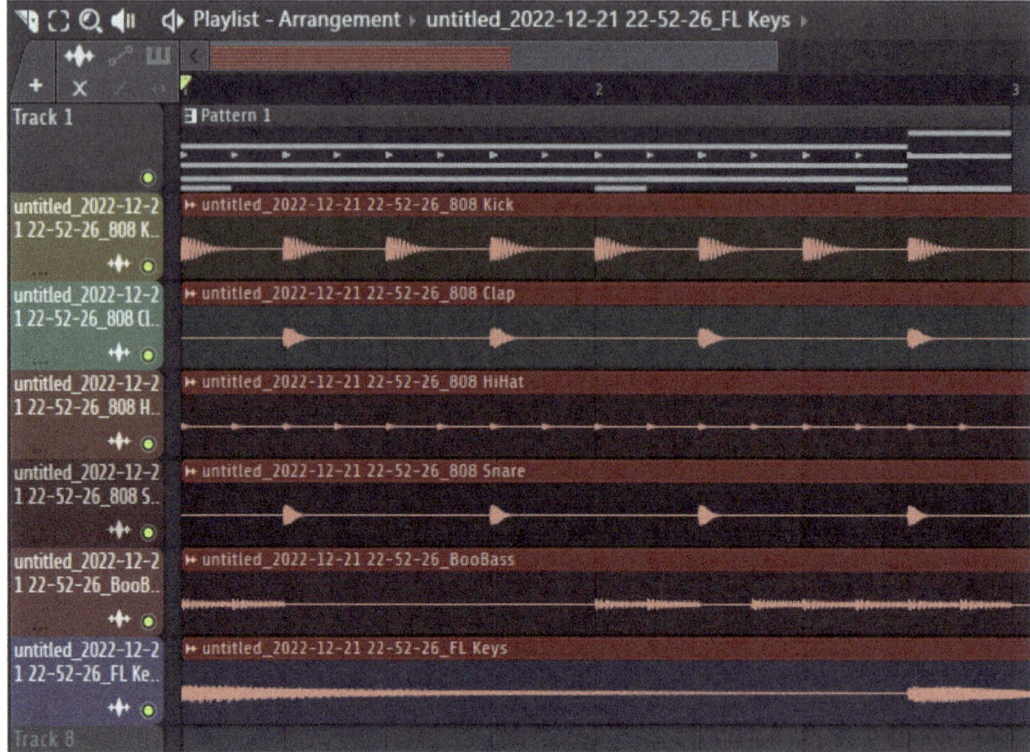

Figure 4.40 – Rendered audio clips

The audio clips will appear in the **Playlist**. You now know how to render any mixer track into an audio clip.

Summary

In this chapter, we learned about the Mixer console. The Mixer console is where you combine your sounds, blend them together, and apply effects to them. We learned how to route audio and instruments to the Mixer. We learned about the components that make up the Mixer and what they're used for. We also learned how to apply automation to our plugin controls to change them over time. We learned how to repurpose the automation clips for multiple effects, and also how to gain fine control over editing the automation. Finally, we learned how to render audio in the Mixer into new audio clips.

We will return to the Mixer and explore mixing techniques starting in *Chapter 6*. In the next chapter, we'll learn about sound design and audio envelopes.

Get this book's PDF version and more

Scan the QR code (or go to `packtpub.com/unlock`). Search for this book by name, confirm the edition, and then follow the steps on the page.

Note: Keep your invoice handy. Purchases made directly from Packt don't require an invoice.

Part 2

Music Production Fundamentals

In this second section of the book, you'll take your musical ideas and polish them through mixing, sound design, and effects processing. You'll begin by learning the fundamentals of how sound works. We'll discuss topics such as what exactly sound is, how we hear things, and how instruments create music. These concepts will give you a behind-the-scenes look at how music plugins work. Next, you'll dive into essential mixing techniques using compression, equalization, sidechaining, and limiting to tame dynamic ranges and craft balanced, polished sounds. From there, you'll explore stereo imaging techniques like panning, reverb, delay, and chorus effects to create depth and space in your mixes. You'll learn vocal processing, how to use vocoders and create vocal chops, learn to build custom instruments and effects chains, and delve into sound design using tools like pitch shifting, frequency manipulation, and granular synthesis. By the end of this section, you'll have the knowledge to apply professional-grade effects and processing to create radio-ready music.

This part of the book includes the following chapters:

- *Chapter 5, Fundamentals of Sound Design*
- *Chapter 6, Mixing Basics – Compression, Sidechaining, Limiting, and Equalization*
- *Chapter 7, Stereo Width – Panning, Reverb, Delay, Chorus, Flangers, and Distortion*
- *Chapter 8, Recording Live Audio and Vocal Processing*
- *Chapter 9, Understanding Vocal Effects*
- *Chapter 10, Glitch Effects and Creating Your Own Instruments and Effects*
- *Chapter 11, Intermediate to Advanced Mixing Topics and Sound Design Plugin Effects*

5

Fundamentals of Sound Design

In this chapter, you'll learn the foundations of how sound works. We'll learn what sound is, how it's manipulated, and how instruments create sound. We'll also discuss what an audio envelope is and how to adjust its parameters. Once you understand how sound is created, you'll be able to quickly learn instrument plugins and effects and have an intuition behind how they work.

Lastly, we'll look at how to take any song and break it down into its individual stem components using an AI tool called **Extract stems from sample**. This will allow you to take any song and extract the **bass**, **drums**, **instruments**, and **vocals**. This is useful for analyzing songs for learning, for remixing songs, and as material for DJs to use.

In this chapter, we'll explore the following topics:

- What is sound?
- What causes a note's pitch?
- How do we hear things?
- How do instruments create sounds with different pitches?
- What are sound envelopes, and how do you modify them?
- Extracting stems from samples using AI

What is sound?

In the following chapters of this book, we will learn how to use plugins that manipulate sound. But what exactly is sound? When we talk about sound design, what exactly are we designing? Most music books simply dive into making music without explaining the science behind it. Most physics textbooks on sound go super deep on the math, but do very little to help musicians relate to it. While music books excel at teaching how to make music and physics texts thoroughly explain the mechanics of sound, I believe musicians will benefit most from combining the two perspectives. In this chapter, we bridge the two worlds together and explain the physics of music in a way that is understandable for musicians without a math background. Then, in later chapters, when you're tinkering with music plugin effects, you'll have a deeper appreciation for what the effects are actually doing to create your sounds.

Sound is a form of energy like electricity and light. Sound is made when molecules vibrate and move in a wave pattern, which we call sound waves. Air is able to support many sound waves simultaneously, which is why you can hear multiple sounds at once. When you clap your hands, your clapping causes energy to move outward into the air. The air molecules vibrate, bump into neighboring molecules, and transfer energy, causing them to vibrate. This energy is sent outward from the source, around the room, and continues until the energy is equally dispersed. The energy gets weaker as it gets distributed over a wider area. This is why there's no sound in outer space. There are no air molecules vibrating to support sound waves.

Molecules don't move around the room with sound. Instead, energy is transferred between molecules. A molecule moves from its original position, transfers energy to a neighboring molecule, and then returns to its resting point. This movement of the molecule is what we call vibration or oscillation.

The following figure shows how molecules vibrate in a wave pattern:

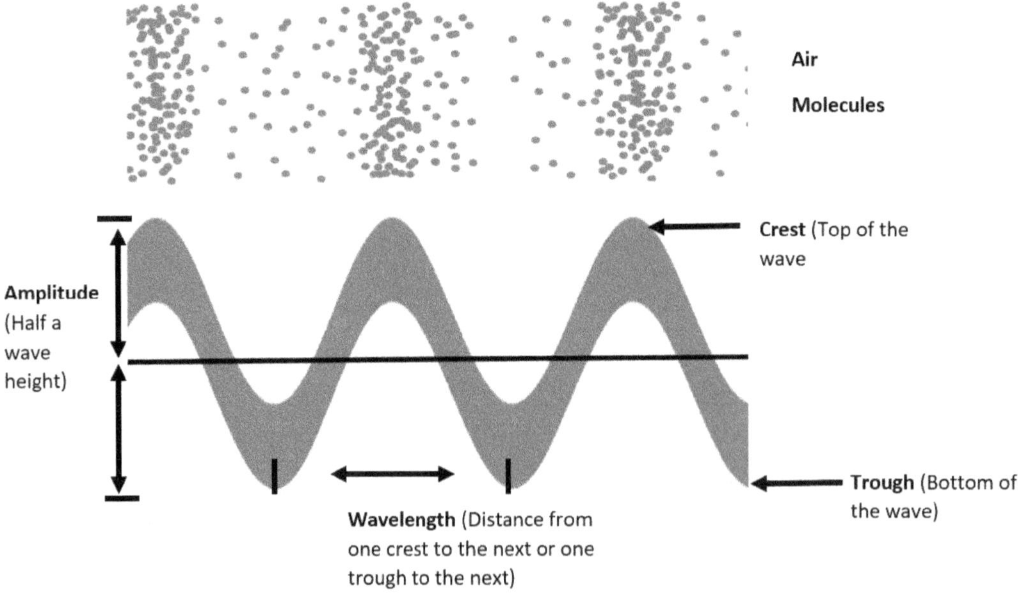

Figure 5.1 – Sound wave

The preceding diagram shows an example of how molecules bunch up together while vibrating. They collect in some places and are less frequent in others. This can be visualized as a wave. The top of the wave indicates that there are more molecules, and the bottom of the wave indicates that there are fewer molecules.

One of the factors dictating what the wave sounds like is the amplitude of the wave. The amplitude of a wave is the distance from the point of rest (the middle) to the crest (top of the wave). The amplitude is the same distance from the middle to the trough of the wave. The amplitude is what we think of as volume loudness. The larger the amplitude, the louder the sound.

There are two kinds of waves:

- Transverse waves are where the oscillation is perpendicular to the direction that the wave is traveling in. Imagine a water wave moving up and down.
- Longitudinal waves are where the oscillations happen in the same direction that the wave travels, similar to what you see when a spring compresses. Imagine a spring moving horizontally back and forth. Sound is a longitudinal wave.

We've learned that sound is energy that travels between molecules and can be visualized as a longitudinal wave. Next, let's learn what distinguishes one sound from another.

What causes a note's pitch?

When you think of **pitch**, you think about how high or low a sound feels. The pitch of a sound is determined by the frequency of the vibrations. **Frequency** is how many wave cycles pass through a given point per second. The more vibrations per second, the higher the frequency and the higher the pitch. The following figure shows an example of high and low frequency:

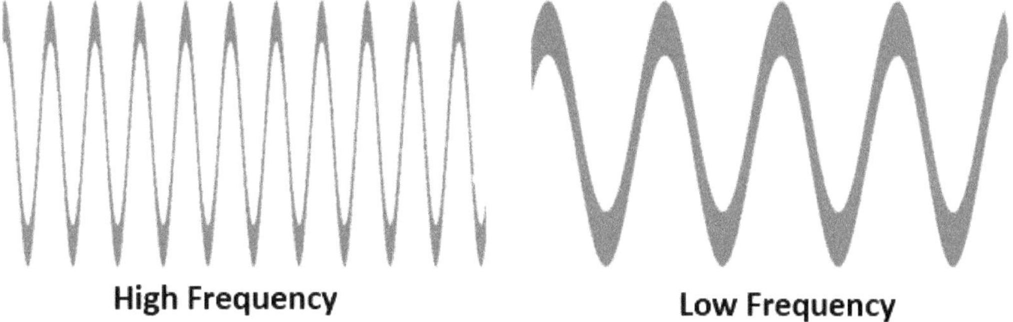

Figure 5.2 – High and low frequency

The higher frequency will have a higher pitch, and the lower frequency will have a lower pitch. An example of a pitch is a middle C note, which has a frequency of 261.63 Hz.

Human ears can pick up frequencies between 20 and 20,000 Hz. Hz is the unit to measure how many wave cycles pass per second. As you get older, your ears lose the ability to pick up higher-pitch sounds. Sounds that are higher than this range are called **ultrasonic**. Sounds that are lower are called **infrasonic**. Some animals can hear sounds outside of this frequency range. Dogs hear sounds that are higher, which is why they can hear dog whistles. Elephants and whales can hear sounds that are lower.

We now know that sound has something to do with wave patterns, amplitudes, and frequencies, but how do these fit together so that we can hear sound?

How do we hear things?

Sound causes air to expand and contract. Air expands under low pressure and compresses under high pressure. Changes in air pressure are useful because we can use devices to measure air pressure. Microphones detect changes in air pressure. Microphones are made up of a diaphragm stretched over a metal plate. As sound waves pass over it, the changes in high and low pressure cause the diaphragm to move back and forth and vibrate. This movement is measured by the device and converted into audio data. The data is then interpreted by your computer. The following figure shows an example of a microphone:

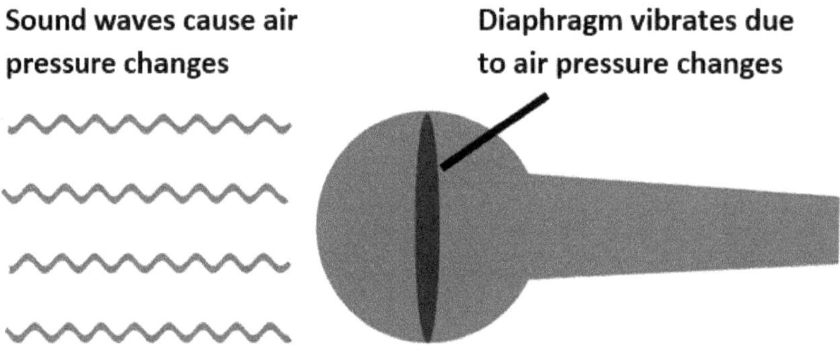

Figure 5.3 – Microphone

Your ears work in a similar fashion to a microphone. Your eardrums encounter air pressure changes, which cause them to vibrate. Your brain interprets these vibrations as sound. We

Learned about how sound travels and is received, but what happens when multiple sounds encounter each other?

When audio waves meet, they can react to one another. This can result in the following effects:

- **Constructive interference** is where two sound wave crests combine to make one crest with a higher amplitude than the original one. This makes the sound seem louder.
- **Destructive interference** is where the crest and the trough of two sound waves encounter each other and cancel each other out.

Noise cancellation technology in headphones works by analyzing the sound around you and generating a sound wave that destructively interferes with the original sound wave to cancel it out. Essentially, one sound makes another sound quieter. It's also why detuning layers of sound creates movement or makes it sound muddy.

Increases in loudness are not linear. Sound needs to be about 10 times the intensity in order for it to appear twice as loud. Decibels (dB) are the units measuring the loudness of a sound. Take the following examples:

- Near total silence: 0 dB
- A whisper: 15 dB
- Normal conversation: 60 dB
- A lawnmower: 90 dB
- A car horn: 110 dB
- A rock concert or a jet engine: 120 dB
- A gunshot or firecracker: 140 dB

Sounds around 120–130 dB are painful to humans, and instant hearing damage starts around 140 dB. The maximum loudness you can generate in air is around 194 dB. In water, it's around 270 dB. Why? Remember that sound is energy, and sound waves exert pressure. So, when we say 194 dB in air, we're talking about a huge amount of pressure. Anything higher than that, and the medium that the sound is traveling through starts to break down, making the measurement no longer meaningful. Sound loudness isn't necessarily constant; your placement relative to the sound will change how you perceive loudness. This is better known as the Doppler effect.

The **Doppler effect** is when the pitch of a sound changes as you get closer to or farther away from the sound. As you get closer, the pitch of the sound increases, and it decreases as you move farther away. Imagine the siren of a police car. As the car approaches you, the sound gets louder, and the pitch gets higher. As the car gets farther away, the sound gets quieter, and the pitch gets lower. Some instrument effect plugins mimic the Doppler effect. They do this by simulating how the loudness and pitch appear to increase as the object gets closer. This effect is frequently used in movie sound effects.

How do instruments create sounds with different pitches?

In order to understand how instruments create pitches, we need to understand how instruments create sound waves. There are two types of sound waves:

- **Traveling waves** are observed when a wave *is not confined* to a given space. If you were to shake an unattached, loose rope, the resulting random ripple in the rope would be a traveling wave. The wave could have any wavelength, as nothing is restricting the length.
- **Standing waves**, on the other hand, are observed when a wave *is confined* to a fixed space in a medium. The medium restricts the wavelength to recurring wavelengths and frequencies. If you were to shake a string that's attached to a pole, the resulting constrained ripple due to the medium restriction produces a regular wave pattern that repeats, called a standing wave (as though it were standing still).
  Musical instruments are designed to produce standing waves, so this chapter will focus on standing waves rather than travelling waves. You can see an example of a standing wave in the following figure:

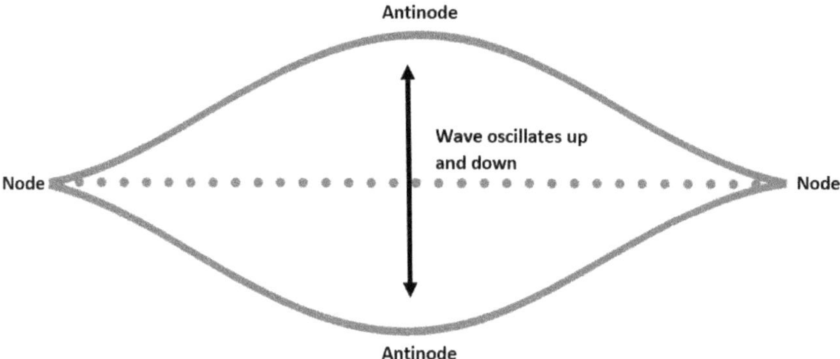

Figure 5.4 – Standing wave

You can think of a standing wave as a guitar string. The string is attached to both ends of the guitar, so each string end has no movement. Only the middle of the string can move. Physicists call the point of no movement on a wave a **node**. The part of a wave that moves is called the **antinode**. The wave appears to vibrate in a repeating movement in which only the amplitude of the wave is changing.

If you tune a guitar, you tighten the string, restrict the wavelength, and cause the string to vibrate a certain number of times per second. What you're doing by tuning the guitar string is shaping the frequency of the wave. When you hear the frequency of the wave, you recognize the sound as a specific pitch. When you press down on the guitar string in different places, you cause the active part of the string to change length, resulting in a new note pitch.

In wind and brass instruments, there are no strings to vibrate to create sound. Instead, the air molecules are restricted within the space of the pipe. This space confines the size of the wavelength and amplitude. The shape of the pipe dictates the nature of the standing wave. The following figure shows a wave confined within a pipe:

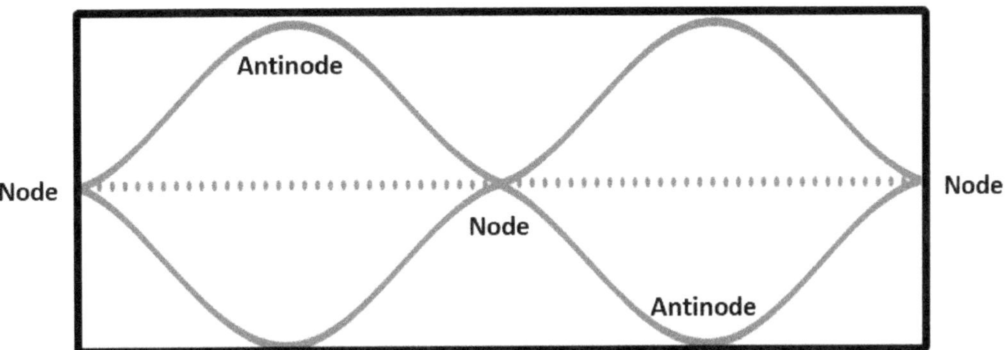

Figure 5.5 – Standing wave in a pipe

In a pipe (like a woodwind or brass instrument), the end of the pipe acts as the fixed node. The wave reflects back off the end of the pipe and creates the waveform. An open-ended pipe can reflect a wave too, even if there isn't a solid surface for the wave to reflect off of.

There are a number of variables to play around with that can shape the wave, such as how long the pipe is, whether the pipe is open or closed, and how many openings are open or closed. Imagine a flute. When you blow into a flute, the sound changes depending on how many holes you cover up. The pitch is dictated by the number of open holes.

If we adjust the medium the wave is traveling through (such as making the pipe longer or shorter), we can get a different number of wave nodes and antinodes. This is a way to change the pitch we hear. The lowest number of nodes and antinodes that can exist in a wave is two nodes and one antinode. We call this the **first harmonic**, also known as the **fundamental**:

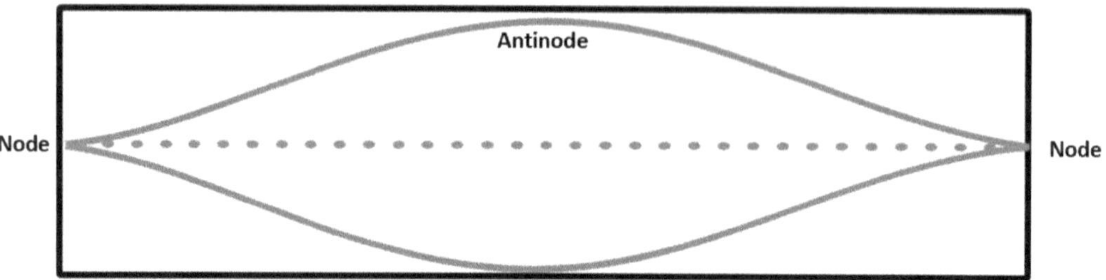

Figure 5.6 – First harmonic (fundamental)

If we add a single node and antinode to our wave, we get a wave like the one in the following figure. You can see that there are now three nodes and two antinodes:

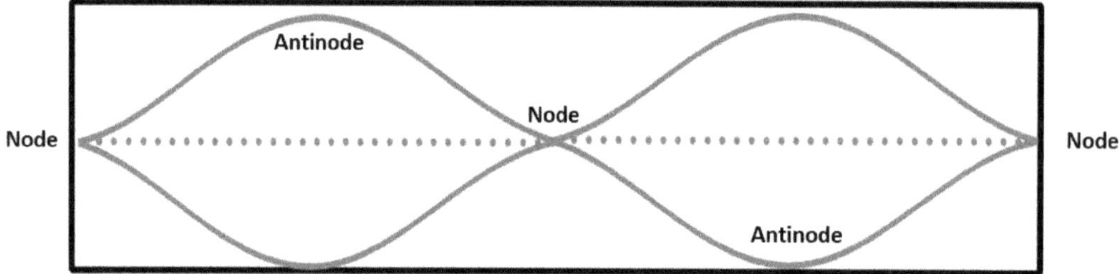

Figure 5.7 – Second harmonic (first overtone)

We call this the **second harmonic**. Another name for this is the **first overtone**. Music theory often uses the term **harmonic**. Physics often uses the term **overtone**, but they both mean the same thing. Notice we have increased the frequency of the wave. The first harmonic only had half a wavelength, while the second harmonic had a full wavelength, but it's the same total distance. This means the pitch of the sound would be higher. How much higher? Exactly one **octave**. If, for example, our fundamental had a pitch of middle C, meaning it had a frequency of 261.6 Hz, the second harmonic/first overtone would be 523.2 Hz, or a C note that is exactly one octave higher.

If we add another node and antinode, we get a wave as shown in the following figure:

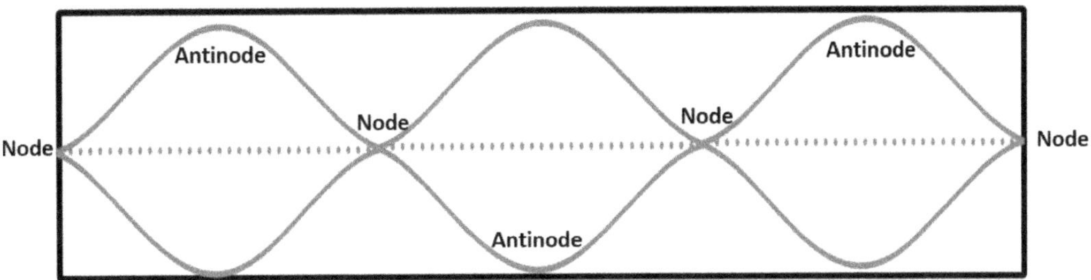

Figure 5.8 – Third harmonic (second overtone)

A wave with four nodes and three antinodes is known as the third harmonic, also called the second overtone. Note that the frequency has increased again, raising the pitch by another octave.

Put simply, harmonics are frequencies that occur at multiples of the fundamental frequency. For example, doubling the frequency (2×) gives you an octave higher, tripling it (3×) results in an octave plus a perfect fifth, and quadrupling it (4×) produces a pitch two octaves above the fundamental.

All of this means that instruments can create different pitches by modifying the wavelength and frequency of the sound wave.

Why do different instruments playing the same pitch sound different?

Different instruments emphasize different harmonics/overtones. They emphasize some overtones louder than others. The waveforms of different instruments have different amplitudes, which also shape the sound. Also, remember that air is able to support many sound waves simultaneously. This variation in the combination of waveforms played simultaneously also shapes the sound we hear.

In our diagram examples, we've looked at **sine waveforms**. There are many kinds of waveforms. Instrument plugins can generate different types of waves, such as **square waves**, **saw waves**, and any sort of strange concoction developers can think up. The type of waveform will affect the resulting sound. For example, a sine wave sounds pure and flute-like, a square wave is hollow and similar to a clarinet, a saw wave is aggressive like strings or brass, a triangle wave is soft, and noise resembles percussion or breathy sounds.

When you experiment with synthesizer plugin instruments, the plugin creates different wave shapes. It adjusts the wavelength, amplitude, frequency, harmonics, and the combination of waveforms it plays. Once the waveform is created, there are additional ways to modify sound waves using what are called **sound envelopes**.

Now that you understand how sound is created and shaped, let's explore how we control its movement and character over time using envelopes.

What are sound envelopes, and how do you modify them?

A **sound envelope** is a term describing how sound changes over time. When playing around with instrument plugins, you may come across the acronym **ADSR**. This stands for **attack**, **decay**, **sustain**, and **release,** and refers to the four stages of a sound envelope.

The best way to understand a sound envelope is to modify one yourself. Reading alone will not teach you to understand; you must tweak the controls and listen to how the sound changes:

1. Grab a single sound sample and load it up into the **Channel rack** (note that I say *Channel rack*, not *Playlist*. It's important that you don't drag the sample directly into the **Playlist** at this stage, as you won't be able to see the envelope controls). Later on, after we've adjusted the sample envelope, we'll add it to the **Playlist**. I'm going to use an acoustic guitar sample, as shown in the following screenshot:

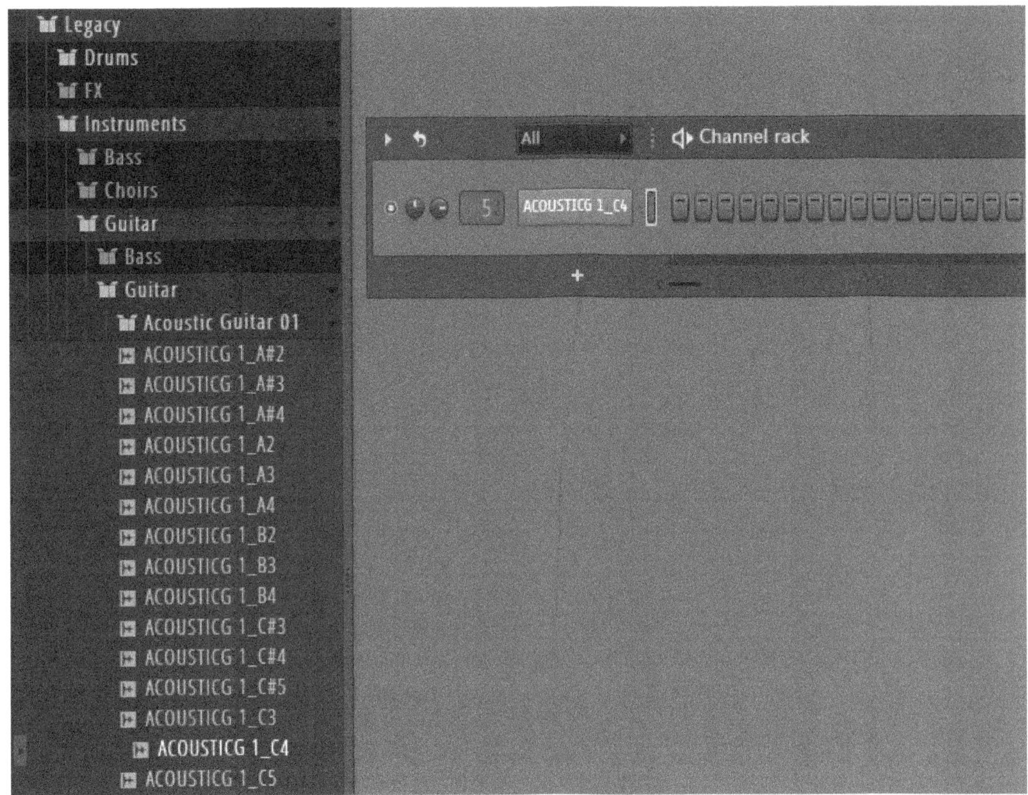

Figure 5.9 – Guitar sample

Once loaded, left-click on the sample in the **Channel rack** to bring up the sample properties. Select the **envelope/instrument settings toggle button** at the top left of the window, as shown in the following screenshot:

Figure 5.10 – Envelope settings

You will now be able to see the sample envelope as shown in the preceding screenshot. By default, the volume envelope is highlighted. Directly underneath the **Volume** button, you can see a set of knobs with controls for changing the volume envelope.

You can think of an envelope as a container for sounds. Imagine you have a bunch of objects that are all different, but they're shipped in a standard format container, just like how boats ship items overseas. The container itself has a bunch of properties regardless of what it carries, such as how long it is or how quickly it gets delivered. The container has an influence on how we interact with the object inside. An audio envelope is a little like that. The envelope allows us to interact with the sound using some universal controls.

2. Experiment with changing the delay (**DELAY**), attack (**ATT**), hold (**HOLD**), decay (**DECAY**), sustain (**SUS**), and release (**REL**) knobs while playing the sample at the same time. You'll be able to hear how the envelope manipulates the sound.

Here's a brief description of the **Envelope** controls in order from left to right:

- **Delay**: It is the silence before the envelope starts rising.
- **Attack**: The time it takes for the note to reach its maximum level (in this case, volume). By increasing the attack, you'll hear the sound become more punctuated.
- **Hold**: How long to hold the maximum level.
- **Decay**: The time taken from the attack level to the sustain level.
- **Sustain**: The level at which the note is held.
- **Release**: The time it takes for the note to fall from the sustain level to silence after being released.
- **Tension**: The first **TENSION** knob adjusts the time between the delay and the attack. The second **TENSION** knob adjusts the time between the sustain and the release. Tension controls adjust the shape of the attack and release curves in an envelope, changing how quickly or gradually the sound starts and stops. By changing the tension, you can make the attack or release feel snappier and more abrupt, or smoother and more gradual, depending on the sound you want.

When dealing with envelope controls in plugins, you may come across a term known as a **transient**. Transients refer to the initial, high-energy portion of a sound, such as the attack of a drum hit or the pluck of a string. Modifying the attack and release controls of a sound volume envelope can increase or decrease the prominence of transients. If increased, this will make the sound more punctuated. If decreased, it will make the sound less punctuated and less intense.

Any sample can have its audio envelope manipulated in this fashion. Most instrument plugins include envelope controls. Understanding the terminology described so far in this section will allow you to learn instrument plugins and effects much more quickly. We've learned how to manipulate the envelope of a sound. Next, let's learn how to break apart elements of a sound and extract them using AI.

Extracting stems from samples using AI

Music **stems** are groups of audio files that represent parts of a song, such as drums, vocals, bass, or guitars. Instead of exporting every individual track separately, stems combine related sounds into a smaller set of files, making the song easier to remix, perform live, or adjust in mastering. For example, breaking a song into stems might give you one file for vocals, one for drums, one for bass, and one for instruments, which can then be mixed and balanced independently.

FL Studio has a tool that can take any song and break it apart into its individual stem components using AI. The tool can extract the drums, bass, instruments, and vocals from the song. This is a very handy technique with many use cases. The most common scenario is that you want to extract the vocals from a song to use in a remix of another song. The extraction tool will give you just the vocals, which you can then remix into a new song. Note that for copyright reasons, you need to obtain permission to use someone else's vocal/sample before you can use a song commercially.

For DJs, breaking a song into its stem components is extremely useful. DJs often want songs' stem components prior to performing their sets. This way, a DJ can slowly bring in parts of a song piece by piece. For example, first they play just the vocals, then slowly fade in the volume of the instruments, and then at a pivotal moment of anticipation, bring in the drums and bass/drums. It also allows them to mix and match stems between different songs. For example, if I have song A and song B, I might want to play the drums and bass from song A and use the instruments and vocals from song B. The freedom to swap around stems gives DJs lots of room to play around with the songs.

Stems are useful for musicians analyzing songs to learn how they were made, for remixing pre-existing songs, or for DJs assembling tracks for DJ sets. Let's learn how to extract music stems from any song sample:

1. Load any song into the FL Studio Playlist. You can drag a song from the **Browser** or from a File Explorer into your Playlist, whichever you prefer. The following screenshot shows an example where I've dragged a song I created, *"Creatures of the Night,"* into the **Playlist**.

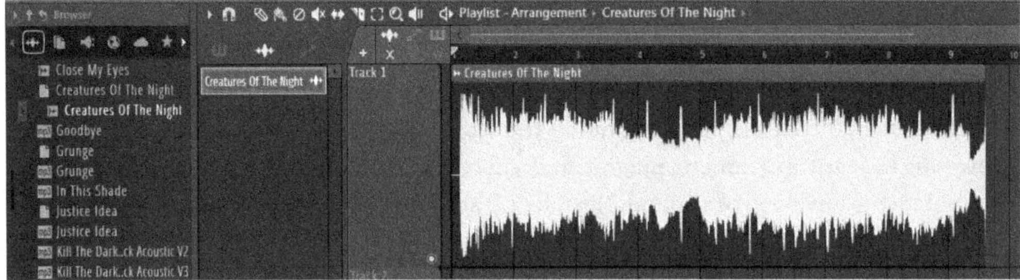

Figure 5.11 – Load sample into Playlist

You now have your song audio in the **Playlist**.

2. On the top left of the sample, left-click to view the sample options, then choose the option **Extract stems from sample** as shown in the following screenshot:

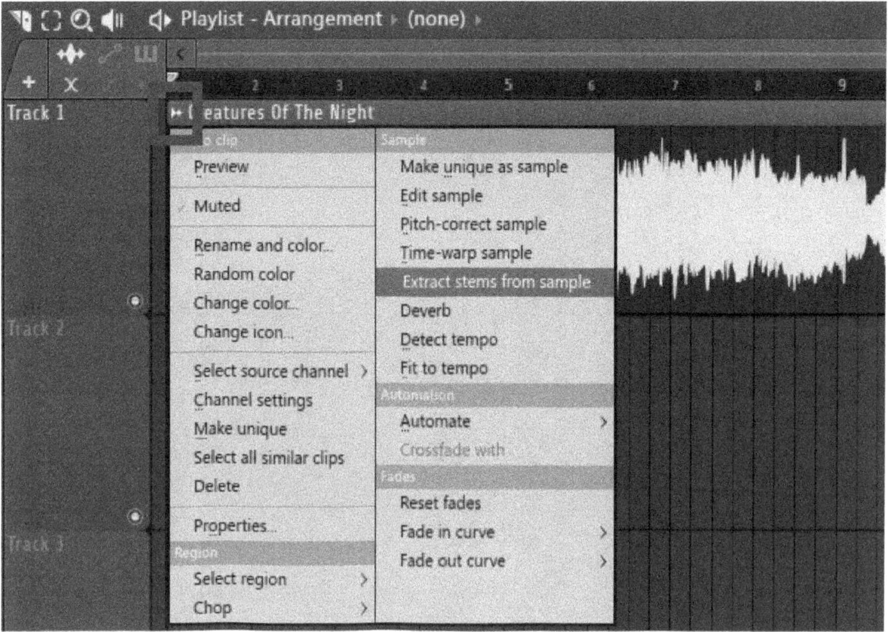

Figure 5.12 – Extract stems from sample

This will bring up the **Extract stems from sample** window.

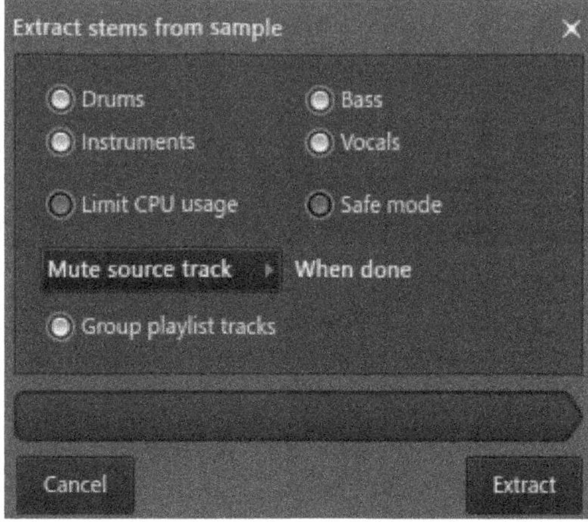

Figure 5.13 – Choose stems to extract

Here you can choose which stems to extract. I want all the stems, so I'll leave the default options as they are and click the **Extract** button. The tool then uses AI to extract the drum, bass, instrument, and vocal elements from the sample. The **Drums**, **Bass**,

Instruments, and **Vocals** stems of the song sample will appear in the **Playlist**. You can now manipulate these new sample stems as you like.

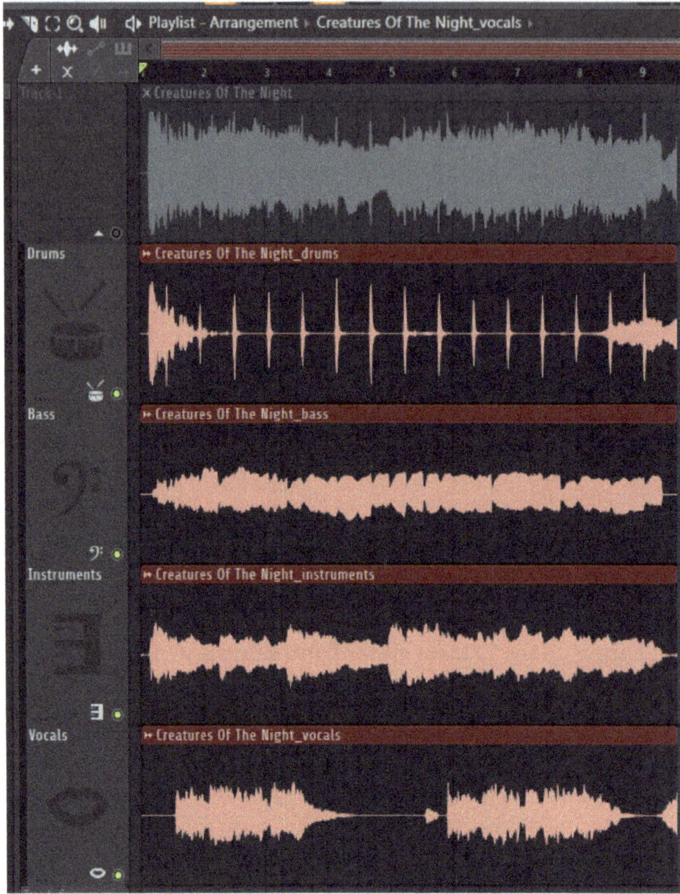

Figure 5.14 – Drums, Bass, Instruments, and Vocals extracted

Analyzing stems is a great way for you to learn about your favorite songs. You can now listen to the individual pieces and try to figure out why a sound is good. What was the composer doing with the drums? You can hear the individual parts more clearly and distinctly once you've removed all the other distracting elements.

If you want to immediately export the stems as they are without further changes (such as if you are using the stems for a DJ mix), there's an easy way to export the song from FL Studio. Go to **File | Export | All playlist tracks | From song start...**.

Figure 5.15 – Export song stems

This will export a new audio file for each playlist track. So if you have 4 stems, then it'll export 4 audio files, one for each stem. You now know how to break any song sample into its stem components of drums, bass, instruments, and vocals.

Summary

In this chapter, we explored how sound works. We learned about sound waves, how we hear sounds, and how instruments create sounds. We learned about audio envelopes and how to adjust the audio envelope of any audio sample. With this information, you will be able to learn instrument plugins quickly and have an intuition for how they work.

We also learned how to extract the drum, bass, instrument, and vocal stems from any song sample using an AI tool. This is useful for dissecting songs into their individual components, whether for learning about songs, remixing song components, or use by DJs.

In the next chapter, we will learn about music mixing techniques and explore plugin effects that can be applied to your sounds.

Get this book's PDF version and more

Scan the QR code (or go to `packtpub.com/unlock`). Search for this book by name, confirm the edition, and then follow the steps on the page.

Note: Keep your invoice handy. Purchases made directly from Packt don't require an invoice.

6

Mixing Basics – Compression, Sidechaining, Limiting, and Equalization

When you hear music performed live, there's variation in the volume. Some sounds are loud, some are quiet. Some may be muffled, distorted, shrill, or filled with echo, but you probably won't notice when you're enraptured by the performance visuals. If you were to record the performance live on your phone and play it back later, you'd notice that the sound quality of the recording is poor. There's background noise, the lyrics are hard to make out clearly, and the bass sound likely overpowers the higher instrument sounds.

When you prepare a song for production, you want to achieve the highest quality sound you can get. You want the audio to be as clear as possible, emphasize the best parts of your sounds, and reduce the unpleasant parts.

Mixing is the name of the process we use to polish our sounds. It includes combining and grouping recordings of instruments in a tool called the **Mixer**. The Mixer balances the volumes of each instrument relative to the others and applies effects to your sounds. The two categories of effects that you can apply to your sounds are **compression** and **equalization**. These are broad categories. There are several types of compression: **simple compression**, **gating**, **sidechaining**, and **limiting**.

In this chapter, you'll learn mixing techniques with **compressors** and **equalizers**. Compressors allow you to tame extremes in your sounds and make your sounds appear balanced and fuller. Equalizers allow you to shape and refine your sounds. Sidechaining reduces the volume of a sound based on the input of a second sound source. Limiting creates a cap on the volume of a sound, constraining the volume to a certain value threshold. These concepts might seem a bit unclear right now, but don't worry, we'll explore them in depth as we go through this chapter.

In this chapter, we'll cover the following topics:

- Understanding compression
- Applying gates and expanders
- Applying sidechaining
- Using limiters
- Applying equalization

Understanding compression

When mixing, we call the range in volume from loud to quiet, the **dynamic range**. Compression is an effect applied to a sound to reduce the dynamic range. After compression is applied to a sound, the loudest parts of the sound become quieter relative to the quieter parts. The volume of the whole sound is then raised. Reducing dynamic range means that you have less change between the quietest and the loudest parts of your sound.

Why would you want to use compression? Imagine you were having a conversation with someone and wanted someone else to hear the recording. In the recording, some parts of the dialogue might be really loud while others might be quiet. You might whisper in some parts and yell in others; you might move close to or further away from the microphone. All of these factors will affect the volume of the end result of the recording. For someone listening to the recording, you don't want them to be struggling to hear the whispering and then having their ears blasted off in the louder parts. You want to have a consistent volume throughout to ensure an easy listening experience.

Applying compression to a sound can help to remove these problems. By applying compression, the volume of the loud parts of your audio will be brought down so that they don't overpower your listener. After compressing, we can bring up the volume of the whole sound, including the quiet parts. The volume of the whispering parts will be increased to a level that is comfortable to hear. The overall result is a recording that's easy to listen to, with the loud peaking parts tamed and the quiet parts made more audible.

Let's see what compression looks like visually. The following figure shows the waveform of a kick drum audio sample before it is compressed:

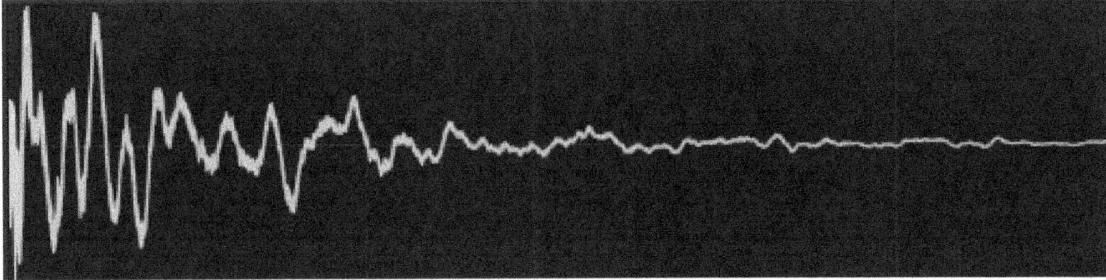

Figure 6.1 – Uncompressed kick drum sample

The following figure shows the waveform of the same sample after it has been compressed:

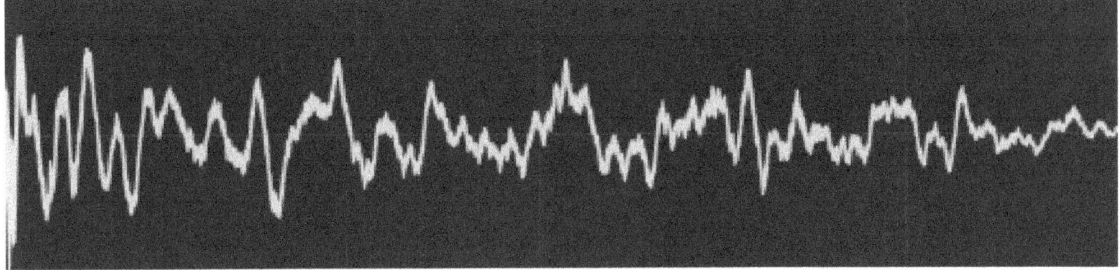

Figure 6.2 – Compressed kick drum sample

The amplitude (height) of the waveform indicates the loudness. In *Figure 6.1*, you can see that the dynamic range is large. It's loud in the beginning, but tapers off over time until it becomes nonexistent.

In *Figure 6.2*, you can see that the dynamic range is smaller. It's loud in the beginning, and the volume stays high throughout the duration of the sound. The volume of the loud part at the beginning has decreased, and the quiet tail end of the sound has increased.

When we compress, we bring the loud and quiet parts closer together so that there is less variation between the highs and lows (less dynamic range), and then usually increase the overall volume of the sound.

Applying compression with Fruity Limiter

Let's learn how to apply compression to a sound. To illustrate the examples in this chapter, we will use **Fruity Limiter**, a plugin that comes with FL Studio. Fruity Limiter has multiple tools, including compression, gating, sidechaining, and limiting. We will explore these topics in detail in the upcoming pages. Understanding how to use these tools will give you generally applicable skills used in many synthesizer plugins and effects.

Let's get started with applying compression with Fruity Limiter:

1. Drag any audio recording sample into the **Playlist** and route the audio to a **Mixer** channel. In my example, I'm using a single kick sound sample found in the `Pack` folder in the **Browser**. If you need a refresher on routing audio to Mixer channels, see *Chapter 4*.
2. In the **Mixer** channel you routed your sample to, insert the **Fruity Limiter** effect plugin, and select the **COMP** setting (which stands for compression), as shown in the following screenshot:

Figure 6.3 – Fruity Limiter

Fruity Limiter is made up of several components: the **LOUDNESS** section, the **ENVELOPE** section, and the **NOISE GATE** section.

The **LOUDNESS** section is a compressor. The following are descriptions of the controls from left to right:

- **GAIN**: Increases or decreases the overall volume. After applying compression to the sound, the louder parts will be quieter. This means the loud and quiet parts of the sound are closer together in amplitude. You can then increase the volume of the sound as a whole by increasing the gain.
- **SAT** (saturation): This is a form of mild distortion. It affects the louder parts (higher amplitude) of the sound more than the quieter parts. In electrical hardware, this occurs by overloading the electrical component. The more signal you apply, the more the sound gets saturated. If you combine saturation with compression, the compression brings down the volume of the louder parts. This results in the quieter parts of the sound being closer in amplitude to the louder parts and allows more of the sound to receive saturation.
- **THRES** (threshold): This sets the level above which the signal will be compressed. If the threshold is set to 0 dB, it disables the threshold, and no compression will be applied.
- **KNEE**: This determines the transition between no compression and full compression. It allows you to fade in the amount of compression.
- **RATIO**: This determines how much compression should be applied once the threshold is exceeded.

To apply compression, do the following:

1. Have the sample playing while applying the compression.
2. Set the **THRES** control level to a value below `1.0` (you can always check values for your controls in the top left of FL Studio). This determines what volume to start applying compression at. Anything above the threshold level will have compression applied to it. You can set the **KNEE** control if you want the compression to fade in instead of coming in abruptly. The lower the value you set the threshold to, the more you will notice the sound of the compression.
3. Set the **RATIO** level to a value greater than `1.0:1`. This will determine how much the sound is compressed. If the ratio is set to `2.0:1`, this means that for every dB in volume, the signal will be reduced to half. If the ratio were `3.0:1`, then the signal would be reduced by a third, and so on.
4. Increase the **GAIN** level of the sound. After adjusting the threshold and ratio controls, the volume of the sound has decreased. The loud parts of the sound have been lowered

to a level closer to the volume of the quieter parts. We now apply what is called **makeup gain**. This will increase the overall volume and result in an ending sound where the quieter and louder parts are brought closer together. This makes the sound appear fuller with less dynamic variation.

Congratulations, you just applied compression to your sound!

Let's continue exploring the Fruity Limiter plugin. To the right of the **LOUDNESS** section, you can see the **ENVELOPE** section, as shown in the following screenshot:

Figure 6.4 – Envelope

The **ENVELOPE** controls affect the transients of a sound. **Transients** are the short bursts of energy that you hear at the start of any sound. The **ENVELOPE** provides control over the **ATT** (attack), **REL** (release), and **SUSTAIN** levels of the transients.

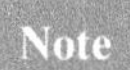

> The **ENVELOPE** section here is applied to the compression. You won't hear any difference when you use these controls unless you compress the sound first.

By decreasing the attack, you cause the compression to come in quicker. This will reduce the punchy articulation of the sound. By decreasing the release time, the sound becomes shorter and brings focus to the loud, punchy peaks of the sound. By increasing the release time, the sound becomes longer, and you can hear more of the compressed tail after the makeup gain. The **SUSTAIN** control allows the compression to last longer or shorter.

In the bottom-right corner of **Fruity Limiter**, you can see two circle icons with arrows called **store in spare state**. These buttons allow you to flip between two states of the plugin to give you a before-and-after comparison.

Fruity Limiter contains several presets in the top-right corner of the plugin. I encourage you to experiment with the presets to see examples of compression.

Any sound with extreme peaks in dynamic range may benefit from compression. After applying compression, sounds generally appear thicker and fuller, which is desirable. The trade-off with using compression is that you won't have as much contrast between loud and quiet sounds. If you compress your sound too much, you might remove all the punchy transients that exist in the original sound. There is a way to get around this issue called parallel compression, which we will discuss next.

Understanding parallel compression

If you look up the term compression online, you may come across the term **parallel compression**. Parallel compression is where you have two identical sounds being played simultaneously. One of the sounds has compression applied to it, while the other doesn't. You have a compressed sound and an uncompressed sound.

The benefit is that you get the emphasized part of the compressed sound without losing the original transients. When you compress a sound, you make a trade-off. You lose the impactful loudness peaks of the original sound and trade them for a thicker, fuller-bodied sound that emphasizes more of the quieter parts. The hope is that the fuller-bodied compressed sound is more pleasing to the ears.

In parallel compression, you don't have to make this trade-off. You layer the uncompressed version with the transients over the compressed sound that doesn't contain the transients. You gain all of the benefits of compression while leaving the delicate transients intact. The result is a thicker, fuller sound that still maintains the punchy articulations. Parallel compression is most often used on drum instruments to maintain transient punchiness.

Applying parallel compression sounds complicated, but it's actually really quite simple. All you need to do is route your instrument track to two Mixer channels. On one of the mixer tracks, you add a compressor, and on the other track, you don't. Then you just decide the output volume you want of the two mixer tracks. Here's an example:

Figure 6.5 – Parallel compression

In the preceding screenshot, we can see that the instrument track is routed to two mixer tracks. One of them is labeled **With Compression**, and the other is labeled **No Compression**. On the track **With Compression**, you could add a compressor plugin. Using this technique, you would be able to compress the instrument sound while still maintaining any transients that would normally be lost due to compression.

So far, we've covered simple compression and parallel compression. Let's look at another type of compression, called a **gate**.

Applying gates and expanders

Gates and **expanders** are useful tools for music producers and can be used in a wide variety of situations. They can be used independently of the rest of the controls in Fruity Limiter.

To understand gating, let's compare it to simple compression. Simple compression works by reducing the loudest parts of a sound that are above a threshold level.

Gates and expanders do the opposite. Gates completely remove the audio below the threshold (*don't* allow anything through the gate). Expanders reduce the audio below the threshold, but don't eliminate it completely. A gate acts like an on/off switch for quiet sounds, cutting them out entirely, while an expander works more like a dimmer, fading the sound down instead of turning it off. From here on, we will refer to examples using gates, but the same overall concept is used with expanders too.

Why would you want to use a gate? Imagine you had a dialog recording in a room. In addition to the dialog, there might also be some ambient room noise. Perhaps a gentle hum, some subtle static, a little wind: these undesired sounds detract from the overall focus of clearly hearing the dialogue. Gating allows you to remove the undesired background noise. Gating reduces sounds that are not the desired focus.

To the right of the **ENVELOPE** section in **Fruity Limiter**, we can see the **NOISE GATE** section:

Figure 6.6 – Noise Gate

To use the **NOISE GATE**, do the following:

1. Set the **THRES** (threshold) level to a value below 0 dB. This is the level below which sound will be reduced. If your sample has some background noise you want to remove, set the threshold level slightly above the volume of the unwanted sound but still below the sound of the main subject. For example, if the dialog volume is at least -10 dB, you could set your threshold to somewhere below -10 dB.
2. Decrease the **GAIN** level. This will reduce the volume of the sound below the threshold level and make the unwanted sound quieter.
3. Adjust the **REL** (release) control. This will determine how long you want the gating effect to be applied for after the initial reduction.

The end result of using a gate is that we are able to remove unwanted background noise, leaving behind just the desired louder noise.

When to use gating

Gating is always the first effect that you should apply in a series of effects. You want effects to be applied only to your desired sound and not to unwanted background noise.

You want to use noise gating in any situation where you have unwanted background noise. For example, when you record live vocals or a live instrument, before applying any other effects to your sound, you should consider applying a gate. Unless you have a soundproof studio, there will usually be some unwanted background noise that can be reduced through gating.

So far, we've learned how to use compressors and gates. Next, let's learn about sidechaining.

Applying sidechaining

Sidechaining (also known as **ducking**) is a compression technique where you use the input of one sound source to determine when to compress a second sound. This technique is used extensively in pop and electronic dance music to sidechain bass instruments whenever a kick drum sound occurs. The result is a rhythmic pumping bass sound associated with the urge to tap your feet and bob your head.

Sidechaining in electronic dance music uses the following rationale: sidechaining the bass sound reduces the bass sound when the kick drum comes in. This frees up space to allow the kick sound transient to punch through and focuses your ear's attention more on the kick.

It should be noted that sidechaining can be applied to any sound and doesn't have to involve percussion at all. A sidechain pumping sound of an instrument can be used on its own. For example, you may want to sidechain the bass instrument even if you don't have any percussion playing.

The fastest way to understand sidechaining is to use it in an example. In order to do the following example, you will need a bass instrument and a kick sound sample. You can use any bass instrument and kick sound sample you like. In my example, I will be using the FL Studio Harmless synthesizer and using the default instrument setting when the plugin is loaded. The kick sample used is a kick sample that comes with FL Studio in the `Pack` folder found in the **Browser**:

1. Load your kick sample and bass instrument into the **Channel rack**. Create a clone of the kick sound sample in the **Channel rack**. This cloned kick is going to be the kick sound that we use for sidechaining. If you need a refresher on loading instruments, we covered it in *Chapter 2*.
2. Add a note every 1/4 bar for both kick samples.
3. Add the pattern to the **Playlist** and name it `Kicks`.
4. Route all channels in your **Channel rack** to the **Mixer**. We covered how to do that in *Chapter 4*. Consider coloring your instruments and patterns for visual convenience. After completing these steps, your **Playlist** and **Channel rack** should look similar to the following:

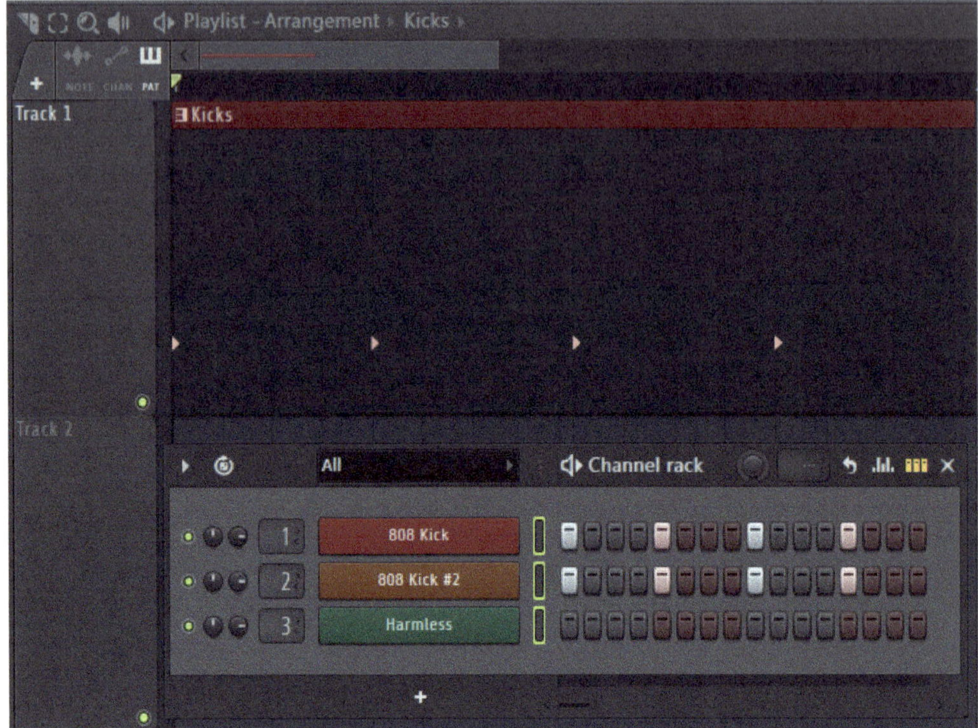

Figure 6.7 – Kick drum setup

5. Create a new pattern and name it `Bass`.
6. For the bass instrument (in my case, Harmless), add notes every 1/4 bar. Aim to have the low bass sound by decreasing the pitch until the sound of the instrument is low. For a Harmless example, notes in the pitch of C3 are low enough. After adding bass instrument notes, your screen should look similar to the following:

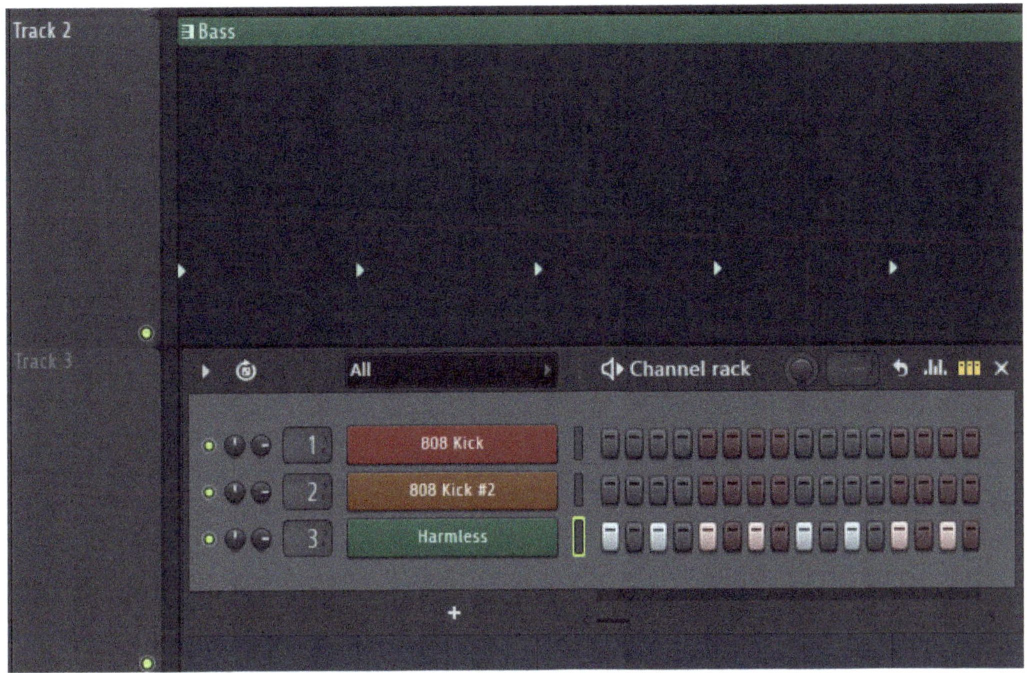

Figure 6.8 – Bass instrument setup

7. Add the pattern with the bass instrument to the **Playlist**. Your **Playlist** should look similar to the following, with both the Kicks pattern and the Bass pattern added as shown in the following screenshot. Note how the **Kick** and **Bass** notes line up each bar:

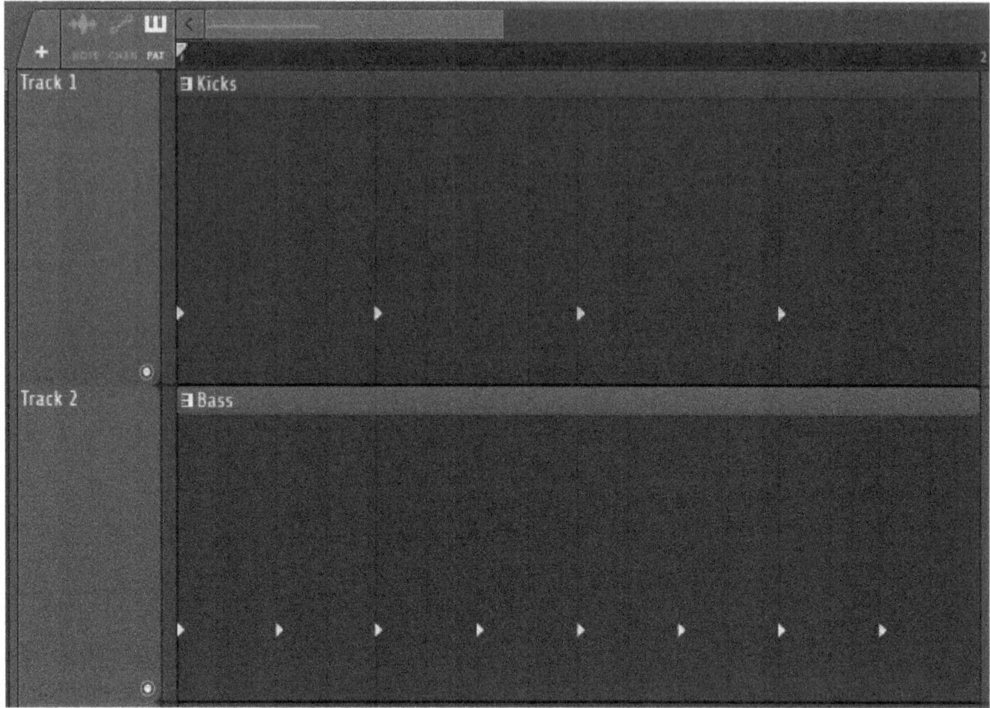

Figure 6.9 – Playlist with both the bass instrument and kick

You can now play the Playlist and hear the bass instrument and the kick sounds.

8. Next, we're going to apply sidechain compression to the bass instrument. This will cause the volume of the bass instrument to decrease whenever the kick drum occurs.
9. It's time to sidechain the bass instrument to the kick. In the **Mixer**, select one of the kick channels. Then, right-click on the arrow at the bottom of the bass instrument channel (Harmless) and select the **Sidechain to this track only** menu drop-down option.

Figure 6.10 – Sidechaining kick to the bass instrument

What we've done is told the signal of the kick drum to no longer route to the **Master** channel. The signal from the kick sample is now being sent exclusively to the bass instrument channel to be used as an input for sidechaining.

10. Add the Fruity Limiter plugin to the Harmless Mixer (**Mixer – Harmless**) channel. Select **COMP** in **Fruity Limiter**.
11. In the **SIDECHAIN** control of **Fruity Limiter**, scroll to select **1**. This will tell Fruity Limiter to listen for the kick audio. Your screen should look similar to the following:

Figure 6.11 – Fruity Limiter now accepts kick as a sidechain source

12. Play the song. At the same time, under the **LOUDNESS** and **ENVELOPE** sections of **Fruity Limiter**, add compression to your sound using the techniques we learned earlier in this chapter. The exact compression control adjustments will depend upon the sounds you are using, but when you're done, it could look similar to the following:

Figure 6.12 – Fruity Limiter LOUDNESS and ENVELOPE sidechain settings

In the **LOUDNESS** and **ENVELOPE** controls, we've added compression to the sound. Remember, compression reduces the loudness of the sound.

We used a kick sound as an input for sidechaining. This is a little different from the simple compression we did in an earlier example. We're using sidechaining to cause the bass instrument to compress only at certain times, rather than constantly throughout. The bass instrument gets compressed when it receives input from the sidechained kick channel. When the bass channel receives signal input from the kick channel, it starts the compression.

If you've done everything correctly, when you play your Playlist, you should be able to hear a rhythmic pumping action of your bass instrument that ducks every time the kick drum sound occurs.

You may have wondered, why did we need 2 kick samples? Couldn't we have used sidechaining with a single kick sample and still heard the bass get sidechained? The answer is yes. However, using 2 kick samples and sidechaining just one of them gives you an additional advantage: the sidechaining of the bass is not restricted to the timing of the audible kick. You can have the bass sound sidechained regardless of whether the sound of the kick is audible or not. Sometimes all you may want is the sidechained bass sound and not to hear any kick sound at all. Using the setup provided, you have complete freedom to control when to hear sidechaining or not.

Congratulations, you've successfully used sidechaining! Next, let's learn how to use **limiters**.

Using limiters

So far, we've discussed simple compression, parallel compression, and sidechain compression. Fruity Limiter offers another tool called a limiter. Limiters are tools that lower the amplitude peak of a sound. Limiters have a threshold level, and when it's reached, the average volume of the audio is compressed and then raised until it reaches the threshold. The result is that the overall sounds appear louder but are contained under the threshold.

The difference between a compressor and a limiter is that in a compressor, you set the compression ratio to an exact value (for example, reduce by a 3:1 ratio), whereas in a limiter, the ratio is not specifically set by you. The ratio of compression adapts until the overall volume is raised up to the threshold.

Why would you use limiters? One reason to use limiters is to prevent unwanted distortion. If the volume of your final audio exceeds 0 dB, unwanted distortion occurs. In hardware, this causes a signal overload. Limiting reduces your audio signal to prevent this.

Another reason to use limiters is to increase the overall perceived volume of your completed song. Audio that appears louder is easier to hear and is preferred.

A limiter is used on your Master channel. Limiters are used to bring up the overall volume of the finished song in the mastering process. Before exporting your final song for mastering, the last plugin effect that the sound is processed through is always a limiter.

Let's use a limiter in our project:

1. Add Fruity Limiter to your **Master** channel.

Figure 6.13 – Fruity Limiter loudness and envelope sidechain settings

Under the **LOUDNESS** section, you can see three controls: **GAIN**, **SAT** (saturation), and **CEIL** (ceiling). **GAIN** and **SAT** perform the same function as they do in a simple compressor. The **CEIL** control sets the maximum level that the volume of the sound can reach. Any sound that reaches the ceiling is compressed until it no longer exceeds the ceiling level. By default, the ceiling level is set to 0 dB. This means the maximum volume that can be reached is 0 dB. Anything above 0 dB could result in unwanted distortion, so you never want to set the ceiling above 0 dB. You can leave the ceiling at the default of 0 dB in most cases.

2. Increase **GAIN** slightly. You'll need to experiment with how much to increase the gain. If you increase the gain too much, you'll find your overall sound feels squashed. Increase the gain until you find a comfortable balance between making your song as loud as you can while still maintaining the desired dynamic range.

The end result of using a limiter is that our sound is louder and easier to hear. We will go into a more in-depth exploration of limiters when we get to *Chapter 12*.

We've covered the main types of compression. Next, let's look at equalizer plugins.

Applying equalization

In *Chapter 5*, we learned that frequencies are related to the pitches we hear. By increasing the frequency, we increase the pitch of a sound.

Equalization (shortened to **EQ**) is a category of filter effect used to increase or decrease targeted frequencies of a sound. EQ is used to enhance the frequencies of sounds you like and reduce those you don't.

One way that EQ can be used is to clean up muddy mixes. When multiple instruments are playing, they may sound like they're trying to play over one another. The overlapping of sounds makes it difficult to hear any of the competing instruments clearly. This is known as **mud in the mix** and is undesirable. EQ can help fix muddy mixes by removing competing frequencies of instruments playing at the same time. This helps to designate an area of frequency space for each instrument so that you can hear each one clearly. This is known as cleaning up the mix or removing the mud. The result is a desirable, clearer sound.

FL Studio comes with an excellent EQ plugin called **Fruity parametric EQ 2**. It has lots of features to satisfy most of your EQ needs. Let's use Fruity parametric EQ 2 to demonstrate how to apply EQ to your sounds:

1. Route an instrument or sound sample to an empty mixer track and add the **Fruity parametric EQ 2** effect.
2. Play your sound. When your sound is played, your plugin will look as shown in the following screenshot:

Figure 6.14 – Fruity parametric EQ 2

The EQ plugin visually shows the frequencies of the sound as orange/pink vertical lines. Louder frequencies will appear brighter and quieter ones duller. Directly below the frequency visual, you can see a scale of frequencies ranging from **20** Hz to **10k** Hz. Above the frequency visual, you can see the note pitches and labels associated with the corresponding frequencies.

Along the horizontal line in the middle of the frequency visual, you can see circle icons with the numbers **1** to **7**. Each of these icons represents a frequency range known as a **band**. You can drag these band icons with the mouse to move them. The bands allow you to increase or decrease the sound of frequencies at the corresponding position.

3. While playing your sound, left-click on one of the EQ bands and drag it upward. You'll notice that the sound increases in volume in the area of the affected frequency. This is known as boosting the frequency. Dragging the band down will decrease it. This is known as **cutting the frequency**.
   When used in practice, you want to experiment with increasing and decreasing EQ bands to boost frequencies that you like the sound of and cut those that you don't.

   A way to determine offensive frequencies is to select a band and increase the value. Then, move the band (sweep it) left and right to find the frequency that is most offensive. For example, you may find that at a certain position, you hear undesired shrill whistling. At this position, experiment with decreasing the level of the band below 0 dB. The amount to reduce will depend on your specific scenario. The hope is that this will cut out the offensive frequency sound.

4. On the EQ band that you moved upward in position, hover over the band and scroll with your mouse wheel. Doing so will adjust the slope of the EQ band fading in. The slope makes the change in frequency more or less abrupt. The terminology associated with adjusting the slope is known as **bandwidth** (**Q**). You can adjust the slope (bandwidth) to make it wider or narrower.
5. Right-click on the same EQ band. A menu of additional option features will appear, as shown in the following screenshot:

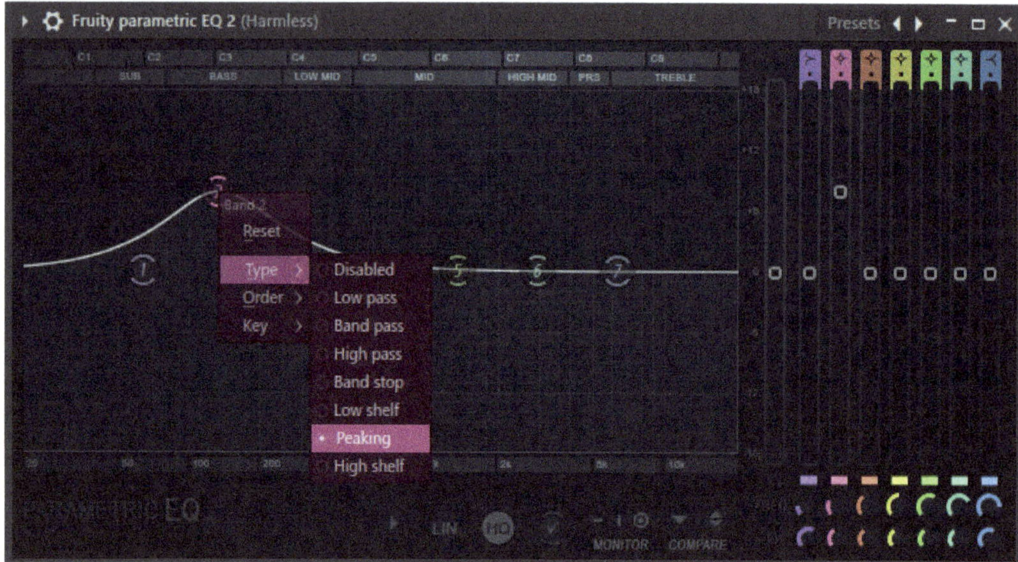

Figure 6.15 – EQ pass and shelves

By default, the type of EQ band is set to **Peaking**, which allows us to add or reduce specific frequencies. You can see that there are other option types for **pass**, **stop**, and **shelf**.

A pass is a filter that restricts which frequencies are allowed. Only frequencies within the pass filter range will be heard. A **low-pass filter** only allows frequencies that are below the filter. A **high-pass filter** only allows frequencies that are above the filter. A stop is where all frequencies in the chosen band are removed. A shelf is where you increase all frequencies that occur within the shelf filter range.

Passes are very useful. Instruments are intended to occupy a specific frequency range. The scale above the frequency visual has labels for common frequency ranges: **Sub**, **Bass**, **Low**

Mid, **Mid**, **High Mid**, **Prs**, and **Treble**. Outside of the frequency range, instrument frequencies may be competing with other instruments, which could result in muddy mixes. In such cases, it is advised to consider adding a pass to remove the unneeded frequencies. This can help prevent muddy mixes. For example, a sub-bass instrument likely benefits from a low-pass filter. This removes high frequencies from the instrument and helps prevent the sub-bass instrument sound from overpowering the sounds of higher instruments.

The **Band** menu has an option with the **Order** category.

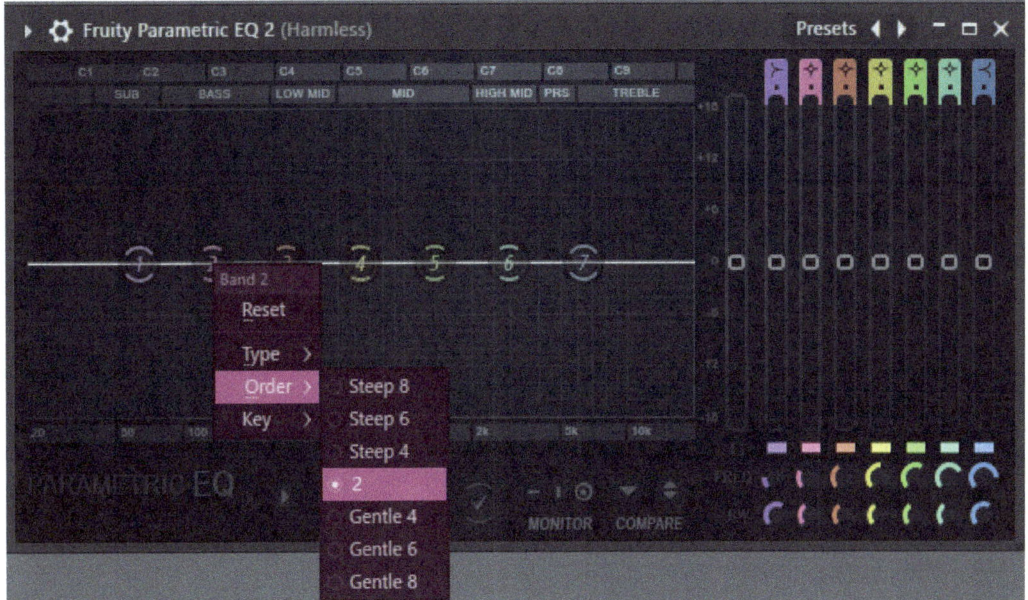

Figure 6.16 – EQ Order

Order lists various slopes in the band. This does the same thing as hovering over the EQ band and scrolling with your mouse wheel.

The final Band menu option is the **Key** category. Since frequency is the same thing as pitch, you can choose to increase or decrease specific pitches. By selecting a specific pitch in the menu, you can set an exact pitch position for an EQ band.

The right side of **Fruity parametric EQ 2** has knob controls for precise control over individual bands. Moving the sliders up or down allows you to move the frequency bands.

At the top right of **Fruity parametric EQ 2**, you'll see a menu of presets. I encourage you to experiment with presets to see examples of EQ possibilities.

At the bottom of the plugin, you'll see the options and settings. One worth mentioning is the **COMPARE** button. This allows you to flip back and forth between two states of the plugin. It can be used to show a before-and-after state to see whether the EQ improved your sound.

EQ best practices

At its core, EQ is about shaping the tone and space of your mix – carving out room for each element so everything can shine without fighting for attention.

The fewer instruments you have playing at any given time, the less likely you are to run into competing frequencies. If you add in a lot of instruments playing simultaneously, you're going to have to spend more time with the EQ to carve out and create frequency space for each instrument.

Your ears pay more attention and can more easily detect changes in high frequencies than in lower frequencies. You only ever want to have one instrument at a time playing in the sub-bass frequencies. Your ears won't be able to distinguish multiple melodies going on in the sub-bass region. Consider using a high-pass filter on everything that is not a bass instrument.

Here are some general EQ suggestions:

- Cut frequencies if you're trying to make things sound better. The best results are usually achieved by eliminating offensive elements in a mix.
- Boost frequencies if you're trying to distinguish sounds from each other.
- Find the most important element in a song and emphasize it. Everything else acts as support. Remove competing frequencies. This leading instrument element may change throughout the course of the song, for example, from vocals to a guitar solo. You'll usually want to create frequency space for the vocals and favor them over other instruments.

When two instruments are playing at the same volume and occupy the same frequency range, they are competing for attention. To fix this, consider the following potential solutions:

- Consider one of the instruments in a different section. Mute one competing instrument and bring it in later.
- Set one of the instruments further back through the use of reverb. We discuss reverb in the next chapter.
- Focus each instrument on its own frequency and tailor the offending instrument to focus on a different frequency range.
- Pan the competing instruments to different locations.

The following is a list of terminology commonly associated with frequency ranges. For example, if an audio engineer says that a sound feels muddy, they're probably referring to the range around 250 Hz:

Frequency Octave Range	Popular Definition
31 Hz	Sub-Bass
63 Hz	Bottom
125 Hz	Boom, Thump, Warmth
250 Hz	Fullness or Mud
500 Hz	Honk
1 kHz	Whack, Nasal
2 kHz	Crunch
4 kHz	Edge
8 kHz	Sibilance, Definition, *Ouch*
16 kHz	Air

Figure 6.17 – Frequency range terminology

If you hear a musician use this terminology, you now understand which frequency range they're referring to.

In this section, we explored Fruity parametric EQ 2, which is a parametric equalizer. Parametric means that you have continuous control over the frequencies and can adjust any chosen frequency.

Summary

In this chapter, we learned about various types of compressors and equalizers. These are tools to help tailor every sound that you use to emphasize the best parts and minimize the poor parts. Compressors can make your sounds appear thicker and fuller. Gates can reduce unwanted background noise. Sidechaining can be used to give your bassline a pumping groove. Limiters can be used to raise the volume of your mix. Equalizers can be used to enhance desired frequencies and reduce unwanted ones.

In the next chapter, we will investigate additional mixing techniques involving stereo width.

Get this book's PDF version and more

Scan the QR code (or go to `packtpub.com/unlock`). Search for this book by name, confirm the edition, and then follow the steps on the page.

UNLOCK NOW

Note: Keep your invoice handy. Purchases made directly from Packt don't require an invoice.

7

Stereo Width – Panning, Reverb, Delay, Chorus, Flangers, and Distortion

Imagine you're at a rock concert. The sound feels huge. The stage itself is large. There are echoes and reverberations throughout the theater. Every sound you hear echoes throughout the room. It's an impressive experience. When mixing music for production, we want to recreate that feeling. How can we make our music sound huge when the listener is listening in a small environment? If the audience is listening with headphones, the actual space that sound can bounce off is tiny. What we have to do is trick our ears into thinking the sound is in a space much larger than it is.

Stereo width describes the perceived width of a sound. By increasing stereo width, your sound gains the impression of being in a larger space. This can be done with several tools that we will explore in this chapter. We will discuss the tools in isolation, but you can, and should, consider layering these tools on top of each other to increase the stereo width further.

At the end of this chapter, we will discuss **mix buses**, which are a fundamental tool in **mixing**.

They allow you to apply effects to multiple sounds at the same time.

In this chapter, we will cover the following topics:

- Panning audio
- Using reverb
- Using LuxeVerb
- Using delay effects

- Using chorus effects
- Using flanger effects
- Using phaser effects
- Understanding distortion effects
- Stereo widening effects with Spreader
- Understanding mix buses

Panning audio

The simplest tool to increase stereo width is a technique called **panning**. Before we can explain panning, we need to understand what **mono** and **stereo** mean.

Monophonic sound (known as mono) is the term used when different audio channels play the same sound equally. Regardless of whether you are listening out of your right or left speaker/headphone, the audio is identical. Mono is used for radio talk shows and telephone calls.

When identical audio is played out of two audio speakers, as with mono, your ears perceive the sound as originating from a location in the middle of the two sources. This is known as a **phantom center**.

Stereophonic sound (known as stereo) means you have different sounds coming out of each audio channel. If your left speaker/headphone has a different sound coming out of it than the right, your sound is said to be in stereo. The benefit of stereo sound is that it creates the illusion of audio coming from multiple directions, just like real life. If you were to watch a band playing live, the instruments are positioned on the stage at different locations. The audio reaches each ear at different intensities depending on how close each instrument is. Stereo sound is used extensively in films to create a sense of motion. For example, when you see something on the right side of the screen, the audio may come from just the right speakers.

Panning means choosing the direction that sound comes out of audio channels. We can set audio to pan left, meaning that the audio comes out of our left channel, or pan right, so the audio comes out of our right channel. In film score mixing, you may have additional pan controls to include up and down as well, but this requires a special speaker setup, such as a movie theater with speakers surrounding the listener above and below them, as well as to the left and right.

By default, audio coming out of any channel in the Mixer is set to monophonic. If you were to have two identical sounds where one is panned all the way right, and one is panned all the way left, you would hear a mono sound. Duplicating a track and hard panning each in opposite directions does not make a sound stereo. In order to hear a stereo sound, you need to have different sounds playing out of the left and the right audio channels.

Let's pan some audio:

1. Load any instrument and add some notes to it. Route the instrument to a channel in the **Mixer**.
2. While playing your audio, left-click on the panning control knob and drag left or right. As you drag, you'll be able to hear the audio volume if you focus on the speaker you're panning toward.

Figure 7.1 – Panned audio

You can pan any sound in the **Mixer** in a similar fashion.

Panning best practices

Panning is one of the most underrated tools in music production; it's what turns a flat, two-dimensional mix into an immersive sonic landscape. While EQ and compression shape tone and dynamics, panning shapes space. It decides where each sound lives in the stereo field and how listeners experience your mix. Done thoughtfully, panning brings clarity, balance, and excitement; done poorly, it can make everything sound lopsided or confusing.

Low-frequency sounds instinctively get associated with larger objects. Biologically, this makes sense, as a lion makes a much deeper and larger sound than a bird, which makes a higher frequency and smaller sound.

You want your low-frequency sounds (sub-bass and bass) to be centered in your mix, meaning you want them to be mono. Your higher frequency sounds can be panned out more to the left or right.

If you have an instrument panned to the right, you should have another instrument panned to the left to balance out the mix. You want to avoid scenarios where you have an instrument hard-panned to one side for long durations of time, and nothing panned to the other side. This would result in the mix feeling off-center and sounding unpleasant to users wearing headphones.

If you have two similar sounds occupying the same frequency range playing simultaneously, consider panning the instruments in different directions to spread them out. This can result in the instruments sounding like they are playing off each other and adds a sense of distinction between them.

Lead vocals should be centered in your mix (mono). Backup vocals and harmonies can be panned and spread out in the mix.

Panning in combination with other stereo width tools can create interesting effects. For example, using automation to pan a guitar to the right while gradually panning a delay of the guitar to the left can make it appear as if the guitar sound is bouncing off a wall and echoing to the opposite ear.

Panning becomes even more powerful when combined with automation. **Static panning** works, but **dynamic panning**, where sounds move slightly over time, can add motion, and excitement. For instance, you can automate a synth pad to drift slowly from left to right, or let a delay echo bounce across the stereo field. These small shifts keep a listener's attention and make the mix feel fluid and three-dimensional.

Panning also works hand in hand with EQ and reverb to create depth. You can think of panning as the left-right dimension, EQ as the tonal balance (up-down), and reverb as front-to-back space, which we will discuss next. Together, they form the full 3D image of your mix. A bright, panned sound will feel closer, while a darker, reverberant one will seem farther away. Use this interplay to guide the listener's focus and create contrast between foreground and background elements.

Panning is the simplest tool to create stereo width. Next, let's look at a technique called reverb.

Using reverb

Natural reverb occurs when sound waves bounce off a surface and reflect back to a listener. The timing and amplitude of the reflected audio exhibit some variation compared to the original. Over time, the amplitudes and frequencies in the sound wave decrease, and the sound dissipates.

You can think of reverb as making your sound feel further away. The more reverb you add, the further away your sound will feel and the larger the space the sound appears to exist in. Reverb is actually a separate sound that is played (you can play just the reverb of a sound without hearing the original source), but our ears get tricked and interpret the original and the reverb as if they are connected as a single sound.

In general, reverb is the last effect you want to apply in the signal chain to your sound.

There are two kinds of reverb: **algorithmic digital reverb** and **convolution reverb**. Let's take a look at each of these.

Applying digital reverb with Fruity Reeverb 2

Algorithmic digital reverb plugins work by generating delayed versions of the original sound. The number of reflections in the reverb is determined by sending the delays through a feedback loop. In a natural environment, your ear expects to hear sound echoing throughout the room and to hear echoes of echoes. Feedback resembles echoes of echoes. Unless specifically labeled otherwise, reverb plugins are digital algorithmic types and not convolution types.

Fruity Reeverb 2 is a plugin effect that creates **algorithmic reverb**. Let's take a look at using reverb with Fruity Reeverb 2:

1. Load up a sample or an instrument with notes and route it to a new mixer track.
2. Apply the **Fruity Reeverb 2** effect to the Mixer channel and play your sound. The easiest way is to left-click on any empty slot in the **Mixer** and then choose the effect plugin you want to apply. In the example screenshot, I have selected the Mixer channel that I want to add the effect to, and then I am selecting the effect plugin **Fruity Reeverb 2**.

Figure 7.2 – Adding the effect Fruity Reeverb 2

This will add the effect plugin to the Mixer channel. Now you'll see the effect plugin **Fruity Reeverb 2**.

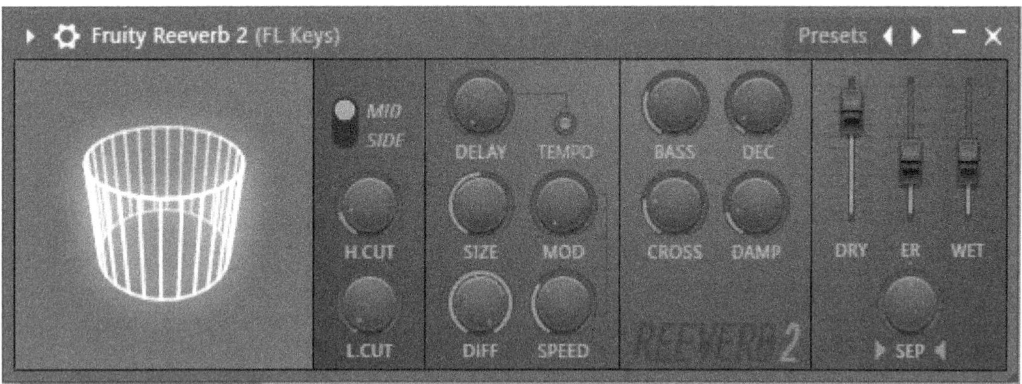

Figure 7.3 – Fruity Reeverb 2

While playing your sound, you'll notice it has echoes and the appearance of being further away.

3. Click on the cylinder image to the left of the reverb plugin and drag the image around. You'll notice the cylinder changes shape and the reverb controls adjust accordingly.

Let's take a look at the reverb controls (from left to right):

- **MID/SIDE**: Determines how your reverb affects your sound in mono or stereo. By default, it is set to **MID**, meaning the reverb is mono. If you have a sound that is panned to the right or left, you should use the **SIDE** option. This will affect your left/right stereo field, but leave your center untouched so it doesn't wash your sound out.
- **H.CUT**: Stands for **high cut** and allows you to remove high frequencies before applying reverb.
- **L.CUT**: Stands for **low cut** and allows you to remove low frequencies before applying reverb. Effective when used on drums to remove low rumble muddiness.
- **DELAY**: The more delay you add, the longer it takes to hear an echo, and the further away the sound will appear. There is a **TEMPO** button to sync the echo to fit it to the song's BPM.
- **SIZE**: Determines the space of the reverb. A higher setting means a larger reverb sound.
- **MOD**: Stands for **modulation** and removes metallic reverb ringing sounds that can occur.

- **DIFF**: Stands for **diffusion** and determines the density of sound reflections. Low values make the reflections appear spread out; high values make the reflections appear more concentrated, as though coming from a more central place.
- **SPEED**: Determines the speed of the modulation control.
- **BASS**: Determines the amount of bass frequencies in the reverb.
- **DEC**: Stands for **decay** and determines how long it is before a sound dissipates. Smaller values give the impression of a smaller room, while larger values sound like larger rooms.
- **CROSS**: Determines the threshold below which bass frequencies get boosted.
- **DAMP**: Stands for **high damping** and is the rate at which high frequencies decay. Turning this to maximum bypasses (turns off) the high-damping control.
- **DRY**: Sets the input signal level. Turning it all the way down lets you hear just the reverb on its own without the original source.
- **ER**: Stands for **early reflections** and sets the level of the first reflections.
- **WET**: Sets the overall level of the reverb.
- **SEP**: Stands for **stereo separator** and pans the reverb. The dry signal is unaffected.

So far, we've discussed **digital reverb**. There is another type of reverb called convolution reverb.

Applying convolution reverb with Fruity Convolver

Convolution reverb is more realistic than digital reverb. To create convolution reverb, software developers travel to physical locations and collect audio recordings of sounds reflecting around the space. By measuring the impulse timings, developers can recreate a simulated environment that mimics the real one. Then, when a sound is sent into the simulated environment, it reflects off the surroundings just like it would in a real space. This creates very realistic reverbs but can potentially be more CPU-intensive.

FL Studio has a convolution reverb effect plugin called **Fruity Convolver**. This will apply the effect of convolution reverb to your sound. Let's apply a convolution reverb with Fruity Convolver:

1. Load up a sample or an instrument with notes and route it to a new mixer track.
2. Add the **Fruity Convolver** effect to the Mixer channel and play your sound.

Figure 7.4 – Fruity Convolver

3. In the top-right corner of the **Fruity Convolver** plugin window, left-click on the **Presets**. You will see the list shown in the following screenshot:

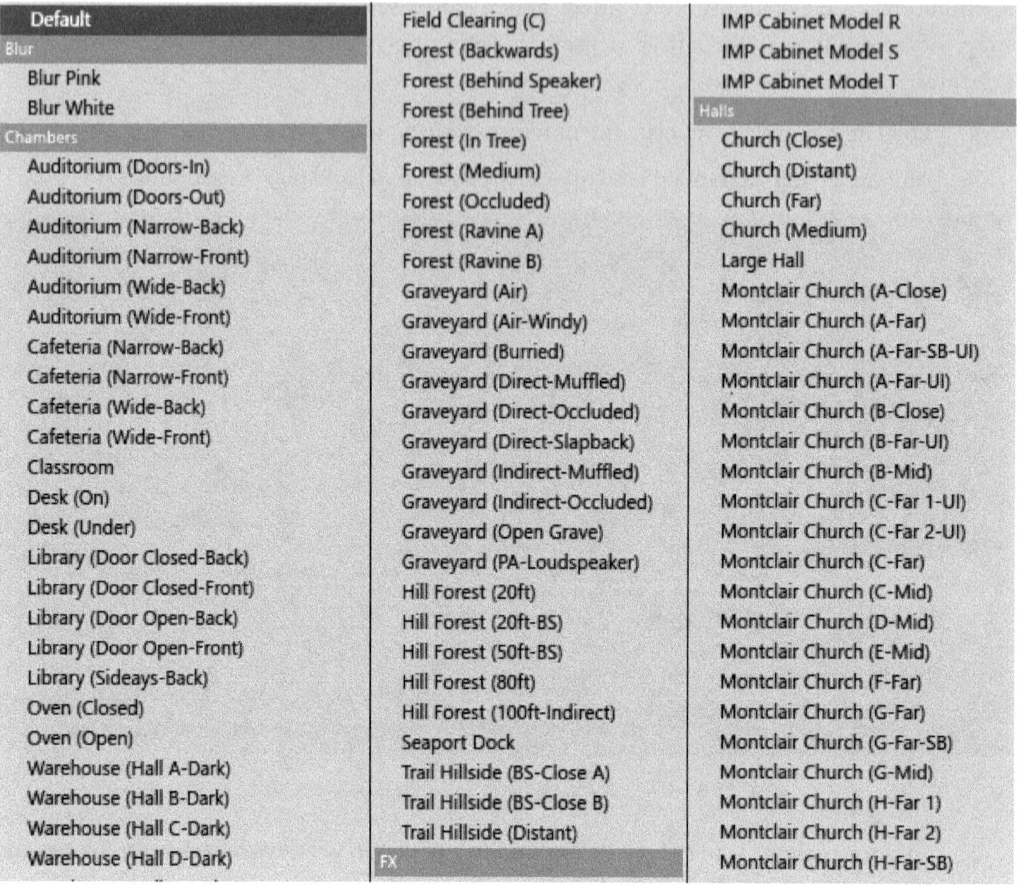

Figure 7.5 – Fruity Convolver room presets

Here you can see a list of reverb room presets with various room types to choose from.

4. Select one of the presets. A reverb will be applied to your sound that simulates how your sound would echo if it were played in the chosen room.

   For most users, these presets will supply more than enough reverb options. For those who want more, though, Fruity Convolver offers a vast array of features that extend beyond the scope of this chapter. For example, the **impulse** section of Fruity Convolver allows you to record a sound and simulate your own custom reverb room.

Note

For a detailed breakdown of all Fruity Convolver features, see the Image Line documentation videos at `http://support.image-line.com/redirect/FruityConvolver_Videos`.

Next, let's explore the FL Studio reverb plugin **LuxeVerb**.

Using LuxeVerb

LuxeVerb is a cutting-edge reverb plugin that comes with FL Studio *All Plugins Edition*. With LuxeVerb, you can adjust the pitch and dynamics of the reverb. Let's take a look at the controls of LuxeVerb.

Figure 7.6 – LuxeVerb

As always, in the top right, you'll find a list of **Presets** to explore. I encourage you to check out the presets, as they will give you a shortcut to exploring how the plugin can be used.

By default, LuxeVerb is split into a top blue **REVERB** section and a bottom black **ENVELOPE** section. You can choose to hide the **ENVELOPE** section by clicking the bottom edge and dragging upwards.

Let's take a look at each section, starting with the **INPUT** and **REVERB** sections.

Figure 7.7 – LuxeVerb INPUT and REVERB panels

Here's a description of the controls:

- The **INPUT** panel:
  - **WET GAIN**: Controls how much input sound to feed into LuxeVerb.
  - **HIGH CUT**: Filter to remove high frequencies.
  - **LOW CUT**: Filter to remove low frequencies. Low frequencies can make your sound muddy when applying reverb. Consider using it when you automate to pitch down, as this can create an over-the-top rumbling sound.
- The **REVERB** panel:
  - **DECAY**: Controls how long you want the reverb to last in seconds. Longer decay times create a bigger, more atmospheric space, while shorter times sound tighter and more controlled.
  - **BRIGHTNESS**: Controls how pronounced you want the high frequencies to be present in the reverb tail. 100% will simulate a space with hard surfaces. By decreasing the value, you simulate an environment with soft surfaces, which will reduce high frequencies. This helps you shape the tone of the reverb to match anything from a bright hall to a warm, muffled room.
  - **SIZE**: Increases the space between echoes of the reverb. 0–10 values simulate a small plate-sounding space, 10–50 simulate an acoustic space, and >50 simulate an over-the-top large space. Adjusting this changes how *big* or *close* the virtual room feels.

- **DIFFUSION**: Simulates obstacles in the room in the path of the echoes. Creates more irregularity in the echo. Higher diffusion makes the reverb smoother and denser, while lower diffusion makes reflections more distinct and echo-like.
- **CHARACTER**: Values of 0.5 create a smooth, diffuse reverb tail. Values <0.5 create more prominent echoes. Values >0.5 allow reverb to collect and create a fuzzy echo effect. You'll hear a stronger effect if you increase the **SIZE** value. This control shapes the personality of the reverb from clean and polished to gritty and textured.
- **P. DELAY**: This is the predelay. You can enable tempo sync, which usually sounds better. This sets the gap between the dry sound and the start of the reverb, helping maintain clarity and space in the mix.
- **MOD AMP**: Modulates delay line lengths. Creates a **chorus effect** in the reverb. You'll hear the effect more when the **CHARACTER** control is all the way up or down. This adds subtle movement or shimmer to the reverb tail, making it feel more alive.
- **MOD FREQ**: It is the frequency of the modulation delay line lengths. Controls how fast the modulation moves, changing the speed of the chorus-like motion within the reverb.
- **FREEZE MODE**: Allows infinite reverb duration. 3 modes: This feature turns reverb into a sustaining pad or ambient texture.
  - **NORMAL**: As standard, Freeze mode is disabled. The reverb behaves as usual, fading naturally over time.
  - **FREEZE**: Uses current input and sustains reverb at the moment when **FREEZE** control is enabled. Sound sustains until **FREEZE** control is disabled. Ideal for capturing and holding a moment of sound for atmospheric effects.
  - **SUSTAIN**: Same as **FREEZE**, but allows input to continue so sound will build. This creates a lush, evolving wash of sound that keeps growing as new audio is added.

- **HQ**: On gives higher resolution on higher frequencies. Off makes a grittier sound where high frequencies die out faster. More noticeable when **FREEZE** or **SUSTAIN** are in use. Turning it on makes the reverb more detailed and pristine, while turning it off gives it a vintage or lo-fi character.

Next, let's look at the **FEEDBACK** and **OUTPUT** panels.

Figure 7.8 – LuxeVerb FEEDBACK and OUTPUT panels

The **FEEDBACK** panel is where you can do **pitch shifting effects**:

- On the far right, you'll see an enable and disable control for the panel.
    - **HIGH CUT**: Filter to remove high frequencies from being fed back into the plugin.
    - **LOW CUT**: Filter to remove low frequencies. Otherwise, the output can get muddy when pitching down.
    - **PITCH SHIFT**: Feeds reverb output back as input audio with pitch shifting. Values of 12+ create ethereal rising sounds. Value of 0 is normal. Values of -12 create dark, evil sounds. You can automate this control to hear the reverb pitch of your sound increase or decrease.
    - **GAIN**: Amount of gain on feedback. Value of 0 means no feedback.
    - **DELAY**: Controls the amount of delay to apply. Tempo sync can be enabled, which usually sounds better.
    - **REVERB MIX**: Controls how much effect to feed back into the loop.
- The **OUTPUT** panel:
    - **DRY**: Amount of original input sound to output.
    - **WET**: Amount of effect to apply.
    - **PEAK FREQ**: Peaking filter center frequency.
    - **PEAK GAIN**: Allows you to add gain.

- **PEAK Q**: Sets the resonance peak. Values of 1 result in an octave-wide peaking filter. Values of 2 create a half octave wide filter. The greater the value, the smaller the filter peak.
- **WIDTH**: Amount of stereo width. The value of 1.25 is the default. Larger values create more width.

In the lower section of **LuxeVerb**, you'll find the **ENVELOPE** section.

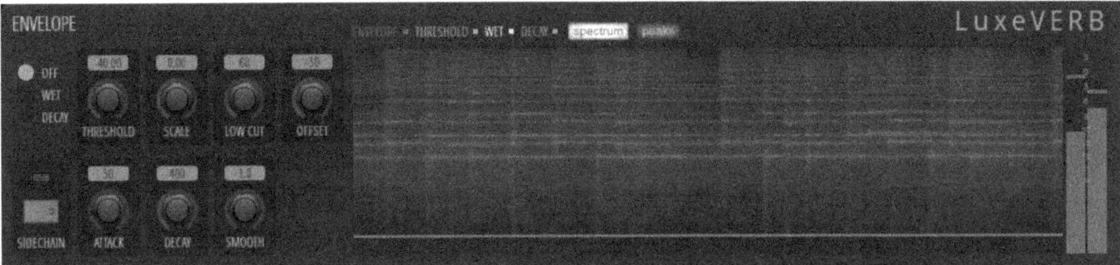

Figure 7.9 – LuxeVerb ENVELOPE

The **ENVELOPE** section is there to allow you to shape the attack and decay of the reverb. Here you'll find controls to manipulate the reverb output. This allows you to create gated or sidechained sounds.

Figure 7.10 – LuxeVerb ENVELOPE controls

Let's take a closer look at the controls:

- **MODE**: Type of modulation. This determines how the reverb's sound is dynamically changed over time, influencing its movement and texture.
  - **OFF**: No modulation. The reverb remains static and consistent without any pitch or volume movement.

    - **WET**: Output is modulated. The modulated effect is applied only to the reverb tail, creating subtle motion and shimmer in the reflections.
    - **DECAY**: Decay time is modulated. This makes the reverb tail dynamically lengthen or shorten, adding variation and liveliness to the space.
- **SIDECHAIN**: Lets you choose which insert track to use as a sidechaining source. In order to use this, you must previously route a mixer track to the same mixer track as LuxeVerb. See *Chapter 4* if you need a refresher on how to route mixer tracks. This allows the reverb to react to another sound (like ducking when a kick hits), helping keep the mix clean.
- **THRESHOLD**: The threshold value where any audio above gets modulated, just like how a compressor works. It sets the level at which the modulation starts responding to the input signal's volume.
- **SCALE**: Controls the amount of envelope to apply. Positive values create a gated reverb, usually used to make space for percussion sounds. This helps shape how much the modulation affects the reverb, controlling its punch and dynamics.
- **LOW CUT**: Filter to remove low frequencies. This cleans up muddiness in the reverb by reducing low-end buildup.
- **OFFSET**: Value of 0 gives mono-polar modulation. If value>0, then bipolar modulation. This changes how the modulation moves around its center point, affecting whether it only goes one direction or oscillates evenly up and down.
- **ATTACK**: Controls when the audio gets affected. Usually, we leave this alone. It determines how quickly the modulation or envelope begins after the input passes the threshold.
- **DECAY**: Controls decay, how long before reverb level drifts back down to input level. Longer values make the modulation linger, while shorter ones make it more snappy.
- **SMOOTH**: Controls smoothness, with high values increasing smoothness and low values allowing more fluctuations. This affects how fluid or choppy the modulation sounds, helping you fine-tune between natural and rhythmic movement.

At the bottom right, you'll find the display panel.

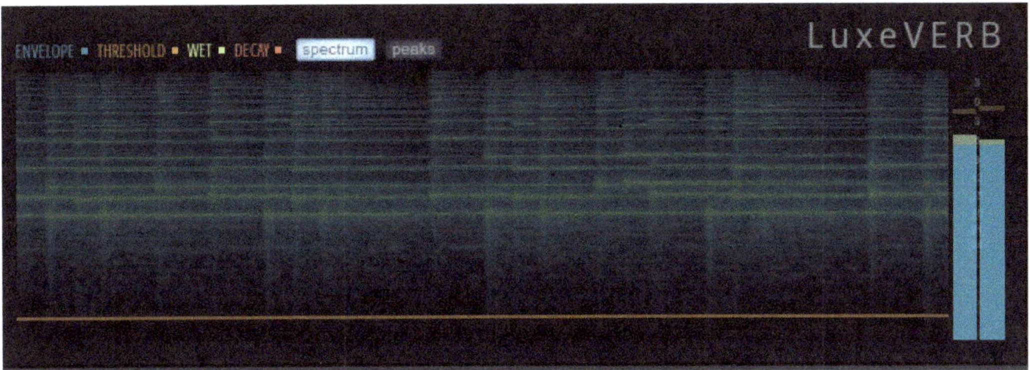

Figure 7.11 – LuxeVerb display panel

Here's a description of the **ENVELOPE** display. This will show you how your sound changes depending on the control parameters you set:

- **ENVELOPE** (Blue): The input signal or the sidechain signal (if selected). This controls how the reverb reacts dynamically, letting louder or sidechained sounds influence the effect more strongly.
- **THRESHOLD** (Orange): Level above which modulation begins. Only signals that exceed this level will trigger modulation, allowing precise control over when the effect engages.
- **WET** (Green): Shows modulation of output. The **MODE** switch determines if the **WET** or **DECAY** is modulated. Changing the **SIZE** control affects how the modulation alters the reverb's presence in the mix.
- **DECAY** (Red): Shows modulation of decay. The **MODE** switch determines if the **WET** or **DECAY** is modulated. Adjusting this lets you control how the reverb tail length changes dynamically, adding movement or evolving textures.

We've looked at the reverb plugins we can use to increase stereo width. Next, let's look at using **delay** to increase stereo width.

Using delay effects

A **delay** is the repeat of a sound played back after a few milliseconds. That's it, pretty simple, right? With a delay plugin, you can control how long to wait before hearing the echo. It can be synced to the tempo of your project.

The following terminologies are used to describe certain types of delays:

- **Straight delay**: Delaying the original material.

- **Slapback delay**: Delay times of between 70 ms and 120 ms. Generally, this complements dry sounds.
- **Doubling delay**: Delay times of between 20 ms and 50 ms. Generally, this creates an artificial doubling of the track.
- **Ping-pong delay**: Creates a call-and-response reaction between the repeats of the delay. For example, the initial call is 300 ms, and the follow-up call is 600 ms.
- **Stereo-widening delay**: Short delays around 10 ms. Sounds like the original sound to the listener, but spreads out more in the stereo field.

Applying delay effects with Fruity Delay 3

Fruity Delay 3 is a delay plugin effect that comes with FL Studio. It is a beast of a plugin and offers above and beyond the **delay effects** that you will need for your projects.

Let's apply a delay effect to our audio using Fruity Delay 3:

1. Load up a sample or an instrument with notes and route it to a new mixer track.
2. **Fruity Delay 3** is an analog delay plugin. It has the ability to sync with the BPM of your song. It offers filtering and distortion effects and allows self-feedback to create special effects. Add the Fruity Delay 3 effect onto your Mixer channel. When you play your instrument, you will be able to hear a delay effect.

Figure 7.12 – Fruity Delay 3

Check out **Presets** in the top-right corner of the plugin for examples of delay effects.

Each section of the delay plugin is labeled; let's take a look at each section. As you read the control descriptions, make sure you play with the plugin to hear how the sound changes:

- **INPUT**: Determines the *dryness* or *wetness* (the level of audio input into the delay plugin). You can create an automation to turn on and off audio being input so that only certain parts of the audio receive the delay.

- **DELAY TIME**: Determines the time between echoes.

  The **TIME** knob allows you to adjust the delay from 1 ms to 1,000 ms. **TEMPO SYNC** limits the values of the **TIME** knob to fixed intervals. Having **TEMPO SYNC** on and the **TIME** knob set to 4:0 is generally pleasing for most cases, so this is likely the setting you'll want most of the time. As the **TIME** knob changes values, the pitch will adjust. You can maintain the pitch with the **KEEP PITCH** button. **SMOOTHING** determines how fast the pitch changes. Long values create a **tape-style delay**. **OFFSET** controls the panning of the delay. It depends on the **DELAY MODEL** setting.

- **DELAY MODEL**: Lets you choose how panning effects are used with the delay.

  Mono creates delays in mono, where the audio is the same out of all speakers. The offset creates a left-right bouncing panning effect. **Stereo** creates stereo delays. **Offset** controls pre-delays for left-right bouncing effects. **Ping pong** is a type of stereo delay. The left and right channel audio outputs flip back and forth in isolation, creating a bouncing effect. **Off** is for no delay; you can still use filters, saturation, limiting, sample rate, bit reduction, and tone effects later on in the plugin. The **STEREO** spread knob controls how much of the mono or stereo effect is applied to the sound.

- **FEEDBACK**: Works by sending a signal output from the plugin back into the plugin to be processed again. **LEVEL** controls how much delay is sent into the feedback. **CUTOFF** allows you to limit the frequencies sent into the feedback. How you limit is determined by the filter types. The following options for filter types are available:

  - **LP**: Stands for low-pass filtering, and it allows only frequencies below the cutoff value
  - **HP**: Stands for high-pass filtering and allows only frequencies above the cutoff value
  - **BP**: Stands for band-pass filtering, and it allows only frequencies around the cutoff value
  - **Off**: No filtering

  RES stands for resonance, and it creates a boost in the frequency at the point of the cutoff value, drawing attention to it. This will increase feedback.

  SMP RATE stands for sample rate and removes rumbles created by feedback. **BITS** stands for bit depth, and it controls the number of bits used in the waveform file. At maximum values, your audio retains its original quality. Lower values add a crunchy, grainy character to the sound. If you want to make your sound feel like it is coming from an old, degraded device, this can be one way to create that effect. The effect becomes more noticeable at lower values.

- **MODULATION**: This offers controls affecting delay timing and feedback.

RATE sets the modulation time, from 0 to 20 Hz. **TIME** determines how much modulation to apply to the decay time. Increasing this value results in flanging and chorus effects. **CUTOFF** modulates the feedback cutoff value.

- **DIFFUSION**: Controls the blending of the delay sound.
  LEVEL smears the echoes, and **SPREAD** sets the time of the smearing.
- **FEEDBACK DISTORTION**: Distorts the delay each time that it's passed back into the plugin. You can choose between the following two types of distortions:
  Limit sets the maximum level value of the waveform. If this is selected, you won't hear much distortion.

  Sat, or saturation, determines the maximum level of the distortion. This is affected by the **KNEE** and **SYMMETRY** controls. **KNEE** controls how extreme the transition is between non-distorted and distorted audio. **SYMMETRY** controls the waveform properties, making the distortion equal in the positive and negative waveform cycles. **LEVEL** determines the value at which limiting or saturation starts. The lower the value, the quieter the sound.
- **OUTPUT**: Controls the level of sound output from the plugin.
  WET controls the output signal level. **TONE** sets a low- or high-pass filter for the wet signal. Finally, **DRY** determines how much of the original sound to output. If you set this to 0, you can hear the delay on its own without the original sound.

Delay effect best practices

Unless you're trying to go for a crazy effect, you generally want to apply compression to your sounds before you apply delay.

- Apply delay effects before reverb effects. You want to have the reverb of a delay, as this will sound realistic, but not the delay of a reverb. When you use delay with reverb, try adding EQ to the delay signal. Cutting out the low frequencies with a high-pass filter helps prevent the mix from sounding too thick or muddy.
- Short delays under 100 ms make the original sound appear larger and help to fill empty space.
- Single sounds, such as orchestral hits, explosions, and impacts, benefit from delay effects to make them feel huge.
- Delays can be used to add grooves to your melodies when used at intervals of 8th or 16th notes.
- Use the delay of a sound on its own by using the wet signal and removing the dry signal. Effects can be applied to delay sounds, including phasers, flangers, pitch correction, and

automation to create movement. Then you can tame harsh frequencies down with EQ and compression to make it sound appealing.

- EQing your delay can clean up the mix. Rolling off the low end keeps echoes from muddying the bass, while trimming a bit of high end makes the repeats sit behind the main sound instead of jumping out. Think of it like putting the delay in its own pocket of the frequency spectrum so it complements, rather than crowds, the original track.
- Stereo placement can also take your delay game to the next level. Panning your delay slightly opposite the dry signal creates a natural sense of width and movement. Dual delays, where each side has slightly different timing or feedback, can make the sound feel alive and three-dimensional.
- Automation is your friend when it comes to delay. Automating the feedback, mix, or timing can turn a static effect into a dynamic storytelling tool. For example, you might fade in a long, washy delay during a vocal outro, or automate feedback to build tension at the end of a phrase. These small moments of evolution give your mix personality and emotional momentum.
- As with any effect, the secret to great delay use is context. What sounds epic in solo might clutter the mix when everything else comes in. Always dial in your settings while listening to the full track. The best delay treatments often go unnoticed; they simply make the music feel more spacious, more alive, and more finished.

We've discussed using echoes and delay to increase stereo width. Next, let's look at how playing with the waveform itself can increase stereo width.

Using chorus effects

In *Chapter 5*, we discussed **phase cancellation** and **interference**. This is where multiple waveforms interact with each other and cause the sound to become louder or quieter. In-phase audio makes the sound louder, while being out of phase causes the sound to become quieter. These are the two extreme phase possibilities, but there is a range between them. Plugins that play with sound phase include chorus plugins, flangers, and phasers. We will discuss each of these over the next few pages.

A **chorus effect** makes it sound like multiple voices or instruments are playing the same part at once. It does this by taking the original sound, making delayed copies of it, and slightly changing their pitch. When these slightly detuned copies are mixed back with the original sound, they create the rich, shimmering "chorus" effect. It's similar to a choir, where no two singers are perfectly in sync or exactly on the same pitch, giving the sound a fuller, more natural feel.

Chorus plugins play with the signal phase. A chorus plugin creates duplicates of the audio signal, using the same phase position, amplitude, and frequency. The copied signal is delayed to create a difference in phase. With this delayed sound, we can adjust a number of properties such as the timing or pitch.

Next, we'll look at several chorus plugin effects that come with FL Studio. We'll start with the simplest legacy plugin called **Fruity Chorus**. Then take a look at the new chorus plugins, **Hyper Chorus** and **Vintage Chorus**.

Using Fruity Chorus

Let's apply a chorus effect to an instrument:

1. Load up a sample or an instrument with notes and route it to a new mixer track.
2. Add the Fruity Chorus effect. When you play your instrument, you will be able to hear a chorus effect.

Figure 7.13 – Fruity Chorus effect

3. To hear examples of chorus effects, left-click on **Presets** in the top right of the plugin.

Here's a description of the **Fruity Chorus** plugin controls:

- **DELAY**: Determines the time to wait before playing the copy of the audio. This sets the spacing between the original sound and its delayed version, which forms the foundation of the chorus effect.
- **DEPTH**: Sets the range for the delay. The chorus effect sweeps back and forth between the **DELAY** and **DELAY** + **DEPTH** values. Higher depth values create a more pronounced, wider-sounding chorus.
- **STEREO**: Controls stereo image width. Increasing this spreads the effect across left and right channels, making the sound feel larger and more immersive.
- **LFO FREQ** (short for frequency): determines the modulation speed. Faster LFO rates create rapid movement, while slower rates produce a gentle, sweeping effect.
- **LFO WAVE**: Lets you choose the waveform. Different wave shapes change how the modulation moves, from smooth sine sweeps to more abrupt, dramatic variations.

- **CROSS TYPE**: Lets you choose whether to work on the low or high area of the sound frequency. This allows selective modulation, so you can target specific frequency ranges for the chorus effect.
- **CROSS CUTOFF**: Sets the cutoff frequency value for use in **CROSS TYPE**. This determines the boundary between low and high frequencies that the modulation will affect.
- **WET ONLY**: Lets you choose whether to allow the original audio to be outputted or not.

Using Hyper Chorus

My favorite chorus effect in FL Studio is the **Hyper Chorus effect**. It's great for creating extremely wide and lush sounds, such as for **Super Saw sounds**, and for adding movement and depth to pads, vocals, or guitars. Use it whenever you want an aggressive chorus sound.

Let's apply a hyper chorus effect to an instrument:

1. Load up a sample or an instrument with notes and route it to a new mixer track.
2. Add the Hyper Chorus effect. When you play your instrument, you will be able to hear a chorus effect.

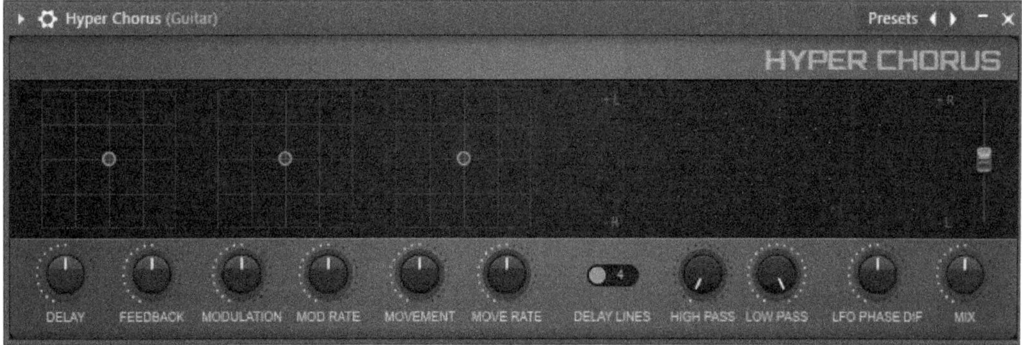

Figure 7.14 – Hyper Chorus

3. To hear examples of chorus effects, left-click on **Presets** in the top right of the plugin.

Here's a description of the Hyper Chorus plugin controls:

- **X/Y Pad 1**: This controls the delay (left/right), feedback (up/down):
  - **DELAY**: Controls how long each chorus delay is. This sets the basic spacing between the original signal and its copies, shaping the overall thickness of the effect.
  - **FEEDBACK**: Controls how much of the effect's output loops back into itself. Higher values create a swirling, flanging, or more intense chorus texture.

- **X/Y Pad 2**: This controls the modulation (left/right) and mod rate (up/down):
    - **MODULATION**: Controls the amount of pitch wobble. Turning it up makes the detuning effect stronger and more dramatic, giving a richer chorus character.
    - **MOD RATE**: Controls the speed of the pitch wobble. Faster rates create a more energetic shimmer, while slower rates produce gentle movement.
- **X/Y Pad 3**: This controls the movement (left/right) and move rate (up/down):
    - **MOVEMENT**: Determines how far the delay pans across the stereo field. Larger movement values make the chorus feel wider and more immersive.
    - **MOVE RATE**: Controls how fast the panning motion occurs. Faster rates create lively, animated stereo effects; slower rates feel smoother and more spacious.
- **DELAY LINES**: Choose 4 or 8 delay voices. Using 8 voices produces a fuller, richer, and more extreme chorus sound.
- **HIGH PASS**: Cuts low frequencies from the *effected* (wet) signal. This prevents the chorus from muddying the low end of the mix.
- **LOW PASS**: Cuts high frequencies from the *effected* (wet) signal. This softens harsh highs and makes the chorus sit more smoothly in the mix.
- **LFO PHASE DIF**: Spreads out the starting points of the modulation for each delay line. Higher values create a wider, more complex stereo effect.
- **MIX**: Controls how much of the effect you want to hear. Adjusting this balances the processed signal with the dry sound for subtle or extreme chorus.
- **Display scaling**: Zooms in/out on the stereo scope display, which shows the stereo width, panning, and phase relationship.

Using Vintage Chorus

FL Studio *Signature Edition* has a chorus effect plugin called **Vintage Chorus**. Vintage Chorus is a chorus effect plugin that emulates the *Roland Juno 6's* **bucket brigade delay** (**BBD**) chorus effect.

1. Load up a sample or an instrument with notes and route it to a new mixer track.
2. Add the Vintage Chorus effect. When you play your instrument, you will be able to hear a chorus effect.

Figure 7.15 – Vintage Chorus

As usual, there is a list of **Presets** in the top right corner of the plugin to get you started. Let's take a look at the components of Vintage Chorus.

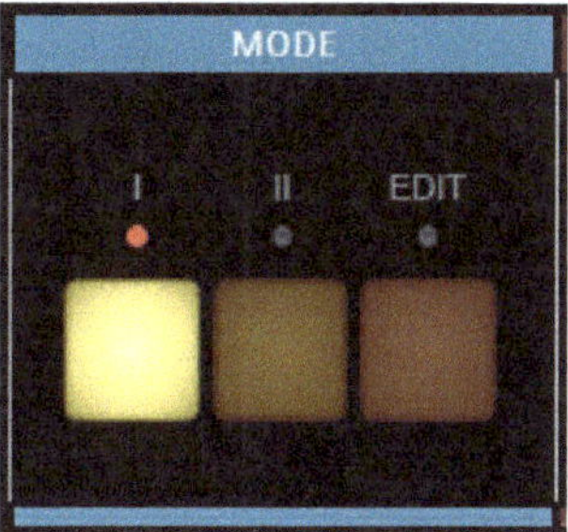

Figure 7.16 – MODE

In Vintage Chorus, there are 3 modes to choose from. These modes are various chorus effects that can be applied. By default, Mode **I** is selected.

MODE **I** creates the **Juno 6 Chorus I** effect. MODE **II** creates the **Juno 6 Chorus II** effect. You can apply both MODE **I** and **II** effects at the same time by left-clicking MODE **I** and holding *Shift* while left-clicking on MODE **II**.

If MODE **I** or **II** is selected, the **DELAYS** and **MODULATION** panels will be disabled. If you select the **EDIT** mode, then you'll be able to edit the **DELAYS** and **MODULATION** panels.

Let's take a look at the **DELAYS** panel.

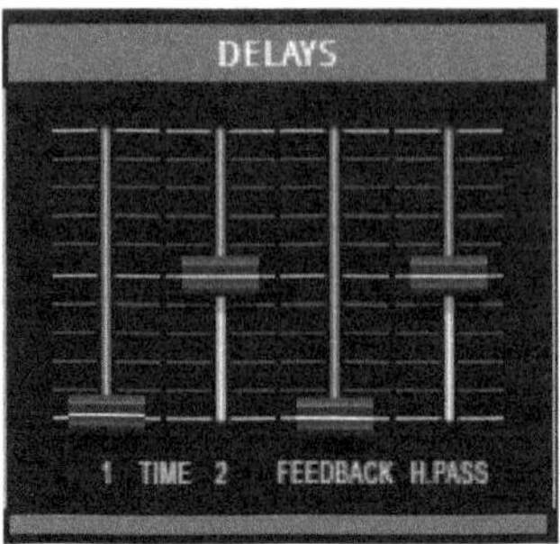

Figure 7.17 – DELAYS panel

Here's a description of the **DELAYS** controls:

- **TIME 1**: Sets delay time 1. This determines the starting point of the chorus modulation, affecting how thick or spacious the effect sounds.
- **TIME 2**: Sets the delay time 2. The chorus modulates between **TIME 1** and **TIME 2**, creating movement and richness in the sound.
- **FEEDBACK**: Creates feedback from the output audio back into the input audio. Higher values produce a more intense, flanger-like chorus with swirling or resonant tones.
- **H PASS**: Sets a high-pass filter cutoff. This prevents low-frequency sounds from being affected by the chorus, keeping the bass clear and focused.

The next panel is the **MODULATION** panel.

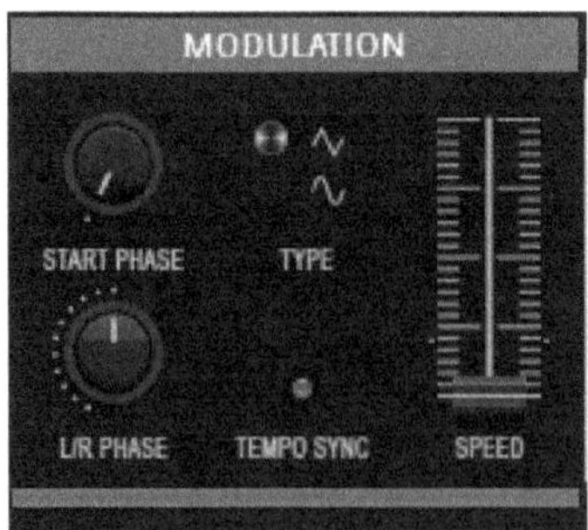

Figure 7.18 – MODULATION panel

Here's a description of the controls:

- **START PHASE**: Sets the time for when to restart the LFO phase. Adjusting this changes the timing of the modulation and how the chorus evolves over time.
- **L/R PHASE**: Phase difference between left and right channels. Larger values increase the stereo width, making the chorus feel wider and more immersive.

- **TYPE**: Allows you to choose between a saw and a sine wave for the LFO. Different waveforms change how the pitch modulation moves, from smooth (sine) to more dramatic or edgy (saw).
- **TEMPO SYNC**: Syncs the LFO waveform to the project tempo. This ensures the modulation stays in rhythm with your track for a cohesive sound.
- **SPEED**: Changes the speed of the chorus LFO. Faster speeds create energetic movement, while slower speeds give a gentle, sweeping effect.

The last panel is the **LEVELS** panel.

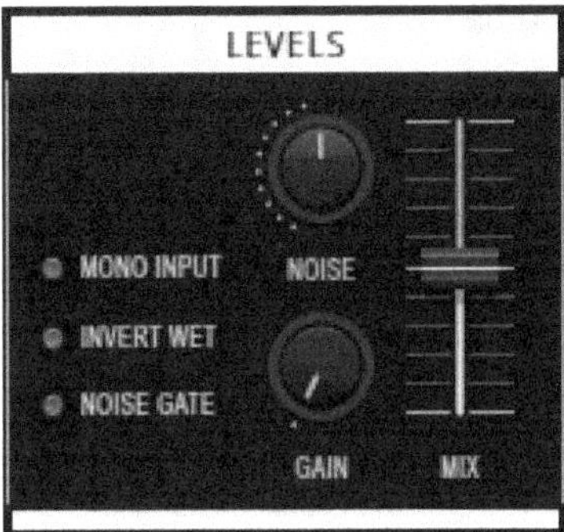

Figure 7.19 – LEVELS panel

Here's a description of the controls:

- **MONO INPUT**: Creates a mono sound. This collapses the input to a single channel, which can help center the effect or simplify the stereo field.
- **INVERT WET**: Inverts the audio polarity of the *effected* signal. This can produce phase cancellations or interesting interactions with other audio.
- **NOISE GATE**: Adds a noise gate to remove hissing sounds when no audio is playing.
- **NOISE**: Controls the amount of added hissing noise.
- **GAIN**: Adjusts the loudness of the output signal.
- **MIX**: Controls how much of the chorus effect is applied.

Chorus effect best practices

Chorus effects can be great on accompanying instruments to surround your lead instrument or vocal. As a general guideline, consider applying chorus effects on guitars, electric pianos, snare drums, bass guitars, and backing vocals. Adding chorus effects increases the perceived stereo width of a sound, making it appear larger.

When chorus effects are applied to vocals, they sound similar to vocal doubling. Natural vocal doubling is when a singer's vocals are repeated by backup singers. With natural vocal doubling, there is a variation in timing and pitch with the backup vocals. A chorus effect resembles this sound by also creating variation in timing and pitch. The overall effect is a larger-sounding vocal.

When mixing, you want to place chorus effects before your delay and reverb effects in the signal chain.

Next, let's look at another plugin that plays with phase: flangers.

Using flanger effects

Flanger effects are similar to chorus effects and create a copy of the original sound, adjusting the delay times. The copied sound is usually delayed between 5 and 25 ms. A low-frequency modulator is applied to the delay time to oscillate between shorter and longer delay times. Since the waveforms are the same, wave interference occurs as discussed in *Chapter 5*. At certain interfering frequencies, resonances are created. You can think of a **resonance** as an intense tone made more pronounced than other frequencies. The low-frequency oscillator moves around the waveform to find different resonances. We call this sweeping resonance sound a **flanger**. Flangers take advantage of the feedback to resend the output sound back into itself and create additional resonances.

As a general guideline, consider applying flanger effects to hi-hats, guitars, and pads. When mixing, you want to place flanger effects before delay and reverb effects in the signal chain.

Let's apply a flanger effect to an instrument:

1. Load up a sample or an instrument with notes and route it to a new mixer track.
2. Add the **Fruity Flanger** effect. When you play your instrument, you will be able to hear a flanger effect.

Figure 7.20 – Fruity Flanger

3. To hear examples of flanger effects, left-click on **Presets** in the top right of the plugin.

The following is a description of the Fruity Flanger plugin controls:

- **DELAY**: Controls the minimum time to wait before playing the copied delayed sound. This sets the base spacing between the original signal and its delayed version, forming the foundation of the flanger effect.
- **DEPTH**: Controls the modulation of the wait before playing the delayed sound. Higher depth values create a more pronounced sweeping effect.
- **RATE**: Adjusts the speed of the modulation. Faster rates create rapid, intense flanging, while slower rates produce gentle, evolving movement.
- **PHASE**: Widens the stereo image. Increasing this spreads the delayed signals across left and right channels, making the effect feel larger and more immersive.
- **DAMP**: Allows you to filter the selected frequencies. This lets you soften harsh tones or focus the flanger effect on a specific frequency range.
- **SHAPE**: Adjusts the shape of the low-frequency modulator between a sine wave and a triangle LFO. Sine waves are smooth, while triangle waves produce more abrupt pitch changes for a sharper effect.
- **FEED** (Feedback): Sets the level of feedback on the sound fed back into Fruity Flanger. More feedback intensifies the swirling, resonant character of the effect.
- **INV FEEDBACK/INV WET**: Allows you to invert the output signal phase. This can create phase cancellations or unique interactions with other sounds in the mix.
- **DRY/WET/CROSS**: Control the level of the output signal. These let you balance the original and *effected* signals for subtle modulation or a fully processed flanger effect.

Next, let's discuss phaser effects.

Using phaser effects

Phasers sound similar to chorus and flanger effects and are used in almost the same way. In phasers, a copy of the original sound is moved in and out of phase with the original. The focus of a phaser is to sweep frequencies across the spectrum.

When mixing, you want to place **phaser effects** before your delay and reverb effects in the signal chain.

Let's apply a phaser effect to an instrument:

1. Load up a sample or an instrument with notes and route it to a new mixer track.
2. Add the **Fruity Phaser** effect. When you play your instrument, you will be able to hear a phaser effect.

Figure 7.21 – Fruity Phaser

3. To hear examples of phaser effects, left-click on the **Presets** in the top right of the plugin.

The following is a description of the Fruity Phaser plugin controls:

- **SWEEP FREQ.** (Frequency): Sets the frequency of the low-frequency modulator. This determines how fast the phaser sweeps through its notches, affecting the movement and rhythm of the effect.
- **MIN DEPTH** and **MAX DEPTH**: Choose the range for the phaser to sweep in. Larger depth values create more pronounced pitch modulation and a stronger sweeping effect.
- **FREQ. RANGE**: Sets the range for the sweeping frequency.
- **STEREO**: Controls the stereo image width. Higher values spread the phaser across left and right channels, making it feel wider and more immersive.

- **NR. STAGES** (number of stages): Sets the number of phases the signal goes through. Increasing the stages intensifies the effect, creating a more dramatic sound.
- **FEEDBACK**: Sets how much output is fed back into the phaser. More feedback increases resonance at the notches, producing a sharper, more pronounced sweep.
- **DRY-WET** Controls the level of phaser output.
- **OUT GAIN** Allows you to increase the output signal.

Using Vintage Phaser

FL Studio *Signature Edition* comes with a phaser plugin called **Vintage Phaser**. It's modeled after the **Electro-Harmonix Small Stone Phase Shifter** guitar pedal. As with other phaser effects, it works by mixing a sound with a slightly delayed version of itself, creating a characteristic *whooshing* or *jet plane* sound as certain frequencies fade in and out. The delay time is modulated, which produces the sweeping effect.

Let's explore **Vintage Phaser** and add a phaser effect to an instrument:

1. Load up a sample or an instrument with notes and route it to a new mixer track.
2. Add the Vintage Phaser effect. When you play your instrument, you will be able to hear a phaser effect.

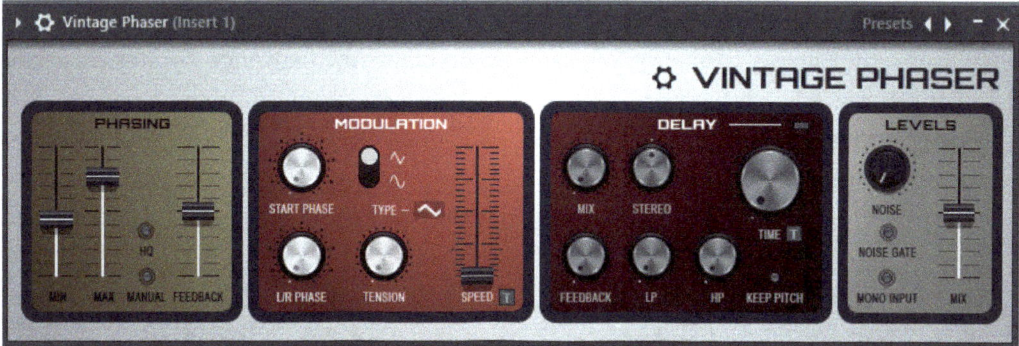

Figure 7.22 – Vintage Phaser

Let's learn about the controls. The layout is very similar to the layout of the FL Studio plugin **Vintage Chorus**. The **PHASING** panel lets you change the modulation range.

Figure 7.23 – Vintage Phaser PHASING panel

It has the following controls:

- **MIN**: lets you set the minimum frequency for the oscillator.
- **MAX**: Lets you set the maximum frequency for the oscillator.
- **HQ**: Allows **oversampling**. Oversampling is when the plugin converts the audio to a higher sample rate. This helps remove negative artifacts from the audio such as aliasing. This produces a cleaner, more detailed phaser sound.
- **MANUAL**: Swaps out the **MIN** and **MAX** controls with a knob that lets you manually adjust the phaser frequency. You can then automate the frequency if you want precise control.

The **MODULATION** panel lets you change the modulation speed/choose how the phase moves between the min and max frequencies.

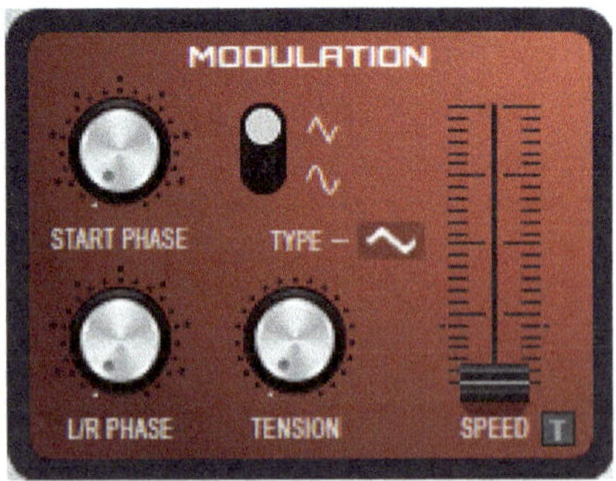

Figure 7.24 – Vintage Phaser MODULATION panel

It has the following controls:

- **START PHASE**: Chooses where to restart the phase from.

- **TYPE**: Lets you choose between a triangle and a sine wave. Different wave shapes change the character of the modulation.
- **L/R PHASE**: If increased, it will increase the stereo effect. This spreads the phaser across the left and right channels, creating a wider and more immersive sound.
- **FEEDBACK**: Lets you choose how much output sound is fed back into the input. More means a larger phasing effect. Increasing feedback intensifies the sweeping notches, producing a more dramatic phaser.

The **DELAY** panel controls delay effects.

Figure 7.25 – Vintage Phaser DELAY panel

It has the following controls:

- **ACTIVATE**: Turns on delay effects. This allows you to engage or bypass the delay without affecting other settings.
- **MIX**: Adjusts the amount of delay effect. This controls how prominent the delayed signal is compared to the original sound.
- **FEEDBACK**: Feeds delay output back into the input to increase the delay effect. Higher feedback values create longer, more pronounced echoes.
- **HP/LP**: Controls high-pass and low-pass filters to cut off frequencies. This shapes the tonal range of the delayed signal by removing unwanted lows or highs.
- **KEEP PITCH**: Allows you to maintain pitch when delay modulation changes. This prevents pitch-shifting artifacts when using modulation on the delay.
- **TIME**: Sets the delay time. This determines the spacing between the original signal and the delayed copies, affecting rhythm and groove.
- **TEMPO SYNC**: Sets delay time in beat units instead of milliseconds. This ensures the delay stays in time with the project's tempo.

The **LEVELS** panel controls output.

Figure 7.26 – Vintage Phaser LEVELS panel

It has the following controls:

- **NOISE**: Simulates noise that the analogy device would normally produce.
- **NOISE GATE**: Allows analog noise only when there is an active sound being fed into the plugin. Otherwise, it will create phasing effects without input sound.
- **MONO INPUT**: Sets input to mono.
- **MIX**: Controls how much effect to output.

Selecting the **advanced options gear icon** unlocks additional controls.

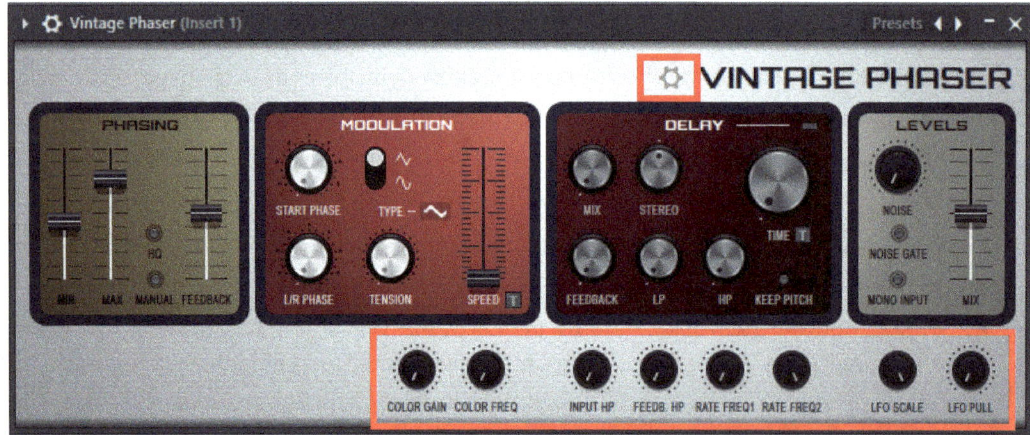

Figure 7.27 – Vintage Phaser advanced options

The original guitar pedal was battery-powered and sounded different depending on the amount of remaining battery level. The phaser sound was richer and crisper when the battery level was high, and more crunchy and laggy when on low battery. The additional controls allow you to create sounds similar to how the pedal effect changed due to battery level.

Figure 7.28 – Vintage Phaser additional controls

Let's learn about them:

- **COLOR GAIN**: Sets the gain. This controls the overall loudness of the phaser's colored frequencies, making the effect more or less prominent.
- **COLOR FREQ**: Sets the frequency. This determines which part of the spectrum the phaser emphasizes, shaping the tonal character of the effect.
- **INPUT HP**: Sets a high-pass filter on input audio. This prevents low-frequency content from being affected by the phaser, keeping the bass clean and focused.
- **FEEDBACK**: Sets how much output audio to feed back into the phaser input to increase the effect. Higher feedback values intensify the sweeping motion and resonance of the phaser.
- **RATE FREQ 1**: Maximum frequency value. This sets the top boundary of the phaser's **LFO** sweep, controlling how fast the highest modulation points occur.
- **RATE FREQ 2**: Minimum frequency value. This sets the bottom boundary of the phaser's **LFO** sweep, controlling how low the modulation dips during the sweep.
- **LFO SCALE**: Sets how much to lower the volume as the frequency increases. This allows for a more natural-sounding sweep by reducing intensity at higher frequencies.
- **LFO PULL**: Controls the strength of the LFO modulation, making the phaser sweep more or less pronounced.

Next, let's discuss applying **distortion effects**.

Understanding distortion effects

Distortion is an audio effect created by overloading audio. It changes the waveform and compresses sound in a way often described as *warm or dirty-sounding*.

Not all distortion is the same. Distortion can be good or bad depending on the type and how it is used. There are several types of distortion. Some of these definitions in the following list overlap, so if you're thinking "hey, these definitions sound very similar to each other," it's because they are.

- **Clipping** occurs when your audio is louder than the sound system can handle. Unintended clipping is an unpleasant sound to the ear. You've heard clipping whenever you hear audio feedback from phone or video calls. This type of audio can occur when audio gain is turned above 0 dB. Unintended clipping distortion is undesirable; however, many kinds of desirable distortion can be used in creative effects for your music to add a unique character to your sounds. For this chapter, we will be talking about intended distortion being used as a creative effect, rather than unintended clipping distortion.
- **Harmonic distortion** is when an audio signal is altered so that new frequencies, called harmonics, are added. These harmonics are multiples of the original sound's frequency – for example, if the original note is 100 Hz, harmonics might appear at 200 Hz, 300 Hz, and so on. This changes the tone of the sound, making it richer, warmer, or sometimes more aggressive.
- **Saturation distortion** effect is a gentle kind of distortion that makes a sound warmer and fuller. Saturation means pushing the gear too hard, like tape or tubes, so it starts to compress and soften the peaks. When a sound is pushed a little too hard, it naturally adds harmonic distortion.
- **Tube distortion** is the warm, rich type of distortion created when audio is pushed through vacuum tubes (like in old amps and studio gear). When the signal gets too strong, the tubes can't handle it perfectly, so they smoothly round off the peaks instead of clipping them harshly. This produces extra harmonics that sound natural and warm.
- **Bit crushing** reduces the sample rate and bit depth. You can think of it as though you are reducing the resolution of the sound. A comparison might be watching a 240-resolution video instead of a 1080-resolution video. Why would you want this? Sometimes you want to create a retro sound where less precision in sound is desirable.
- **Overdrive distortion/Fuzz distortion** makes your audio sound more aggressive. This is what you think of when you hear a metal band playing guitars with lots of distortion effects. Overdrive makes a sound warm, slightly crunchy, and "pushed," like when a guitar amplifier is turned up loud and starts to break up naturally. It gently clips the audio signal, adding extra harmonics that give the sound more character and richness, while still keeping the original tone mostly clear. It keeps most of the original note clear while adding subtle extra tones, making the sound richer and more expressive. Fuzz, on the other hand, is much more extreme. It's like the sound has been completely smashed and reshaped into a square wave, creating a buzzy, saturated, and splattery texture – think of a loud radio station that's completely lost its signal.

Using Distructor

FL Studio has a distortion effect plugin called **Distructor**. Distructor is an effect rack that takes effects from several FL Studio plugins and groups them together conveniently in an easy-to-use interface.

Let's apply a distortion effect to an instrument using Distructor:

1. Load up a sample or an instrument with notes and route it to a new mixer track.
2. Add the **Distructor** effect. When you play your instrument, you will be able to hear a distortion effect:

Figure 7.29 – Distructor

Distructor is a collection of 4 modules of effects. Distructor contains distortion, filter, chorus, and speaker effects. Upon loading, Distructor populates with four effects that work on the audio chain from left to right. For example, in the initial setup, the audio passes through the **DISTORTION** module, which then passes the audio to the **FILTER** module, then **CHORUS**, and finally the **SPEAKER**. As usual, in the top right corner of the plugin, you'll find **Default** effect presets, which you can instantly apply to your audio.

You can swap out the type of module by left-clicking the module title and choosing the effect module you want to use, as shown in the following screenshot.

Figure 7.30 – Swap the module in Distructor

All Distructor effect modules have the same bottom panel buttons, allowing you to control how much input audio and output audio you want the effect to use. These are controlled by the **IN**, **MIX**, and **OUT** knobs. Each knob has a volume meter to the left to help you visualize the levels.

Below the **IN**, **MIX**, and **OUT** knobs are the **move module left** and **move module right** option. These allow you to rearrange the order of the effects applied to your audio. For example, using the **options** button, you can completely delete an effect module from the rack.

Below that is the **SOFT CLIP OUTPUT** button, which helps to stop audio from peaking above 0 dB, and the **SHOW PEAKMETERS** button, which enables you to toggle the audio volume visual on or off.

Let's take a look at each of the Distructor effects. First up is the **DISTORTION** effect module.

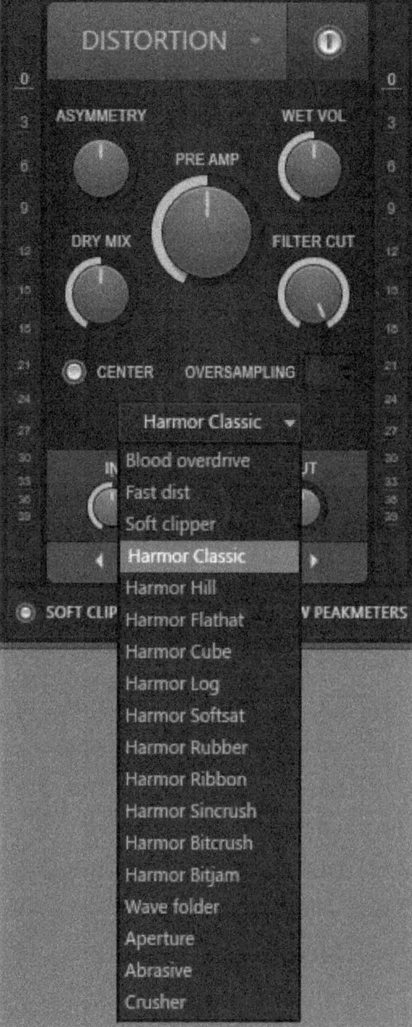

Figure 7.31 – DISTORTION effect module

In the preceding screenshot, we've clicked on the algorithm section, which reveals a dropdown menu of various distortion presets. The controls in the effects module change depending on which preset is selected.

- **Blood overdrive**: Creates an overdrive distortion that produces compressed soft sounds.
- **Fast dist**: Creates a gritty, punchy effect.
- **Soft clipper**: Avoids clipping by applying a soft knee compression to the audio. It can cause saturation distortion when the audio exceeds the threshold level.

The following are some distortion effects taken from the **Harmor** plugin that are reused in the Distructor module (Harmor is another synthesizer plugin available in FL Studio).

  - **Classic**: Traditional distortion, adds harmonics and crunch.
  - **Flathat**: Produces a flatter, more compressed distortion.
  - **Cube**: Applies cubic distortion, resulting in a more pronounced, edgy sound.
  - **Log**: Uses a logarithmic curve for subtle, musical distortion.
  - **Softsat**: Soft saturation, for gentle warmth.
  - **Rubber**: Bouncy, rubbery distortion character.
  - **Ribbon**: Smooth, ribbon-like distortion character.
  - **Sincrush**: Sine-based distortion character, can sound metallic or digital.
  - **Bitcrush**: Reduces bit depth, creating digital artifacts and a lo-fi effect.
  - **Bitjam**: Adds jittery, glitchy digital noise.

- **Wave folder**: Folds the waveform back on itself when it exceeds a threshold, creating complex, harmonically rich distortion. Great for aggressive, modular-style sounds.
- **Aperture**: Warps the waveform in a unique way, introducing unusual harmonics and textures. Useful for experimental sound design.
- **Abrasive**: Modulates the signal with noise, resulting in a harsh, gritty, and abrasive distortion. Perfect for industrial or experimental genres.
- **Rate crush**: Reduces the sample rate of the signal, introducing aliasing and digital artifacts. This creates a crunchy, retro digital sound.
- **Bit crush**: Lowers the bit depth, adding graininess and digital noise. This is the classic lo-fi, video game-style distortion.

The next Distructor module is the **FILTER** module:

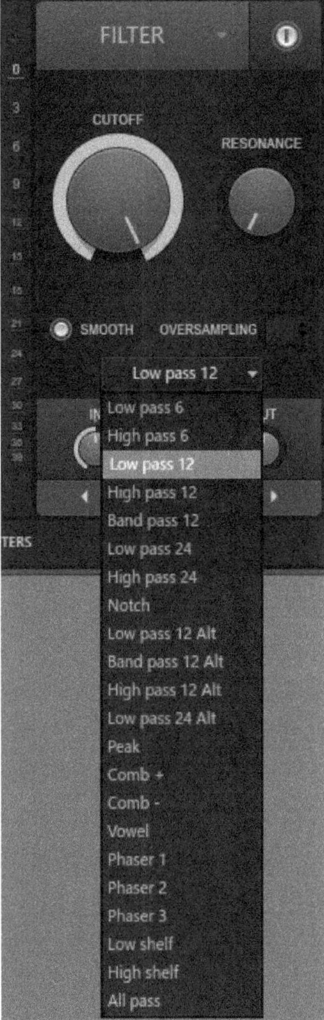

Figure 7.32 – FILTER effect module

The **FILTER** module contains a variety of presets and provides a **CUTOFF** and **RESONANCE** knob to adjust control values.

In general, the **CUTOFF** control allows you to select which frequency the filter acts on. The **RESONANCE** control lets you choose what peak to use for the cutoff frequency. Here's a description of the controls:

- **Low pass** filter: Only allows frequencies below the filter value to be heard. This makes the sound darker or more muffled as higher frequencies are removed.

- **High pass** filter: Only allows frequencies above the filter value to be heard. This makes the sound thinner or brighter by cutting out the low end.
- **Low shelf**: Boosts or cuts frequencies below the cutoff value. It's often used to add warmth or remove boominess from a mix.
- **High shelf**: Boosts or cuts frequencies above the cutoff value. It is perfect for adding sparkle or taming harsh highs in your sound.
- **Notch**: A band of frequencies where frequencies are cut at the cutoff frequency. The **RESONANCE** knob controls the width of allowable frequencies. Great for removing unwanted tones or resonances without affecting the rest of the signal.
- **Peak**: A band of frequencies where frequencies are allowed to pass through. The **RESONANCE** knob controls the boost. Useful for emphasizing specific frequencies to make a sound stand out.
- **Phaser 1**, **2**, **3**: Phaser effects. These create a sweeping, whooshing motion by shifting phase across frequencies.
- **Vowel**: Makes the sound like a spoken vowel sound. **CUTOFF** knob controls A, E, I, O, U sounds. Resonance parameter controls shifting/offsetting. It gives your sound a human-like "talking" or formant quality.
- **Comb+**: Series of band peaks looking like a comb. Produces a metallic, resonant tone often used for flanging or robotic textures.
- **Comb-**: Series of band cuts looking like a comb. Creates hollow or phasey effects by removing evenly spaced frequencies.
- **All pass**: Changes phase of sound frequencies. **RESONANCE** knob controls the width. Alters the tone subtly without changing overall volume, adding movement or depth.

You can always see what value a control is set to by clicking the control and looking at the top left corner of your screen to see the hint panel, as shown in the following screenshot.

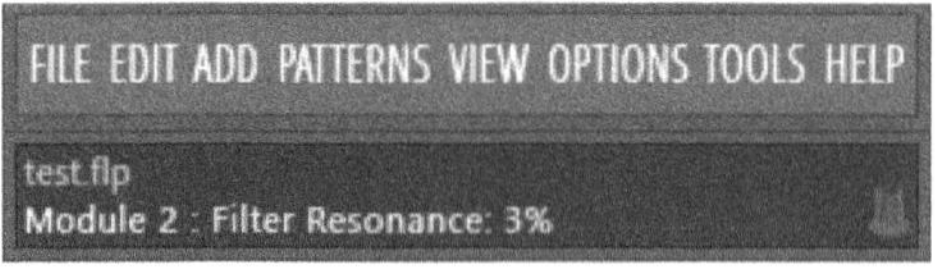

Figure 7.33 – Control value

Next, let's look at the **CHORUS** effect module.

Figure 7.34 – CHORUS effect module

Chorus effects are created by delaying copies of a sound and detuning them.

- **DELAY**: Controls the minimum delay. This sets the base time difference between the original signal and its copies, shaping how spacious or tight the chorus sounds.
- **FEEDBACK**: Controls how much you want the original sound to be mixed with the delayed sound. Increasing this makes the effect more intense and can create swirling or resonant textures.
- **SPEED**: Chooses modulation speed. Higher values create faster, more energetic movement, while lower values produce a gentle, slow shimmer.
- **DEPTH**: High values create a stronger modulation of the voice delay. This increases the pitch variation and makes the chorus sound wider and more dramatic.
- **BLUR**: Controls the number of chorus voices. More voices create a thicker, ensemble-like effect, while fewer voices sound cleaner and more subtle.
- **COLOR**: Left creates a **low-pass filter**, right creates a **high-pass filter**. This lets you darken or brighten the chorus tone to fit better in the mix.
- **MONO**: Creates chorus voices that are in mono, making the audio the same in the left and right speakers. This produces a focused, centered effect that blends easily.
- **STEREO**: Creates chorus voices that are set to stereo, allowing differences between audio from the left and right speakers. This gives a more spacious and immersive sound.
- **WIDE**: Creates a wide stereo chorus effect. It exaggerates the stereo field, making the sound feel large and surrounding.

Next, let's look at the **SPEAKER** effect module:

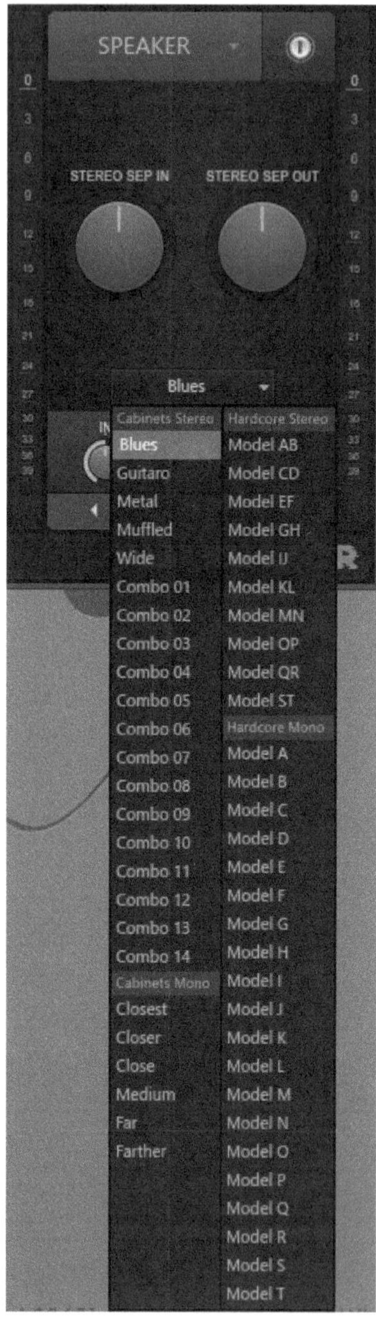

Figure 7.35 – SPEAKER effect module

The speaker effect module creates reverb effects using convolution technology. The idea is that it replicates an environment for your sound and plays your audio in the environment to simulate the reverb. The presets are effects taken from the Fruity Convolver plugin.

- **STERO SEP IN**: Controls the stereo amount of the input sound.
- **STEREO SEP OUT**: Controls the stereo amount of the output sound.

Distortion best practices

Adding distortion effects is useful when you want to make your sounds more aggressive, warm, or to cut through the mix. Brass instruments can sometimes benefit from sounding a little more aggressive with the aid of a little distortion.

Distortion is often added for guitar and bass/808 instruments. It can be used on vocals depending on the genre of music you're trying to make. If used on vocals, it's recommended that you add distortion to the vocals on a parallel mixer track to your vocals so that you retain all your vocals' original nuances without losing them.

Why apply distortion in parallel? This preserves the clarity and punch while letting you dial in as much dirt and energy as you want. You may want to filter before and after distortion. High-pass filtering before the distortion effect prevents low-end frequencies from becoming messy, and EQing afterward helps tame harsh resonances introduced by the process.

Distortion also interacts strongly with dynamics, so paying attention to the volume changes is important. Make sure your input level isn't too hot or too weak – small adjustments can completely change the character of the distortion. Different distortion types behave differently. Tube or tape emulations give warmth and smoothness, while digital or bit-crushing distortion adds sharp, edgy textures – each has its place depending on the vibe you're going for.

So far in this chapter and the previous chapter, we've discussed applying effects to individual instruments. Next, let's discuss how to apply effects to multiple instruments at once.

Stereo widening effects with Spreader

Wider sounds are generally desirable. A wider sound creates a more immersive listening experience. FL Studio has a plugin called **Spreader** that can make your existing sounds feel wider.

It increases the difference between the left and right channels (using **MID/SIDE** processing), which makes the audio sound wider and more spacious. The plugin gives you control to keep low frequencies centered and mono-compatible, ensuring your mix remains solid and translates well to all playback systems.

Let's increase the stereo width of a sound using Spreader:

1. Load up a sample or an instrument with notes and route it to a new mixer track.
2. Add the **Spreader** effect plugin. When you play your instrument, you will be able to hear a widening effect.

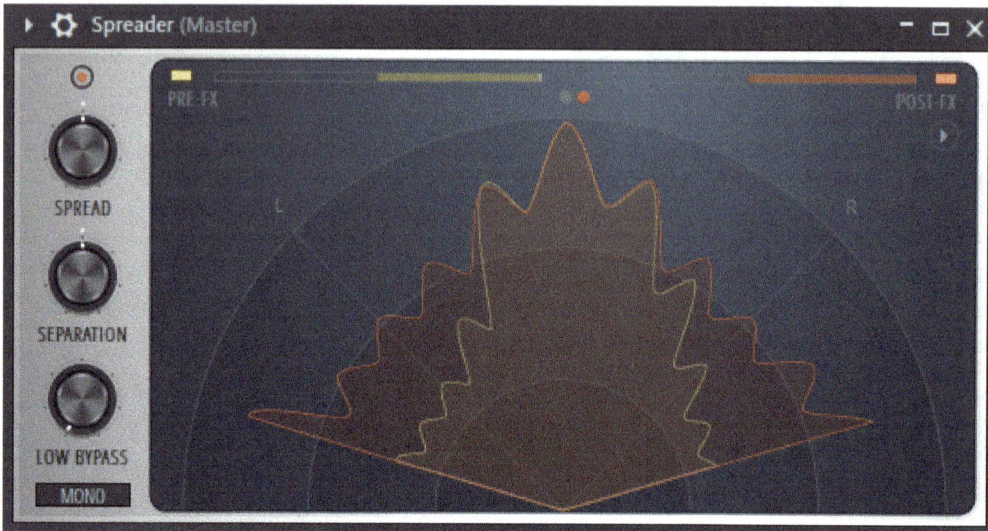

Figure 7.36 – Spreader effects plugin

The plugin itself is minimal in the number of controls. It's designed to do one thing: make your existing sounds feel wider, and it does so very well. There are controls on the left side of the plugin and a visual vector scope display on the right to help you see the difference in the sound before and after the effect has been applied. Let's discuss the controls on the left side.

- **ENABLED**: Toggles between turning the plugin effect on or off so you can compare the difference.
- **SPREAD**: This knob increases the difference between the left and right channels. This makes sounds that are already panned or have stereo information appear even wider. It boosts the **SIDE** (difference) component relative to the **MID** (center/shared) component of the audio.
- **SEPARATION**: This knob lets you blend from mono (no stereo width) to fully separated (maximum stereo width). This is similar to the **STEREO SEPARATION** knob on the **Mixer** and works by adjusting the balance between the **MID** and **SIDE** signals. Happens after the **SPREAD** control.

- **LOW BYPASS**: Removes low frequencies (range of 10Hz to 10,000Hz) from the stereo widening process. This keeps bass frequencies in mono (centered). This is important because wide bass can sound weak or phasey on some systems.
- **MONO**: Collapses the frequencies you removed in the **LOW BYPASS** control to mono. This ensures a solid, centered low end. This lets you remove stereo width from a sound for the bass frequencies so that your bass sounds will sound good on large speaker systems with mono bass channels. When you use stereo widening tools like Spreader, it's important to check how your mix sounds in mono. Sometimes, widening effects can cause key elements to disappear or become less clear when the mix is collapsed to mono. To avoid this, briefly switch your master output to mono and make sure all important parts of your track are still present and balanced.

You now know how to increase the stereo width of your sounds to make them feel wider. Applying effects to one sound at a time is only one way to apply effects. You can apply effects to multiple sounds simultaneously. Let's learn how to apply effects to multiple sounds at once using Mix Buses.

Understanding mix buses

When you have two or more Mixer channels routed into a single Mixer channel, we call the combined audio a bus, also known as a **mix bus**. Buses are useful for combining sounds together and making them appear related to one another.

The master channel is a type of bus that collects audio from all the other Mixer channels. Most of the time when we talk about a bus, we aren't referring to the master channel, though.

You can generally think of a bus as a checkpoint along the way to the master channel. Does the audio coming out of the bus sound good so far up to this point? In most songs, you will have a bus for your drums, a bus combining the layering of your instruments, and a bus for your vocals.

Using mix bus effects

Using mix bus effects is where a track starts to feel cohesive, polished, and alive. A mix bus acts as the control room for shaping the overall tone, dynamics, and glue of your song. The key to effective bus processing is subtlety: you're not trying to fix individual instruments here; instead, you're enhancing the whole mix.

Let's set up a mix bus in our Mixer:

1. Load up two instruments in the **Channel rack**, add some notes, and copy those notes to both instruments.
2. Route both instruments to separate new Mixer channels.

3. In the **Mixer**, select both mixer tracks. You can select multiple Mixer channel tracks at once by pressing *Ctrl* + *Shift* + left-clicking on the desired mixer tracks.
4. With the mixer tracks still selected, right-click on the arrow at the bottom of the mixer track you would like to make into a bus, as shown in the following screenshot. In this case, the pop-up is covering up the mix bus that we are routing to. There is an arrow hidden underneath the pop-up. You right-click the arrow to see the pop-up.

Figure 7.37 – Mix bus

The audio signals from your two instrument channels have been sent to be combined in a Mixer channel. You've just created a mix bus.

5. Make it easy for yourself to identify that the mixer track is being used as a bus. Right-click on the mix bus channel and change the name and color by selecting the **Rename, color and icon...** option. This will make it easy for you to organize:

Figure 7.38 – Rename and color your mix bus

6. In this bus Mixer channel, add any effect plugin. The effect plugin will affect all instrument sounds routed to the bus. In the following screenshot, we can see that I've added the **Fruity Delay 3** plugin. This will apply a delay effect to both instruments routed to the bus channel:

Figure 7.39 – Adding the Fruity Delay 3 plugin

Mix bus best practices

Compression effects should be applied to the bus to gain a sense of cohesion among the instruments. For example, drum instruments are often grouped together in a bus and then given compression. Note that the compressor is going to change the volume and frequencies of all instruments sent to the bus. To save yourself some time, if you know you're going to be adding bus compression, add the compressor first before doing additional mixing, such as volume and EQ tweaks.

You can apply EQ effects to a bus. You can create low- or high-pass filters to avoid your instruments interfering with instruments in other buses. For example, you can add a high-pass filter to remove the sub frequencies from your non-sub-bass instruments. This will make any remaining bass instruments' sub frequencies stand out unimpeded.

You can make subtle EQ cuts, such as at around 200 Hz, to remove muddiness. If you find yourself making large EQ cuts, you should probably be doing EQ on the individual instruments themselves rather than on the bus.

When reverb effects are applied to a bus, it gives the impression that all instruments in the bus exist in the same physical space. Consider applying convolution reverb at this stage to make your instruments feel like they all exist together.

Adjusting the volume of a bus will change the volume of all instruments in it at once. This can be useful when balancing the volume of different instrument groups. For example, you can adjust the volume of the drum bus relative to the vocal bus.

Congratulations, you've created a bus and used it to apply effects to multiple instruments at once! You now know how to group your instruments together and apply effects that make the grouped instruments sound more cohesive.

Summary

In this chapter, you learned how to make your sounds feel large and trick your ears into thinking your digital instruments were played in actual physical environments. This will make your sounds feel natural and more enjoyable to listen to.

We discussed stereo width and effects you can use to make your sounds feel larger. We explored tools used to manipulate stereo width, including panning, digital reverb, convolution reverb, delay effects, chorus effects, flangers, and phasers. We learned how to use distortion effects. We learned how to increase the stereo width of your sounds using the Spreader plugin. Finally, we discussed how to use mix buses to combine your instruments together. This allows you to apply effects to all sounds in the mix bus at once.

In the next chapter, we'll jump into recording live audio and best practices for vocal processing.

Get this book's PDF version and more

Scan the QR code (or go to `packtpub.com/unlock`). Search for this book by name, confirm the edition, and then follow the steps on the page.

UNLOCK NOW

Note: Keep your invoice handy. Purchases made directly from Packt don't require an invoice.

8

Recording Live Audio and Vocal Processing

Vocals are the most recognizable part of a song and can single-handedly determine whether people love it or hate it. For this reason, you'll want to devote attention to making sure you get the best-sounding vocals possible. In this chapter, we will learn how to record live audio and process vocals with effects to make them sound as polished and professional as possible.

In the pages ahead, we'll discuss the setup and preparation you need before recording. We'll look at how to record into FL Studio. We'll learn how to mix your vocals and discuss best practices for applying effects.

In this chapter, we'll cover the following topics:

- Understanding microphones
- Setting up your recording environment
- Recording audio into FL Studio
- Vocal denoising in Edison using AI
- Removing reverb in Edison using AI
- Using pitch correction with NewTone
- Retiming samples with NewTime
- Vocal effects processing best practices

Technical requirements

To follow the examples in this chapter, you will need the FL Studio *Producer Edition* or higher. You will also need headphones and a microphone to record into.

Understanding microphones

You need a microphone to record live audio. What are microphones? Microphones are electronic devices you use to record audio. They contain a material called a **diaphragm** that vibrates when struck by sound waves. They convert the sound waves into an electrical current that can be played by devices that replay sound.

If you were to Google search *what* microphone should I buy?, you may feel overwhelmed by the number of search results. There are many competing brands of microphones, each with its own advantages. Prices range from tens of dollars to thousands of dollars.

Personally, in my experience, if you do a good job in terms of recording, mixing, and applying effects to your audio, most listeners won't be able to tell how expensive the microphone you used to record is. The thing you record and what you do with it is much more important than the price of the mic you use. That said, there are different types of microphones you will come across, and they are used for different purposes.

Let's discuss the types of microphones available so you can make an informed choice when selecting one for yourself.

Dynamic microphones

Dynamic microphones are microphones intended for use in stage performances. They consist of a wire coil coupled with a diaphragm. A minimum amount of energy is required to initially cause the diaphragm to vibrate from sound waves. The diaphragm is subject to inertia in that once it starts vibrating, it continues to vibrate. This inertia problem means the microphone won't be able to pick up subtle transients as they are too brief.

Dynamic microphones can be used to record loud sounds, such as sounds from drums and guitar amps. They record audio from one direction and reject incoming sound from other directions. This allows them to focus on a singer/instrument and ignore background noise. If placed further than 1 foot away from the sound source, the sound becomes thin, so you need to place them close to the source. They are materially tough as they are expected to withstand being roughly handled onstage. They can withstand extreme sound pressure without distorting. If you're doing live shows, a dynamic mic is the right choice for you. If you're recording in a studio, a dynamic microphone is the wrong choice for you.

Condenser microphones

Condenser microphones are intended to be used in quiet recording environments. They consist of a diaphragm next to a metallic alloy. Sound pressure causes the diaphragm to vibrate. The vibration changes the space between the two surfaces, and an electrical charge accumulates between the two. The discharge is translated into electrical current, which is interpreted later as sound. They are more expensive than dynamic microphones and are delicate and sensitive to nuanced tones. If recording in a studio, a condenser microphone is a good choice for you.

Ribbon microphones

Ribbon microphones are delicate and fragile microphones that are usually quite expensive. They too need to be placed within 1 foot of the source to avoid sounding thin. They record audio bi-directionally and pick up all sound in their proximity. If placed close to the audio source, they may receive an increase in bass frequencies. They consist of a ribbon (of conductive material) between two magnets. The ribbon functions as both a diaphragm and a conductor. As a result, ribbon mics are not subject to the inertia problem of dynamic microphones. This means they can pick up subtle transients. If recording in a studio, a ribbon mic is another good choice.

> Note
>
> Condenser microphones and ribbon microphones require a device called a **microphone preamp** or an audio interface to plug your microphone into. These devices provide electrical power to the microphone, known as **phantom power**, to increase the volume of the recorded audio. Without phantom power, your microphone's audio will be too quiet to use. If you use a condenser or ribbon microphone, you will need to investigate how to connect to phantom power. The phantom power device will then have an output that can be connected to your computer.

USB microphones

USB microphones are a special type of condenser microphone. These are mics you can plug directly into your computer via a USB port. This makes it easy to record audio, as you don't need to worry about getting a microphone preamp. They tend to be cheap and beginner-friendly, but offer less control over recording compared to the higher-priced condenser mics. If you are new to music production and just playing around, unsure of whether you want to get serious or not, get a USB mic. They're cheap, and you can just plug them into a computer and use them right away without worrying about phantom power. When you need to record professionally, look into getting a condenser or ribbon mic.

Setting up your recording environment

Before recording your audio, you want to be in a location free from background sounds. Ideally, you would be in a soundproof environment.

If you record audio and find there is some consistent background static or hum, it's not the end of the world. If the unwanted sound is at a low volume level, you may be able to remove the unwanted noise using a **gate plugin** effect. We discussed **gates** in *Chapter 6*. We will also explore tools to isolate your vocals from background noise and reverb in this chapter using AI with the **Edison** tool.

You'll need to obtain headphones so you can listen to your music playing while you are recording your instrument or vocals. You don't want to hear your song playing in the background on speakers while you're recording sounds, or else the background noise will appear in the recording.

Recording instruments

Recording instruments appears simple on paper, but takes a surprising amount of effort to do. If you're recording an acoustic instrument, position the microphone as close as you can to the instrument and record. With electric instruments, position the microphone close to the instrument amp/speaker.

The following photo shows an example of how you can set up a microphone to record an electric guitar amp:

Figure 8.1 – Recording guitar amp

Note that the microphone is positioned slightly off the center of the speaker. Each speaker has a sweet spot in terms of where the best sound comes from, and it's usually not directly smack dab in the center. You will need to experiment with the positioning of your microphone to find the best-sounding spot.

Recording drum kits

Drum kits are fiddly for recording. When recording a drum kit, you want to designate a microphone for each drum kit item. This way, you can record each part in isolation, which allows you the freedom to play with individual sounds when mixing. It's a bit of an art arranging the microphones so that they are close to the drums but don't impede the drummer when playing the drum kit.

The following photo shows an example of how you could position your microphones to record a drum kit. You can see that each drum and cymbal has its own dedicated microphone.

Figure 8.2 – Drum kit microphones

In addition to recording each instrument, you also want to record the instrument in the context of the room to hear the natural reverb. To do so, place microphones some distance away from the instrument as shown in the following photo:

Figure 8.3 – Drum kit room microphones

In the preceding photo, on the far left and right, you can see microphones recording the drum kit at a distance. These microphones capture the room reverberations of the drum kit. The same idea applies to any instrument. Ideally, you would record both close to the instrument and further away to capture the natural reverb.

Preparing to record vocals

Before recording your vocals, make sure your body is physically prepared. You're going to record many takes of the song and then mix and match the best parts from all the takes. Recording vocals takes a while and is energy-intensive. You should warm up beforehand. Consider doing some of the following activities before recording vocals to get your lungs and throat into peak performance condition:

- Go for some brief cardio exercise beforehand, such as a quick run to get the blood circulating.
- Hum a little.
- Consider doing vocal exercises such as singing scales.

- Take a hot shower.
- Drink a hot beverage.

Using pop filters

When recording vocals, you should obtain a **pop filter**. A pop filter is a mesh screen used to filter your vocals while recording. Pop filters help to remove undesired popping sounds created while talking. You can get pop filters cheaply. Any kind of mesh fabric can work as a pop filter; you can even create your own at home by following a YouTube tutorial. You can see a pop filter in the following photo:

Figure 8.4 – Pop filter

In the image, the black circular object is a pop filter. To use a pop filter, place it directly in front of the microphone and sing into the pop filter while recording.

So far, we've discussed microphones, recording instruments, and getting ready to record vocals. Next, let's record audio into our digital audio workstation.

Recording audio into FL Studio

Let's record audio into FL Studio:

1. Select the position in the Playlist of your song where you want to begin recording from. Left-click to place your cursor on the **Playlist** timeline.
2. Check that the **countdown before recording** button is selected as shown in the following screenshot. This will give you a few seconds to prepare when you are recording:

Figure 8.5 – Record countdown

3. Open your **Mixer** and left-click on a new mixer track to select it. When you record, your audio will be recorded into this audio Mixer channel and then sent to the **Playlist**. If you have effect plugins on the Mixer channel, like **pitch correction** plugins such as **Autotune**, these will be applied while recording the audio file. We will discuss pitch correction in further detail later in this chapter.
   Usually, you'll want to apply effects later in mixing, but it is possible to do so at this point. If you're going to record with audio effects, it's recommended to record on two channels simultaneously (one channel with the effect applied and another to capture the raw audio).
4. Once you've chosen your Mixer channel, ensure that **Song** is selected on the **Transport** panel, and then press the **record** button at the top of the screen as shown in the following screenshot:

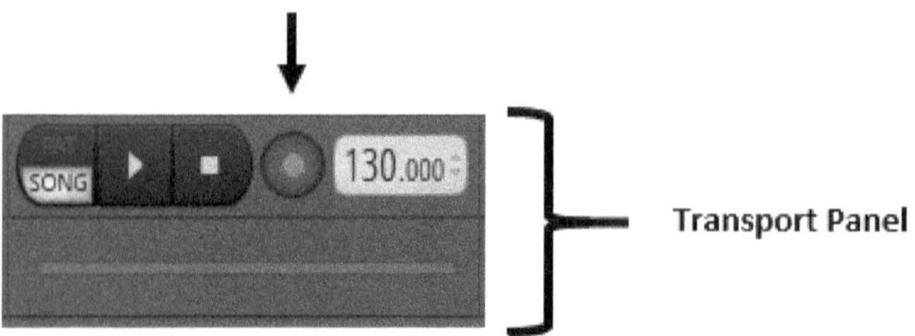

Figure 8.6 – Record button

After hitting **Record**, a menu will pop up as shown in the following screenshot:

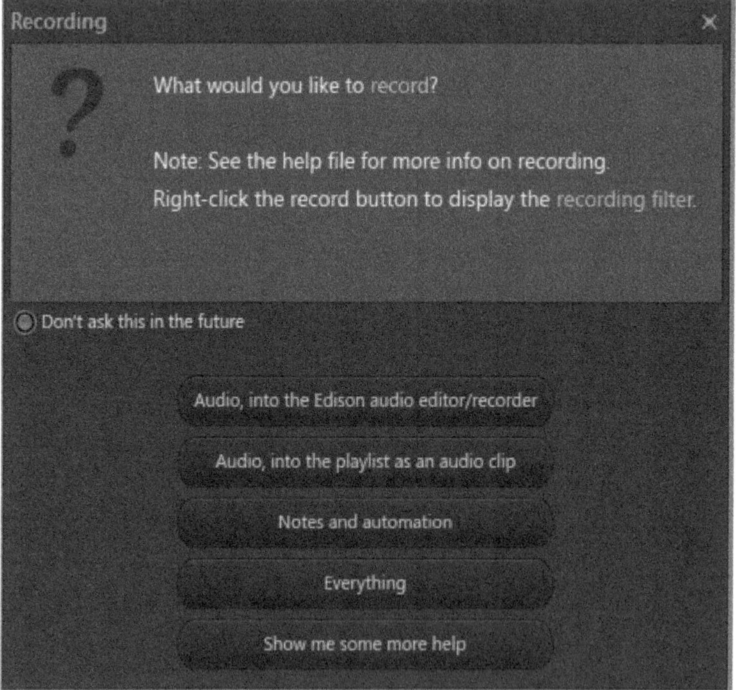

Figure 8.7 – Recording options

5. The simplest recording option is to select **Audio, into the playlist as an audio clip**. Once you do this, you will be prompted with a list of all available microphones in a dropdown menu on the right of the **Mixer**.

Figure 8.8 – Choose a microphone to record with

Once you've selected a microphone, your recording will begin and the song will start playing and recording.

If you record into the **Playlist** and you have **BLEND NOTES** and **LOOP RECORD** both engaged (in the **Transport** panel), your audio takes will be on a loop, and you can then hear one take after another. After pressing **stop**, you can delete the takes you don't want.

When you press the **stop** button, which is next to the **record** button in the **Transport** panel, your song will stop playing and your recorded audio will appear in the **Playlist**.

Your recorded audio is saved as a file on your computer. You can see all audio recordings in the **Browser** under a folder called **Recorded**. Unless you delete these audio files, they will continue to accumulate throughout your projects. Over the years, this could result in a large amount of memory being used, so you should occasionally check for and delete unused files. If you want to remove all unused audio samples in a single project, go to **Tools** | **Macros** | **Purge Unused Audio Clips**.

Congratulations! You now know how to record audio.

Recording with Edison

Edison is an audio editor and recorder available with FL Studio. It's an alternative to the previous recording method and has many additional features to give you fine control over your audio recording, such as removing background noise and reverb.

1. To record with Edison, go into the **Mixer** and load **Edison** onto a **Mixer** channel. Alternatively, you can click on a **Mixer** channel and press *Ctrl* + *E*. At the top right of the **Mixer**, choose the microphone you want to use to record into Edison. The following screenshot shows **Edison** having been loaded onto a mixer track and the selection of a microphone to use:

Figure 8.9 – Loading Edison

2. In **Edison**, press the **record** button. Now play your song in the **Playlist** (press **play** on the **Transport** panel). As the song plays, **Edison** will record audio.
3. **Edison** will continue to record until you tell it to stop. This means that you can play your song, pattern, or selected segment of the **Playlist** on repeat multiple times and continue to record in **Edison** throughout. When you're finished recording, press the **record** button again in **Edison** to stop. An audio wave will appear in **Edison**.
   Alternatively, select the **drag/copy sample/selection** button and hold left-click to drag and drop the audio into any other FL Studio window.

Congratulations, you've just recorded audio with Edison.

Loop recording with Edison

In Edison, you can loop a segment of your Playlist and record over that segment to get multiple takes before choosing the best one. To do this, execute the following steps:

1. In your **Playlist**, highlight the segment you want to loop and record over by left-clicking and dragging on the **Playlist** timeline.
2. Press the **loop recording** button at the top of the screen. This will keep the Playlist looping through your song.
3. In the preceding screenshot of **Edison** (*Figure 8.9*), to the right of the **record** button at the top, you can see the text **ON INPUT**. If you click on that text, you can see some more recording options. Select the option that says **On Play**.
4. Hit **record** in **Edison** and press play in your **Playlist**. As the Playlist loops through the selected segment, **Edison** will record multiple takes of your recording.
5. Press **record** again in Edison to stop recording. You'll see that the recording in **Edison** has been split up into multiple takes. You can see an example of how your audio might look in the following screenshot:

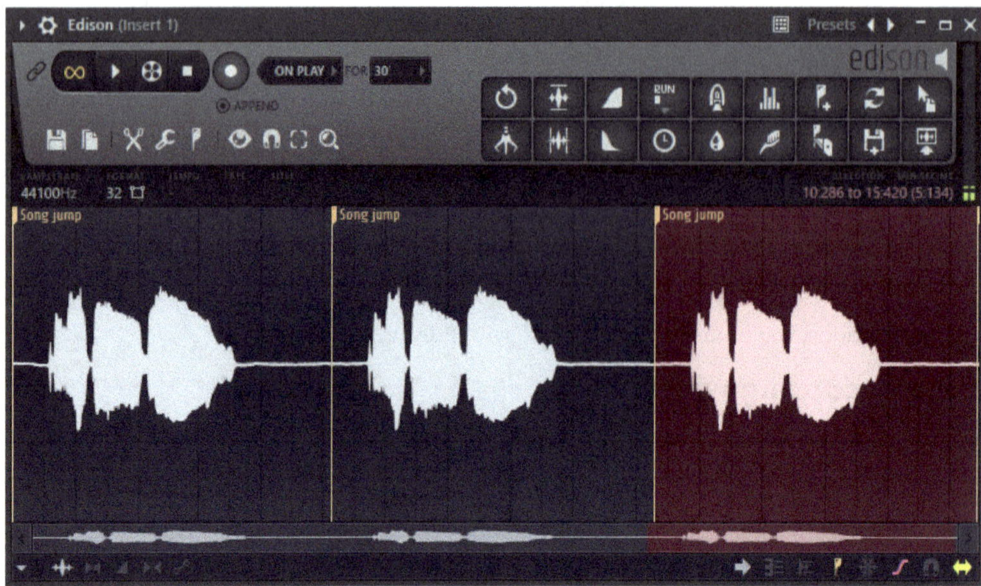

Figure 8.10 – Multiple takes recorded on Edison

6. Choose which recording take you like best by pressing the *left* and *right* arrow keys on your keyboard. If you press *Delete*, a recording take will be removed. You can press *Shift* + *C* to send your audio take to the **Playlist**.

Exporting audio from Edison

When you're happy with your audio recording, you can export the audio clip from **Edison**, as shown in the following screenshot:

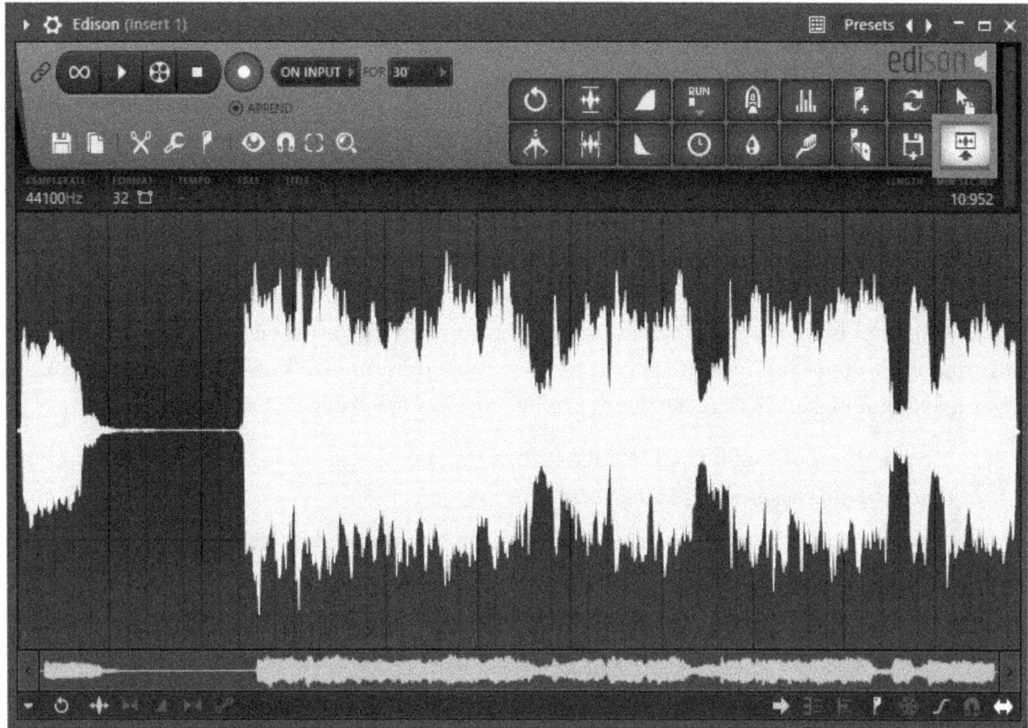

Figure 8.11 – Export from Edison

In the preceding screenshot, we can see the **send to Playlist as audio clip/to channel** button. Clicking this sends your audio clip to the **Playlist** as an audio sample.

Congratulations, you've just recorded multiple audio clips and chosen the best one using Edison.

Vocal denoising in Edison using AI

So far, we've recorded audio into Edison. Once you're happy with your recording take, and you're certain you have the clip you want to use, you can now improve the recording. Edison has AI-powered tools that allow you to remove background noise or undesired reverb from any recording.

First, let's check out the AI-powered denoising tool. Edison can remove unwanted background noise from your vocal recordings or do the opposite and remove vocals while only keeping the music. This tool blew my mind when I first saw it in action. You used to have to spend ages tinkering with denoising tools, trying to remove background noise from recordings. FL Studio made a tool that makes this so easy that it can be done in a few seconds. Let's try it.

1. To use this tool, you'll need to have loaded into Edison an audio recording that has both background noise/music and a vocal.
2. Click the **tools** button and choose the option **Vocal denoise/isolator**, as shown in the following screenshot:

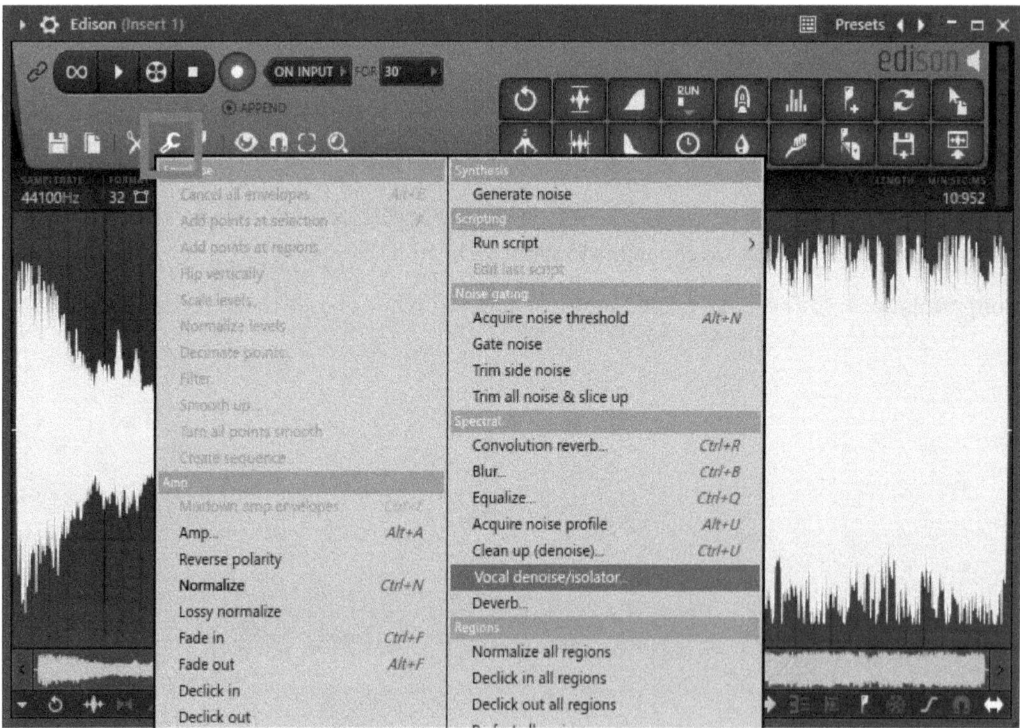

Figure 8.12 – Vocal denoise/isolator in Edison

The **Vocal denoiser** plugin will appear.

Figure 8.13 – Vocal denoiser

In the tool, you'll see a fader knob that ranges from -100 (only **Noise**) to 100 (only **Vocal**). In the preceding screenshot, it's showing a value of **38**. If the value is set to 0, then the tool is not making any changes to the audio.

3. If you hear background audio in your vocal recording that you want removed, move the knob to the right. The tool will analyze your audio and remove the undesired sound.

   The tool has the ability to do the opposite as well. It can remove vocal sounds from a recording to leave only the background music. If you want to remove a vocal from the audio, turn the knob to the left.

You can hear the sound after the effect has been applied by clicking the **preview** button (play arrow symbol) at the bottom. When you're happy with your effect changes, click **Accept**.

Removing reverb in Edison using AI

Similar to the ability to remove background noise from a vocal recording, Edison can also remove reverb sounds from audio. It uses AI to analyze your sound sample and isolate the reverb. Before AI tools came around, removing reverb from audio samples was extremely difficult, if not impossible. If you had reverb in your original audio recording and didn't want it, your only option was to record it again. Thanks to the miracle of AI tools, this is no longer the case. Let's learn how to remove reverb from your audio recordings.

1. To use this tool, you'll need to have loaded into **Edison** an audio recording that has a sound with reverb in it. You can pick any sound; it doesn't have to be a vocal. For instance, it could be an instrument sound.
2. Click the **tools** button and choose the **Deverb...** option as shown in the following screenshot:

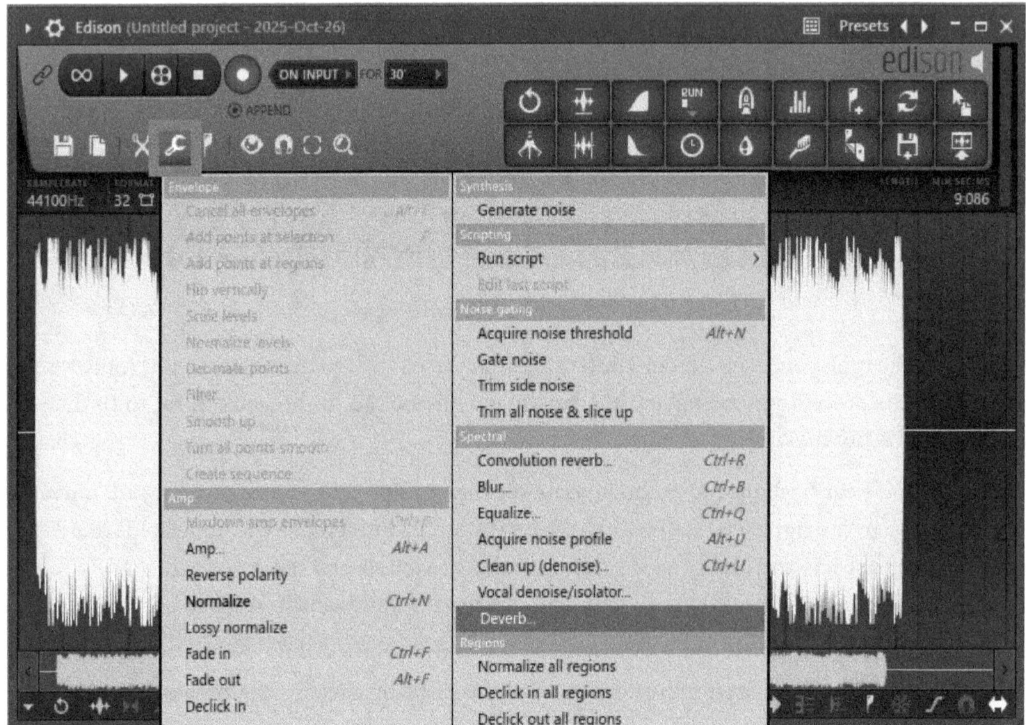

Figure 8.14 – Deverb

The **Deverb** plugin will load up and ask you to choose a profile for the source material. If it's a vocal with reverb, you'll choose the **Voice** option. If your sample is any other instrument, you'll want to choose the **General** option.

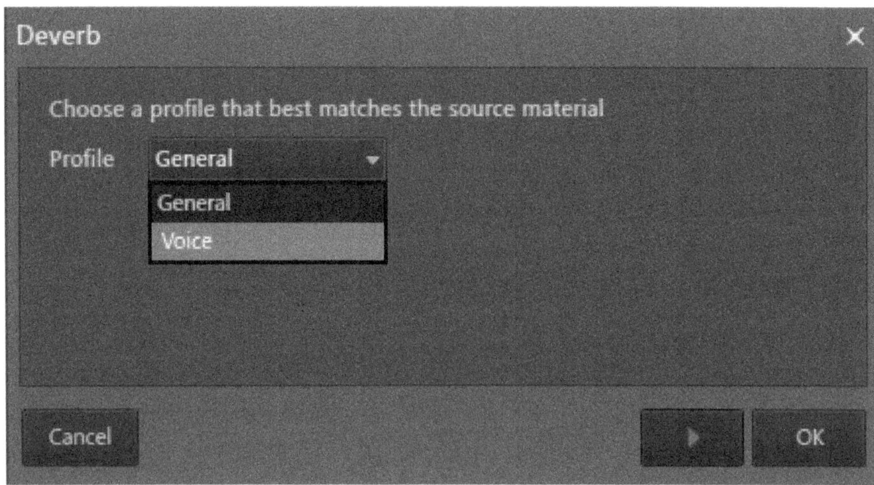

Figure 8.15 – Deverb Voice

Once you've chosen the description that best describes your audio, select **OK**.

The **Deverb** plugin loads up with a similar visual layout to the **Vocal denoiser** plugin. There's one central knob that turns the Deverb effect on the more you turn it to the right. If you turn it all the way to the left, you will just hear the original sound. Turning it all the way to the right will remove all the reverb.

Figure 8.16 – Choose Noise Profile

You'll notice that turning the knob all the way likely will damage the sound, so you'll want to experiment with turning the knob to somewhere in the middle. Remove just as much reverb as you can without ruining the sound.

We've covered the features that I personally use in Edison. However, there are lots more features you can dive into. If you want to go further, check out the FL Studio documentation or the YouTube channel *In The Mix* for tutorials on using Edison at`www.youtube.com/c/inthemix`.

Using pitch correction with NewTone

When you are recording, a singer's melody will sometimes drift out of pitch from the song scale. Usually, this is undesired and makes the vocal sound bad. **Pitch correction** is a tool used to bring note pitches back into the song scale. There are several pitch correction tools on the market. Some well-made pitch correction plugins include *Antares's* Autotune and *Celemony's* **Melodyne**. The most widely known and used pitch correction tool in the industry is Autotune by *Antares*. If you have money to spend, Autotune is the optimal choice. It is a little pricey for beginners, though. If you're interested in purchasing Autotune, visit `www.antarestech.com`.

FL Studio has a pitch correction plugin called **NewTone** that comes with the FL Studio *Signature Edition*. If you are new to processing vocals and don't have access to Autotune or Melodyne, NewTone is a beginner-friendly option to give you an introduction. It offers the ability to adjust pitch in a timeline graphical mode, as well as allowing you to convert audio to **MIDI** notes.

Let's pitch correct with NewTone. Add a vocal sample to the **Playlist** and route it to a new **Mixer** channel. Left-click on the top left corner of the audio sample and select the option **Pitch-correct sample**. This will import the audio into **NewTone**.

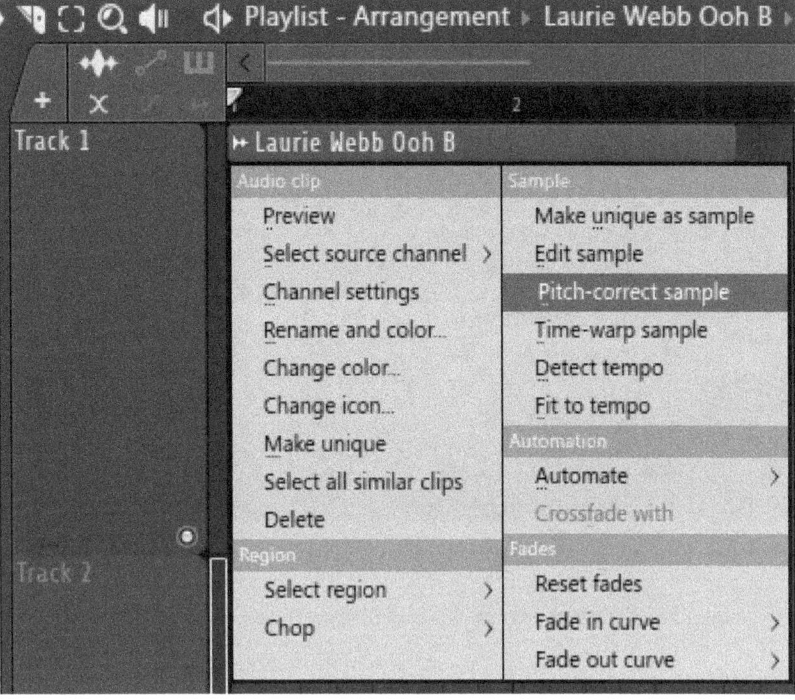

Figure 8.17 – Importing audio into NewTone

The method described in the preceding screenshot is what I find to be the easiest method of getting audio into **NewTone**. Alternatively, you can load a sample in NewTone directly by opening **NewTone** as an effect in the **Mixer** by clicking **File** | **Load Sample** and finding your audio sample.

Once the sample is loaded into **NewTone**, it automatically divides the audio into note pitches. You can click on any of the notes and change the pitch by dragging the note up or down. If you click on the left or right edge of a note, you can shorten or lengthen the note. You can also delete a note by left-clicking on it and pressing *Delete* on your keyboard.

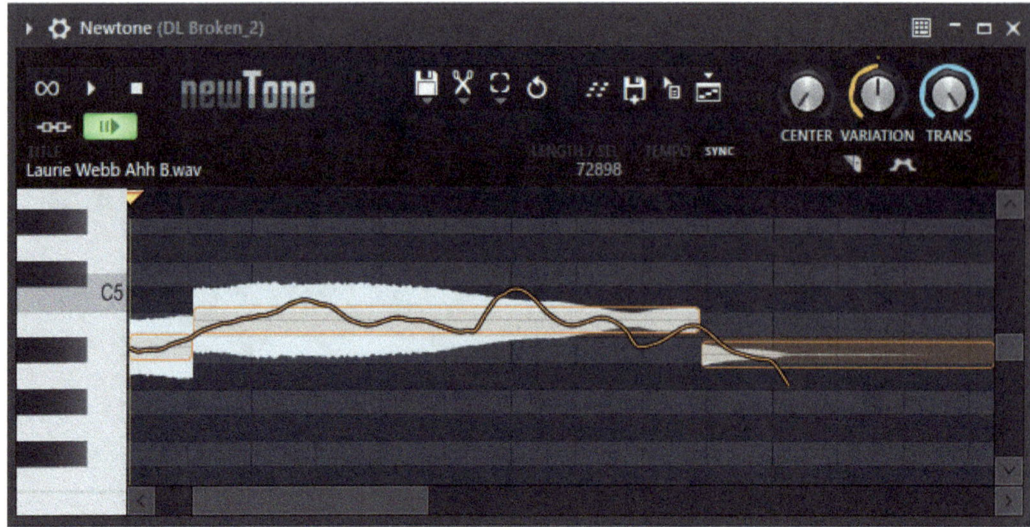

Figure 8.18 – Audio divided into note pitches in NewTone

The following screenshot shows the control panel of NewTone:

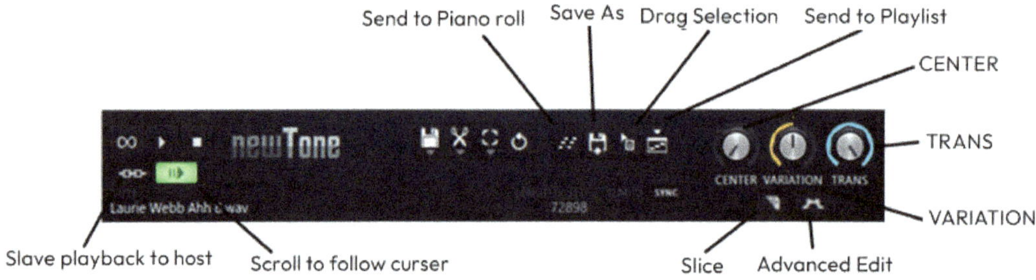

Figure 8.19 – NewTone controls

Let's take a look at the controls in the top-right corner of NewTone from left to right:

- **Send to Piano roll** identifies the note pitches used in the audio and creates MIDI notes in the **Piano roll**.
  To use this feature, select an instrument in the **Channel rack** that you want to send notes to. Press **Send to Piano roll**. MIDI notes will appear for the instrument you selected in the **Channel rack** and **Piano roll**. You can then go into the **Piano roll** and edit the notes.
- **Save As** saves the file.
- **Drag Selection** allows you to drag audio after editing in **NewTone** to a new location, such as a **Mixer** channel.

- **Send to Playlist** sends the audio to the **Playlist**.
- **CENTER** adjusts note pitches in the audio to force fixed pitch intervals. This control affects the entire audio sample.
- **VARIATION** increases or decreases the amplitude of the waveform to control how drastic pitch jumps are. If **VARIATION** is turned all the way down, it sounds robotic. This control affects the entire audio sample.
- **TRANS** (transition) controls the speed of moving between notes. This control affects the entire audio sample.
- **Slice** allows you to chop notes into smaller pieces.
- **Advanced Edit** allows access to an additional set of pitch control options. When **Advanced Edit** is enabled, you can click on a note, and you'll be able to edit the volume and pitch variation.
- **Slave playback to host** syncs **NewTone** with the Playlist timing. When you play your playlist, **NewTone** will play at the corresponding time.
- **Scroll to follow curser**, when selected, moves along the **NewTone** timeline as the audio plays.

Pitch correction best practices

Let's learn some pitch correction best practices that will apply to any pitch correction tool.

- If you have fast retune speeds in your pitch correction plugin, you will hear stronger pitch correction and a more robotic vocal sound. This may be a desired effect and is used intentionally in a lot of trap music. If you want more natural-sounding vocals, you'll want to reduce the retune speeds. A lower speed will have a more natural, relaxed sound, letting the vibrato of the vocal through.
- Pitch correction won't turn a bad voice into a good voice. Pitch correction is best used to assist vocals that are already near the correct pitch. If your vocal is significantly out of pitch, pitch correction likely won't make the vocal sound great. Great singers combined with Autotune can sound amazing. Bad singers using Autotune still sound bad. If your vocals don't sound good before going into pitch correction, you should get some better vocals.
- Never tune a double, harmony, or stacked vocal in isolation. Instead, tune them as a unit. Align their micro-pitch movements and vibrato speeds so they feel glued but still breathe. When tuning harmonies, don't make them identical to the lead; rather, use a slight detuning (2–5 percent difference) to create that lush, wide blend.
- On many pitch correction plugins, you may come across the term **formant**. In audio pitch correction, formants are the resonant frequencies of the vocal tract that define a

voice's tone and vowel character (the *color* of the sound). Tools like Auto-Tune or Melodyne include formant preservation to keep these resonances constant while adjusting pitch, maintaining a natural sound. Disabling formant correction, on the other hand, is often used intentionally for creative or stylistic vocal effects.

This probably sounds confusing. Let's look at an example. With a human vocal, the shape of the throat, chest, and nasal cavity all contribute to the individual's voice tone to give it a distinctive character. It's tricky to adjust the shape of your body, but with a formant plugin, you can achieve what it would sound like if your body were a different shape. This can be used to make your vocals appear higher, like a chipmunk, or much deeper. Many electronic dance music artists use an extensive amount of formant effects on their vocals to achieve their signature sound. An FL Studio plugin that uses formants is Pitcher. We will cover Pitcher in *Chapter 9*.

- Always experiment with the before and after of your tuned vocal against the untouched take. You'll be surprised how often the raw version has more life – and when it doesn't, you'll know exactly why your tuning improved it.
- Timing and phrasing come before pitch. Many producers make the mistake of tuning first, then realizing the rhythm feels off. Fix timing and breath placement before pitch correction, because re-timing after tuning can warp your edits. This leads us into our next topic: retiming.

Next, let's learn to improve the timing of our audio recordings.

Retiming samples with NewTime

When recording live audio or importing samples, sooner or later, you'll find that audio clip timings don't match up with the rest of your song. Audio mistiming can be corrected using the FL Studio plugin **NewTime**.

NewTime allows you to map out the key moments in your audio sample and adjust the timing to better fit your song. Let's retime audio samples using NewTime:

1. You'll first need an audio sample clip to retime. Load up an audio clip sample in the **Playlist**. Any audio sample will do. In my example, we'll use a drum sample that comes with FL Studio, but you can use any sample that you like. If this is your first time, I recommend finding a drum loop sample, as this is the easiest way to see clear retiming results. The following screenshot shows where you can get a drum sample that comes with FL Studio:

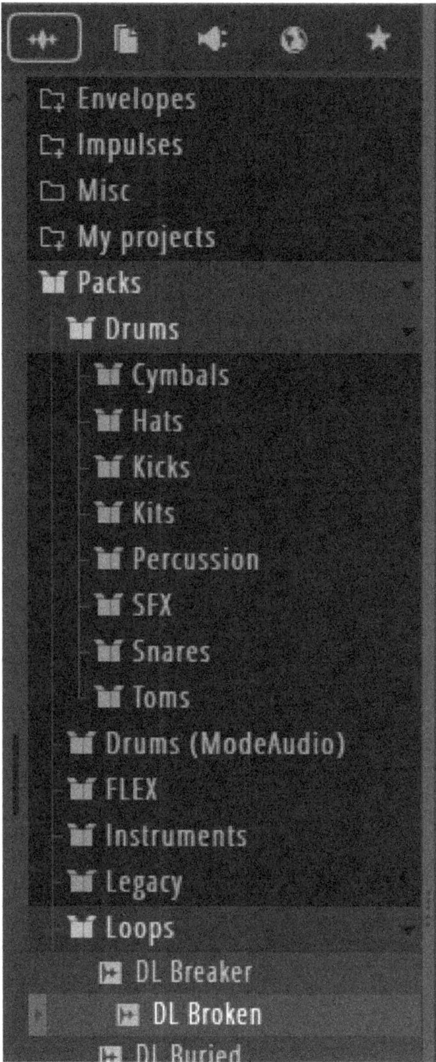

Figure 8.20 – Drum sample

2. In the **Playlist**, left-click on the top left corner of the sample to see the options and choose the **Time-warp sample** option. To clarify, you're clicking on the very left of the sample name. This will bring up the options dropdown menu.

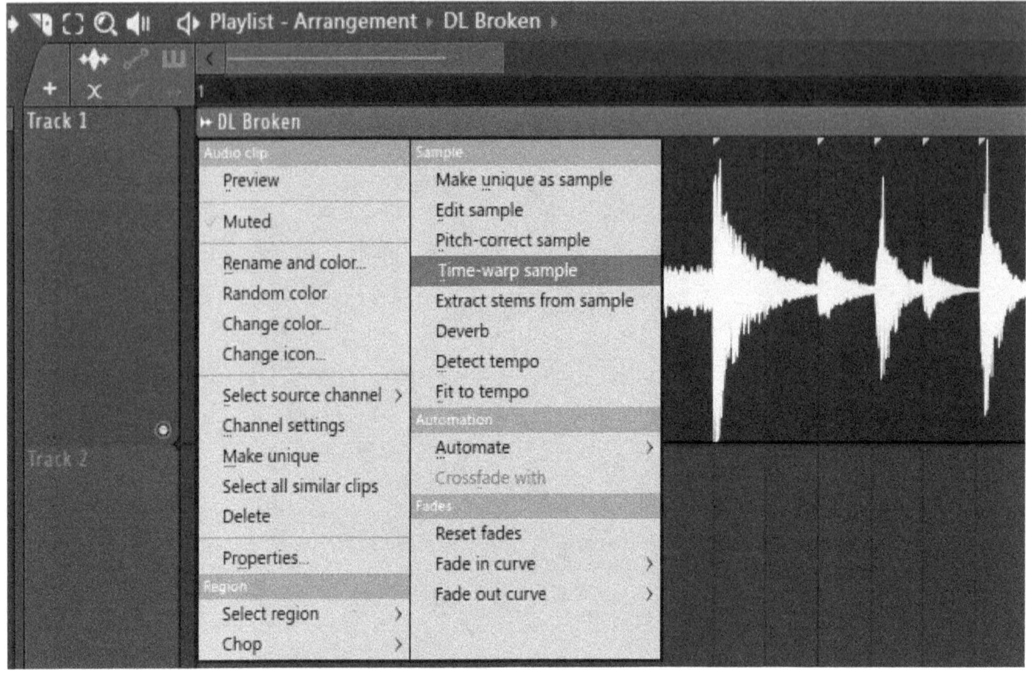

Figure 8.21 – Time-warp sample option

This will load the sample in NewTime. You'll see NewTime load the audio clip, similar to the following screenshot:

Figure 8.22 – Loaded sample in NewTime

NewTime splits audio into sections based on transients. It assigns markers (called **warp markers**) that you can move around to retime the audio.

The interface is very similar to FL Studio's NewTone plugin, with many of the same controls.

3. Enable the **slave playback to host** button to sync the NewTime audio playback with your playlist. Once enabled, any time you play the playlist, NewTime will play the audio in sync. You'll likely want to keep playing the song in the **Playlist** from now on when editing the sample in NewTime. This way, you'll be able to hear the changes as you edit the sample in real time.

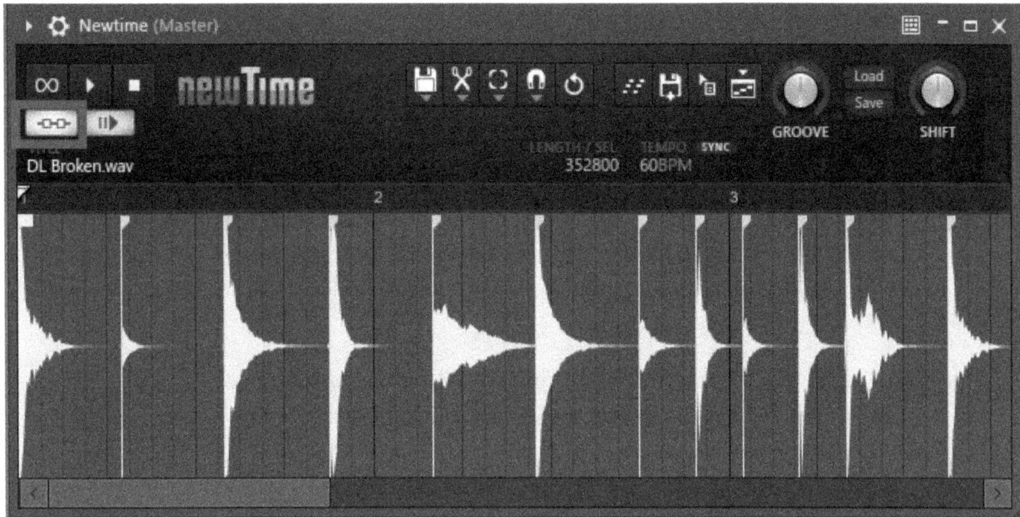

Figure 8.23 – Slave playback to host in NewTime

NewTime can attempt to match the sample timing to the tempo in the **Playlist**.

4. Select **Tempo Sync**. NewTime will attempt to fit the sample to match the project tempo. The following screenshot shows the selection of the **Tempo Sync** button:

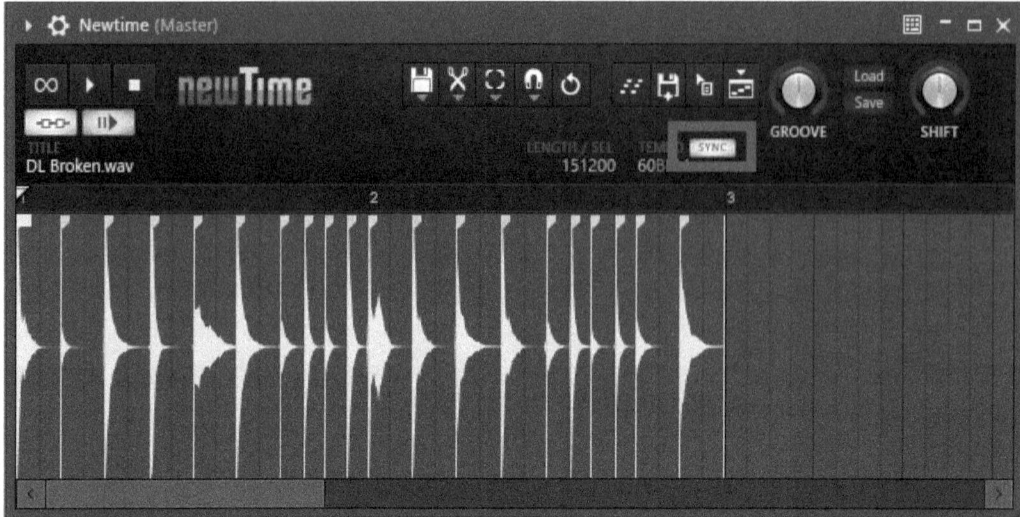

Figure 8.24 – Select Tempo Sync button

The more rhythmic your audio sample, the more likely NewTime will correctly retime the audio sample. The less rhythmic, the more likely you'll have to manually retime the audio.

The markers (warp markers) can be dragged left or right to retime the audio. This is how you can retime your audio manually. Simply move the markers around until you feel that the sound matches the rest of your song.

Tip

By default, the first marker will be highlighted in green to indicate that it is the downbeat marker. The downbeat marker helps with beat detection. If your melody doesn't start on the first beat of the bar, you can reassign the downbeat marker by right-clicking on a marker, which will reassign the downbeat marker.

If you hold *Alt* while dragging a marker, it will temporarily disable snapping to the grid.

You can double-click anywhere in the grid to add more warp markers.

After left-clicking once in the waveform, you can hold down *Shift* while hovering over the audio wave to display a line that helps with fine-tuning placement.

You can select multiple marker clips at once by holding *Ctrl*. Then you can drag them all at once.

5. NewTime comes with built-in **groove** presets available to manipulate your samples. Grooves are another way of saying adjusting the timing of the sample by a preset. Select the **Load** button as shown in the following screenshot to load a groove pattern:

Figure 8.25 – Load groove pattern

Once you've chosen a groove, several of the markers will be selected in yellow.

6. Adjust the **GROOVE** knob to determine how much groove effect you want applied to the sample. An example is shown in the following screenshot:

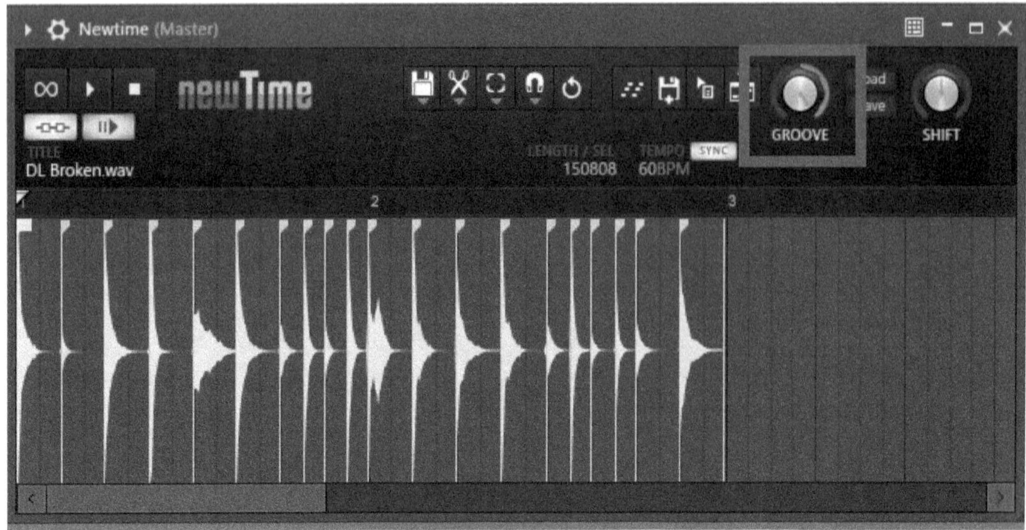

Figure 8.26 – Adjust GROOVE knob

I encourage you to experiment, trying out different grooves and seeing how they sound with the rest of your song.

7. You've finished tweaking the timing of your audio sample. Now it's time to export it out of NewTime and back into the rest of your song. There are multiple options for exporting from NewTime, as shown by the four buttons on the left of the following screenshot:

Figure 8.27 – Export audio sample from NewTime

- **Send to Piano roll** sends the MIDI timing of the NewTime markers to the **Piano roll**. This is useful if all you care about is the timing but not the audio itself. This might be useful if you want the groove to be played by an instrument.
- **Save as** allows you to save the audio as a file.

- **Drag selection** allows you to drag the NewTime audio into any other plugin that requires an audio sample.
- **Send to Playlist** sends the audio into the **Playlist**. This is usually the option that you'll want to use.

You now know how to retime your audio samples.

Vocal effects processing best practices

Let's discuss some best practices for processing your vocals.

It's best to record dry vocals without any effects. You can always add in and swap out effects later. If you need to hear how an effect will sound for reference while recording (such as when using Autotune or Vocoder), record the dry vocals at the same time as the *effected* vocals on two separate channels so you end up with access to the dry vocals in addition to any *effected* vocals.

When applying effects to vocals, there's an order that's usually followed. It's a suggestion, not a mandatory rule, but you may find it helpful. If you find any of the following terminology confusing regarding compression or EQ, revisit *Chapter 6*.

Here's a suggested order for applying effects to vocals in the **Mixer**:

1. Pitch correction corrects pitch and adjusts mistiming.
2. Gate or expander effects remove background and unwanted noises. For example, **Fruity Limiter** can be used as a gate.
3. A compressor balances out the dynamic range of the vocal and reduces the difference between the loud and quiet parts of the vocal. The amount of compression used is down to personal taste and depends on the genre of music you are making. You may also consider using parallel compression if you want to preserve vocal transients.
4. A **de-esser** plugin removes sibilance, makes surgical resonant cuts, and tames and controls harsh frequencies. **De-essing** is done using a multiband compressor. It compresses common problem-frequency areas. On the FL Studio **Maximus** plugin, there is a preset for de-essing that can help you get started.
5. Vocal effects. Examples of special vocal effects are harmony creation, vocoders, and saturation effects, to name a few. We discuss vocoders in *Chapter 9*.
6. EQ cuts out unwanted frequencies and boosts desired ones. You can add an **EQ high-pass filter** to remove the sub-bass frequencies that are not the focus of the vocal. This high-pass filter is usually placed around 80 Hz to 120 Hz. FL Studio's **EQ2** has a vocal preset that can get you started.

   You may want to make an EQ boost somewhere around 12 kHz to 16 kHz. If there are unwanted resonances in your vocals, you may want to cut somewhere in the low-mid to high-mid frequencies to remove them. Where and how large the cut or boost is will depend on the vocal you are working with.

The following screenshot shows an example of how your EQ curve may look when applied to vocals:

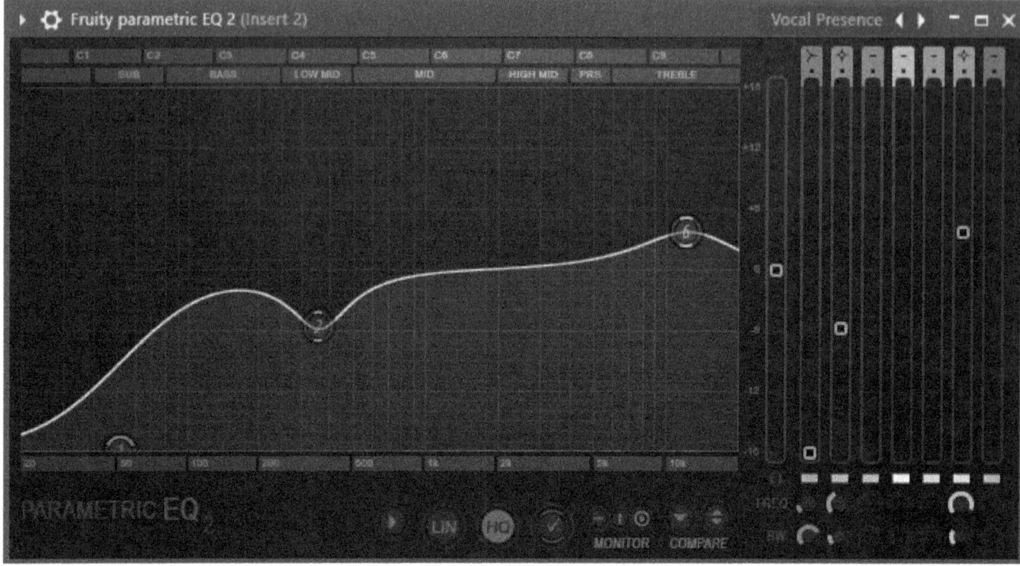

Figure 8.28 – EQ curve on vocals

In the preceding screenshot, you can see we've rolled off the low-end frequencies, created an EQ cut around 350 Hz, and a boost around 12 kHz. This is not a fixed rule to blindly apply, though. Your vocal EQ curve will look a little different in every situation.

7. **Delay**, if desired, adds additional stereo width. Pan out your delay to achieve side delays so that they don't conflict with the lead vocal frequencies in the center.
8. Reverb makes the vocal sound as though it were in a realistic environment. Some mixing engineers like to have minimal pitch correction on the original dry vocal and another hard pitch-corrected version with the speed set to full to use on the vocal reverb.

Next, let's learn best practices for vocal effects.

Backing vocals effects best practices

Backing vocals are mixed the same as lead vocals, with a few subtle differences:

- With the backing vocals, you don't need to hear as much breathiness as the lead vocal because it may distract from the focus.
- Backing vocals, if desired, can be subtly panned out left and right, whereas the lead vocal you want to leave directly mono in the center.
- Have more relaxed pitch correction on the backing vocals than the lead vocals. Harder pitch-corrected vocals are generally more noticeable, and you don't want your backing vocals to take focus away from the lead.

Once you've set up your effect plugins in your **Mixer**, you can save the project as a template to save time and reuse it. Create a template by saving the project under `C:\Program Files (x86)\Image-Line\Data\Templates`. Then, in the future, you can reopen the template by going to **File** | New from your template and selecting your project. Your exact folder location may differ depending on your computer.

We've covered best practices for vocal processing. Congratulations, you now know how to mix vocals.

Summary

In this chapter, we learned about recording audio so you can record your instruments and vocals. We learned about microphones and how to prepare for recording. We learned how to record in FL Studio. We learned how to denoise your audio to remove background noise or a vocal using AI in Edison, and how to remove the reverb from a sound using AI. We learned about pitch correction and how to pitch correct using NewTone. We learned how to retime audio samples using NewTime. Finally, we learned a series of tips and best practices for mixing your vocals.

In the next chapter, we will learn about special effects that you can create with your vocals using **vocoders** and **vocal chopping**. This will allow you to turn your vocals into an instrument and create cutting-edge effects used by popular musicians.

Get this book's PDF version and more

Scan the QR code (or go to `packtpub.com/unlock`). Search for this book by name, confirm the edition, and then follow the steps on the page.

UNLOCK NOW

Note: Keep your invoice handy. Purchases made directly from Packt don't require an invoice.

9

Understanding Vocal Effects

This chapter explores creative vocal effects using **vocoders** and techniques for making **vocal chops**. You'll learn what vocoders are and how they blend voice with synthesizers to create robotic, textured sounds. Understanding MIDI fundamentals will help you control vocoders precisely. You'll also learn to use FL Studio's powerful **Vocodex** plugin for advanced **vocoding** effects. Finally, you'll discover how to create catchy, rhythmic vocal chops that add energy and interest to your productions.

In this chapter, we'll cover the following topics:

- Understanding vocoders
- Using vocoders
- Using Vocodex
- Creating vocal chops

Understanding vocoders

What are vocoders? If you've heard a voice that has been transformed to sound like a robot, then you've probably heard a vocoder. They sound awesome and are my favorite weapon to wield when making music. Vocoding is used extensively in electronic dance music, especially in the house, electro, and dubstep genres. If you're unsure about what a vocoder effect sounds like, consider checking out the following songs:

- *Daft Punk – Harder, Better, Faster, Stronger*
- *Don Diablo – You're Not Alone ft. Kiiara*

Vocoders create effects that modulate an existing sound. The input sound (usually a vocal) is split into frequency bands and analyzed for its frequency level and content. We call this first input sound the **modulator**. The vocoder breaks this information down into a series of **band-pass filters** to be used later. In other words, the vocoder figures out what frequencies were used in the vocal.

A second sound (usually an instrument) is fed into the vocoder. We call this the **carrier**. We use this as the sound that we're going to modify. We use the modulator filter to filter the incoming carrier audio. In other words, we allow the instrument sound to play frequencies that line up with our vocal frequencies.

If you find this confusing, you can think of your own voice as a vocoder. Your throat and mouth shape act as a vocoder, modulating the sound in the air as it leaves your body. As you adjust the shape of your mouth, the sound changes.

There are several vocoder plugin effects on the market. If you like the ones that are demonstrated in this chapter and want to buy more vocoders, I recommend the following:

- The best one I've found is iZotope's **VocalSynth plugin**, available at `www.izotope.com`.
- **RAZOR** is another excellent vocoder plugin by Native Instruments, available at `www.native-instruments.com`.

In order to use vocoders, we need to first know how to use the **Musical Instrument Digital Interface** (**MIDI**).

Understanding MIDI

MIDI is a way for software and electronic devices to pass music information from one device to another so that the new device knows what notes to play. In *Chapter 3*, we discussed how to record MIDI information to the Piano roll. Once entered, notes in the Piano roll act as MIDI information that can be passed between instrument plugins.

Passing MIDI information between plugins is useful in a few scenarios:

- Passing MIDI information is how you can communicate with hardware instrument devices. Hardware instruments use MIDI to give and receive information to and from your computer. If you want to play notes directly from FL Studio to or from your hardware device, you use MIDI. FL Studio has documentation and video tutorials to help connect your hardware MIDI devices at `http://support.image-line.com/redirect/MIDI_Out`.

- MIDI notes defined in one place can be sent to one or more instrument plugins at once. For example, **Channel rack** layers allow you to use the same MIDI notes for multiple instruments.
- Some plugins require external MIDI input to work. Vocoders usually require the use of MIDI to operate. We will explore this feature extensively in this chapter.

Using vocoders

In this section, we will prepare MIDI for use in plugins. Then we'll route the MIDI notes into additional instruments and effects, such as vocoder effects. Although we specifically discuss vocoders in this chapter, any plugin that uses MIDI as an input will follow the same steps.

In our examples, we assume that you are using a vocal audio sample to feed into the vocoder. You do have the option of using any sound at all instead of a vocal, such as a guitar, and this can be used to create interesting effects.

Harmonizing vocals with Pitcher

To illustrate vocoding, we will use a built-in FL Studio plugin called **Pitcher**, which comes with FL Studio *Signature Edition* and higher. Although it's not advertised as a vocoder, it has vocoder features and most closely resembles how you use other vocoder plugins on the market. Let's learn how to use Pitcher:

1. Load up a vocal sample in the **Playlist**. Either use an existing vocal sample or record a new audio vocal. We covered recording audio in *Chapter 8*. This vocal will be the source that we will modulate in the vocoder.
2. Route the vocal to a free mixer track.
3. Let's create **chords** so that we have some MIDI notes. Load an instrument, such as **FL Keys**, in the **Channel rack** and create some chords in the **Piano roll** for the instrument.
4. Route the instrument to a free Mixer channel.

   The following screenshot shows an example of the chords you could create in the Piano roll:

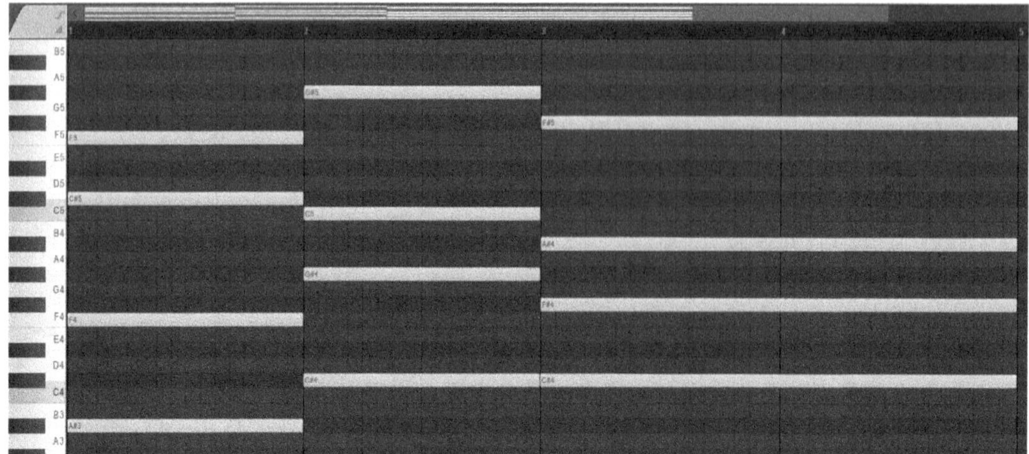

Figure 9.1 – Piano roll chords

The notes used in the chords should be in the same key as the rest of your song. When you play the notes, they should complement any other instruments playing. If the chords don't fit the rest of the song, your vocoding will not sound good when finished.

The chords must complement the song. The vocal, however, can be in any key (even one from a different scale). It doesn't matter what note pitches the vocal uses, as they will be changed by the vocoder. To re-emphasize, the only notes that matter are the notes that the vocoder plays, not the notes used by the vocals.

5. Add the vocal and the Piano roll notes to your **Playlist** so that they are in time with each other. Your **Playlist** will now look something like the following screenshot:

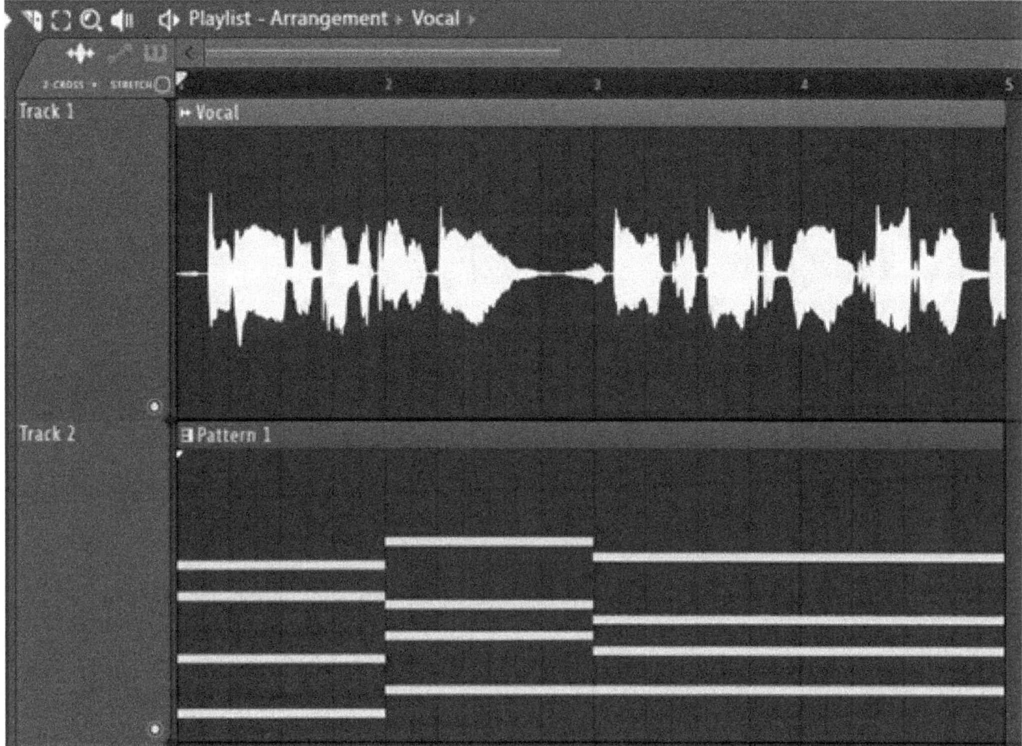

Figure 9.2 – Vocal and chords

In the preceding screenshot, we can see a vocal running in time with the chords that we just created.

In the previous chapters of this book, we thought of the Piano roll notes as belonging to the instrument playing them. It turns out that we can take these notes and send them anywhere, such as to plugin effects. We can do so with the **MIDI Out** plugin.

6. In the **Channel rack**, load the **MIDI Out** plugin, as seen in the following screenshot:

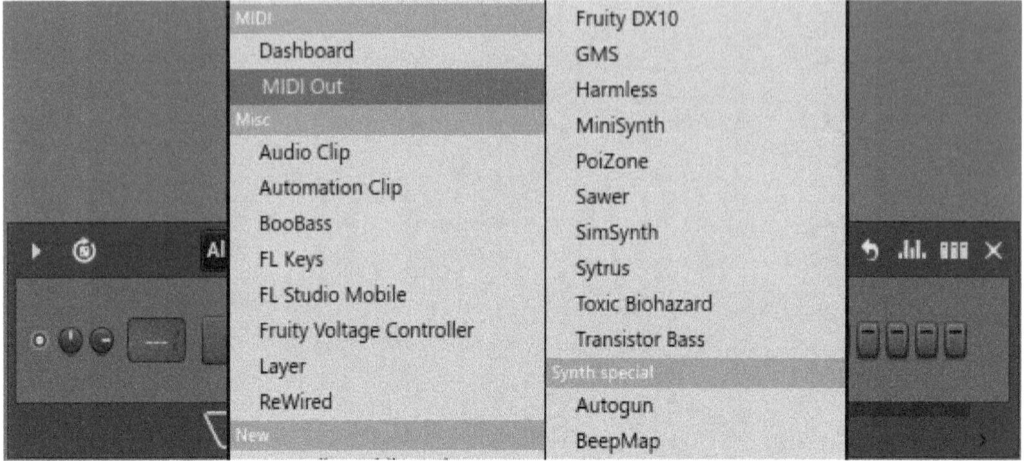

Figure 9.3 – Load the MIDI Out plugin into the Channel rack

7. Copy the chord notes from your **FL Keys** to **MIDI Out**. You can do so by selecting (left-clicking) the instrument that you want to copy in the **Channel rack**. In the following screenshot, the **FL Keys** instrument has a clickable box highlighted beside its name to indicate it's selected. Then press *Ctrl+C* to copy.

Figure 9.4 – Copy notes from the instrument

Next, select the **MIDI Out** instrument where you want to paste the notes. In the following screenshot, we have selected the **MIDI Out** instrument. Left-click the box beside the name **MIDI Out** and press *Ctrl + V* to paste the notes.

Figure 9.5 – Paste notes to MIDI Out

8. The **MIDI Out** instrument should now have the copied notes, the same as your **FL Keys** instrument. You will see the following plugin if you left-click on **MIDI Out**:

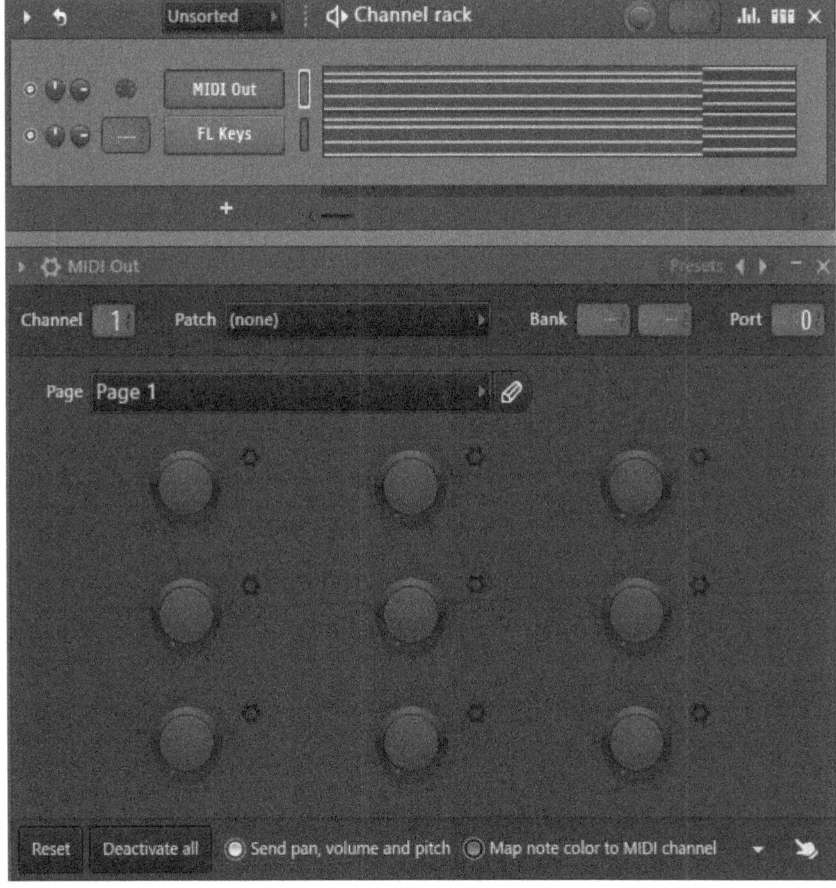

Figure 9.6 – MIDI Out

> **Note**
>
> MIDI Out does not make any sound when you play it, as it is not an instrument. Rather, it's a controller that sends notes to other plugins.

9. At the top right of **MIDI Out**, you can see a **Port** value. Change this **Port** to a value other than 0. Any MIDI notes played in **MIDI Out** will become available to any instrument or effect that receives from that port value.

Figure 9.7 – Assigning a port value

In the preceding screenshot, you can see I've chosen a **Port** value of **1**. Remember the port value that you've chosen; you will need it in a moment.

10. In the **Mixer**, load up your choice of vocoder instrument effect into an empty Mixer channel and name it `Vocoder`. I am going to use FL Studio's **Pitcher**, as shown in the following screenshot:

Figure 9.8 – Loading Vocoder

11. Route the signal from the **Vocal** channel to the **Vocoder** channel. Do this by first selecting the **Vocal** channel, then right-clicking on the **Vocoder** Mixer channel arrow and choosing the **Route to this track only** option, as shown in the following screenshot:

Figure 9.9 – Routing the Vocal to the Vocoder

Our **Vocal** has been routed to the **Vocoder** channel and is accessible to the Pitcher plugin. Now we need to notify our vocoder plugin about the MIDI notes that are available to be used.

> **Note**
>
> In this example, the instrument is not routed to Pitcher, only the vocals. This is very important.

12. Open up the **Pitcher** plugin.

Figure 9.10 – Pitcher plugin

13. Left-click to press down each of the **MIDI**, **OCTAVES**, and **HARMONIZE** buttons, as shown in the preceding screenshot.
14. At the bottom of **Pitcher**, the text **MIDI Input Port Number:** ... will appear. Left-click on **...** and drag to change the value to the MIDI Out **Port** value you chose earlier. In my case, the value is **1**. It could be something different depending on how you routed it.
15. Play your Playlist and be blown away by how **Pitcher** harmonizes your vocals.

Whoa, that sounds cool! What just happened to my vocals? Pitcher is a pitch-correction plugin. When it comes to generating harmonized vocals to MIDI, it's spectacular. It allows you to generate up to four voices controlled by the MIDI note melodies.

Pitcher uses the MIDI notes as filters. It generates copies of the vocals that are fed into it and filters them to hit only the MIDI note pitches.

Let's take a closer look at some of the Pitcher harmonizing controls, as shown in the following screenshot from left to right:

Figure 9.11 – Pitcher harmonizing controls

- **VOICE PANNING** allows you to pan the vocals left or right, from the highest-pitched MIDI note to the lowest. Panning the vocals will increase the stereo width and make the harmonies appear larger.
- The **REPLACE MIX** switch allows you to hear the original vocals or just play the harmonized vocals.
- **VEL** (velocity) controls the harmonized vocal velocity. You must turn off **OCTAVES** for this feature to work.
- **STEREO SPREAD** allows you to increase the overall mono or stereo effect.
- **GENDER** allows you to control the formant effect. Turning left will make the vocal deeper, turning right will make the vocal sound higher. **FORMANT** turns the gender control on or off. If you see a bright orange light on the **FORMANT** button, then this means it's on.
- **FINE TUNE** adjusts the output tuning of the plugin.

So far, we've looked at how you can generate harmonies for your vocals using vocoding. We've had an introduction to vocoding. Now let's really get our hands dirty with another vocoder. Next, we'll explore the FL Studio plugin Vocodex.

Using Vocodex

Vocodex is a traditional vocoder and allows you to modulate a vocal. It comes with FL Studio *Producer Edition* and higher. It is used a little differently than most vocoder plugins, though, as it doesn't require MIDI Out to operate. Instead, you can directly use an instrument sound in the **Mixer**.

Let's begin using Vocodex:

1. To start, you will need to already have a vocal and an instrument playing chords, with MIDI notes routed to the **Mixer**. Specifically, you need to have your MIDI notes in the **MIDI Out** instrument and the **MIDI Out** instrument routed to the **Mixer**. We already did this in *steps 1–6* in the preceding section on *Harmonizing vocals with Pitcher*; go through those steps first if you haven't already.

   In the **Vocoder** Mixer channel that we created earlier, mute any other effects and add the **Vocodex** plugin, as shown in the following screenshot:

Figure 9.12 – Adding Vocodex

2. Select the **FL Keys** Mixer channel and the **Vocal** Mixer channel and route them to the **Vocoder** channel by right-clicking on the **Vocoder** Mixer channel arrow and selecting the **Route to this track only** option, as shown in the following screenshot:

Figure 9.13 – Routing the instrument and vocal to the Vocoder

3. Open **Vocodex**. At the top, you'll see the modulator sidechain input port numbers next to the text **L-R ENCODING**. These are waiting to receive the modulator (instrument sound) and the carrier (vocal sound).

   L-R ENCODING refers to the left and right channels in your **Mixer**. Right-click on one of the sidechain input number boxes and you'll see your available options. Choose the **Vocal for the Modulator sidechain** input number box and the **instrument for the Carrier sidechain** input number box:

Figure 9.14 – Setting up ports in Vocodex

When you play your sound, you'll hear your vocals harmonized using the MIDI notes, with vocoding effects applied to them. There are lots of controls that you can use to tweak the vocoder sound.

The following is the summary of the controls starting from the top:

1. **WET** controls the amount of vocoding that is applied. **SG** (**Sound Goodizer**) applies compression as used in the Sound Goodizer plugin. **MOD** (**Modulation**) controls how much of the original vocal (modulator signal) is mixed into the output; increasing its level will allow more of the dry vocal through.

   Modulator High Pass Filter sets the cutoff frequency for the vocal input. Frequencies below this point are removed, so only higher-frequency content drives the vocoder.
2. **CAR** (Carrier) pass-through low-pass frequency (**low-pass filter**) sets the low-pass filter threshold cutoff. Only sounds lower than the threshold of the carrier are used.
3. **Carrier added noise high pass frequency** (**HP**) allows noise to pass through. A little noise can help make speech easier to understand.
4. **Contour** turns the volume envelope on the modulator and carrier on or off. **DRAFT** lowers CPU usage but may result in lower quality. **THREADED** allows multi-core processing.
5. Under the **Options** (down arrow) in the top right of Vocodex, you'll see the **Detect modulator noise level**, which generates a noise mapping from the source to try to identify the background noise. Use this on a quiet section of your audio, then you can select the subtractive denoising option to denoise the background noise.
6. Back on the left side, you'll see the **HOLD**, **ATT**, and **REL** time controls, which adjust the sound envelope. **HOLD** allows the note to play for a longer length of time. The attack determines how quickly the carrier responds to the modulator. Increasing the value will create a smoother sound. The release determines how long the vocoder effect will last. **PEAK** and **RMS** determine whether you want the envelope to respond to the audio peaks or the RMS level (more of an average sound).
7. The **bandwidth** control determines how wide the frequency bands are. Smaller values create a thinner sound. Larger values create a fuller sound. The **modulator bandwidth multiplier** adds more resonance at a low level and airy sounds at higher levels.
8. The **modulator pitch shift** increases the **FORMANT** value. The **modulator unison shift** allows you to add layers of voices. Drag on the **Modulator unison order** box to increase the number of voices.
9. The **unison panner** allows you to pan the unison voices. **ORDER** allows you to choose how much you want the vocoder to sound like a synth or a human vocal.

10. **Bands - Distribution** sets the number of bands to be used. Lowering the band distribution will make the vocoder sound more synthetic. A higher value will make it sound more like a human.
11. **Band gain multiplier** allows you to set the volume for selected frequencies.

Below **Envelope Follower**, you can see the text **Band gain multiplier**. This is a dropdown option that is preselected. It is only one of several options, though.

Figure 9.15 – Vocodex Editor target dropdown options (Band gain multiplier)

Here is a brief description of the options in the dropdown:

- **Band gain multiplier** allows you to choose the volume for selected frequencies.
- **Band panning** allows you to pan the sound for selected frequencies.
- The **band gain offset** allows you to choose how much of the carrier sound you want to hear for selected frequencies. Increasing it will allow you to hear more of the carrier sound.
- The **modulator noise level** determines the minimum threshold level that needs to be reached before you can hear the sound. By default, it's set to 0.
- **Modulator-pass through** determines how much of the modulator you can hear.
- **Envelope Follower** contains envelope controls for setting the hold, attack, and release.
- **Band distribution** allows you to choose how many bands are used for selected frequencies.
- **Bandwidth** allows you to determine the size of the bands around selected frequencies.
- **Modulator pitch shift** allows you to adjust the pitch of selected frequencies.
- **Saturation mix** allows you to add distortion.
- **Carrier Tone** provides you with several filter sounds that can be used to shape the carrier sound.

Vocoder best practices

Here are some tips that you can use with any vocoder plugin:

- Vocoders are an excellent way to design creative vocal instruments. If you want a song to stand out and be instantly recognizable, using a vocoder effect is a way to do so.
- Vocoder vocals tend to take center focus of the listener's attention. If you're using vocals, plan for them to be the lead melody or layered with the lead melody.
- When subtly layered and played at the same time with a regular vocal, vocoder sounds can add thickness to the lead vocal. You can also layer vocoded instruments.

- If you find that your vocoder sound is not quite right, consider changing the instrument used as the carrier sound.
- Vocoder effects on vocals work really well when combined with **vocal chopping**, which we will discuss next.

Creating vocal chops

In this section, we'll learn how to create vocal chops. Vocal chops are chopped-up fragments of vocal samples. You hear them most often in electronic dance music, and they are often applied to vocal samples after those samples have been processed through a vocoder.

If you're unsure what vocal chops are, consider listening to some of the following songs that use vocal chops:

- *Porter Robinson & Madeon – Shelter*
- *Skrillex – First Of The Year (Equinox)*
- *Skrillex – Summit (feat. Ellie Goulding)*

In the upcoming section, we will assume that you are creating vocal chops, but the same techniques can be used to chop up any audio sample. For example, you can just as easily slice up a guitar or drum audio sample.

If your aim is simple, you could slice and dice samples on the **Playlist** just by cutting up a sample manually with the slice tool.

On any sample in the **Playlist**, you can quickly chop up the sample by left-clicking the top-left corner of a sample, navigating to **Chop**, and then choosing one of the chopping presets.

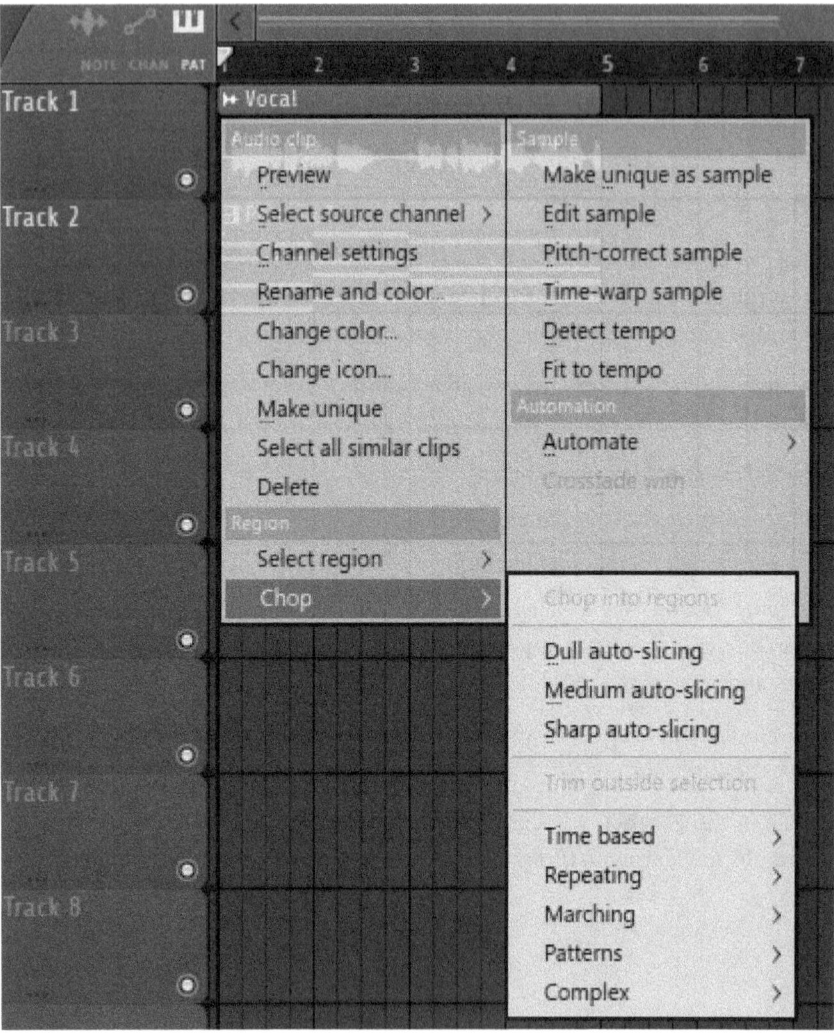

Figure 9.16 – Quickly chopping samples

You have options for **Medium auto-slicing** (good if you just need simple chopping)**, Time based**, **Repeating**, **Marching**, **Patterns**, and **Complex** vocal chopping presets. If you just need some quick glitchy sounds, this chopping approach may be all you need. They can quickly break your sample into pieces that you can rearrange as you see fit.

There are tools, such as **Fruity Slicer 2** and **Slicex**, that provide you with more precise control over chopping samples. More specifically, they give you control over how the chopping is done and the pitch of the vocal chop. We will explore Fruity Slicer 2 and Slicex next.

Using Fruity Slicer 2 to create vocal chops

Fruity Slicer 2 is an FL Studio plugin included in all FL Studio editions that is intended for **slicing** and **dicing** audio samples (breaking samples into smaller pieces). It's especially useful for creating vocal chops. You can chop up any sample, but this tool is most noticeably used for chopping up vocal samples. Vocal chops used to be a major chore and pain to create. Fruity Slicer 2 takes all the fiddly pain away and makes vocal chopping extremely easy to do. The plugin works by loading an audio sample and breaking it apart into pieces based on perceived transients. You can then manipulate each of the chopped samples individually, such as playing just a single sample chop.

Once you're happy with your vocal chops, you navigate to the **Piano roll** and play the sample chops as though they were any other instrument loaded into the **Channel rack**. A MIDI note in the Piano roll will trigger the audio chop to play. So you'll spend some time deciding where the audio chop will best fit in with the rest of your song. We will show you the full process of taking a sample to be chopped up in Fruity Slicer 2, and then later editing it in the **Piano roll**.

Let's create vocal chops with Fruity Slicer 2:

1. Create a new pattern and add it to the **Playlist**.
2. In the **Channel rack**, insert the **FRUITY SLICER 2** plugin. Make the **FRUITY SLICER 2** plugin detached by going to the top-left corner of **FRUITY SLICER 2**, clicking the plugin option down arrow button, and then choosing **detached**.
3. There are three ways to get your audio sample into **FRUITY SLICER 2**:
    a. Drag your chosen audio sample (such as a vocal) into **FRUITY SLICER 2**. One way is to drag it directly from the **Browser**. I recommend this way as it's the easiest.
    b. Another way is to load the sample directly into **FRUITY SLICER 2** by finding its location on your computer and dragging it in.
    c. A third fiddly, cumbersome way is to double-left-click on the audio sample in the **Playlist** to reveal the waveform and drag the audio from there into **FRUITY SLICER 2**, as shown in the following screenshot:

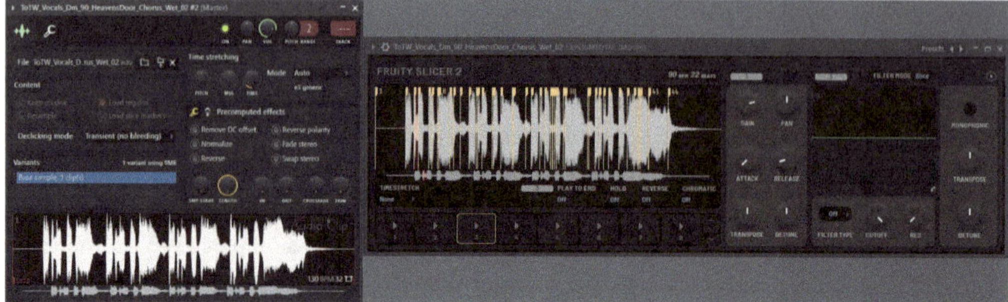

Figure 9.17 – Dragging the sample into FRUITY SLICER 2

4. Once you've dragged in your audio sample, **FRUITY SLICER 2** will attempt to automatically slice up the sample if there are obvious **transient sounds**. **FRUITY SLICER 2** will have your audio sample loaded and look something like the following:

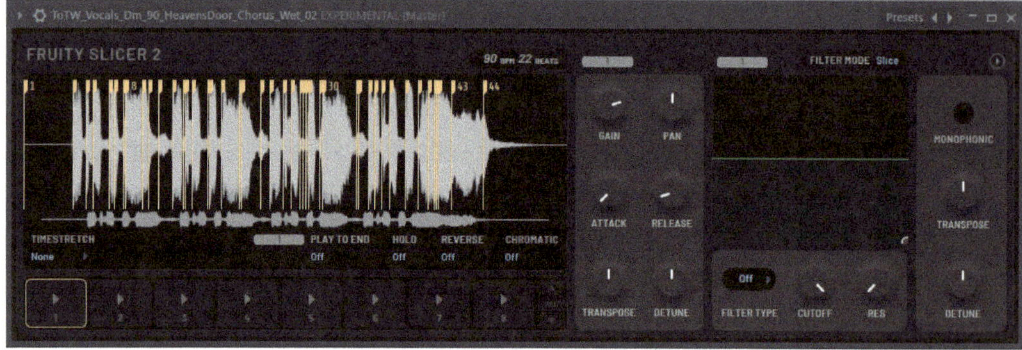

Figure 9.18 – Audio sample loaded in Fruity Slicer 2

The **FRUITY SLICER 2** interface contains two main sections. On the left, you'll see a visual of the audio sample sliced up with markers that can be rearranged to adjust their timing. Below are buttons to play each individual slice.

On the right side are controls to apply effects to the audio slices. There are controls to apply effects to individual sample slices or to globally affect all the slices at once.

Let's take a look at the left-side controls first.

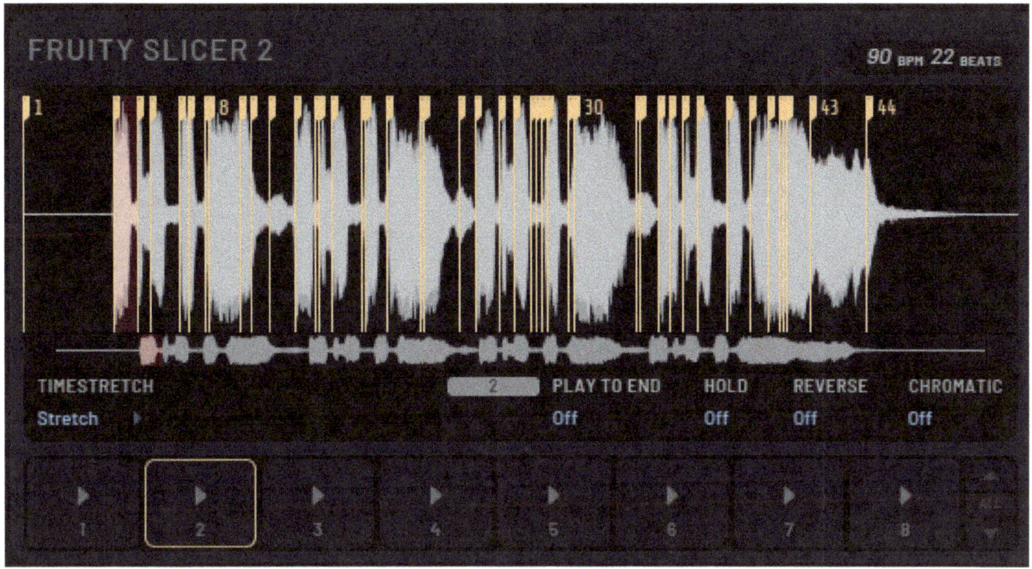

Figure 9.19 – Left-side controls on Fruity Slicer 2

In the preceding screenshot, we can see the sample has markers placed throughout the sample, numbered from 1 to 44. These are chops auto-created by analyzing the sample by transients. You can move the markers around to retime the samples if you desire. Usually, Fruity Slicer 2 does a pretty decent job straight out of the gate, so you might not need to move the markers around too much.

Below you'll find several controls:

- **TIMESTRETCH**: How slices behave when pitch is changed:
  - **None** (default): No stretching.
  - **Resample**: Pitch and duration change together.
  - **Stretch**: Preserve pitch/duration using the **Elastique algorithm**.
- **PLAY TO END**: Play from the slice start to the end of the sample (or just the slice if off). Usually, you'll want to leave this set to **Off**.
- **HOLD**: Always plays slice to the end, regardless of note release. Usually, you'll want to leave this set to **Off**.
- **REVERSE**: Plays slice backward. Fun for creative effects.
- **CHROMATIC** mode: When enabled for a Pad controller, you can play it chromatically (like a sampler) via Piano roll or MIDI controller. This is also something you usually can leave as **Off**.

Below these controls are the numbered slices. If pressed, they will play the sound of the audio sample.

Figure 9.20 – Right Side controls in Fruity Slicer 2

At the top, you'll see a **FILTER MODE** which can toggle between **Slice** and **Global**. If set to **Slice**, the controls adjusted will only target the specific audio slice selected. If set to **Global**, the controls will affect all sample slices at once. Then there are other controls:

- **GAIN** (Volume): Make it louder or quieter.
- **PAN**: Move the sound left or right.
- **ATTACK**: Make the sound fade in slowly.
- **RELEASE**: Make the sound fade out slowly.
- **TRANSPOSE/DETUNE**: Change the pitch (higher or lower).

- **FILTER TYPE**: Some minimal EQ controls.
    - **Off**: No change to the sound.
    - **LP12** (Low-pass): Removing high frequencies.
    - **HP12** (High-pass): Removing low frequencies.
    - **BP** (Band-pass): Keeping only a narrow *slice* of sound in the middle, removing both highs and lows.
- **CUTOFF**: Tells the filter where to start cutting the sound. For example, with a low-pass filter, turning the cutoff down removes the high frequencies. Turning it up lets more highs through. With a high-pass filter, turning the cutoff up removes more bass.
- **RES** (Resonance): This boosts the sound right at the cutoff point, making it stand out. Turning up the res control can make a *peaky* or *whistling* sound.

The following three controls are always global controls, so they affect all vocal slices at once.

- **MONOPHONIC**: Only one note plays at a time. By default, it's not enabled, which means it's possible to play multiple chop slices simultaneously. For example, if you have multiple chops playing at the same time in the **Piano roll**.
- **TRANSPOSE**: This control moves the pitch of your slice up or down in big steps called "**semitones**" (like moving up or down keys on a piano). For example, if you set **TRANSPOSE** to +2, your slice will sound two notes higher.
- **DETUNE**: This control makes tiny changes to the pitch, measured in "cents" (there are 100 cents in one semitone). **DETUNE** is for fine-tuning the pitch, not big jumps. It's useful if something sounds just a little bit off and you want to adjust it slightly. For example, you can use **DETUNE** to make a slice sound a bit sharper or flatter or to create a subtle difference between slices for a thicker sound.

Directly to the right of the **FILTER MODE**, you'll find a drop-down arrow. This gives you options to choose how to break up your sample slices in the **Piano roll**.

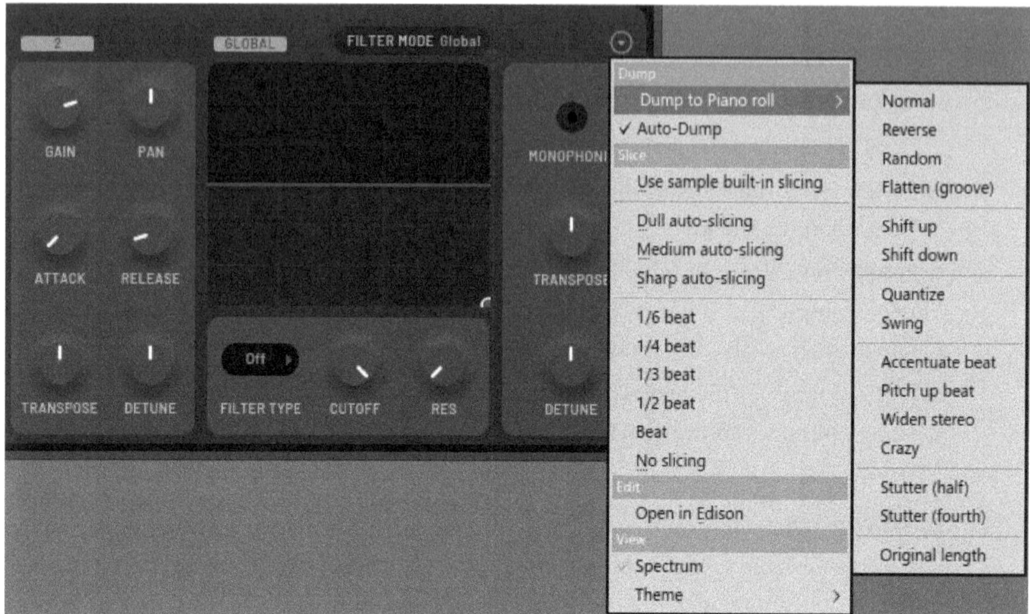

Figure 9.21 – Dump to Piano roll drop-down on Fruity Slicer 2

FRUITY SLICER 2 is an instrument in the **Channel rack** and is intended to be played like an instrument. The drop-down options in the preceding screenshot choose how to break up your slices. By default, **Medium auto-slicing** is selected, which is usually the best for chopping up a vocal sample. If you are dealing with a sustained sound, you may want to experiment with other options such as **1/6**, **1/4**, **1/3**, **1/2**, or beat slices. These options will chop up your sample into differently timed pieces.

Dump to Piano roll chooses how you want the slices to be initially arranged in the **Piano roll**. Here are some of the options available:

- **Normal**: Puts the slices in order, matching the original loop's rhythm.
- **Reverse**: Puts the slices in order, matching the original loop's rhythm, but the order of the slices is flipped (plays backward).
- **Random:** Puts the slices in random order, but the rhythm stays the same.
- **Flatten (groove)**: Keeps the rhythm, but plays the same slice for every note.
- **Shift Up / Shift Down**: Moves all slices up or down by one, keeping the groove.
- **Quantize / Swing**: Adjusts the timing to be more "on the grid" (quantize) or add a swing feel.

- **Accentuate Beat**: First slice in each beat is given a higher velocity. I usually find that this option makes the vocal chop sound best. It's my go-to selection.
- **Pitch up beat**: Gives a higher pitch to each slice belonging to an odd-numbered beat.
- **Widen stereo**: Alternates panning for each slice.
- **Crazy**: Randomly assigns pan, pitch, and velocity values for each slice.
- **Stutter (half)/Stutter (quarter)**: Breaks slices into 2 or 4 pieces for a stuttering effect.
- **Original length**: Matches loops original speed at current tempo.

Composing melodies with vocal chops

You've chopped up your audio sample using Fruity Slicer 2. Now it's time to navigate to the **Piano roll** to edit the melody and timing of the chops you've created.

1. Open up the **Piano roll** and make sure your vocal chopped (**Vocal Chops**) sound from **FRUITY SLICER 2** is selected as shown in the following screenshot:

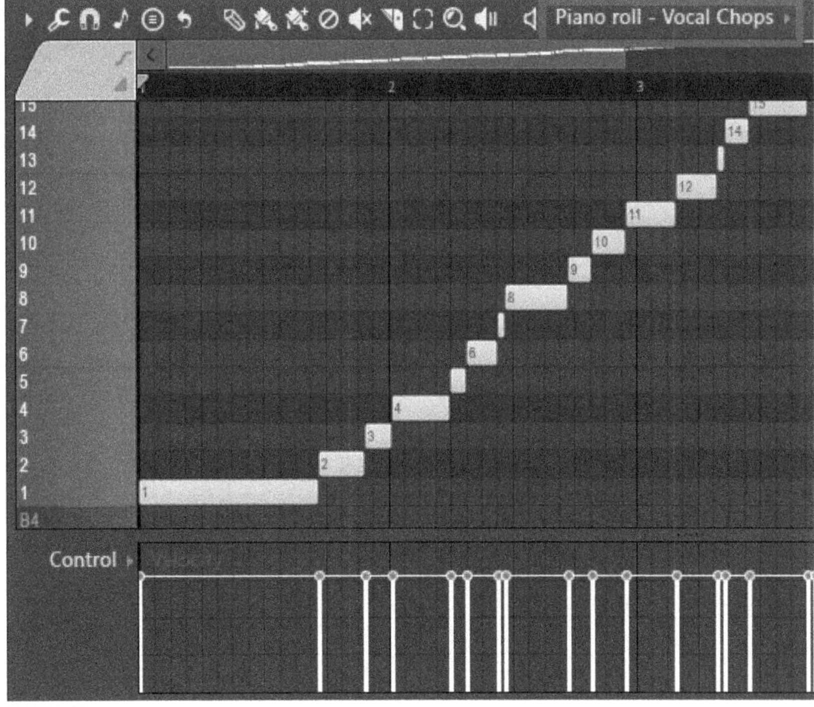

Figure 9.22 – Vocal chops in the Piano roll on Fruity Slicer 2

If you play your pattern, you'll see and hear your vocal chops being played. You can now manipulate the MIDI notes in the **Piano roll**, and you'll hear the vocal chops being triggered with each MIDI note. You'll notice on the left side the numbers ascending from **1** upwards. These correspond to the vocal chops you created in **FRUITY SLICER 2**.

2. Find the groups of slices that sound good to you and rearrange them as you see fit. Vocal chops often benefit from repetition. An example of how you might arrange your vocal chops is shown in the following screenshot:

Figure 9.23 – Example of how you might arrange your vocal chops in the Piano roll

In the preceding screenshot, I've selected a few chops that sound pleasant to me and timed them out in the **Piano roll** into three groups of notes. You should experiment with arranging your vocal chop notes and timings in the **Piano roll**. Often, I find that matching the start of the vocal chop pairs well with the start of each beat. If you pretend that a vocal chop is similar to a percussive instrument and time it similarly, you're likely to create pleasant-sounding vocal chops.

You'll notice in the preceding screenshot that the chop notes are in an ascending fashion. Based on the way the auto-slicing in Fruity Slicer 2 chopped up the sample, a single phrase of notes was broken into several chops. To play the whole phrase, I keep the slices together. As the chop notes play through on the **Piano roll**, it will sound like a single phrase. Alternatively, you may want to consider combining these chops together before they get to the **Piano roll** so that you don't have several chops for each phrase. This can sometimes result in better-sounding vocal chops, but it does require more manual effort. This is a little tricky to do in Fruity Slicer 2. However, there is a tool designed exactly for this purpose called Slicex, which we will discuss later in this chapter.

Using Slicex to create vocal chops

Slicex is another tool to create vocal chops. Most of the time, I can do everything I would ever want to in Fruity Slicer 2 already. But if you want even more control, Slicex will provide you with fine-grained manipulation over each vocal chop. You can think of it as a heavy-duty Fruity Slicer 2.

Before creating vocal chops, you need to have a vocal audio sample. You can use any audio sample. Once we have it, let's start creating vocal chops with Slicex:

1. Create a new pattern and add it to the **Playlist**.
2. In the **Channel rack**, insert the **Slicex** plugin. Make the Slicex plugin detached by going to the top-left corner of **Slicex**, clicking the plugin option down arrow button, and then choosing **detached**.

   If you're like me, the first time you see **Slicex**, you instantly feel overwhelmed. What is this monstrous, beastly plugin? Don't worry – you won't need to use most of these features, except in very special cases where you want to tinker with the finest details. Most of the time, chopping vocal samples is a very straightforward task, and we'll look at the easiest way.

3. You add audio to **Slicex** the same way you did with Fruity Slicer 2. Drag your chosen audio sample (such as a vocal) into **Slicex**. One way is to drag it directly from the **Browser**. Another way is to load the sample directly in Slicex by finding its location on your computer and dragging it in. A third way is to double-left-click on the audio sample in the **Playlist** to reveal the waveform and drag the audio from there into **Slicex**, as shown in the following screenshot:

Figure 9.24 – Dragging the sample into Slicex

Once you've dragged in your audio sample, **Slicex** may attempt to automatically slice up the sample. This occurs if there are obvious transient sounds. If this doesn't occur automatically, you can force Slicex to do an auto-slice by clicking the **Medium auto-slicing** option, as shown in the following screenshot:

Figure 9.25 – Auto-slicing using the Medium auto-slicing option

Auto-slicing may or may not do a good job of slicing. Maybe this is good enough for you. If not, you will have to go in and manually assign markers to create chops, which we will discuss next.

If you play your pattern, you'll see the cursor in **Slicex** move through the slices of sampled audio.

Every time you see a marker, this is the start of a new chop. Slicex contains many controls that can be used to place markers and choose where a chop begins and ends. For example, on the waveform, you can left-click and drag to move the position of a marker left or right. You can right-click at the top of a marker to see the available options, such as deleting the marker.

4. By right-clicking on the waveform, you can play a selected sample chop. You can replay the sample by pressing *Space* on your keyboard. You can then move forward and backward through the chops by using your left and right keyboard arrows.
5. Once you're happy with the chops themselves, we can arrange the chop timing. In the **Channel rack**, find the **Slicex** plugin and open it up in the **Piano roll**.

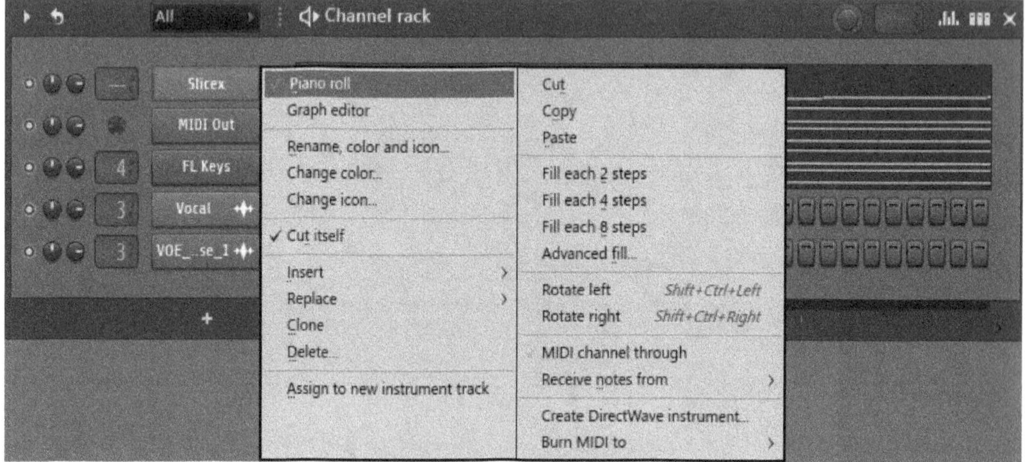

Figure 9.26 – Slicex in the Piano roll

In the **Piano roll**, you'll see that the audio sample has been sliced up by markers, as shown in the following screenshot:

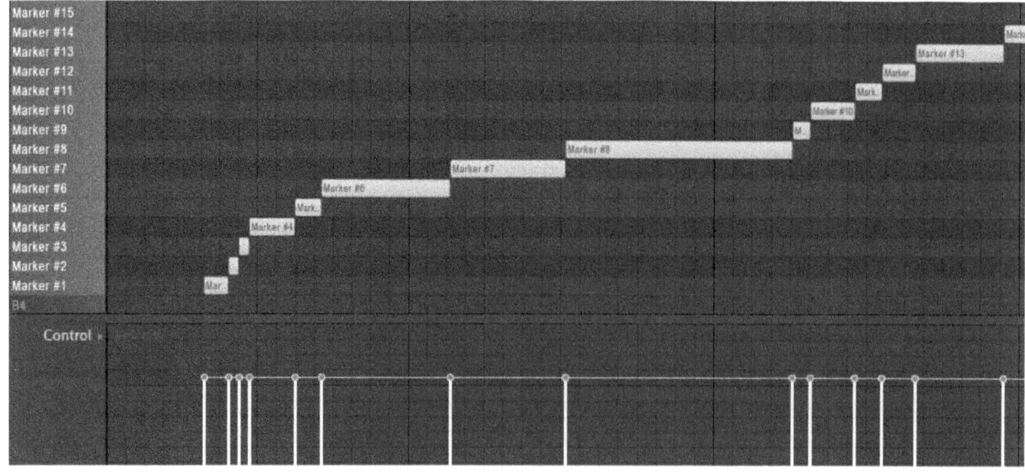

Figure 9.27 – Vocal chopping in the Piano roll

6. Play the pattern.

   You'll see that the vocal chops play just like instrument notes moving from left to right. Each marker represents a chop. You can trigger chops to play by adding notes. You can trigger a chop to occur multiple times by adding additional notes. For example, in the following screenshot, we can see that I've triggered **Marker #1** chops by playing the same note three times:

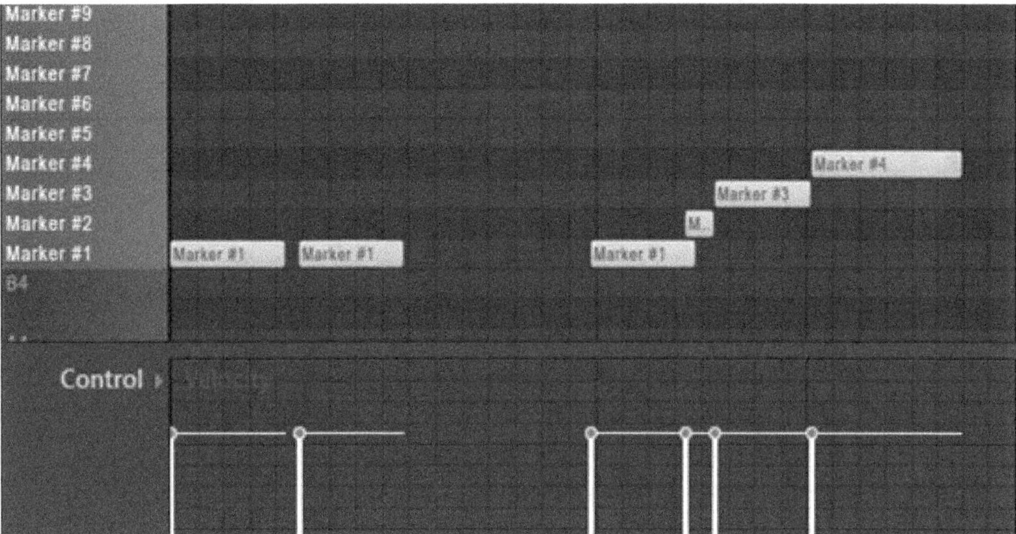

Figure 9.28 – Retriggering a vocal chop

7. By arranging the timing of your chops, you can create rhythmic vocal chop melodies. For the icing on the top, you can adjust the pitch of any given vocal chop. To do so, left-click on the **Control** button at the bottom left of the **Piano roll** and choose the **Note fine pitch** option.

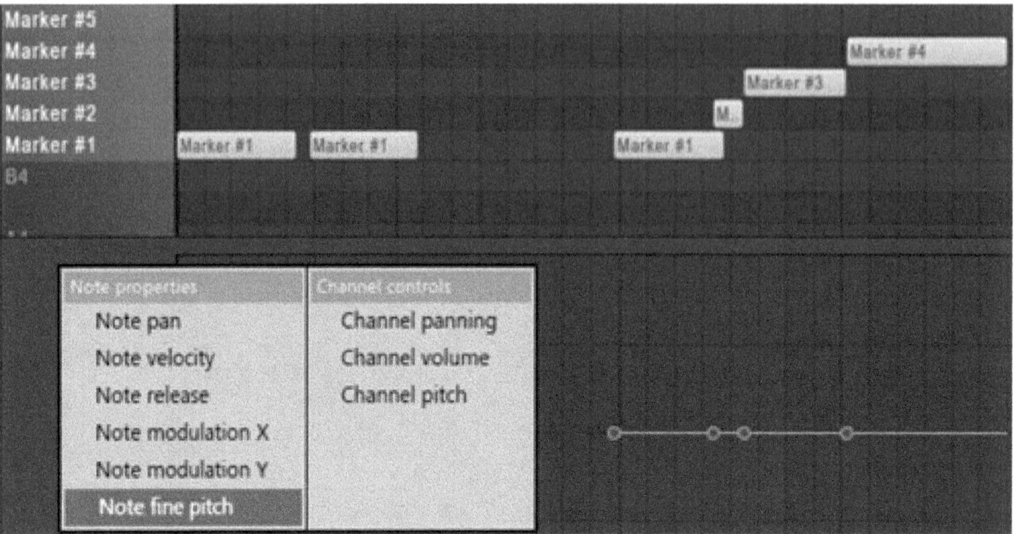

Figure 9.29 – Note fine pitch option

8. You can adjust the pitch of notes by left-clicking in the **Event Editor**. Anything higher than its default position will increase the pitch; anything lower will decrease the pitch. You can see an example of this in the following screenshot:

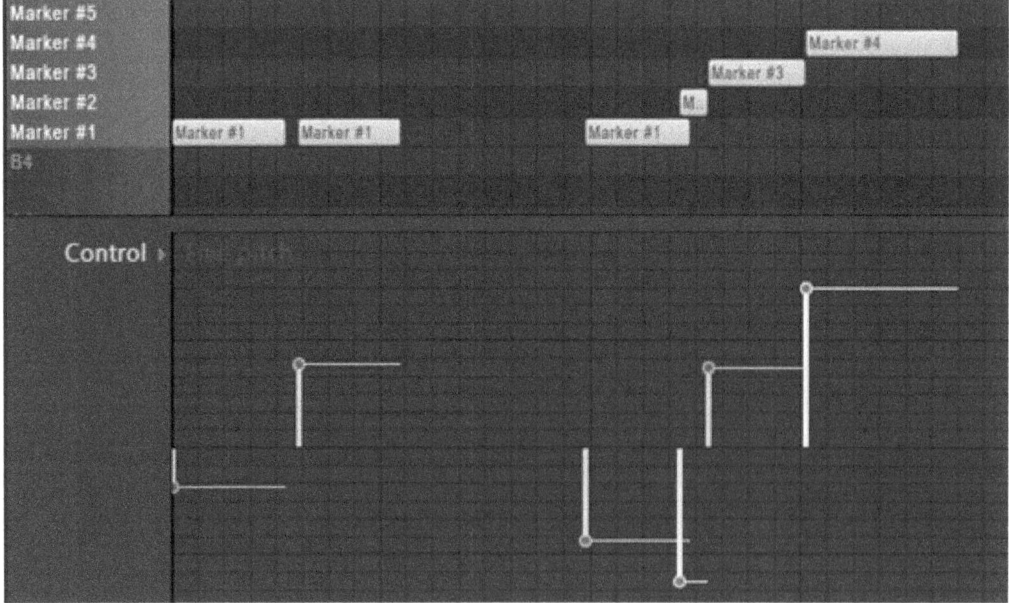

Figure 9.30 – Adjusting note fine pitch

You can see the amount of pitch change in the hint panel at the top left of the screen. In the following screenshot, you can see that we've adjusted the pitch by 700 percent:

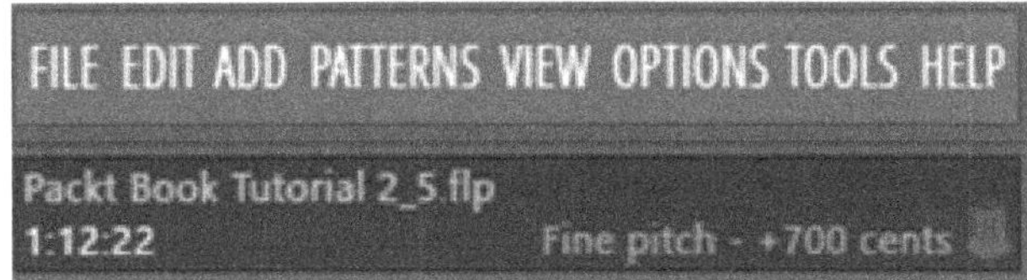

Figure 9.31 – Pitch change value

100 percent means 1 pitch higher, so 700 percent means 7 pitches higher than the original sample pitch.

This is all you need to create vocal chops. You could stop here and have more than enough to work with. For the ambitious, though, there are lots of additional controls in Slicex.

Let's take a brief look at some of the most useful features.

Drag/Copy sample/selection allows you to take any highlighted chops as individual audio samples and drag them anywhere, such as the **Playlist**. In the following screenshot, you can see that **Marker #29** has been selected and can now be dragged:

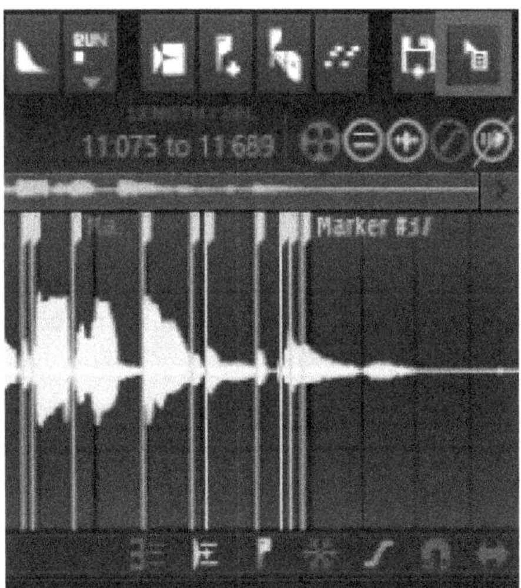

Figure 9.32 – Dragging the chop

Tip

Why might you want to drag an individual chop? Sometimes, you may find it easier to edit the timing of a vocal chop in the **Playlist**. Dragging a chop into the **Playlist** can make it easier to arrange the timing of the sample, rather than having to create an additional Slicex pattern each time you want to use the chop.

At the top of Slicex, you can see the global effects that get applied to all chops in Slicex.

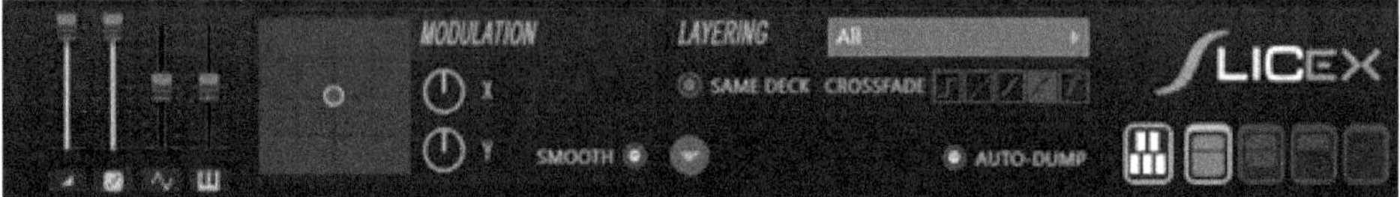

Figure 9.33 – Slicex global controls

- **Master level** adjusts the output volume level.
- **Master randomness level** increases any randomness effects applied in the audio editor.
- **Master LFO** increases any Low Frequency Oscillator (LFO) effects applied in the audio editor.
- **Master pitch** changes all slice pitches.
- **MODULATION X** and **Y** controls automate and link to parameters later on in the plugin.
- The **LAYERING** section allows you to create multiple decks of sample chops if you want to play a drum pad with samples.

The audio editor section contains controls that allow you to manipulate the sound of individual vocal chops. In the following screenshot, we can see that we're looking at a chop labeled **Marker #29**:

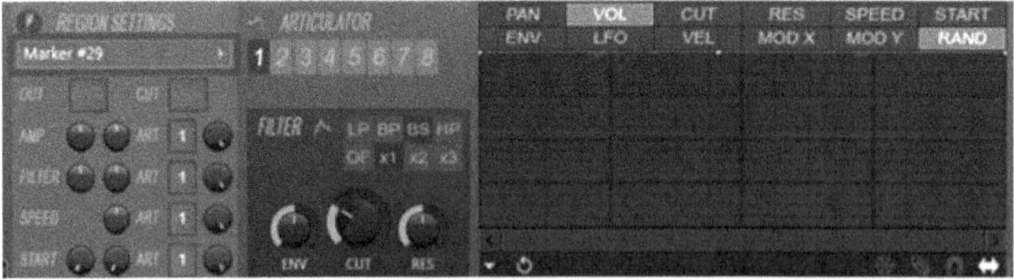

Figure 9.34 – Region settings

All the following settings will be applied to that specific chop sample:

- **AMP** (panning) allows you to control the panning. The knob to the right of the panning button lets you control the volume.
- The **FILTER** knobs let you control the frequencies and resonance.
- **SPEED** controls the pitch.
- **START** controls the delay time for when the sample begins.
- To the right of **AMP**, **FILTER**, **SPEED**, and **START**, you can see the word ART (articulator), which allows you to assign an articulator variable control value. For each articulator, you can also adjust the envelope. Essentially, this is just there to help you map controls together.

The **FILTER** section provides a series of envelope controls that allow you to choose among different types of filters that can be applied to the sound.

On the right in the editor target section, you can see a visual grid that allows you to automate any of the controls as the sound is played.

The **Tools** button (the wrench symbol) has a list of features, as shown in the following screenshot. I encourage you to experiment with them.

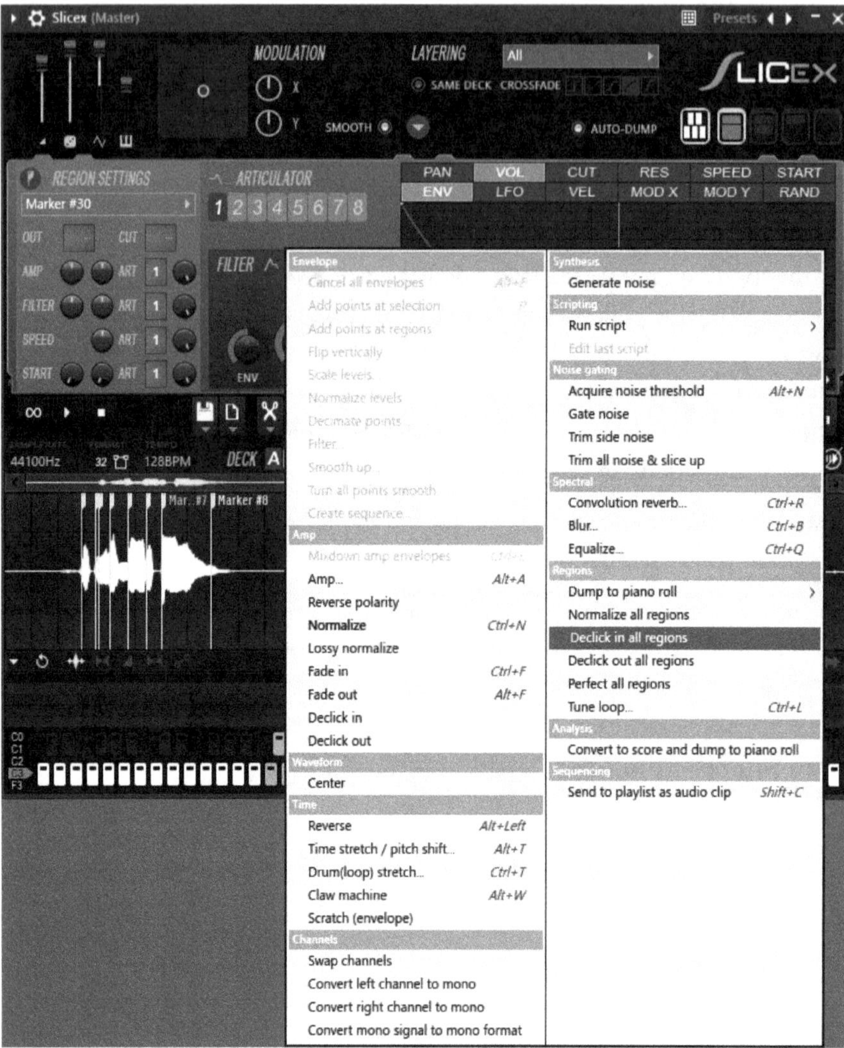

Figure 9.35 – Tools options

Of the many controls listed, here are some of the most important ones:

- **Gate noise** removes unwanted background noise.
- **Trim side noise** removes unwanted noise before or after your chop.
- **Normalize all regions** normalizes your audio volume and increases its loudness level.
- **Declick in all regions** and **Declick out all regions** help remove unwanted clicking sounds that occur when chopping.

Under the **regions** section (marker icon), you can assign the chopped-up sample to another device to be played back, as shown in the following screenshot:

Figure 9.36 – Slicex global controls

Once assigned, you can trigger the playback of individual sample chops on another device, such as an MPC pad. If you like playing live and using hardware, then this is for you.

Vocal chopping considerations

Here are some things you should consider when creating vocal chops:

- Vocal chops tend to take the center focus of the listener. Plan for this accordingly.

- Vocal chops may sound better at different pitches; try transposing the vocal chop pitch higher or lower.
- Try adding distortion effects.
- Apply sidechaining to the vocal chops.
- Apply effects and filters to your samples before chopping them up. In this chapter, we suggested using vocoders before chopping up your samples. This is commonly used in EDM dance music and sometimes can single-handedly make your song sound awesome.
- Chop up any sample, not just vocals.

Congratulations! You now know how to chop up samples.

Summary

In this chapter, we learned about some plugin effects that you can apply to your vocals. These effects can enhance your vocals and give your songs a distinctive quality.

We learned how to route MIDI notes to other instruments and effects. We also learned how to generate harmonies for your vocals using Pitcher. We learned how to use vocoders, such as Vocodex. Finally, we learned how to create vocal chops and slice up your samples using Fruity Slicer 2 and Slicex.

In the next chapter, we will explore glitch effects and create our own instruments and effects.

Get this book's PDF version and more

Scan the QR code (or go to `packtpub.com/unlock`). Search for this book by name, confirm the edition, and then follow the steps on the page.

Note: Keep your invoice handy. Purchases made directly from Packt don't require an invoice.

10

Glitch Effects and Creating Your Own Instruments and Effects

In this chapter, we'll explore a variety of creative plugin instruments and effects. We'll learn how to create glitch effects with sounds. This is a technique commonly used in pop and electronic dance music. We'll learn how to transform samples into playable instruments – essentially, you can build your own instrument. We'll learn how to create real-time looping effects using the **Transporter** plugin. We'll learn how to create custom instruments and effect chains that can be reused in other projects. Finally, we'll learn how to create arpeggiated patterns with **VFX Sequencer**. With these skills, you can build custom sounds and tools for your project.

In this chapter, we will cover the following topics:

- Creating glitch effects with Gross Beat
- Creating instruments with DirectWave
- Using Transporter to create real-time looping effects
- Creating instruments and effects with Patcher
- Using Patcher presets
- Using VFX Sequencer to create arpeggiated patterns

Creating glitch effects with Gross Beat

Glitches are the sound of audio device failure. When a hardware music player fails to work, various sounds can occur, such as stuttering, scratching, stretching, and reversing. When unintended, these indicate that something went wrong. When intended, glitch sounds can be a creative tool to make your sounds feel more artificial and more mechanical.

Glitch effects can be used in a lot of situations, such as the following:

- Transitioning between one song section to another.
- Fading instrument sounds in or out.
- Creating movement within a sound.

Here are some of the best glitch plugins on the market.

- FL Studio's **Gross Beat**, included with FL Studio *Signature Edition* and higher. We'll learn how to use Gross Beat in the upcoming pages.
- Izotope's **Stutter Edit**, available at `https://www.izotope.com/`.
- Dblue's **Glitch 2**, available at `https://illformed.com/`.
- Sugarbyte's **Effectrix**, available at `https://sugar-bytes.de/effectrix`.

Gross Beat is a plugin for creating effects such as beat-synced glitches, stutters, repetitions, scratches, and gating effects.

The easiest way to understand what Gross Beat does is by using it on an audio sample:

1. Add an audio sample to the **Playlist**.
2. Route the audio sample to an empty mixer track.
3. Add the **Gross Beat** plugin to the **Mixer** channel. Open **Gross Beat**. You will see a screen similar to the following:

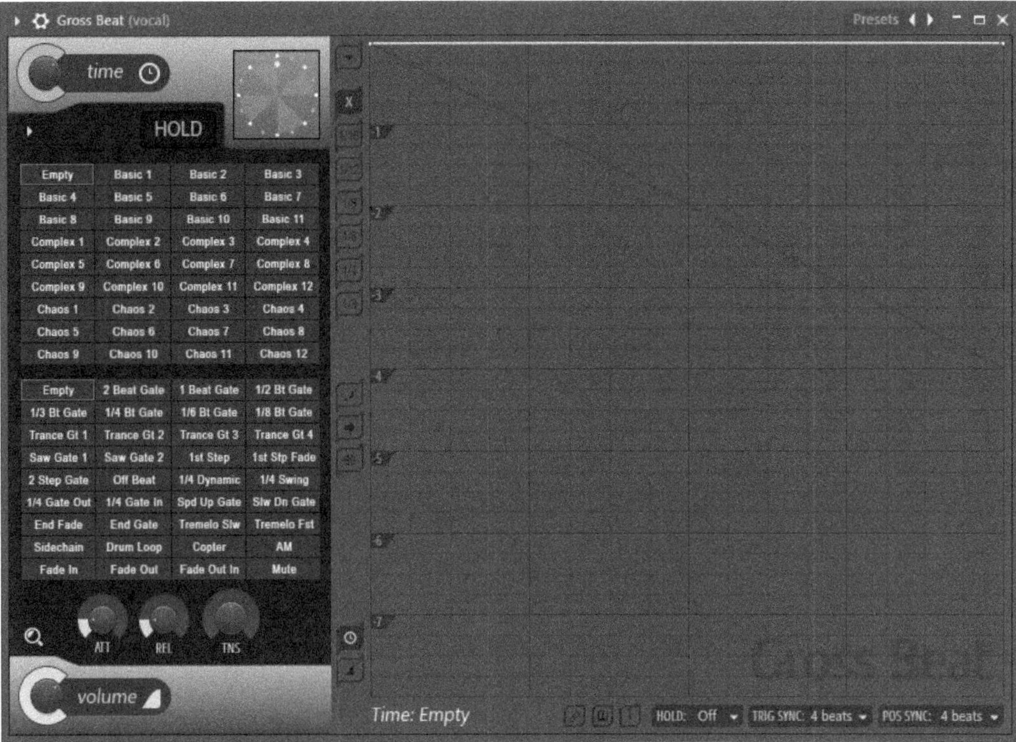

Figure 10.1 – Gross Beat

The left side of **Gross Beat** lists the time and volume effect presets. The right side contains a visual grid that allows you to draw and modify **time-** and **volume**-based effects.

Gross Beat contains two types of effects: **time-travel envelope effects** and **volume envelope effects**. Time-travel effects play with the speed of the audio playthrough. You can speed it up, slow it down, or reverse it with precise control. Volume effects control the level of the audio. They can be used separately or in combination. You can tell which type of effect is currently selected by the symbols and text at the bottom.

In the following screenshot, we can see that the time-travel envelope is currently selected because the **time envelope** symbol is highlighted:

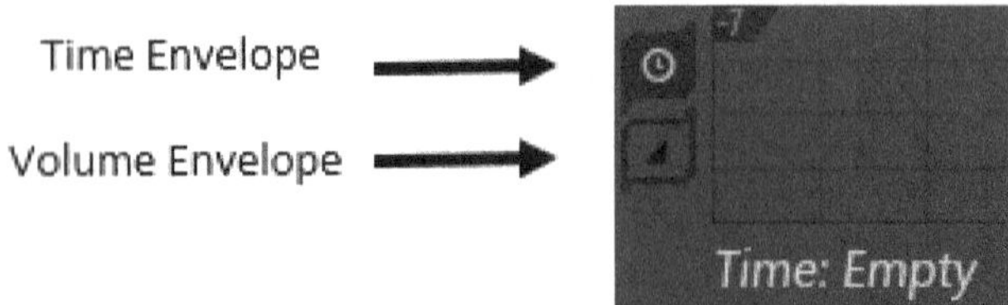

Figure 10.2 – Time and volume

4. **Time** and **volume** effect presets are listed on the left side panel. While playing your sound in the Playlist, left-click on some of the presets to see how they affect your sound. Time-based effects will slow down or repeat previous beats of your sample. Volume effects will add volume variation, such as volume gating effects, sidechaining, or fading. I encourage you to experiment by trying out different effect presets.

Figure 10.3 – Time and volume effect presets

If you want to automate how an effect is turned on and off throughout your song in the Playlist, go through the following steps:

1. Left-click on the **time** or **volume** effect you want to add. Right-click on the preset effect. Menu options will appear. Select **Copy value**; this will copy the effect.
2. Right-click again on the effect preset and select **Create automation clip**, as shown in the following screenshot:

Figure 10.4 – Automating effect

An automation clip will appear in the **Playlist**. By default, the effect is turned on.

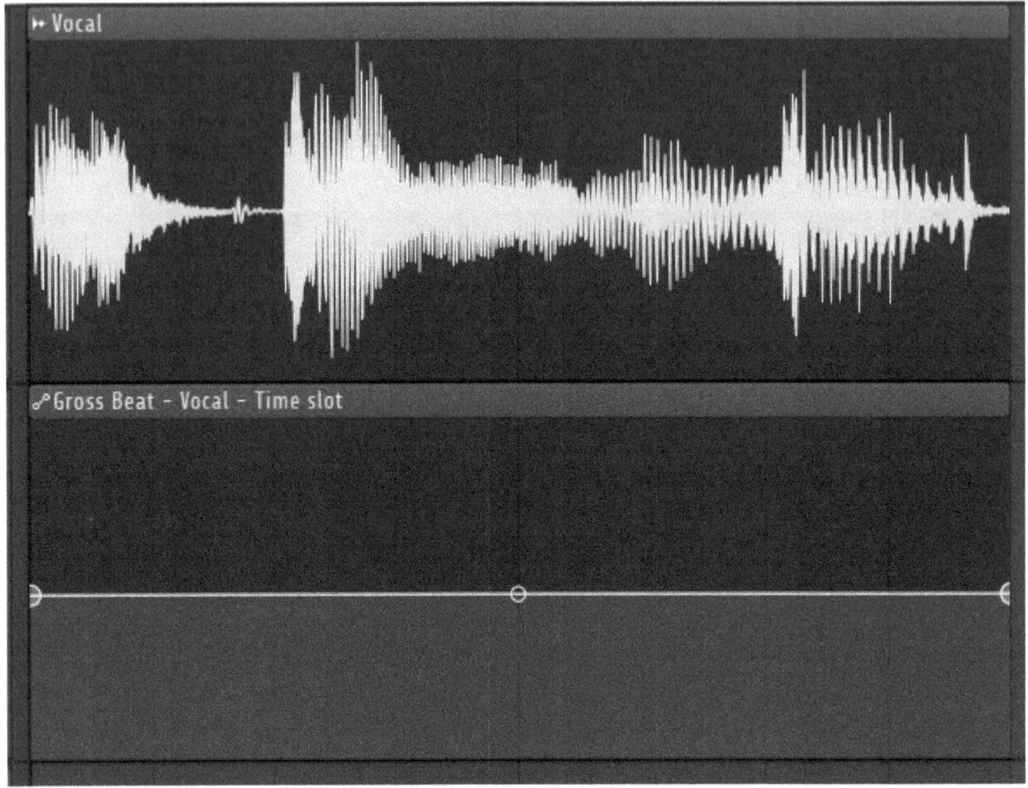

Figure 10.5 – Automation in the Playlist

3. Left-click and drag the automation key points down to **0**, as shown in the following screenshot. You'll notice that the purple line is no longer in the middle of the automation clip but instead is now at the bottom. This will turn the effect off.

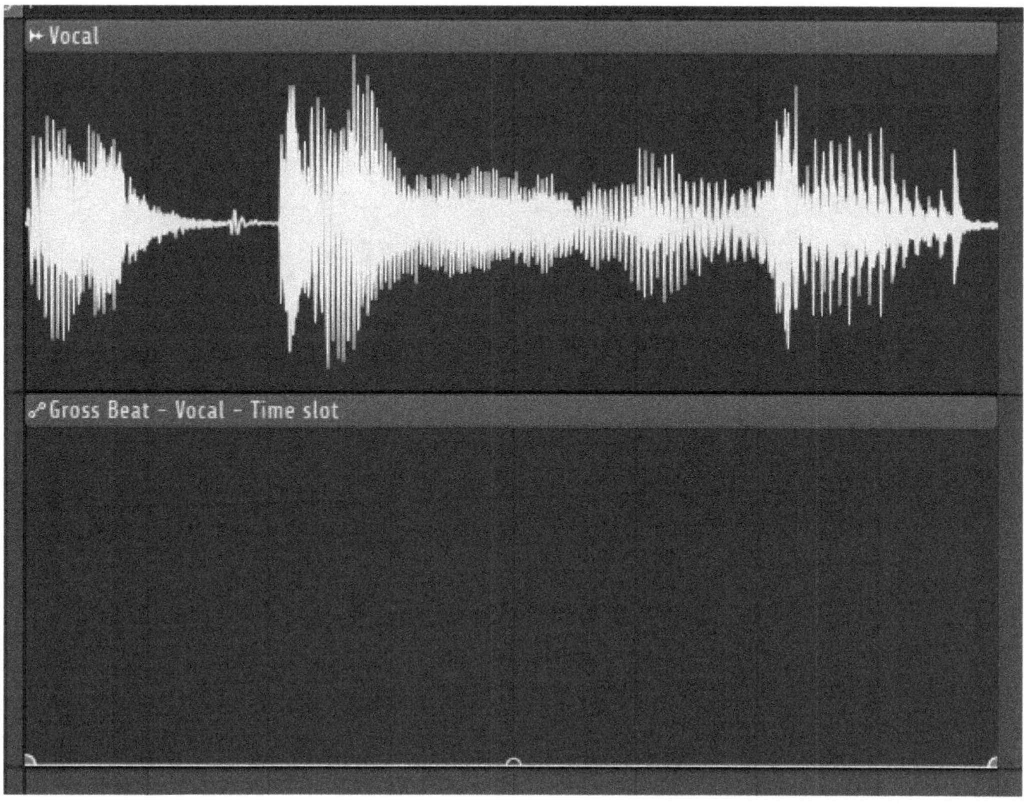

Figure 10.6 – Reduce level to 0

4. At the position where you want the glitch effect to activate, right-click in the automation clip twice and paste the value that you previously copied from **Gross Beat**. This will paste the preset effect you copied earlier.
5. Adjust the automation curve so that it looks like the following screenshot:

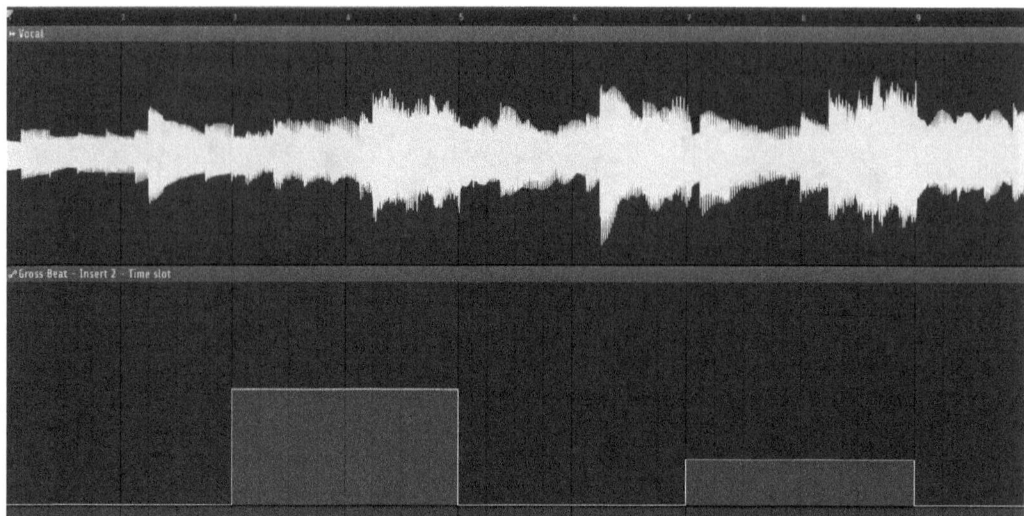

Figure 10.7 – Pasting the value that was copied in Gross Beat

In the preceding screenshot, the **Gross Beat** effect is automated to start off and then turn on at bar **3** until bar **4**, and then again from bar **7** to **9**. This shows an example of how you might turn the glitch effect on for a specific section. You can visually see that the automation values are not the same as each other. The first automated section is higher than the second. This will cause a different effect on Gross Beat to turn on each time. So you can turn on different Gross Beat effects throughout your song using the same instance of Gross Beat.

Congratulations! You can now turn **Gross Beat** effects on and off. Using this method, you can switch between Gross Beat effects at different stages of your song by copying and pasting different effect values. This can be applied anywhere in your Mixer, including in a mix bus, to affect multiple sounds at the same time.

Next, let's learn about some of the many presets that come with Gross Beat.

Gross Beat presets

In the top corner of **Gross Beat**, you'll find the **Presets** dropdown. Clicking it will display a list of presets.

Figure 10.8 – Gross Beat presets

Selecting one of the options will change the dashboard of time and volume effects available to choose from. In the following screenshot, we've selected the **Momentary** preset:

Figure 10.9 – New time and volume effects

On the left side dashboard, a new list of time and volume effect presets will populate. There are a ton of time and volume effects available. I encourage you to explore the dropdown presets to see all the options that are available.

Mapping time and volume effects to a sample

You can drag an audio sample into **Gross Beat**. Doing so will generate **time** or **volume** effects based on the waveform. This is easiest understood by seeing it in action:

1. Find an audio sample in the Browser. Use a drum loop sample or a loop with punctuated transients for the best results.
2. In **Gross Beat**, choose either the **time travel** envelope or the **volume** envelope symbol. This will determine the type of effect we are generating.
3. Left-click and drag the sample audio waveform into **Gross Beat**. Gross Beat will analyze the sample and generate an automation point based on the sample. You can see how Gross Beat looks after you have dragged in a drum sample in the following screenshot:

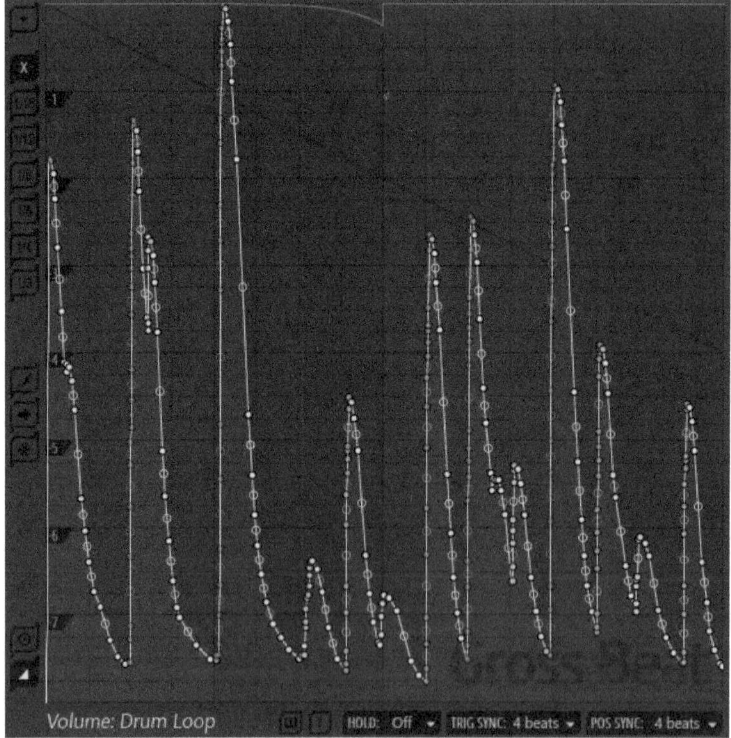

Figure 10.10 – Effect based on a sample

If you play the sample in the Playlist, you'll be able to hear the Gross Beat effect applied.

Gross Beat sequencer

Gross Beat contains a sequence generator that produces automation curves that can be used for **time** and **volume** effects. This allows you to quickly create new effects with ease.

To load up the sequencer, go to **Options** | **Create sequence...** as shown in the following screenshot:

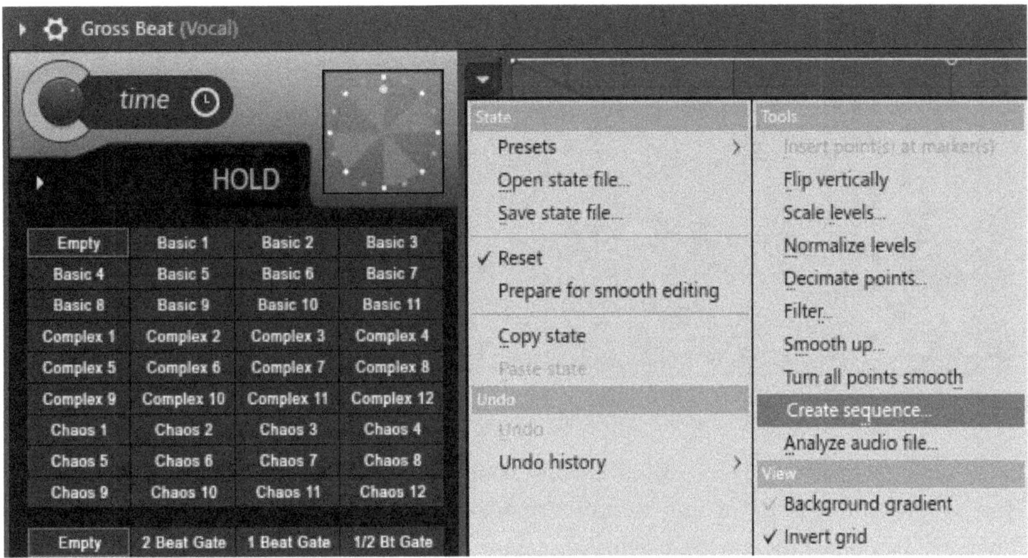

Figure 10.11 – Load Gross Beat sequencer

A window will pop up showing additional controls.

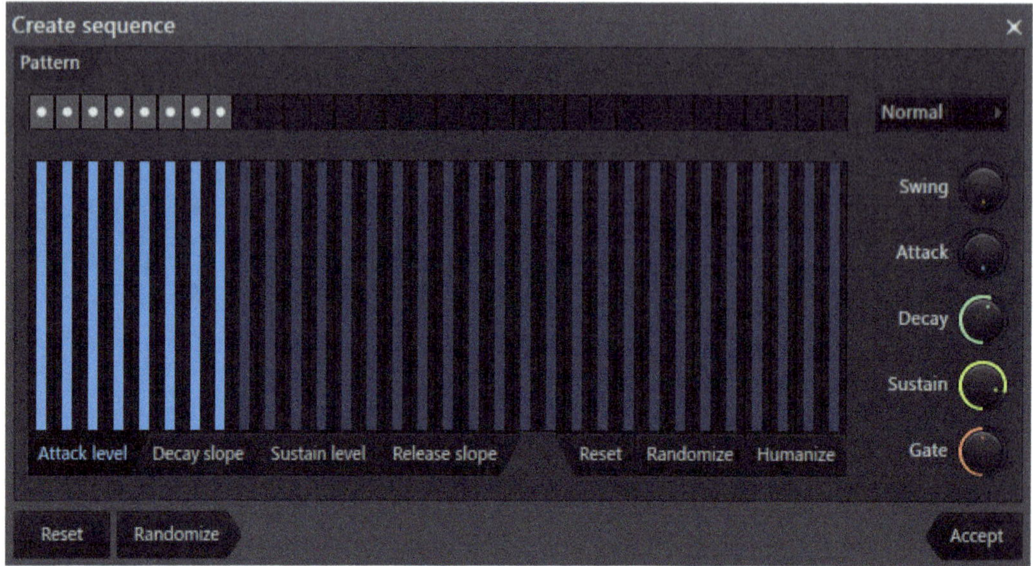

Figure 10.12 – Gross Beat sequencer additional controls

In the sequence generator, you'll discover some controls to create Gross Beat automation curves. Here's a brief description of the controls; these are intuitive, so you will quickly learn their function if you adjust them while playing the sample:

- **Off/on/hold/stick** let you create additional automation curves. You can add or remove them by left-clicking on the buttons.
- **Mode** lets you toggle between a single or double version of the automation curves.
- The **arpeggiator increment** lets you increase the size of the curves. What the curve changes is dictated by the **Attack level**, **Decay slope**, **Sustain level**, or **Release slope** that is selected.
- **Randomize** generates random curves.
- **Humanize** tries to make the automation curves feel less robotic.
- On the far right, you'll see global envelope controls for **Swing**, **Attack**, **Decay**, **Sustain**, and **Gate**.
- At the very bottom, you'll see a **Randomize** button, which generates random settings for all the parameters.

We've just scratched the surface of what Gross Beat can do. If you want more features and examples, check out the FL Studio Gross Beat video tutorials at `http://support.image-line.com/redirect/GrossBeat_Videos`.

We've learned how to create glitch effects. Next, let's learn how to create our own instruments from audio samples.

Creating instruments with DirectWave

DirectWave is a native FL Studio plugin sampler. Among other things, it allows you to take any single audio sample and generate additional pitches for the sound. Let's create instruments with DirectWave:

1. Add the **DirectWave** plugin to the **Channel rack**.
2. Locate an audio sample you'd like to convert into an instrument. This works best with one-shot samples or sampled instruments. You can find a list of samples and instruments intended for use in **DirectWave** in the browser under the **Packs** folder.
3. Drag the sample or sampled instrument into **DirectWave** in the **Channel rack**, as shown in the following screenshot:

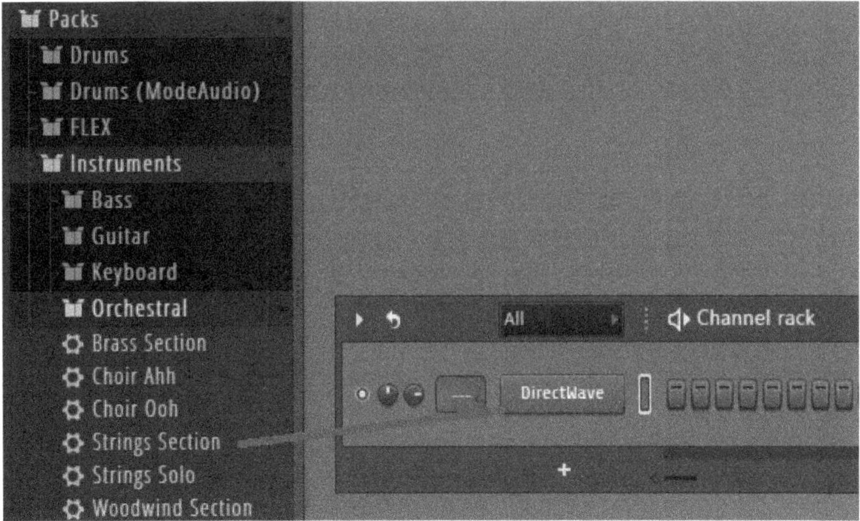

Figure 10.13 – Sampled instrument in DirectWave

If you want to quickly swap out one sample for another, you can do so by clicking on the sample in the browser with the scroll button on your mouse.

Once the sample or sampled instrument has been dragged in, **DIRECT WAVE** will open, as shown in the following screenshot:

Figure 10.14 – DirectWave

If you play some instrument notes on your MIDI instrument or in the Piano roll, you'll hear that DirectWave has analyzed the audio sample and generated transposed pitches above and below the original sample. Essentially, DirectWave created an entire instrument that you can play. This is a big deal. You can go out and record any audio sample, and DirectWave will turn that sound into an instrument by creating additional note pitches.

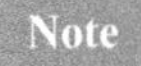

FL Studio has lots of instrument samples that can be imported into FL Studio. To download the samples, go to **ONLINE CONTENT** in the top-left corner of DirectWave.

After DirectWave has created your instrument, it offers a large array of controls to modify the envelope of your sound, as well as a series of effects, as shown in the following **PROGRAM** panel:

Figure 10.15 – PROGRAM panel

The **PROGRAM** panel contains lots of effects to adjust your sampled sound. Of interest is the **PLAY MODE** panel, where you can choose to hear your sound as **Mono** (plays single notes at a time), **Poly** (allows you to play multiple notes at a time), or **Legato** (allows single notes to smoothly glide into the next note). The **GLIDE** panel then controls how smooth the glide between notes is.

We've learned how to create our own instruments. Next, let's learn about an instrument effect that creates looping effects.

Using Transporter to create real-time looping effects

Transporter is a **creative effects plugin**. It gives you the ability to create looping sounds with a variety of controls over how the loops sound. For example, you can make the loops more frequent or less frequent, pitch loops higher or lower, or reverse the sound of the loops. If you find the idea of a loop a little confusing, you may want to picture in your mind the sound of an echo. It's essentially the same sound as the original, just played back slightly after the original sound.

This effect plugin has a very specific use case and will not sound good when applied to every sound. I find the best results come from using this plugin with very simple sounds. For example, repeating chord pluck sounds. The more regular and clearly defined the transients are in the original sound, the more likely the plugin effect will sound good. If this is your first time using this plugin, I recommend using it on only a single instrument rather than applying it to a mix bus. Once you know how this plugin affects simple sounds, your ears will know what to listen for when applying it to multiple sounds at once.

This plugin can only be understood by playing with it and listening to how it affects a sample:

1. Add an audio sample to the **Playlist**. I recommend a simple, repeating chord progression or something else that is very bare and minimal.

2. Route the audio sample to an empty mixer track.
3. Add the **Transporter** plugin to the **Mixer** channel. Open **Transporter**. You will see a screen similar to the following:

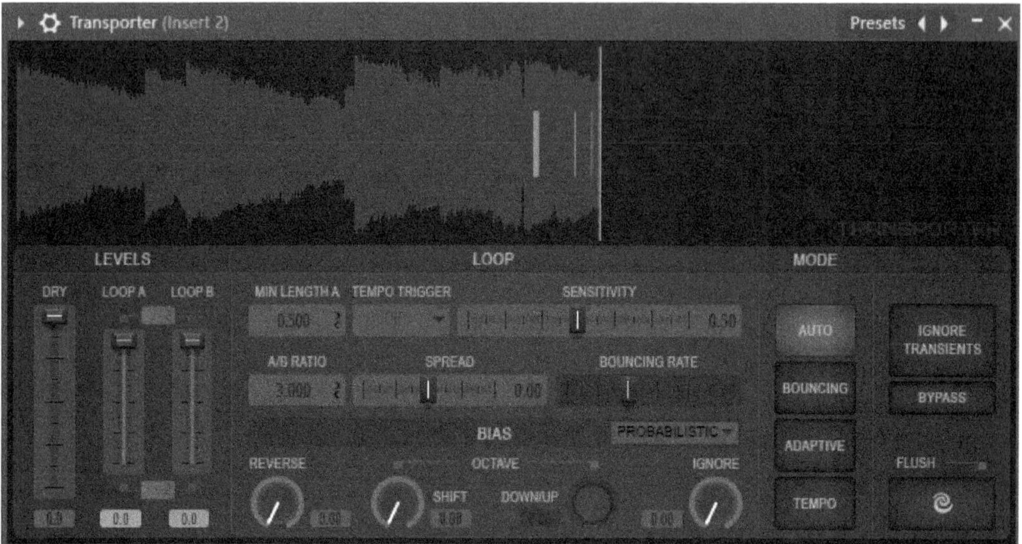

Figure 10.16 – Transporter plugin

Let's take a look at the controls from left to right. On the far left, you'll see the **LEVELS** section.

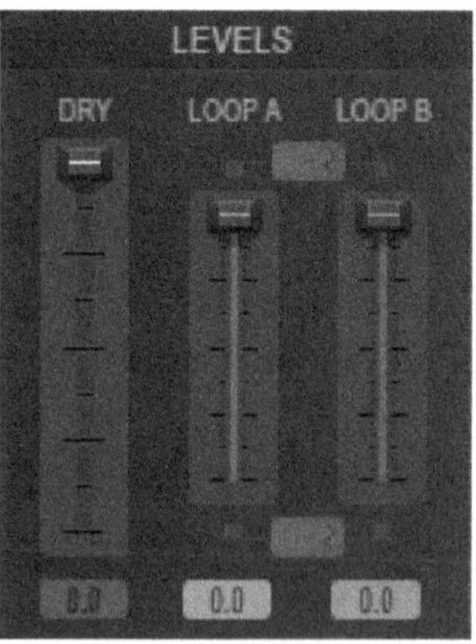

Figure 10.17 – Transporter plugin LEVELS component

- **DRY:** When the plugin is first loaded, the **DRY** knob is set to **0.0**. This means you can hear the original sound as well as the sounds generated from the plugin. For listening ease when trying to learn the plugin, you can pull the **DRY** knob all the way down, and you'll only hear the sounds that are generated from the plugin without hearing the original. Sometimes the sounds generated from the plugin sound good on their own without hearing the original source sound too.

- **LOOP A** and **LOOP B:** Transporter listens for transient sounds in your audio source sound. Based on the transients, when it hears a transient, it creates a loop. This loop sound is essentially a repeat of the original sound. Two of these loops are created. These controls allow you to turn up or down the signal of either of these loops. In other words, you can isolate to hear just one or both of these looping sounds.

  For those already comfortable with the plugin and who really want to experiment, you'll notice a number box above and below **LOOP A** and **LOOP B** that initially shows the number 2. These are there to allow you to sidechain transients from another track to trigger the loop.

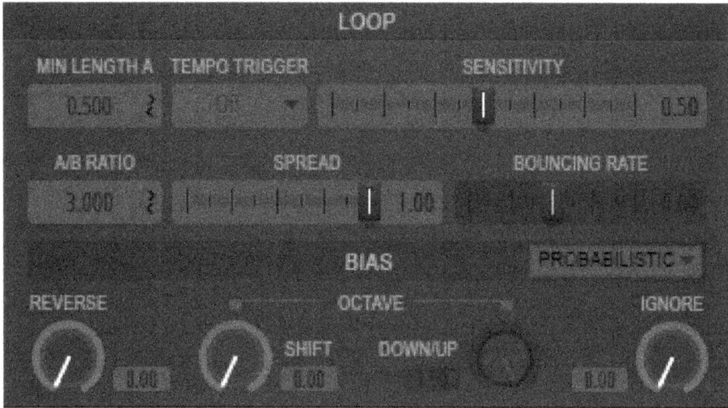

Figure 10.18 – Transporter plugin LOOP component

- **MIN LENGTH A:** This sets the shortest possible length for a loop before it can be triggered again. In **AUTO**, **BOUNCING**, and **ADAPTIVE** modes, this is measured in seconds. In **TEMPO** mode, it's based on your project's **BPM** (short for **beats per minute**). In **BOUNCING** mode, this also sets where the loop starts, and the loop length can grow or shrink each time, depending on the **BOUNCING RATE**. If you manually click on the waveform to trigger a loop, it ignores this minimum time.
- **TEMPO TRIGGER**: In **BOUNCING** and **TEMPO** modes, you can set up automatic loop triggers that happen at regular musical intervals (like every beat or bar).
- **SENSITIVITY**: This controls how easily the plugin detects sudden changes (transients) in your audio. Higher sensitivity means it will react to even small changes, but might trigger too often by mistake. When a transient is detected, the control flashes – use this to check if the timing matches your music.

- **A/B RATIO**: This sets how long **LOOP B** is compared to **LOOP A**. For example, if **LOOP A** is 1 second and the ratio is 2, **LOOP B** will be 0.5 seconds. Changing this ratio changes the groove or rhythm of the loops. Try different values for creative effects.
- **SPREAD**: This controls how the two loops are panned left and right in the stereo field. Move the slider right for fixed left/right panning. Move it left for automatic panning that moves back and forth, controlled by a sine wave (from 0 to 10 Hz).
- **BOUNCING RATE**: In **BOUNCING** mode, this controls how the loop length changes each time. Positive values make the loop get longer each cycle (accelerating). Negative values make the loop get shorter each cycle (decelerating). The starting length is set by **MIN LENGTH A** and the **A/B RATIO**, and it changes each time a loop is triggered.
- **BIAS**: This controls how predictable or random your loops are. If you want loops to repeat in a steady, regular way, set it for more predictable behavior. If you want loops to keep changing and evolving, set it for more randomness.
- **PROBABILISTIC** Mode: The plugin makes random choices for each loop, so the sound keeps changing and never repeats exactly the same way. Great for experimental or evolving textures.
- **DETERMINISTIC** Mode: The plugin's choices depend on where you are in the audio, so the pattern is more predictable and can repeat the same way each time. Great if you want loops to sync up with other events or automation.
- **REVERSE**: Sets how likely it is that a piece of audio will play backwards. Higher values mean you hear more reversed sounds.
- **SHIFT**: Sets how likely it is that a piece of audio will be shifted up or down by one octave instead of playing at its normal pitch. The direction (up or down) is controlled by the **DOWN/UP** setting.
- **DOWN/UP**: Sets whether octave shifts go up or down. If **SHIFT** is set to 0 (no octave shifts), this does nothing.
    - 1 = all shifts go up
    - 0 = all shifts go down
    - 0.5 = equal chance of up or down
- **IGNORE**: Sets how often the plugin will skip updating the loop, no matter what triggers it (like transients, manual clicks, or tempo sync). This can make the timing less regular, adding variation even if your triggers are steady.

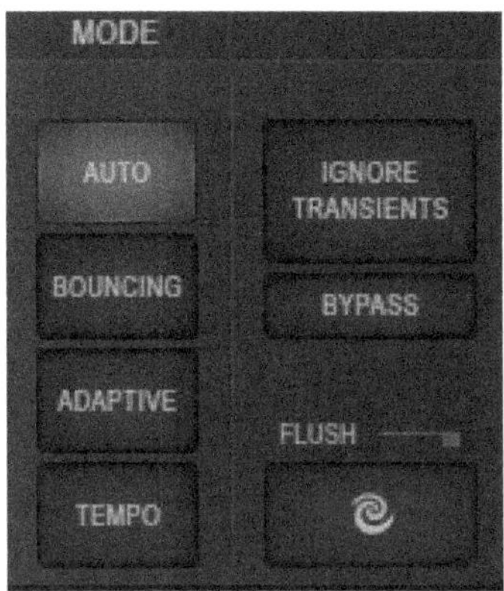

Figure 10.19 – Transporter plugin MODE component

- **AUTO**: Loops start when the plugin hears a beat in your audio.
- **BOUNCING**: Loops get longer or shorter each time, like a bouncing ball.
- **ADAPTIVE**: Loop length changes depending on how many beats are in your audio. More beats = shorter loops (if **MIN LENGTH A** is small).
- **TEMPO**: Loops follow your project's tempo. Loop length is set by your BPM.
- **IGNORE TRANSIENTS**: Turns off beat detection. Loops keep going the same way until you change them or click to trigger a new loop.
- **BYPASS**: Turns off the effect. This allows you to hear just the original sound source.
- **FLUSH**: Resets everything and starts the loop over.

Transporter suggestions for getting better results

If you're not getting nice results out of the plugin, I recommend trying the following:

1. Pick a source sound that is a simple melody/chord progression. Overly complex sounds tend to feel a little cluttered.
2. Turn the **DRY** control to **-INF**. This will allow you to hear only the loops generated and omit the original source sound. I find this also helps to remove overwhelming, cluttering noise.

3. For most sounds with irregular transients, the optimal Mode is **AUTO**, and the optimal **BIAS** will be **PROBABILISTIC**. If, on the other hand, your sound sample is very repetitive, the **TEMPO** mode will likely give you better results, along with setting the **BIAS** to **DETERMINISTIC**.
4. Play around with the **REVERSE**, **SHIFT**, and **DOWN/UP** controls.

Transporter can be used to generate transitions between sounds when used at the end of a musical section. For example, if applied to drums, it can create drum fill-like sounds. Use automation to turn the plugin effects on and off.

We've learned how to use the Transporter plugin to create real-time looping effects. Next, let's learn how to create your own instruments and effects.

Creating instruments and effects with Patcher

Patcher is an FL Studio plugin that allows you to chain instruments and effects together. Patcher allows you to create your own custom instrument and effect chains, link everything together, and save them for reuse in other projects. Patcher is related to modular synthesis. **Modular synthesis** involves having individual instrument and effect components and linking them together to connect everything. You literally plug one instrument or effect into another. The sound coming out of one instrument or effect is then passed on to the next plugin to be manipulated.

Patcher can be loaded into the Channel rack or onto a Mixer channel. If loaded into the Channel rack, you can load instrument plugins, and Patcher will play the instrument using MIDI notes sent to it from the Piano roll. If Patcher is loaded in the Mixer, it's intended to be used as an effect rather than to play MIDI notes. In the following examples, we assume that you want to use Patcher as an instrument and accept MIDI notes, and have loaded Patcher into the Channel rack:

1. In the **Channel rack**, load up **Patcher**. Open it up, and you'll see the following screen:

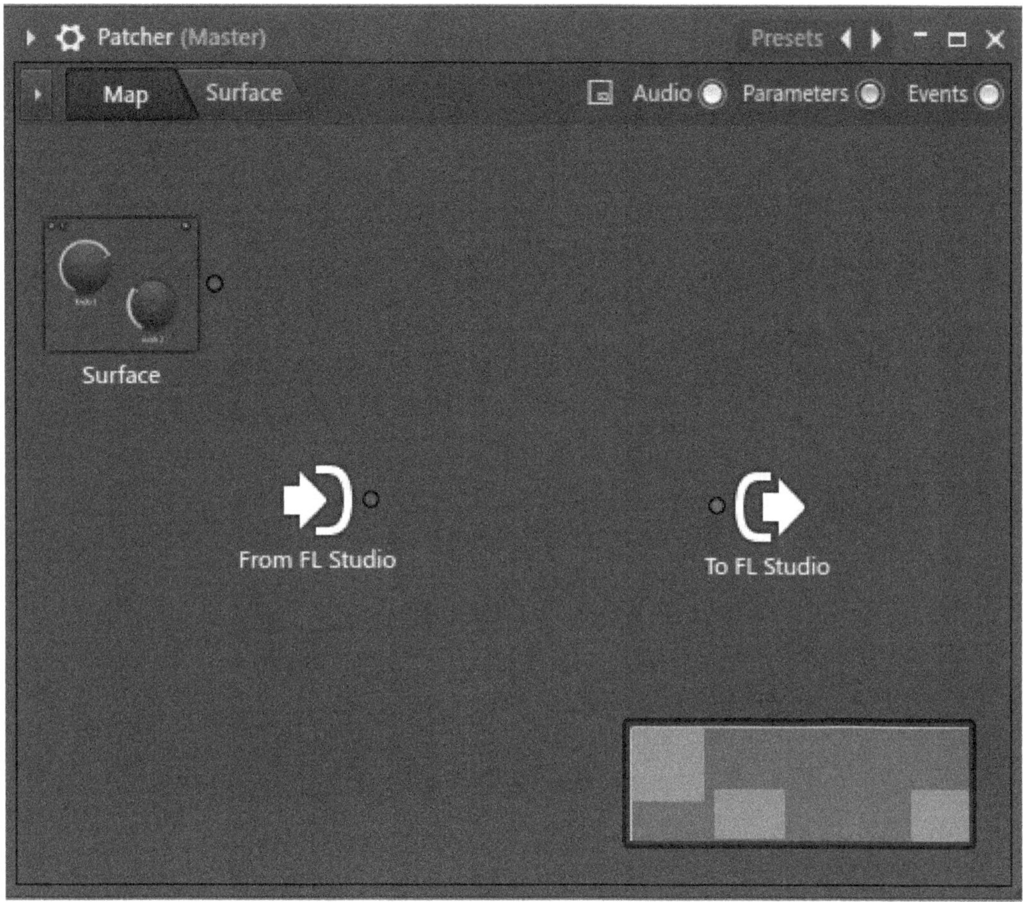

Figure 10.20 – Patcher

2. To add a synthesizer, right-click on an empty space in **Patcher**, select **Add plugin** from the menu options that appear, and select a synthesizer plugin. In my case, I'm going to add the **FLEX** plugin, as shown in the following screenshot:

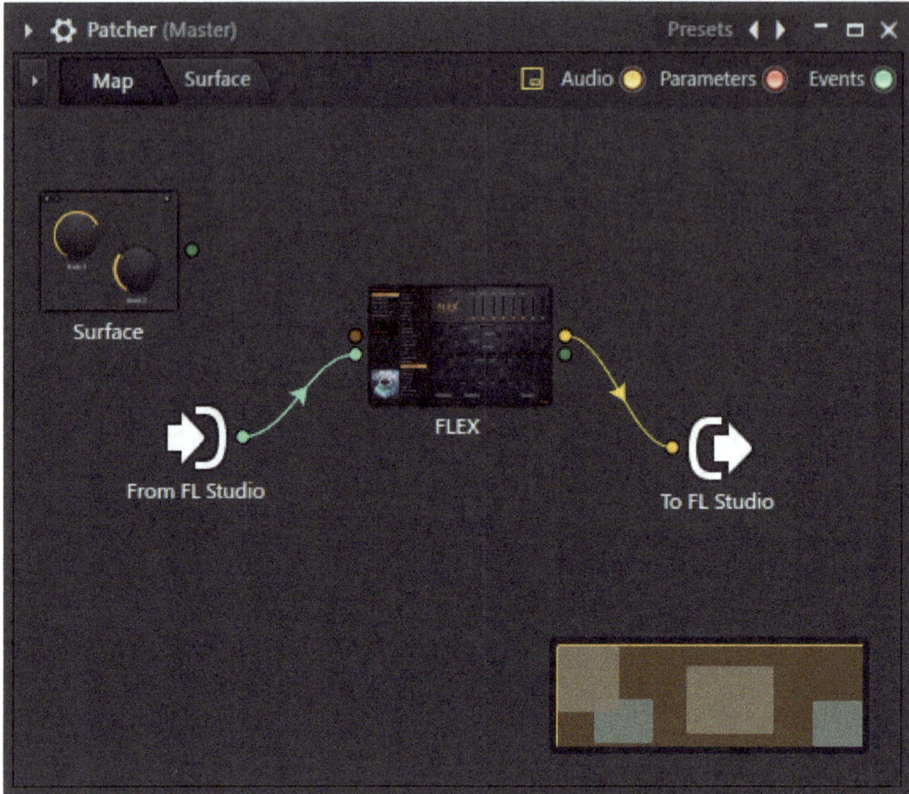

Figure 10.21 – Added FLEX

You'll notice that a blue arrow line and a yellow arrow line have been added. The blue line indicates that MIDI input coming from FL Studio is being sent to **FLEX**. If you don't see this, it means you opened **Patcher** in the Mixer as an effect and not in the **Channel rack**. The yellow line shows where the audio is going. In this case, audio is leaving **FLEX** and being sent back to the **Channel rack**.

If you play some MIDI notes, you will hear **FLEX** play. If you left-click and drag the yellow line, you can adjust the output level (volume).

3. If you double-left-click on a plugin in **Patcher**, it will open up. You can then tweak any controls you like.

You can add effects or multiple synthesizers. Once you've added them, choose where you want MIDI or audio to be routed. Let's look at a quick example.

Add an effect plugin, such as **Fruity Convolver**, in the same way that you added the **FLEX** instrument. Redirect audio from **FLEX** to it by left-clicking the yellow audio arrow from **FLEX** and dragging it to **Fruity Convolver**. In the following screenshot example, I've added the **Fruity Convolver** effect and redirected the audio from **FLEX** to go to **Fruity Convolver**. I then routed the audio from **Fruity Convolver** to return to FL Studio.

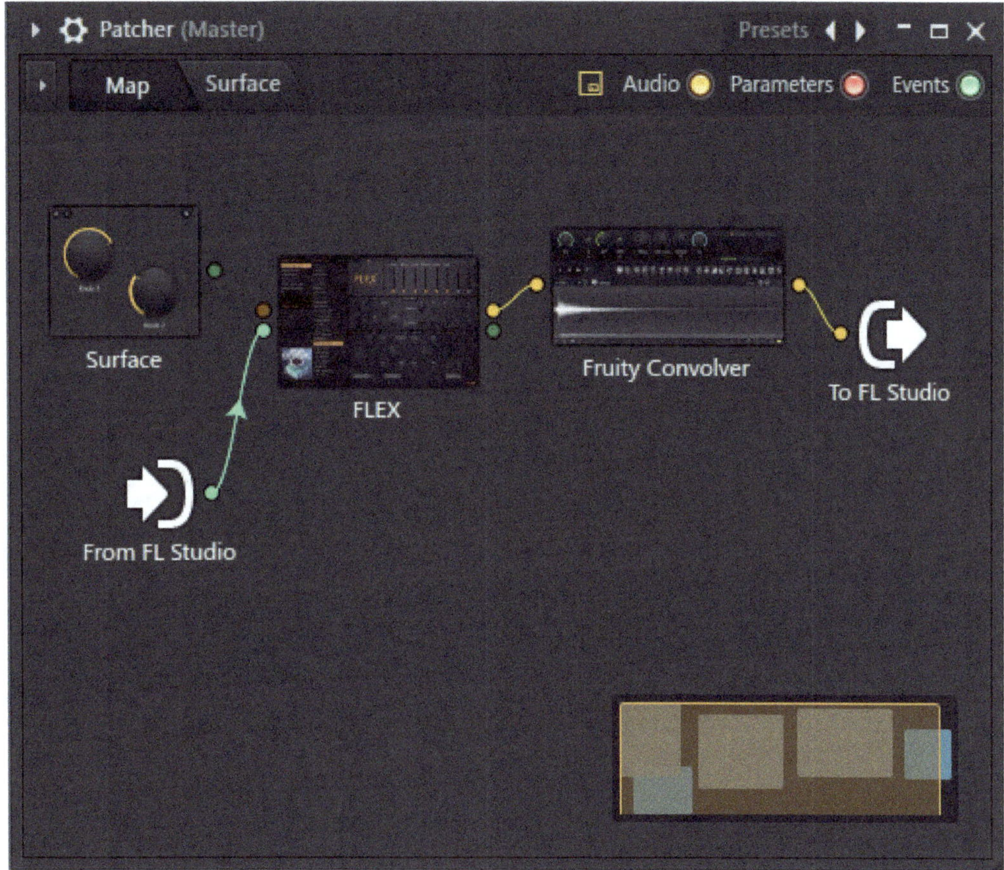

Figure 10.22 – Routing audio from FLEX to Fruity Convolver

If you play some MIDI notes, you can hear the notes played by **FLEX** with an effect added by **Fruity Convolver**.

Next, let's learn how to create a dashboard in Patcher so you can interact with your custom effects chain with ease.

Creating custom dashboards in Patcher

In **Patcher,** you can create dashboards with gadgets to navigate your instruments and effects. The benefit of using a dashboard is that you have a list of custom controls and effects in one place instead of opening up plugins one at a time. This is useful when you're playing live, and you want to change your instruments and effects all in one place. It also unlocks automation abilities within Patcher, as you can automate controls added to the dashboard. To understand this, let's look at an example:

1. Go to the **Surface** tab at the top of **Patcher**.
2. Click the plus sign icon. A menu will pop up showing you the controls that you can add. There is also an option called **Control creator**, which allows you to design your own controls.

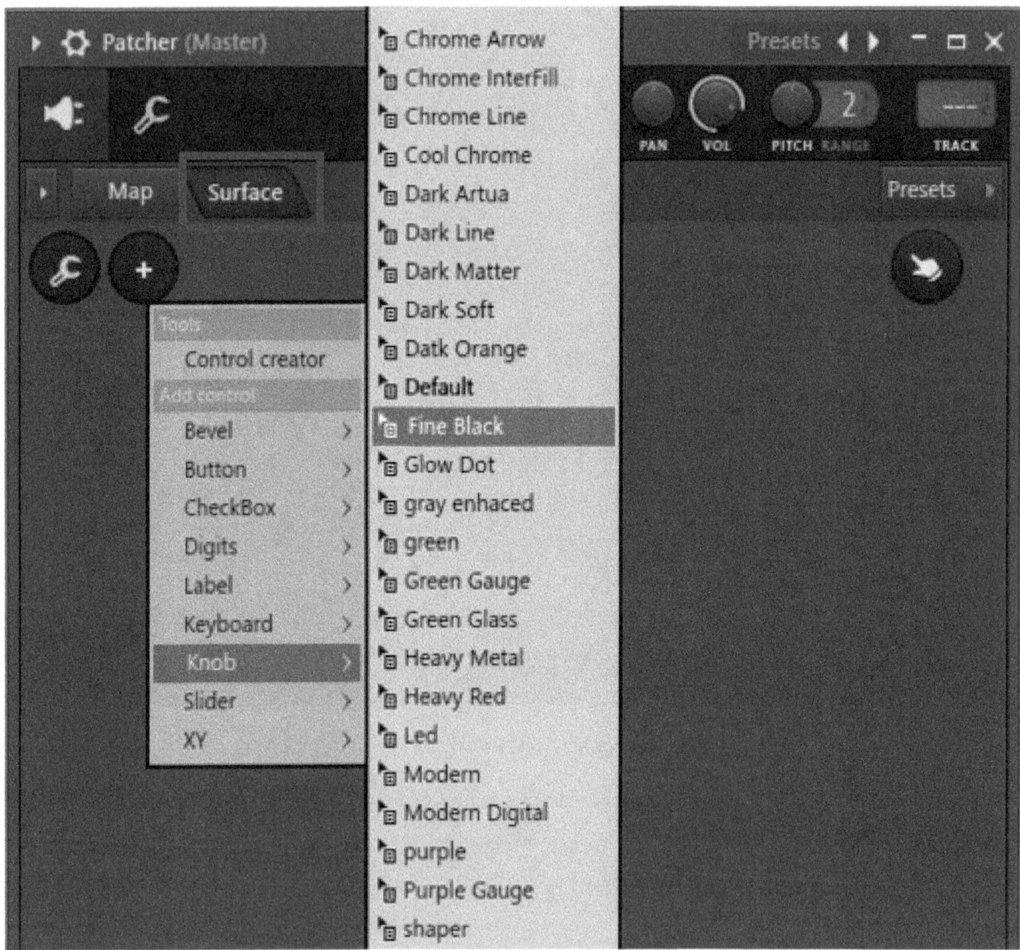

Figure 10.23 – Adding a knob

Select a knob. In the preceding screenshot, I've chosen one called **Fine Black**. A knob will appear.

3. Left-click on the **wrench** symbol at the top left of **Patcher** to finish placing the knob. We've created a gadget. Now we need to tell the gadget to connect to a plugin control so it knows what to do.
4. Click the **Map** tab at the top left to return to your instruments and effects. You'll see that a red circle appears to the right of the **Surface** object. This is the output port of the dashboard and is connected to the knob that we just created:

Figure 10.24 – Surface object now has an additional output

5. We're now going to connect our knob to a control in an instrument. Double-left-click on the **FLEX** instrument in **Patcher**. **FLEX** will open up.
6. Right-click on any control in **FLEX**. A menu will appear. Choose the **Activate** option. This will tell Patcher that we want an input port to lead to this control. This is shown in the following screenshot:

Figure 10.25 – Activating a control

7. Close **FLEX**. Back in **Patcher**, you'll see that a red circle has appeared to the left of the **FLEX** instrument. This is the input controlling the knob we just activated.

Figure 10.26 – New input to FLEX

8. Left-click on the red circle output of the **Surface** object and drag it onto the **FLEX** red input port circle we just created. When you're done, it will look like the following screenshot:

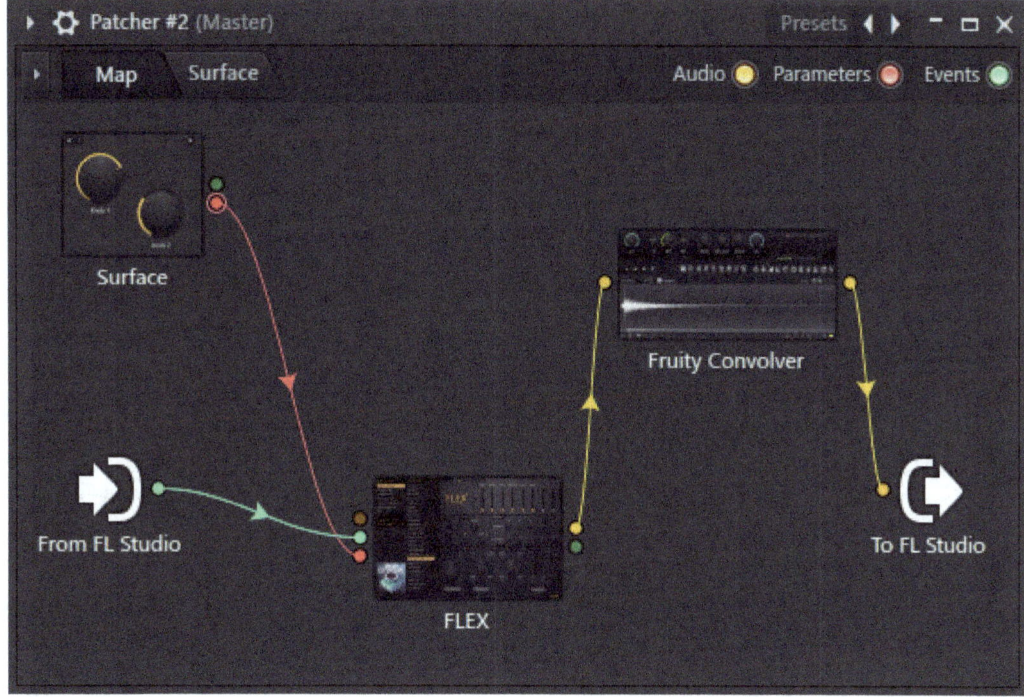

Figure 10.27 – Connecting the knob on the Surface dashboard to FLEX

What we've just done is connect the knob that we added to the **Surface** dashboard to the control in **FLEX**. The knob in the **Surface** dashboard now manipulates the control in **FLEX**.

9. Left-click the **Surface** tab again to return to the **Surface** dashboard. Then you can click the little arrow pointing symbol on the right side to enable interaction with the dashboard. The following screenshot shows the **Surface** dashboard:

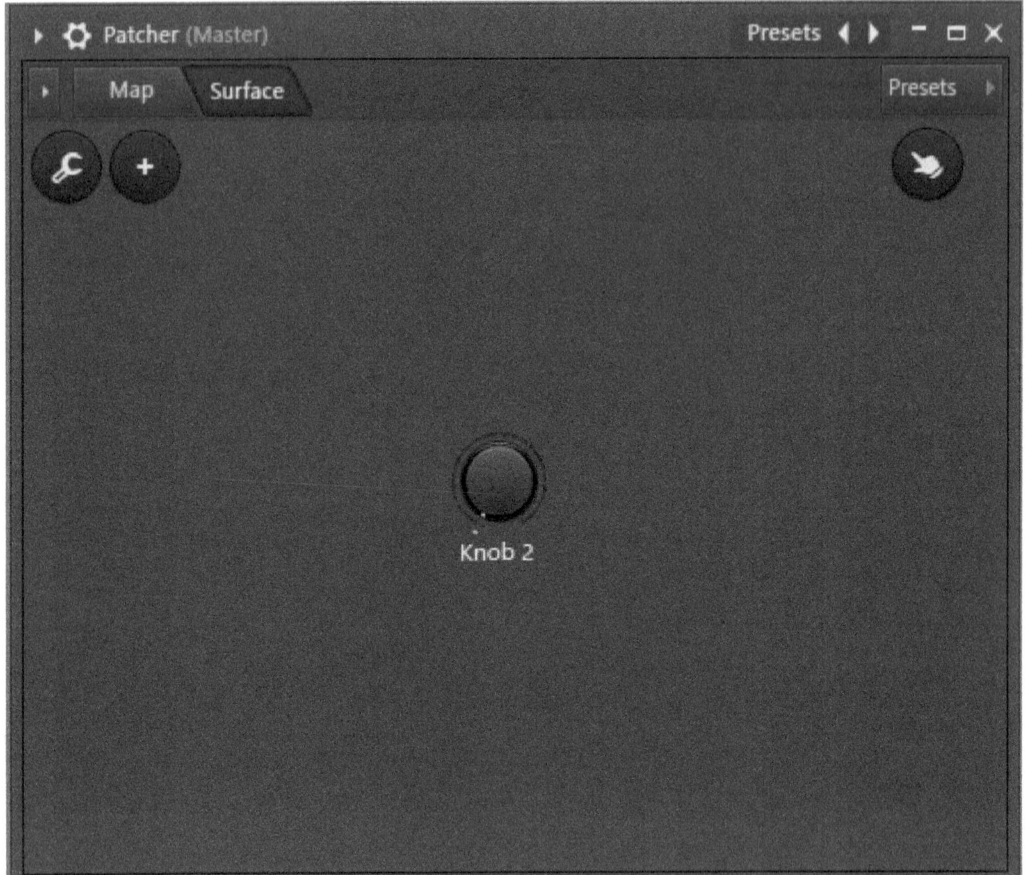

Figure 10.28 – Surface dashboard

From now on, anytime you want to adjust the control in **FLEX**, instead of opening **FLEX**, you can play with the knob on the **Surface** dashboard. Play some MIDI notes and adjust the knob in the **Surface** dashboard; you will hear the **FLEX** control adjusting as the instrument plays. When you're finished adding and routing instruments and effects, it's time to save Patcher.

10. To save it, go to the drop-down arrow at the top left of **Patcher** and choose **Save preset as** to save your preset.

Later on in any project, you can go to the drop-down arrow again and load your Patcher effects chain. You can even send the Patcher preset to another musician, and they'll be able to open your Patcher preset, assuming that they have access to the same plugins you do.

You now know how to create your own instrument and effect chains in Patcher. But what can you put into Patcher? Can you put any instrument? Why yes, yes you can.

Send any instrument into Patcher

There's a very easy way to send any **vst** plugin into Patcher using the **Patcherize** option. This will allow you to easily start creating chains of instruments and effects.

1. In order to send an instrument into **Patcher**, first load an instrument in the **Channel rack**.
2. Right-click on the **Channel rack** instrument and select the **Patcherize** option as shown in the following screenshot:

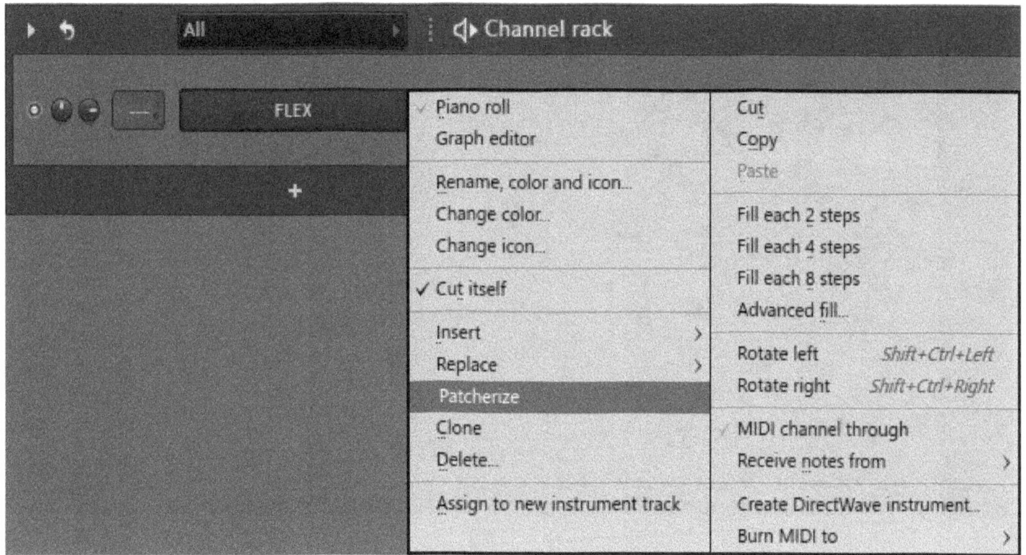

Figure 10.29 – Patcherize option

Patcher will open with the instrument loaded, ready to go.

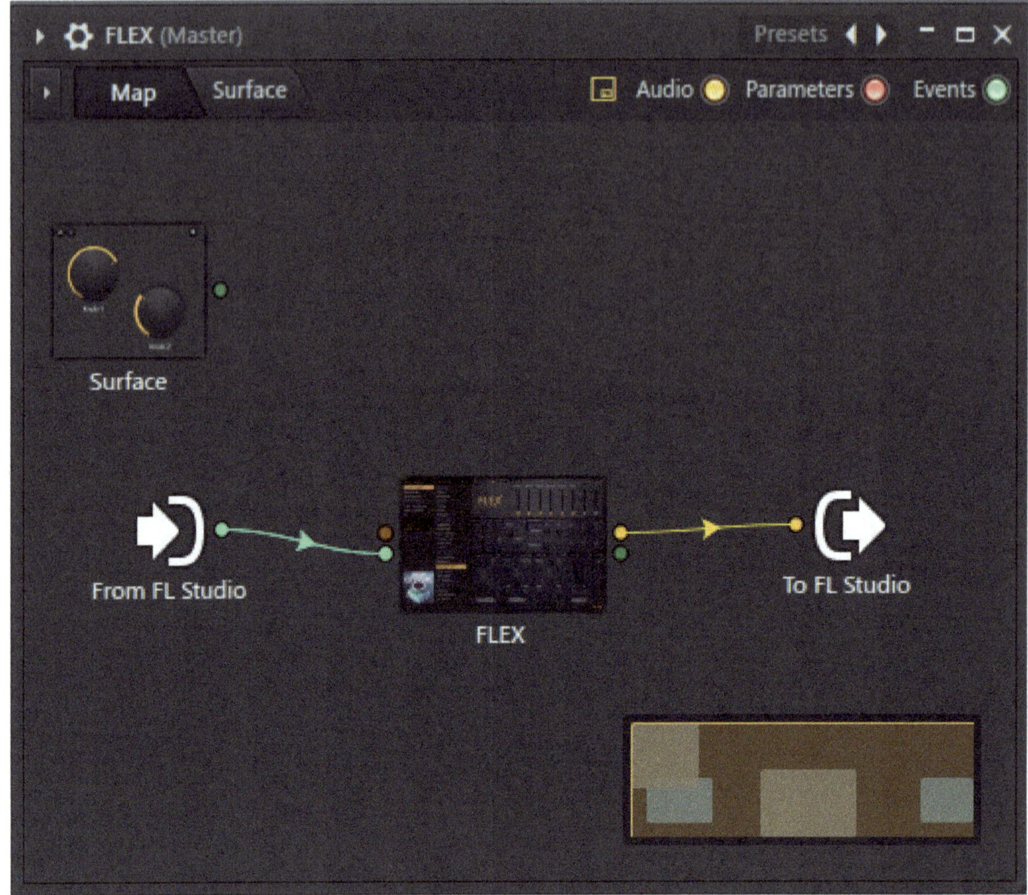

Figure 10.30 – Instrument sent to Patcher

You're not restricted to just using FL Studio instruments and effects inside of Patcher. You can even send non-native plugins into Patcher using the **Patcherize** option.

We've learned how to load instruments into Patcher; next, let's check out Patcher's presets.

Exploring Patcher presets

Patcher presets in FL Studio are pre-configured instrument and effect chains that can be loaded directly into a project. These presets cover a wide range of sounds and functions, including instruments, drum machines, and effects tools. By exploring the available Patcher presets, you can quickly access complex setups without manual configuration. This section outlines a number of presets that are included.

1. In the **Channel rack**, load an instance of Patcher.
2. In the top right corner of the **Patcher** plugin, select the **Presets** drop-down.

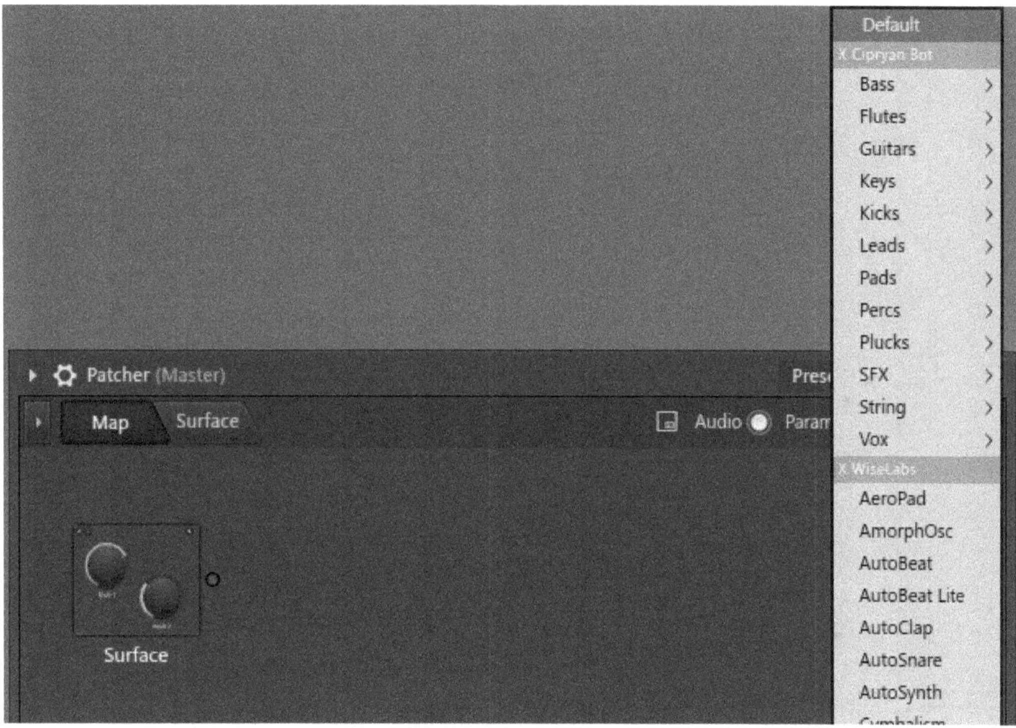

Figure 10.31 – Patcher presets

First in the presets is a list of instrument presets: **Bass**, **Flutes**, **Guitars**, **Keys**, **Kicks**, **Leads**, **Pads**, **Percs**, **Phucks**, **SFX**, **String**, **Vox**.

They keep adding presets with new editions of FL Studio, so this list of presets is ever-expanding. The following are the plugin presets included in Patcher: AeroPad, AmorphOsc, AutoBeat, AutoBeat Lite, AutoClap, AutoSnare, AutoSynth, Gymbalsm, DardmPad, DrumBass, Infinitom, KickMachine, LayerMor, Magic Hat, MeloScape, MidiVore, PercSeed, Plucker, ProbaBeat, ProbaBeat Lite, APR, APR UIE, Randomless, Reezor, RisenShine, SplitKit, Unblocker, Vocatcher, Wobbler, YottaSaw.

These presets are customized versions of Patcher. There are lots of Patcher presets, and I recommend you browse through them. There are too many to discuss all of them in this book, but we'll briefly touch on a few.

AeroPad is an ambient pad generator. Select the first preset and load up **AeroPad**, and you'll see the following:

Figure 10.32 – Patcher AeroPad

On the top right, you'll see a tab called **Presets**. Anytime you want, you can save a custom preset of Patcher for easy reloading later on. Saving a custom preset will remember the exact knob and effect positions of your Patcher instance.

At the top middle is a tab that says **Help**. By selecting this, you'll find a detailed set of instructions for what each button does in the preset.

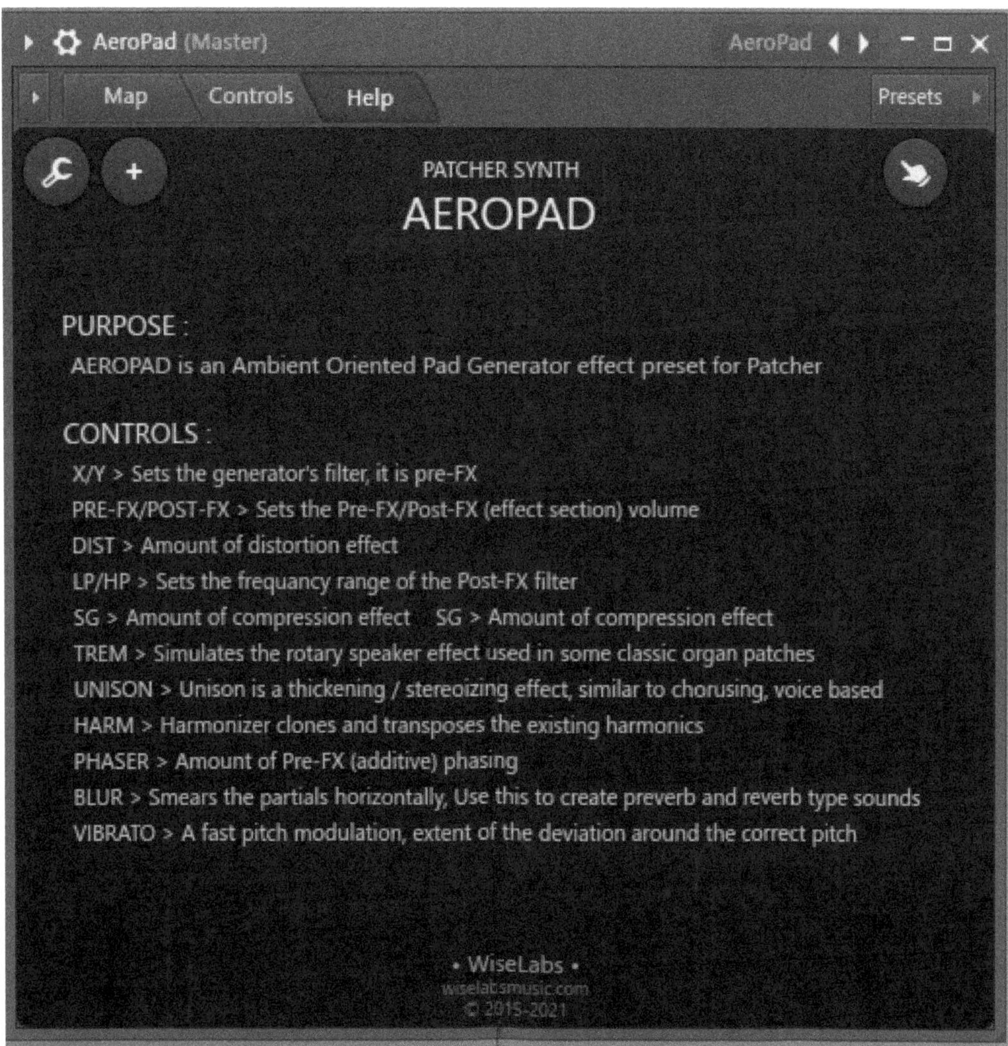

Figure 10.33 – Patcher Help tab

Most of the plugin presets have a **Help** tab, so make sure to check that out for tips on how to use the plugin. Also, using the AI **Gopher** help tool can sometimes shed light on advice.

Here's a brief description of some of the Patcher instrument presets:

- AutoClap, AutoSnare, Cymbalism, DrumBass, Infinitom, KickMachine, Magic-Hat, and PercSeed are percussion plugins that create percussion sounds. SplitKit is a full drum kit with different instruments assigned to each keyboard MIDI note.

- MidiVore is a key scale plugin that allows you to select an instrument scale. When you play MIDI notes, it will shift the notes received into notes that fit the selected instrument scale. If you're wondering what different scales might sound like, this is an easy way to experiment with playing notes from different scales.
- Plucker is a key-based plucked chord generator.
- ProbaBeat is a drum machine. QDR is a drum instrument.
- Randomless is based on the Harmless plugin. It generates new random presets depending on a random seed value you set.
- Reezor is a bass lead synth generator.
- Vocatcher is one of my favorites and is seen in the following screenshot. It's a vocal synth generator allowing you to create a synth sound like a vocal with many customizable parameters.

Figure 10.34 – Patcher Vocatcher

Lots of trap music uses synths that sound like vocals. If you've been looking for a great vocal synth, look no further than **Vocatcher**.

- Wobbler is a wobble machine generator. It creates wobble sounds that are often heard in dubstep music.

Figure 10.35 – Patcher Wobbler

For the control nut, the real beauty of Patcher is the endless automation and control capabilities. Remember earlier in this chapter, in *Figure 10.25*, we created a knob from scratch as a dashboard and hooked the knob to control our FLEX synth plugin. You can do the same thing with any Patcher preset.

In the case of Wobbler and some of the other presets, you can automate controls directly to the **Channel rack**. In Wobbler, if you right-click inside **OSC**, you can "**Create automation** Clip" as shown in the following screenshot.

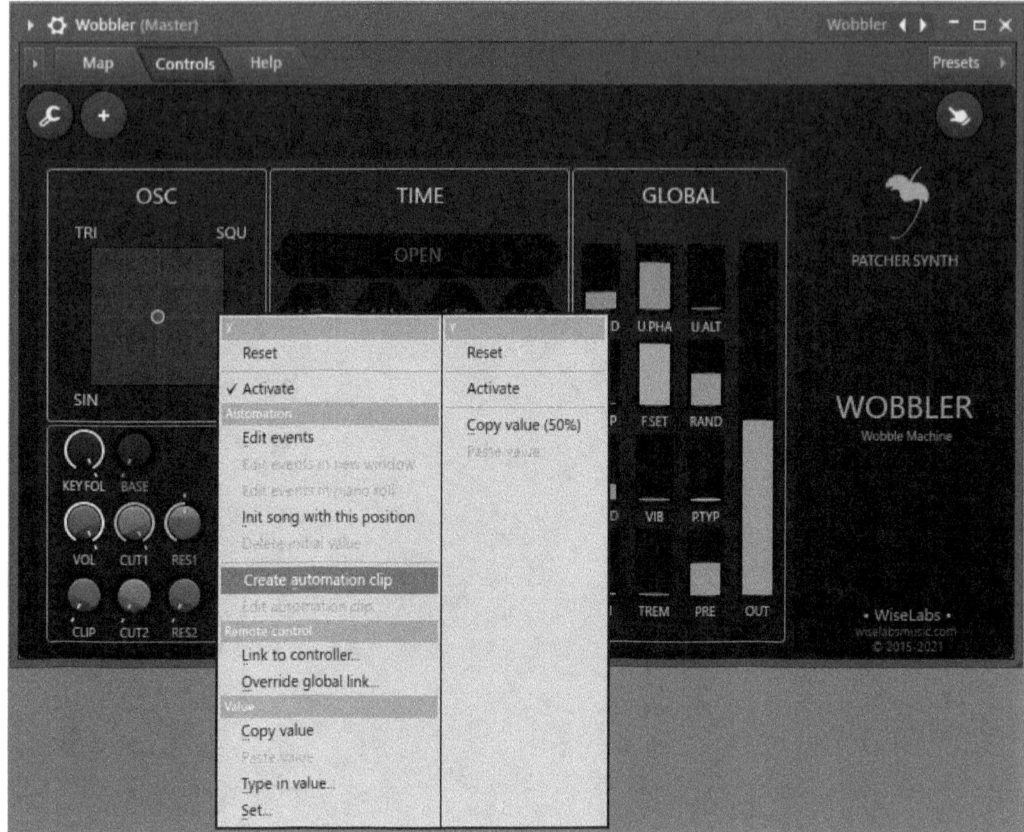

Figure 10.36 – Patcher Wobbler automation

This will create an automation clip in the Playlist that you can then adjust.

- YottaSaw is another of my favorite Patcher presets. It's a key-based chord generator.

Figure 10.37 – Patcher YottaSaw

With YottaSaw, regardless of what note you hit, the plugin will create a full saw chord out of the note. You can then customize the sound.

The great thing about Patcher presets is that, although you can endlessly customize them inside of Patcher, at the end of the day, they're just instruments that exist in the Channel rack. So you can treat them just like any other instrument in the Channel rack. You can add MIDI notes for them to play in the Piano roll and later add effects in the Mixer.

We've explored some of Patcher's presets. That said, we've only just scraped the surface. All of the Patcher presets we looked at were from using Patcher in the Channel rack. However, if you load up Patcher in the Mixer and check out the presets, you'll discover a massive list of additional effects.

Figure 10.38 – Patcher presets when loaded into the Mixer

There are too many presets to dive into in this book, but I encourage you to check them out on your own.

Next, let's look at a powerful **Patcher arpeggiator plugin** called **VFX Sequencer**.

Using VFX Sequencer to create arpeggiated patterns

VFX Sequencer is a powerful MIDI sequencer plugin that runs inside Patcher.

In general, **arpeggiators** play a series of notes whenever they receive a MIDI note. For example, you could play a chord, and the arpeggiator could then cycle between playing notes inside the chord. A **sequencer** is an advanced arpeggiator, giving you lots of control over how the note patterns are created.

VFX Sequencer allows you to generate MIDI notes for any instrument. Let's explore VFX Sequencer:

1. Open up an instance of Patcher in the **Channel rack**.
2. Inside **Patcher**, right-click and select the option **Add plugin**.

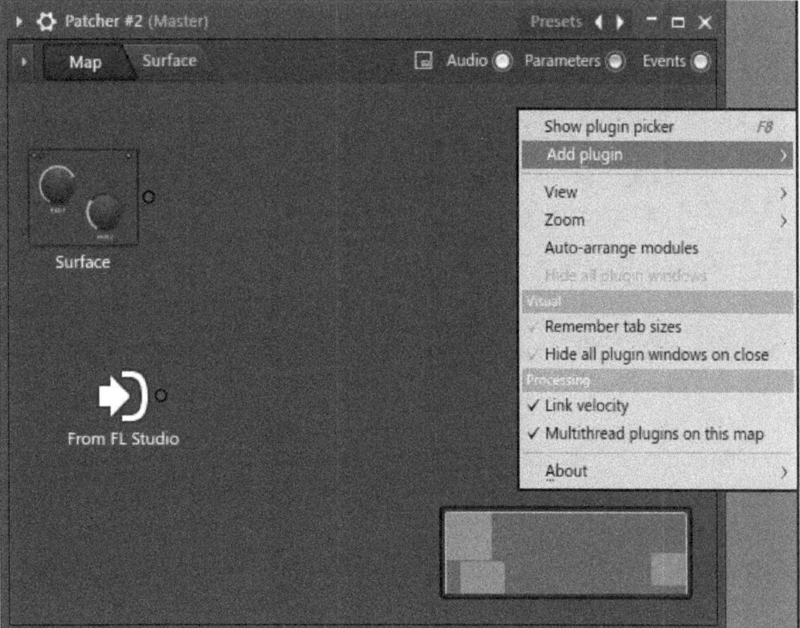

Figure 10.39 – Add plugin option in Patcher to add VFX Sequencer

3. Locate **VFX Sequencer** and select it. You'll see that **VFX Sequencer** is added to **Patcher** as shown in the following screenshot.

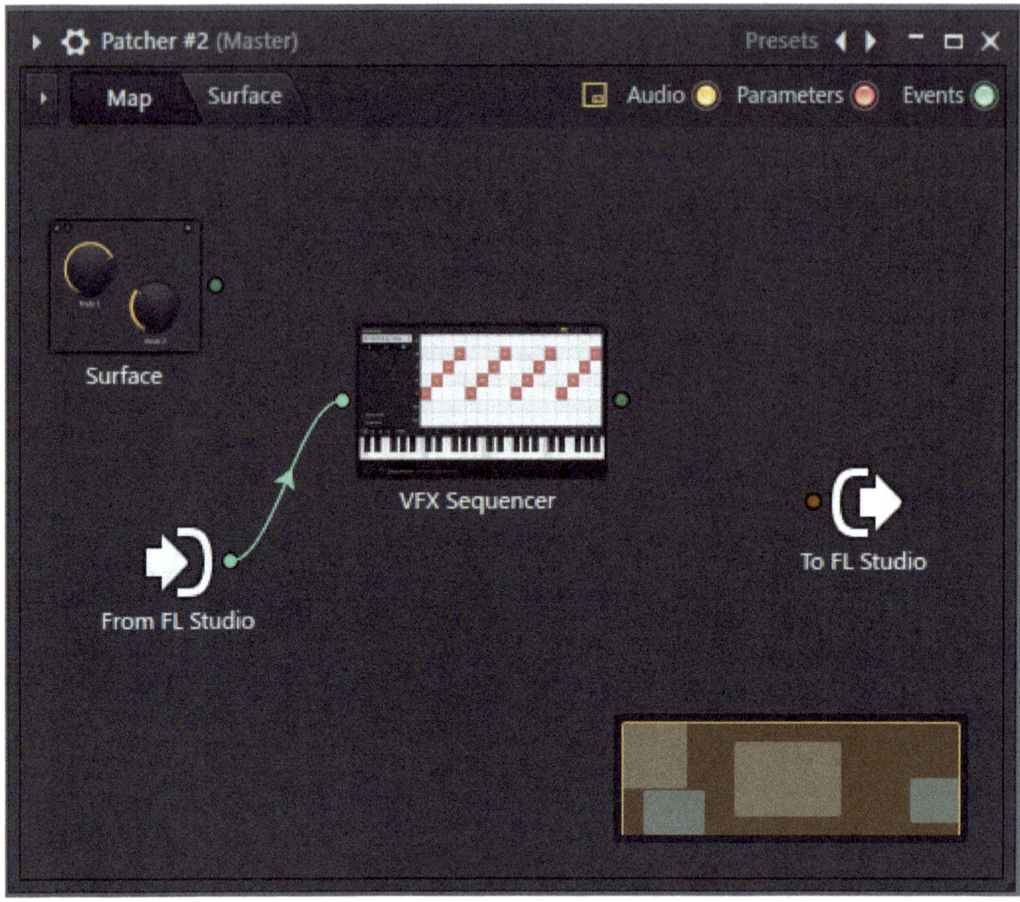

Figure 10.40 – VFX Sequencer added to Patcher

You'll notice by default that VFX Sequencer doesn't output audio the way that synthesizer plugins like FLEX do. Hitting MIDI notes won't make any sound by default. This is because VFX outputs MIDI notes, but doesn't output audio. VFX generates MIDI sequences to be played by a synthesizer plugin. We need to add an instrument for the VFX Sequencer to generate notes for. Let's do that next.

4. Right-click on the green circle to the right of **VFX Sequencer** as shown in the following screenshot. Add a synthesizer plugin of your choice. In the following example, I'm using the FL Studio plugin **FL Keys**, but I encourage you to try with FLEX, Harmless, or another synth plugin.

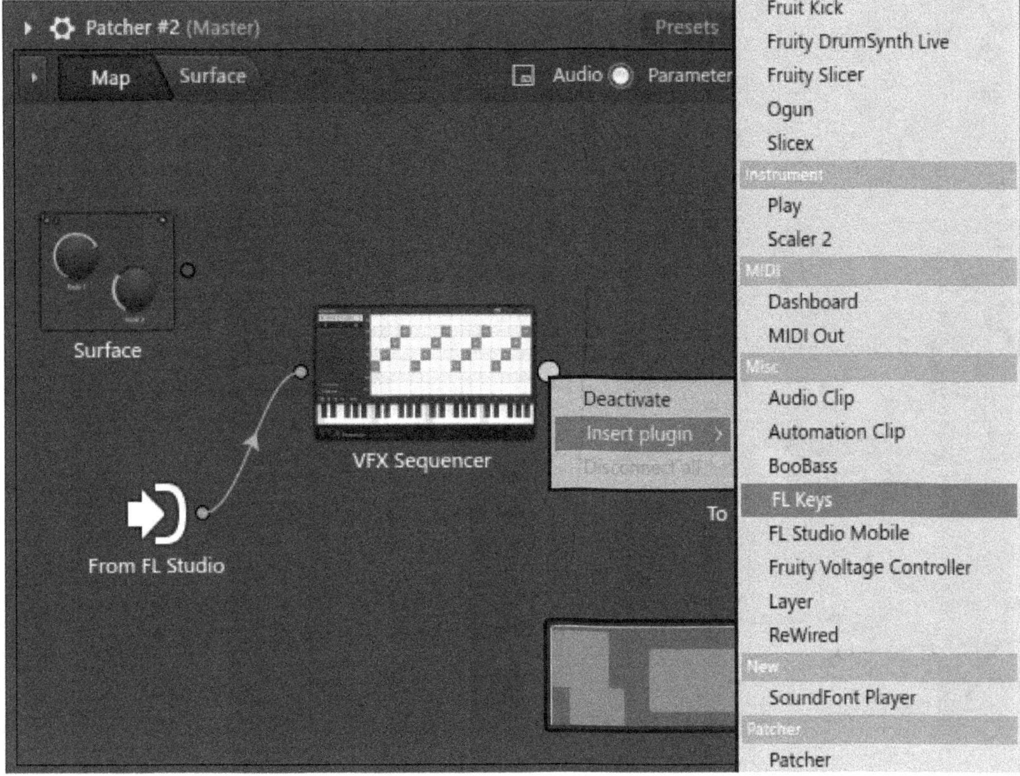

Figure 10.41 – Add instrument for VFX Sequencer

This will create an instrument synthesizer inside Patcher and automatically set up the MIDI routing. It will route any MIDI output from VFX and send it to the new instrument before routing the Patcher audio to the Patcher output. The result is shown in the following screenshot:

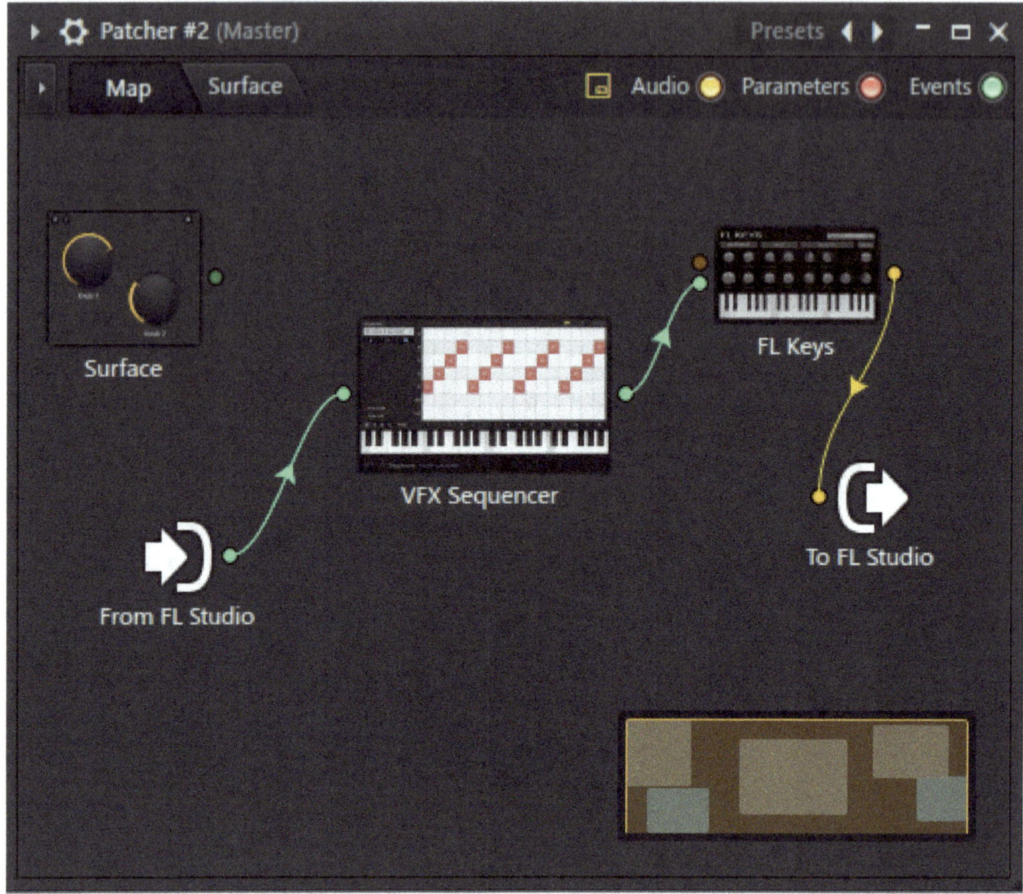

Figure 10.42 – VFX Sequencer MIDI data routed to instrument

In the preceding screenshot, we can see that MIDI notes are received from the Piano roll. This is what **From FL Studio** means. The MIDI notes are passed to the VFX Sequencer. VFX Sequencer performs any arpeggiation transformations it wants to and then passes the MIDI information along to **FL Keys**, which plays the MIDI notes and creates audio, which is then output from Patcher and sent through **To FL Studio** to be sent to the Mixer.

Okay, we're all set up and ready to get started using VFX Sequencer. Let's check out the arpeggiation abilities of VFX Sequencer. Double right-click on VFX Sequencer to open the plugin.

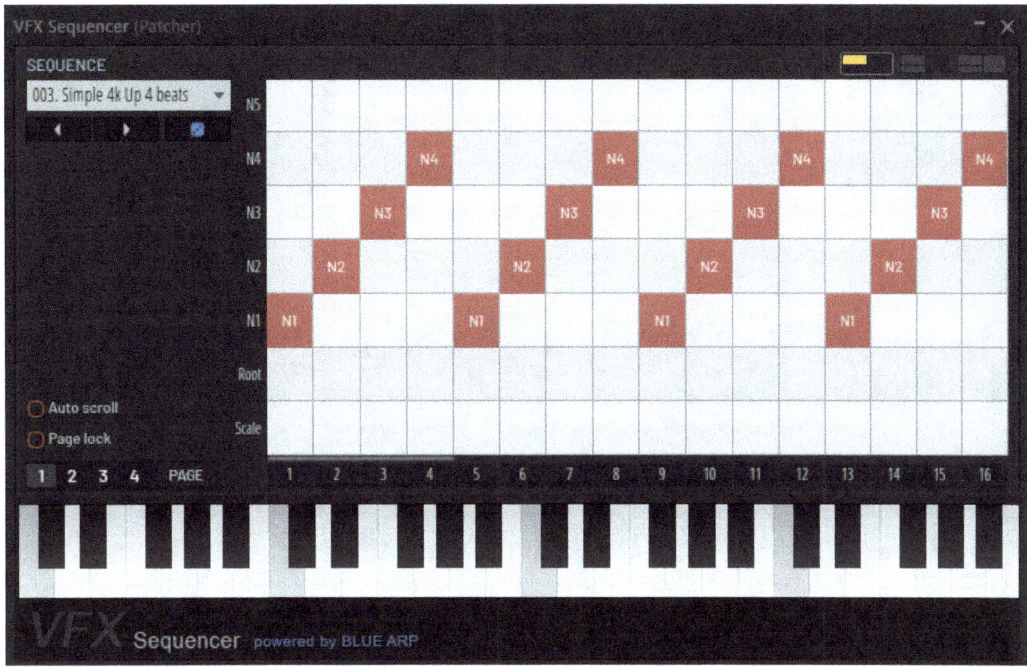

Figure 10.43 – VFX Sequencer single panel

By default, VFX Sequencer opens up in single panel mode. If you left-click on one of the keyboard notes, you'll hear the VFX Sequencer playing an arpeggio starting with the selected note.

In the middle, you'll see the grid of notes for VFX Sequencer to play. You can left-click on blank spaces in the grid to change the arpeggio being played.

At the top left, you'll see a drop-down menu of various arpeggio presets that can be selected. Below are arrows to go to the next sequence preset, previous sequence, or to generate a random sequence of notes.

At the top right of VFX Sequencer, you'll see various display modes. Select the **DISPLAY MODE COMPLETE**. You'll see the following:

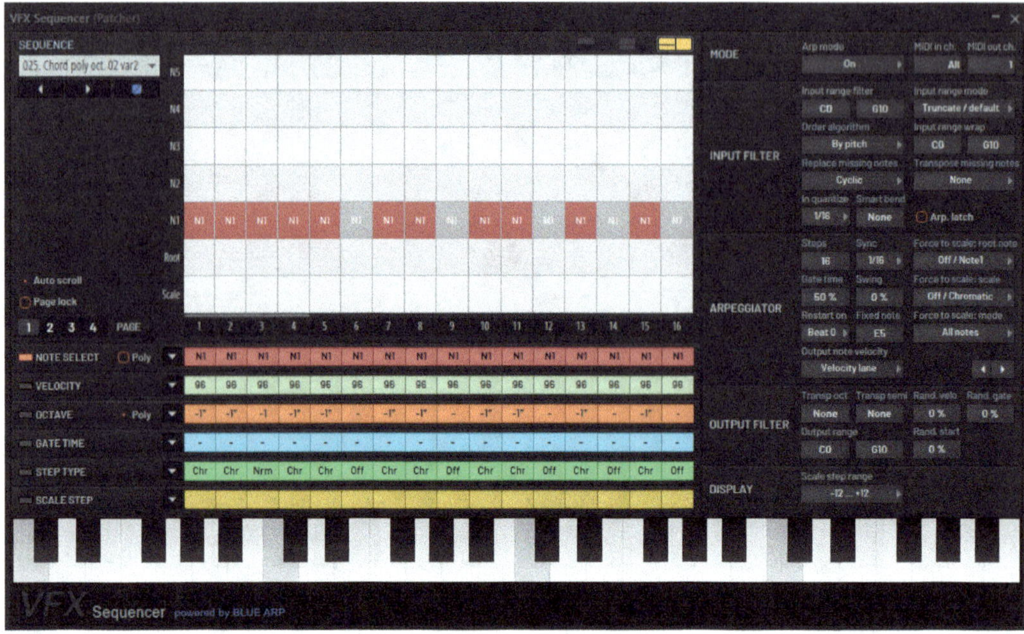

Figure 10.44 – DISPLAY MODE COMPLETE

This will unlock additional panels. Let's take a look at the panel in the bottom left.

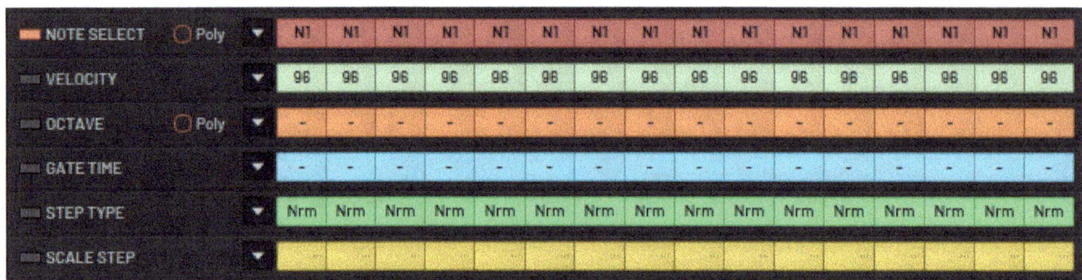

Figure 10.45 – Additional panel with controls – NOTE SELECT by default

On the left side, you'll see the controls: **NOTE SELECT**, **VELOCITY**, **OCTAVE**, **GATE TIME**, **STEP TYPE**, and **SCALE STEP**. As you select one of these, you'll see the display change to give you a view of the control. By default, you're seeing **NOTE SELECT**. If you select a different control, the display will adjust accordingly.

The colored bands of notes to the right of the controls allow you to scroll or drag to change the values of individual arpeggio note parameters.

NOTE SELECT and **OCTAVE** have an enabling button for **Poly**. This allows you to enable multiple notes to be played simultaneously instead of the default single note. To the right of the controls are dropdown options that allow you to create global changes to your arpeggio notes, affecting all the notes at once instead of accessing them individually.

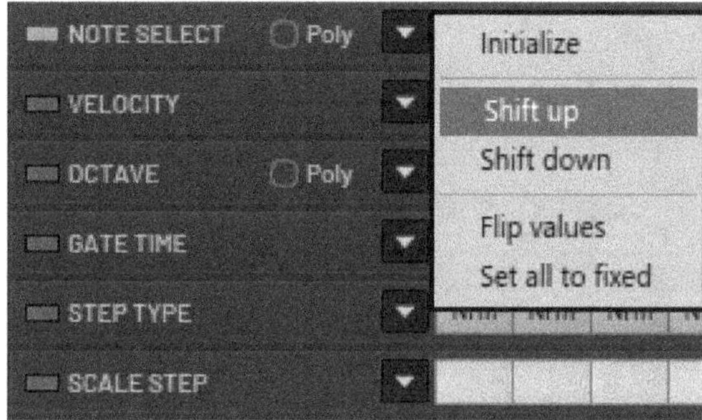

Figure 10.46 – Dropdown options

Next, let's check out the right side panels.

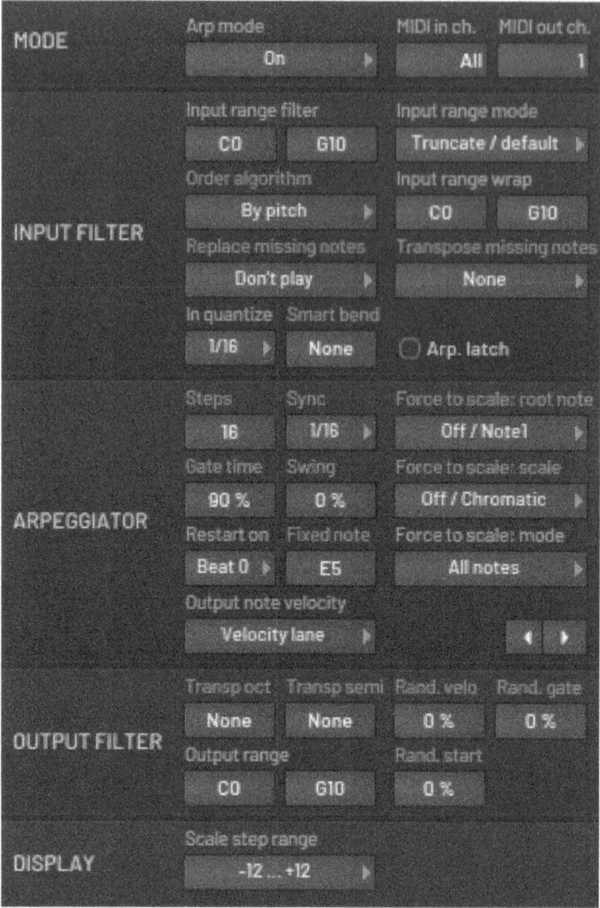

Figure 10.47 – VFX Sequencer advanced controls

Here's a description of the controls. They're a little confusing to understand by just reading them. If you want to understand them, I recommend playing some arpeggiated notes while toggling between the settings.

- **MODE**:
  - **Arp mode**: Chooses how to arpeggiate. Options are:
    - **On**
    - **Off**: Ignore any input.
    - **Thru**: Allow notes, but don't arpeggiate. Still allow other settings such as **Input Range**, **Output Range**, **Transpose**, and **Force** to scale.

        - **2/3 auto on/off**: Only play when 2 or 3 notes are being played, or otherwise turn off.
        - **2/3 auto on/thru**: When 2 or 3 notes are played, the arpeggiator runs or otherwise allows single notes to pass without arpeggiation.
    - **MIDI in ch.**: Use MIDI input channel (All/Omni or 1 to 16).
    - **MIDI out ch.**: Use MIDI output channel (All/Omni or 1 to 16).
- **INPUT FILTER**:
    - **Input range filter**: Sets the range of notes for the arpeggiator to play within.
    - **Input range mode**: Options are:
        - **Truncate**: Only arpeggiates notes within the selected range.
        - **Pass thru**: Notes within the range are not arpeggiated.
    - **Input range wrap**: Transpose notes up or down an octave until they fit within range. For example, with a bass instrument, you'd want to keep notes in the lower range.
    - **Order algorithm**: Set how to order notes: Options are:
        - **By pitch**: Lowest note is N1.
        - **By pitch desc**: Last note set is N1.
        - **As played**: Plays chords from low to high.
        - **As played desc**: N1 is played last.
        - **By velocity**: Max velocity is N1.
        - **By velocity desc**: Minimum velocity is N1.
        - **Chord (normalized)**: Ignore chord inversions.
        - **Chord (as played)**: Allow chord inversions.
    - **Replace missing notes**: Decide what to do when there are multiple input notes simultaneously. Options are:
        - **Don't play**: Mute notes for arpeggiation.
        - **Cyclic**: Cycle between notes for arpeggiation.
        - **First key**: Use the first note for arpeggiation.
        - **Last key**: Use the last note for arpeggiation.
        - **Fixed key**: Use a fixed note for the arpeggiation set under **ARPEGGIATOR**.

- **Transpose missing notes**:
    - **None**: Don't transpose notes.
    - **+1 / -1 Octave**: Replace notes an octave relative to the input.
- **In quantize**: Allows you to re-time notes.
- **Smart bend:** Works with **Force to scale: scale**. Adjusts notes to fit into the selected scale. If **Force to scale** is set to **Off**, then it is a chromatic scale.
- **Arp latch – OFF**: arpeggiator stops when input stops. **ON**: arpeggiator keeps playing the last input notes. Can assign a switch to a keyboard pedal to activate it for live performance with a little tinkering.

- **ARPEGGIATOR**:
    - **Steps**: 0-64.
    - **Sync**: Step fraction of a bar.
    - **Force scale: root note - Off/Note1**: Create a chord from the N1 pitch.
    - **Force to scale: scale**: Set scale. Works with **Force to scale: root note**.
        - **Off/chromatic**
        - **Detect from chord:** Use input notes to create a scale.
        - **Explicit options:** Choose from a list of scales.
    - **Force to scale: mode**: Works with the **Force to scale: scale**.
        - **All notes**: Transposes everything.
        - **Semi-transposed**: Steps with **'Scale Step > '-'' (no change)** selected won't be transposed.
    - **Gate time**: Select a step with a range of 1 to 125%.
    - **Swing**: Select a swing range. Swing shifts the timing of even steps.
    - **Restart on**: Select when to restart the pattern. Options:
        - **Beat 0**
        - **Notes**: Whenever a new input note is received.
        - **1st note**: Continues until FL Studio playback is restarted.
        - **Play**: Play upon FL Studio playback.
    - **Fixed note**: Using the **NOTE SELECT** lane on the far left of VFX Sequencer allows you to replace input notes with a fixed key value instead.

    - **Output note velocity**: Velocity can be thought of as how much emphasis you're using on a percussive sound. More velocity means you're hitting the instrument note harder. Velocity options are:
        - **Velocity lane**: Use velocity lanes.
        - **Input note**: Use input note velocities.
        - **Lane + input note**: Scale input by velocity lane.
    - **Pattern shift**: Rotate the pattern. Useful if the pattern doesn't fit the downbeat.
- **OUTPUT FILTER**:
    - **Transp oct**: Transposes sequence by octaves.
    - **Transp semi**: Transposes sequence by semitones.
    - **Rand. vel**: Randomly assigns velocities within range. Creates some realism, so note velocities are less repetitive.
    - **Rand. gate**: Randomly assigns gate values within range.
    - **Output range** (wrap): Notes outside the range will be transposed until fitting into the range.
    - **Rand. start**: Randomizes note start times within the selected range.

You now know how to use VFX Sequencer to create arpeggiated patterns for any instrument.

Summary

In this chapter, we learned how to create glitch effects using Gross Beat so that you can come up with creative sound effects. We learned how to create our own instruments from samples using DirectWave. We learned how to create real-time looping effects using the Transporter plugin. Finally, we learned how to create our own instrument and effect chains with Patcher. We learned about various presets available in Patcher, and we learned about the VFX Sequencer in Patcher.

In the next chapter, we will learn about postproduction.

Get this book's PDF version and more

Scan the QR code (or go to `packtpub.com/unlock`). Search for this book by name, confirm the edition, and then follow the steps on the page.

Note: Keep your invoice handy. Purchases made directly from Packt don't require an invoice.

11

Intermediate to Advanced Mixing Topics and Sound Design Plugin Effects

In this chapter, we'll cover some of FL Studio's latest plugins. For the ambitious and eager to explore cutting-edge sound design, FL Studio offers an abundance of tools. This chapter explores advanced FL Studio plugin effects for those who feel they already have a decent grasp of FL Studio and want fine control over their sound design. These are advanced topics, so don't feel discouraged if they go a little over your head the first time you read about these topics.

In this chapter, you will learn how to create real-time pitch-shifting effects using **Pitch Shifter**. You will explore how to create metallic sounds and shift frequencies with **Frequency Shifter**. You will also learn how to stretch audio waves to create complex sound textures with **Fruity Granulizer**. In addition, you will discover how to create delay effects with **Multiband Delay** and how to use **Frequency Splitter**, a tool designed to provide precise control over multiband processing in the Mixer. You will learn how to enhance the bass in your sounds using **Low Lifter**. Finally, you will learn how to play the synthesizer plugins **Kepler** and **Kepler Exo**.

In this chapter, we will cover the following:

- Real-time pitch shifting with Pitch Shifter
- Shifting frequencies with Frequency Shifter
- Creating granular synthesis with Fruity Granulizer
- Creating delay effects with Multiband Delay
- Multiband processing with Frequency Splitter
- Adding harmonics to bass frequencies using the Low Lifter plugin

- Learning to play the Kepler synthesizer
- Learn to play the Kepler EXO synthesizer

Real-time pitch shifting with Pitch Shifter

Pitch Shifter is a pitch-shifting effect that comes with FL Studio *All Plugins Edition*. It is used to change the pitch of audio in real time. This means you can make sounds higher or lower without affecting their speed, or creatively manipulate vocals and instruments for effects like harmonization, pitch correction, or experimental sound design. It contains two pitch shift algorithms, one for **monophonic sounds** (single notes at a time) such as vocals, and one for **polyphonic sounds** (multiple notes at a time). In my opinion, Pitch Shifter creates a more natural and better pitch-corrected result than the FL Studio plugin **NewTone**, which was discussed in *Chapter 8*.

In the following subsection of Pitch Shifter, we will first discuss how to apply effects to polyphonic sounds, then to monophonic sounds like vocals, and finally, how to use controllers with **MIDI** notes to manually dictate which pitch notes are used.

Let's get started using Frequency Splitter.

1. Load up an audio sample in the **Playlist** and route it to the **Mixer**.
2. Apply the **Pitch Shifter** effect to the **Mixer** channel and play your sound. You'll see **Pitch Shifter** load up as shown in the following screenshot:

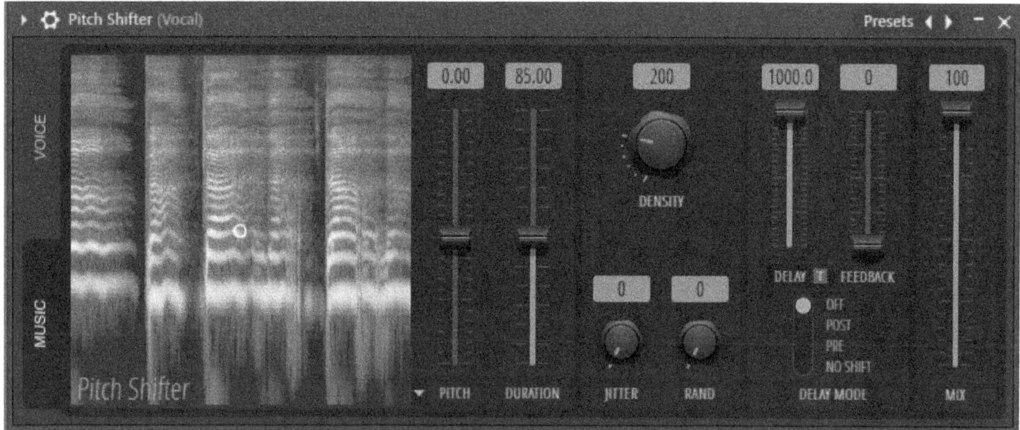

Figure 11.1 – Pitch Shifter

On the far-left side, you'll see the tabs **MUSIC** and **VOICE**. **MUSIC** is for polyphonic sounds. **VOICE** is for the **monophonic pitch shifting algorithm**. You'll usually want the **VOICE** setting if you're applying pitch shifting effects to vocals. You'll see a different plugin interface depending on whether the **VOICE** or **MUSIC** tab is selected. By default, the **MUSIC** tab is selected.

When the **MUSIC** tab is selected, a *granular* **pitch-shifting engine** is used. Incoming audio is sliced into waves, which can be looped. **Loops** are called **grains**. Pitch is controlled by the speed of playback of the grains. Playing a granular loop faster will increase its pitch. Playing it slower will decrease its pitch. Duration can lengthen the sound by repeating grains or shorten it by skipping grains.

There are plugin presets in the top right corner of the plugin, which I encourage you to check out. Moving from left to right, here's a summary of the controls.

- **PITCH**: Controls the pitch of the audio. If you want to change the pitch of the audio, this is the knob that you'll want to automate. You can automate by right-clicking and choosing the option **Create Automation Clip**.
- **DURATION**: Length of the grain buffer. Longer buffers work better with low-pitched audio; shorter buffers work better with higher-pitched audio.
- **DENSITY**: How much smoothness to apply to sound. Larger values smooth the sound more.
- **JITTER**: Adds randomness to the timing grains. At a value of 0, there is no randomness added. If you want to hear more artifices, you can increase the value.
- **RAND**: Adds randomness to the start position of each grain.
- **DELAY**: Amount of delay time to add.
- **FEEDBACK**: Amount of output signal to feed back into Pitch Shifter.
- **DELAY MODE**: In the Pitch Shifter plugin, it determines how the delay effect interacts with the pitch-shifting process. There are several delay options:
    - **OFF**: no delay effects.
    - **POST**: signal is delayed, and then pitch shifted.
    - **PRE**: audio is pitch-shifted and then delayed.
    - **NO SHIFT**: deactivate feedback.
- **MIX**: How strong an effect to apply.

On the far left, if you select the **VOICE** tab, you'll see the interface turn blue, and some new controls appear (**PITCH**, **FORMANT**, and **PITCH ANALYSIS**) as shown in the following screenshot:

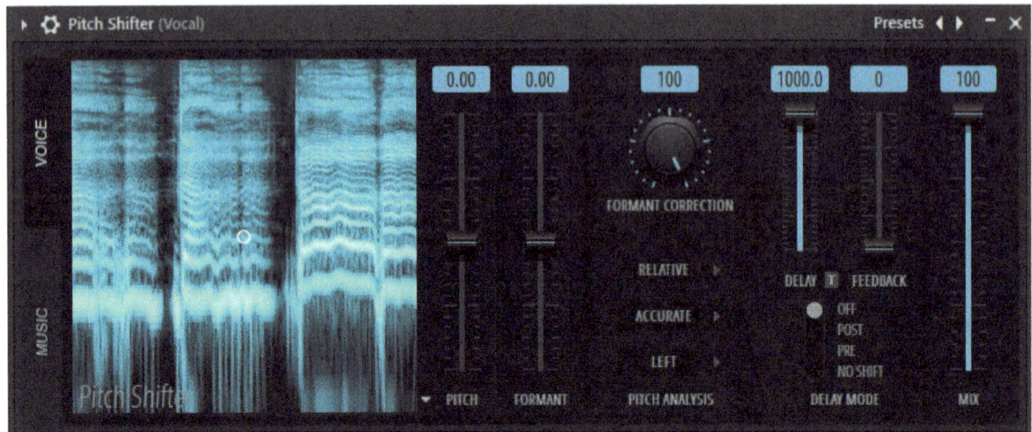

Figure 11.2 – VOICE tab

Here's a description of the Pitch Shifter **VOICE** tab controls:

- **PITCH**: Controls the pitch of the audio. You can right-click and select **Create Automation Clip** to automate the control. You can also control this through a keyboard controller or envelope controller. If so, you'll want to enable the **Absolute Pitch** mode on the plugin. We'll discuss this further in a moment.
- **FORMANT**: Creates the impression of a larger or smaller sound. When you adjust the pitch, you may find the audio sounds unnatural; you can adjust the formant to attempt to compensate. For example, as you adjust the pitch up, you can adjust the formant effect lower. Alternatively, many musicians enjoy the sound of playing with the formant effect on its own, regardless of any changes in pitch.
- **PITCH ANALYSIS**: In this panel, you'll find controls for **FORMANT CORRECTION** and three drop-down menus: **Pitch Mode**, **Pitch Detector**, and **Analysis** channel. In the screenshot above, although they aren't labeled, you see the text **RELATIVE**, **ACCURATE**, and **LEFT**. These are the initial selections in the drop-down menus.
    - **FORMANT CORRECTION**: Automates formant correction. If set to 0%, it produces the most natural sound. If set to 100%, you'll get the most variability and the least natural sound. Normally, formants don't change with pitch, so having formant to compensate automatically sounds unnatural, but could be a creative effect if desired.

- **PITCH MODE** dropdown menu:
  - **RELATIVE**: Incoming pitch is preserved.
  - **ABSOLUTE**: Incoming pitches are flattened to C notes. The intended purpose of this is for the pitch knob to be controlled by an automation clip, keyboard controller, or envelope controller. This will repatch the audio into a new melody. We'll discuss an example next.
- **PITCH DETECTOR** dropdown menu:
  - **FAST**: Keeps live input and pitch-shifted signals in sync. May struggle with lower frequencies below 100Hz. In general, you should use **FAST** unless you hear problems.
  - **ACCURATE**: May be more accurate when detecting frequencies below 100Hz.
- **ANALYSIS CHANNEL** dropdown menu: Chooses which channel for pitch analysis. **LEFT**, **RIGHT**, or both (**LEFT + RIGHT**). This can be useful if one stereo channel is clearer than the other.

Controlling Pitch Shifter effects with a controller

You can adjust the pitch effect of the Frequency Shifter using a keyboard controller or envelope controller. This allows you to use MIDI notes to decide what pitch frequency to hit. This gives you much more precise control than using an automation clip. Let's control the pitch using a keyboard controller or envelope controller.

1. Load up an audio sample in the **Playlist** and route it to the **Mixer**.
2. Apply the Pitch Shifter effect to the **Mixer** channel and play your sound.
3. Select the **VOICE** tab on the left side of **Pitch Shifter**. This will turn the interface blue and show formant controls.
4. In the **Playlist**, create a new pattern that is the length of the audio sample. Your **Playlist** should look similar to the following screenshot:

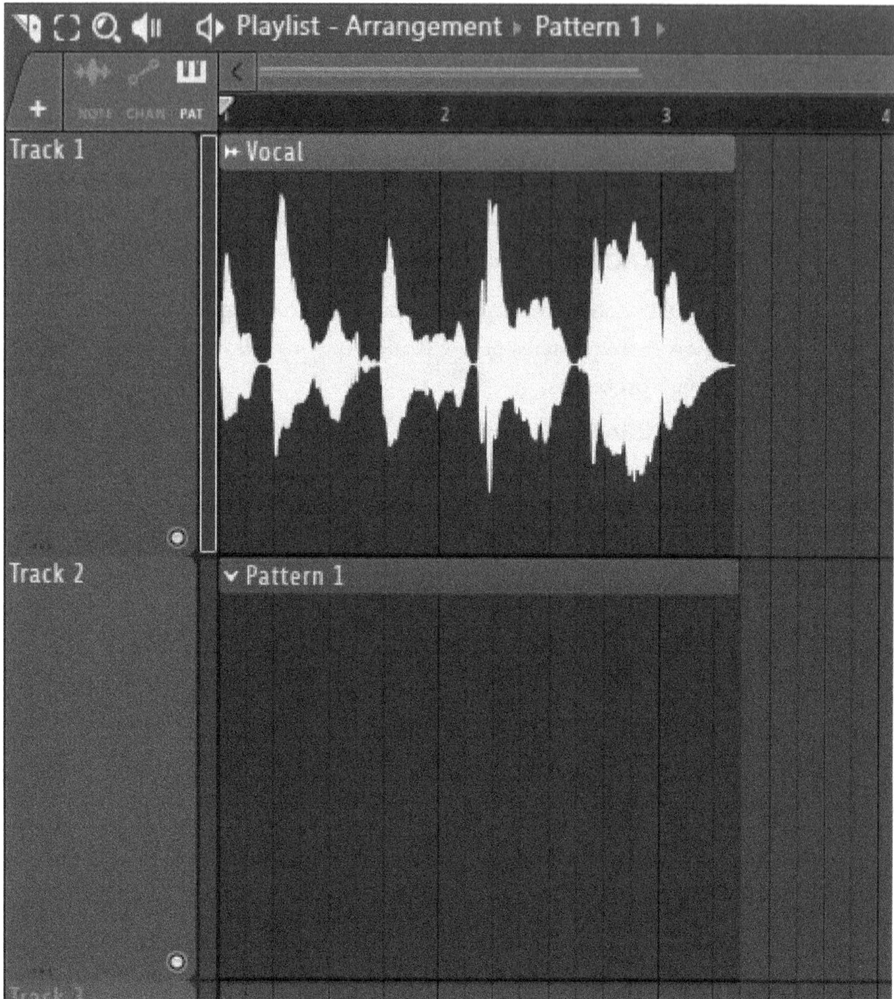

Figure 11.3 – New pattern in the Playlist

5. In the **Channel rack** pattern, load up an instance of **Fruity Keyboard Controller** or **Fruity Envelope Controller**. Right-click the controller you added and select **Piano roll**.

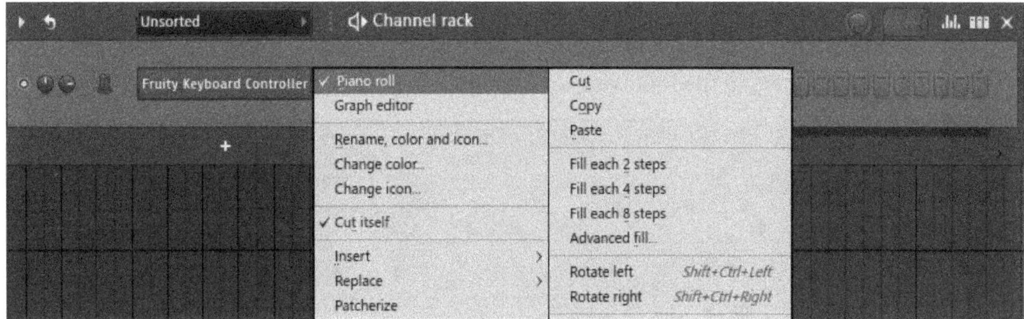

Figure 11.4 – Selecting Piano roll

6. In the **Piano roll**, left-click in the grid to add some MIDI notes for your controller to play. These will be the pitches that Pitch Shifter will force the audio to use. An example is shown in the following screenshot:

Figure 11.5 – Add MIDI notes

In the preceding screenshot, we can see that we've added MIDI notes to the **Fruity Keyboard Controller**. In the **Playlist**, the pattern playing MIDI notes is placed side by side with the vocal so they play at the same time.

7. Open up **Pitch Shifter**. Make sure that **ABSOLUTE** is selected under **FORMANT CORRECTION**. Then right-click on the pitch slider and select **Link to controller...**. An example is shown in the following screenshot:

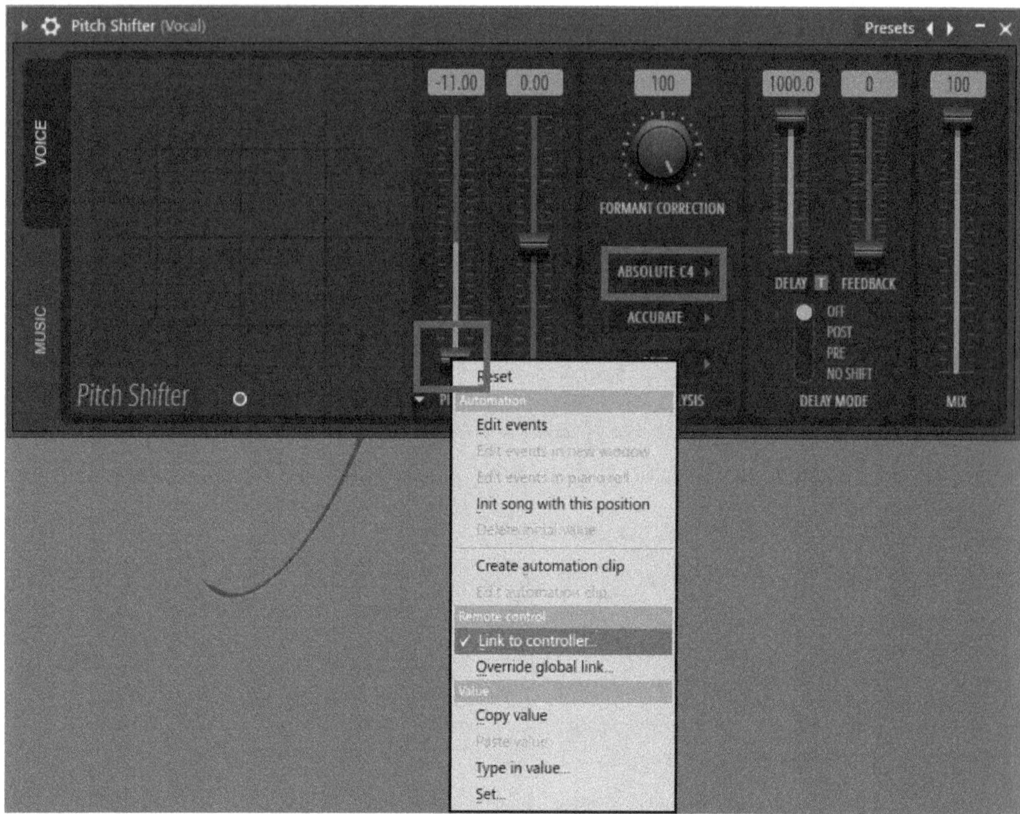

Figure 11.6 – Selecting Link to Controller option

A pop-up will appear with the **Remote control settings**.

Figure 11.7 – Remote control setting - Internal Controller

8. Select the dropdown under **Internal Controller**. You'll see the controller that you added in the **Channel rack**; select it.

From now on, whenever you play your audio, the Pitch Shifter will be controlled by the MIDI notes that you set in the Piano roll for the controller. This is a very convenient way to control pitch shifting. You now know how to use Pitch Shifter.

We've learned how to adjust the pitch of music and voice. Next, let's learn about another pitch-altering plugin called Frequency Shifter.

Shifting frequencies with Frequency Shifter

Frequency Shifter is a special effect plugin that comes with FL Studio *Producer Edition* and higher that shifts all frequencies of a sound by the same amount. It operates similarly to the FL Studio plugin Pitch Shifter, except that it doesn't preserve the **pitch key** when shifting frequencies. Pitch key refers to the specific MIDI note (key) that plays a sample or instrument at its original, unaltered pitch. Instead of altering the pitch key, Frequency Shifter increments by whatever exact value you tell it to use. It doesn't force specific pitches the way Pitch Shifter does.

Frequency Shifter effects are much stronger on lower frequency sounds than higher frequency sounds. Why? If you have a starting frequency at 100 Hz and shift by 400 Hz, the result is 500 Hz. If you have a starting frequency at 10,000 Hz and the shift is 400 Hz, the result is 10,400 Hz. The relative change is much smaller for the higher frequencies compared to the relative change for the lower frequencies. This is different from how other Pitch Shifters work, as they multiply the frequencies by a value instead of just adding. How does this affect the sound? Audio affected by Frequency Shifter effects will sound more dissonant and metallic. This is great for creating **dark dubstep bass sounds**.

Let's get started using the Frequency Shifter.

1. Load up an audio sample in the **Playlist** and route it to the **Mixer**.
2. Apply the Frequency Shifter effect to the **Mixer** channel and play your sound. You'll see **Frequency Shifter** load up as shown in the following screenshot:

Figure 11.8 – Frequency Shifter

There are plugin presets in the top right corner of the plugin that I encourage you to check out.

Here's a description of the controls:

- **FREQUENCY**: Amount in Hz to add to the original sound.
    - **20 kHz**: use for extreme effects.
    - **200 Hz**: default effect.
    - **TEMPO**: adds a frequency multiple of the song tempo. A cool effect to consider if you plan on changing the song tempo, as it will adjust accordingly.
- **FREQ. SHIFTER**: This is the standard frequency shifting mode. It shifts all frequencies in the input signal by a fixed amount (in Hz), which can create unique effects such as metallic sounds or phasing.
- **FREQ. SHIFTER HQ**: This is the high-quality version of the frequency shifter. It reduces aliasing noises that can occur when applying dramatic frequency shifts, resulting in a cleaner and more accurate effect.
- **RING MOD**: Enables sidechaining input to influence effects. This is discussed further in the next section.
- **SIDECHAIN**: Used in **RING MOD**.
- **SIDEBAND L/R**: Gives control over whether the frequency shift occurs in just the left or right channel. Left and right can be linked to move simultaneously.
- **ST. PHASE** (Start Phase): Sets the start phase for the sine wave oscillator.
- **L/R PHASE**: Sets the difference between the Left and Right phase. The effect sounds stronger when the frequency parameter is 5Hz or lower.
- **FEEDBACK**: Controls how much output to feed back into Frequency Shifter. This increases the shifting effect.
- **MIX**: Amount of effect
- **STEREO**: Amount of stereo width.

If you enable the **RING MOD** setting, you'll notice the interface changes color, as shown in the following screenshot:

Figure 11.9 – RING MOD enabled

What is **ring modulation**? Ring modulation multiplies the amplitude of one audio signal by the amplitude of another signal. When modulated by a slow source, a **tremolo effect** is heard; when modulated by a fast source, new tones are created.

The input source is taken from the sidechain. You'll need to sidechain another audio source to the Frequency Shifter mixer track to use this feature.

Frequency modulation can get deep and technical. If you want a further deep dive into the specifics of Frequency Shifter, *Convolva's* YouTube channel does an in-depth tutorial.

We've learned how to apply creative pitch and frequency effects. Next, let's learn how to apply granular synthesis effects using **Fruity Granulizer**.

Creating granular synthesis with Fruity Granulizer

Fruity Granulizer is an effect that uses **granular synthesis**. Granular synthesis splits a source audio into small pieces called **grains**. These grains are then looped and played back based on the plugin settings.

Fruity Granulizer is a great effect for bass sound design and for transitions such as risers and falling sound effects. You can design evolving textures, soundscapes, glitch, and stutter effects by adjusting grain parameters. It enables time-stretching (changing tempo without affecting pitch) and pitch-shifting (changing pitch without affecting duration). The effects of panning, LFO modulation, and randomness add movement and unpredictability. Consider using this plugin for ambient, cinematic, experimental music, and unique transitions.

Let's get started with Fruity Granulizer:

1. Create a new pattern and add it to the **Playlist**.
2. In the **Channel rack**, insert the new instrument **Fruity Granulizer**.

Figure 11.10 – Fruity Granulizer

3. Load a new sample into **Fruity Granulizer**, such as by clicking in the **CLICK TO LOAD SAMPLE** area and navigating to an audio sample you want to use. Alternatively, you can drag and drop a sample from the **Browser** into **Fruity Granulizer**.

Figure 11.11 – Fruity Granulizer loaded with a sample

4. We need MIDI data to tell Fruity Granulizer when to play the sample, so we need to add some MIDI notes in the **Piano roll**. Open the **Piano roll** with **Fruity Granulizer**, as shown in the following screenshot:

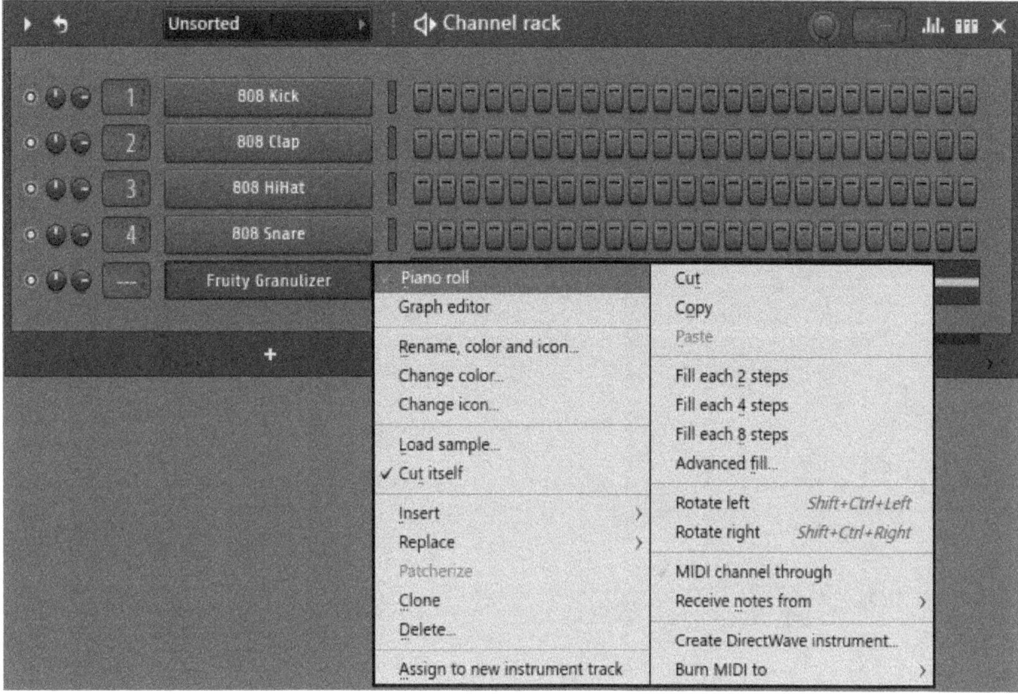

Figure 11.12 – Open Piano roll with Fruity Granulizer

5. In the Piano roll, add some MIDI notes; an example is shown in the following screenshot:

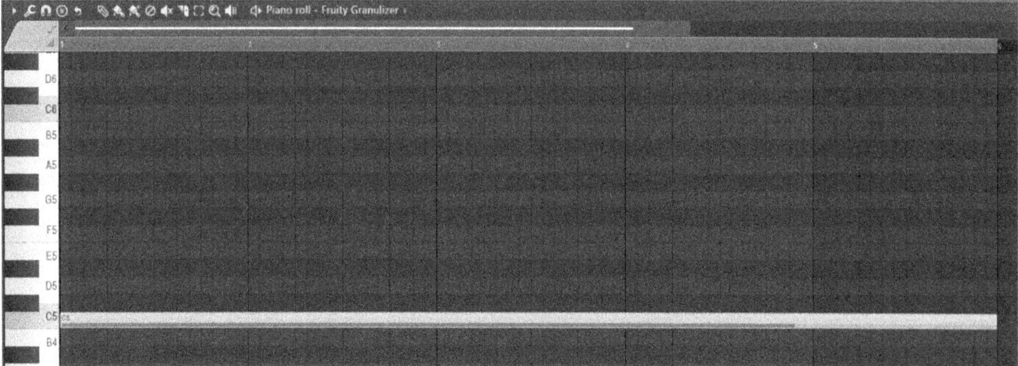

Figure 11.13 – Added MIDI notes in the Piano roll

Your pattern in the **Playlist** should now show the MIDI note you added for Fruity Granulizer. It should look something like the following screenshot:

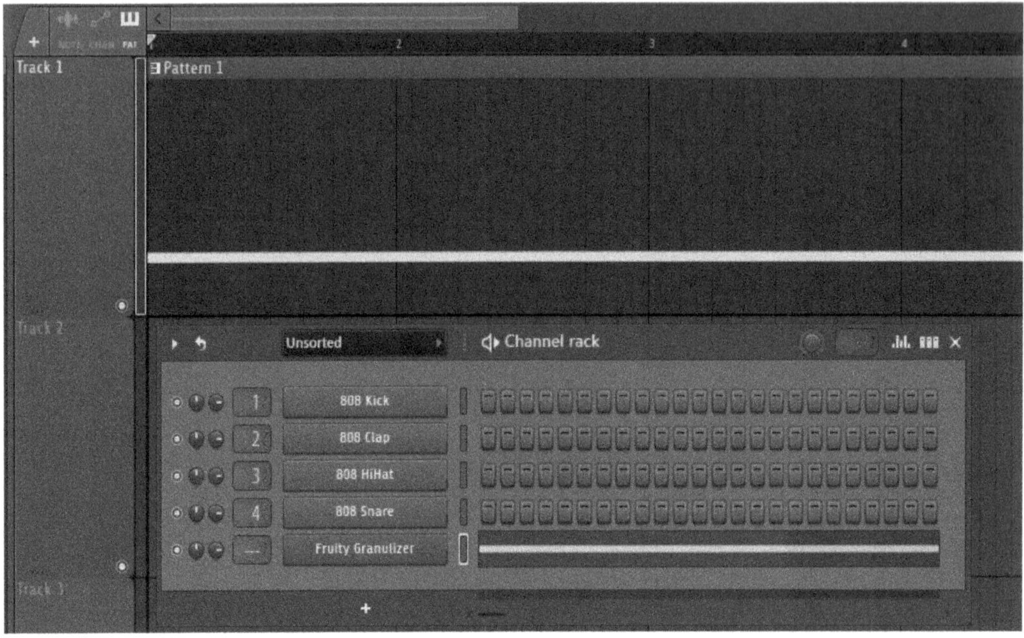

Figure 11.14 – Added Fruity Granulizer pattern to the Playlist

Now whenever you play your song, it will tell Fruity Granulizer to play the MIDI notes. A quick recap: we added an audio sample into Fruity Granulizer, and then told the Playlist when to play Fruity Granulizer as if it were any other instrument. Okay, we're set up; now we can play with the Fruity Granulizer settings.

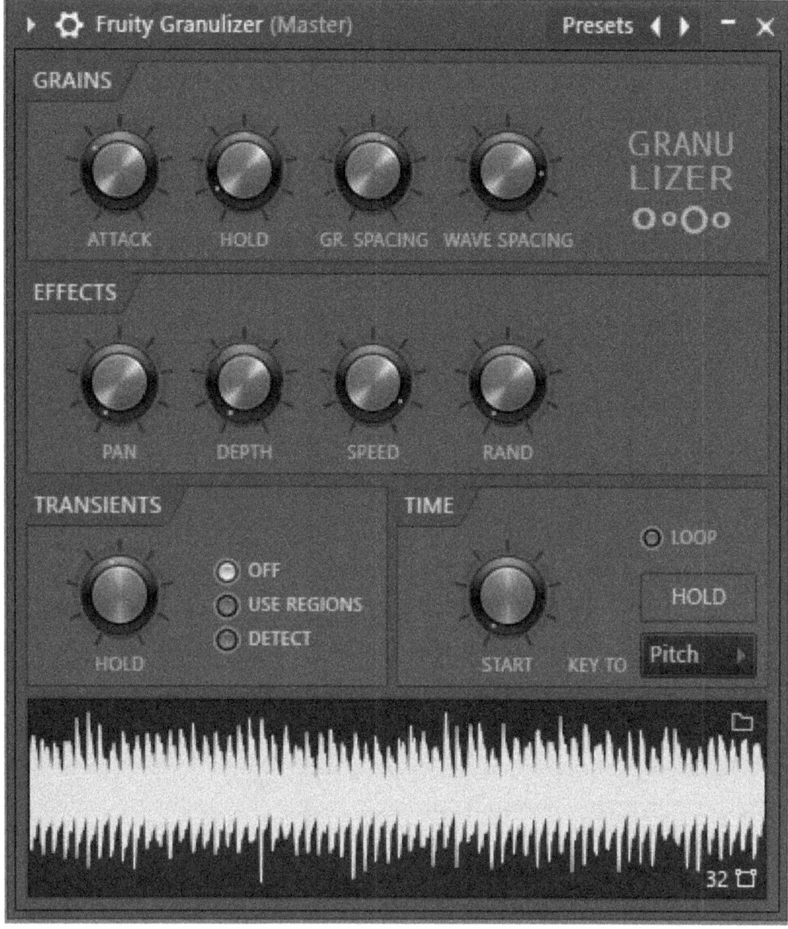

Figure 11.15 – Fruity Granulizer controls

You should play your song while tweaking Fruity Granulizer so you can hear the effect as it is applied to your audio. This is a plugin where the settings can sound a little confusing. The best way to understand this plugin is to tweak knobs while looping over the audio.

There are **Presets** available at the top right of the plugin, which I encourage you to check out.

Here's a description of the controls:

- **GRAINS**:
  - **ATTACK**: Values for the attack length of grain. It is added to the fade in and out of the grain. Higher values make each grain start and end more smoothly, reducing

clicks and making the sound softer or more blurred. Lower values make grains start and stop abruptly, resulting in a sharper, more percussive sound.

  - **HOLD**: How long a grain is held before moving to the next grain. Increasing hold makes each grain last longer, which can make the sound smoother or more stretched. Decreasing hold shortens each grain, making the sound more choppy or stuttered.
  - **GR. SPACING**: Spacing of grain. Increasing spacing raises the space between grains, slowing down playback and creating a more spaced-out, stretched effect. Decreasing spacing lowers the space, making playback faster and more continuous.
  - **WAVE SPACING**: Number of grains created from audio. Small values mean more grains are used. Negative values reverse the playback of the grains. Note that this doesn't mean the audio is reversed.
- **EFFECTS**:
  - **PAN**: Higher values increase panning. Odd grains are panned left. Even grains are panned right. Increasing pan creates a wider stereo effect, making the sound move between the speakers. Turning pan down centers the grains, reducing stereo movement.
  - **DEPTH**: Amplitude of LFO applied to wave spacing. Higher depth values make the LFO effect more pronounced, causing more dramatic movement in the playback position of grains. Lower depth values reduce the modulation effect.
  - **SPEED:** Controls the speed of the LFO. Higher speed values result in quicker, more pronounced movement in the sound. Lower speed values slow down the modulation, creating more gradual and subtle changes.
  - **RAND**: Randomizes the order that grains are played back. Increasing the randomness makes the sound more chaotic and unpredictable, adding texture and complexity. Lower rand values keep the playback order more regular and predictable.
- **TRANSIENTS**:
  - **HOLD**: Determines the length of the grain transient
  - **Switches**:
    - **OFF**: disable transients.

        - **USE REGIONS**: use slices loaded from the sample if existing (it's possible to set transient markers onto samples).
        - **DETECT**: autodetect transients.
- **TIME**:
    - **LOOP**: Loops wave when enabled.
    - **HOLD**: Playing position won't change if pressed. Same effect as setting the wave spacing to 0.
    - **KEY TO** (opens dropdown menu):
        - **KEY TO** - **Pitch**: maps keys to pitch. This is the default setting.
        - **KEY TO** - **Percent**: C5 to C7 are equivalent to 0% - 100%. So you can hit C6 to start at 50%.
        - **KEY TO** - **Step**: Keys C5 and higher offset the sample start with a step (C6 offsets 12 steps, C7 – 24).
        - **KEY TO** - **Transient**: Keys C5 and higher trigger the sample starting from a specific slice. This assumes that you have previously built transient slices into the audio.
    - **START**: Determines what position to start playing the sample from.

You now know how to create Granular Synthesis with Fruity Granulizer. Next, let's learn about a plugin that allows you to apply advanced delay effects.

Creating delay effects with Multiband Delay

Multiband Delay is a sound design delay effect. It works by splitting up audio into 16 frequency bands. For each frequency band, you can adjust the volume, delay, and panning.

The effect is more noticeable on some sounds than others. For example, the effect is noticeable on flat-sounding acoustic instruments. I recommend trying it with flat piano chords to hear the effect clearly.

Here are some ways you might consider using Multiband Delay:

- Creating rhythmic, multi-layered echoes that move across the stereo field.
- Designing wide, immersive stereo effects by panning different frequency bands.
- Adding movement and complexity to vocals, synths, drums, or any audio.
- Producing glitchy, experimental effects by randomizing band settings.

Let's get started using Multiband Delay.

1. Load up an audio sample or instrument in the **Playlist**, and route it to the **Mixer**.
2. Apply the Multiband Delay effect to the **Mixer** channel and play your sound. You'll see **Multiband Delay** load up as shown in the following screenshot:

Figure 11.16 – Multiband Delay

The main idea behind Multiband Delay is that you can set delay, volume, and panning values for individual frequency bands. You can save your band settings in a **Bank** preset. If desired, you can then morph from one preset bank to the next.

There are plugin presets in the top right corner of the plugin, which I encourage you to check out (in the preceding screenshot, it's the button labeled **Default**).

The main display shows 16 vertical bands, each representing a slice of the frequency spectrum from 20 Hz (left) to 20 kHz (right). For each band, you can select whether you want to edit delay (**DELAY**), volume (**VOL**), or pan (**PAN**) using the **band mode selector**. When editing delay, the top of a band means maximum delay (up to 1000 ms or 100 ms, depending on the scale range), and the bottom means no delay. For volume, the top is full volume, and the bottom is silent. For pan, the top is left, the bottom is right, and the center is center-panned. You can adjust these bands individually with **Pencil mode**, draw straight lines with **Line mode**, or create smooth curves with **Curve mode**. Each band also has a switch at the top to turn it on, off (bypassed), or lock it to prevent changes.

In the middle, we find the following controls:

Figure 11.17 – Multiband middle controls

Let's discuss these controls left to right:

- **Options** dropdown arrow brings up the following options:
    - **Random Curve**: Create a random curve for the frequency bands.
    - **Reset**: Reset the curve.
    - **Interpolate 1 to 8**: Use the curves from Bank 1 and Bank 8 to generate intermediate steps in between.
    - **Wave visualization**: Enable/disable wave display.
- The **dot** symbol, **slash** symbol, and ^ buttons:
    - (**dot** symbol) **Pencil** mode: Control individual bands.
    - (**slash** symbol) **Line** mode: Allows you to left-click and drag lines.
    - (^ symbol) **Curve** mode: Allows you to draw smooth curves.
- **DELAY** (Delay): Changes the display visual to show the amount of delay. The top of the band is 1000ms delay, and the bottom is 0ms delay.
- **VOL** (Volume): Changes the display visual to show the volume with the range 0 to 100%.
- **PAN** (Panning): Changes the display visual to show panning. The bottom is panning left, the top is panning right.
- **BANK Values 1-8**: Each number is a saved setting known as a bank. You can later move between banks (transition between settings) using the **MORPH** knob.

Let's move on to the bottom panel of controls and discuss these controls left to right.

Figure 11.18 – Multiband Delay bottom controls

- There are three filter type controls:
    - **GENTLE**: Wider bands. Allow frequencies to appear in more than one band. Result in a smeared or blurry sound, especially with short delays. Great for lush, ambient, or washed-out effects where you want the bands to blend together.

    - **STEEP**: Use narrower bands with steeper crossovers, so there's less frequency spill between bands. Cleaner separation between bands, less blur. Useful for rhythmic, percussive, or clearly defined delay effects where you want each frequency band to stand out.
    - **LINEAR PHASE**: Use linear phase to split frequencies while maintaining perfect phase alignment. Will create the most identifiable pitched sounds.
- **SCALE**: Use for delay times -100% to 100%. Quickly stretch, shrink, or invert all band delay times for creative effects or rhythmic changes.
    - **x0.1** Scale Range Off: 100ms range. On: 100ms range. Use for tighter, more resonant or comb-filter-like effects (short range) or for longer, echo-style delays (long range).
    - **Harmonic scale** (**music** symbol): Sets delay times in semitone steps (+/- 24), so each band's delay time corresponds to a musical pitch. It creates harmonic resonances and pitched delays that fit musically with your track.
    - **Harmonic weighting** (**w** icon): Extends the decay time of higher frequencies, making their resonances more audible and balanced with lower frequencies.
    - **FEEDBACK**: Sends output back into the plugin to increase the effect.
    - **SMOOTHING TIME**: Smooths out abrupt changes when adjusting the Scale control. Prevents clicks, pops, or abrupt jumps in the delay effect when automating or tweaking the **SCALE** parameter.
    - **KEEP PITCH**: Maintains the pitch of the signal even as delay times are changed. Useful for time-based effects where you don't want pitch shifting (e.g., when automating delay time for creative effects).
- **MORPH**: Sweeps between the settings of Bank 1 (left) and Bank 8 (right). Consider adding automation to transition smoothly. Allows for smooth, automated transitions between different delay setups, great for evolving effects or builds.
- **WET** panel:
    - **COMP**: Compresses the delayed (wet) signal to control dynamics.
    - **SAT**: Adds soft, analog-style distortion for warmth.
    - **CLIP**: Allows the signal to clip, creating harsher, digital distortion.
    - **HP (high-pass filter)**: Filters out low frequencies from the output. Prevents low-end buildup and keeps the delay effect clean, especially useful on vocals or melodic instruments.
    - **MIX**: Controls how strong of an effect to apply.

In general, when not using Multiband Delay, you want to have the lower frequencies in mono, and the higher frequencies can be panned more left and right. You usually also have the low and high frequencies with less delay applied to them than the mid frequencies. However, Multiband Delay gives you the freedom to break the rules and explore new stereo width options. The whole point of this plugin is to make your ears notice the changes in stereo width. So this is a plugin where you can break the rules and move your sounds around the stereo field with ease.

We've learned how to create and perform sound design delay effects. Next, let's learn about **multiband processing** with the plugin Frequency Splitter.

Multiband processing with Frequency Splitter

Frequency Splitter is an effects plugin that separates audio into low, mid, and high-frequency bands. Once the frequency bands are split, you can route them to different mixer tracks for additional processing.

Splitting audio into frequency bands has a wide range of applications. Some use cases are as follows:

- In its simplest form, it can be used to perform simple EQ.
- It allows you to perform band pass sweeping effects.
- It allows you to isolate frequency bands to duck when sidechaining instead of sidechaining the entire sound. For example, reduce the bass frequencies when percussion comes in while still retaining the upper frequencies. More generally, apply different effects to low, mid, or high frequencies of a sound.
- It can be used to duck instrument frequencies when a vocal comes in so that it can maintain focus on the vocal.
- Use it in mastering to isolate frequencies so that you can increase effects such as stereo width, compression, and saturation to each frequency band separately.

Let's get started using Frequency Splitter:

1. Load up a sample or instrument with MIDI notes, and route it to a new mixer track.
2. Apply the Frequency Splitter effect to the **Mixer** channel and play your sound:

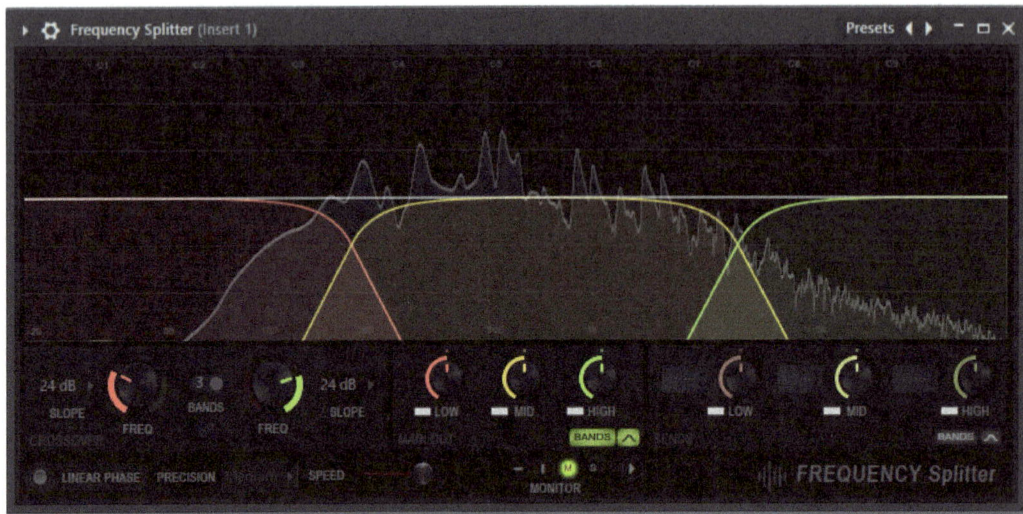

Figure 11.19 – Frequency Splitter

Frequency Splitter shows a visual representation of splitting frequencies into frequency bands, with red representing the lower frequencies, yellow for the mids, and green for the high.

There are plugin presets in the top right corner of the plugin, which I encourage you to check out. The far left panel controls which frequencies make up the bands, as shown in the following screenshot:

Figure 11.20 – Frequency bands, far left panel

From left to right:

- The slope will determine the steepness of the frequency curve.
- Control which frequencies are contained within a band by adjusting the Low/Mid frequency and Mid/High frequency knobs. These adjust the cutoff frequencies for the band.
- The **BANDS** allows you to have either 2 bands or 3 frequency bands.
- The **link** icon connects the frequency knobs so that adjusting one knob will move the other. This is great for when you want to create band pass sweeping effects.

The level (loudness) of audio in the frequency band is controlled in the center panel, as shown in the following screenshot:

Figure 11.21 – Frequency bands, center panel

Adjusting one of the knobs will increase or decrease the audio output level of the frequency band. By selecting the checkbox, you can mute/solo the frequency band.

The **options** arrow at the bottom provides options to view different visualizations of the audio.

On the right panel, you'll find the frequency send controls, as shown in the following screenshot:

Figure 11.22 – Frequency Splitter send controls, right panel

To use the frequency sends, you'll want to sidechain the audio from the mixer track that contains Frequency Splitter to another mixer track. You select the track that has Frequency Splitter, then right-click on the arrow at the bottom of the mixer track that you want to sidechain to and select the option **Sidechain to this track**. An example is shown in the following screenshot:

Figure 11.23 – Sidechain to this track option

Once you've done this, audio from the Frequency Splitter bands will be routed to the sidechained mixer tracks. Back in Frequency Splitter, you'll need to order the frequency band sends, with the lowest number being the leftmost mixer track. In the following screenshot, **1** is the **LOW** frequency band:

Figure 11.24 – Order frequency band sends

From now on, Frequency Splitter will split audio into frequency bands and send it to the designated mixer track. You've isolated the audio into lows, mids, and highs. Now you can perform effects on the mixer tracks targeting only specific frequency ranges.

Using Frequency Splitter for mastering

Frequency Splitter is a great tool for **mastering**, as you can mix each frequency band separately and chain a series of effects. To do so, you'll want to load Frequency Splitter inside of **Patcher**.

If used inside **Patcher**, you add send outputs by right-clicking on Frequency Splitter and adding an output. An example is shown in the following screenshot:

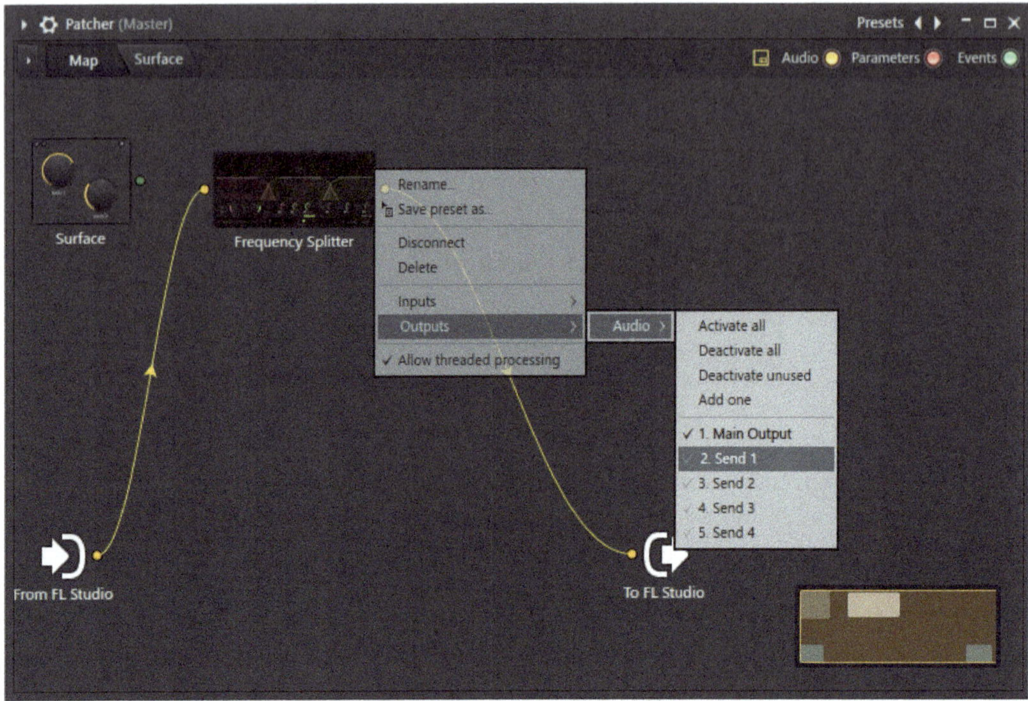

Figure 11.25 – Adding outputs to Frequency Splitter in Patcher

Once you've added output for Frequency Splitter, you can now apply compression, saturation, and stereo effects to each frequency band separately. For example, consider the following:

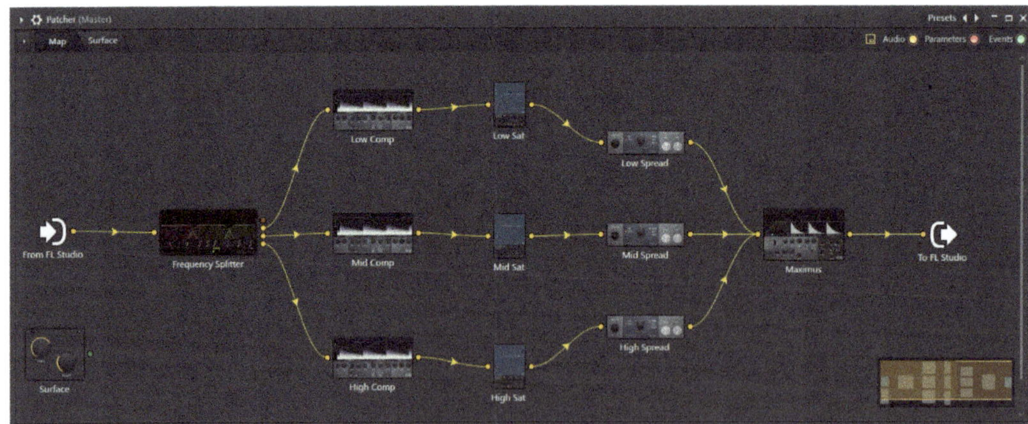

Figure 11.26 – Mastering chain

In the preceding screenshot example, we have different effects applied to the low, mid, and high frequencies.

How you want to master will depend on the song you're working with. The preceding screenshot is just an example of a mastering chain you could come up with; the details aren't important here. You now know how to use Frequency Splitter.

Next, let's learn how to sound design your bass frequencies using Low Lifter.

Adding harmonics to bass frequencies using the Low Lifter plugin

Low Lifter is an effect plugin that comes with FL Studio *Signature Edition* and higher. Low Lifter dynamically adds harmonics to bass frequencies, making the bass sound stronger and more present. The bass will sound stronger even on small speakers or headphones that can't reproduce deep sub-bass.

Low Lifter works by finding the lowest bass sounds in your music and creating extra harmonics (higher-pitched notes) above the bass notes. These notes trick your ears into thinking the bass is louder and deeper. It's an optical illusion for your ears. Instead of boosting the bass itself, extra frequencies are added above the bass, and your ears interpret this as being a louder bass.

Let's get started using Low Lifter:

1. Load up an audio sample or instrument in the **Playlist**, and route it to the **Mixer**.
2. Apply the Low Lifter effect to the **Mixer** channel and play your sound. You'll see **Low Lifter** load up as shown in the following screenshot:

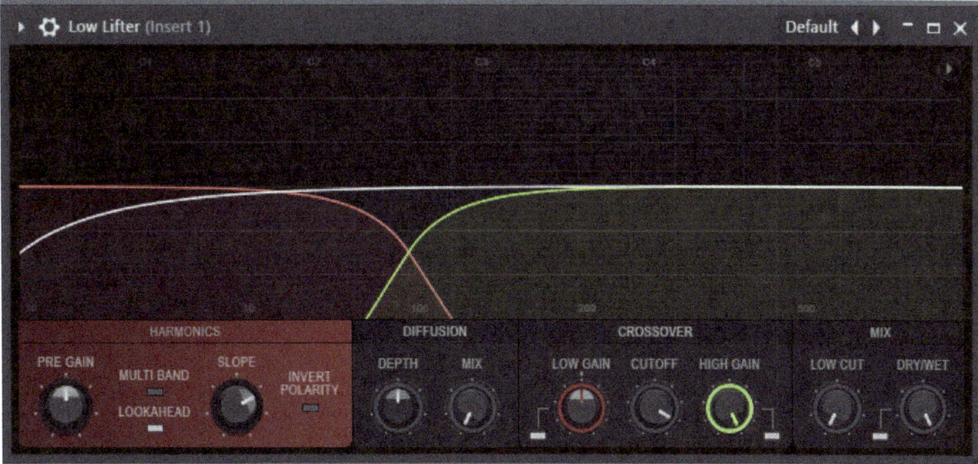

Figure 11.27 – Low Lifter plugin

Here's a breakdown of the controls from left to right, which is also the way you should interact with this plugin. You can think of the sound as moving from the controls starting on the left and moving to the right of the plugin.

- **HARMONICS** section: This section is where the plugin analyzes your low frequencies and generates new harmonics (higher-frequency content) based on them.
    - **PRE GAIN:** Sets how much low-frequency signal is sent into the harmonic generator (more input = more harmonics). Slowly increase Pre Gain while playing your bass track. Listen for the bass to become fuller and more present. Stop increasing when the bass enhancement sounds good, but before it gets muddy or distorted.
    - **MULTI BAND:** Shapes how quickly the added harmonics fade as they move up the frequency spectrum. Enable for a cleaner, more transparent enhancement.
    - **LOOKAHEAD:** Lets the plugin "peek ahead" to prevent sudden loud spikes (clipping) when boosting bass. Enable for cleaner limiting if you hear distortion or want a more controlled sound.
    - **SLOPE:** Controls how quickly the added harmonics fade out as they go up in pitch. Lower values = harmonics extend further into higher frequencies (brighter, more pronounced effect). Higher values = harmonics fade out quickly (darker, subtler effect).
    - **INVERT POLARITY:** Flips the phase of the bass. Sometimes this makes the bass feel even louder, depending on your mix. If the bass sounds punchier, leave it on.
- **DIFFUSION** section: The sound generated from the **HARMONICS** section can sometimes sound harsh or artificial. The **DIFFUSION** section randomizes the timing of the harmonics so they don't build up or cancel each other out. Increase to smooth out the harmonics if they sound harsh or artificial.
    - **DEPTH:** Controls how much the harmonics are randomized. More = smoother.
    - **MIX (DIFFUSION):** Blends the diffused (smoothed) harmonics with the regular ones.
- **CROSSOVER** section: Splits your audio into low and high bands, letting you focus the processing exactly where you want it.
    - **LOW GAIN:** Sets how loud the processed bass (low band) is after the effect.

    - **CUTOFF:** Sets where the plugin splits the bass from the rest of the sound (the crossover point). Set higher for more of your sound to get bass enhancement; lower for just the deepest bass.
    - **HIGH GAIN:** Sets how loud the higher frequencies (above the cutoff) are. Use this to balance the highs if the bass boost makes the rest sound quieter.
- **MIX** section: Controls how the processed signal is balanced with the original sound and allows you to fine-tune the final output. Use this to clean up excessive low-end and blend the effect into your mix.
    - **LOW CUT:** Removes the very lowest bass after processing (high-pass filter). Use this if your mix gets too boomy or rumbly.
    - **DRY/WET:** Blends between your original sound (dry) and the processed sound (wet).

Here are some general practical tips for using Low Lifter:

- Just turning up **PRE GAIN** and **DRY/WET** can make a big improvement.
- If the bass gets muddy, use **LOW CUT** to clean up the lowest rumble.
- For punchier bass, try toggling **INVERT POLARITY**.
- On full mixes, **MULTI BAND** mode is usually safer and cleaner.
- If the effect sounds weird, lower **DEPTH** or **MIX** in the **DIFFUSION** section.
- Always compare. Bypass the plugin now and then to make sure you are improving the sound, not just making it louder.

We've learned how to add harmonics to bass frequencies using the Low Lifter plugin. Next, let's learn how to create sounds using the Kepler Synthesizer.

Learning to play the Kepler synthesizer

Kepler is a recreation of the **Roland JUNO-6**™ vintage synthesizer that comes included with FL Studio *Producer Edition* and higher. The JUNO-6™ is a classic analog synthesizer originally produced by Roland in the early 1980s. It is renowned for its warm, rich sound and iconic chorus effect, making it a favorite among electronic musicians and producers.

Let's learn how to use Kepler. In the **Channel rack**, insert the Kepler plugin. You'll see the plugin load as in the following screenshot:

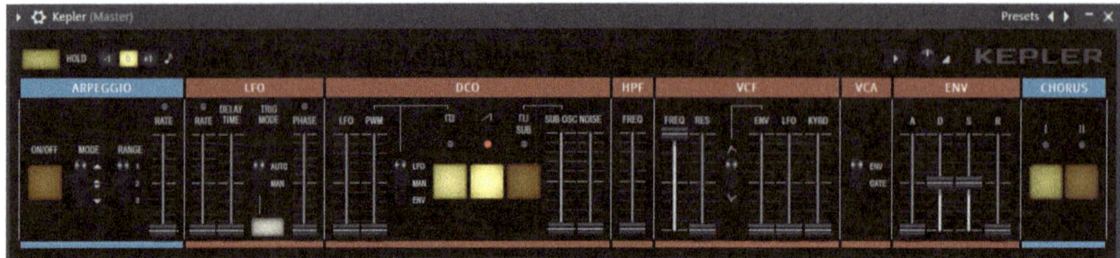

Figure 11.28 – Kepler plugin

The first place to start is to check out the preset library found in the top right corner of the plugin. Explore those, and then come back and take a look at the control parameters.

Here's a breakdown of the controls. The logical place to start in the plugin is the **DCO**, **HPF**, and **VCF** section, as this is where the sound first gets generated. Let's look at that first.

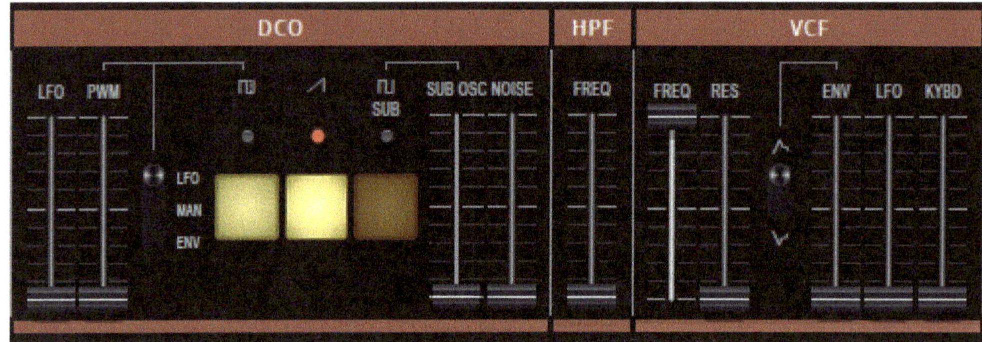

Figure 11.29 – DCO section (sound generation) and filtering sections

- DCO (short for **digitally controlled oscillator**) section:
    - **Waveform Buttons** (**Pulse**, **Saw**, **Sub**): Select which waveforms are active. Use to shape the basic character of your sound (saw = bright, pulse = hollow, sub = deep bass).
    - DCO **SUB OSC**: Controls the level of the sub oscillator (deep bass). Use to add weight to basses or thickness to leads.
    - **NOISE** volume: Controls the amount of white noise. Use for percussive sounds or to add texture.

    - **LFO**: Controls the amount the LFO modulates pitch (vibrato). Use for vibrato or pitch movement.
    - **PWM** (short for pulse width modulation): Controls the shape of the pulse wave. Use for richer, evolving sounds.
    - DCO **PWM** Source:
        - **LFO**: LFO modulates pulse width (moving sound).
        - **MAN**: Manual control (static sound).
        - **ENV**: Envelope modulates pulse width (dynamic attack). Use **LFO** for movement, **MAN** for steady, and **ENV** for evolving attack.
- **HPF** (short for **high-pass filter**):
    - **FREQ**: Removes low frequencies below the cutoff. Use to thin out sounds or remove bass rumble.
- **VCF** (short for **voltage-controlled filter**):
    - **FREQ**: Sets the cutoff frequency (how much high end is filtered out). Use to make sounds darker or brighter.
    - **RES**: Resonance, boosts frequencies at the cutoff for squelchy, sharp, or "acid" sounds.
    - **VCF** Polarity: Sets whether the envelope moves the filter up or down. Use to invert how the envelope affects the filter.
    - **ENV**: Sets how much the envelope affects the filter. Use for filter sweeps or plucky sounds.
    - **LFO**: Sets how much the LFO modulates the filter. Use for rhythmic filter movement.
    - **KYBD**: Sets keyboard tracking. Higher notes open the filter more. Use for natural-sounding leads and basses.

Next, let's look at the plugin panels to the right, as shown in the following screenshot:

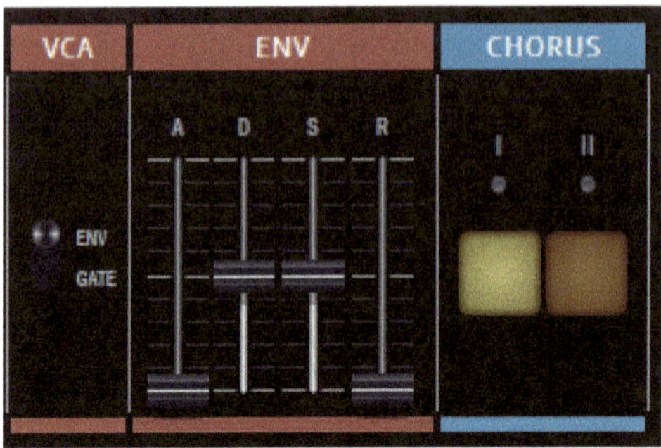

Figure 11.30 – VCA, ENV, and CHORUS sections

- **VCA** (Amplifier section):
  - **ENV**: Volume is controlled by the envelope section in the panel to the right.
  - **GATE**: Volume is on/off with key press. Use for organ-like, instant sounds.
- **ENV** (Envelope): Shape the amplitude or filter envelope with Attack (**A**), Decay (**D**), Sustain (**S**), and Release (**R**) sliders.
- **CHORUS**:
  - **I/II**: Emulate classic Juno chorus modes for lush, wide sounds. You can even combine both for a third mode (*Shift + Click*).

Next, let's explore the top controls.

Figure 11.31 – Top controls, ARPEGGIO and LFO sections

- **HOLD**: Keeps notes playing after you let go of the keys. Use when you want sustained sounds without holding down keys (great for pads or drones).

- **Octave**: Shifts the keyboard up or down by one octave.
- **MENU** options:
  - **Quantize first arpeggiator** step: Makes the arpeggiator start exactly on the beat.
  - **Velocity to Volume**: Makes how hard you play affect loudness.
  - **Align sub oscillator phase**: Changes the phase of the sub oscillator. Use for subtle changes in bass character.
  - **Chorus Noise/Chorus Noise Gate**: Adds/gates noise in the chorus effect. Use for vintage, noisy textures.
  - **HQ Mode**: Improves sound quality (less aliasing). Use for cleaner, more accurate sound.
- **Volume**: Master output level.
- **ARPEGGIATOR**:
  - **ON/OFF**: Turns arpeggiator on or off.
  - **MODE**: Sets direction of arpeggio (up, down, up & down).
  - **RANGE**: Number of octaves the arpeggio covers.
  - **RATE**: Speed of the arpeggio.
- **LFO**:
  - **RATE**: Speed of LFO (how fast it modulates). Use for slow sweeps or fast tremolo/vibrato.
  - **DELAY TIME**: Time before the LFO effect fades in. Use for sounds that start steady, then get wobbly.
  - **TRIG MODE** (Trigger mode): Use **AUTO** for continuous movement, **MAN** (manual) for triggered effects.
    - **AUTO**: LFO always runs.
    - **MANUAL**: LFO only runs when triggered.
    - **PHASE**: Sets the starting point of the LFO wave.

Kepler can make some fun sounds, but it's really just an introduction to the fully featured Kepler Exo synthesizer, which we'll explore next.

Learning to play the Kepler Exo synthesizer

Kepler Exo is a synthesizer plugin that comes with FL Studio *All Plugins Edition*. It's inspired by classic analog synths like the Roland JUNO-6™ and **Jupiter-8**™. The Jupiter-8™ is an analog synthesizer originally produced by Roland in the early 1980s. It has been used in many classic electronic, pop, and film scores.

Kepler Exo offers a wide range of sound design possibilities, from lush pads and classic basses to aggressive leads and experimental textures. It's a beast of a plugin with huge possibilities for the sounds you can create. One of its strengths, by design, is the ability to have envelopes and LFO controls in one part of the plugin affect the controls in other parts of the plugin. So, changes you make in one control section of the plugin can be reused over and over again.

Let's learn how to use Kepler Exo. In the **Channel rack**, insert the Kepler Exo plugin. You'll see the plugin load as in the following screenshot. Yours may look different color-wise depending on the theme option chosen for Kepler.

Figure 11.32 – Kepler Exo plugin

As with all synthesizer plugins in FL Studio, I recommend checking out the presets in the top right corner of the plugin to get an idea of the sounds that can be created.

Let's do a breakdown of the controls from left to right. At the top of the plugin, you'll see the top controls.

Figure 11.33 – Kepler Exo plugin: top controls

Here's a breakdown of the controls shown in the preceding image from left to right. The buttons don't have labels, but the descriptions correspond to the buttons in the image.

- **HOLD**: When activated, notes are sustained as if you're holding down keys on a keyboard.
- **Octave**: Transposes the sound by -1, 0, or +1 octave.
- **Options** menu (**arrow** icon):
    - **Arp 1st Step Quantize**: Start arpeggiator playback on the next step, always quantized.
    - **HQ Mode**: Enable a higher quality filter mode.
    - **Enhanced Oscillators**: Enable a higher quality algorithm to reduce aliasing artifacts (slightly higher CPU usage).
    - **Theme**: Choose the color scheme for the interface.
- **X/Y** knobs: Modulation offsets for X/Y parameters, assignable in the Piano roll.
- **Master Tune**: Fine-tune the pitch in cents (1/100th of a semitone).
- **Volume**: Master output level.
- **Pan**: Master stereo panning.

Kepler Exo follows a classic subtractive synthesis structure, moving from sound generation to shaping and then effects. It uses the following flow, so we'll explore the panel controls in the same order: **Oscillators** (DCO 1 & 2) | **Mixer** | **Filter** (VCF) | **Amplifier** (VCA) | **Effects** (Saturation, Hyperchor, EQ, Delay, Reverb)

Let's look at the oscillator **DCO2** Mixer panels.

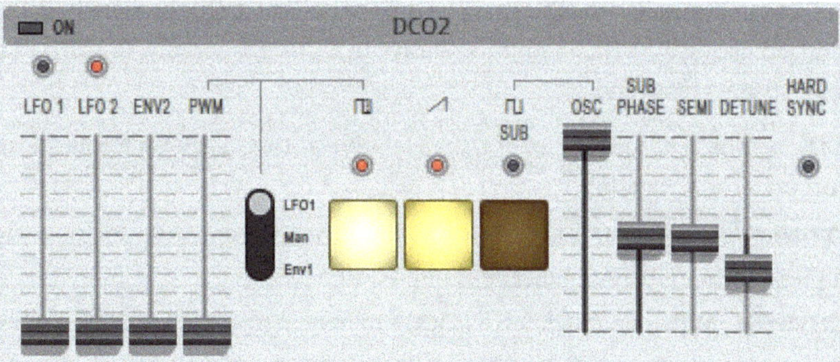

Figure 11.34 – Kepler Exo plugin: DCO2

DCO stands for **digitally controlled oscillator**, inspired by classic Roland™ Juno™ synthesizers. Each of the two main oscillators (**DCO1** and **DCO2**) in Kepler Exo has a set of controls that let you shape the core sound. We will skip discussing the **DC01** panel, as the **DC02** panel is the same but with a few additional buttons.

- **LFO 1 & LFO 2**: Control how much **LFO 1** and **LFO 2** modulate the pitch. When both are active, their effects are combined for more complex modulation.
- **ENV**: Control how much of the **ENV** effect is applied, as set in the **ENV** panel further down in the plugin. The effect of this control depends on the settings in the **ENV** panel.
- **PWM** (short for pulse width modulation): Changes the pulse width of the oscillator when pulse is active. At 50%, it's a standard square wave. Lower or higher values create brighter or mellower tones.
- **DCO PWM SOURCE**: Selects the modulation source for **PWM**:
    - **LFO**: Uses LFO (another panel in the plugin) to modulate pulse width.
    - **Man**: Manual control via the PWM slider.
    - **Env**: Uses envelope (another panel in the plugin) to modulate pulse width.
- **WAVEFORM SELECTORS**: Multiple waveforms can be active at once for a richer sound.
    - **PULSE**: Activates a pulse wave. The pulse width can be modulated for classic analog movement.
    - **SAW**: Adds a sawtooth wave.
    - **SUB**: Adds a square sub-oscillator (one octave below). Adds weight and depth.
- **DCO SUB VOLUME**: Controls the level of the sub-oscillator (square wave, -1 octave). Adds depth and weight to your sound.
- **DCO SUB PHASE**: Sets the phase of the sub-oscillator.

The following controls exist on the **DC02** panel, but not on the **DC01** panel. These controls allow for interaction, adjusting how DC02 sounds relative to DC01. Essentially, the former panel affects how the second panel will sound.

- **SEMI**: Sets the semitone offset of DCO2 relative to DCO1. Allows for harmonies, octaves, or interval-based layering.
- **DETUNE**: Fine-tunes DCO2 relative to DCO1 in percent. Allows for a thicker, more complex sound by introducing slight pitch differences.
- **HARD SYNC**: When enabled, forces DCO2 to restart its waveform cycle whenever DCO1 completes a cycle. Produces harmonically rich, sharp, and sometimes aggressive sounds. For **HARD SYNC** to be audible, DCO1 and DCO2 must have different pitch or phase (use **DETUNE** and **SEMI**).

Looking to the left is the **CROSS MOD** panel. **CROSS MOD** stands for **cross-modulation**, which is a form of frequency modulation in which one oscillator modulates the frequency of another. This can create complex, harmonically rich, and sometimes metallic or bell-like sounds.

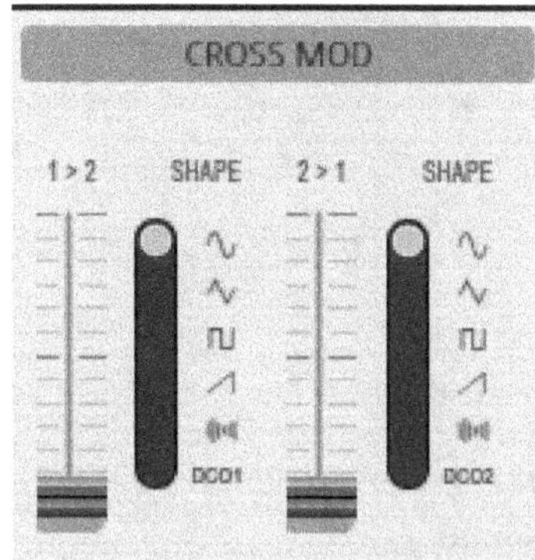

Figure 11.35 – Kepler Exo plugin: CROSS MOD

- **1 > 2**: Controls how much Oscillator 1 affects the pitch of Oscillator 2. Turn it up for more dramatic, complex sounds.
- **SHAPE** (on the left): Picks the type of wave used for the effect from Oscillator 1 to Oscillator 2. Different shapes give different sound flavors.
- **2 > 1**: Controls how much Oscillator 2 affects the pitch of Oscillator 1. Turn it up for more effect in the other direction.
- **SHAPE** (on the right): Picks the type of wave used for the effect from Oscillator 2 to Oscillator 1.

To the right of the DC02 panel is the **DCO 1-2 MIXER** panel. This panel lets you mix the levels of both main oscillators and noise, and also add amplitude modulation for richer, more dynamic timbres. Adjust these controls to shape the core blend and character of your sound.

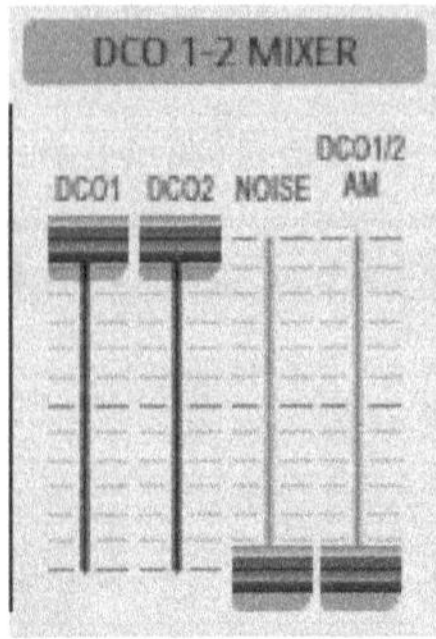

Figure 11.36 – Kepler Exo plugin: DCO 1-2 MIXER

- **DCO1**: Controls the volume level of Oscillator 1 (DCO 1). Use this to blend in more or less of DCO 1 in your overall sound.
- **DCO2**: Controls the volume level of Oscillator 2 (DCO 2). Use this to blend in more or less of DCO 2.
- **NOISE**: Controls the level of the noise generator (adds hiss or white noise). Useful for adding texture, percussive elements, or simulating analog synth noise.
- **DCO1/2 AM**: Controls the amount of **amplitude modulation** (**AM**) applied between the two oscillators. The level of DCO 2 will modulate the amplitude of DCO 1. This creates new harmonics and more complex, evolving timbres. By increasing the **DCO1/2 AM** knob, you introduce more amplitude modulation, resulting in richer and sometimes more metallic or bell-like sounds, depending on the oscillator settings.

Then, we have the **VCF**, **HPF**, and **VCA** panel controls.

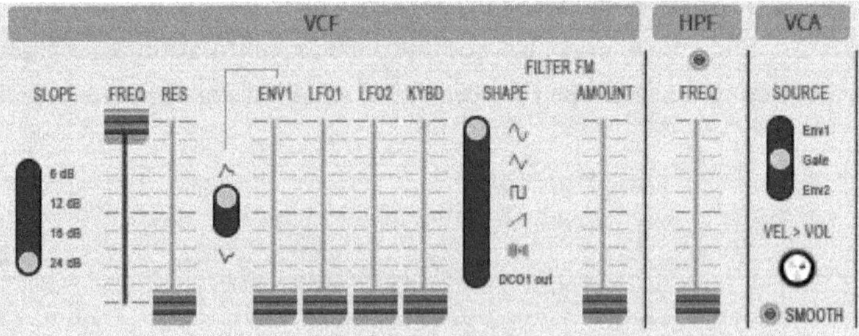

Figure 11.37 – Kepler Exo plugin: VCF, HPF, and VCA

- **VCF** panel controls:
    - **SLOPE**: Determines how sharply the filter cuts off sound above the cutoff point. Lower values (like 6 dB) = gentle, smooth filtering. Higher values (like 24 dB) = strong, dramatic filtering.

- **FREQ** (cutoff frequency): Determines the point where the filter starts to remove high frequencies. Turn it down for a darker sound. Turn it up for a brighter sound.
- **RES** (resonance): Boosts the sound right at the cutoff point, making it more pronounced or "squelchy." Higher values mean a more pronounced, sharper sound.
- **VCF Polarity** (toggle): Decides if the envelope (Env) moves the filter cutoff up (positive) or down (negative) as the envelope plays.
- **ENV** (envelope amount): Controls how much the filter cutoff moves according to the envelope shape (like attack, decay, etc.). Higher values = more movement in the filter as the note plays.
- **LFO** (low frequency oscillator amount): Controls how much the filter cutoff moves up and down automatically, creating effects like "wah-wah" or pulsing. Higher values = more noticeable movement.
- **KYBD** (keyboard tracking): Makes higher notes open the filter more than lower notes, useful for keeping high notes bright and low notes dark.

- **HPF** (high-pass filter) panel:
  - **On/Off** (switch): Bypasses the filter completely when not needed.
  - **FREQ**: Sets the cutoff frequency of the high-pass filter. Frequencies below this point are removed, allowing only higher frequencies to pass.
- **VCA** (voltage controlled amplifier) panel:
  - **ENV1**: Controls the VCA (amplifier envelope).
  - **GATE**: Controls the VCA. The sound is only heard when a note is held.
  - **ENV2**: Also controls the VCA.
  - **VEL>VOL** (velocity>volume): Determines how much velocity (how hard you play a note) influences the output level.

Next, we have the **ENV1**, **ENV2**, **LFO1**, and **LFO2** panels.

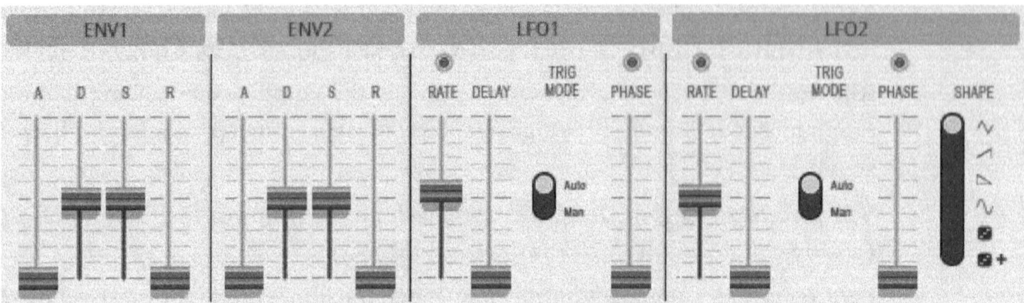

Figure 11.38 – Kepler Exo plugin: ENV1, ENV2, LFO1, and LFO2 panels

ENV1 and **ENV2** panels are envelope generators that shape how certain parameters change over time, using standard **ADSR** (Attack, Decay, Sustain, Release) controls found on most synthesizers.

The ADSR controls let you set:

- Attack (**A**): Time taken to reach the maximum level after a note is pressed. Short attacks make the sound more percussive.
- Decay (**D**): Time taken for the level to fall from the maximum to the sustain level.
- Sustain (**S**): Level held while the note is sustained.
- Release (**R**): Time taken for the sound to fade out after the note is released.

ENV1 and ENV2 are used in other parts of the plugin as modulation sources. So whatever changes you make in the **ENV1** and **ENV2** panels will affect other parts of the plugin:

- In the DCO 1 & 2 sections, ENV modulates the pitch of the oscillators.
- ENV can be set as the PWM source, allowing ENV to modulate the pulse width of the oscillator.
- The **modulation matrix** allows you to assign ENV as sources to modulate various destinations (such as filter cutoff, pitch, etc.). This is a flexible way to use the envelopes throughout the synth.

To the right of the ENV panels, you'll see the **LFO1** and **LFO2** panels. We know **LFO** stands for low frequency oscillator. Think of an LFO as a slow, repeating wave that you can use to automatically move (modulate) other controls in the synth. Imagine it turning a knob back and forth for you. LFO1 and LFO2 are two separate LFOs, so you can have two different types of automatic movement happening at once.

- **RATE**: How fast the wave moves (slow or fast wobble).
- **DELAY**: How long before the LFO starts after you play a note.

- **TRIG MODE**: Decide if the LFO restarts every time you play a note or just keeps running.
    - **Auto**: restart every time you play a note
    - **Man**: keeps LFO running if the **LFO TRIG** control is enabled (yellow button in the bottom left of the plugin shown in *Figure 11.32*)
- **PHASE**: Where in the wave the LFO starts.

You can use LFO1 and LFO2 to automatically move (modulate) different parts of the synth:

- **Oscillator pitch**: Make the pitch of your sound wobble up and down for vibrato effects. In the DCO 1 & 2 section, you'll see sliders for LFO1 and LFO2. Move these to decide how much each LFO affects the pitch.
- PWM: Make the shape of the pulse wave change over time, creating a richer, moving sound. You can set the LFO as the source for this movement in the **DCO1** or **DCO2** panel. Look next to the **PWM** slider; you'll find the **PWM Source selector**. Here, you can choose between three options: **LFO**, **Man**, **Env**. Set this selector to **LFO** to use the LFO as the source for PWM.
- **Filter cutoff**: Make the filter open and close automatically, like a *wah-wah* effect. To use the LFO to control this, look in the **VCF** panel for the sliders labeled **LFO1** and **LFO2**.
- **Modulation matrix**: If you want even more control, you can use the modulation matrix to send **LFO1** or **LFO2** to almost any parameter you want.

At the bottom left of Kepler Exo, you'll see the following controls:

Figure 11.39 – Kepler Exo plugin: ARPEGGIATOR section

- **LFO TRIG**: When **LFO TRIG** is enabled, the LFO will be retriggered (start from the beginning of its waveform) each time a new note is played. This is useful if you want the modulation (such as vibrato or filter movement) to always start in the same way for each note, making the sound more predictable and consistent. If **LFO TRIG** is off, the

LFO runs freely and does not restart with each note, so the modulation phase will be different depending on when you play the note.

- **PORTA MODE**: Sets the style of portamento (glide between notes).
    - **EXP** (exponential): The pitch glides faster as the distance between notes increases, keeping the glide time more consistent.
    - **LINEAR:** The pitch glides at a constant rate, regardless of the distance between notes.
- **PLAY MODE**: Controls how notes are played and how envelopes are triggered.
    - **MONO:** Only one note can play at a time (monophonic).
    - **LEGATO:** When playing overlapping notes, the sound glides smoothly from one note to the next without retriggering the envelope.
    - **RETRIG:** The envelope restarts every time a new note is played.
    - **RELEASE:** The envelope resets when you release a note.
- Arpeggiator **ON/OFF**: Activates or deactivates the arpeggiator.
- **MODE**: Sets the pitch cycle direction. Options include:
    - Up
    - Up & Down
    - Down
    - Random (3 sequences)
    - As played (play notes in the order you press them)
- **RANGE**: Sets the octave range for the arpeggiator (1 to 3 octaves).
- **RATE**: Sets the playback speed of the arpeggiator. There is a red LED switch above the slider to synchronize the rate to the song tempo.
- **GATE**: Controls the note length (how long each note is held).

Then, we have the **MODULATION MATRIX** and **CHORUS** panels.

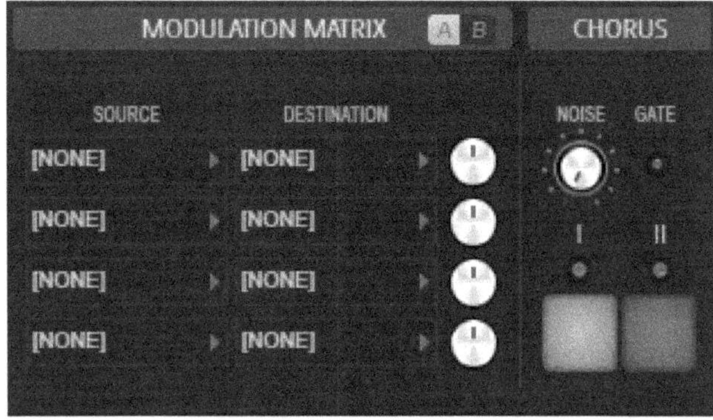

Figure 11.40 – Kepler Exo plugin: MODULATION MATRIX and CHORUS panels

The modulation matrix lets you route modulation sources (like LFOs, envelopes, velocity, etc.) to various parameters in the synth. This allows for complex, dynamic sound movement.

- **SOURCE**: Choose what will do the modulating (e.g., LFO1, LFO2, Envelope, Velocity).
- **DESTINATION**: Choose which parameter will be affected (e.g., filter cutoff, pitch, pulse width, etc.).
- **Amount**: Set how much the source will affect the destination (positive or negative values).

Here's an example of how you might use the modulation matrix. You could set **LFO1** as the source, filter cutoff as the destination, and adjust the amount so the filter opens and closes automatically.

The **CHORUS** panel adds a classic, lush chorus effect to your sound, inspired by vintage analog synths.

- **NOISE**: Adds noise to the output signal only when one or both chorus modes are selected.
- **I**: Emulates the Juno 6 chorus I mode.
- **II**: Emulates the Juno 6 chorus II mode.

- Chorus **I+II**: (*Shift* + *Click* the disabled chorus mode) to engage both modes at once. This combines the two chorus circuits for a thicker effect.

Now, let's see the **SAT** panel.

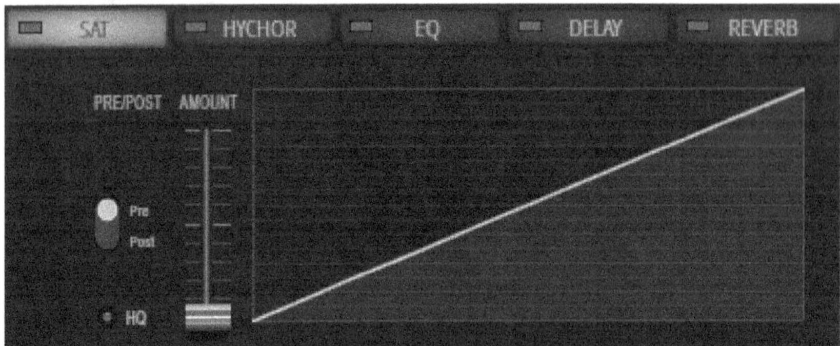

Figure 11.41 – Kepler Exo plugin: SAT effect panel

The **SAT** panel provides a soft-saturation distortion effect, shaping your sound by mapping input levels (horizontal axis) to output levels (vertical axis). This adds warmth, harmonics, and character to your signal.

- **PRE/POST**: Choose where in the signal path the saturation is applied, affecting how it interacts with other effects.
    - **Pre**: Apply the saturation at the beginning of the effects chain.
    - **Post**: Applies the saturation at the end of the effects chain.
- **Amount of saturation** (curve): The curve visually represents how input waveforms are transformed. You can adjust the curve to control the intensity and character of the saturation/distortion.
- **HQ** (high quality): When enabled, this mode reduces aliasing (unwanted digital artifacts), resulting in a cleaner, higher-quality saturation effect.

Beside it is the **HYCHOR** panel.

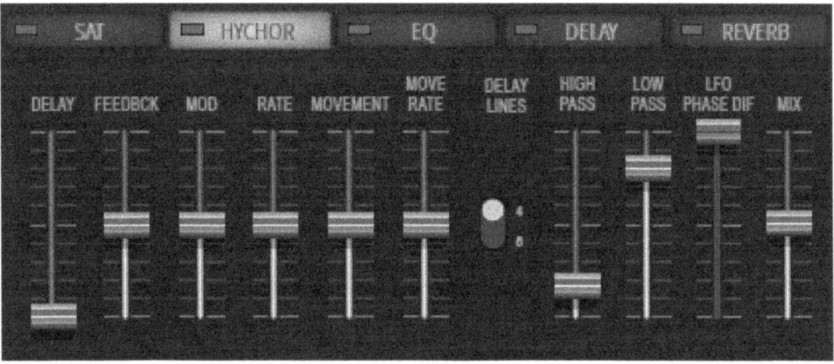

Figure 11.42 – Kepler Exo plugin: HYCHOR effect panel

- **DELAY**: Sets the length of the chorus delay line. This affects the depth and character of the chorus effect.
- **FEEDBACK**: Sets how much of the chorus output is fed back into the input. Higher feedback values can create a more pronounced, flanging-like effect.
- **MOD** (modulation): Sets the amount of LFO (Low Frequency Oscillator) modulation applied to the delay lines, detuning them for a thicker sound.
- **RATE** (mod rate): Sets the speed of the LFO modulation, changing how quickly the chorus effect moves.
- **MOVEMENT**: Sets the auto-pan speed, making the delay lines move across the stereo field for a wider, more animated sound.
- **MOVE RATE**: Sets the speed at which the delay lines are panned (the rate of the "movement" parameter).
- **DELAY LINES**: Sets the number of delay lines to either 4 or 8. More delay lines result in a denser and more extreme chorus effect.
- **LOW PASS**: Removes high frequencies from the chorus effect, making the sound darker or less bright. This is useful for taming harshness or creating a smoother, more vintage chorus character.
- **LFO PHASE DIF**: Increasing the phase difference spreads the modulation cycles apart, making the chorus effect wider and more animated. Lower values make the modulation more uniform across delay lines, while higher values create a more complex, swirling stereo image.
- **MIX**: Controls how much chorus effect you want to hear.

Next is the **EQ** panel.

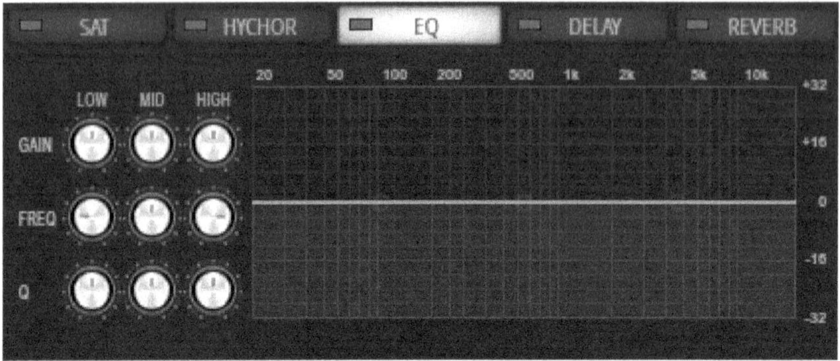

Figure 11.43 – Kepler Exo plugin: EQ

The **EQ** panel provides you with a simple equalizer to shape the tonal balance of your sound. You can use the **LOW**, **MID**, and **HIGH** controls to boost or cut specific frequency ranges and shape your sound to fit your mix. **Equalization** is covered in depth in *Chapter 6*, so we won't repeat it here. Let's look at the **DELAY** panel now.

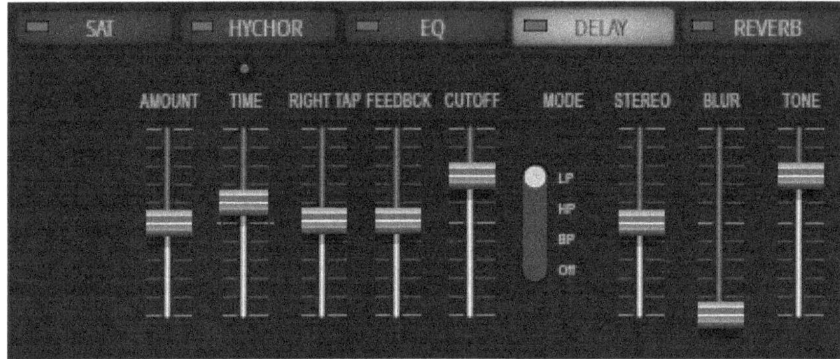

Figure 11.44 – Kepler Exo plugin: DELAY panel

- **AMOUNT**: Sets the level of the input signal sent to the delay effect. Higher values mean more of your sound is processed by the delay.
- **DELAY BPM SYNC:** Switches the delay time between free (milliseconds) and tempo-synced (musical divisions) modes. When enabled, delay times lock to your project's BPM for rhythmic echoes.
- **TIME**: Set smaller values to create quick, slapback-style echoes. Set longer values to produce more spaced-out, pronounced echoes.
- **RIGHT TAP**: Adjusts the delay time for the right channel relative to the left. Creates stereo or ping-pong delay effects by offsetting the right side.

- **FEEDBACK**: Controls how much of the delayed signal is fed back into the delay input. More feedback means more repeats and a longer echo tail.
- **CUTOFF**: Sets the cutoff frequency for the delay's filter. Shapes the tone of the echoes by filtering out high or low frequencies.
- **MODE** (**LP**, **HP**, **BP**, **OFF**): Selects the filter type for the delayed signal:
  - **LP (LOW PASS):** Removes high frequencies for darker echoes.
  - **HP (HIGH PASS):** Removes low frequencies for thinner echoes.
  - **BP (BAND PASS):** Allows only a band of frequencies through.
  - **OFF:** No filtering; echoes remain unfiltered.
- **STEREO**: Adjusts the stereo spread of the echoes. Higher values make the delay wider in the stereo field; lower values make it more mono.
- **BLUR**: Adds a smearing or diffusion effect to the echoes. Higher blur values make repeats softer and more ambient.
- **TONE**: Controls the brightness or darkness of the delay effect, helping the echoes sit better in your mix or avoid muddiness.

Finally, we have the **REVERB** panel.

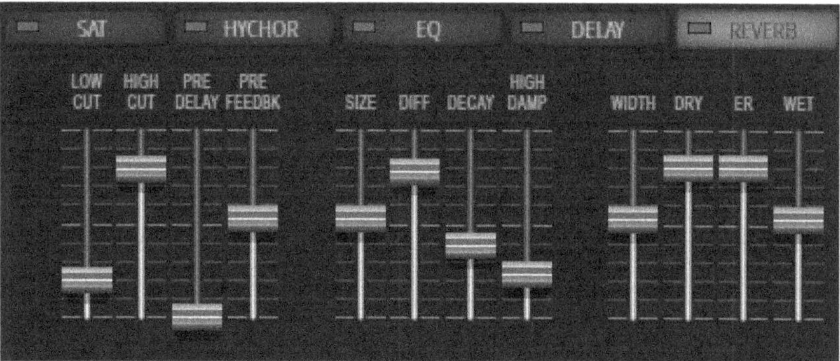

Figure 11.45 – Kepler Exo plugin: REVERB panel

- **LOW CUT**: Removes low frequencies from the input before reverb, preventing muddiness.
- **HIGH CUT**: Removes high frequencies from the input before reverb, making the effect darker.
- **PRE DELAY**: Sets the time between the dry signal and the onset of reverb, adding a sense of space.

- **PRE FEEDBACK**: Adds feedback to the pre-delay, creating more complex early reflections.
- **SIZE**: Adjusts the virtual room size, from small/tight to large/spacious.
- **DIFF** (diffusion): Adjusts the density of reflections; low = distinct echoes, high = smooth tail.
- **DECAY**: Sets how long the reverb lasts; longer decay = larger space.
- **HIGH DAMP** (high damping): Controls how quickly high frequencies fade, making the reverb warmer.
- **WIDTH**: Adjusts the stereo spread of the reverb.
- **DRY**: Sets the level of the original (unprocessed) signal.
- **ER** (early reflections): Sets the level of initial reflections, adding clarity and spatial definition.
- **WET**: Sets the level of the processed (reverb) signal.

Summary

This chapter dived into some of the more complex effects and instrument plugins that come with FL Studio. These allow you to perform creative sound design on your songs to help your songs stand out.

We learned how to use Pitch Shifter to apply pitching effects in real time. We learned how to create frequency shifting effects with Frequency Shifter. We learned how to use Fruity Granulizer to break audio into grains, which can then be looped over. We learned about Multiband Delay to break up audio into frequency bands and apply individual delay effects. Finally, we learned about multiband processing with Frequency Splitter. This allows us to isolate frequency bands, which we can then apply effects to. We learned how to add harmonics to bass frequencies using the Low Lifter plugin to make your bass easier to hear, regardless of the speaker playing your sound. Finally, we learned how to play the Kepler Synthesizer and the more advanced Kepler EXO synthesizer instruments.

We've finished covering topics on composing and mixing your music. In the next chapter, we'll learn how to master your music to get it ready for publishing.

Get this book's PDF version and more

Scan the QR code (or go to `packtpub.com/unlock`). Search for this book by name, confirm the edition, and then follow the steps on the page.

UNLOCK NOW

Note: Keep your invoice handy. Purchases made directly from Packt don't require an invoice.

Part 3

Postproduction and Publishing Your Music

In this final part of the book, you'll prepare your finished music for the world and build a sustainable music career. You'll begin by mastering your tracks, learning the critical final production steps to ensure your music sounds professional and translates well across all playback devices. You'll learn techniques like equalization, compression, stereo imaging, and limiting to get your song ready for release. Following production, you'll shift focus to promotion and business, learning how to craft your brand identity, establish your online presence through websites and social media, and leverage content creation and AI tools to expand your reach. You'll explore practical marketing strategies, learn to create professional album artwork and visuals, and understand how to engage audiences on platforms like YouTube and TikTok. Finally, you'll navigate the business side of music by registering your work with performance rights organizations, properly tagging your files, distributing your music to streaming platforms and online stores, and claiming royalties from multiple sources. By completing this section, you'll have the tools to start your career as an independent artist, ready to share and monetize your creations globally.

This part of the book includes the following chapters:

- *Chapter 12, Mastering Fundamentals*
- *Chapter 13, Marketing, Content Creation, and AI for Music Production*
- *Chapter 14, Publishing and Selling Music Online*

12

Mastering Fundamentals

In this chapter, we will learn about **mastering**. Mastering is the process taken to ensure our music is at a production-level quality and prepared for distribution. We'll learn the theory behind mastering and the generally applicable techniques you can use when mastering music. Everything you've learned so far in this book has been about creating your music. Now that your music is created, it's time for the final processing steps before releasing it to the world. By the end of this chapter, you'll know how to master your music so that it is ready for distribution.

In this chapter, we'll cover the following topics:

- What is mastering?
- Equalization in mastering
- Understanding stereo imaging with vectorscopes
- Adjusting song dynamics
- Understanding limiters
- Mastering with single-band compressors (Emphasis plugin)
- Mastering with multiband compressors (Maximus plugin)
- Mastering music with AI
- Formats to export your songs
- Exporting audio for third-party mixing and mastering

What is mastering?

When your song is finished being mixed, before publicly releasing it, you take it through a series of steps to enhance it called mastering. Mastering is an all-encompassing term for post-production activities that include the following:

1. Making the song sound consistent with other songs in the album.
2. Editing out flaws.
3. **Equalization** to ensure a well-balanced frequency range.
4. **Compression** to balance dynamic range.
5. Stereo width enhancement.
6. Limiting to raise the overall volume of the mix.
7. Listening to the audio on different devices and ensuring that there is a consistent quality of sound heard across them.
8. Any other adjustments necessary to prepare the music for distribution.

You should always master your song before publicly releasing it. Mastering should always make your music sound better than it did before mastering.

Can you master music yourself?

I personally say yes, or you should at least learn enough about mastering so that you know what you're paying for if you use a third party.

Learning to master will help tune your ears, and as a byproduct, help you become better at **mixing**. The activities involved in mastering audio force you to look at your music from a different perspective than when composing. It makes you imagine how your music will be received from the perspective of a third party. It helps you to hear your music the way your audience will hear it.

I note that you can't do a good job of mastering your music without decent music production speakers. If you don't have a decent speaker setup, you'll need to invest in some if you want to do it yourself.

When should you master your music?

Master your music when you're done mixing and ready to publicly release it. If possible, try to give yourself time (at least a day) after finishing mixing the song before you start mastering. This will allow you to approach the song with fresh ears.

How do I get good at mastering?

If you want to get good at mastering, master a lot of music. Just like playing an instrument requires muscle memory in your fingers, mastering requires you to fine-tune your ears. You need to develop a sense of what could be done to improve a song, and to know this, you need to experience what mastering can do. It's not something you can memorize; rather, it's something that you listen to and then make tweaks based on what you want to hear. To master a lot, you either need to make a lot of music and master it or master other people's music. Theory is not the goal in mastering; it's more of a muscle and technical skill that you need to build up.

What equipment do I use to master music?

To do a good job at mastering, you need mastering plugins. Mastering plugins include the following tools:

- **Equalizers/dynamic equalizers**
- **Saturators/harmonic exciters**
- **Multiband compressors**
- **Stereo imagers**
- **Limiters/maximizers**
- (Optional) reference tracks

The order of plugins in the effects chain while mastering is usually as follows:

1. The EQ or equalizer
2. Stereo FX – such as widening or mastering reverb
3. Compressors
4. Limiting

We'll learn about mastering concepts in a generally applicable way, so that you can use the techniques with any mastering plugin.

I personally use iZotope's *Ozone* suite of tools to master my music. If you are looking for a cutting-edge, all-encompassing mastering suite, iZotope's Ozone is an excellent choice. If you're interested in learning about Ozone, go to `https://www.izotope.com/`.

Let's learn about mastering concepts first, and then learn about the mastering tools that come with FL Studio. The first concept we need to touch on is equalization.

Equalization in mastering

When mastering, you will use a **parametric equalizer**. We learned how to use a parametric equalizer in *Chapter 6*, so refer to that chapter if you need a refresher. Parametric equalizers show audio levels at each frequency and have **band filters** to apply EQ to selected frequencies. A band filter is a tool used to isolate certain frequency ranges and reject frequencies outside its range. You can then perform effects on elected frequencies in the band filter. The following is an example of a parametric equalizer:

Figure 12.1 – Parametric equalizer

Parametric equalizers break up audio frequencies into multiple filter bands. You can then either increase or decrease the level of a band. By increasing, you'll boost a sound. By cutting, you'll reduce selected frequencies. Boosting the frequencies of a sound brings the sound more into focus. Cutting frequencies is useful for removing undesirable or offensive sounds.

You may be thinking, I used compressors and equalizers in the mixing stage, so how is mastering different? When you use compressors and equalizers in the mixing stage, you're tailoring individual sounds as well as combining sounds together. You can make extreme cuts and pass filters to shape your instrument sounds. You fix clashing instruments and balance individual sounds against each other.

When we apply compressors and equalizers in the mastering stage, we're thinking about the mix as a whole and balancing overall dynamics and frequencies. We're thinking about the entire combined sound, rather than individual sounds. We're no longer isolating frequencies; instead, we're choosing frequency areas to emphasize over others. While mastering, any changes you make will affect the entire mix. Your boosts and cuts will need to be more subtle than when mixing.

Let's discuss how you can EQ your song in the mastering stage.

Diagnosing frequency problems

Equalization is all about listening and then making EQ adjustments based on what you hear. When trying to find problematic frequencies, it helps to start by boosting a frequency band. Once you've found an area that sounds unpleasant, you can lightly cut frequencies at that position.

Here are examples of fixes you can do with equalizers:

- Some mastering engineers like to add a high-pass filter, cutting all frequencies below 20Hz–30Hz, as some speakers struggle to reproduce frequencies in that region.
- If the sound is too muddy, try cutting somewhere between 100 and 300 Hz.
- If the sound is too nasal-sounding, try cutting somewhere between 250 and 1,000 Hz.
- If the sound is too harsh, try cutting somewhere in the range of 2,000 to 2,500 Hz.
- If you are cutting more than 4 dB, you probably have an issue that needs to be fixed in the mixing stage rather than the mastering stage, and should go back and make mixing tweaks first.

Once you've made a change, always flip back and forth, turning effects on and off to see whether you made the sound better. Also, make sure you compare the ending track after mastering to the pre-mastered track to see whether you made it sound better.

Understanding spectrograms

Spectrograms are tools that allow you to visualize audio frequencies. You use them when applying equalization and place them after the EQ plugin on the effects chain. They allow you to visualize differences made from EQ cuts or boosts.

If you load up the FL Studio **Wave Candy** plugin on the master channel and choose the built-in **Spectrum** preset, it will load a spectrogram. In the following screenshot, we can see a spectrogram displaying audio frequencies and energy levels at each frequency:

Figure 12.2 – Wave Candy spectrogram

In the example in the preceding figure, we can see that the highest energy level appears to be in the 200 Hz to 500 Hz range. I've adjusted the scale knob to fit my audio, as seen in the preceding screenshot. You can adjust your scale knob to fit your music.

Spectrograms are useful when you're trying to troubleshoot low frequencies that are hard to hear with your ears. For example, let's say you noticed there was some issue in the bass frequencies but weren't sure what was causing the problem. You could look at a spectrogram to try to identify where frequency peaks are occurring.

We've learned that you can use spectrograms to diagnose frequency issues. Next, we'll learn about tools to diagnose stereo width issues.

Understanding stereo imaging with vectorscopes

Stereo imaging is a way to visualize how your sound is heard out of the left and right channels. You can think of this as how your sound is balanced to come out of your left or right speaker. Stereo imaging helps you troubleshoot any issues that may occur, such as sounds unintentionally focused on one side or the other.

A **vectorscope** is a tool to identify where your sounds are positioned in the stereo field (how much mono or stereo). If your goal is to create more stereo width (more spread out), the vectorscope lets you see how much stereo width has been created.

The following is an example of FL Studio's Wave Candy plugin using the built-in **Vectorscope** preset. It shows the stereo image of your audio.

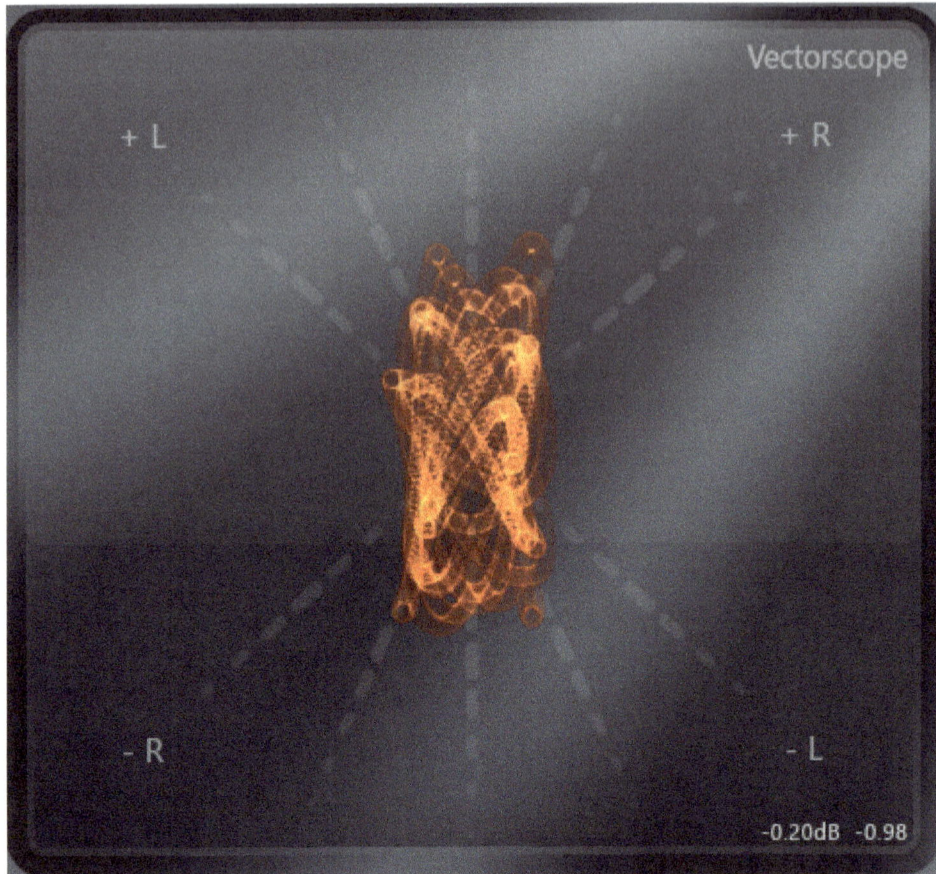

Figure 12.3 – Vectorscope

L stands for left audio channel and *R* for right. In the center, you can see a visual of the audio. If the audio is centered, it will appear up and down as shown in the screenshot. You can think of this as a mono sound, where you have equal sound coming out of the left and right channels. If the visual shows a leaning toward the left or right, it means that there is a different sound in the left and right channels.

Stereo imaging best practices

You want most of your sounds to be centered in the stereo field. Why? A lot of the time, your music will be played on a mono device, where the same sound comes equally out of all speakers. In such a case, any panning sounds will appear as mono to the listener. Also, if your audience is positioned far from the speakers, the overall impression is still mono.

Does this mean the goal of your music is to be mono? No. It's just important that your song sounds good in mono before you think about stereo effects. Stereo imaging is more like the icing on the cake, you can add. Stereo imaging plugins usually come with the ability to increase the stereo width. You can then spread selected frequency ranges out.

Sounds that are centered in the stereo field usually include kicks, snares, lead vocals, and bass instruments. Other higher-frequency sounds may be directed away from the center to give the impression that the sound exists in a larger space.

You can't do stereo imaging adjustments while wearing headphones. It can only be done on speakers. Headphones will make sounds seem much wider than they would on speakers.

Generally, when mastering, most songs have a very narrow stereo width in the lower frequencies. The mid frequencies have some stereo width, and the high frequencies have the most.

We've learned how to analyze the stereo width of your song. Next, let's learn how to adjust the dynamics of your song for mastering.

Adjusting song dynamics

Dynamic range refers to how loud or quiet your sound is. When mastering, you need to find a comfortable dynamic range for your listener. If a song has no dynamics, the song will appear flat and lack variety. If too much dynamic range is present, the listener will need to keep changing the volume to hear clearly, which is an undesirable experience.

One part of mastering is processing the dynamic range of your audio. You want to find a balance between loud and quiet sections of your song. More specifically, we want to find a balance in dynamic range throughout your frequency ranges. You don't want your low-end frequencies to overpower your high-end ones, or your high-end frequencies to overpower your low-end ones. You want everything to have clarity while drawing attention to your leading melody.

Listening to your audio in different environments

Another goal of mastering is ensuring your song quality is consistent across various devices. For example, does your song sound good coming out of a car radio, earbuds, TV speakers, and any other devices that you can find? Does your music sound good when played on suboptimal speakers? Everything sounds better on amazing speakers, but does your song hold up when played on bad speakers?

How do we control dynamics while mastering and ensure that our song sounds great across various devices? For that, we need to learn about a tool called limiters.

Understanding limiters

The idea behind **limiting** is that you choose a threshold volume and compress audio volume peaks that reach the threshold level. Then, you can raise the overall volume of the sound close to the threshold level without going over. This results in your ending sound appearing louder overall to your listener. In general, if your sound is louder, listeners will be able to hear your sound more easily and have a more enjoyable listening experience.

Without a limiter, you risk having your audio go above 0 dB, which can result in uncontrolled distortion on speakers. A limiter ensures that the final sound is contained below a threshold to help prevent unwanted distortion.

In theory, you can set a limiter ceiling to 0 dB. In practice, there's a chance that the speaker playing the audio may distort when playing the sound, especially if the file format is changed due to file compression. To be safe and ensure there's no peaking, some mastering technicians choose to give a little headroom and set the ceiling threshold somewhere between -0.3 dB and -3 dB, and some as much as -6 dB. In other words, your goal is to find a balance between increasing the volume as much as you can before you lose too much dynamic range.

We've learned about the concepts that are used in mastering. Next, let's put theory into practice and learn some mastering tools.

Mastering with single-band compressors (Emphasis plugin)

You can master your music using **single-band compressor** tools or multiband compressor tools. We will discuss both of these options in this chapter. We will discuss single-band compressors first using the **Emphasis** plugin, and then we will discuss multiband compressors using the **Maximus** plugin.

Let's take a moment to clarify some confusing terminology. What is a single-band and multiband compressor? A **band** refers to a specific range of frequencies. So a "band" compressor means a compressor that operates on a specific frequency range. If it's a single-band compressor, that means the compressor affects all the frequencies. If it's a multiband compressor, that means the compressor operates on each range of frequencies differently.

Single-band compressors are intended to be simpler than multiband compressors. Single-band compressors like Emphasis are good for quick, transparent, and musical loudness maximization with minimal fuss. This is good if you want a fast loudness boost with minimal setup.

Multiband compressors like Maximus are useful when you need deep dynamic control and are willing to spend more time fine-tuning your sound. This is good when you need detailed control over different frequency bands or want to address specific mix issues (e.g., tighten bass, tame harsh highs).

Let's look at single-band compressors. Emphasis is a single-band mastering limiter designed to enhance loudness and sound while preserving dynamics. It's great for making your tracks sound louder, punchier, and more polished quickly with minimal effort.

1. Before using Emphasis, you'll need to have a sound to apply **single-band compression** to. If you have a song already mixed and ready to be mastered, add it to the **Playlist**.
2. Insert Emphasis on the **Master** channel. Place Emphasis as the last effect on your master mixer track (or on a group bus). The mastering limiter (Emphasis) should be the final processor in your signal chain so that it can control the absolute peak level of everything that comes before it.

Figure 12.4 – Emphasis plugin

3. On **Emphasis**, you'll see a set of controls. We'll work our way through the controls from left to right, starting with **INPUT GAIN**. Adjust the **INPUT GAIN** control to set how much signal is sent into the plugin. Input level has a significant impact on how much processing occurs. The input gain determines how much signal is sent into the limiter. The goal is to find a balance where you achieve the desired loudness without introducing unwanted artifacts. Higher input pushes the signal harder into the limiting stage, making it louder.

4. In the **ENHANCEMENT** tab, select a **MODE** that fits your material:
    - **TRANSIENT**: Emphasizes punch and attack, which is good for drums or percussive material.
    - **STEADY**: Focuses on sustained sounds, which is useful for pads, vocals, or smooth genres.
    - **VERSATILE**: Adapts, balances loudness and transparency. Great starting point for most music.
    - **LOUD**: Maximizes loudness, increases aggression. Best for electronic, dense, or competitive genres.
5. Adjust **EMPHASIS** Amount (if available). Use the **EMPHASIS** amount control to set how much loudness and dynamic shaping is applied. Lower values = more natural, subtle enhancement. Higher values = more loudness and shaping. This will be auto-applied if the **MODE** is set to **VERSATILE** or **LOUD**, or you can manually set it if the **MODE** is set to **TRANSIENT** or **STEADY**.
6. Set the **HARDNESS** control. It controls the transition from soft, transparent limiting to hard, aggressive clipping. Lower values = softer, more transparent. Higher values = harder, more aggressive.
    - At low **HARDNESS** values (near 0): The limiting is very gentle and transparent. The plugin avoids any clipping, so peaks are controlled smoothly, preserving the natural shape of the audio. As you increase **HARDNESS**, the limiting curve becomes steeper. The plugin starts to act more like a clipper, sharply cutting off peaks that exceed the threshold. This introduces more distortion and makes the sound more aggressive.
    - At maximum **HARDNESS** (9): The plugin acts as a hard-clipper. Any part of the signal that exceeds the threshold is cut flat, resulting in a very "hard" and pronounced limiting effect, which can add harmonics and make the sound more "in your face."
7. Set the **ENVELOPE** control. It shapes how the plugin responds over time to changes in your audio's level. At low **ENVELOPE** values, the attack and release curves are more gradual and natural. The plugin responds smoothly to changes, affecting a broader portion of each transient (the initial hit of a sound). This results in a more natural, louder output because more of the transient is emphasized. At high **ENVELOPE** values, the attack and release curves become more S-shaped and pronounced. The plugin reacts more sharply, focusing its processing on a smaller slice of the transient. This creates stronger, more dramatic dynamic shifts, emphasizing only the very start of hits and making the sound punchier but less natural.

8. Set the **ROUTING** to either **L/R** or **M/S**:
    - **L/R** (left/right) mode: The plugin treats the left and right sides of your stereo sound separately. Example: If something is louder on the left, only the left side is affected.
    - **M/S** (mid/side) mode: The plugin splits your sound into "Mid" (the center, like vocals or bass) and "Side" (the edges, like reverb or stereo effects). This lets you control the center and the sides of your mix differently.
9. Set the **LINKING** level value: This knob decides if the plugin treats both channels (L/R or M/S) together or separately. At low linking values, the plugin works on each channel by itself. This can make your mix sound wider, but sometimes the balance can shift if one side is much louder. At high linking values, the plugin treats both channels as one, applying the same effect to both. This keeps your stereo image stable and balanced.
10. Set **OUTPUT** level: Use this control to set your final output ceiling, typically between -1 dB and 0 dB.

At the bottom of **EMPHASIS**, you'll notice a few additional optional controls:

- **DC BLOCK**: Removes any DC offset (a constant "zero Hz" signal) from your audio by applying a gentle high-pass filter. This recenters the waveform around zero, which helps the limiter work more efficiently and can allow your track to be made louder without unwanted artifacts.
- **INSTANT RECOVERY**: Changes how quickly the limiter "lets go" after reducing the volume of a loud sound.
    - **OFF** (default): The limiter adapts its release speed based on the music, aiming for a natural, transparent sound and preserving dynamics.
    - **ON**: The limiter releases instantly, maximizing loudness and punch but with less focus on preserving the original dynamics. This is useful if you want your track as loud as possible.
- **TRUE PEAK**: Makes the limiter look for the "real" highest peaks in your audio, not just the ones at the sample points. It oversamples the signal to catch inter-sample peaks, helping to prevent digital clipping and distortion that might not show up on a regular peak meter.
- **OVERSAMPLING FACTOR**: Sets how much the plugin oversamples the audio internally (Off, 2x, 4x, 8x, or 16x). Higher oversampling reduces distortion and aliasing, especially when pushing the limiter hard, but uses more CPU. If your FL Studio project is already set to a high sample rate (like 192 kHz), you usually don't need extra oversampling in the plugin.

- **BYPASS**: This switch temporarily turns off the effect, letting you hear the original, unaffected sound. It is useful for quickly comparing your processed sound with the original ("A/B testing") to decide if your changes are actually improving the audio.
- **DELTA**: Lets you listen to just the difference between the original and processed audio (what the plugin is changing or removing). It is useful for hearing exactly what the limiter is doing to your sound – great for fine-tuning settings or checking for unwanted artifacts.
- **LEVEL MATCHING**: When enabled, this automatically adjusts the output loudness so that the processed and original signals are equally loud (based on RMS, or perceived loudness). This is important because louder sounds often seem "better" even if they aren't. Level matching helps you make fair comparisons by removing loudness differences from your judgment.

We've learned how to master using single-band compressors. Next, let's learn how to master using multiband compressors.

Mastering with multiband compressors (Maximus plugin)

Let's discuss the theory behind using a multiband compressor and then show an example using FL Studio's Maximus plugin. Multiband compressors allow you to isolate frequency ranges and apply **compression** to each region. This way, you can bring up or down the level of the low, mid, or high frequencies separately. For example, say your low-frequency sounds need compression but not the rest of your frequencies – a multiband compressor allows you to do this.

When you use a multiband compressor, you'll do the following steps:

1. First, split the audio into filter bands based on a frequency range. Usually, there are three or four bands for your lows, mids, and highs. Essentially, we're saying let's break up our audio and look at each frequency area separately.
2. Within each filter band, solo the band so that you can hear the frequencies and level of audio in just that range.
3. Apply compression just to your chosen frequency range. This will help balance out the loud and quiet parts within the band. You can then choose to either raise or lower the volume level.

I realize this is very confusing without a visual. Let's do the steps described with a multiband compressor plugin.

Applying multiband compression with Maximus

Maximus is a multiband compressor, limiter, **noise gate**, **expander**, **ducker**, and **de-esser**. Maximus comes with FL Studio *Signature Edition* and higher. Although you may or may not use Maximus, it is a great tool to learn about multiband compression and works similarly to other multiband compressors on the market, so we'll use it in our examples. Let's apply multiband compression using Maximus:

1. Before using Maximus, you'll need to have a sound to apply multiband compression to. If you have a song already mixed and ready to be mastered, add it to the **Playlist**.
2. On the **Master** channel, add the Maximus plugin and play your sound. You'll see something like this:

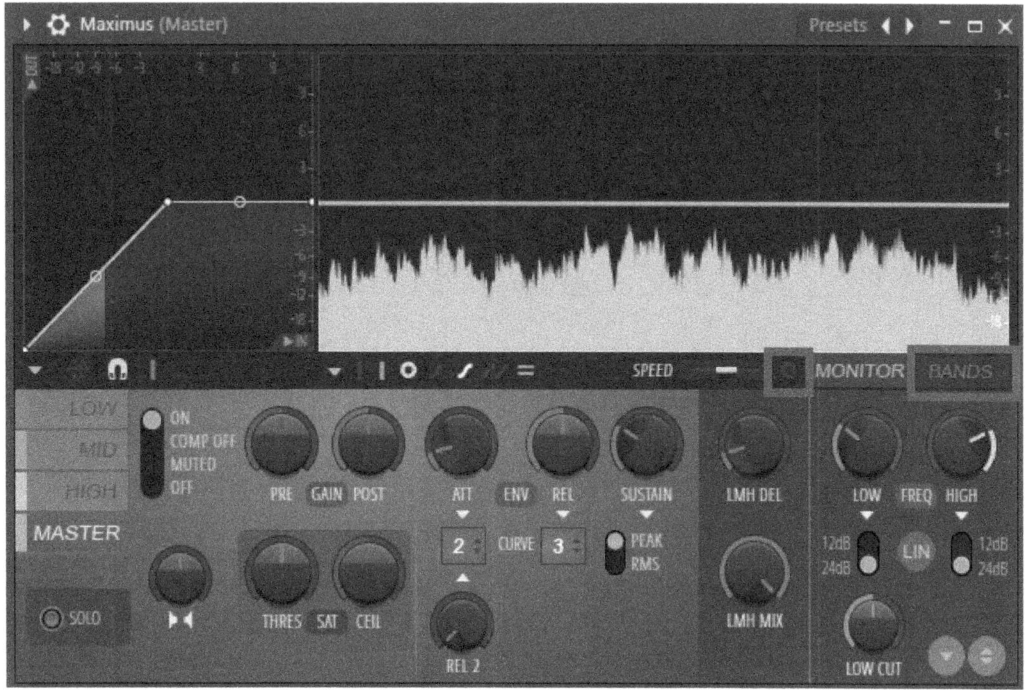

Figure 12.5 – Maximus plugin

Maximus allows you to break up your audio into three frequency bands and apply individual compression to each of them. To apply multiband compression, we first need to break up the audio into frequency filter bands.

3. On **Maximus**, select the **BANDS** tab as shown in the preceding screenshot.

4. Check the **show output spectrogram** button directly to the left of the **MONITOR** button. This will allow you to visually see the frequency level.

   You'll see the visual on the right side of the plugin display three distinct colors. These represent the three frequency band filters and are shown from left to right as red, orange, and yellow. Red represents low frequencies, orange represents mid frequencies, and yellow represents high frequencies. This is shown in the following screenshot:

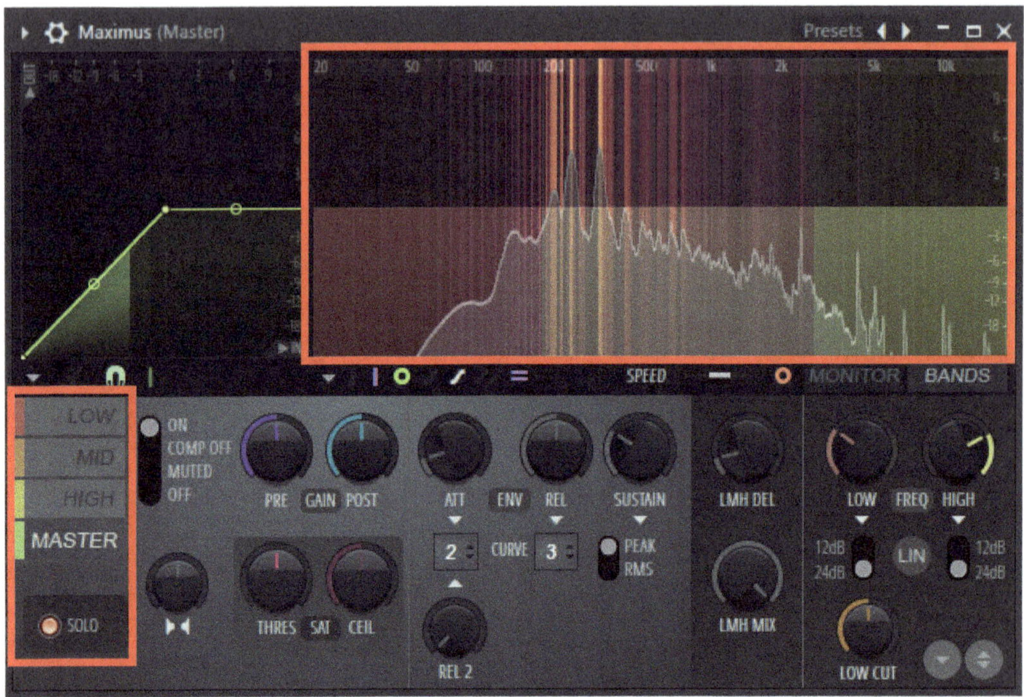

Figure 12.6 – Frequency bands

On the left side of **Maximus**, you can see four tabs – **LOW**, **MID**, **HIGH**, and **MASTER** – with the corresponding red, orange, and yellow colors. These tabs allow you to switch between frequency ranges. The **MASTER** tab is the resulting combined sound of any effects applied to the **LOW**, **MID**, and **HIGH** bands.

5. Let's choose a range for a filter band. Left-click to select the **LOW** tab. This will select the low-frequency band.
6. Left-click on the **SOLO** button. You will now be listening to just the frequencies that exist in the **LOW** filter band.

7. Now, we need to customize our frequency bands. While the **LOW** tab is selected, left-click on the low filter band visual and drag it around. By dragging, you resize the filter band. The goal here is to isolate the low frequencies of your audio. For example, you could drag until you hear just the sub-bass sounds. Dragging the band will automatically adjust the **LOW** and **pregain** (**PRE**) knobs.

Figure 12.7 – Adjusting the low-frequency band

8. Left-click on the **MID** tab on the left, and adjust the filter band as you did in the previous step until you hear just the mid frequencies.

   When you drag a filter band around, you'll notice that the **PRE** knob will adjust. This is the volume of your audio before it is compressed. You may be wondering whether it's better to increase or decrease **PRE**. This is something you'll have to discover for yourself. Whether to increase or decrease the volume before compressing will depend on your specific situation. It's a matter of playing around to see whether your sound is improved or not.

   You have successfully broken down your audio into three filter bands. Next, you can apply individual compression to these filter bands.

9. While the **LOW** tab is selected, we can apply compression to the low frequencies. On the left side, you'll see a visual as follows:

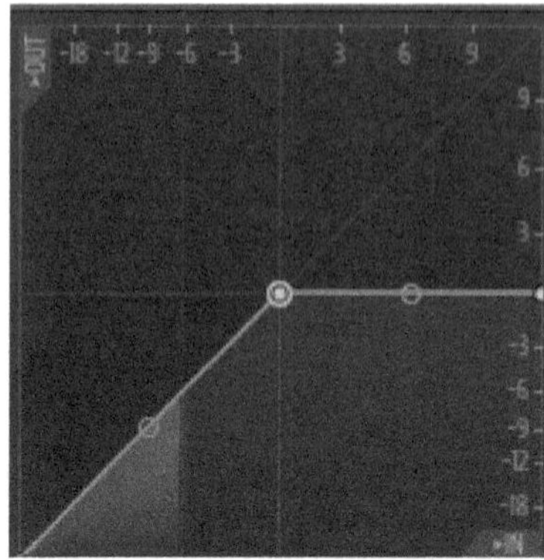

Figure 12.8 – Limiting

By default, limiting is applied at a threshold of 0 dB. By left-clicking and dragging the key points on the visual, you can change how compression is applied.

You can drag points on the line around, add new points, and add curves. This will compress the audio in various ways. An example is shown in the following screenshot. Notice the difference in curve shape between *Figure 12.8* and *Figure 12.9*:

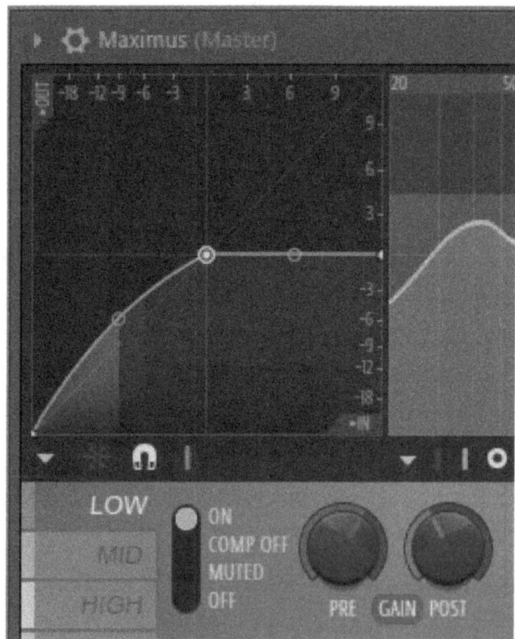

Figure 12.9 – Applied compression

Remember that compression can be used to bring the loud and soft parts of a sound closer together. If we like, we can then increase the overall volume of the compressed sound with a makeup gain. On Maximus, makeup gain is done with the **POST** knob, as shown in the preceding screenshot. In other words, if you want to increase or decrease the volume of your compressed sound, you use the **POST** knob. For example, say after you compressed your sound you discovered that it was too quiet. You could fix this by increasing the **POST** gain.

Repeat applying compression to the mid and high frequencies in the **MID** and **HIGH** tabs.

You're probably thinking that the sound difference is quite subtle, and maybe you don't really hear much of a difference. You're right. Compression in the mastering stage is very subtle. Compression removes dynamic range, so you're hearing the absence of dynamic range.

10. When using a multi-compressor plugin, a good place to start is to select one of the mastering presets, listen to the different possibilities available, then go back and tweak the filter bands and controls to your liking.
    Maximus comes with several presets. On Maximus, select a preset by clicking **Presets** in the top-right corner.

Figure 12.10 – Maximus presets

In the **Presets** menu in the screenshot, under the **Mastering** label, you can see presets for **Clear master** and **Clear master RMS**. These presets can give your mastering some initial controls to get started.

I've compressed my sound, now what?

The release time of the compressor is an important tool. A fast release time could cause distortion or a pumping sound. A slower release time allows the compressor to compress after the loud peaks pass. You'll likely want your low-end frequency sounds to be compressed differently from your high-end frequency sounds.

Some examples of using multi-compressors are as follows:

- Set different attack and release times for different frequencies. Use shorter attack times for high frequencies, such as hi-hats, or avoid compressing the hi-hat frequencies altogether. In general, use shorter attack and release times for high frequencies than for low frequencies.
- Compress the bass sounds more than other frequencies if you want to increase the loudness of your track but not have the bass sounds overpower.

There is a trade-off made between making your sound louder and how much dynamic range your sound retains. Overcompressing your mid and high frequencies can ruin transient sounds. Transients are the punctuated bursts when a sound first hits. Think about a snare drum hit. In a rock song, you want that to break through the mix and be clearly heard. You don't want the transients to be overcompressed. The way to avoid overcompressing transients is to adjust the release time to be shorter for a less noticeable pumping effect. Maximus contains some presets that can be used to add punchiness to your drums.

This isn't a one-rule-fits-all situation, though. You may have scenarios where you want your transients to smear together, in which case you'll want less punchy transients. Your decision comes down to a case-by-case basis for what you want your sound to feel like. This is why **reference tracks** can be helpful, as you have a guide for what you want your song to sound like.

Using reference tracks

Prior to working, some mastering engineers collect songs they like that are similar to the song being mastered. When mastering the song, they will swap back and forth between the song being mastered and the reference tracks. The goal of reference tracks is to give the mastering engineer a reference point to compare with.

If you want your mastered track to sound similar to an existing song, you can use reference tracks. Instead of applying mastering presets, you compare your song to other similar songs that you'd like your song to mimic. You then tweak your equalization and compression to create a similar mastered sound.

Using reference tracks is easy to do. Simply find some songs that you'd like your song to sound like and periodically compare listening to the two while mastering. Some mastering plugins, like Izotope's Ozone, allow you to quickly switch between the mastered track and the reference song without having to leave the plugin.

You now know how to use multiband compressors. Next, let's learn how to master using AI.

Mastering music with AI

FL Studio offers a tool to use artificial intelligence to master your music. You can find the Master tool by going to **File** | **Export** | **Master**, or through the keyboard shortcut *Ctrl* + *Alt* + *M*. This will bring up the following window:

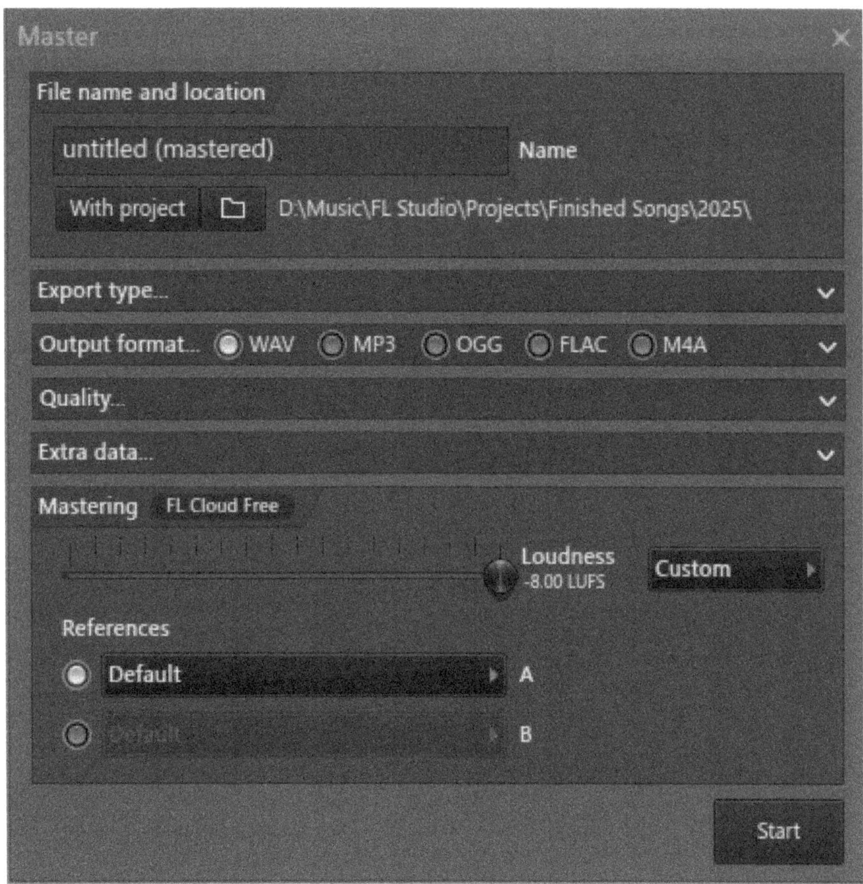

Figure 12.11 – Master tool window

In the preceding screenshot, you can see a control for **References**. Depending on whether you have an **FL Cloud** subscription or not, you will be able to see additional genre presets. In the preceding screenshot, the **Default** preset is selected. These presets apply different AI algorithms to master your music. Simply click **Start,** and FL Studio will master your music for you.

Unlike other mastering tools in this section, there aren't really any controls to play around with. AI makes all the decisions and choices about how your music should be mastered.

Using AI to master your music provides an alternative to compare against your own mastering efforts. Then you can see which mastered version of the song you prefer. Using AI, of course, doesn't give you any fine-tuned control, so if you don't like what it did, then you'll have to master it the old-fashioned way.

We've mastered our song. Now it's time to export the song. When you export the song, you need to choose a format for export.

Formats to export your songs

Depending on the type of medium (vinyl, streaming, CD, cassette, and so on) you are exporting to, you may have to choose a different bit depth. Higher bit depth values will give better audio resolution but result in larger file sizes. Usually, you can export at 16- or 24-bit depths. Also, make sure your final master has a resampling rate of 64 points or higher.

This may sound complicated, but it's just a matter of choosing an export setting when you're exporting your finished track, as shown in the following screenshot:

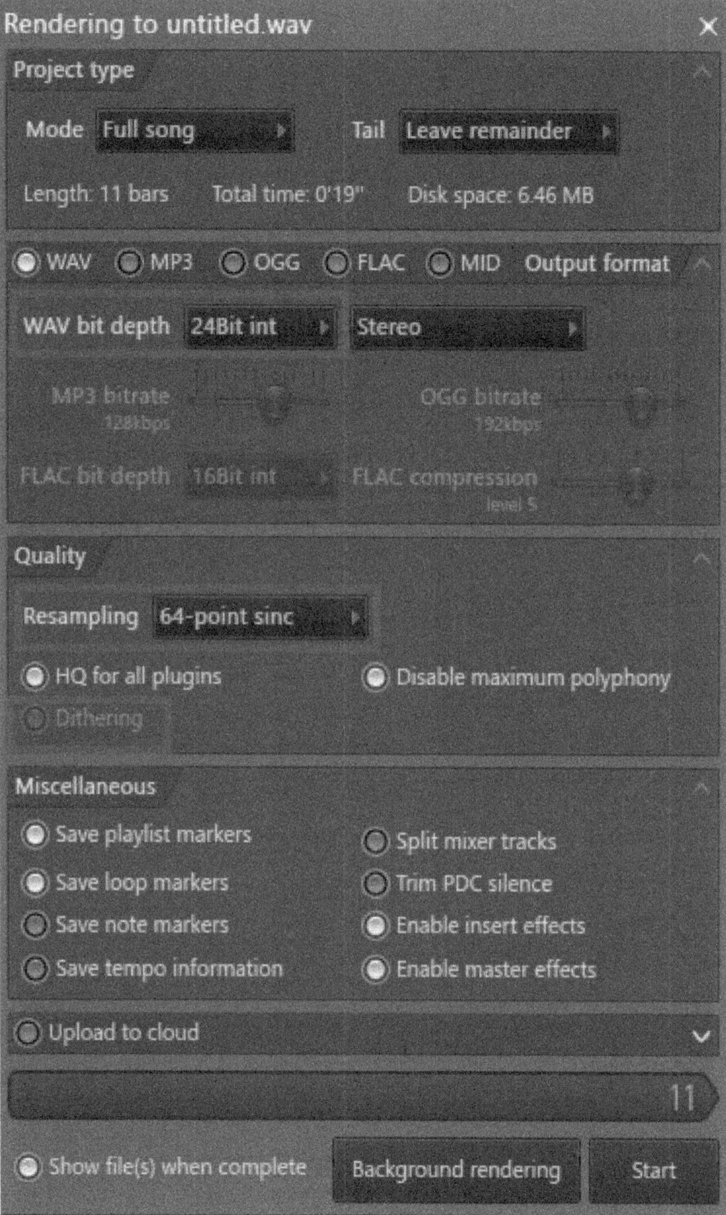

Figure 12.12 – Export settings

If you have a bit depth of 16 bits, turn on **Dithering** on the final master when exporting. How **dithering** works is beyond the scope of this book, but the general gist is that it makes it appear that your audio is higher in resolution than it actually is.

We've learned skills to master your music yourself. Next, we'll learn about mixing and mastering using third parties.

Exporting audio for third-party mixing and mastering

If you want your music mastered, but don't think you have the skills or plugins to do it yourself, one option is to hire a mastering engineer. One benefit a mastering engineer can provide is an independent set of ears. They will hear your song from an outsider's perspective and may pick up on flaws or ways to enhance your music that you wouldn't think of.

If you want to send a song to a third party to mix or master your music, you should send all the audio from the Mixer channels in your project. This way, the third party can apply additional effects to your sounds. To export each Mixer channel as an individual audio file, including the Master channel, ensure that you're exporting **WAV** files and that **Split mixer tracks** is checked when exporting, as shown in the following screenshot:

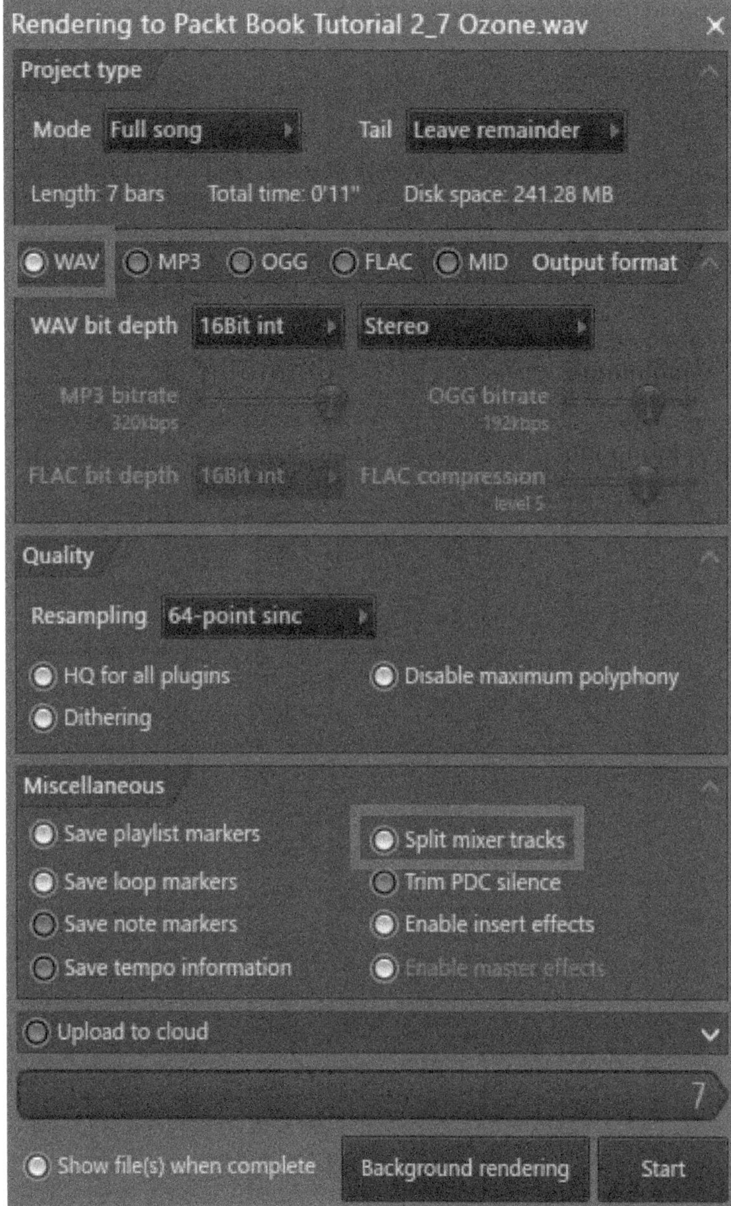

Figure 12.13 – Split mixer tracks

Once they're exported, WAV files will be generated from the audio output of each Mixer channel. You now know how to export your music for editing by third parties.

Summary

In this chapter, we learned about the post-production mastering process so that you can successfully master your music. We learned what mastering is and techniques to master your music, including equalization, stereo imaging, limiters, single-band compressors, multiband compressors, and AI tools to master your music. Finally, we learned how to export your song as individual audio stems for use by third parties.

In the next chapter, we'll learn about marketing your music and promoting yourself as an artist.

Get this book's PDF version and more

Scan the QR code (or go to `packtpub.com/unlock`). Search for this book by name, confirm the edition, and then follow the steps on the page.

Note: Keep your invoice handy. Purchases made directly from Packt don't require an invoice.

13

Marketing, Content Creation, and AI for Music Production

Learning to produce music is just the beginning. To build a real career, you need to get your music heard and connect with listeners. That's where branding, marketing, and promotion come in. Sharing your work, building an audience, and making genuine connections are just as important as the music itself.

This chapter gives you practical strategies for getting your music out there. You'll learn how to shape your brand, set up your online presence, and use marketing basics to reach more people. We'll cover how to create content that reaches your audience, add visuals to your releases, and use platforms like **YouTube** and live shows to grow your followers. You'll also see how AI tools can support your music production and promotion.

In this chapter, we will discuss the following topics:

- Marketing essentials
- Creating a brand identity
- Making the most of your live performances
- Making the most of YouTube
- TikTok for musicians
- Creating album artwork with AI
- Creating music visuals with ZGameEditor Visualizer
- AI tools for music production
- Creating entire songs with Suno AI
- Have AI tools replaced musicians?

Marketing essentials

How much you're able to earn as an artist is directly connected to how well you're able to market yourself. To market yourself, at a minimum, you'll want to have the following:

- A brand identity.
- A musician's website featuring you and your products.
- A Facebook page for your brand.
- A YouTube channel.
- A Google email account for business-related inquiries. Give it a professional name.
- Optional but potentially useful; **SoundCloud**, **Patreon**, **X** (formerly **Twitter**), **Instagram**, **TikTok**, and/or **Twitch** accounts.

Building a brand isn't something that happens overnight. It takes months or years for you to develop it. So, if you don't have the previously listed items yet, now is the time to get started.

Creating a brand identity

Time for the fun part...choosing your identity. What do you want to be known as? How would you like to be recognized? Think about the visuals, logos, genres, and so on. If you don't know what kind of artist you want to be yet, start thinking now.

The more specific you get with your brand image, the easier it becomes to generate content. By narrowing your options and choosing some rules to work within, it becomes easier to create. This applies to any creative artistic expression. Once you know what direction you'd like to go in, you'll start discovering lots of opportunities to get there.

Making decisions to advance your career can be intimidating and overwhelming when you first start, as there are countless paths you could take. Creating a brand makes decision-making easier. Think about how you want to look visually: what clothing, hairstyle, atmosphere, and tone you'd like to convey. Once you pick a style, you'll instinctively start looking for inspiration and tools to help you get there. Your style will help shape the type of live show you deliver when performing and the type of content you want to create when promoting yourself online.

Choosing your artist name

Unless you want to use your real name, you need a professional artist name or band name that you can use when performing. For picking a name, here are two recommendations:

- Pick a name that's easy to spell and pronounce. If people can't remember your name, they'll struggle to search for you, and it becomes harder to become famous.
- Pick a name that's unique. Do a Google search beforehand to see if someone else already has a name similar to yours. Pick a name that isn't too similar to something else. Also, check that the website domain name hasn't already been taken. Picking a unique name will help immensely when dealing with search engine optimization, as you'll have less online competition.

Creating a website

To promote your brand, you'll want to have a website to showcase your work, enable fans to buy your products and services, and provide contact information for business opportunities.

When creating a website, there are several options available to you. If you have no website-making experience whatsoever, there are website templates and website builders. These will guide you through the process of creating a musician's website, and you don't have to worry at all about what's going on in the website backend. If you choose this option, it's easy: just pay money every month, and you're done.

If you don't mind getting your hands a little bit dirty and want more customization than what a website builder can offer, I recommend looking into using WordPress. WordPress allows you to import a template of your choosing and then customize the template. It does require some effort to get your template customized, your website hosted, and your **SEO** optimized, but it is cheaper than using a website builder, and you end up with a website that has as many features as you desire. Lots of reasonably priced WordPress templates are available at `https://elements.envato.com/`.

If you choose to go the WordPress route, you can test your website and host it on your own computer before paying for hosting and publicly deploying it. You can test WordPress sites using a service called Local, available at `https://localwp.com/`.

When you're ready to deploy your WordPress website, you'll need to look into a service that can host it. There are lots of companies dedicated to providing web hosting. At the time of writing, I am using a service called *IONOS by 1&1* for my web hosting. I end up paying about $100 a year for the hosting with the domain name included. IONOS by 1&1 services are available at `https://www.ionos.ca/`.

A website is important for conveying the brand identity you want to portray. In addition to being the place for fans to find you, your website will also shape the types of future business opportunities that come your way. Next, let's learn about performing live.

Making the most of your live performances

If you're a live-performing musician, that means you're an entertainer. That means you should be thinking about how to entertain. It's not enough to just stand up and play an instrument. In order to stand out, you need to deliver a full show. The music, although important, is only one piece of the act. If someone is watching your show, you need to find ways to keep them engaged. Why should they watch you? Give them compelling reasons.

Think about visuals you can create to captivate your audience. Although you may not be able to control the venue itself since it changes with each performance, there are many parts of your act that you can control, even when you're first starting out with little to no budget. Here are some suggestions:

- Find a costume visual that is pleasing to look at. You might consider incorporating costume changes throughout your show.
- Think about what kind of movement/dancing you could do if you're singing. Perhaps come up with some signature dance moves.
- Think about how to make the instrument part of the act if you're playing an instrument. Can you dress up the instrument? Can you incorporate it into dance moves? Can you do flashy tricks with it?
- Have some banter ready to help bridge the gap between songs. If you don't do this, you'll soon discover that the room becomes awkwardly silent, and you'll lose any momentum you built up. Plan out some interesting stories you can share. Consider humorous banter between your band members. Perhaps include recurring gag bits you can bring back again throughout the show.
- Consider short games where you interact with your audience members. Prizes and contests are easy and repeatable. For example, a prize could be an autographed piece of merchandise that you're selling after the show. This will also help advertise that you have merchandise available for sale.
- Consider duets or any other form of collaboration with other artists.
- If you're a DJ, you'll want to look into learning VJ software (video jockey software) to create animated visuals for your performances.

You've prepared a performance, now it's time to book your show.

Booking your first gigs

Booking gigs when you're relatively unknown can be a lot of work. You'll have to find bars and venues and send them emails to book stage time. Music venues want to make money. If you want a music venue to let you play a show at their venue, you need to convince them that you're going to bring them customers. If you're wondering why the world isn't beating down your door to give you gigs, it's because you haven't yet proven yourself to be a reliable generator of money for other people.

There's an old saying that goes like this:

> *"You need money to make money."*

In the music and film business, the saying should be a little different. You don't need to start off with money, but you need to show that you're able to generate money. The saying should go like this:

> *You need to show you can make other people money to make money.*

If you want to increase your chances of booking a slot at a music venue, it helps to have a show that consists of multiple artists. Music venues want an event that will attract a crowd. A larger crowd means more ticket and drink sales. A show package consisting of several acts increases the likelihood that more people will come to the venue.

So, if you're struggling to get booked at venues, consider teaming up with other musicians. You can then go to a music venue and tell them you have a whole evening of acts ready to play. Even better, tell them how many audience members you expect your show will bring in and what you'll do to help promote the show. When you do that, you're helping venues see the monetary value you can deliver.

Filming your shows

Every time you perform in front of a live crowd, you should consider recording your performance. You can use the footage in the future for your music videos and post the photos on your social media accounts and website. It's simple enough to do. You just need to get someone to film and take photos periodically throughout your show. Some artists have created music videos entirely from fan footage taken by audience members. It's a good idea to periodically post short clips of your live shows on TikTok/Instagram/YouTube Shorts.

Streaming performances online

If you're considering filming your show, why not take the next step and live-stream your show as well? You can live-stream on YouTube or Twitch. Twitch is a video platform for recording live video streaming rather than edited videos. If you live-stream your video, you have the benefit of live audience engagement. You can deliver online performances, chat with your audience throughout your show, give live Q&As, and receive donations directly. You can visit Twitch at `https://www.twitch.tv/`.

When you build your brand as an artist, it really helps to have a clear idea, almost like a thesis, that ties your story together. This gives people something real to connect with. These days, streaming sessions are one way to let your true personality shine through. When you go live, fans get to see who you are beyond the music: your quirks, your process, even your off-the-cuff thoughts. That kind of authenticity draws people in and makes them want to stick around, not just for your songs, but for you as a person. Over time, this genuine connection can turn casual listeners into a loyal community.

Another tool to consider is Patreon. Patreon is essentially a YouTube channel that you charge viewers to access. On Patreon, users pay a subscription fee to you. In return, you provide videos, written media, lessons, or whatever else you want to offer your subscribers. It's free to upload videos, but Patreon takes a small percentage of the profits from your subscribers. You can visit Patreon at `https://www.patreon.com/`.

You now know how to get the most out of your performances. Next, let's talk about marketing yourself on YouTube.

Making the most of YouTube

YouTube is generally the biggest platform for musicians to promote themselves. Contrary to expectation, creating a successful YouTube channel isn't done through luck, timing, or hoping a single upload suddenly goes viral. Posting a video and crossing your fingers is no better than buying a lottery ticket. What separates channels that grow consistently from those that fade away is a clear strategy. Successful creators know exactly who they're making videos for, what their audience cares about, and how to keep viewers engaged from the first second to the last.

When you understand your YouTube audience on a deeper level, you will be able to create content that resonates with them. If you know how they think, what motivates them, what problems they want solved, and what entertains them, you can create videos that feel tailor-made for them. Pair that with studying successful creators in your niche, analyzing your own content, and improving your titles, thumbnails, and storytelling, and you'll develop a repeatable system for growth.

The following steps walk you through how to understand your audience, study your niche, plan stronger content, and create a community of loyal viewers who want to keep watching what you make. Whether you're just starting out or looking to improve what you already have, following a structured process will give you a path to long-term success on YouTube.

1. Start by writing out the basic details of your ideal viewer, also known as your viewer persona. Include their age or generation, gender, income range, education level, location, and relationship status. If you already have videos on your channel, you can find much of this information in the analytics of your YouTube channel. If you're just starting and don't have data yet, create a projected viewer persona based on who you expect your audience to be. Make one version for a male viewer and another for a female viewer.
2. Write down your viewer persona's online behavior. This includes the types of media they consume, what they watch for personal interest versus pure entertainment, and the kinds of channels they subscribe to. Outline their offline behavior. Describe how they shop, the habits they have, the hobbies they enjoy, and where they spend their time when they're not online. Include details about what motivates them, the values they care about, their attitudes and lifestyle, the fears they have, and the goals they want to achieve. When you've done your research, you should have a clear idea of who your niche audience is. A niche is *who the channel is for, why they watch, and what problem or desire you serve.*
3. Research at least ten successful creators in your niche. Take note of the things they have in common, such as their style, video structure, or the way they engage with their audience. Watch their top-performing videos carefully and look for patterns in how they plan, create, and edit their content. Pay attention to elements like pacing, storytelling, visuals, thumbnails, titles, and calls to action. Understanding these patterns will give you valuable insights into what works in your niche and help you apply similar strategies to improve your own videos. Sort their videos by *Most Popular* and select six to ten of their highest-viewed videos.

Figure 13.1 – Sort YouTube videos by popularity

Take notes on each one, including the title, thumbnail style, number of views, number of likes, number of dislikes, and how long the video is.

4. Pay close attention to whether these creators use a story arc in their videos. Notice how they grab viewers' attention with a strong hook at the beginning and keep them engaged with moments that re-capture interest throughout. Look at how they set up the main content, build toward a climax, and deliver a satisfying conclusion. Also, pay attention to any extra value they provide at the end, such as tips, resources, or bonus content. Understanding these storytelling techniques can help you structure your own videos in a way that keeps viewers watching from start to finish.
5. Check your local area to see if there are other YouTube creators nearby. Look for meetups or creator groups you can join. If none exist, consider starting your own small group and meeting on a regular basis to share ideas and help each other grow.
6. Come up with ten potential title ideas for your next video. Then narrow them down to your best three. Make sure each title is memorable, easy to say, and simple for others to share. For each chosen title, brainstorm three to four thumbnail concepts. Use YouTube and Google Images for inspiration to make your ideas stronger. Choose the best thumbnail strategy and sketch a rough version of it.
7. YouTube provides analytics data on your video performance. Review the videos you've posted in the last 90 days. Write down your top performers and analyze each one using the *Four Ws* (*Who*, *What*, *Where*, and *Why*). Look for patterns that show what your audience responds to. Review your three videos with the highest *Average View Duration* and *Average View Percentage*. Look closely at where viewers stick around and where they drop off. Try to spot any patterns in those moments.
8. Go through your video library and group similar videos together by topic. Give each group a clear label, creating your own channel's content categories. Many channels use similar naming on their videos to quickly group together similar topics. Study the titles and thumbnails in each category, paying attention to patterns in the videos with the highest *Click-Through Rate* and longest *Average View Duration*, which you can see in your YouTube analytics. Finally, plan, create, and upload a new video that fits into one of these content categories.
9. Using your viewer persona (ideal viewer for your content), create a plan to build a community with your most loyal followers. Decide how you will engage with your audience each month and what actions you could propose to your followers to stay engaged.

10. Take a close look at your YouTube analytics to see what other videos your audience is watching. This can give you valuable insight into the types of content they enjoy and the creators they follow. Based on this research, make a list of five to ten creators you think would be a good fit for collaborations. Consider creators whose style, audience, or niche complements your own, and think about how working together could bring value to both channels. Collaborating with the right creators can help you reach new viewers, build relationships within your niche, and grow your community.
11. An important way to monetize your subscribers is to collect your fans' email addresses and phone numbers. Give links that direct your viewers to subscribe to your email list. This gives you direct access to your audience, so you're not dependent on platforms like YouTube or social media. When you own your list, you can launch products, sell music, or offer services on your own terms. Even a small, dedicated list can lead to big results.

Building a strong YouTube channel takes a lot of work, but it is potentially the biggest way to market yourself and build a fan base. We've learned how to get more results from YouTube; next, let's learn how to promote your band on TikTok.

TikTok for musicians

TikTok is a video platform for phone and the web. It's a useful tool for artists to promote their content and build their fan base.

How does TikTok work? When a video is uploaded to TikTok, the video is randomly shown to a group of users, slipping the video into the video feed between popular videos. If users engage with the video, such as watching, commenting, sharing, or downloading it, then the video is promoted to more viewers. Due to the way the algorithm promotes new content, videos on TikTok can potentially reach a high number of viewers even if you have no prior existing followers.

When a user first opens the app, they are shown the *For You* page, which is a feed of videos that TikTok recommends to them. The more you use the app, the more personalized the video recommendations become. The algorithm recommends videos to you based on your interaction with videos, accounts followed, comments you posted, and content you created. It also takes into consideration captions, sounds, hashtags, language settings, and country location.

Here are some general guidelines and suggestions for musicians creating video content for TikTok:

- Find a niche. TikTok algorithm identifies content that viewers have previously watched and shows them similar content.
- Identify trending content and create a related video to join in on the trends. Follow the #trendalert and `#TikTokchallenge` hashtags to figure out what the current trend is.
- Create music video teaser videos.
- Perform duets.
- Creating music out of household objects.
- Dancing to your own music.
- Demo versus the final version of your song so people can hear the before and after.
- The story behind your song.
- Consider replying to user comments in a video.
- Show behind-the-scenes footage of your show or music video.

You now know how to promote yourself through collaboration and social media. Next, let's learn how to create visuals.

Creating album artwork with AI

Whenever you release a song, you need artwork. Great artwork can be instrumental in promoting the song on social media. There are many traditional ways to create album artwork, but I want to direct your attention to a recent method using artificial intelligence. The current industry leader in AI art generation is a tool called **Adobe Firefly**.

Adobe Firefly is a tool to create AI-generated content. It can generate photos, videos, speech, sound effects, mood boards, and soundtracks, have AI avatars read out text, and translate audio and video. The tools it offers keep expanding, so by the time you read this, it may offer many more. It is a paid service; however, they provide you with free credits to try out the product and generate a limited number of images for free every month. Let's learn how to use Adobe Firefly to generate album art or other social media artwork.

1. Go to the website `https://www.adobe.com/ca/products/firefly.html`. On the site, you'll be prompted to create an account. Once you've signed in, you'll see a home page such as the following:

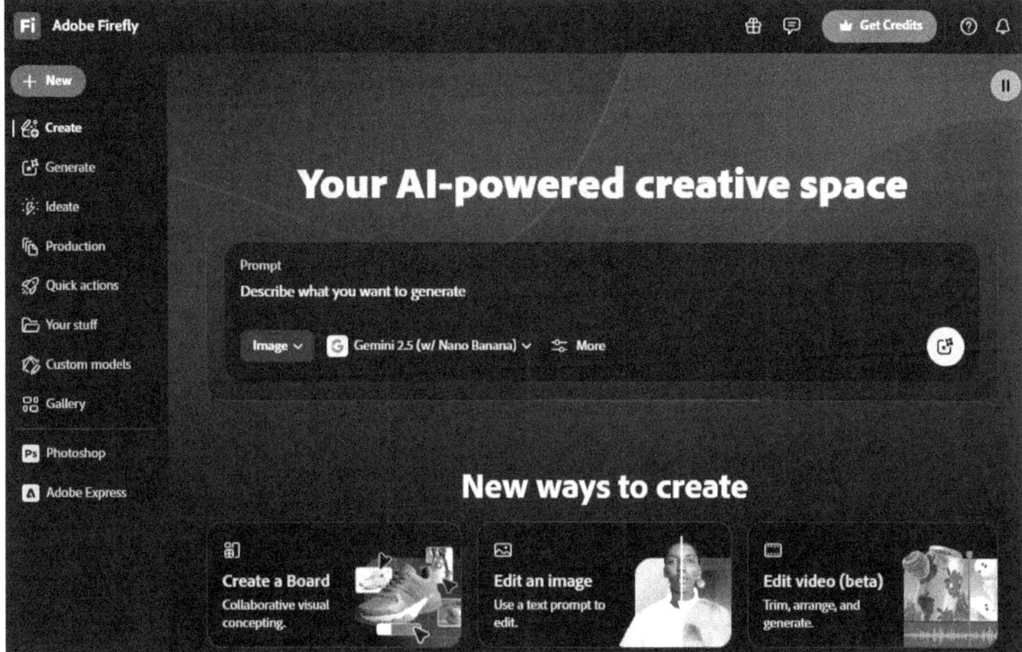

Figure 13.2 – Adobe Firefly dashboard

2. On the left side of the screen, you'll see a **Generate** tab. Click that, and you'll see options for generating images. Click the **Generate image** option.

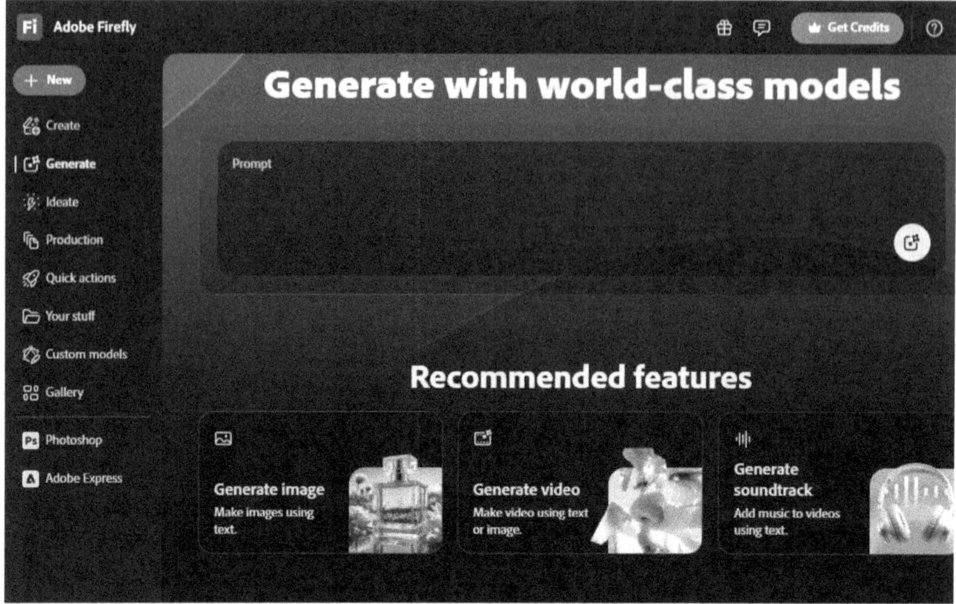

Figure 13.3 – Generate image option

3. You will be directed to a page with tools to generate your images. You'll find a text input prompt allowing you to enter the type of art you want to create. Type in the artwork you want to create and submit.

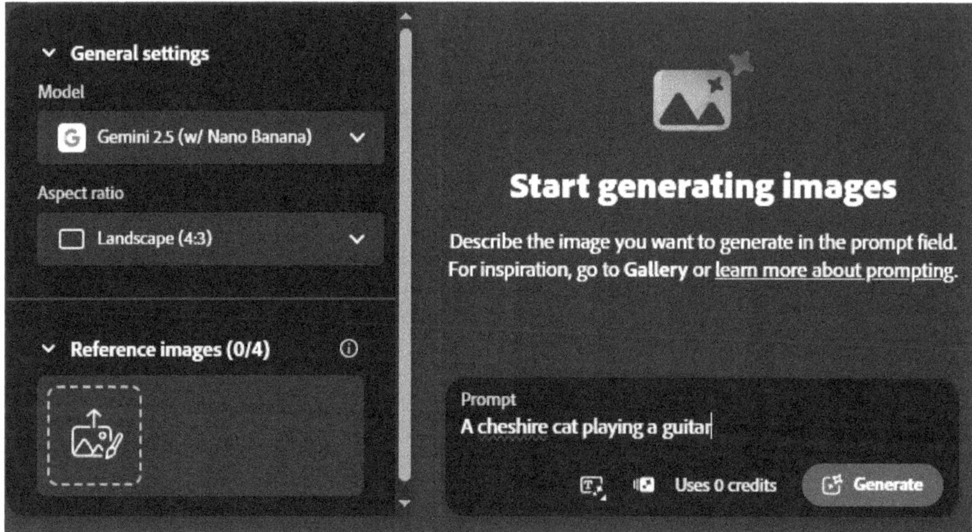

Figure 13.4 – Enter text prompt for image

4. Enter a text prompt for the art you want to create. Once you've finished typing your prompt, press the **Generate** button, and it will start creating your art. An example prompt could be "`A cheshire cat playing a guitar`," shown as follows:

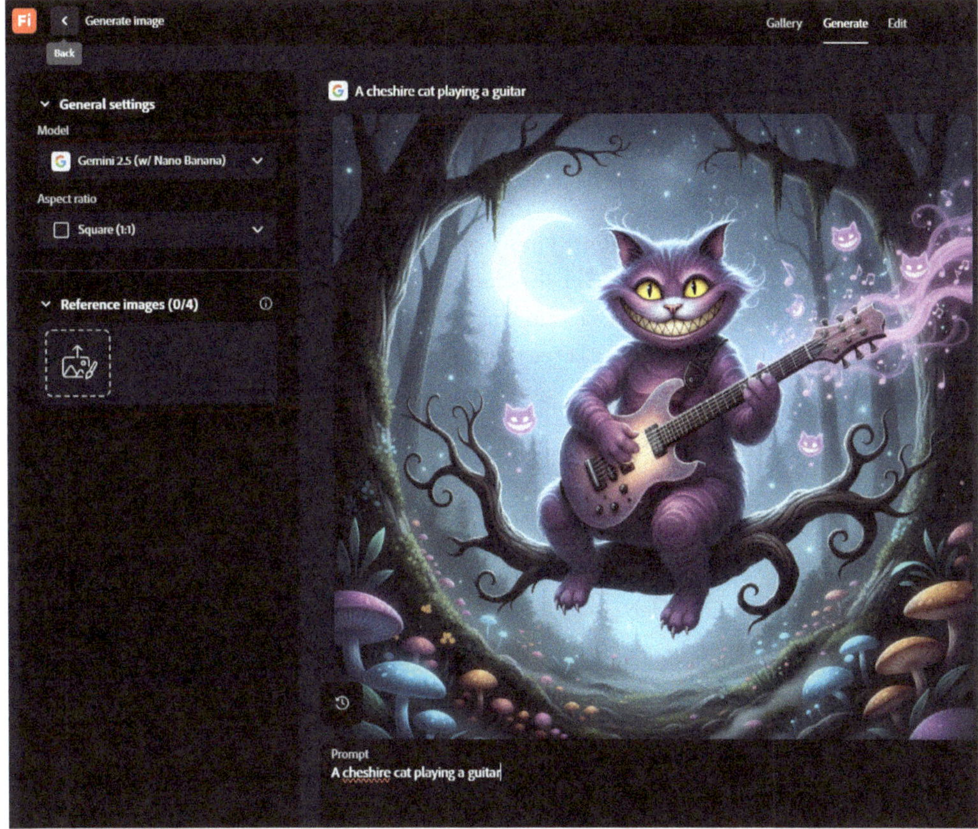

Figure 13.5 – Art generated using a prompt

Tada! Artwork has been generated.

The type and quality of the images depend on the word choice of the prompt you enter. There are lots of options for changing the image dimensions and AI model used. Different AI models will give different results with the same text prompt. Some models give you additional options for customizing the style of artwork created. In the preceding screenshot above, you can see an option to insert a reference image. If you use this tool, the image model will try to produce an image with similar traits to the reference image you upload.

If you want assistance inputting better prompts to get better art results, there are lots of examples of art that were generated by other people and the prompts they used. Examples can be found at `https://firefly.adobe.com/gallery`.

There are other options besides Adobe Firefly on the market. For example, there's **Midjourney**, which is also a paid service, and free open-source AI generator tools such as **Stable Diffusion**. If you're interested in learning more about Stable Diffusion, I teach a course on it available at `https://chestersky.com/stable-diffusion-masterclass`.

We've learned how to create static album art. Next, let's learn how to create music video visuals with **ZGameEditor Visualizer**.

Creating music visuals with ZGameEditor Visualizer

When you're playing a song, you always need a visual. In the long term, you'll need to invest time and effort in learning about video creation or collaborate with someone who does.

In the short term, when you're just getting started, there's a free tool in FL Studio that can easily generate decent animations called ZGameEditor Visualizer. It allows you to sync your music to video and text and add visual effects.

Let's learn how to create animations with ZGameEditor Visualizer:

1. Create a new project and import your finished song into the **Playlist**. You'll want a new FL Studio project, as ZGameEditor Visualizer can be quite CPU-intensive.
2. On the master bus **Mixer** channel, load up the ZGameEditor Visualizer effect plugin.

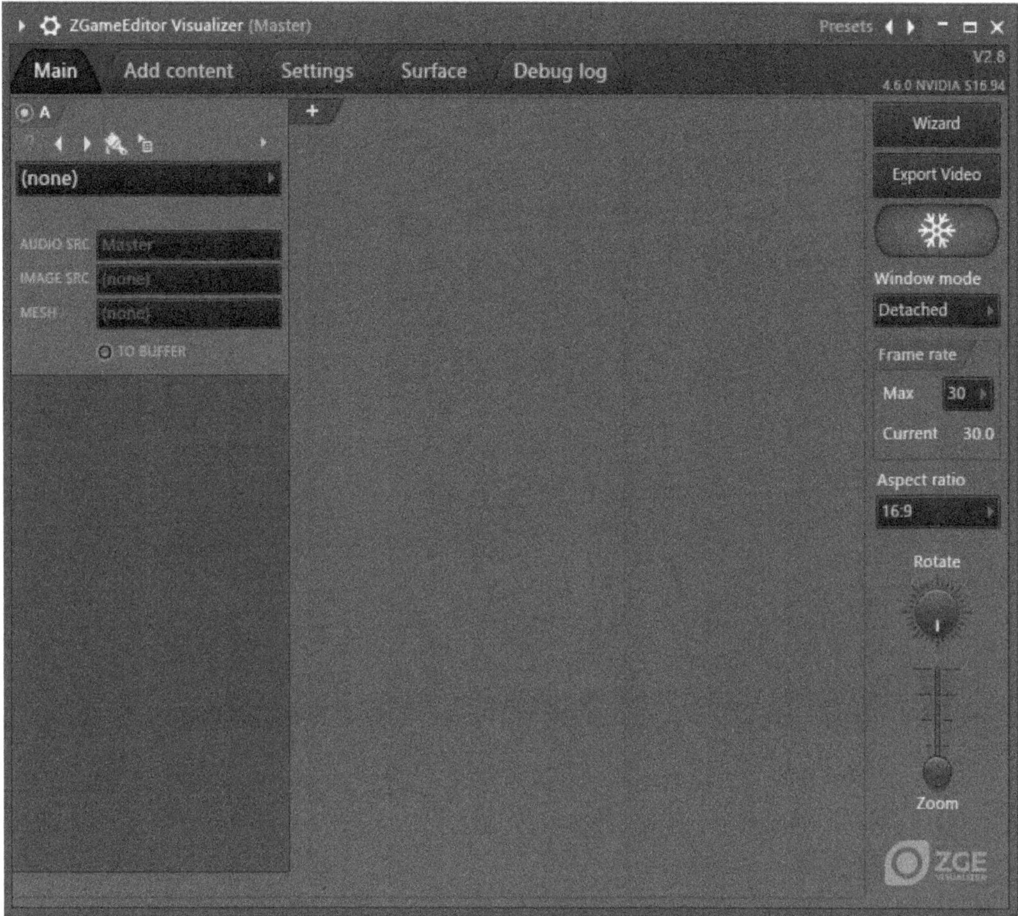

Figure 13.6 – ZGameEditor Visualizer

ZGameEditor Visualizer allows you to load videos, images, and effects in layers. Although you could create animations from scratch, there's an easy way to get up and running quickly using the wizard.

3. Click on the **Wizard** button in the top-right corner. You'll see a window pop up similar to the following screenshot:

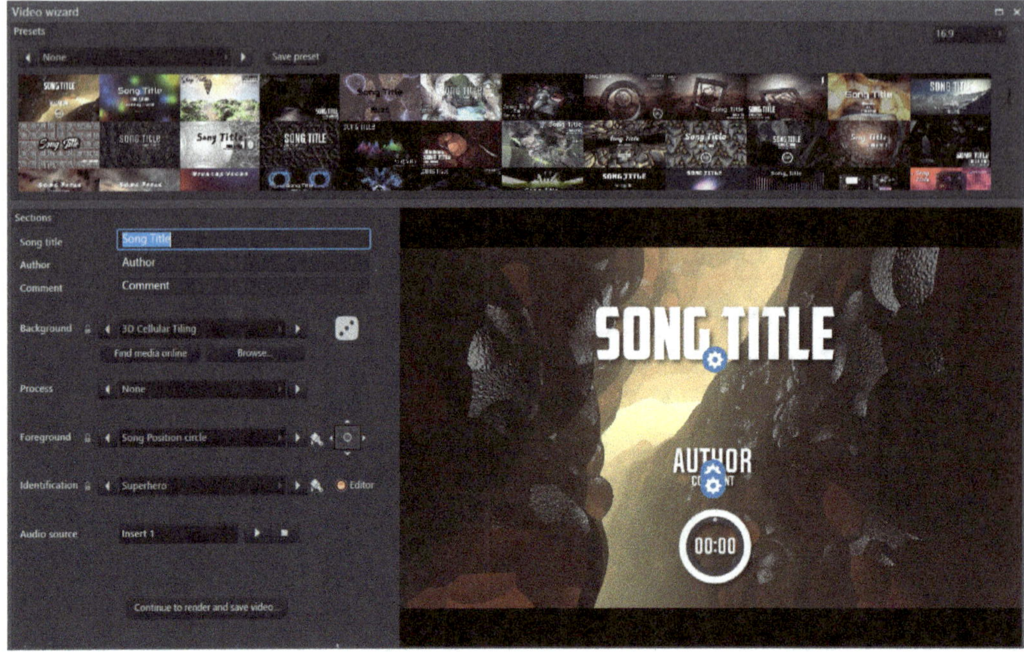

Figure 13.7 – Video wizard

The **Video wizard** allows you to easily add a video or image background and overlay it with a foreground animation and text.

4. At the top, you can see a list of presets that you can scroll through. Under the **Sections** header, you can add your **Song title**, **Author**, and **Comment** settings. **Background** lets you choose between using a picture or video on your computer or selecting media online. If you choose **Find media online**, you'll see a window with free photo and video media that you can use in your visuals, as shown in the following screenshot:

Figure 13.8 – Search media online

When you've chosen your image, you'll see a pane of controls.

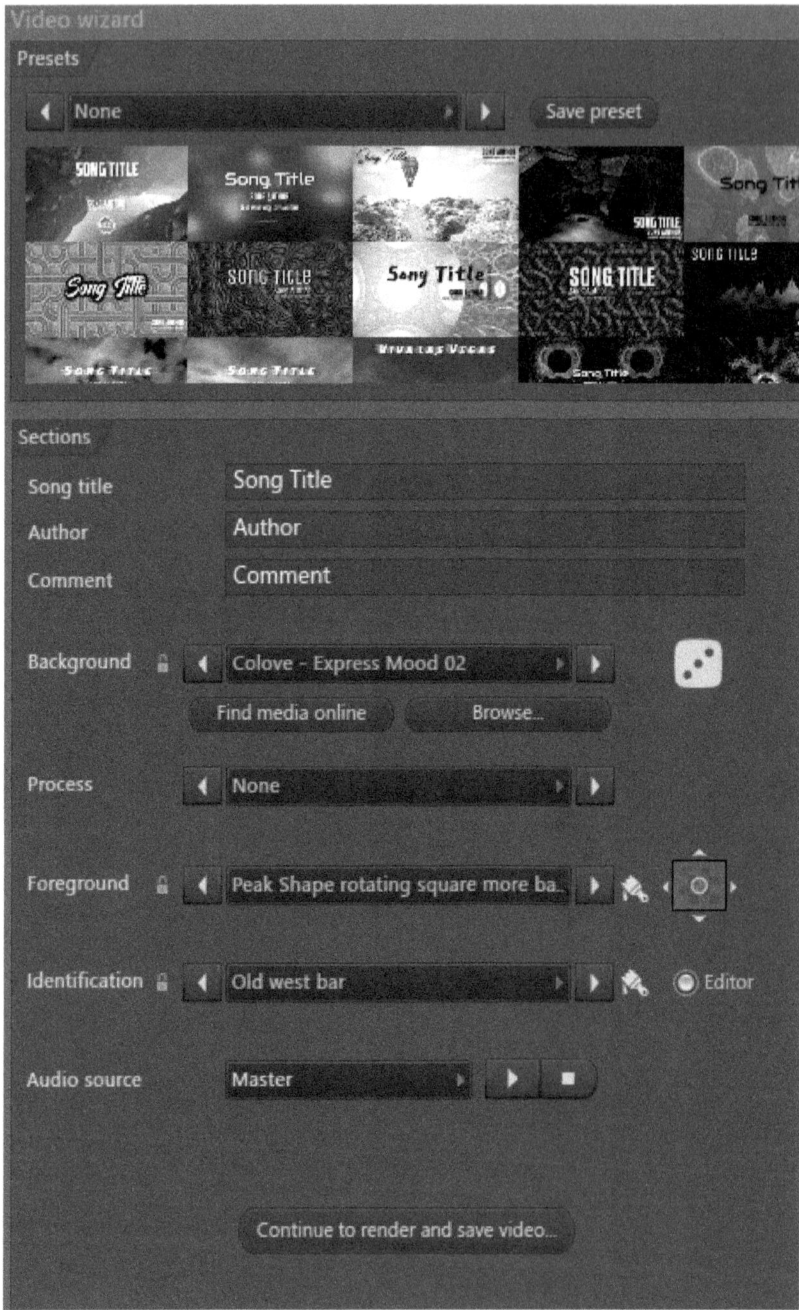

Figure 13.9 – Video wizard controls

Process throws an effect onto your visual. **Foreground** lets you choose an audio-reacting animation visual. To the right of the **Foreground** presets, you can see a **select color** paintbrush icon to let you choose your color and an **X/Y Position** control to let you choose where to position the animation on the screen.

Identification lets you choose the type of font you want for your text. To the right of the font presets, you can use the **select color** paintbrush icon to choose a color for your font. **Audio source** lets you choose which audio source you want to use.

Your visual doesn't have to be perfect yet; you can customize everything in a minute. Just find something that you like; that's good enough for now.

5. When you're finished, select the **Continue to render and save video...** option at the bottom of the panel. The following window will pop up, allowing you to choose your export video format:

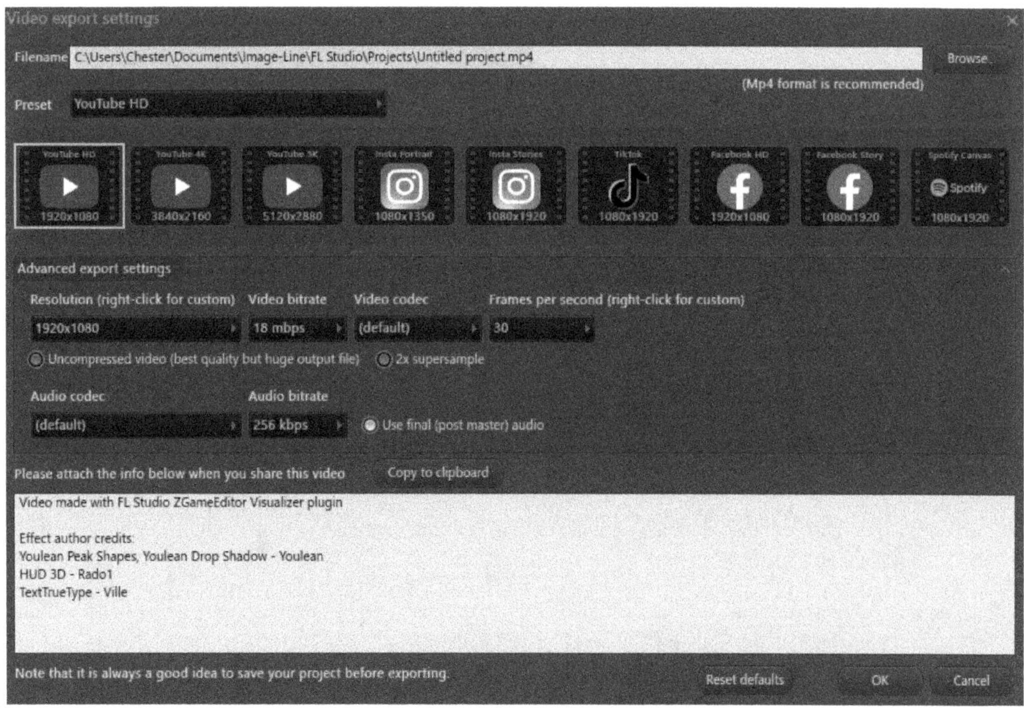

Figure 13.10 – Video export settings

6. Choose the **Filename** location. Under **Advanced export settings**, there are additional controls:
    - Higher **Resolution** and **Video bitrate** values will result in better video quality but larger video files.
    - **Video codec** allows you to choose between `H.264` and `MPEG-4` files. `H.264` files result in higher video quality.
    - The **Uncompressed video** button results in no video compression and huge file sizes. Don't select this.
    - **2x supersample** results in better video quality but takes longer to render.
    - **Audio codec** uses `MP3` by default, but can use `FLAC` for lossless audio if you plan to use it in another video editor.
    - Higher **Audio bitrate** results in higher audio quality but a larger file size.
7. If you're happy with the video footage, you can choose your desired export format and select **OK**, and your video will begin exporting. If you want to customize your visual more, select **Cancel**. You'll return to the **Main** tab.
8. You'll notice that the **Main** tab of **ZGameEditor Visualizer** has become filled with effects. These effects were added based on what you chose in the **Video wizard**.

Figure 13.11 – Main tab with effects loaded

You can customize any of these effects. The effect layers apply from left to right, with the rightmost layer affecting the layers to the left of it.

9. At the top of each effect, you can see the effect selector, as shown in the preceding figure. Here, you choose the effect to apply.
   AUDIO SRC sets the audio to use in the effect.

   IMAGE SRC sets the media to use in your effect. Here you can view images or videos that have already been imported into **ZGameEditor Visualizer**. If you want to use new media, you'll need to navigate to the **Add content** tab and import your media there.

   MESH applies 3D meshes that you may have imported. Underneath **MESH**, you'll see the list of effect controls. You can adjust the controls to customize your visual. For any control, you can right-click on it and automate it in the Playlist to turn a control up or down throughout your song.

10. In the **Add content** panel, you'll see a list of options, as in the following screenshot:

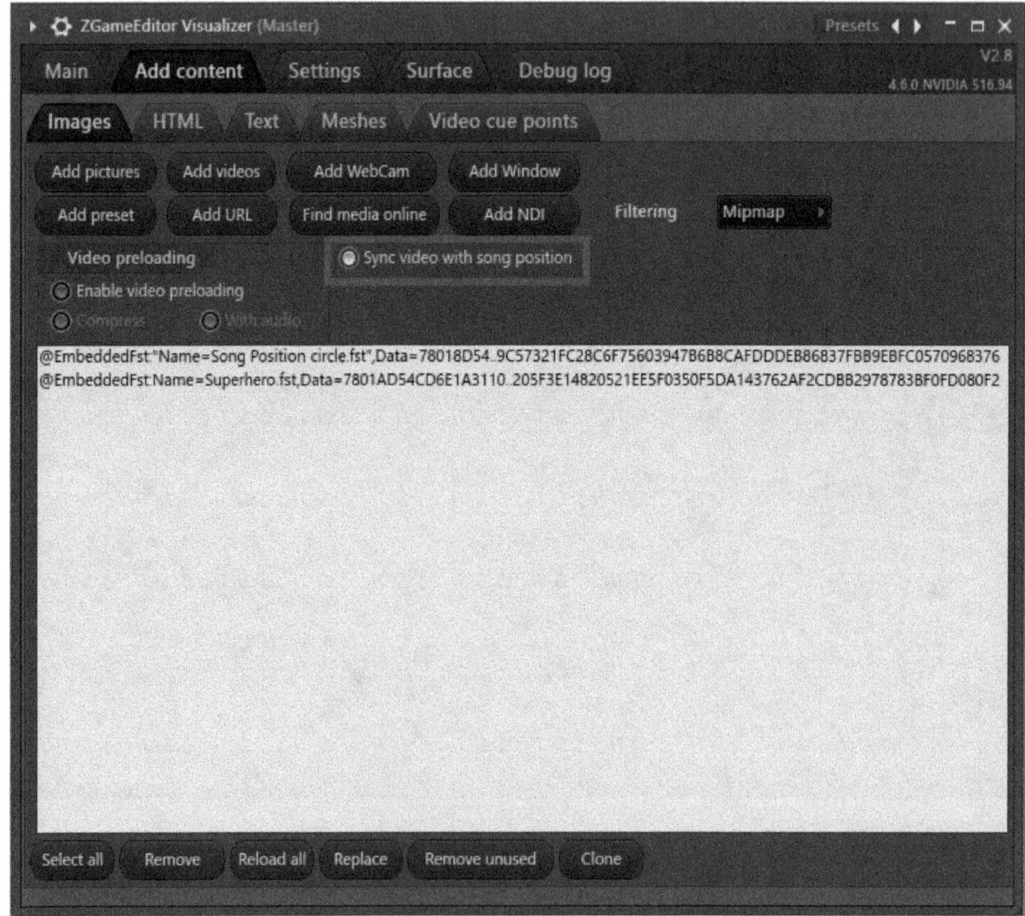

Figure 13.12 – The Add content panel

Here, you can import images, videos, or even record your webcam for media to be used in your effects on the **Main** tab. If you choose the **Add URL** option, you can grab an image online. There's also an option called **Add Window**, which lets you grab a video playthrough of your Mixer, Playlist, Piano roll, or Channel rack while the song is playing.

Note that you'll want to make sure that the **Sync video with song position** setting is selected so that your video always plays in time with your music.

11. When you're finished, go back to the **Main** tab and choose the **Export Video** button on the far right to export.

Congratulations, you now have visuals for your songs. Next, let's learn how to utilize cutting-edge artificial intelligence tools to assist your music production.

AI tools for music production

Artificial intelligence tools are everywhere, and music production is no exception. There are many AI tools to speed up your music production workflow, generate sounds and melodies, or even create entire songs from scratch. In this book so far, we've already discussed many AI tools in FL Studio, such as the *Piano roll chord progression* tool in *Chapter 3*, *extracting audio stems from a sample* in *Chapter 5*, *denoising and deverbing audio* in *Chapter 8*, and *using FL Cloud's AI to master music* in *Chapter 12*. In this section, we will cover a few third-party plugins. We'll start with tools used to assist your production and then move on to tools that can generate entire songs from scratch. Let's talk about music production assistance tools.

First up is the iZotope company. iZotope offers a full suite of mixing and mastering tools. They are industry heavyweights.

iZotope offers several AI-enabled music production tools. They use intelligent audio analysis and machine-learning-assisted workflows. **Ozone** is iZotope's flagship mastering suite. Ozone includes an **AI-powered Master Assistant** that listens to your track and suggests a custom mastering chain. It then applies **EQ**, dynamics, and stereo settings tailored to your music so you have a polished starting point you can refine yourself. This smart Assistant analyzes frequency balance, dynamics, and loudness targets to guide your mastering decisions.

Neoverb is iZotope's intelligent reverb plugin that uses an **AI-assisted Reverb Assistant** to help you quickly dial in the right ambience for vocals and instruments. The Assistant listens to incoming audio and proposes reverb settings in real time. You can blend multiple reverb types visually, while the plugin's smart pre- and post-EQ sections help the effect sit well in a mix.

Nectar focuses on vocal production and uses machine-learning tools to streamline tasks like leveling and layering voices. It includes modules like **Auto-Level** to keep vocal volume consistent, **Voices** for harmony and doubling, and a **Vocal Assistant** that analyzes your vocal track and suggests processing chains (EQ, **compression**, **de-essing**, **pitch correction**, etc.) optimized for clarity and presence within the mix.

RX is iZotope's audio repair and restoration suite. It leverages advanced machine learning throughout its modules. Tools include **Repair Assistant**, **Dialogue Isolate**, **Music Rebalance**, and other spectral tools to detect and reduce noise, clicks, hum, and other imperfections in recordings. The intelligent Assistants automate many cleanup tasks that used to require detailed manual editing, making RX very useful for preparing tracks before mixing and mastering.

You can learn more about iZotope's individual products at `https://www.iZotope.com/`.

The iZotope company merged with the company Native Instruments. So, if you purchase Native Instruments bundles, you'll get iZotope products included, which is much cheaper.

You can learn more about Native Instruments at `https://www.native-instruments.com/en/`.

We've learned about music production tools; now let's learn about tools that can create entire songs from scratch.

Creating entire songs with Suno AI

AI music generators have become extremely good in the last 2 years. There are multiple competitors popping up, and the capabilities of AI get better every day, so there may be better alternatives by the time you read this book. Some of the big names at the moment are:

- **Suno**, available at `https://suno.com/`.
- **Udio**, available at `https://www.udio.com/`.

Suno and Udio faced lawsuits for training their AI on music without permission from the artists. However, Warner Music Group bought out Suno, resolving lawsuits with Suno for the moment.

Registration of AI-generated music with performing rights organizations is a grey area that is still in the process of being sorted out. At the time of writing, you can register songs created with AI assistance, but not songs that are entirely created with AI tools. For more information, check out the following news press release from ASCAP: `https://www.ascap.com/press/2025/10/10-28-ai-registration-policies`.

Let's learn how to make music using Suno (`https://suno.com/`). The same approach can be used with other AI music generation tools.

1. Once you've created an account and logged into Suno, you'll see a website similar to the following:

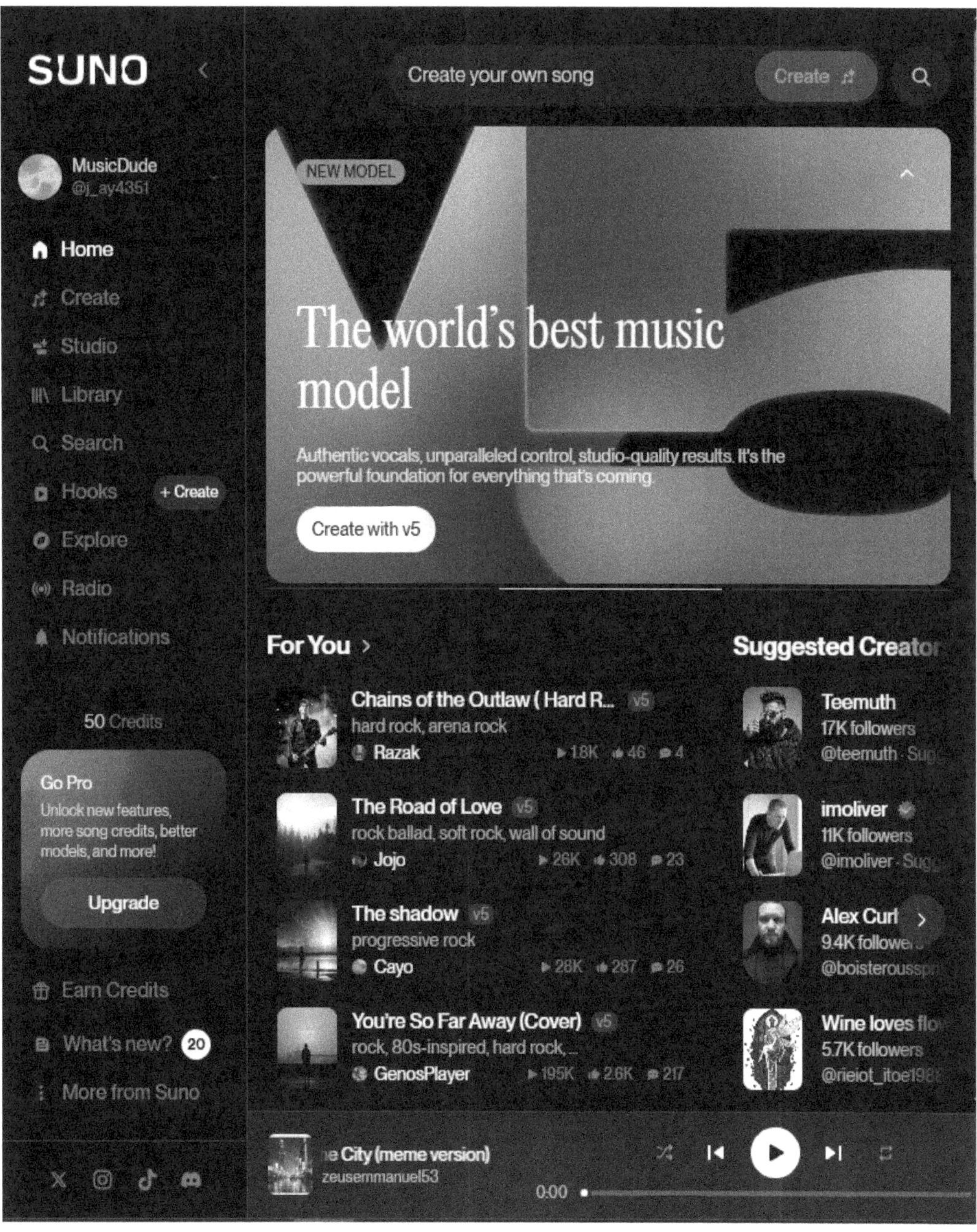

Figure 13.13 – Suno homepage

Here you'll see songs generated by other users. You can click on the songs to see music other users have created.

2. On the left-hand side, you'll see several tabs, including the **Create** tab. Click the **Create** tab, and you'll see a text prompt appear. It is set to **Simple** by default.

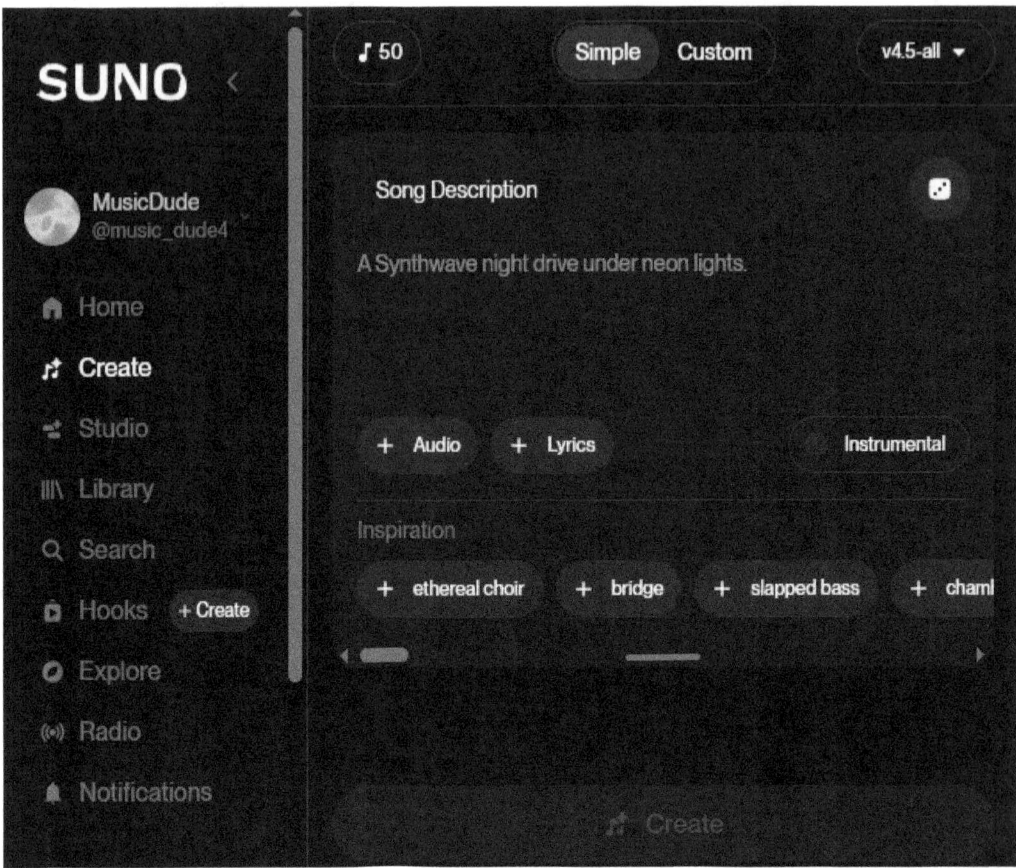

Figure 13.14 – Suno Simple create

3. At the top, you'll see a toggle option to change from **Simple** to **Custom**. Toggle this, and you'll see additional options to customize your song.

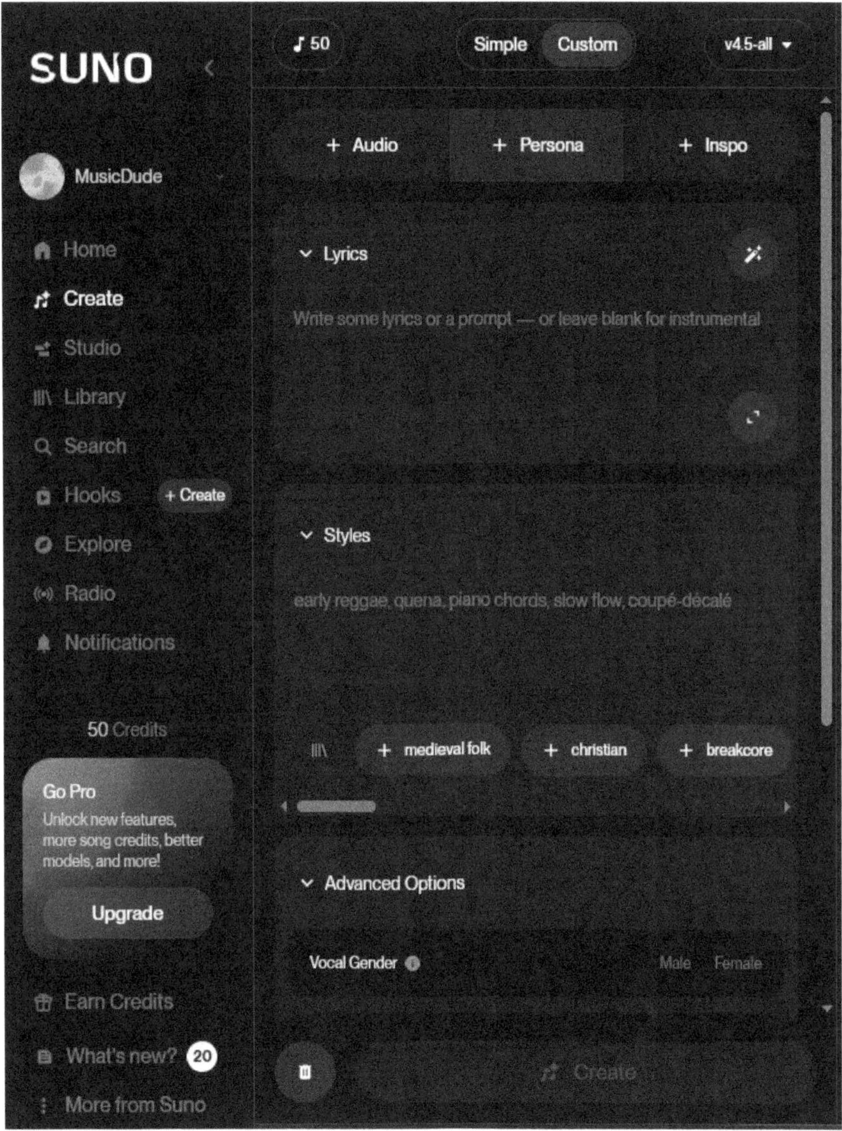

Figure 13.15 – Suno Custom create

4. At the top, you'll see options for **+Audio**, **+Persona**, and **+Inspo**. These are ways to give inputs to the song generation process, telling Suno to use an existing audio file as a reference. This way, the song you generate will be similar to the audio you upload to Suno.

You can input song lyrics for the AI to sing or ask for the song to be instrumental without lyrics. You can choose the genre of the song that you want to create. You can give the song instructions on what style to play.

5. When you're ready, type in the prompt text for the song description in either the **Simple** or **Custom** tab and click the **Create** button.

   After your songs are generated, you'll see your generated songs appear. Here you can download the generated songs.

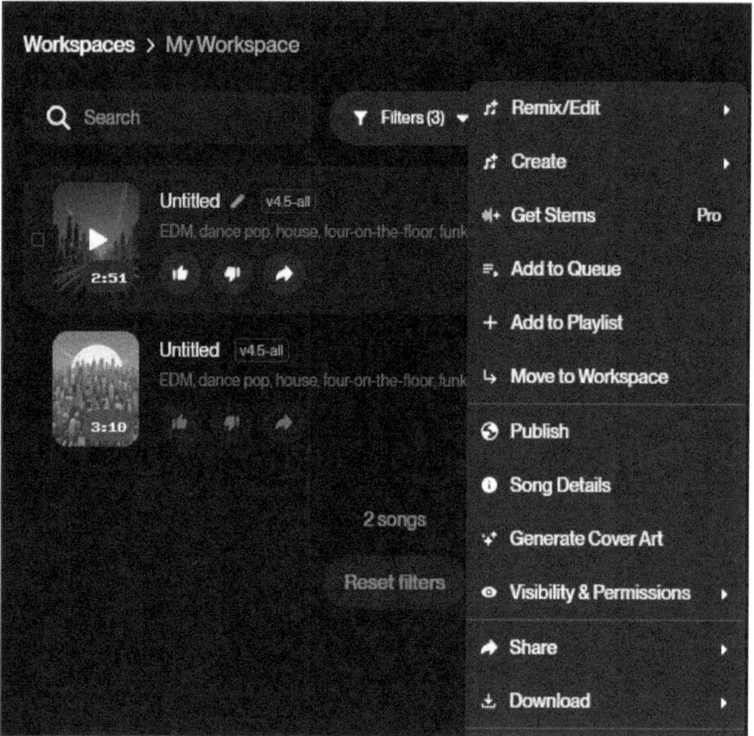

Figure 13.16 – Suno download song

In the preceding screenshot, you'll see a **Download** option that lets you download your song as an audio file.

You can see an option for **Remix/Edit**. This gives you the ability to regenerate the song with edits such as making the song longer, adjusting the lyrics or styles used, replacing sections of the song, or changing the speed of the song.

You'll also see an option for **Stems**. This feature lets you download the song in pieces rather than just as a single file.

6. When you download the stems, you'll get the vocals, drums, bass, and instruments as separate audio files. You can then import those into FL Studio and manipulate the tracks individually.

You now know how to generate music using AI tools. But before you go all in on creating AI-generated music, you should take a step back and consider whether doing so will help you in your music career or actually hinder you. Let's discuss this.

Have AI tools replaced musicians?

AI music generator tools are incredibly good at creating music, perhaps a little too good. With just a text prompt suggestion, you can generate an entire song from scratch. You can tell the song what lyrics to use, and an AI will sing the lyrics. AI voices and instrumentation are so realistic that you can't tell whether they were sung by a real person or not. This brings up the question: why bother to put all the work into learning music production skills if an AI can just create the music in a few seconds? I've wrestled with this problem a lot, but I still believe that music production skills are just as relevant and necessary as before. However, effort spent producing music needs to be directed differently now that AI can generate music in an instant.

If all you need is generic background music sound with minimal to no customization, AI is more than capable. There are things that AI can do better than you, and in those areas, it doesn't make sense to compete. AI can produce generic music in seconds for the cost of next to nothing.

Should you just abandon music production and publish AI-generated music? Will that make you rich and famous beyond your wildest dreams? I highly doubt it. Why? Because everyone can create AI-generated music. People with zero music and performance skills can create an AI song in seconds, just like you. So there's nothing that would distinguish your music creation with AI from any other musician using AI tools. Using AI tools on their own means that you aren't adding any value to the music creation process. And if that's true, why should anyone listen to your music over anyone else's? Streaming platforms are being bombarded by a staggeringly high number of AI-generated songs every day. But what do people predominantly listen to on streaming platforms? Their favorite artists.

The reason that people should listen to your music is that you are connecting with your audience. You need to craft a signature sound that resonates with you and encompasses the style of artist you want to be recognized for. If all you're making is the same sounds that AI can produce, then there's no value being added by you.

Music is only a small part of why people listen to you. Your brand adds value to your music. Your audience could be predisposed to liking or disliking your music before they ever hear it due to your brand. Your distinctive voice and instrument preference in your songs, the story behind why you made the music, the visuals of your artwork for albums and social media, the visuals you choose for your music videos, how you dress and act publicly, how you conduct your live performances, and how you interact with your fans in building a community – these characteristics are what set you apart from AI. AI has made even more apparent the importance of carefully curating a brand for yourself. Your brand is your competitive advantage over other artists and AI-generated music.

If I haven't convinced you to focus on brand yet, perhaps this will: do it because that's where the money is. The biggest reason to put the focus on your brand is that it's the financially smart thing to do. The really big money in the music industry doesn't come from people listening to your music. The money that comes from streaming platforms to artists is tiny. The real big money comes from doing live shows, selling products, and project collaborations. Those benefits only come from building a dedicated fan base of people who want to see you and are willing to pay.

Summary

In this chapter, we learned about branding and promotion. The more effective you are at these, the more publicity and interest you will generate for your music and your business.

We discussed choosing an artist identity and choosing an artist name. We discussed preparation for live show performances and booking gigs. We looked at tips for creating content on social media platforms such as YouTube. We looked at creating album artwork and music video visuals using FL Studio's ZGameEditor Visualizer. Finally, we discussed using AI tools for music production.

In the next chapter, we'll look at monetizing, selling, and registering your music.

Get this book's PDF version and more

Scan the QR code (or go to `packtpub.com/unlock`). Search for this book by name, confirm the edition, and then follow the steps on the page.

UNLOCK NOW

Note: Keep your invoice handy. Purchases made directly from Packt don't require an invoice.

14

Publishing and Selling Music Online

It's never been easier to sell music and collect royalties. **Performance Rights Organizations** (**PROs**) help you collect royalties from music performances. Digital distribution companies help you sell and stream your music online. In a few minutes, you can release your music online to the world and collect royalty revenues. In the upcoming pages, you'll learn how.

This chapter guides you through the essential steps of getting your music officially published and monetized online. You'll learn how to register your music properly to protect your rights and how to tag your tracks accurately to ensure they're easily discoverable on digital platforms. You'll explore the best practices for selling your music on online stores and streaming services and discover how to claim revenue from your songs on YouTube using **AdRev**, helping you generate income from your creative work.

In this chapter, we'll discuss the following topics:

- Registering your music
- Tagging your music in preparation for distribution
- Selling music on online stores and streaming services
- Selling music as an independent artist
- Claiming revenue from songs on YouTube using AdRev

Registering your music

Before uploading your songs and selling them online, you should first register your music with a collection society. From a legal standpoint, it proves that you are the creator of the song and settles any disputes that could potentially arise if someone uses your song without your permission. More importantly, registering your music is how you get paid royalties.

There are different types of royalties that you can collect. How these royalties get retrieved by PROs can be very complex and goes beyond the scope of this book. However, it's straightforward to collect royalties. To ensure you're fully covered for global royalty collection, you should register your music on four platforms that we will introduce you to in this chapter. If you register with all four of these, you should be able to fully collect royalties:

- Register your music as a songwriter with a collection society/**Performance Rights Organization** (**PRO**). Whenever your music is played in a television show, commercial, movie, video game, or live venue, royalties are paid. PROs collect these royalties. Using the information that you input on the PRO website, PROs trace the music back to you, and then the PRO distributes the royalty payments to you.
  PROs are how you collect royalties from live performance usage. However, this isn't how you collect most of the royalties from online sales or streaming. We'll come to that later in this chapter.

  On a PRO website, you will be asked to create an account and list information about your songs. For example, they'll ask you for the song name, when it was created, and who was involved in the creation of the song.

  The PRO you register with will depend on the country you are located in. For example, in the United States, you would register as both a publisher and a writer with one of the following organizations:

  - **The American Society of Composers, Authors and Publishers** (**ASCAP**): `https://www.ascap.com/`.
  - **Broadcast Music, Inc.** (**BMI**): `https://www.bmi.com/`.
  - **Global Music Rights** (**GMR**): `https://globalmusicrights.com/`.

You only need to pick (BMI):reference link">idx_d3df959f one of these organizations to register your music. Which one should you pick? They offer different features and cater to different clients. Here's a blog comparing them: `www.infamousmusician.com/ascap-vs-bmi-vs-sesac-vs-gmr`.

In Canada, you register with the **Society of Composers, Authors and Music Publishers of Canada** (**SOCAN**) (`http://www.socan.com/`). This still registers you with either BMI or ASCAP at the end of the day, but you need to go through SOCAN if you are Canadian.

If you are in another country, you need to look up the relevant PRO for your geographic region.

- Register your music on **SoundExchange** to collect digital royalties such as those on **Pandora**, **SiriusXM**, and webcasters. Depending on your geographic region, SoundExchange collects digital performance royalties generated by master recordings on behalf of master owners and performers. When digital content is played online, such as on Pandora, SiriusXM, and webcasters, digital royalty fees are allocated to the rights holders and featured artists. SoundExchange collects these royalties for you.
- Register your music with a publishing administrator to collect from global performance and mechanical societies such as **SongTrust** or, alternatively, get signed with a record label that will manage your publishing royalties.
  SongTrust registers songs on behalf of songwriters/publishers with PROs, mechanical collection societies, and digital services worldwide to collect publishing royalties for you.
- Register with a digital distributor (for example, **DistroKid** and **CD Baby**) to release your song on streaming platforms and online stores.

Note

SongTrust is available at `https://www.songtrust.com/`.

SoundExchange is available at `https://www.soundexchange.com/`.

An article discussing whether SongTrust is a good investment for you can be found at `https://passivepromotion.com/what-artists-should-know-about-songtrust`.

We've discussed how to register your music. Now, let's discuss how to prepare your music before submission.

Tagging your music in preparation for distribution

Before uploading your music online, you should correctly **tag** it. What's a tag? If you navigate to a song on your computer or phone, you'll see a list of information about the song, such as the name, track number, album, artist, and so on. That information is imprinted upon the file. These are tags, also known as metadata. In the following screenshot, you can see tag information on songs:

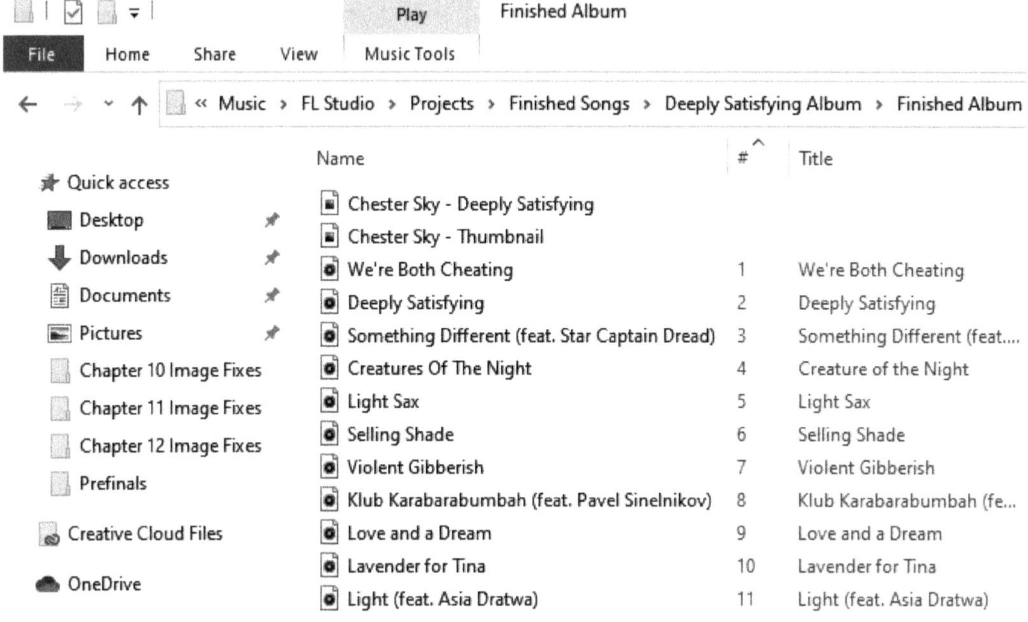

Figure 14.1 – Song tags

You can add custom tags for your songs. The easiest way to do so is with tagging software. I recommend the free tag editor **MP3Tag** for your songs, which is available at `www.mp3tag.de/en`.

When you open up MP3Tag, you'll see a screen like the following:

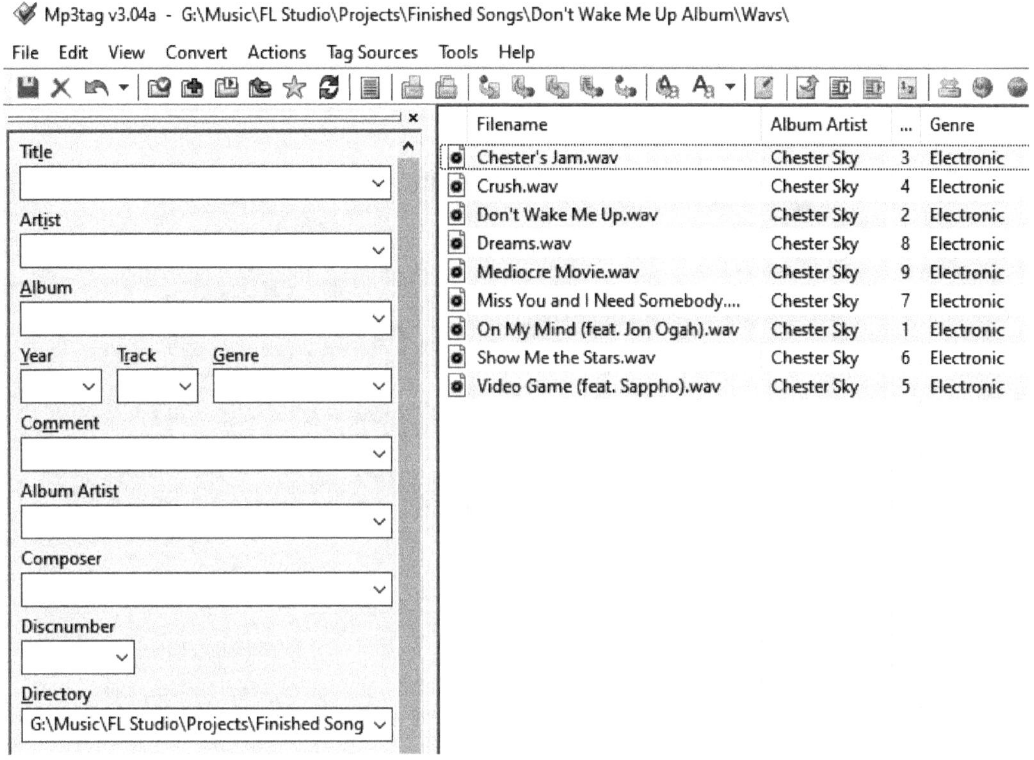

Figure 14.2 – MP3Tag

MP3Tag allows you to add tags for your songs, such as the **Title**, **Artist**, **Album**, and cover image. The cover image should be square. The image you use for the cover image should have a small file size. The size of the image is added to the size of the song. Every time you try to send the song, the image is sent along with it, so for speed and convenience's sake, keep your cover image file size small.

You've registered your songs with a PRO and tagged them. Now you're ready to upload your songs for online distribution.

Selling music on online stores and streaming services

Let's talk about selling your music. To sell your music, you have two main options: get signed by a major label/publisher or use a digital distribution company. Labels and publishers each have their own unique way of operating, so I can't speak for them. Let's discuss getting signed by a label first.

Get signed to labels using LabelRadar

If you're interested in getting your songs signed by a label, one way to get the attention of labels is to use the song submission service **LabelRadar**. Here is the LabelRadar website (`https://www.labelradar.com/`).

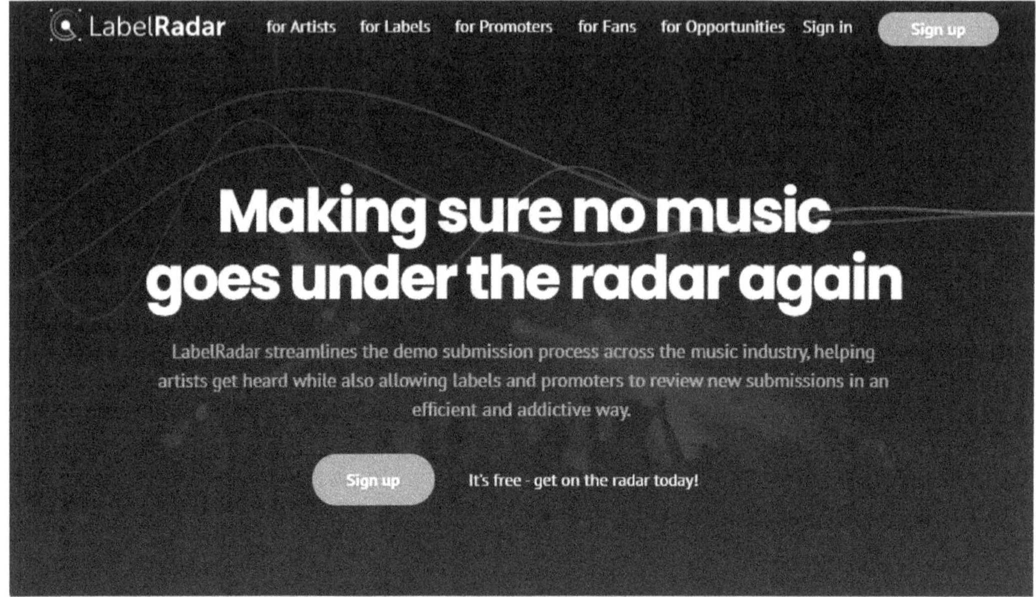

Figure 14.3 – Homepage of www.labelradar.com

LabelRadar is an online service that allows you to upload and submit your songs. Once you've created an account, you can upload a song and submit it to labels or music promoters. The site gives you credits every month, allowing you to submit songs to labels and promoters. If you need more credits than what are provided free, you can pay to get more credits.

If you don't want to pay to submit a song, there is another option. If you're interested in a specific label, the site gives you links to label websites so that you can do more research and reach out to them individually.

Some big-name labels listen for music submissions on the platform, including **Monstercat**, **Armada Music**, **Ninety9Lives**, **CloudKid**, **Blanco y Negro Music**, **Soave Records**, and **Anjunabeats/Anjunadeep**. If you're a label or a music promoter, you can use LabelRadar to receive new song submissions.

Here's a list of music labels that you can submit songs to using LabelRadar: `https://www.labelradar.com/our-labels`.

Alternatively, if you don't want to submit a song to a label but just want some music promotion, LabelRadar offers a list of music promoters to whom you can submit your music. Here's a list of music promoters using LabelRadar: `https://www.labelradar.com/our-promoters`.

You can create or apply to music contests, such as song remix contests. Contest rewards are usually monetary prizes, music gear, song and artist promotion, and getting your name out to labels.

You can increase your chances of being considered by labels by building up a strong artist portfolio and web presence ahead of time. Labels are more likely to want you if you have some fan base and following, and this will put you in a better negotiating position when they reach out to you. If you want long-term success, you should focus on building your brand as discussed in *Chapter 13*. LabelRadar is a tool that can help, but it's just one of many tools you should use. Don't rely on it exclusively and expect miracles.

We've discussed finding record labels to sell your music. Next, let's discuss how to sell your music without a record label.

Selling music as an independent artist

What if you don't want to submit your songs to record labels and want to try self-releasing your music as an independent artist?

In the past, when you wanted to get your music into an online store, you had to upload your songs manually one store at a time. Those days are gone. These days, you upload your songs to a digital distribution company. The digital distribution company publishes your music to lots of online stores and streaming services at once, collects the revenue, and pays it out to you. There are lots of online services that can do this for you. Here are some examples of them:

- **DistroKid** (`https://distrokid.com/`)
- **LANDR** (`https://www.landr.com/`)
- **CD Baby** (`https://cdbaby.com/`)
- **TuneCore** (`https://www.tunecore.com/`)
- **Ditto Music** (`https://www.dittomusic.com/`)
- **Loudr** (`https://www.crunchbase.com/organization/loudr`)
- **Record Union** (`https://www.recordunion.com/`)
- **Reverbnation** (`https://www.reverbnation.com/`)
- **Symphonic** (`https://symphonicdistribution.com/`)
- **iMusician** (`https://imusician.pro/en/`)

- **The Orchard** (they work with labels only) (`https://www.theorchard.com/`)
- **AWAL** (selected applications only) (`https://www.awal.com/`)

All of these services essentially do the same thing, and you only need one of them. They allow you to upload your music, distribute the songs to online stores and streaming platforms, and collect the revenue for you. I recommend comparing the features they offer before enrolling, as each has its own niche.

At the time of writing, I use the digital distribution company DistroKid. It seems to be one of the cheapest options for me personally. It lets you upload an unlimited number of songs for a fixed annual fee and lets you keep 100% of the royalties that DistroKid receives. The store selling the music takes a cut of the royalties, but that's before it gets to DistroKid. If you want, DistroKid allows you to split up the royalties it receives by percentage and send them to collaborators you worked with on your songs.

If you choose to use DistroKid, the following link provides you with a discount on your first year: `https://distrokid.com/vip/seven/701180`.

DistroKid walkthrough

Let's take a tour of a digital distribution company service so you know what you're getting yourself into. In this demo, we'll use DistroKid. If you pick a different service from DistroKid, your layout will look different, but the same overall features will be present.

DistroKid allows you to upload your songs and release them on online stores and streaming services. You can upload your music, album art, song details, and song lyrics. It allows you to track earnings from each service and distribute earnings to song collaborators.

So, let's take a look:

1. When you sign in to DistroKid, you'll see a list of all the albums and songs you've released.

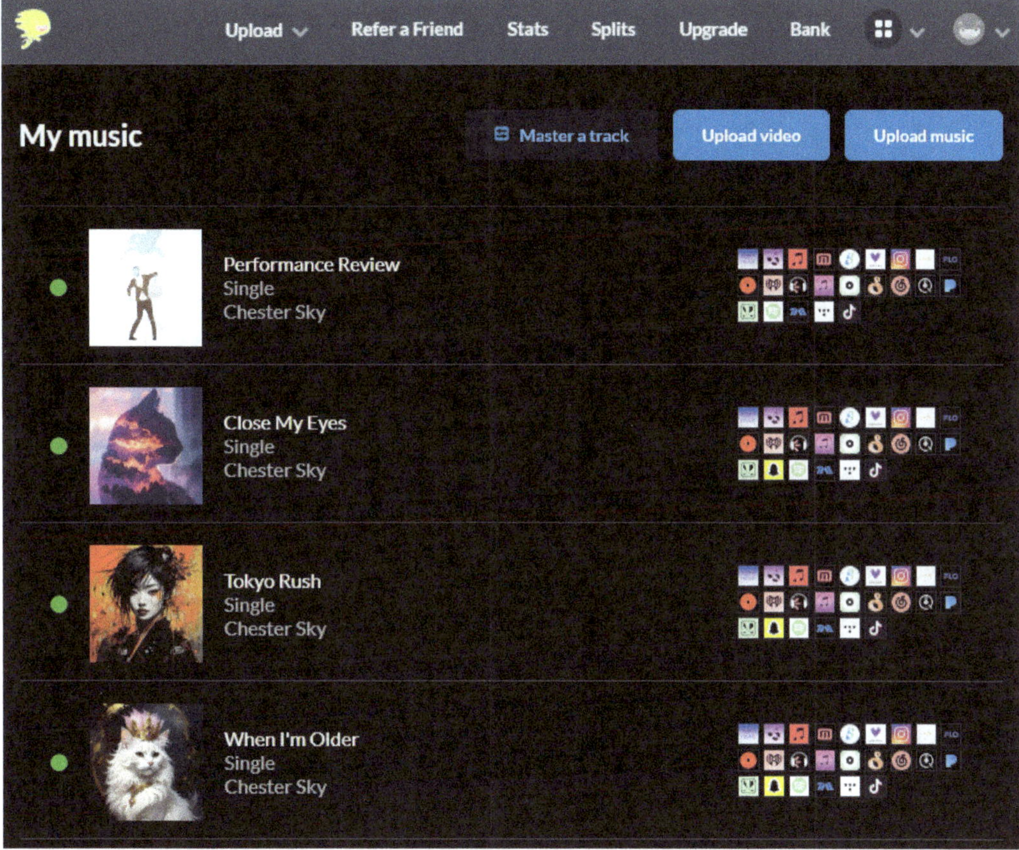

Figure 14.4 – DistroKid dashboard

2. If you go to the **Upload** tab, you'll see a page allowing you to upload songs to online stores and streaming platforms.

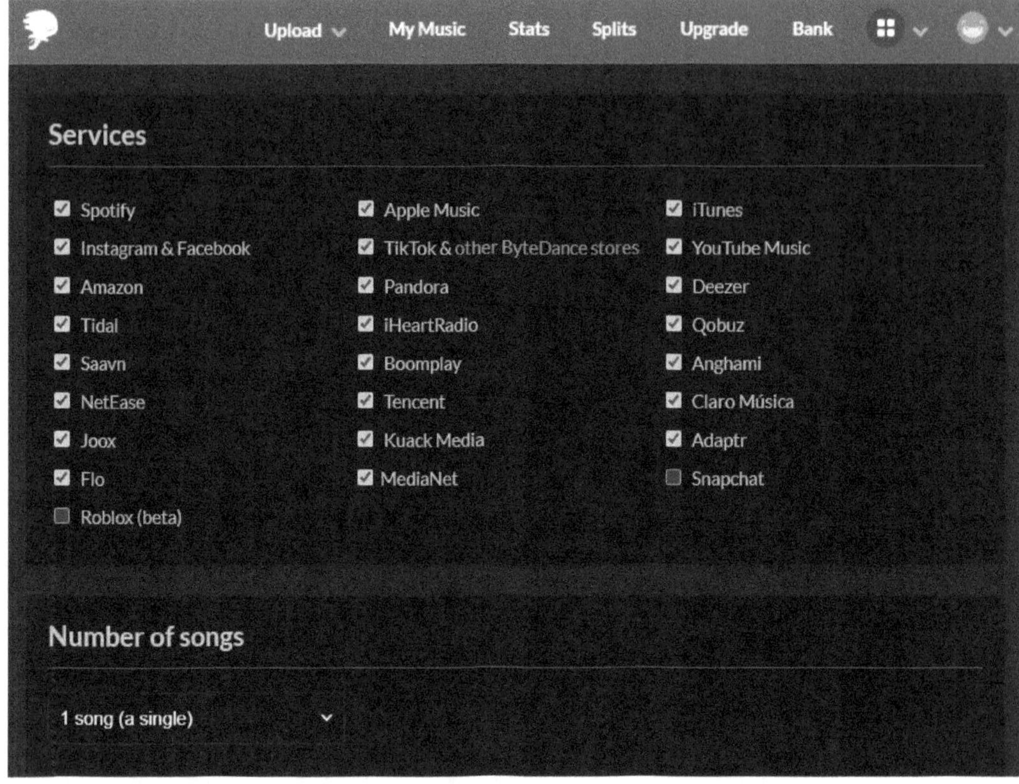

Figure 14.5 – Uploading a song

3. DistroKid lets you enter information related to the song description, such as its name, whether it features any collaborators, and genre, so online stores can categorize it.
4. If you go to the **Bank** tab, you can see information related to how much money your songs are making. There's an option to view your royalties in excruciating detail and reveal your royalty earnings down to fractions of a cent.

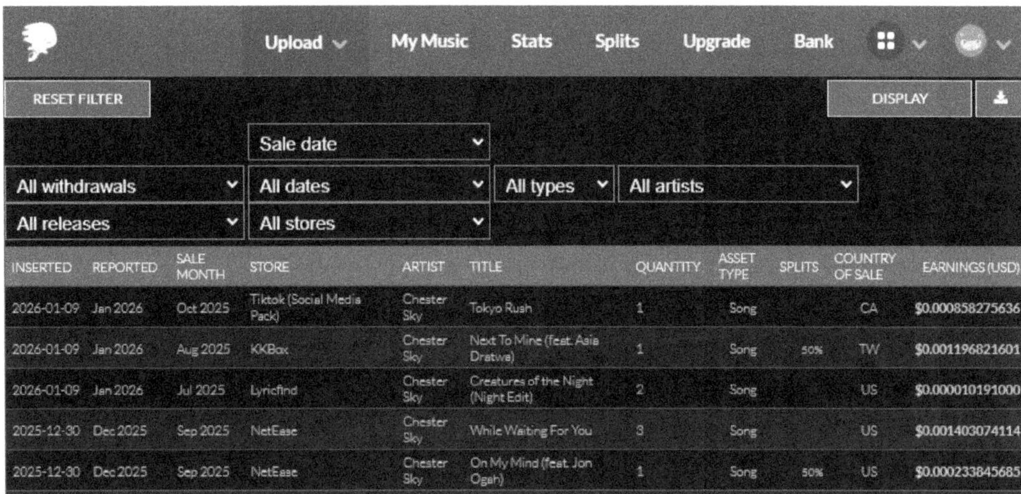

Figure 14.6 – Royalties earned

5. You can filter by date, artist, album, and type of store, and download the information to an Excel sheet.

You now know how to sell your songs through digital distribution companies. Next, let's discuss how to collect music royalties from videos that use your music on YouTube.

Claiming revenue from songs on YouTube using AdRev

When someone plays a video on YouTube that uses your song without obtaining permission, you can claim revenue from the video. You don't have to do any of the work yourself. YouTube algorithms behind the scenes detect when your song is playing in a video and mark the video as using your song. Any ad revenue the video was generating then gets collected for you. If you're looking for more information about this, YouTube uses the terminology **ContentID** to refer to claiming revenue from videos.

ContentID monetizing is done using a service called AdRev. It's the official service for registering music on YouTube. Some digital distribution companies may include YouTube AdRev in their features, but if not, you can do this yourself for free.

> **Note**
>
> If you signed up for SongTrust, SongTrust can claim revenue for you, and you don't have to register your music on AdRev.
>
> AdRev is available at `https://adrev.net/`.

Contacting AdRev support is also how you notify YouTube not to claim the ad revenue from a video (for example, if someone paid you to use your music in a video and got your permission). On AdRev, you can whitelist your own YouTube channel so that it doesn't interfere with any YouTube channel revenue. Whitelisting means that AdRev won't claim monetization on a specific video or YouTube channel. If you want to submit your music to music-promoting YouTube channels, they'll likely want you to whitelist their YouTube channels to play your songs.

Note that if you start claiming monetization whenever a YouTube video plays your song, it might dissuade YouTubers from using your song in their videos. So there's a tradeoff you'll have to consider. If you want to be paid every time someone plays your song on YouTube, AdRev is the tool for you. If you don't mind people freely using your music and just want your song to get out there, maybe you don't need AdRev.

What's the risk? If you don't register your music on AdRev, there is always the risk that some unscrupulous person may register your song on AdRev and try to claim the monetization even though they didn't create the song. This scenario happened with musician TheFatRat. People registered his songs and claimed YouTube monetization on his songs. If this is something you want to avoid, then you should register your songs with AdRev before releasing them. You can always whitelist an individual YouTube channel through AdRev.

On AdRev, you will come across an option for uploading songs to YouTube Premium. Be aware that your digital distribution company may already have uploaded songs to YouTube Premium. If so, you don't need to do it here. In addition, if you upload to YouTube Premium using AdRev and also through your digital distribution company, you will see duplicates of your songs on YouTube.

When you log in to AdRev, you'll see a screen like the following, where you can upload your songs:

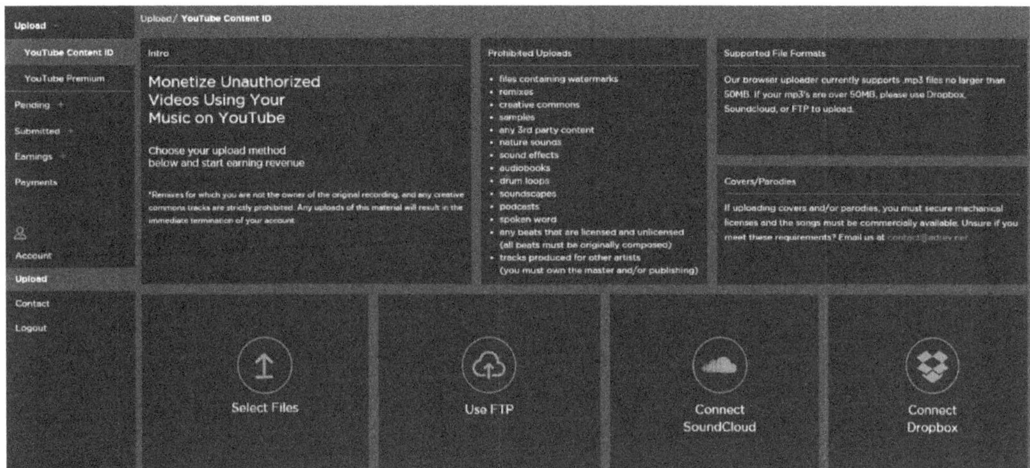

Figure 14.7 – AdRev

Once you've uploaded your songs, you'll need to enter information about your songs, such as the following:

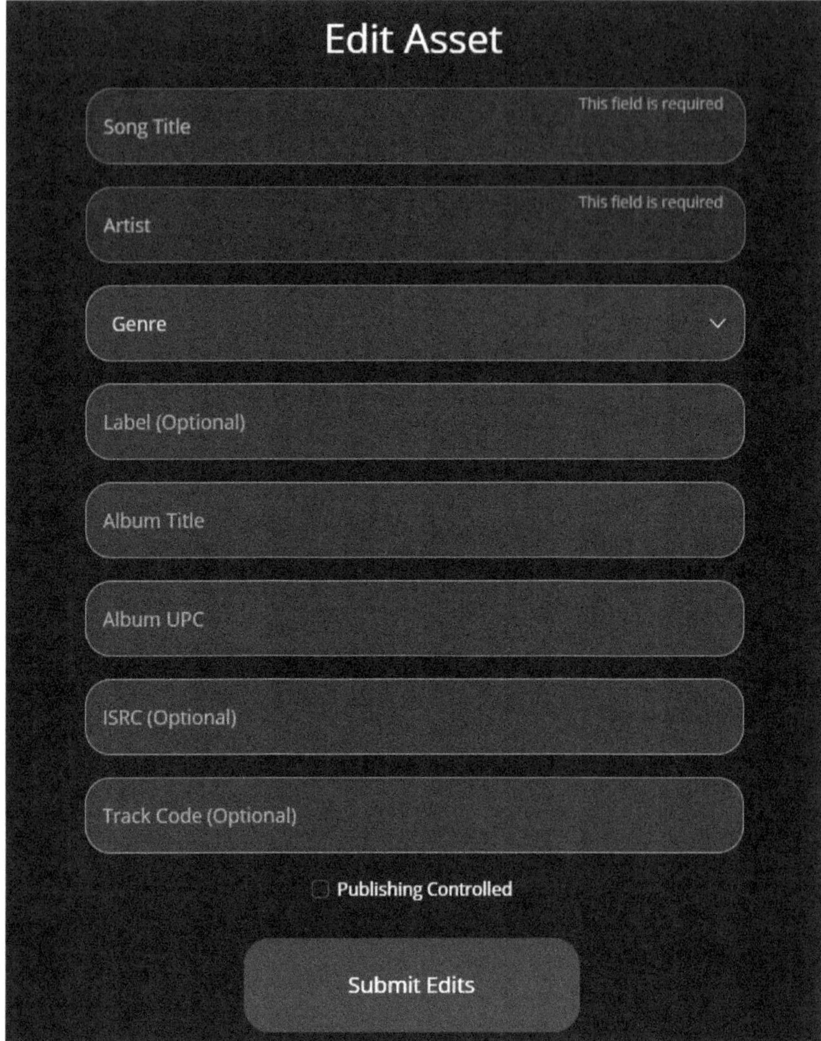

Figure 14.8 – Editing song information

On the form, two of the form boxes are for **Album UPC** and **ISRC**. You can find this information on your digital distribution company's (such as DistroKid) website. Your digital distribution company automatically assigns ISRC numbers and UPC numbers to your songs and albums when you upload the songs.

What are ISRC, ISWC, and UPC codes?

ISRC, ISWC, and UPC numbers help PROs and music distributors identify songs to trace song usage. You can think of them as your song barcode numbers.

ISRC stands for International Standard Recording Code. Every song receives a unique ISRC number. If you have a label or publisher, they handle getting the code. If you use an online distribution company service such as DistroKid, they provide the ISRC code. Here's an example of one of my songs' ISRC codes: `QZ-K6H-20-73696`.

The first two characters stand for the country code. The next three characters are issued by the ISRC agency and may reflect the record label/distributor or release number. The next two digits refer to the issue date; in this case, it was released in the year 2020. The last five digits are a unique identifier for the person or company.

ISWC stands for International Standard Musical Work Code. It's assigned by a collection society such as ASCAP in North America. It refers to a specific musical work. It's used to identify a song title, songwriters, music publishers, and song splits. If you need to figure out what your ISWC number is, contact your country's collection society.

UPC stands for Universal Product Code. It's the code printed on products for identifying them and is used to scan at the checkout counter at stores. Your digital distribution company website usually assigns your released album a UPC code. Here's an example of one of my albums' UPC values:`195596 62921 3`

The first six digits identify the manufacturer of the product. The next five digits are the item's unique identifier. The last digit is called the check digit and is used in calculations to confirm to the checkout scanner that the UPC is valid.

You now know how to sell your music online and claim revenue.

Summary

In this chapter, you learned about publishing and selling music online. You learned how to register your music to collect royalties from live performances. You learned how to tag music to prepare it for distribution. You learned how to sell your music on online stores and streaming services. Finally, you learned how to claim revenue from YouTube videos using your music.

Share your music

If you'd like to share your music with other readers and students and ask for feedback, feel free to post your music in the following Facebook group: `https://www.facebook.com/groups/musicproducerandcomposercommunity`.

Conclusion

Our book has come to an end...but your music journey has just begun. You can now produce songs like a pro and kick off your music career.

I hope you had a fascinating time learning music production throughout this book. You're now up to date with the latest and greatest cutting-edge tools on the market. A few decades ago, people couldn't even imagine doing what you're now capable of.

A few final thoughts:

- Music is meant to be shared. You can take influences from lots of sources and combine them to make something original. If you need ideas, try combining genres.
- When you make something, be proud of it. Having a little ego at stake makes you strive to be better. Make something that you care about.
- If your music isn't connecting, try changing the context in which the music is delivered. For example, consider experimenting with different names and visuals. Often, the presentation of your music shapes how it gets received.
- Create lots of music, it's the only way to get good. If you make something that you or others don't like, don't dwell on it. It's okay, just learn from it and start thinking about what you want to make next.

Remember, making music should be fun. If it doesn't feel like fun, you're doing it wrong. Good luck.

More from the author

Feel free to get in touch and check out the rest of my courses and products:

- Website: `https://www.chestersky.com/`
- Facebook: `https://www.facebook.com/realchestersky`
- Instagram: `https://www.instagram.com/iamchestersky`
- Twitter: `https://twitter.com/realchestersky`

If you liked this book, you'll like my book "Music for Film and Game Soundtracks with FL Studio" (`https://www.amazon.com/dp/180323329X`).

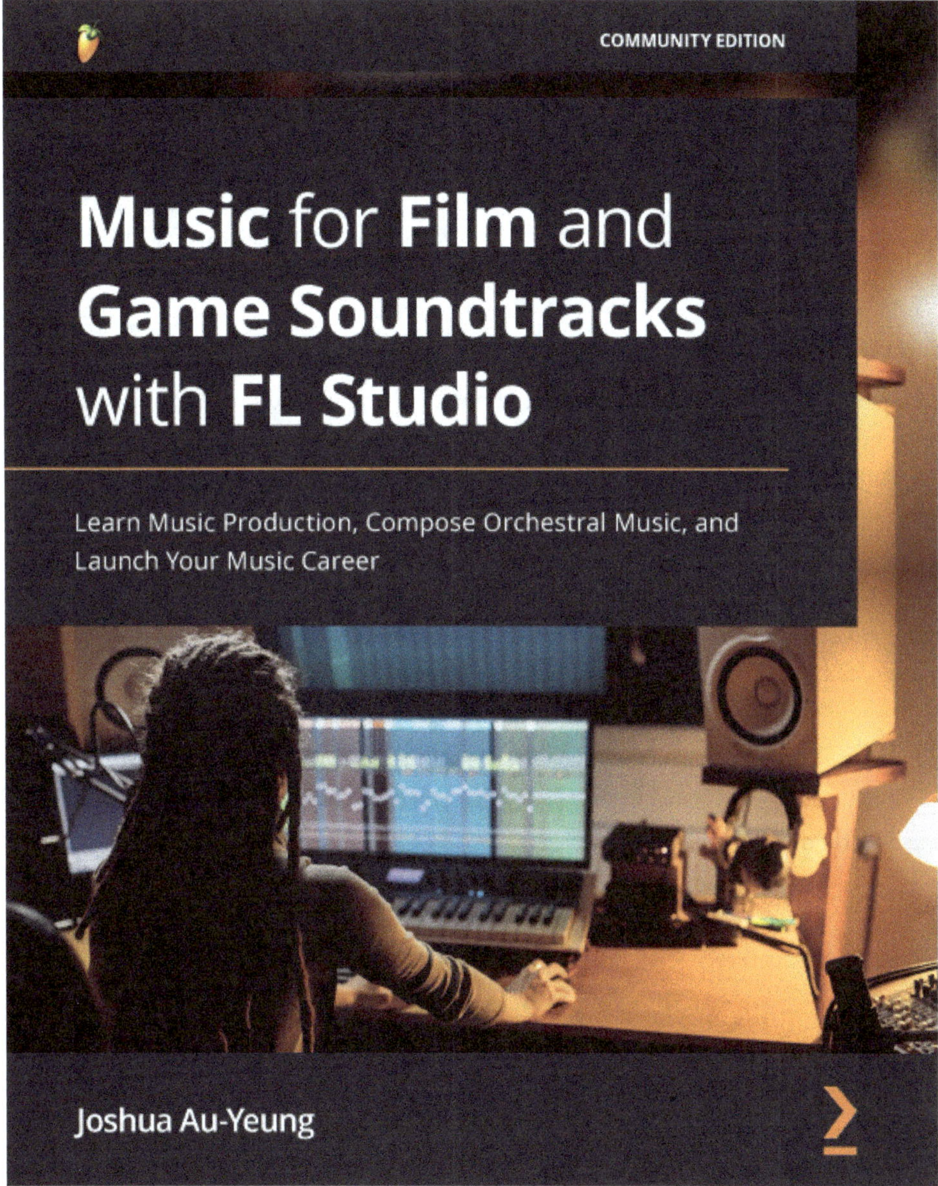

Figure 14.9 – Music for Film and Game Soundtracks with FL Studio

In the book, you'll learn the business of composing, how to communicate, score, market your services, land gigs, and deliver music projects for clients like a professional. Next, you'll set up your studio environment, navigate key tools such as the **Channel rack**, **Piano roll**, **Playlist**, **Mixer**, and **Browser**, and export songs. The book then advances to show you how to compose orchestral music using **MIDI** (**musical instrument digital interface**) programming, with a dedicated section on string instruments. You'll create sheet music using **MuseScore** for live musicians to play your compositions. Later, you'll learn about the art of Foley for recording realistic sound effects, creating adaptive music that changes throughout video games, and designing music to trigger specific emotions, for example, scary music to terrify your listener. Finally, you'll work on a sample project that will help you prepare for your composing career.

By the end of this book, you'll be able to create professional soundtrack scores for your films and video games.

Further reading

If you want to go further and learn more about the business side of a music career, I highly recommend the book *How to Make It in the New Music Business: Practical Tips on Building a Loyal Following and Making a Living as a Musician* by Ari Herstand. This book is hands down the best book I've read on the music business. I cannot recommend it enough.

You may be wondering, how exactly do royalties get collected, and what share of royalties do you get? On the surface, this sounds like a simple question. It turns out the legal details are really complex. If you want to learn how royalties are collected, read the book *All You Need to Know About the Music Business* by Donald Passman.

Get this book's PDF version and more

Scan the QR code (or go to `packtpub.com/unlock`). Search for this book by name, confirm the edition, and then follow the steps on the page.

Note: Keep your invoice handy. Purchases made directly from Packt don't require an invoice.

15

Unlock Your Exclusive Benefits

Your copy of this book includes the following exclusive benefits:

Follow the guide below to unlock them. The process takes only a few minutes and needs to be completed once.

Unlock this book's free benefits in 3 easy steps

Step 1

Keep your purchase invoice ready for *Step 3*. If you have a physical copy, scan it using your phone and save it as a PDF, JPG, or PNG.

For more help on finding your invoice, visit `https://www.packtpub.com/en-us/unlock?step=1`.

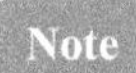

Note: If you bought this book directly from Packt, no invoice is required. After *Step 2*, you can access your exclusive content right away.

Step 2

Scan the QR code or go to `packtpub.com/unlock`.

On the page that opens (similar to *Figure 15.1* on desktop), search for this book by name and select the correct edition.

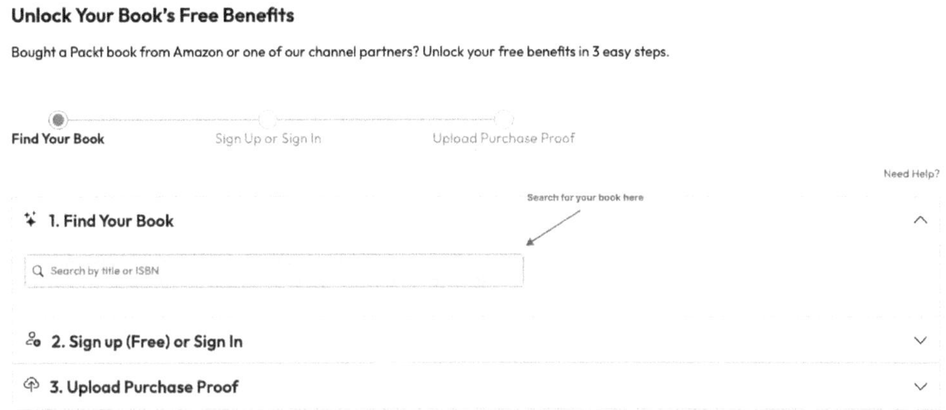

Figure 15.1: Packt unlock landing page on desktop

Step 3

After selecting your book, sign in to your Packt account or create one for free. Then upload your invoice (PDF, PNG, or JPG, up to 10 MB). Follow the on-screen instructions to finish the process.

Need help

If you get stuck and need help, visit `https://www.packtpub.com/unlock-benefits/help` for a detailed FAQ on how to find your invoices and more. This QR code will take you to the help page.

Note

Note: If you are still facing issues, reach out to `customercare@packt.com`.

packtpub.com

Subscribe to our online digital library for full access to over 7,000 books and videos, as well as industry leading tools to help you plan your personal development and advance your career. For more information, please visit our website.

Why subscribe?

- Spend less time learning and more time coding with practical eBooks and Videos from over 4,000 industry professionals
- Improve your learning with Skill Plans built especially for you
- Get a free eBook or video every month
- Fully searchable for easy access to vital information
- Copy and paste, print, and bookmark content

At `www.packtpub.com`, you can also read a collection of free technical articles, sign up for a range of free newsletters, and receive exclusive discounts and offers on Packt books and eBooks.

Other Books You May Enjoy

If you enjoyed this book, you may be interested in these other books by Packt:

Video Editing Made Easy with DaVinci Resolve 20

Lance Phillips

ISBN: 978-1-83620-883-9

- Edit and add effects to your videos quickly using the Cut page
- Export videos to various social media platforms
- Fix common video issues, such as stabilizing footage and syncing audio
- Enhance video visuals with green screen and other simple visual effects techniques
- Utilize AI in DaVinci Resolve Studio to speed up your work
- Understand common filmmaking terms, including codecs and video compression types

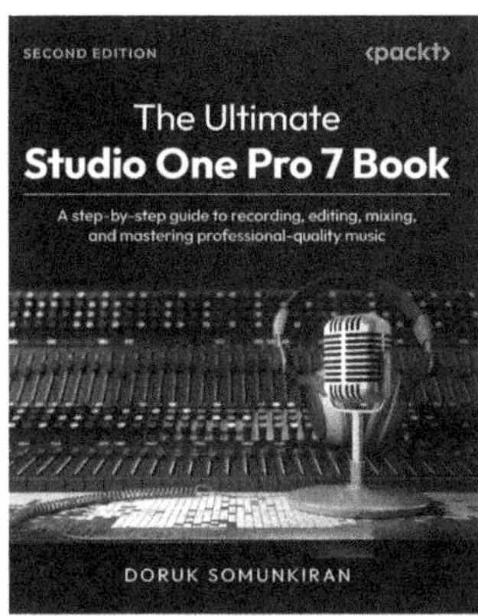

The Ultimate Studio One Pro 7 Book

Doruk Somunkiran

ISBN: 9781836200970

- Set up and optimize Studio One for a smooth and efficient production workflow
- Record and edit MIDI with precision using advanced manipulation tools
- Capture high-quality audio recordings and refine them with Melodyne and Audio Bend
- Create dynamic arrangements with Studio One's comprehensive suite of built-in virtual instruments
- Mix songs like a professional using stock effects and processing tools
- Master tracks seamlessly in the Project window for a polished, release-ready sound
- Explore immersive audio features to produce Dolby Atmos-compatible mixes

Packt is searching for authors like you

If you're interested in becoming an author for Packt, please visit `authors.packt.com` and apply today. We have worked with thousands of developers and tech professionals, just like you, to help them share their insight with the global tech community. You can make a general application, apply for a specific hot topic that we are recruiting an author for, or submit your own idea.

Share your thoughts

Now you've finished *The Music Producer's Ultimate Guide to FL Studio 2025*, we'd love to hear your thoughts! Scan the QR code below to go straight to the Amazon review page for this book and share your feedback or leave a review on the site that you purchased it from.

`https://packt.link/r/1806384418`

Your review is important to us and the tech community and will help us make sure we're delivering excellent quality content.

Index

N

O

P

Q

R

S

W

Y

Z

www.ingramcontent.com/pod-product-compliance
Lightning Source LLC
LaVergne TN
LVHW081255100826
845148LV00005B/884

* 9 7 8 1 8 0 6 3 8 4 4 1 9 *